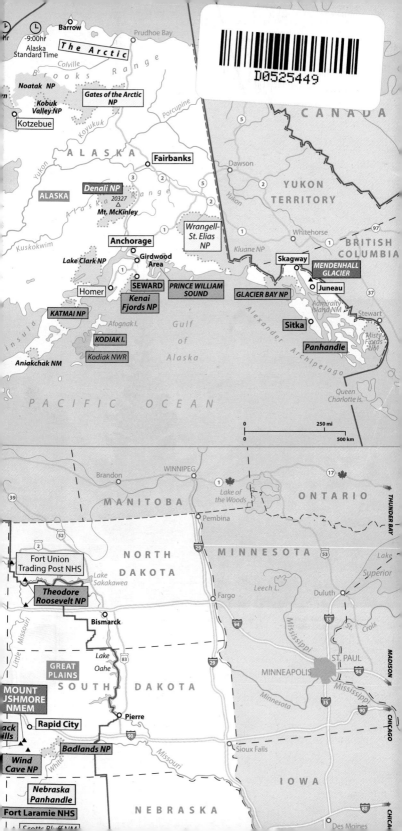

The Arctic

-9:00hr
Alaska
Standard Time

Barrow

Prudhoe Bay

Colville

Brooks Range

Noatak NP

Kobuk Valley NP

Koyukuk

Porcupine

CANADA

Kotzebue

5

ALASKA

Fairbanks

Dawson

YUKON TERRITORY

2

Yukon

2

Denali NP

Alaska Range

Mt. McKinley
20327 △

ALASKA

Whitehorse

97

BRITISH COLUMBIA

Kuskokwim

1

Anchorage

Wrangell-St. Elias NP

Kluane NP

1

Skagway

MENDENHALL GLACIER

37

Lake Clark NP

Girdwood Area

1

Juneau

Stewart

Homer

SEWARD

PRINCE WILLIAM SOUND

GLACIER BAY NP

Admiralty Island NM

Kenai Fjords NP

KATMAI NP

Afognak I.

Gulf of Alaska

Sitka

Alexander Archipelago

Panhandle

Misty Fjords NM

Aniakchak NM

KODIAK I.

Kodiak NWR

insula

PACIFIC OCEAN

Queen Charlotte Is.

0   250 mi
0   500 km

Brandon

WINNIPEG

MANITOBA

Lake of the Woods

1

7

ONTARIO

17

THUNDER BAY

39

Pembina

52

2

Fort Union Trading Post NHS

NORTH DAKOTA

Lake Sakakawea

29

MINNESOTA

53

Lake Superior

Theodore Roosevelt NP

Fargo

Duluth

Bismarck

94

Mississippi

St. Croix

35

Little Missouri

Lake Oahe

83

SOUTH DAKOTA

GREAT PLAINS

29

ST. PAUL

MINNEAPOLIS

MADISON

MOUNT RUSHMORE NMEM

Pierre

Minnesota

94

Mississippi

CHICAGO

ack ills

Rapid City

90

90

Badlands NP

90

Missouri

Sioux Falls

IOWA

Wind Cave NP

White

Nebraska Panhandle

Fort Laramie NHS

NEBRASKA

Des Moines

20

CHIC

Scotts Bluff NM

Glacier National Park, Montana
© Gwen Cannon/Michelin

THEGREENGUIDE
USA West

How to...

Green Guides - Discover the Destination

Main sections

PLANNING YOUR TRIP
The blue-tabbed section gives you **ideas for your trip** and **practical information.**

INTRODUCTION
The orange-tabbed section explores **Nature, History, Art and Culture** and the **Region Today.**

DISCOVERING
The green-tabbed section features Principal Sights by region, **Sights, Walking Tours, Excursions,** and **Driving Tours.**

Region intros

At the start of each region in the Discovering section is a brief introduction. Accompanied by a regional map, the intro provides an overview of the main tourism areas and their background.

Region maps

Star ratings

Michelin has given star ratings for more than 100 years. If you're pressed for time, we recommend you visit the three or two star sights first:

★★★ Highly
      Recommended
★★   Recommended
★   Interesting

Tours

We've selected driving and walking tours that show you the best of each town or region. Step by step directions are accompanied by detailed maps with marked routes. If you are short on time, you can follow the star ratings to decide where to stop. Selected addresses give you options for accommodation and dining en route.

Addresses

We've selected the best hotels, restaurants, cafes, shops, nightlife and entertainment to fit all budgets. See the Legend on the cover flap for an explanation of the price categories. See the back of the guide for an index of where to find hotels and restaurants.

Other reading

- Green Guide California
- Must Sees Alaska
- Must Sees Grand Canyon & Arizona
- Must Sees Hawaiian Islands
- Must Sees Pacific Northwest
- North America Road Atlas

Welcome
to USA West

The vast, varied territory of the American West offers boundless opportunities for exploration and recreation. Seventeen mainland states plus the remote states of Alaska and Hawaii occupy the fascinating landscape of plains, deserts, mountain ranges and coastlines west of the Mississppi River. They are grouped in this guide according to the following eight geographical regions and states:

California and Nevada ◆ Southwest and Canyons ◆ Rockies ◆ Texas ◆ Great Plains ◆ Northwest ◆ Alaska ◆ Hawaii

Canyon de Chelly, Arizona © Leslie Forsberg/ Michelin

Planning Your Trip

Introducing USA West

Discovering USA West

California and Nevada

Regions of USA West

California and Nevada (pp114-215)

Nicknamed the Golden State, California well merits its reputation as a tourist mecca, thanks to its sun-baked beaches, dynamic and diverse cities, gloriously scenic landscapes and legendary history. A land of geographical extremes, California harbors both the highest and lowest points in the US as well as lush forests and arid deserts. Iconic Hollywood, sun-drenched San Diego, ever-popular Disneyland and Universal Studios theme parks, and cosmopolitan San Francisco, with its enticing setting and cutting-edge cuisine, all delight visitors. Neighboring Nevada boasts sights of the Old West silver rush as well as Las Vegas, undisputed capital of gaming and glitz.

Badwater Basin, Death Valley National Park, California
© Andy Selinger / age fotostock

Southwest and Canyons (pp216-293)

Home to deep and colorful canyons, contorted rock formations and vast desert dunes and plateaus, the southwestern states feature some of the nation's most breathtaking natural scenery. The Grand Canyon, Bryce and Zion Canyons, Arches National Park, Canyon de Chelly and Monument Valley all entice and amaze visitors with their strange and wondrous beauty. Taos, Santa Fe and nearby New Mexico communities preserve the intriguing remnants of ancient cultures, while fostering a vibrant arts scene. In the southeast part of the state, the Carlsbad Caverns make up one of the world's largest cave systems. Arizona's cities of Sedona, Phoenix and Tucson offer man-made delights in the form of luxurious spa resorts, guest ranches and lushly irrigated golf links amid stunning desert scenery.

View from West Rim Drive, Grand Canyon National Park
© National Park Service

Rockies (pp294-371)

Famed Colorado resorts at Vail, Aspen, Breckenridge and Telluride draw skiers (and celebrities) to well-groomed slopes of majestic peaks, upscale shopping meccas and fine-dining spots. The regional capital of Denver exudes a modern, high-tech atmosphere, while nearby Boulder and Colorado Springs bask in exquisite settings thanks to surrounding mountains and rock formations. The region's national parks—Glacier, Yellowstone, Grand Teton, Rocky Mountain and Mesa Verde—preserve matchless natural and cultural heritage.

Texas (pp372-409)

Immense and sprawling in geography and personality, the Lone Star state enjoys a thriving modern economy that funds an outstanding array of high-quality museums and cultural institutions in the vast metropolitan areas of Houston and Dallas-Fort Worth. Seekers of Old West scenery and history head for colorful San Antonio and its Alamo, while the lively capital of Austin, with its large population of university students, nurtures an active music and cultural scene.

PUBLIC MARKET CENTER

FARMERS

Great Plains (pp410-446)

Land of wide open spaces and amber waves of grain, the Great Plains occupy the western American heartland. Corn, wheat, and other grain crops flourish in this region's rich black soil, while cattle graze on acres of prairie grass. Massive hills rise in the Dakotas to the north. Lush forests cloak the famed Black Hills, home to dramatic Mount Rushmore and sacred Sioux heritage sites; limestone caverns lurk below the earth's surface. To the south, Oklahoma treasures its Native American heritage, its cowboy persona, and its modern cultural institutions in urban centers like Tulsa and Oklahoma City.

Northwest (pp447-485)

Washington, Oregon and Idaho, northwesternmost of the lower 48 states, are blessed with dynamic cities, abundant recreational opportunities and spectacular scenery, thanks to the proximity of the Pacific Ocean and the volcanic peaks of the Cascade Range. The scenic Columbia River snakes its way through western

Oregon to the friendly and progressive city of Portland in the shadow of snow-capped Mt. Hood. Seattle, Washington's lively cultural capital, boasts an active population of sports enthusiasts, top-notch cuisine and a trendsetting high-tech ambience in its rain-kissed waterside setting. Lovers of the outdoors target Idaho for its fabulous skiing at Sun Valley, and undeveloped parklands like Hells Canyon.

Alaska (pp486-503)

A peninsular knob extending from the northwest corner of North Amerca, Alaska is a land of extremes. It's both the largest and least-populated state; its vast size produced the Native name Alyeska, meaning "Main Land." The 16 highest US mountain peaks rise within its boundaries. Magnificent glaciers, torrential rivers and abundant wildlife mark its immense expanse. Alaska is a popular cruise ship destination; the state's vast distances and utter remoteness make travel by air and sea an appealing option. With a quarter of its territory preserved as parkland, Alaska is tailor-made for seekers of adventure in the great outdoors.

Glacier Bay National Park, Alaska
©Bill Eichenlaub/National Park Service

Hawaii (pp504-527)

Part of an archipelago stretching west into the Pacific, the eight main Hawaiian islands are a tropical paradise of coral reefs, colorful flora, majestic volcanic landscapes and broad black-sand beaches fanned by gentle ocean breezes. Deluxe resorts dot the beach areas; Waikiki Beach, near the state capital of Honolulu on the island of Oahu, draws throngs of surfers and sunworshippers, while less-developed Kauai and Maui boast gorgeous botanical gardens and parks. The "Big Island" of Hawaii offers Polynesian history and native culture along with excellent deep-sea fishing. Come to these beautiful isles to experience traditional luau feasts, hula dances, music as graceful as the islands themselves, and Hawaii's aloha welcome, complete with flower leis.

Iolani Palace, Honolulu, Hawaii
© Rolf Schulten / age fotostock

Planning
Your Trip

Planning Your Trip

*Getty Villa main courtyard,
Pacific Palisades, California*
© Jamie Pham/Alamy

Inspiration

WHAT'S HOT

–**San Francisco**'s striking new waterfront Exploratorium opened in 2013 on Pier 15 (p184).

– **Oakland**'s completed (2013) eastern span of the San Francisco-Oakland Bay Bridge is the world's widest such bridge (p187).

– Petersen Automotive Museum's exciting new exterior debuts in **Los Angeles** in 2014 (p129).

–**Seattle**'s Great Wheel (2012) is the largest observation Ferris wheel on the West Coast (p455).

–The recently opened (2012) Mob Museum in **Las Vegas** (p163) is already a popular attraction, and a new SLS hotel will open in 2014.

– **Tucson**'s new (2013) aquarium at the Arizona-Sonora Desert Museum highlights the Colorado River (p259).

– The recently unveiled (2012) Perot Museum of Nature and Science in **Dallas** is drawing in the crowds (p379).

San Carlos Borromeo de Carmelo Mission, Carmel, California © Paul Giamou/iStockphoto.com

Michelin Driving Tours

Outlined below are tours that take in highlights of the West, from California's Hollywood, Yellowstone's Old Faithful, and Mount St. Helens in Washington to The Alamo in San Antonio, Texas. Be sure to be familiar with the state's driving regulations and have an idea of the weather forecast.

CALIFORNIA DREAMING
15 days; about 1,800mi.

California has a bit of everything, from surf-washed beaches, alpine resorts and cosmopolitan cities to ghost towns. This tour begins in **San Francisco**, keeper of the Golden Gate, with its cable cars scaling the hills from **Fisherman's Wharf** to **Chinatown**. Drive south to **Monterey** with its aquarium anchoring Cannery Row. Highway 1 weaves a cliff-side path along the wild **Big Sur** coast to emerge at eclectic **Hearst Castle**. From the charming mission town of **Santa Barbara**, boats provide access to Channel Islands National Park. Stay long enough in sprawling **Los Angeles** to spot movie stars in **Hollywood** or **Beverly Hills**; spend an afternoon at the **Getty Center** or another renowned art museum. Revisit your childhood at **Disneyland**, the popular amusement park. Subtropical **San Diego** is a delight for animal lovers with its world-famous zoo, wild animal park and **SeaWorld**. Loop back to L.A. via Pacific Coast Highway (Rte. 1) through Laguna Beach and **Long Beach**, permanent home of the **Queen Mary**.

Northbound I-5 runs up the Central Valley, the richest farmland on earth, and lures outdoor lovers to the big trees of **Sequoia and Kings Canyon National Parks** and to the deep glacial valley and waterfalls of **Yosemite National Park**.

Across the crest of the **Sierra Nevada**, year-round resorts surround deep-blue **Lake Tahoe**. A short drive from the casinos of **Reno**, Nevada, is historic **Virginia City**, built in the 1860s and 70s on the fabulously rich Comstock Lode. West lies the **Gold Country**, many of whose towns—like quaint **Nevada City** and bustling Auburn —date from the 1850s gold-rush era. Miners traveled upriver from **Sacramento**, now the state capital. In the **Wine Country** of Napa and Sonoma Counties, dozens of wineries welcome tasters.

An easy drive down the Marin County coast, to rugged **Point Reyes National Seashore** and majestic **Muir Woods National Monument**, leads back to San Francisco.

CANYONS AND CASINOS
15 days; about 1,800mi.

Las Vegas is the high-energy 24-hour gateway to the spectacular canyon country of the Southwest.

From **Las Vegas**, cross the great **Hoover Dam** and continue east via I-40 to the vast and colorful **Grand Canyon**. Earth's best-known chasm is a mile deep, 10mi wide, 277mi long and 2 billion years in the making. From Grand Canyon Village, touring roads extend east and west; dizzying trails descend to the canyon floor.

Delightful **Sedona**, in **Red Rock Country** south of **Oak Creek Canyon** via Rte. 89A, is a magnet for artists and New Age spiritual seekers. National monuments preserve ruins of ancient civilizations. **Canyon de Chelly** and Navajo National Monuments are north and east on the broad Navajo Indian Reservation. Surrounded by Navajo lands, Hopi reservation residents pursue ancient cultural traditions. The landscape of **Monument Valley** is well-known from myriad Western movies. US-191 continues to **Moab**, a center for mountain biking and rafting, and gateway to **Canyonlands** and **Arches National Parks**—the former, a stunning canyon wilderness, the latter preserving more than 2,000 sandstone arches. Southwest, drivers skirt the beautiful backcountry of **Capitol Reef National Park** en route to **Bryce Canyon National Park**, a fairyland of rock spires and pinnacles. Two hours farther, **Zion National Park** encloses a steep canyon adorned with waterfalls and hanging gardens. Returning to "Lost Wages," you now can gamble unspent cash in lavish casinos. On the celebrated **Las Vegas Strip**, you'll "find" the Eiffel Tower and Statue of Liberty, King Arthur's castle and King Tut's tomb.

HEART OF TEXAS
8 days; about 1,100mi.

Texas is the largest US state after Alaska. This tour, which starts and ends at the Dallas-Fort Worth airport, samples its vast diversity.

Begin in **Fort Worth**. The **Stockyards National Historic District** brings to life the cowboy days of yore in western-wear stores, a rodeo arena and the world's largest honky-tonk. The **Kimbell Art Museum's European collection** is outstanding. South via I-35 **Austin**, the state capital, boasts the famous Sixth Street Entertainment District. The **Lyndon Baines Johnson**

Durango & Silverton Narrow Gauge Railroad Train, Southwest Colorado, founded by the Denver & Rio Grande Railway in 1879

© Matt Inden/Weaver Multimedia group/CTO

Presidential Library and Museum on the University of Texas campus pays homage to a native son further remembered at historical parks in the nearby **Hill Country**. Settled by Germans, **Fredericksburg** retains a touch of Germanic heritage.

San Antonio, rich in Hispanic tradition, is the cradle of Texas freedom. **The Alamo** canonizes 189 pioneer Texans who died in its defense. Gondolas cruise past the 2.5mi **River Walk**, lined with shops and cafes. Southeast via I-37, on the Gulf Coast, **Corpus Christi** is the gateway to **Padre Island National Seashore**, a favorite of birdwatchers. East of San Antonio via I-10 rises **Houston**, fourth-largest city in the US and home to **Space Center Houston**, where US space research and astronaut training take place. Oil wealth helps to support Houston's superb Museum District, highlighted by the Surrealist works of the **Menil Collection** and the energy exhibits of the **Houston Museum of Natural Science**. Seaside **Galveston** has a notable 19C historic district.

North via I-45 lies **Dallas**. Shoppers love the Dallas Market Center, world's largest wholesale merchandise market. The **Sixth Floor Museum at Dealey Plaza** commemorates the life of President John F. Kennedy and analyzes his assassination there in 1963.

PEAKS AND PUEBLOS
13 days; about 1,500mi.
From the heights of the Rocky Mountains to the secrets of ancient pueblo heritage, this tour highlights Colorado and New Mexico.
Start and finish in **Denver**, urban center of the Rockies. The **LoDo** district is a landmark of historic preservation; the **Denver Art Museum** has a renowned Native American collection. Climb across the Continental Divide on I-70. Colorful Victorian architecture in the thin air of **Breckenridge** and **Leadville** bears testimony to a silver-mining heritage.

The ski resort of **Vail** is a playground for high society; chic **Aspen**, which nestles near the beautiful **Maroon Bells**, has a delightful 19C downtown. Continue west to the stark geology of the **Colorado National Monument** and **Black Canyon of the Gunnison National Park**, then follow spectacular US-550 through the San Juan Mountains to **Durango**, with its fine historic railway. At nearby **Mesa Verde National Park**, visitors walk through five major cliff dwellings dated AD 750-1300. New Mexico's **Chaco Culture National Historical Park** embraces ruins that formed a 9-12C trade and political hub. South, off I-40, cliff-top **Sky City at Acoma Pueblo** has been continually inhabited since the 11C. The **Indian Pueblo Cultural Center** at **Albuquerque** represents 19 communities; the **National Atomic Museum** details the nuclear age. Enchanting **Santa Fe** begs a lengthy stay. See its **Palace of the Governors**, in use since 1610, and the **Georgia O'Keeffe Museum**, displaying the artist's works. Marvel at the spiral staircase in the **Loretto Chapel** and take in a performance at the **Santa Fe Opera**. Meander north to the artists' colony of Taos, packed with galleries, historic homes, the remarkable **Taos Pueblo** and the adobe **San Francisco de Asis Church**.

En route back to Denver via I-25, pause in **Colorado Springs**. Take a railway to the 14,110ft summit of **Pikes Peak**, learn about broncos at the ProRodeo Hall of Fame, and stand beneath the spires of the Cadet Chapel at the **US Air Force Academy**.

ROCKY MOUNTAIN HIGH
13 days; about 1,900mi.
Several of America's most famous national parks and historic sites are a part of this high-elevation tour.
Salt Lake City fascinates visitors intrigued by the religion and culture of the Mormons. Take I-80 east to the historic mining town of **Park City**, site of many events in the 2002 Winter Olympics, then head north. US-89

leads through **Jackson**, renowned for its cowboy ambience and its **National Museum of Wildlife Art**, and **Grand Teton National Park**, embracing a dramatic range of craggy mountains. US-89 continues into **Yellowstone National Park**, whose unparalleled natural attractions—geysers, hot springs, canyons and rich wildlife—demand several days.

Turning east on US-14, pause in **Cody** to explore the **Buffalo Bill Historical Center**, then proceed directly across the Big Horn Mountains to the fluted monolith of **Devils Tower National Monument** and into the **Black Hills**. After paying homage to the stone images of US presidents at **Mount Rushmore National Memorial**, detour to **Wind Cave National Park** and the once-rowdy mining town of **Deadwood**. Swing east through the geological curiosities of **Badlands National Park**, then south across western Nebraska to pick up the **Oregon Trail** near Scotts Bluff National Monument. The historic trail follows US-26 past **Fort Laramie National Historic Site**. Turn south through **Cheyenne**, a quintessential rodeo town; detour via US-34 to pristine **Rocky Mountain National Park**. The tour ends in **Denver**, described in "Peaks and Pueblos."

NORTHWEST PASSAGES
10 days; about 1,700mi.
This tour starts and ends in Seattle and takes in the Cascade Range,

great rivers, redwood forests and an unforgettable Pacific coastline.

The futuristic **Space Needle** towers above **Seattle**, home of Microsoft, Boeing and Starbucks Coffee. The maritime city invites exploration of its **Pike Place Market**, its **Seattle Center** cultural complex, and its museums and gardens. Visitors can view airplanes being constructed at **Boeing's Everett factory**. Alpine roads wind southeast through **Mount Rainier National Park** and fascinating Mount **St. Helens National Volcanic Monument**, which offers perspective on the peak's 1980 eruption.

In the shadow of **Mount Hood** is **Portland**, Oregon's "Rose City." The International Rose Test Garden is one of several gardens in **Washington Park**, which sprawls across hills near downtown. Outside Portland lies the pinot-rich **Oregon Wine Country** and the End of the **Oregon Trail Interpretive Center**, documenting the journey of mid-19C pioneers. Panoramas extend east up I-84 through the **Columbia River Gorge**, host to myriad windsurfers and ribbon-like Multnomah Falls.

The hub of central Oregon is Bend, southeast of Portland on US-97. Drive the **Cascade Lakes Highway** en route to **Crater Lake National Park**, where a cobalt-blue lake, deepest in the US, fills a collapsed caldera. Continue southwest via Rte. 62 to taste the Shakespearean persona of Ashland, the 19C gold-rush flavor of **Jacksonville** and the labyrinths of **Oregon Caves National Monument**. Ease into northwest California on US-199 to see giant redwood trees in **Redwoods National and State Parks**. Then proceed up the coast, a gorgeous three-day drive on US-101 via **Oregon Dunes National Recreation Area** and the noted Oregon Coast Aquarium in Newport. **Olympic National Park** dominates Washington's Olympic Peninsula home to **Hoh Rain Forest** and **Hurricane Ridge**. See the Victorian seaport of Port Townsend, then take a ferry back to Seattle.

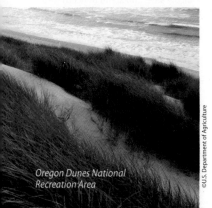

Oregon Dunes National Recreation Area

©U.S. Department of Agriculture

DISTANCE CHART

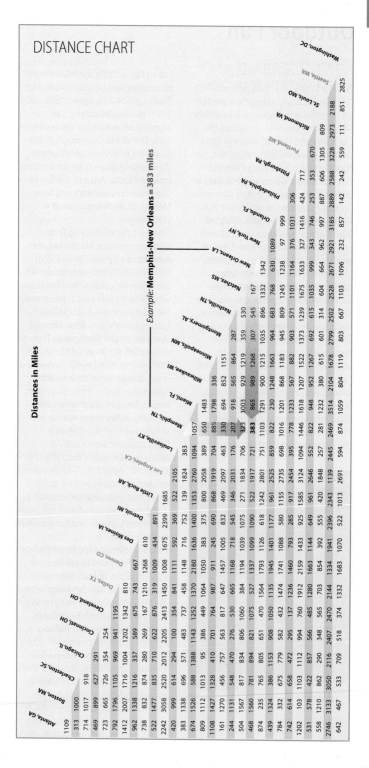

Distances in Miles

Example: Memphis–New Orleans = 383 miles

Outdoor Fun

ADVENTURE TRAVEL AND MULTI-SPORT EXCURSIONS

The varying geography of the western US provides opportunities for outdoor adventure—from surfing along the California and Hawaii coasts to cross-country skiing in Yellowstone National Park or the birch forests of Alaska. Contact state tourism offices (pxxx) for information about activities in specific areas, or consider an organized tour. **Gorp** is an online website affiliated with *Outside* magazine that catalogs responsible adventure travel (www. gorp.com). REI also offers an extensive list of trips and adventures (www.rei. com). *The following is a sampling of tour providers and programs available:* For extensive **all-inclusive vacations** involving activities such as bicycling, hiking and kayaking, contact **Backroads** (✆510-527-1555 or 800-462-2848; www.backroads.com). Programs include destinations in Alaska, Arizona, California, Colorado, Hawaii, Idaho, Montana, New Mexico, Utah, Washington and Wyoming. For adventures on **horseback** throughout the USA West, including

Snowboarding

Comstock, INC

riding tours, cattle drives and visits to working ranches, contact **Hidden Trails** (✆604-323-1141 or 888-987-2457; www.hiddentrails.com).

Multi-sport vacations are available from **The World Outdoors** (✆303-413-0938 or 800-488-8483; www. theworldoutdoors.com). Destinations include Alaska, Arizona, California, Colorado, Hawaii, Montana, New Mexico, Utah, Washington and Wyoming.

Covering the western US from Alaska to Arizona, **Austin-Lehman Adventures** (✆406-586-3556 or 800-575-1540; www.austinlehman. com) provides multi-sport vacations with expert guides for active travelers. National parks are a special focus. Rafting adventures, on wilderness rivers across the West, range from half-days to full weeks at **OARS** (✆209-736-4677 or 800-346-6277; www.oars. com); www.northernalaska.com). Adventures in the Arctic, from the Brooks Range to Barrow, are the specialty at **Northern Alaska Tour Co.** in Fairbanks (✆907-474-8600; www.northernalaska.com).

Wilderness Inquiry, Inc. (✆612–676–9400 or 800–728–0719; www. wildernessinquiry.org) catalogs tours that include activities such as kayaking in Alaska's fjords, rafting in the Grand Canyon, and horsepacking in the Rockies.

All but the most experienced **whitewater rafters and kayakers** book expert guides to lead them down Western rivers. The following veteran outfitters are experts on rivers in their home states: **All-Outdoors California Whitewater Rafting** (✆925-932-8993 or 800-247-2387; www.aorafting.com); **Colorado's Dvorak Expeditions, Inc.** (✆719-429-6851 or 800-824-3795; www. dvorakexpeditions.com); **ECHO: The Wilderness Company** (✆800-652-3246; www.echotrips.com) in Idaho and Oregon; and **R.O.W.–River**

Odysseys West (☏208-765-0841 or 800-451-6034; www.rowinc.com) in Idaho, Oregon, Montana and Alaska; and Alaska kayaking with Backcountry Safaris in Seward (☏907-222-1632 or 877-812-2159; www.alaskakayak.com). In Hawaii: **Kayak Kaua'i** (☏808-826-9844 or 800-437-3507; www.kayakkaui.com).

SKIING THE WEST
From the Rockies to the Cascades and Sierra Nevada, ski areas are abundant, ranging from small local hills to international resorts. Most western states, except those of the southern Great Plains, boast at least one ski area; associations count more than 160, including 31 in California and 27 in Colorado. SkiTown (www.skitown.com) has details on every North American resort.

Major destination areas – with at least eight lifts and a 2,000ft vertical drop – include these:

Alaska: Alyeska Resort (☏907-754-1111; www.alyeskaresort.com).

California: Heavenly Valley (☏775-586-7000; www.skiheavenly.com), Kirkwood (☏209-258-6000; www.kirkwood.com), Northstar-at-Tahoe (☏530-562-1010; www.northstarattahoe.com), Sierra-at-Tahoe (☏530-659-7453; www.sierraattahoe.com), Squaw Valley (☏530-583-6985; www.squaw.com), June Mountain (☏760-648-7717; www.junemountain.com), Mammoth Mountain (☏760-934-2571; www.mammothmountain.com).

Colorado: Aspen/Snowmass (☏970-925-1220; www.aspensnowmass.com), Crested Butte (☏970-349-2323; www.skicb.com), Purgatory (☏970-247-9000; www.durangomountainresort.com), Telluride (☏970-728-7350; www.tellurideskiresort.com), Steamboat Springs: Steamboat (☏970-879-6111; www.steamboat.com), Breckenridge (☏970-453-5000; www.breckenridge.com), Copper Mountain (☏970-968-

2882; www.coppercolorado.com), Keystone (☏970-496-4111; www.keystoneresortcom), Beaver Creek (☏970-476-9090; www.beavercreek.com), Vail (☏970-754-8245; www.vail.com), Winter Park (☏970-726-1564; www.skiwinterpark.com).

Idaho: Schweitzer Mountain (☏208-263-9555; www.schweitzer.com), Sun Valley (☏208-622-4111; www.sunvalley.com).

Montana: Big Sky (☏406-995-8000; www.bigskyresort.com), Red Lodge Mountain (☏406-446-2610; www.redlodge.com), Whitefish (☏406-862-2900; www.skiwhitefish.com).

New Mexico: Santa Fe Ski Basin (☏505-982-4429; www.skisantafe.com), Ski Apache (☏575-464-3600; www.skiapache.com), Taos Ski Valley (☏505-776-2916; www.skitaos.org).

☺ Safety Tips ☺

Thunderstorms
- If outdoors, take cover and stay away from trees and metal objects.
- If riding in a vehicle, remain inside until the storm has passed.
- Avoid being in or near water.
- If in a boat, head for the nearest shore.
- Do not use electrical appliances, especially the telephone.

Tornados
- If indoors, move to a predesignated shelter (usually a basement or stairwell); otherwise find an interior room without windows (such as a bathroom).
- Stay away from windows.
- Do not attempt to outrun the storm in a car; get out of the automobile and lie flat in a ditch or low-lying area.

Oregon: Mt. Bachelor (☏541-382-2442; www.mtbachelor.com), Timberline Lodge (☏503-231-7979; www.timberlinelodge.com).

Utah: Alta (☏801-359-1078; www.alta.com), The Canyons (☏435-649-5400; www.thecanyons.com), Deer Valley (☏435-649-1000; www.deervalley.com), Park City (☏435-649-8111; www.parkcitymountain.com), Snowbasin (☏801-399-1135; www.snowbasin.com), Snowbird (☏801-742-2222; www.snowbird.com).

Washington: Crystal Mountain (☏360-663-2526; www.skicrystal.com).

Wyoming: Grand Targhee (☏307-353-2300; www.grandtarghee.com), Jackson Hole (☏307-733-2292; www.jacksonhole.com).

GUIDES AND OUTFITTERS

A list of accredited **mountaineering organizations** and guides can be obtained from the nonprofit **American Mountain Guides Association** (☏303-271-0984; www.amga.com). **America Outdoors** (☏865-558-3595; www.americaoutdoors.org) offers an outfitter database on its website.

NATURE AND SAFETY
Wildlife

In publicly protected natural areas, tampering with plants or wildlife is prohibited by law. Although the disturbance caused by a single person may be small, the cumulative impact of a large number of visitors may be disastrous. Avoid direct contact with wildlife; any animal that does not shy from humans may be sick or dangerous. Some wild animals,

GOLF: HITTING THE LINKS

Following is a list of some top-rated public-access courses in the western US:

COURSE	LOCATION	☏
Troon North	Scottsdale AZ	480-585-7700
Sedona	Sedona AZ	520-284-9355
Tahquitz Creek	Palm Springs CA	760-328-1005
Pebble Beach	Pebble Beach CA	800-654-9300
Meadows del Mar	San Diego CA	858-792-6200
Pasatiempo	Santa Cruz CA	831-459-9155
The Broadmoor	Colorado Springs CO	719-577-5790
The Prince	Kauai HI	808-826-5000
Mauna Kea Beach	Kohala Coast HI	808-882-7222
Coeur d'Alene	Coeur d'Alene ID	208-765-0218
Pumpkin Ridge	Cornelius OR	503-647-9977
Angel Park	Las Vegas NV	888-446-5358
Edgewood Tahoe	Stateline NV	775-588-3566
Piñon Hills	Farmington NM	505-326-6066
Del Lago	Conroe TX	409-582-7570
Horseshoe Bay	Burnet TX	830-598-2511
Las Colinas	Irving TX	972-717-2441
Entrada at Snow Canyon	St. George UT	435-674-7500
Teton Pines	Jackson WY	307-733-1733

Many websites list courses, including www.golflink.com.

particularly bears, may approach cars or campsites out of curiosity or if they smell food. *Never offer food to wild animals—doing so is extremely dangerous, and illegal.*

Food storage safety: when camping, hang food 12ft off the ground and 10ft away from a tree trunk, or store in a car trunk or in lockers provided at many campgrounds. Improper storage of food is a violation of federal law and subject to a fine. If a wild animal approaches, stand tall and talk firmly to attempt to deter it. Do not run; instead, back away calmly. Never approach a mother with young, as she may attack to protect her offspring (this warning applies to bears, moose, bison, elk and other wild creatures).

Wildlife parks: Numerous parks and outdoor zoos throughout the West invite visitors to watch both indigenous and exotic animals. Only those certified by the Association of Zoos and Aquariums (www.aza. org) practice humane husbandry and adhere to ethical exhibit standards. This guide includes only certified wildlife parks and zoos.

Beach and Water Safety

In the strong sun of coastal areas where white sand and water increase the sun's intensity, visitors run the risk of sunburn, even in winter. Apply sunscreen even on overcast days, as ultraviolet rays penetrate cloud cover. During summer months, when temperatures may be extreme, avoid strenuous midday exercise and drink plenty of liquids.

Along public beaches warning flags may be posted: blue flags signify calm waters; yellow flags indicate choppy waters; **red flags** indicate dangerous swimming conditions such as riptides, strong underlying currents that pull swimmers seaward. Take precautions even when venturing into calm waters: never swim, snorkel or scuba dive alone; and supervise children at all times. Most public beaches employ lifeguards seasonally; take care when swimming at an unguarded beach. Stinging creatures such as jellyfish, Portuguese men-of-war and sea urchins can inhabit shallow waters. Although most jellyfish stings produce little more than an itchy skin rash, some can cause painful swelling. Treating the affected area with papain-type meat tenderizer will give relief. Stingrays and Portuguese men-of-war can inflict a more serious sting; seek medical treatment immediately. Before beginning any water sports activity, check with local authorities for information on water and weather conditions. If you rent a canoe or charter a boat, familiarize yourself

Black Bear munching on dandelions, Alaska

NPS/Melinda Webster

29

with the craft, obtain charts of the area and advise someone of your itinerary before setting out. **Life jackets** must be worn when boating. Many equipment-rental facilities also offer instruction. Be sure to choose a reputable outfitter. Boating while intoxicated is illegal.

Earthquake Precautions

Although severe earthquakes are infrequent, they are also unpredictable, making earthquake preparedness a fact of life in California and other Pacific-coast states. If you are **outside** when a quake occurs, stay clear of trees, buildings and power lines. If you are in a **vehicle**, pull to the side of the road and stop. Do not park on or under bridges; sit on the floor of the vehicle if possible. If you are in a **building**, stand inside a doorway or sit under a sturdy table; stay away from windows and outside walls. Be alert for aftershocks. If possible, tune to local radio or TV stations for advisories.

Desert Safety

When traveling through desert areas, particularly in summer, certain precautions are essential. Before driving or hiking in remote areas, notify someone of your destination and your planned return time. Have plenty of water with you.

For Your Vehicle

Always stay on marked roads; many remote roads are suitable only for four-wheel-drive vehicles. As service stations may be far apart, it is wise to keep your gas tank at least half full, and carry extra radiator water. If the vehicle is running hot, turn off the air conditioning. Do not use your air conditioner while climbing long hills. If it overheats, pull to the side of the road, keep the engine running and turn on the heater; remove the radiator cap with extreme caution, then slowly pour water over the radiator core. Refill the radiator after the engine has cooled.

In the event of a breakdown, do not leave your vehicle to seek help; instead, raise the hood of your car to indicate help is needed, use your cell phone and stay with the vehicle while waiting for help to arrive. If responding to another's breakdown, never loan your cell phone, but rather make the call yourself, keeping your phone in your possession at all times.

For You

Summer temperatures can reach above 120°F (48°C). It is imperative to carry plenty of water and drink it freely, at least once an hour. Do not lie or sit in direct sunlight. Always wear loose-fitting clothes (preferably long-

WORLD HERITAGE IN THE WEST

These places in the US West have a UNESCO World Heritage Site designation: Page numbers refer to description in this guide.

Alaska: Glacier Bay/Kluane/Tatshenshini parks complex (p494)

Arizona: Grand Canyon (p221)

California: Redwood National Park (p194); Yosemite National Park (p209)

Colorado: Mesa Verde National Park (p326)

Hawaii: Hawaii Volcanoes National Park (p527); Papahānaumokuākea

Montana: Glacier/Waterton International Peace Park (p363)

New Mexico: Chaco Culture National Historic Park (p293); Carlsbad Caverns (p275); Taos Pueblo (p290)

Washington: Olympic National Park (p464)

Wyoming: Yellowstone National Park (p342).

© NPS

Park Avenue Pass, Arches National Park

sleeved), a broad-brimmed hat and sunglasses.

Heat exhaustion is caused by overexertion in high temperatures. Symptoms include cool, clammy skin and nausea. If experiencing either of these symptoms, rest in the shade and drink plenty of fluids.

Symptoms of **heat stroke** include hot, dry skin, dizziness or headache; victims may become delirious. To treat these symptoms, try to lower the body temperature with cold compresses or cool baths (do not use analgesics) and seek medical assistance.

Abandoned mines are common in desert and mountain areas, and all are potentially dangerous. Never enter a tunnel without a flashlight. Watch for loose rock and do not touch support timbers. Be watchful for sudden storms that may produce flash floods.

Mountain Safety

Take particular care if you are traveling at high altitudes, whether driving across Trail Ridge Road at 12,183ft in Colorado's Rocky Mountain National Park or taking the cog railway to the 14,110ft summit of Pikes Peak. Your body does not immediately acclimate to the reduced oxygen level and lowered atmospheric pressure. One to four days may be necessary to fully adjust. Restrict activity to moderate exertion, get plenty of rest, avoid large meals, and drink lots of water. Senior citizens, pregnant women and travelers with a history of heart problems should consult their physicians before climbing heights.

Especially if you are hiking or skiing above 8,000ft, you may suffer altitude sickness caused by overexertion. Symptoms include headache, shortness of breath, appetite loss or nausea, tingling in fingers or toes (which may progress to swelling in feet and legs) and general weakness. If experiencing any of these symptoms, rest and eat high-energy foods such as raisins, trail mix or granola bars; take a couple of aspirin and slow your pace. If symptoms become more severe, descend to a lower altitude; if they do not disappear in 2-5 days, seek medical attention.

As the sun's rays are more intense at higher elevations, they cause sunburn more quickly, especially in winter when they reflect off snow. A good sunblock is essential.

It is important to keep yourself warm and your clothing dry at any time of year. Hypothermia poses the greatest threat in winter, but even midsummer temperatures can drop below freezing at high altitude—and hypothermia can occur well above freezing.

Snow is possible at high elevations in the West any time of year, and blizzards are potential travel hazards November through April. Heed weather warnings and do not attempt travel, especially across more remote regions, when bad weather is forecast. Do not rely on GPS devices to find safe roads in bad weather.

NATIONAL AND STATE LANDS

The US has an extensive network of federal and state lands, including national and state parks, national monuments, recreation preserves and wildlife refuges, that offer year-round recreational opportunities such as camping (pxx), fishing, horseback riding, cross-country skiing, wildlife watching and boating. Public lands are widespread throughout the West, especially in Alaska, where more than half the state is federal property. US federal land-management agencies support a comprehensive online database (www.recreation.gov) that supplies information on all recreation areas through a variety of search options and Internet links. The National Park Service provides a listing of all lands under its jurisdiction on its website (www.nps.gov).

Both national and state parks offer **season passes** (disabled travelers p xx). The **US national recreational lands pass** ($80) is good for one year and includes admission to all national parks and other federal lands that charge admission, parking fees and so on. The pass may be purchased at any park entrance area or online (www.nps.gov). Most parks have information centers equipped with trail maps and informative literature on park facilities and activities. Contact the following agencies for further information:

Sunset Crater Volcano National Monument

© Gwen Cannor/Michelin

Federal Lands
◆ **US Department of the Interior Bureau of Land Management.** www.blm.gov

Wildlife Refuges
◆ **US Fish and Wildlife Service.** www.fws.gov

National Forests
◆ **US Department of Agriculture Forest Service**, National Headquarters, 1400 Independence Ave., Washington DC 20250. ℘202-205-1680. www.fs.fed.us

National Parks
◆ **US Department of the Interior National Park Service**, Office of Public Inquiries, 1849 C St. NW Washington DC 20240. ℘202-208-6843. www.nps.gov

State Park Divisons
◆ **Alaska Division of Parks & Outdoor Recreation.** ℘907-269-8400. www.dnr.alaska.gov/parks.
◆ **Arizona State Parks.** ℘602-542-4174 or 800-285-3703. www.pr.state.az.us.
◆ **California Dept of Parks & Recreation.** ℘916-653-6995 or 800-777-0369. www.parks.ca.gov.
◆ **Colorado Parks.** ℘303-297-1192. www.parks.state.co.us.
◆ **Hawaii Division of State Parks.** ℘808-587-0300. www.hawaiistateparks.org.
◆ **Idaho State Parks & Recreation Department.** ℘208-334-4199. http://parksandrecreation.idaho.gov.
◆ **Kansas Dept of Wildlife & Parks.** ℘620-672-5911. www.kdwpt.state.ks.us.
◆ **Montana Parks Division.** ℘406-444-2535. http://fwp.mt.gov.
◆ **Nebraska Game & Parks Commission.** ℘402-471-0641. http://outdoornebraska.ne.gov
◆ **Nevada State Parks.** ℘775-684-2770. http://parks.nv.gov.
◆ **New Mexico State Parks Division.** ℘505-476-3355 or 888-667-2757. www.emnrd.state.nm.us/spd.

• **North Dakota Parks & Recreation Department.** ☎701-328-5357. www.parkrec.nd.gov.

• **Oklahoma Parks Division.** ☎405-521-3411. www.travelok.com/state_parks.

• **Oregon State Parks & Recreation Department.** ☎503-986-0707 or 800-551-6949. www.oregonstateparks.org.

• **South Dakota Park & Recreation Division.** ☎605-773-3391. gfp.sd.gov.

• **Texas Parks & Wildlife Department.** ☎512-389-4800 or 800-792-1112. www.tpwd.state.tx.us.

• **Utah Parks & Recreation Division.** ☎801-538-7220. http://stateparks.utah.gov.

• **Washington State Parks & Recreation Commission.** ☎360-902-8844. www.parks.wa.gov.

• **Wyoming Division of State Parks & Historic Sites.** ☎307-777-6323. http://wyoparks.state.wy.us.

Historic and Scenic Trails

The National Park Service, US Forest Service and Bureau of Land Management administer national scenic and national historic trails in the US. Some are for hikers, others (historic) for car travelers. For information, obtain the *National Trails System Map and Guide* ($3) from the federal publications office (http://publications.usa..gov); download it at www.nps.gov; or contact agencies listed below.

Continental Divide National Scenic Trail

• Mountain trail for wilderness hikers, 3,000 miles from New Mexico to the Canadian border. **Continental Divide Trail Society, www.cdtsociety.org; or Continental Divide Trail Coalition,** ☎720-340-2382. www.continentaldividetrail.org.t

Juan Bautista de Anza National Historic Trail

• Spanish pioneer explorer led 240 settlers from southern Arizona to San Francisco Bay in 1775-76. ☎415-623-2344. www.nps.gov/juba.

Lewis and Clark National Historic Trail

• Thomas Jefferson sent Meriwether Lewis and William Clark west to explore the newly-purchased Louisiana Territory from 1804-1806; they were the first Americans to cross the continent. **Lewis and Clark Trail Heritage Foundation,** ☎406-454-1234. www.lewisandclark.org.

Mormon Pioneer National Historic Trail

• Brigham Young led the first band of Mormons 1,300 miles from Illinois to Utah to escape persecution in 1846; eventually 70,000 Mormons used the route. ☎801-741-1012. www.nps.gov/mopi.

Nez Perce (Nee-Me-Poo) National Historic Trail

• Chief Joseph led his Nez Perce tribe members on a 1,170-mile trek from Eastern Oregon to Montana in a failed attempt to escape to Canada. ☎208-476-8334. www.fs.usda.gov/npnht.

Oregon National Historic Trail

• More than 400,000 pioneers emigrated westward along the Oregon Trail between 1842 and 1870. ☎801-741-1012. www.nps.gov/oreg.

Pacific Crest National Scenic Trail

• Mountain trail for wilderness hikers, 2,650 miles through California, Oregon and Washington. **Pacific Crest Trail Association,** ☎916-285-1846. www.pcta.org.

Santa Fe National Historic Trail

• The Santa Fe Trail was an early 19C route from Spanish New Mexico to the young United States. Santa Fe Trail Assn., ☎620-285-2054. www.santafetrail.org.

Trail of Tears National Historic Trail

• Historic route tracing the Cherokee people's banishment from North Carolina to Oklahoma. National Park Service, ☎505-988-6888. www.nps.gov/trte.

Spectator Sports

See listings below.
Tickets can be purchased online, at the individual venue or via the local
Ticketmaster office (www.ticketmaster.com).

BASEBALL	APR–OCT	
MLB (Major League Baseball) www.mlb.com		
TEAM	**VENUE**	✆
Anaheim Angels	Edison International Field	714-634-2000
Arizona Diamondbacks	Bank One Ballpark, Phoenix	602-514-8400
Colorado Rockies	Coors Field, Denver	800-388-7625
Houston Astros	Minute Maid Park	713-259-8000
Kansas City Royals	Kauffman Stadium	816-921-8000
Los Angeles Dodgers	Dodger Stadium	323-224-1448
Oakland Athletics	Network Associates Coliseum	510-762-2255
San Diego Padres	Qualcomm Stadium	619-881-6500
San Francisco Giants	Pacific Bell Park	415-972-2000
Seattle Mariners	Safeco Field	206-346-4001
Texas Rangers	The Ballpark in Arlington	817-273-5222

BASKETBALL	OCT–APR	
NBA (National Basketball Association) www.nba.com		
TEAM	**VENUE**	✆
Dallas Mavericks	American Airlines Center	877-316-3553
Denver Nuggets	Pepsi Center	303-405-1212
Golden State Warriors	Arena in Oakland	510-986-2200
Houston Rockets	Compaq Center	713-627-3865
Los Angeles Clippers	Staples Center	213-742-7500
Los Angeles Lakers	Staples Center	213-480-3232
Phoenix Suns	America West Arena	602-379-7867
Portland Trail Blazers	Rose Garden	503-231-8000
Sacramento Kings	ARCO Arena	916-928-6900
San Antonia Spurs	TSBC Center	210-554-7773
Seattle SuperSonics	KeyArena	206-281-5800
Utah Jazz	The Delta Center, Salt Lake City	801-355-3865

FOOTBALL	SEPT–JAN	
NFL (National Football League) www.nfl.com		
TEAM	**VENUE**	✆
Arizona Cardinals	Sun Devil Stadium, Tempe	602-379-0102
Dallas Cowboys	Texas Stadium	972-785-4800
Denver Broncos	Mile High Stadium	720-258-3333
Kansas City Chiefs	Arrowhead Stadium	816-920-9300
Oakland Raiders	Network Associates Coliseum	800-225-2277
San Diego Chargers	Qualcomm Stadium	619-220-8497
San Francisco 49ers	3Com Park	415-656-4900
Seattle Seahawks	Seahawks Stadium	888-635-4295

HOCKEY	OCT–APR	
NHL (National Hockey League) www.nhl.com		
TEAM	**VENUE**	✆
Colorado Avalanche	Pepsi Center, Denver	303-405-1111
Dallas Stars	American Airlines Center	214-467-8277
Los Angeles Kings	Staples Center	888-546-4752
Mighty Ducks of Anaheim	Arrowhead Pond	714-703-2545
Phoenix Coyotes	America West Arena	480-563-7825
San Jose Sharks	Compaq Center	408-287-9200

Entertainment

The best source for entertainment, nightlife and events listings is the local newspapers in each city. Daily papers focus on mainstream offerings, while weekly papers include more offbeat and unorthodox arts and culture. Each paper maintains a website, though some require free registration by users for unlimited access. Consult each area's official visitor information website for names of local papers and their websites. The most comprehensive events listings covering the US are available at www.citysearch.com.

The West's most notable symphony orchestras are in Dallas, Houston, Los Angeles, San Francisco and Seattle. Opera companies of international renown are in Houston, San Francisco, Santa Fe (summer only) and Seattle (globally famed for its triennial Ring Cycle). Austin, San Francisco, and Seattle are famous live-music locales; Portland is a national center for blues and jazz, as is Kansas City.
Here is a selection of popular venues in the West:

Ahmanson Theatre, 135 N. Grand Ave. Los Angeles, CA
American Conservatory Theater 405 Geary St., San Francisco, CA
The Old Globe, 1363 Old Globe Way, San Diego, CA
Chandler Center for the Arts, 250 N. Arizona Ave., Chandler, AZ
Sarofim Hall, The Hobby Center, 800 Bagby St., Houston, TX
Winspear Opera House, AT&T Performing Arts Center, 2403 Flora St., Dallas, TX

Sightseeing & Tours

NATIONAL AND CITY TOURS

Several national tour companies provide all-inclusive packages for motorcoach tours of the US (🕭 see opposite). The scope of tours may vary among tour operators, but most offer packages of varying length, geographic coverage and cost.

TrekAmerica (🕾973-983-1144 or 800-221-0596; www.trekamerica.com) caters to travelers who prefer small groups, varied sightseeing/sporting activities and flexible itineraries. For those interested in more educational offerings, **Smithsonian Study Tours**, sponsored by the Smithsonian Institution, offer single- and multi-day thematic tour programs covering topics such as architecture, history, the performing arts and cuisine. Educators specializing in related fields lead tours. For more information: 🕾202-633-6088 or 855-330-1542; wwwsmithsonian journey.org.

CityPass is a discount admission scheme that provides entry to top attractions in Seattle, San Francisco, Southern California and Houston; visit www.citypass.com.

Information on **city tours** can be obtained from convention and visitors bureaus in most large US cities. **Gray Line Tours** provides half- and full-day sightseeing motorcoach tours for more than 70 cities: Gray Line Worldwide (🕾303-433-9800 or 800-472-9546, www.grayline.com).

NATIONAL TOUR COMPANIES

✦ **Globus and Cosmos**, Littleton, CO. 🕾877-245-6287. www.globusandcosmos.com.
✦ **Mayflower Tours**, Downers Grove, IL. 🕾800-323-7604. www.mayflowertours.com.
✦ **Tauck Tours**, Norwalk, CT. 🕾800-788-7885. www.tauck.com.
✦ **Trafalgar Tours**, New York City. 🕾866-513-1995. www.trafalgar.com.

Activities for Kids

Sights of particular interest to children are indicated with a 👫 symbol. Many of these attractions offer special children's programs. Most offer discounted (if not free) admission to visitors under 12 years of age. In addition, many hotels, airlines and theme parks offer family packages that often include free or steeply discounted travel for children. Most restaurants have a children's menu.

Books

Cannery Row (1945), *The Grapes of Wrath* (1939), *East of Eden* (1952).
John Steinbeck. These three novels portray the West in terms so real and human that they won Steinbeck a Nobel Prize.

The Way West (1949).
A.B. Guthrie. A Pulitzer-prize novel about the Oregon Trail.

The Man Who Walked through Time (1968).
Colin Fletcher. A journey through the Grand Canyon on foot.

Bury My Heart at Wounded Knee: An Indian History of the American West (1970).
Dee Brown. Best-seller documenting the Cheyenne, Dakota, Sioux and

other tribes' views of the massacres by, and broken treaties of, whites.

Western Forests; Pacific Coast (1985). Audubon Society. These books are the best natural history guides to the West's nature and wildlife.

The Good Rain (1990). Timothy Egan. The New York Times Northwest correspondent explains the delicate ecology of the Northwest.

Lonesome Dove (1985). Larry McMurtry. Widely considered the best fictional depiction of the cattle drive era.

Undaunted Courage (1996). Stephen Ambrose. Prize-winning story of the Lewis & Clark expedition.

Great Plains (2001). Ian Frazier. A humane modern look at the vast high plains of the West.

I Feel Earthquakes More Often Than They Happen (2006). Amy Wilentz. A transplanted New Yorker looks at life in California in the 21C.

Walt Disney: Triumph of the American Imagination (2006). Neal Gabler. A complete and even-handed look at the pioneer who created two key Disneyland and animated film.

Films

Shane (1953), George Stevens.
The Ballad of Little Jo (1993), Maggie Greenwald.
Set amid incomparable mountain scenery, the tale of gunfighter Shane's epiphany is a Western classic. By contrast, Little Jo, the fact-based story of a woman pioneer who masqueraded as a man, is a "stinging rebuke to the Hollywood myth of the Old West," in the words of one critic.

North by Northwest (1959), Alfred Hitchcock.
Famed director Alfred Hitchcock's thriller starring Cary Grant includes an unforgettable chase by a crop-dusting plane and a scuffle atop Mt. Rushmore.

Cheyenne Autumn (1964), John Ford.
Ford's elegaic portrait of the tragedy of the Cheyenne is one of the earliest films to consider the Indian perspective.

The Endless Summer (1966), Bruce Brown.
Filmmaker and surfer Bruce Brown initiated global surfing travel with his watershed film about the quest of two native Californians to find the perfect wave in Hawaii, Australia and elsewhere.

High Plains Drifter (1971),
Unforgiven (1992) Clint Eastwood.
The iconic star's earliest directorial effort and his two-decades-later Oscar winner both offer an unvarnished looks at the classic Western theme of vengeance.

Chinatown (1974), Roman Polanski,
Quinceanera (2006), Richard Glatzer and Wash Westmoreland.
Polanski's classic film focuses on the water-grab that created Los Angeles; *Quinceanera* portrays the multicultural diversity of Los Angeles today.

Lonesome Dove (1989), Simon Wincer.
Starring Robert Duvall and Tommy Lee Jones.
The TV series adaptation of Larry McMurtry's book is the quintessential depiction of a Western cattle drive, in this case, all the way from Texas to Montana.

The Descendants (2011), Alexander Payne.
George Clooney stars as a lawyer living in Honolulu who must deal with challenges in his family life and as trustee for a sizable tract of pristine land in Kauai, Hawaii, ripe for development. Film was shot in Honolulu and Kauai.

Festivals & Events

For information about these events, access the official tourism office of the city shown.

SPRING

MARCH

Academy Awards, Los Angeles CA
Pole, Pedal, Paddle Triathlon; Jackson Hole WY
Mariachi Conference, Tucson AZ
Mar or Apr: Easter Pageant, Phoenix AZ

APRIL

Houston International Festival, Houston TX
Azalea Festival, Muskogee OK
Merrie Monarch Hula Festival, Hilo HI
Cowboy Festival, Santa Clarita CA
International Wildlife Film Festival, Missoula MT
Toyota Grand Prix, Long Beach CA
Fiesta San Antonio, San Antonio TX
Fiesta Broadway, Los Angeles CA
Doo Dah Parade, Pasadena CA
Newport-Ensenada Yacht Race, Newport Beach CA

LATE APRIL–EARLY MAY

Buccaneer Days, Corpus Christi TX
Orange Blossom Festival, Riverside CA
Cherry Blossom Festival, San Francisco CA
Apple Blossom Festival, Wenatchee WA
Ramona Pageant, Hemet CA

MAY

Molokai ka Hula Piko, Molokai HI
Helldorado Days, Las Vegas NV

1 MAY

Lei Day, Honolulu HI

5 MAY

Cinco de Mayo, cities throughout the West
Art Car Parade, Houston TX
Mayfest, Fort Worth TX
California Strawberry Festival, Oxnard CA
Tejano Conjunto Festival, San Antonio TX

Kerrville Folk Festival, Kerrville TX
Bay to Breakers Foot Race, San Francisco CA
Calaveras County Fair & Jumping Frog Jubilee, Angels Camp CA
Elkfest and Antler Auction, Jackson WY

LATE MAY

CityArts Festival, Dallas TX
Fine Arts Festival, Austin TX
Carnaval, San Francisco CA
Spring Arts Festival, Santa Fe NM
Sacramento Music Festival, Sacramento CA
Northwest Folklife Festival, Seattle WA

JUNE

Seattle International Film Festival, Seattle WA
King Kamehameha Day, all islands HI
Portland Rose Festival, Portland OR
Mormon Miracle Pageant, Manti UT
Red Earth Native American Cultural Festival, Oklahoma City OK

MID JUN

Juneteenth African-American Festivals, major cities
Telluride Bluegrass Festival, Telluride CO
Smoky Hill River Festival, Salina KS
Cannon Beach Sand Castle Contest, Cannon Beach OR
La Jolla Festival of the Arts & Food Faire, La Jolla CA

SUMMER

JUNE

Medora Musical, Medora ND
Aspen Music Festival and School, Aspen CO
Cody Nite Rodeo, Cody WY
Jun–early Sept
The Britt Festivals, Jacksonville OR

LATE JUNE

Summer Solstice Celebration, Fairbanks AK
Fremont Solstice Festival, Seattle WA
Little Big Horn Days, Hardin MT
Lewis & Clark Festival, Great Falls MT

Lesbian/Gay/Bisexual/Transgender Pride Celebration, San Francisco CA, Seattle WA

LATE JUN–EARLY AUG
Central City Opera, Central City CO

LATE JUN–LATE AUG
Santa Fe Opera, Santa Fe NM

LATE JUN–EARLY SEPT
Utah Shakespeare Festival, Cedar City UT

JULY

Cherry Creek Arts Festival, Denver CO
Days of '47, Salt Lake City UT
Taos Pueblo Powwow, Taos NM
Green River Rendezvous, Pinedale WY

4 JULY
Independence Day Celebrations, every city and town
Independence Day Fireworks, Mt. Rushmore SD
Pikes Peak International Hill Climb, Manitou Springs CO
North American Indian Days, Browning MT

MID JUL
Cable Car Bell-Ringing Competition, San Francisco CA
California Rodeo, Salinas CA
International Climbers Festival, Lander WY

MID JUL
Cheyenne Frontier Days Rodeo, Cheyenne WY

LATE JULY
World Eskimo-Indian Olympics, Fairbanks AK
Days of '76, Deadwood SD
Last Chance Stampede, Helena MT
US Open Surfing Championships, Huntington Beach CA
Oregon Brewers Festival, Portland OR
Gilroy Garlic Festival, Gilroy CA
Spanish Market, Santa Fe NM

24 JULY
Pioneer Day, Utah

JUL–AUG
Colorado Music Festival, Boulder CO
Flagstaff Festival of the Arts, Flagstaff AZ
Festival of Arts & Pageant of the Masters, Laguna Beach CA
Grand Teton Music Festival, Jackson WY

MID JUL–MID AUG
Seafair Festival, Seattle WA

AUGUST

Hawaiian International Billfish Tournament, Kailua-Kona HI
World's Oldest Continuous Rodeo, Prescott AZ
Texas Folklife Festival, San Antonio TX

EARLY AUGUST
Sturgis Rally and Races, Sturgis SD
Festival of the Arts, Bigfork MT
Old Spanish Days, Santa Barbara CA
Park City Kimball Arts Festival, Park City UT

JUNE: Portland Rose Festival, Portland, Oregon

Courtesy the Portland Rose Festival Foundation

Steinbeck Festival, Salinas CA
Hot August Nights, Reno NV
Cabrillo Festival of Contemporary Music, San Diego CA
Burning Man, Black Rock Desert (near Reno) NV

EARLY–MID AUG
Inter-Tribal Indian Ceremonial, Gallup NM

MID AUG
Indian Market, Santa Fe NM

MID AUG–MID OCT
State Fairs, every state

LATE AUG
World Body Surfing Championships, Oceanside CA

SEPTEMBER

Grand Canyon Music Festival, South Rim, Grand Canyon AZ
Cherokee National Holiday, Tahlequah OK
Fleet Week, San Diego CA
Moab Music Festival, Moab UT

EARLY SEPT
Fiesta de las Flores, El Paso TX
A Taste of Colorado, Denver CO
All-American Futurity Race, Ruidoso NM
Chokecherry Festival, Lewistown MT
Sausalito Art Festival, Sausalito CA
La Fiesta de Santa Fe, Santa Fe NM
Bumbershoot, Seattle WA
Virginia City International Camel Races, Virginia City NV

MID SEPT
Mexican Independence Day, cities near Mexican border
Navajo Nation Fair, Window Rock AZ
Fiestas Patrias, Houston TX
Pendleton Round-Up, Pendleton OR
United Tribes International Pow Wow, Bismarck ND
San Francisco Blues Festival, San Francisco CA
Monterey Jazz Festival, Monterey CA
Wooden Boat Festival, Port Townsend WA
National Championship Air Races, Reno NV
Jackson Hole Fall Arts Festival, Jackson WA

FALL

LATE SEPT
Elk Fest, Estes Park CO
River City Roundup & Rodeo, Omaha NE

SEPT–OCT
Aloha Festival, all islands HI

LATE SEPT–EARLY OCT
Taos Fall Arts Festival, Taos NM

LATE SEPT–MID OCT
State Fair of Texas, Dallas TX

OCTOBER

Albuquerque International Balloon Fiesta, Albuquerque NM
Oklahoma International Bluegrass Festival, Guthrie OK
Oktoberfest, Fredericksburg TX

MID OCT
Alaska Day Festival, Sitka AK
Ho-Down Mountain Bike Festival, Moab UT
Helldorado Days, Tombstone AZ

LATE OCT
Ironman World Championship, Big Island HI

31 OCT
Halloween, most cities and towns

NOVEMBER

Texas BBQ Festival, Austin
Kona Coffee Festival, Kailua-Kona HI
Death Valley Fall Festival & '49er Encampment, Furnace Creek CA
Wurstfest, New Braunfels TX

LATE NOV

NOV–DEC
Hollywood Christmas Parade, Hollywood CA
Triple Crown of Surfing, North Shore, Oahu HI

LATE NOV–MID DEC
Feria de Santa Cecilia, San Antonio TX

LATE NOV–EARLY JAN
Red Rock Fantasy of Lights, Sedona AZ

EARLY DEC
Bachelor Society Ball & Wilderness Women Contest, Talkeetna AK
National Finals Rodeo, Las Vegas NV

WINTER

DECEMBER
Christmas celebrations, every city and town
Na Mele o Maui, Maui HI
Festival of Lights at the Grotto, Portland OR
Fiesta Bowl Events, Phoenix AZ
Yuletide in Taos, Taos NM

MID DEC
Our Lady of Guadalupe Fiesta, Las Cruces NM
Christmas Boat Parade, Seattle WA, Newport Beach CA

16-24 DEC
Las Posadas, Los Angeles CA

JANUARY
Sundance Film Festival, Park City UT
Seattle International Boat Show, Seattle WA

1 JAN
Tournament of Roses, Pasadena CA

MID JAN:
Winterskol, Aspen CO
National Western Stock Show and Rodeo, Denver CO

LATE JAN–FEB
Chinese New Year Festival, Asian communities (especially CA & HI)
Cowboy Poetry Gathering, Elko NV

FEBRUARY
Flagstaff Winterfest, Flagstaff AZ
Mardi Gras! Galveston, Galveston TX
San Antonio Stock Show and Rodeo, San Antonio TX

EARLY FEB
Winter Carnival, Steamboat Springs CO
Whitefish Winter Carnival, Whitefish MT

MID FEB
Gem and Mineral Show, Tucson AZ
Whale Festival, Maui HI
An Affair of the Heart, Oklahoma City OK

LATE FEB
Fur Rendezvous, Anchorage AK
World Ice Art Championship Fairbanks AK

OCTOBER: Albuquerque International Balloon Festival, New Mexico

©iStockphoto.com/Karen Gentry

National Date Festival, Indio CA
La Fiesta de los Vaqueros, Tucson AZ
Newport Seafood & Wine Festival, Newport OR

LATE FEB–END OCT
Oregon Shakespeare Festival, Ashland OR

MARCH
EARLY MAR
Festival of Whales, Dana Point CA
Iditarod Trail Sled Dog Race, Anchorage to Nome AK
Snowfest, Tahoe City CA

MID MAR
Western Art Week, Great Falls MT
Honolulu Festival, Honolulu HI
Scottsdale Arts Festival, Scottsdale AZ

17 MAR
St. Patrick's Day, many cities

19 MAR
Return of the Swallows, San Juan Capistrano CA

Practical Info

TOP TIPS

Best time to go: Early autumn, or if snowbelt areas, summer.

Best way around: Personal vehicle or rental car, for the most freedom.

Best for sightseeing: Avoid Mondays, when restaurants may be closed.

Most authentic accommodation: Guest ranches, lodges, and spa resorts.

Need to know: Road regulations, if driving, and the weather forecast.

Need to taste: Game (buffalo, venison, elk), sockeye salmon, BBQ brisket, fajitas.

CITY	JANUARY			JUNE		
	avg. high °F / °C	avg. low °F / °C	precip. in. / cen.	avg. high °F / °C	avg. low °F / °C	precip. in. / cen.
ALBUQUERQUE NM	47 / 8	22 / –6	0.4 / 1.1	90 / 32	58 / 14	0.6 / 1.5
ANCHORAGE AK	21 / –6	8 / –13	0.8 / 2.0	62 / 17	47 / 8	1.1 / 2.9
ASPEN CO	32 / 0	0 / –18	1.3 / 3.2	72 / 22	34 / 1	1.4 / 3.4
BILLINGS MT	32 / 0	14 / –10	0.9 / 2.3	78 / 26	52 / 11	2.0 / 5.1
BOISE ID	36 / 2	22 / –6	1.5 / 3.7	81 / 27	52 / 11	0.8 / 2.1
DALLAS TX	54 / 12	33 / 1	1.8 / 4.6	92 / 33	70 / 21	3.0 / 7.6
DENVER CO	43 / 6	16 / -9	0.5 / 1.3	81 / 27	52 / 11	1.8 / 4.5
EL PASO TX	56 / 13	29 / -2	0.4 / 1.0	97 / 36	64 / 18	0.7 / 1.7
GRAND CANYON AZ	42 / 5	18 / –8	1.4 / 3.7	78 / 27	45 / 7	0.5 / 1.3
HONOLULU HI	80 / 27	66 / 19	3.6 / 9.0	87 / 31	72 / 22	0.5 / 1.3
HOUSTON TX	61 / 16	40 / 4	3.3 / 8.4	90 / 32	71 / 22	5.0 / 12.6
KANSAS CITY MO	35 / 2	17 / –8	1.1 / 2.8	83 / 28	63 / 17	4.7 / 12.0
LAS VEGAS NV	57 / 14	34 / 1	0.5 / 1.2	100 / 38	69 / 21	0.1 / 0.3
LOS ANGELES CA	66 / 19	48 / 9	2.4 / 6.1	72 / 22	60 / 16	0.0 / 0.1
MOAB UT	42 / 6	18 / –8	0.6 / 1.4	93 / 34	50 / 14	0.4 / 1.1
OKLAHOMA CITY OK	47 / 8	25 / -4	1.1 / 2.9	87 / 31	66 / 19	4.3 / 10.9
OMAHA NE	31 / -1	11 / -12	0.7 / 1.9	84 / 29	60 / 16	3.9 / 9.8
PHOENIX AZ	66 / 19	41 / 5	0.7 / 1.7	104 / 40	73 / 23	0.1 / 0.3

CITY	JANUARY			JUNE		
	avg. high °F / °C	avg. low °F / °C	precip. in. / cen.	avg. high °F / °C	avg. low °F / °C	precip. in. / cen.
PORTLAND OR	45 / 7	34 / 1	5.4 / 13.6	74 / 23	53 / 12	1.5 / 3.8
RAPID CITY SD	34 / 1	11 / -12	0.4 / 1.0	78 / 26	52 / 11	3.1 / 7.8
RENO NV	45 / 7	21 / -6	1.1 / 2.7	83 / 28	47 / 8	0.5 / 1.2
SACRAMENTO CA	53 / 12	38 / 3	3.7 / 9.5	88 / 31	55 / 13	0.1 / 0.3
SALT LAKE CITY UT	36 / 2	19 / -7	1.1 / 2.8	83 / 28	55 / 13	0.9 / 2.4
SAN ANTONIO TX	61 / 16	38 / 3	1.7 / 4.3	92 / 33	73 / 23	3.8 / 9.7
SAN DIEGO CA	66 / 19	49 / 9	1.8 / 4.6	72 / 22	62 / 17	0.1 / 0.2
SAN FRANCISCO CA	56 / 13	42 / 6	4.4 / 11.0	70 / 21	53 / 12	0.1 / 0.3
SANTA FE NM	47 / 8	14 / -10	1.1 / 2.8	82 / 28	47 / 9	4.4 / 11.1
SEATTLE WA	45 /7	35 / 2	5.4 / 13.7	70 / 21	52 / 11	1.5 / 3.8
TUCSON AZ	64 / 18	39 / 4	0.9 / 2.4	100 / 38	68 / 20	0.2 / 0.6
WEST GLACIER MT	29 / -2	15 / -10	3.4 / 8.6	72 / 22	44 / 7	3.4 / 8.6

Before You Go

WHEN TO GO

The diversity of **California's** geography promotes dramatic variations in climate. Although coastal areas are subject to relatively little variation in seasonal temperatures, these tend to increase with distance from the coast, and drop as elevation increases. Most rain falls between October and April. In San Diego, **winter** temperatures range from 60-70°F; summer temperatures average only 5-10°F more. The Los Angeles basin remains warm and pleasant year-round, while inland areas are hot and hazy during the summer and fall. Average temperatures are 45-65°F in winter and 60-75°F in **summer**. San Francisco Bay Area weather can change suddenly in a single day, from warm and sunny to foggy and chilly. Thick **fog** is particularly common in summer, and the same is true along the coast from Santa Barbara to Oregon.

Inland cities are warmer, sometimes with hot summer temperatures. Average temperatures are 40-55°F in winter and 55-70°F in summer.

West of the Cascade Range, the **Pacific Northwest** experiences very wet winters with strong winds and extensive cloud cover that promotes mild temperatures—40-50°F. Summers are usually sunny and rather comfortable with occasional heat waves reaching 90°F. The interior of the region is colder and drier in winter, hotter in summer. **Southwest** winters produce mild days and cold nights with daytime temperatures typically in the 40s on the Colorado Plateau, and 70s in the Sonoran Desert. Heavy **snows** fall in the mountain areas. Mild winter days give way to long summer days of bright sunshine and hot temperatures that exceed 100°F. In May summers start out dry with little rain, but by mid-July the humidity increases, and the area receives many thunderstorms as summer progresses. Despite this rainfall, temperatures remain hot. Winters in the **Rocky Mountain states** usually include large amounts of snow, and temperatures fluctuate between extreme cold to milder days depending on air currents. In summer, with temperatures around 90°F, days are warm while the nights are cool, with temperatures between 40-50°F. Thunderstorms and hail are common in the summer months. Conditions are similar in the **Northern Great Plains**. In the **Central and Southern Plains**, winters fluctuate between warm, pleasant weather and bitterly cold periods that bring snow and ice. Summers can be similarly unpredictable, often with severe thunderstorms and strong winds. In Alaska, May and early June often bring the best summer weather; widespread rains return by mid-August.

For **Northern Lights** viewing and seeing Denali, March is often the ideal month—daylight is nearing 12 hours, the weather is generally fair and not as cold as deep winter, and snow sports are at their best. Throughout the West, April ,May, September and October, are generally delightful months. The exception is the extreme southern part of the region, from Houston to Las Vegas, where unpleasant heat can occur in those months. Summer travelers to Texas, New Mexico, Arizona and inland California may experience the perverse discomfort of being cold indoors, where excessive **air conditioning** is common. Residents of these areas often bring sweaters to restaurants and other public facilities. *Current weather conditions are online: www.weather.com or www.cnn.com/weather.*

USEFUL WEBSITES
Air Travel
www.orbitz.com; www.travelo city.com; www.expedia.com. Most of the time, US airlines attempt to match the fares available on the search engine sites. Fare-tracking sites include **www.kayak.com; www.bing/travel.com** offers predictions on whether future fares will rise or fall.

Conservation
The Sierra Club is the leading environmental advocacy organization (**www.sierraclub.org**). The Nature Conservancy owns hundreds of private land preserves in the West (www.nature.org). Both organizations sponsor trips and tours.

Dining Out
Lots of recommendations for the big cities can be found in the red-cover *Michelin Guide San Francisco*, the *Michelin Guide Los Angeles* and the *Michelin Guide Las Vegas* plus the ADDRESSES of the *Green Guide California* as well as Michelin Must Sees guides for Hawaiian Islands, Alaska, Arizona and Pacific Northwest.

History
The best source for comprehensive, thoughtful information on Western history is **www.pbs.org**.

Ski Conditions
The two key sites to track ski conditions, updated each morning, are www.onthesnow.com and **www.snocountry.com**.

Western Politics and Culture
High Country News is a highly regarded, independent observer of the West (**www.hcn.org**). The website **www.newwest.net** covers the North part of the Intermountain West, from Bend OR to Boulder CO.

Wine Travel
A private site devoted to wine regions from California to Washington state is **www.winecountry.com**. Oregon's Willamette Valley is covered by **www.oregonwinecountry.org**. In Washington state, consult **www.winecountrywashington.org**.

Searching Searches
www.dogpile.com attempts to catalog search engines of every description – travel, dining, accommodations, and so on.

TOURISM OFFICES

In addition to state and regional tourism offices, visitors from outside the US may obtain information from the nearest US embassy or consulate in their country of residence (see list below). For a complete list of American consulates and embassies abroad, see the US State Department Bureau of Consular Affairs listing on the Internet at http://travel.state.gov.

US Embassies and Consulates

In addition to tourism offices, visitors from outside the US may obtain information from the nearest **US embassy or consulate** in their country of residence (&see details below). For a complete list of American consulates and embassies abroad, access the US State Department on the Internet at: www.usembassy.gov.

- ◆ **Australia**
  Moonah Place, Yarralumla ACT 2600
  ☎02 6214 5600
- ◆ **Belgium**
  27, boul. du Régent, B-1000 Brussels
  ☎(32-2) 811 4000
- ◆ **Canada**
  490 Sussex Drive, Ottawa, Ontario K1N 1G8,
  ☎613-688-5335 (US & Canada)
- ◆ **China**
  55 An Jia Lou Lu, Beijing 100600
  ☎(86-10) 8531 3000
- ◆ **France**
  2, av. Gabriel, 75382 Paris
  ☎01 43 12 22 22 / 01 48 60 57 15
  (Tourism information line)
- ◆ **Germany**
  Clayallee 170, 14191 Berlin
  ☎030 8305-0
- ◆ **Italy**
  Via Vittorio Veneto 121, 00187 Rome
  ☎06 4674 1
- ◆ **Japan**
  1-10-5 Akasaka, Minato-ku Tokyo
  107-8420, ☎81-3-3224-5000
- ◆ **Mexico**
  Paseo de la Reforma 305, Col. Cuauhtémoc, 06500 México, D.F.
  ☎55 5080-2000

- ◆ **Netherlands**
  Lange Voorhout 102, 2514 EJ The Hague, The Netherlands
  ☎70 310 2209
- ◆ **Spain**
  Calle Serrano 75, 28006 Madrid
  ☎91587 2200
- ◆ **Switzerland**
  Sulgeneckstrasse 19, CH-3007 Bern
  ☎31 357 7011
- ◆ **United Kingdom**
  24 Grosvenor Square, London W1K 6AH, ☎0 20 7499-9000

State Tourism Offices

State tourism offices (below) provide information and brochures on points of interest, seasonal events and accommodations, as well as road and city maps. Local tourist offices (telephone numbers and websites shown in infoboxes in Discovering section) provide additional information, free of charge, for accommodations, shopping, entertainment, festivals and recreation. Many countries have consular offices in major cities. Information centers are indicated on maps in this guide by the i symbol.

Alaska (AK)
Alaska Travel Industry Association. www.travelalaska.com.

Arizona (AZ)
Arizona Office of Tourism, Phoenix, AZ. ☎866-275-5816. . http://arizonaguide.com

California (CA)
California Divison of Tourism. ☎916-444-4429 or 877-225-4367. www.visitcalifornia.com.

Colorado (CO)
Colorado Travel and Tourism Office, Denver, CO. ☎800-265-6723. www.colorado.com.

Hawaii (HI)
Hawaii Visitors & Convention Bureau, 2270 Kalakaua Ave., Suite 801, Honolulu, HI 96815. ☎808-923-1811 or 800-464-2924. www.gohawaii.com.

Idaho (ID)

Idaho Division of Tourism, Boise, ID. ☎208-334-2470 or 800-847-4843. www.visitidaho.org.

Kansas (KS)

Kansas Travel and Tourism, Topeka, KS. ☎785-296-2009. www.travelks.com.

Montana (MT)

Montana Office of Tourism, , Helena, MT. ☎800-847-4868 or 406-841-2870. www.visitmt.com.

Nebraska (NE)

Nebraska Tourism Commission, Lincoln, NE. ☎888-444-1867. www.visitnebraska.com.

Nevada (NV)

Nevada Commission of Tourism, Carson City, NV. ☎800-638-2328. www.travelnevada.com.

New Mexico (NM)

New Mexico Department of Tourism, 491 Old Santa Fe Trail, Santa Fe, NM 87501. ☎505-827-7336. www.newmexico.org.

North Dakota (ND)

North Dakota Tourism Division, Bismarck, ND. ☎701-328-2525 or 800-435-5663. www.ndtourism.com.

Oklahoma (OK)

Oklahoma Tourism and Recreation, Oklahoma City, OK. ☎405-230-8400 or 800-652-6552. www.travelok.com.

Oregon (OR)

Oregon Tourism Commission, Salem OR. ☎503-378-8850 or 800-547-7842. www.traveloregon.com.

South Dakota (SD)

South Dakota Department of Tourism, Pierre, SD. ☎605-773-3301. www.travelsd.com.

Texas (TX)

Texas Department of Economic Development, Tourism Division, Austin, TX. ☎512-936-0101 or 800-452-9292. www.traveltex.com.

Utah (UT)

Utah Office of Tourism, Salt Lake City, UT. ☎800-200-1160. www.utah.com.

Washington (WA)

Washington Tourism Alliance, www.experiencewa.com.

Wyoming (WY)

Wyoming Travel & Tourism, Cheyenne, WY. ☎307-777-7777 or 800-225-5996. www.wyomingtourism.org.

INTERNATIONAL VISITORS
Documents

All foreign visitors to the US must present a valid machine-readable **passport** for entry into the country. Citizens of countries participating in the Visa Waiver Pilot Program (VWPP) are not required to obtain a visa to enter the US for visits of fewer than 90 days. They will be required to furnish a current passport, round-trip ticket and the customs form distributed in the airplane.

New rules require that residents of visa-waiver countries must apply ahead for travel authorization online through the **ESTA program** (www.cbp.gov/esta). Travelers may apply any time ahead of their travel; at least three days before departure is strongly recommended. Beware private sites charging extravagant fees, such as "www.esta.us"—though they look official, these are not affiliated with the US government. **Citizens** of countries not participating in the VWPP must have a visitor's visa. For visa inquiries and applications, contact the nearest US embassy or consulate, or visit the US State Department Visa Services Internet site: travel.state.gov/visa.

Customs

All articles brought into the US must be declared at time of entry. The following items are exempt from customs regulations: personal effects; one liter of alcoholic beverages (providing visitor is at least 21 years old); either 200 cigarettes, 50 cigars (additional 100 possible under gift exemption) or 2 kilograms of smoking tobacco; and gifts (to persons in the US) not exceeding $100 in value. Prohibited items include firearms and ammunition (if not intended for legitimate sporting purposes); plant materials, and meat or poultry products. For other prohibited items, exemptions and information, contact a US embassy or consulate, or the **US Customs Traveler Information** page on the Internet (www.customs.gov/travel) or call ✆703-526-4200.

Health
The US does not have a national health program that covers foreign nationals; doctors' visits and hospitalization costs may seem high to most visitors. Check with your insurance company to determine if your medical insurance covers doctors' visits, medication and hospitalization in the US. If not, it is strongly recommended that you purchase a travel-insurance plan before departing. Prescription drugs should be properly identified and include a copy of the prescription.

Senior Citizens
Many hotels, attractions and restaurants offer discounts to visitors age 62 or older (proof of age may be required). Discounts and additional information are available to members of AARP, (✆202-434-3525 or 888-687-2277; www.aarp.org), which is open to people over 50.

♿ ACCESSIBILITY
Full wheelchair access to sights described in this guide is indicated in admission information by ♿. Federal law requires that existing businesses (including hotels and restaurants) increase accessibility and provide specially designed accommodations for the disabled. It also requires that wheelchair access, devices for the hearing impaired, and designated parking spaces be available at newly constructed hotels and restaurants. Many public buses are equipped with wheelchair lifts; many hotels have rooms designed for visitors with special needs. All national and most state **parks** have restrooms and other facilities for the disabled (such as wheelchair-accessible nature trails). Permanently disabled US citizens are eligible for a free **US National Parks and Federal Recreational Lands Pass** (see pxxx), which entitles the carrier to free admission to all national parks and a 50 percent discount on user fees (campsites, boat launches). The pass is available at any national-park entrance fee area with proper proof of disability. For details, contact the National Park Service, Office of Public Inquiries, (✆202-208-3818, www.nps.gov). For information about travel for individuals or groups, and general advice, contact the **Society for Accessible Travel & Hospitality** (✆212-447-7284; www.sath.org).

Travel by Train
Train passengers who will need assistance should give 24hrs advance notice. Making reservations via phone is preferable to booking on-line since passenger's special needs can be noted on reservation by booking agent. The annual publication Access Amtrak providing detailed information on Amtrak's services for disabled travelers is available upon request (✆800-872-7245 and 800-523-6590 TDD) or may be viewed on Amtrak's website (www.amtrak.com).

Travel by Bus
Disabled travelers are encouraged to notify Greyhound at least 48hrs in advance. Greyhound Travel Policies for customers with disabilities are available at www.greyhound.com, or by calling ✆800-752-4841; TDD 800-345-3109.

GETTING THERE AND GETTING AROUND
By Plane

Major US airlines serve most of the West's metropolitan areas. Airports with regular nonstop service to and from European cities include Denver, Dallas-Fort Worth, Houston, Las Vegas, Los Angeles, Phoenix, Portland, Salt Lake City, San Francisco, and Seattle.

Major Airports

Albuquerque NM
Albuquerque International Sunport (ABQ). ℘505-244-7700. www.cabq.gov/airport.

Anchorage AK
Ted Stevens Anchorage International Airport (ANC). ℘907-266-2526. www.dot.state.ak.us.

Billings MT
Billings Logan International Airport (BIL). ℘406-247-8609. www.flybillings.com.

Boise ID
Boise Airport (BOI). ℘208-383-3110. wwww.iflyboise.com.

Dallas/Ft. Worth TX
Dallas/Ft. Worth International Airport (DFW). ℘972-973-3112. www.dfwairport.com.

Denver CO
Denver International Airport (DEN). ℘303-342-2000. www.flydenver.com.

El Paso TX
El Paso International Airport (ELP). ℘915-780-4749. www.elpasointernational airport.com.

Honolulu HI
Honolulu International Airport (HNL). ℘808-836-6411. www.hawaii.gov/hnl.

Houston TX
Houston Intercontinental Airport (IAH). ℘281-233-3000. www.fly2houston.com.

Kansas City MO
Kansas City International Airport (MCI). ℘816-243-5237. www.flykci.com.

Las Vegas NV
Las Vegas McCarran International Airport (LAS). ℘702-261-5211. www.mccarran.com.

Los Angeles CA
Los Angeles International Airport (LAX). ℘310-646-5252. www.lawa.org.

Oklahoma City OK
Oklahoma City Will Rogers World Airport (OKC). ℘405-316-3271. www.flyokc.com.

Oakland CA
Oakland International Airport (OAK). ℘510-563-3300. www.flyoakland.com.

Phoenix AZ
Phoenix Sky Harbor International Airport (PHX). ℘602-273-3300. www.skyharbor.com.

Portland OR
Portland International Airport (PDX). ℘503-460-4234. www.flypdx.com.

Reno NV
Reno/Tahoe International Airport (RNO). ℘775-328-6750. www.renoairport.com.

Sacramento CA
Sacramento International Airport (SMF). ℘916-929-5411. www.sacairports.org.

Salt Lake City UT
Salt Lake City International Airport (SLC). ℘801-575-2400. www.slcairport.com.

San Antonio TX
San Antonio International Airport (SAT). ℘210-207-3433. www.sanantonio.gov/aviation.

San Diego CA
San Diego International Airport (SAN). ℘619-400-2400. www.san.org.

San Francisco CA
San Francisco International Airport (SFO). ℘650-821-8211. www.flysfo.com.

San Jose CA
San Jose International Airport (SJC).
📞408-392-3600. www.sjc.org.

Seattle WA
Seattle-Tacoma International
Airport (SEA). 📞206-787-5388.
www.portseattle.org.

Tucson AZ
Tucson International Airport (TUS).
📞520-573-8100.
www.flytucson.com.

By Ferry

With millions of residents living
around major bodies of water, both
the Seattle and San Francisco areas
rely on public ferries for transport.
These boats are both public
transport and superb visitor activities.
Washington State Ferries is one of
the world's largest such systems;
its white-and-green boats ply the
sparkling waters of Puget Sound on
more than a dozen routes, carrying
cars and passengers back and forth
(www.wsdot.wa.gov/ferries). A ferry
ride is not only the most effective
way to get to the Olympic Peninsula
(for example) it is an economical and
memorable travel experience.
In California, **passenger ferries**
cross from Marin County north of
the Golden Gate to downtown San
Francisco (http://sanfranciscobayferry.
com). In Southern California,
passenger and car ferries cross to
Catalina Island on a daily basis
(www.catalinaexpress.com).

By Train

The Amtrak rail network offers a
relaxing alternative for travelers with
time to spare. Advance reservations
ensure reduced fares and availability
of desired accommodations. On
some trains, reservations are required;
smoking is not allowed. Passengers
may choose from first-class, coach, or
cars with panoramic windows.
The **USA RailPass** offers unlimited
travel within designated regions at
discounted rates; 15-, 30- and 45-day
passes are available. For schedule,
prices and route information:
📞800-872-7245 or www.amtrak.com
(outside North America, contact a
travel agent). In the West, service is
provided along the following routes:

California Corridor
Route: San José–Reno
Along the way: San Francisco,
Sacramento

California Zephyr
Route: Chicago–San Francisco
Along the way: Denver, Salt Lake
City, Sacramento

Cascades
Route: Vancouver–Eugene
Along the way: Seattle, Portland

Coast Starlight
Route: Seattle–Los Angeles
Along the way: Portland, San
Francisco, Santa Barbara

Empire Builder
Route: Chicago–Seattle
Along the way: Minneapolis,

Glacier Park
Heartland Flyer
Route: Oklahoma City-Fort Worth
Along the way: Norman

Southwest Chief
Route: Chicago–Los Angeles
Along the way: Kansas City,
Santa Fe, Phoenix

Sunset Limited
Route: New Orleans–Los Angeles
Along the way: San Antonio,
El Paso, Tucson

The **Alaska Railroad** links Seward,
Anchorage, Denali National Park and
Fairbanks (mid May–mid Sept daily; in
winter, weekends only); for schedule
and reservations: Alaska Railroad
Corp., 📞907-265-2494 or 800-544-
0552; www.alaskarailroad.com.

By Bus/Coach

Greyhound, the largest bus company
in the US, offers access to most
cities and communities. Overall,

Re-designed Greyhound bus

fares are lower than other forms of transportation. Some travelers may find long-distance bus travel uncomfortable owing to a lack of sleeping accommodations, and specific seat reservations are not allowed. Advance ticketing is suggested; contact Greyhound for schedules, prices and route information (📞800-231-2222; www.greyhound.com).

By Car

Limited-access **interstate highways** crisscross the US. North–South highways have odd numbers (I-15, I-25); east-west interstates have even numbers (I-40, I-80). Numbers increase from west to east (I-5 along the West Coast and I-95 on the East Coast) and from south to north (I-8 runs east from San Diego CA; I-94 connects Billings MT with Milwaukee WI). Interstate **beltways** encircle cities and have three digits: the first is an even number and the last two name the interstate off which they branch (I-410 around San Antonio TX branches off I-10). There can be duplication across states (there are I-405 beltways around Seattle WA, Portland OR and Los Angeles CA) and exceptions to this general rule. Interstate **spurs** entering cities also have three digits: the first is an odd number and the last two represent the originating interstate.

A system of non-interstate highways and roads, predating the interstate system, includes US, state, county and Indian reservation routes. **US routes** and **state routes** range from major highways to winding two-lane roads. North-south roads have odd numbers (of one, two or three digits), east-west roads even numbers. County roads, Forest Service and Bureau of Land Management and Indian reservation routes typically are smaller local or connector roads. It's crucial to **check locally** on road and weather conditions before venturing off paved roads in remote rural areas.

Rental Cars

National rental companies have offices at major airports and downtown locations. Aside from the agencies listed below, there also are local companies that offer reasonable rental rates. (See Yellow Pages for phone numbers).

Renters must possess a major credit card (such as Visa/Carte Bleue, American Express or MasterCard/Eurocard), a valid driver's license (international license not required). Minimum age for rental is 21 at most major companies; younger drivers may be charged higher rates. A variety of service packages offer unlimited mileage and discounted prices, often in conjunction with major airlines or hotel chains. Since prices vary from one company to another, be sure to research different companies before you reserve. (To reserve a car from Europe, it is best to contact one of the major

US companies such as Hertz, Avis and so on, directly, or a travel agent.) All rentals are subject to local taxes and fees which should be included in quoted prices. Liability insurance is not automatically included in rental terms. Be sure to check for proper insurance coverage, offered at an extra charge. Most rental companies offer breakdown assistance.

Cars may be rented per day, week or month, and mileage is usually unlimited. Only the person who signed the contract is authorized to drive the rental car (or their spouse), but for an additional fee, and upon presentation of the required papers, additional drivers may be approved. If a vehicle is returned at a different location from where it was rented, drop-off charges may be incurred. The gasoline tank of the car should be filled before it is returned; rental companies charge a much higher price per gallon than roadside gas stations. Some companies offer a fuel-fill option in which you can "buy" a tank of gas at rental, often at advantageous prices, and return the car with any level of gas in the tank.

Rental car **information and reservations** across the US may be accessed on the Internet (www.bnm.com), or by contacting:

◆ **Alamo**
   ☎888-233-8749. www.alamo.com.
◆ **Avis**
   ☎800-633-3469. www.avis.com.
◆ **Budget**
   ☎800-218-7992.
   www.budget.com.
◆ **Dollar**
   ☎800-800-4000. www.dollar.com.
◆ **Enterprise**
   ☎800-261-7331.
   www.enterprise.com.
◆ **Hertz**
   ☎800-654-3131. www.hertz.com.
◆ **National**
   ☎877-222-9058.
   www.nationalcar.com.
◆ **Sixt**
   ☎888-749-8227. www.sixt.com.
◆ **Thrifty**
   ☎800-331-4200. www.thrifty.com.

Recreational Vehicle (RV) Rentals
One-way rentals range from a basic camper to full-size motor-homes that can accommodate up to seven people and offer a bathroom, shower and kitchen with microwave oven. Reservations should be made several months in advance. There may be a minimum number of rental days required. A drop fee is charged for one-way rentals. **Cruise America RV** ☎800-671-8042, www.cruiseamerica.com) offers rentals with 24hr customer assistance.

The **Recreational Vehicle Rental Association** (RVRA) lists a directory of RV rental locations in the US on its website (☎703-591-7130; www.rvra.org). **RV America** (www.rvamerica.com) offers an on-line database of RV rental companies as well as information on campgrounds.

Road Regulations and Insurance
The speed limit on most interstate highways in the western US ranges from 55mph (88km/h) to 75mph (120km/h), depending on the state and location. (Limits drop within urban areas.) On state highways outside populated areas the speed limit ranges from 55mph (88km/h) to 70mph (112kmh). Within cities, speed limits are generally 35mph (56km/h), and average 25-30mph (40-48km/h) in residential areas. Headlights must be turned on when driving in poor visibility, and it's advisable to keep them on at all times. Unless traveling on a divided road, the law requires that motorists in both directions bring their vehicle to a full stop when the warning signals on a school bus are activated. When emergency vehicles approach, cars traveling in both directions must pull over. Parking spaces marked j are reserved for persons with disabilities only.

Anyone parking in these spaces without proper identification will be ticketed and/or their vehicle will be towed.

The use of **seat belts** is mandatory for all persons in the car. Child safety seats are required in all states and are available at rental-car agencies; indicate need when making reservations. In some states, motorcyclists and their passengers are required to wear helmets. Hitchhiking along interstate highways, except at entrance ramps, is forbidden by law. Auto liability insurance is mandatory in all states. It is illegal to drink and drive and penalties are severe everywhere, including immediate surrender of car and driving license in some places. The maximum blood alcohol content is .08 percent. In California it is illegal to smoke in the car when minors are present.

In Case of an Accident

If you are involved in an auto accident resulting in personal or property damage, you must notify the local police and remain at the scene until dismissed. If blocking traffic, vehicles should be moved as soon as possible. Automobile associations such as the **American Automobile Association** (AAA) (✆888-852-0766) provide its members with emergency road service. Members of AAA-affiliated automobile clubs overseas benefit from reciprocal services:

Australia
♦ Australian Automobile Association (AAA),
✆02 6247 7311
www.aaa.asn.au

Canada
♦ Canadian Automobile Association (CAA),
✆613 820 1890
www.caa.ca

France
♦ Automobile-Club de France (ACF),
✆01 43 12 43 12
www.automobileclubdefrance.fr

Germany
♦ Allgemeiner Deutscher Automobil-Club E.V. (ADAC),
✆0 180 2 22 22 22 (landline),
22 22 22 (mobile), www.adac.de
♦ Automobilclub von Deutschland E.V. (AvD),
✆69 6606 300, www.avd.de

Great Britain
♦ The Automobile Association (AA),
✆0906 888 4322 (landline),
84322 (mobile), www.theaa.com
♦ The Camping & Caravanning Club (CCC),
✆024 7647 5448
www.campingandcaravanning
club.co.uk
♦ The Caravan Club (CC),
✆01 342 326 944
www.caravanclub.co.uk

Ireland
♦ The Automobile Association Ireland Ltd. (AA Ireland),
✆01 617 9104 www.theaa.ie

Italy
♦ Automobile Club d'Italia (ACI),
✆06 49 11 15, www.aci.it
♦ Federazione Italiana del Campeggio e del Caravanning (Federcampeggio),
✆55 88 23 91
www.federcampeggio.it
♦ Touring Club Italiano (TCI),
✆840 88 88 02
www.touringclub.it

Netherlands
♦ Koninklijke Nederlandsche Automobiel Club (KNAC),
✆70 383 1612
www.knac.nl
♦ Koninklijke Nederlandse Toeristenbond (ANWB),
✆088 269 22 22, www.anwb.nl

Spain
♦ Real Automóvil Club de España (RACE),
✆902 40 45 45, www.race.es

Switzerland
♦ Automobile Club de Suisse (ACS),
✆031 328 31 11, www.acs.ch
♦ Touring Club Suisse (TCS),
✆0844 888 111, www.tcs.ch

On Arrival

Hotels and Restaurants are described in the Addresses within the Discovering USA West section. For price ranges, see the Legend on this guide's cover flap.

WHERE TO STAY

For a listing of lodging recommendations for areas described in this guide, consult the **Addresses** section in each chapter. Luxury **hotels** are generally found in major cities and resort communities, **motels** in clusters on the edges of towns and along the interstate highways. **Bed-and-breakfast inns** usually are found in residential areas of cities and towns, and in more secluded natural areas. Many properties offer special packages and weekend rates that may not be extended during peak summer months (*late May–late Aug.*) and holiday seasons, especially near ski resorts. Advance reservations are recommended during these times. Rates tend to be higher in cities and near coastal and resort areas. Many resort properties include outdoor recreational facilities such as ski areas, golf courses, tennis courts, swimming pools and fitness centers, as well as gourmet dining and entertainment. Activities such as hiking, mountain biking and horseback riding may be arranged by contacting hotel staff.

In most of the West, high season is June through August. In some very popular areas during this time, such as Yellowstone, Seattle and San Francisco, it is wise to make reservations months in advance. By contrast, high season in the desert resorts of Arizona and inland California is November through February.

Many cities and communities levy a hotel occupancy tax that is added to hotel rates. Contact local tourist offices to request free brochures that give details about area accommodations. (*Telephone numbers and websites are listed under entry headings in each chapter.*)

HOTELS AND MOTELS

Rates for hotels and motels vary greatly according to season and location, and tend to be higher during holiday and peak seasons. For deluxe hotels, plan to pay at least $300 and up/night per room, double occupancy. Moderate hotels usually charge between $100–$200/night and budget motels range from $50–$90/night. In most hotels, children under 18 stay free when sharing a room with their parents. In-room efficiency kitchens are available at some hotels and motels. When reserving, ask about packages including meals, passes to local attractions and weekend specials. Typical amenities at hotels and motels include television, alarm clock, Internet access, smoking/non-smoking rooms, restaurants and swimming pools.

Always advise the reservations clerk of late arrival; unless confirmed with a credit card, rooms may not be held after 6pm. Contact state or local (*phone number in Info in infoboxes in this guide*) tourism agencies for free information on accommodations.

Hotel and Motel Reservation Services

Hotel reservation services are abundant, especially on the Internet. Most airlines now offer hotel bookings along with flights as well. Following is a brief selection.

- **Central Reservation Service**
  800-894-0680.
  www.reservation-services.com.
- **Expedia**
  www.expedia.com.
- **Free Hotel Search**
  210-507-5997 or 800-359-4827.
  www.freehotelsearch.com.

MAJOR US HOTEL CHAINS	PHONE NUMBER, WEBSITE
Best Western	800-780-7234, www.bestwestern.com
Clarion, Comfort Inn, Quality Inn, Sleep Inn	877-424-6423, www.choicehotels.com
Days Inn	800-225-3297, www.daysinn.com
Four Seasons	800-819-5053, www.fourseasons.com
Hampton Inn	800-426-7866, www.hamptoninn.com
Hilton	800-445-8667, www.hilton.com
Holiday Inn	800-465-4329, www.holidayinn.com
Howard Johnson	800-221-5801, www.hojo.com
Hyatt	800-591-1234, www.hyatt.com
Marriott	800-236-2427, www.marriott.com
Omni	800-843-6664, www.omnihotels.com
Radisson	800-967-9033, www.radisson.com
Ramada	800-854-9517, www.ramada.com
Ritz-Carlton	800-542-8680, www.ritzcarlton.com
Sheraton, W and Westin	800-328-6242, www.starwoodhotels.com

- **Hotels.com**
  ℘800-246-8357.
  www.hotels.com.
- **Quikbook**
  ℘800-789-9887.
  www.quikbook.com.
- **Kayak**
  www.kayak.com
- **Travelocity**
  ℘888-872-8356, 210-477-1089.
  www.travelocity.com
- **Trivago**
  www.trivago.com

BED & BREAKFAST AND COUNTRY INNS

Most B&Bs are privately owned historic residences. Bed-and-breakfast inns are typically cozy homes with fewer than 10 guest rooms; breakfast is usually the only meal provided. Country inns are larger establishments, often offering over 25 guest rooms; full-service dining is typically available. Both establishments include a breakfast ranging from continental fare to a gourmet repast; some offer afternoon tea and the use of sitting rooms with cozy fireplaces, or garden spots providing breathtaking panoramas of ocean shores or mountain vistas. Some lower-priced rooms may not have private baths. Especially during holiday and peak tourist seasons, reservations should be made well in advance. Minimum stay, cancellation and refund policies may be more stringent during these times. Most inns will accept major credit cards. Rates vary seasonally but range from $105 to $200 for a double room per night. Rates will be higher for rooms with such amenities as hot tubs, private entrances and scenic views.

Bed & Breakfast and Country Inn reservation services

Numerous organizations offer reservation services for B&Bs and country inns, but the best way to find such accommodations is through the visitors' bureaus wherever you are traveling. Many services tend to be regional; following are some nationwide services. For a complete listing, consult the websites for CVBs in your destinations. Also, the **Select**

© Mark Winfrey/iStockphoto.com

Registry (☎269-789-0393 or 800-344-5244; www.selectregistry.com) publishes an annual register listing B&Bs and country inns by state.

BedandBreakfast.com
  ☎512-322-2710
  www.bedandbreakfast.com

BBOnline
  ☎800-215-7365
  www.bbonline.com

GUEST RANCHES

In the late 19C, working farms and livestock ranches welcomed big-city friends eager to help with chores, or paying guests to help them through tough economic times. The romanticization of the American West to an eastern and European audience lent a mystique to the cowboy and the open range that persists to this day. The "dude ranch," as it became known, provides a unique window on the Western lifestyle. Today's dude ranches, now usually called "guest ranches," vary in style from rustic to posh. Catering to as few as 12 or as many as 125 guests, they may be working ranches that involve guests in cattle drives and branding; outfitting ranches that emphasize horseback riding; or resort ranches, where relaxation is the order of the day. Many guests return to the saddle year after year for spectacular scenery, riding and ranch-style family meals or, at upscale ranches, high-end gourmet cuisine. The greatest guest ranch concentrations are in Montana, Wyoming, Arizona, Colorado and California; consult the websites for each state's tourism agency for listings.

Websites have made these Western vacations accessible to a global market intrigued by the cowboy lifestyle. Organizations that provide information on guest ranches include **The Dude Ranchers' Association** (☎307-587-2339 or 866-399-2339, www.duderanch.org), and **Guest Ranches of North America** (www.guestranches.com). **Top 50** Ranches is a consortium of premium quality guest ranches around the world, with 36 ranches in the Western US; each ranch must meet minimum standards for quality, service and business integrity (☎406-749-9131; www.top50ranches.com).

CONDOMINIUMS

Furnished apartments or houses are more cost-effective than hotels for families with children. Hawaii, in particular, has thousands of condos and rental homes available for visitors. Amenities include separate living quarters, fully equipped kitchen with dining area, several bedrooms and bathrooms, and laundry facilities. Most condos provide televisions, basic linens and maid service. Depending on location, properties may include sports and recreational facilities, patios and beach access. Most require a minimum stay of three nights or one week, especially during peak season. When making reservations, ask about cancellation penalties and refund policies. Chambers of commerce and convention-and-visitors bureaus have listings of local property management agencies that can assist with selection. A variety of private accommodations can be arranged through **Condo Rentals.com** (☏ 817-333-5417; www.condorentals.com). Three global online services include many properties in the Western US, ranging from country estate homes to urban apartments; **HomeAway** (www.homeaway.com); **Vacation Rentals by Owner** (www.vrbo.com); and **Air BnB** (www.airbnb.com). Using these services, guests book directly with the property owner after searching online.

In Hawaii, hundreds of units on every island are available from **Aston Hotels & Resorts** (www.astonhotels.com).

Camping at Mountain Lake, Colorado

©iStockphoto.com/Ben Blankenburg

HOSTELS

A simple, no-frills alternative to hotels and inns, hostels are inexpensive dormitory-style accommodations with separate quarters for males and females. Many have private family/couples rooms, which may be reserved in advance. Amenities include fully equipped self-service kitchens, dining areas and common rooms. Hostelling International members receive discounts on room rates and other travel-related expenses (Alamo car rentals, and local attractions). Hostels often organize special programs and activities for guests. When booking, ask for available discounts at area attractions, rental car companies and restaurants.

Rates average $15–$20 a night, but in big cities $25–$45 a nightFor information and a free directory, contact **Hostelling International USA** (☏ 240-650-2100; www.hiusa.org). For more general information on hostels: www.hostels.com.

CAMPING & RECREATIONAL VEHICLE (RV) PARKS

National and state park listings p XX.
Campsites are located in national parks, state parks, national forests, along beaches and in private campgrounds. The season for camping in the high country usually runs from Memorial Day to Labor Day; in lower elevations, campgrounds are open year-round. Some offer full utility hookups, lodges or cabins, backcountry sites and recreational facilities. Advance reservations are recommended, especially during summer and holidays.

National park and state park campgrounds are relatively inexpensive, but fill quickly, especially during school holidays. Facilities range from simple tent sites to full RV hookups (*reserve 60 days in advance*) or rustic cabins (reserve one year in advance). Fees vary according to season and available facilities (picnic tables, water/electric hookups, used-water disposal, recreational equipment, showers, rest rooms): camping & RV sites $8–$50/day; cabins $30–$150/day. For all US national parks, national forests, BLM campgrounds and so on, contact the park you are visiting or the federal reservation site (☎877-444-6777; www.recreation.gov). For state parks, contact the state tourism office (p xx) for information.

Private campgrounds offering facilities from simple tent sites to full RV-hookups are plentiful. They are slightly more expensive (*$15–$30/day for tent sites, $25–$50/day for RVs*) but may offer more sophisticated amenities: hot showers, laundry facilities, convenience stores, children's playgrounds, pools, air-conditioned cabins and outdoor recreational facilities. Most accept daily, weekly or monthly occupancy. In winter (*Nov–Apr*), some campgrounds may be closed. Reservations are recommended, especially for longer stays and in popular resort areas. **Kampgrounds of America (KOA)** operates campsites for tents, cabins/cottages and RV-hookups throughout the United States. For a directory, view online at Http://koa.com (☎406-248-7414 or 888-562-0000). Directories of campgrounds throughout the US are easily found on the Internet. Following is a sample of some Internet **campground directories** covering the US:

◆ **Camping USA**
www.camping-usa.com

◆ **Go Camping America**
www.gocampingamerica.com

◆ **National Forest Campground Guide**
www.forestcamping.com

SPAS

Modern spas offer a variety of programs: fitness, beauty and wellness; relaxation and stress relief; weight management, and adventure vacations. Guests are pampered with mud baths, daily massages, state-of-the-art fitness and exercise programs, cooking classes and nutritional counseling. Spas offer luxurious facilities in beautiful settings that may include championship golf courses, equestrian centers and even formal gardens. Most offer packages for stays ranging from 2 to 10 nights, which include health and fitness programs, golf and tennis, and image enhancement. Most facilities have age restrictions. Most spas are informal, but check when making reservations.

Prices range from $800/week to $3,500/week (price per person, double occupancy) depending on choice of program and season. All meals, including special diets, use of facilities, tax, gratuities and airport transportation, are usually included.

Spa Finders (☎212-924-6800; www.spafinder.com).

WHERE TO EAT

♿See also Food and Drink in USA West Introduction. Every taste is catered to within the big cities of the western half of the US, with the region's orchards, farms, lakes and coastline providing a wealth of ingredients, often combined to unique effect.

In America, food portion sizes tend to be large. Most restaurants will accommodate special dietary concerns, such as food allergies and vegetarian diets. Kosher meals can be difficult to find outside of major metropolitan areas. When in doubt, call ahead and ask.

♿For a selection of restaurants, see the ADDRESSES within the Discovering USA West section of this guidebook.

Practical A–Z

BUSINESS HOURS

Most businesses operate Mon–Fri 9am–5pm. Banks are normally open Mon–Fri 9am–5:30pm, Sat 10am-1pm. Most retail stores and specialty shops are open daily 10am–6pm. Malls and shopping centers are usually open Mon–Sat 10am–9pm, Sun 10am–6pm.

ELECTRICITY

Voltage in the US is 120 volts AC, 60 Hz. Foreign-made appliances may need AC adapters (available at specialty travel and electronics stores) and North American flat-blade plugs.

EMERGENCIES

Except in remote areas where there is little or no telephone service, the emergency phone number throughout the West is 911.. Visitors in need of urgent non-emergency medical care can visit the emergency room at the closest hospital; or one of many urgent care clinics found in most cities. Patients may be required to demonstrate financial ability to pay. Most cities above 50,000 population have local clinics that provide urgent dental care; and 24 hours pharmacies.

INTERNET

Smart phones and tablets should be able to access the Internet almost everywhere in the US, though coverage can be intermittent in rural or mountainous areas, depending on the service provider. Wi-Fi service is widely available throughout the US. Find free Wi-Fi service at most coffee shops and fastfood restaurants, libraries, and some retail stores. Some hotels offer free Wi-Fi to guests; others bill by the hour or day. Airports and airplanes vary in offering free or paid access.

LIQUOR LAWS

The minimum age for purchase and consumption of alcoholic beverages is 21; proof of age may be required. Local municipalities may limit and restrict sales, and laws differ among states. In many states, liquor stores sell beer, wine and liquor. Beer and wine may also be purchased in package-goods stores and grocery stores. Liquor is available at grocery stores in California. Beer may be purchased in gas station convenience stores in some states. However, in other states, wine and liquor are sold at state-operated shops and beer is sold by licensed distributors. Certain states, such as Utah, do not permit alcohol sales on Sundays, even in restaurants (exceptions usually apply in metropolitan and tourist areas). It is a serious offense for those over 21 to procure alcohol for minors.

MAJOR HOLIDAYS

Banks and government offices are closed on the legal holidays shown in the table below.

New Year's Day	January 1
Inauguration Day	Every four years on January 20
Martin Luther King, Jr.'s Birthday*	3rd Monday in January
President's Day*	3rd Monday in February
Memorial Day*	May 30 or last Monday in May
Independence Day	July 4
Labor Day*	1st Monday in September
Columbus Day*	2nd Monday in October
Veterans Day*	November 11
Thanksgiving Day	4th Thursday in November
Christmas Day	December 25

Many retail stores and restaurants remain open on these days

MAIL/POST

First-class postage rates within the US are: 46¢/letter (up to 1oz) and postcard. To Europe: $1.10/letter (up to 1oz), 90¢/postcard. Most post offices are open Mon–Fri 9am–5pm; some may open Sat 9am–noon. Companies such as UPS-Mail Boxes Etc. and FedexKinko's (*consult the Yellow Pages under Mailing Services or search online*) also provide domestic and international shipping services and sell boxes and packaging material. For photocopying, fax service and computer access, FedexKinko's has locations throughout the US (*℘*800-254-6567; www.kinkos.com) or consult a phone book under Copying Services.

MONEY

The American **dollar** ($1) is divided into 100 **cents**. A **penny** = 1 cent (1¢); a **nickel** = 5¢; a **dime** = 10¢; a **quarter** = 25¢. Most national banks and Thomas Cook (locations throughout the US, *℘*800-287-7362; www. thomascook.com) **exchange foreign currency** at local offices and charge a fee for the service.

The simplest methods to obtain dollars are to use traveler's checks (*accepted in most banks, hotels, restaurants and businesses with presentation of a photo ID*) and to withdraw cash from **ATMs** (Automated Teller Machines) with a debit or credit card. Banks charge a fee ($1–$3) for non-members who use their ATMs. For more information on the ATM network, call MasterCard/Cirrus (*℘*800-424-7787) or visit the Visa/Plus Systemat www.visa.com/atmlocator. In the event you lose your credit card: American Express, *℘*800-528-4800; Diner's Club, *℘*800-234-6377; MasterCard/ Eurocard, *℘*800-307-7309; Visa/Carte Bleue, *℘*800-336-8472; or contact the phone number for your card's issuing bank. You can send and receive cash via **Western Union** (locations in more than 100 countries, *℘*800-225-5227; www.westernunion.com).

SMOKING

Laws vary in most Western states but it is illegal to smoke in public areas in most places such as restaurants, airports, buses, offices open to the public such as banks and retail stores. All US airlines are completely nonsmoking. In California, which continues to expand these policies, it is now illegal to smoke in a private car if children are present, and one California city has banned smoking in apartment buildings. Many beaches in California prohibit smoking, too (to curb litter). For a state-by-state list of restrictions, consult Action on Smoking and Health (www.ash.org). Aside from legal restrictions, it is socially unacceptable to expose other individuals to tobacco smoke. If you are bothered by someone's smoke, it is quite all right to ask them to move, unless you are in a private residence or designated smoking area.

TAXES AND TIPPING

With the occasional exception of certain food products and gasoline, **sales tax** is not included in the quoted price and is added at the time of payment. Sales taxes vary by state and range from 3 to 8.5 percent; Alaska, Montana and Oregon charge no sales tax. Sales tax may often be higher in major cities due to local taxes. In some states, the restaurant tax appearing on your bill when you dine out may be higher than the state tax; also, expect additional hotel and rental car taxes and surcharges. In the US, it is customary to leave a **tip**, a gratuity of cash for services received by wait staff (10-20 percent), taxi drivers (15 percent), bellhops ($1/bag), hotel housekeepers ($1/night).

TELEPHONES

For **long-distance** calls in the US and Canada, dial 1 + area code (3 digits) + number (7 digits). To place **local calls**, dial the seven-digit number without 1 or the area code, unless the local calling area includes several area codes. To place an **international call**, dial 011 + country code + area code + number. To obtain help from an **operator**, dial 0 for local and 00 for long distance. For **information** on a number within your area code, dial 411. For long-distance information, dial 1 + area code + 555-1212. To place **collect calls**, dial 0 + area or country code + number. At the operator's prompt, give your name. For all **emergencies**, dial **911**. Most **hotels** add a surcharge for local and long-distance calls. **Public telephones** cost 50¢ or more for local calls and use coins or a credit card. If visiting the US from another country, check with your **cell phone** service provider to be sure your phone or tablet will function in the US as GSM phones must be unlocked to use a SIM card for a North American network. Companies such as Verizon and AT&T may offer short-term contracts and rental phones. In some cities and states, talking on a cell phone (even when using a handsfree device) while driving is illegal and punishable by a fine, as is sending text messages while driving. Telephone numbers that start with 800, 888, 877, 866 and 855 are toll-free within the US. Numbers starting with 900 charge extra fees, sometimes exorbitant; avoid these.

TIME ZONES

There are three standard time zones in the Western US: Central, Mountain and Pacific, and additional Alaska and Hawaii time zones. Daylight Savings Time is observed in all states, except Arizona and Hawaii, from the second Sunday in March to the first Sunday in November; time is moved forward one hour. Pacific Standard Time (PST) is 8hrs behind Greenwich Mean Time (GMT), or Universal Time (UT); Pacific Daylight Time (PDT) is 7hrs behind GMT.

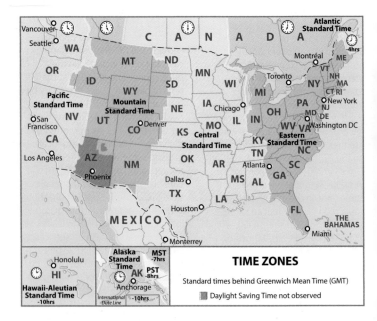

TIME ZONES

Standard times behind Greenwich Mean Time (GMT)

■ Daylight Saving Time not observed

CONVERSION TABLES

Weights and Measures

EU	USA	UK	
1 kilogram (kg)	2.2 pounds (lb)	2.2 pounds	*To convert*
6.35 kilograms	14 pounds	1 stone (st)	*kilograms*
0.45 kilograms	16 ounces (oz)	16 ounces	*to pounds,*
1 metric ton (tn)	1.1 tons	1.1 tons	*multiply by 2.2*
1 litre (l)	2.11 pints (pt)	1.76 pints	*To convert litres*
3.79 litres	1 gallon (gal)	0.83 gallon	*to gallons, multiply*
4.55 litres	1.20 gallon	1 gallon	*by 0.26 (US)*
			or 0.22 (UK)
1 hectare (ha)	2.47 acres	2.47 acres	*To convert*
1 sq kilometre (km²)	0.38 sq. miles (sq mi)	0.38 sq. miles	*hectares to acres, multiply by 2.4*
1 centimetre (cm)	0.39 inches (in)	0.39 inches	*To convert metres*
1 metre (m)	3.28 feet (ft) or 39.37 inches or 1.09 yards (yd)		*to feet, multiply by 3.28; for kilometres to miles,*
1 kilometre (km)	0.62 miles (mi)	0.62 miles	*multiply by 0.6*

Clothing

Women	EU	USA	UK
	35	4	2½
	36	5	3½
	37	6	4½
Shoes	38	7	5½
	39	8	6½
	40	9	7½
	41	10	8½
	36	6	8
	38	8	10
Dresses	40	10	12
& suits	42	12	14
	44	14	16
	46	16	18
	36	6	30
	38	8	32
Blouses &	40	10	34
sweaters	42	12	36
	44	14	38
	46	16	40

Men	EU	USA	UK
	40	7½	7
	41	8½	8
	42	9½	9
Shoes	43	10½	10
	44	11½	11
	45	12½	12
	46	13½	13
	46	36	36
	48	38	38
Suits	50	40	40
	52	42	42
	54	44	44
	56	46	48
	37	14½	14½
	38	15	15
Shirts	39	15½	15½
	40	15¾	15¾
	41	16	16
	42	16½	16½

Sizes often vary depending on the designer. These equivalents are given for guidance only.

Speed

KPH	10	30	50	70	80	90	100	110	120	130
MPH	6	19	31	43	50	56	62	68	75	81

Temperature

Celsius	(°C)	0°	5°	10°	15°	20°	25°	30°	40°	60°	80°	100°
Fahrenheit	(°F)	32°	41°	50°	59°	68°	77°	86°	104°	140°	176°	212°

To convert Celsius into Fahrenheit, multiply °C by 9, divide by 5, and add 32.
To convert Fahrenheit into Celsius, subtract 32 from °F, multiply by 5, and divide by 9.

NB: Conversion factors on this page are approximate.

Introducing
USA West

Cadillac Ranch near Amarillo, Texas, along I-40
between Albuquerque and Oklahoma City

Features

"FOR THE BENEFIT AND
ENJOYMENT OF THE PEOPLE"

YELLOWSTONE
NATIONAL
PARK

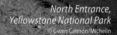

North Entrance,
Yellowstone National Park
©Gwen Cannon/Michelin

USA West Today

The spirit of invention and adventure that has marked the West for centuries continues unabated today. Having absorbed ethnic influences from east, west and south, its cuisine is finding new frontiers in supporting organic foods. Its builders call on the world's most innovative architects; its artists, musicians and filmmakers find novel ways to practice their crafts. Commitment to preserving the natural landscape has never been stronger.

Cowboys, Colorado paddock © World Pictures/Photoshot

Government and Society

The American West has always been perceived as a land of possibility, a place to start anew. Its population is composed largely of immigrants and their descendants, people who set out in quest of the American dream. The West remains one of the most culturally, politically and economically progressive regions on earth, from state governments to the innumerable startup companies that make California's Silicon Valley hum.

FEDERAL GOVERNMENT

Though it has since been copied around the world, when the US created its then-unique federated republic, the concept was radical indeed. The national government consists of three branches—the **executive**, in the office of the president; the **legislative**, which consists of Congress' Senate and House of Representatives; and the **judicial**, which comprises many types and levels of courts, culminating in the Supreme Court. These three bodies guide the vast federal government, which holds sway over national and foreign affairs, and all matters that involve relations between the states. This responsibility includes safeguarding the constitutional liberties Americans enjoy, such as freedom of speech and fair trial guarantees. A federal income tax brings in the bulk of the national budget.

STATE GOVERNMENT

The 50 states, including the 19 covered in this guide, govern themselves in internal affairs such as road construction, criminal and civil law such as requirements for marriage and inheritance standards. All the states are organized along lines very similar to the national government, with an executive, the governor; a legislature (Nebraska, uniquely, has a one-house assembly); and a multilevel judicial system culminating in some sort of supreme court. All 19 Western states are further subdivided into counties (some of which are larger than many European countries) and cities within those counties, divisions which likewise govern some aspects of life within their borders. Some rural Western counties, for instance, do not require building permits for residential home construction. All these levels of government rely on popular vote to select their members, with the exception of judges, some of whom are elected and some appointed. Federal and state elections take place every two years; by and large, governors and senators serve four-year terms, representatives two years.

States, counties and cities raise revenue through various taxes and fees, usually including income and sales taxes. The differences here exemplify the colorful political and cultural diversity of this huge region: Washington state, like several other Western states, has no income tax, and its residents consistently reject any effort to create one. Its neighbor, Oregon, has no sales tax, and its residents consistently reject efforts to create one. In Alaska, there is no property tax, the mainstay of public school funds in every other state.

Political Spectrum

By and large, the three Pacific Coast states, Washington, Oregon and California, are more liberal (socially progressive) than interior states. California, for instance, has led the US (not to mention the world) in restrictions on public smoking. These three states evince an interesting internal dichotomy—the areas nearest the coast, especially the cities, are much more liberal than the inland regions beyond a dividing mountain range. San Francisco is world-famed—and has been for more than a century—as a community tolerant of nontraditional behavior. A gay couple walking down the street in San Francisco holding hands would be commonplace; the same sight would be unheard-of in small towns in far inland California, separated from the liberal coast by not one but two mountain ranges.

It is largely true that individualism and independence enjoy high regard in the Western states—but, as the old axiom has it, what's gospel in one place is heresy in another. Montana was famous during the 90s as the state with no daytime highway speed limit other than "reasonable and prudent." (Under pressure from the national government, the upper limit was made 75 mph in 1999.) Assisted suicide is legal in Oregon and Washington and illegal in every other US state. California allows medical marijuana use; in Alaska, citizens may possess small amounts of marijuana for personal use. Pot is strictly prohibited in most other Western states. A few counties in Nevada have made brothels legal; they are the only such places in the US. The thread of independence that runs through this theme had its birth in the settling of the West by adventurous pioneers, many of whom simply did not fit in elsewhere. Here, as throughout the US, the continuing political ferment over social issues is decided in the privacy of the voting booth, and despite their differences everyone would agree that's best. Alas, fewer than half of Americans vote in most elections.

ECONOMY

The Western economy thrives on the unique American system of free enterprise: a laissez-faire capitalism whereby individuals can create, own and control the production of virtually any marketable good, service or commodity they can conceive. In this arena of inventive enterprise, the Western economy has given rise to industries of global significance, such as high technology and aerospace. Only public services, such as bus and subway systems, are government-owned.

The US West has undergone a profound transformation over the last few generations, from one based on resource extraction to one based on services and manufacturing. Its 21C economy is complex and varied, and its premier example, California, is so large that considered by itself, it would be the 11th-largest in the world. While the 2008 recession hit many Western states hard—especially California and Nevada—recovery has brought near-booms in some places such as Hawaii (tourism) and North Dakota (oil and gas), where employment has rebounded. Other states are recovering more slowly, but show improvement.

Natural Resources

European settlers were first lured westward by an abundance of fur pelts, minerals, fossil fuels, grazing lands, fertile soil, fisheries and timber. Except for furs, these resources still underlie a substantial portion of the Western economy. Private companies engaged in timber harvesting, mining and grazing benefit from favorable contracts for the lease of public lands managed by the US Forest Service or Bureau of Land Management. Altogether, mining accounts for about $225 billion of the US GDP; Nevada is at the forefront of non-fuel production with $6.5 billion annual revenue, mostly from gold, silver and copper. Crude oil is concentrated in pockets along the Gulf of Mexico and in Texas, Oklahoma, California, Alaska, North Dakota and Wyoming, while a vast reserve of undeveloped oil shale underlies the central Rocky Mountains and Colorado Plateau. Fuels production, also largely a Western industry, contributes more than $294 billion to the US GDP.

Though over-fishing threatens wild stocks, commercial fisheries along the West Coast are famed for their catches: San Francisco and Seattle for Dungeness crabs, northern California for abalone, the Pacific Northwest for shellfish and salmon, Alaska for salmon and king crab.

Irrigation has allowed agriculture to thrive despite arid or semiarid condi-

ECONOMIES OF THE WESTERN UNITED STATES

	*GSP (billion$)	Principal Industries
California	$1,959	manufacturing, tourism, crops, oil, film
Texas	1,308	oil, livestock, cotton, manufacturing
Washington	355	fishing, timber, manufacturing, wheat
Colorado	264	tourism, manufacturing, mining, oil
Arizona	258	manufacturing, mining, tourism
Oregon	194	timber, fishing, fruit, manufacturing
Oklahoma	155	natural gas, oil, wheat, livestock
Kansas	131	wheat, corn, livestock, oil, manufacturing
Nevada	130	gambling, tourism, mining, hydroelectric
Utah	124	mining, oil, livestock, manufacturing
Nebraska	94	corn, wheat, livestock, manufacturing
New Mexico	79	mining, manufacturing, livestock
Hawaii	67	tourism, sugar, pineapple, military
Idaho	58	potatoes, wheat, timber, mining
Alaska	51	fishing, oil, natural gas, mining, timber
North Dakota	40	wheat, potatoes, oil
South Dakota	40	corn, wheat, mining, manufacturing
Montana	38	mining, wheat, forage crops, livestock
Wyoming	37	mining, oil, sheep, forage crops

*Gross State Product (2011), from US Bureau of Economic Analysis

tions over much of the West. With over $37 billion in annual sales, California leads the nation in overall agricultural production, followed by Texas with more than $13 billion; Nebraska ranks fourth in the US, after Iowa.

The most diverse Western farmlands are valleys near the Pacific coast. These valleys include Oregon's Willamette Valley, which lured pioneers after being acclaimed by Lewis and Clark. With more sunshine but greater need for irrigation, California's fertile valleys—particularly the Central and Salinas—yield some of the richest harvests in the world. Its Napa and Sonoma Valleys are famed for wine grapes, while elsewhere in the state, farmers produce artichokes, tomatoes, citrus, nuts and other vegetables and fruits. Washington is noted for apples and wine, Oregon for wine and berries, Idaho for potatoes, the Great Plains for wheat and grains. Livestock, especially sheep and cattle, are vital to the economies of several Western states, especially in the Rocky Mountains and Great Plains.

Once known for pineapples and sugar, Hawaii has had to downsize and diversify in the face of foreign competition. A broader threat to agriculture is urban growth and competition for water from expanding cities such as Las Vegas, Phoenix, Denver and Los Angeles.

Travelers in the West would do well to watch for fruit and vegetable stands offering fresh **local produce** – oranges, grapefruits, mandarins, avocados, and strawberries in California, chiefly in winter and spring; peaches, pears, apricots, apples and many kinds of berries from Sacramento north through Washington state, and in Western Colorado and Idaho's Snake River Valley, from July through November.

A delightful visitor experience in agricultural areas can be found at **"U-pick" farms**, where customers stroll the fields and orchards to pick their own fruit, berries and sometimes, vegetables. Buyers pay by the pound for what they pick – but not what they eat while they are picking. California, Oregon, Washington and Western Colorado are centers for this activity.

Diversified Economies

All the classic Western industries—farming and ranching, mining, timber, oil and gas—today contribute less than a quarter of the total USA West Gross

Domestic Product (GDP) of $6 trillion. The growing Pacific coastal cities were the first to diversify from resource- and agricultural-based economies; San Francisco has always been a trade and banking center, and Seattle shifted quickly from timber to trade and manufacturing. During the 20C, manufacturing and service industries inexorably moved to other Western cities. Regional banking centers such as Denver and Reno grew from mining and railroad-supply settlements in the 19C.

Los Angeles has grown into the West's largest, wealthiest, most culturally influential metropolitan area. With an artificial harbor, good railroad connections and ambitious engineering projects that delivered freshwater from the Sierra Nevada, Colorado River and northern California, L.A. set the example for other sprawling, prosperous and economically diversified Western cities such as Houston, Phoenix and Seattle.

The high-technology revolution of the late 20C spread from successful beginnings in Silicon Valley (San Jose), California, to Seattle and other regional centers in Oregon, Texas, Colorado and Idaho.

Service industries are the fastest growing employers in the West. Government is responsible for much of this growth, especially in California, with more than 250,000 federal civilian employees, and Texas, with almost 200,000. Large military bases in Hawaii, California, Nevada, Texas and Washington employ thousands.

Tourism and travel-related services (lodging, restaurants, entertainment, transportation) account for an increasing proportion of US economic activity—approaching $2 trillion in 2013. Tourism engenders close to $120 billion annually in California, followed by Texas ($60 billion), Nevada ($25 billion) and Hawaii ($12 billion).

PEOPLE OF THE WEST

The West remains the fastest growing region of the US. The demographic trend is playing out dramatically in booming communities such as Las Vegas, Tucson, San Antonio and Fort Worth, as the largest cities—Los Angeles, San Diego, Denver, Phoenix, Portland, and the San Francisco Bay and Puget Sound metropolitan areas—continue to drive the West's economic engines. Retirees account for large numbers of new residents here, although many of them are "sunbirds" who depart for cooler climates in summer. Denver, Seattle and Portland have all experienced huge growth as well, driven by technology jobs and a favorable quality of life. Other parts of the West, particularly the Great Basin, the Chihuahuan Desert of west Texas and southern New Mexico, the northern Rockies and Alaska, still contain thousands of square miles that are very sparsely inhabited.

The centuries-old influx of migrants to the West brought a heady mix of cultural traditions. San Francisco, Oakland, Los Angeles and Seattle are

Oil Field, Central Valley, California
©iStockphoto.com/Ian Crockett

among the most ethnically diverse cities in the world, with significant Chinese, Southeast Asian, Japanese, Filipino, Hispanic, Italian, Greek, Portuguese, Eastern European, Native American and African-American populations. The Texas Hill Country has strong ties to Germany. Alaska celebrates Russian heritage in Sitka and Kodiak. Basque sheepherders exert their influence on the hearty restaurants and small hotels of the Great Basin, Idaho and Wyoming. The ubiquitous Irish, who supplied much of the labor force of the early West, have rendered St. Patrick's Day a nearly universal celebration. Mexico's Cinco de Mayo is equally popular, and so is Chinese New Year in coastal cities.

Cowboys and Indians

The mythical picture of the West casts settlement as primarily a contest between Indians and Americans of European heritage. It's a woefully incomplete picture. For instance, a high percentage of cowboys in the late 19C, and rodeo circuit riders of the early 20C, were black. Many others were Hispanic and Indian. And many parts of the West, from southern Texas and Colorado to California, were first settled by Europeans of Hispanic descent centuries before Americans arrived.

Chinese workers represented a large percentage of the miners in the early West, as well as fishermen, railroad workers, road builders and construction workers. Hispanic workers continue to dominate the ranks of migratory field laborers throughout the West, and are key to construction industries as well.

Most Indians today have adopted popular American dress and customs—Indian rodeo, for instance, is hugely popular, quite distinctive and has its own professional circuit (www.aircarodeo.com)—and many have intermarried with other races and moved to urban areas. But a highly visible segment still dwells on reservations throughout the West; many of these tribes are thriving cultural and economic nations. The most traditional are the Hopi, who still live in pueblos on high desert mesas, completely surrounded by the Navajo Reservation. Other tribes and the Navajo maintain a balance between old ways and new, operating dynamic industries that range from timber to tourism. The reservations of the Great Plains and the Pacific slope are less tied to the nomadic or seafaring ways of the past, but likewise are less inclined to welcome tourism. The recent trend to operate casinos on tribal lands has revitalized the economies of many such groups: Indian gaming is a $15 billion enterprise involving more than 230 tribes nationwide. Native prosperity has accompanied a revival of traditional ways such as potlatches and, more commonly, pow-wows. Visitors are often welcome at these gatherings, which take place throughout the West (www.powwows.com).

Cowboys, for their part, are not completely confined to myth and movies. In some parts of the West, small ranchers still drive their cattle herds into the high country in spring and back down in fall, and tourists driving through Nevada, eastern Oregon, parts of Idaho and other interior states may well encounter a cattle drive on back roads. The drovers will, as always, tip their hats and raise a hand in greeting to passersby.

Dynamic—yet Relaxed

Despite the vigor of the Western economy, the region's residents value their time and quality of life as much as they do prosperity. Westerners, compared to the rest of the country, are more likely to work at home all or part of the time and to devote non-working hours to recreation and wellbeing. Seattle, Portland and San Francisco topped a recent survey of cities for "time saving"—ease of travel, access to lifestyle services.

Nine out of the 10 healthiest cities are in the West; Portland is rated most bike-friendly; six of the top 10 outdoor recreation cities are in the West.

Work hard? Sure—at work and life. That's the modern Western lifestyle.

Food and Drink

The food and drink of the West is linked to the staples developed by its peoples during successive waves of immigration: the corn, beans, chiles, squash and tomatoes of Meso-Americans; the salmon and shellfish of coastal peoples; the beef cattle, stone fruits, potatoes and wheat of European immigrants. All these ingredients have been mainstays for centuries. Modern Western cuisine is colored most distinctively by the styles of Hispanic and Asian cooking.

REGIONAL VARIATIONS

The chief regional distinction arises from Hispanic settlement in the Mexican border states (Texas, New Mexico, Arizona and California), where traditional cooking was based on corn (maize) and chiles. The native cuisine of the Indians embraced blue, white and yellow corn. Dried kernels are ground and made into breads, baked in ovens or on hot stones, resulting in the ubiquitous tortilla (which can also be made from wheat). This cuisine is famed for its tacos, tamales and enchiladas, many of which include hot chiles to lend spice. In Texas, such foods are popularized as Tejano or Tex-Mex; one signature dish is chili, a spicy meat stew.

Desert Southwest chefs have taken up traditional Native American foods such as prickly pear and mesquite bean. Bison (buffalo) is widespread inland; travelers might even find buffalo hash in small roadside diners. Game, such as venison and elk (farm-raised) is common in the Rocky Mountains.

Westerners have long been known for their penchant for red meat. Culinary reactions developed in the 1960s. Chief among these was California cuisine, credited to Alice Waters, which emphasized using fresh local ingredients, lightly prepared and presented artistically. Shortly afterward, Seattle and Portland chefs adapted local ingredients to a style known as Northwest Contemporary, which blends seafood with Continental and Asian influences. The most sophisticated dining experiences are still found in large cities and along the coast, especially Los Angeles, northern California, Portland and Seattle. In these areas many chefs, agricultural producers and residents have adopted the precepts of the Italian slow food movement (www.slowfood.org), favoring almost exclusively locally-sourced ingredients.

Elsewhere in the vast rural expanses of the Western hinterland (and in big cities as well) daily cuisine still includes the ubiquitous hamburger, french fries and milkshake, as well as steaks, spaghetti, pizza, tacos, fried chicken, and apple pie with ice cream. Modified ethnic cuisines such as Mexican, Italian, Southeast Asian and Chinese are readily available in nearly every large or medium-size town of the West. Fast-food teriyaki is as popular as hamburgers and french fries in Seattle; sushi holds the same regard in Los Angeles.

Regional differences persist. Seafood is the signature element along the coast, from southern California to Alaska: salmon, crab, oysters, clams and more exotic ingredients such as octopus, sea cucumber and seaweed. Diners seeking quality seafood should inquire about the freshness and origin of their meals; frozen fish is not as good, and some entrées that visitors often think are local are in fact not. With the exception of a very small fishery along the California central coast, for instance, lobster is flown to the West from New England or eastern Canada. Aside from salmon and crab, travelers should sample halibut, lingcod, rockfish, sturgeon, steelhead, sablefish (black cod), and Alaska's delectable but little-known spot prawns. Mexican influences pervade cuisine in

Fog City Diner, San Francisco

Brigitta L.House/MICHELIN

WHAT TO EAT

The culinary revolution begun by Alice Waters at Chez Panisse in Berkeley more than three decades ago has now spread to virtually all corners of the West.

Like most traditional regional cooking, Californian cuisine is based on natural, seasonally and locally available ingredients. Today these essentials are often acquired at farmers' markets and then incorporated using different cooking styles to produce the characteristic fusion style (which might incorporate Mexican and Central American, and Asian and Oceanic influences) that has been readily adapted throughout the West. Here is a brief summary of the signature dishes in several areas:

Texas: barbecued beef shoulder or brisket, roasted plain (no sauce) with hot pecan, mesquite or oak smoke, served on butcher paper.

Oklahoma and Kansas: barbecued pork ribs with tomato-based sauce, smoked 4-6 hours.

Arizona: fajitas, sliced grilled skirt steak served with tortillas.

New Mexico: green chile, spicy pork stew made with chile peppers.

High Plains: Rocky Mountain "oysters" – fried sheep or calf testicles.

Southern California: sushi, particularly the California roll, which is crab, avocado and cucumber wrapped in rice and seaweed; and fish tacos.

Northern California: Fresh Dungeness crab, served whole.

Oregon and Washington state: grilled fresh king, silver or sockeye salmon, cooked just barely firm. Also Dungeness crab; and sauteed geoduck or razor clams.

Dungeness crab, served whole

©iStockphoto.com/Karin Lau

SLOW DOWN, FOOD

Spurred by **Berkeley restaurant owner** Alice Waters' focus on local foods and the West Coast's progressive outlook, Western chefs and residents alike have embraced the ideals represented by the Slow Food movement of Europe. Its proponents promote food that has been produced in a way which respects the environment, human health and animal welfare. Most good restaurants now feature regionally produced ingredients ranging from **natural beef** (cows are grass-fed and not given chemical diets)—even in hamburgers and chili—to sustainably harvested seafood identified as **Oceanwise** (www.vanaqua.org/oceanwise). **Organic** foods range from artichokes to zucchini, and are certified as grown without chemicals. **Sustainably grown** foods might not be certified (which is an expensive process) but are raised with little or no chemicals, usually by small local producers. All these are wise choices, by visitors and residents alike.

Texas, New Mexico, Arizona, Colorado, Utah and Southern California, with local distinctions in each of those places. Asian elements are strong along the coast; Asian curries find their way onto the most sophisticated menus.

Refined tastes for wine have encouraged the increase of acreage planted with grapes, especially in California, Oregon and Washington state. Viticulture has expanded even into the Rockies, the desert Southwest, Texas and Hawaii. Demand for exceptional beer also has fueled the growth of small craft breweries across the West, their products called "microbrews." Portland is a center for this craft.

HISTORICAL FARE

Tomatoes, beans, squash, chillies and corn were all originally cultivated in Central America, but widely distributed in the Southwest and Great Plains when the first Europeans arrived. The dried meats of Plains Indian hunters and the *carne seco* of Southwestern farmers were forerunners of today's popular "jerky" snack.

The stampede of American settlers during gold and silver rushes depended initially upon game for food, but developed a taste for tinned foods and bread. Circumstantial invention produced novelties ranging from the Hangtown Fry (an omelet made from eggs, bacon rind and preserved oysters) to Caesar salad. Immigrants brought such simple recipes as Cornish pasties, Irish stews, Southeast Asian curries and Japanese teriyaki, the latter now ubiquitous.

A scarcity of yeast prompted a method of leavening bread with a large pinch of the latest dough, left in a warm spot to ferment its own. The resultant sourdough bread, descended from the California gold rush, is still baked from San Francisco to Alaska.

The era of the cowboy has associated beef with the West, though wranglers more likely enjoyed beans, stews and organ meats than the tough, stringy steaks. Far tastier beef emerged after a session in the stockyards at the end of the trail drives, to this day giving Kansas City and Omaha a reputation for steaks and barbecue. The Caddo Indians of Texas were smoking meat over smouldering wood 10,000 years ago. Today, barbecue has become a hallmark of Western dining, While grilling over gas fires has replaced using coals or mesquite as the most popular means, the traditional method in Texas is to bury a prepared carcass with the coals, allowing it to cook underground, pit-style.

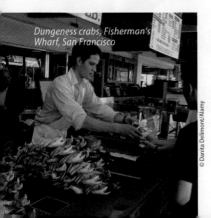
Dungeness crabs, Fisherman's Wharf, San Francisco

© Danita Delimont/Alamy

USA West History

Once a region traversed by nomadic settlers, the US West was one of the last areas on earth exposed to European colonization. Its complex history of peoples in flux led to a frontier spirit that survives in both myth and reality. Those who live "out West," as the phrase goes, pride themselves on their hardiness and adventurous spirit—and the region's colorful past explains why.

Herd of Bison PhotoDisc, Inc

Key Events

Key dates, events, characters, politics, society and cultural shifts in USA West's history: from the early migrations and native inhabitants, European exploration, pioneer settlements and the gold rushes to preservation efforts, World War II and the New Millennium.

THE EARLY MIGRATIONS

Archaeological sites throughout the Americas yield many clues about the origins of Native Americans, but controversy persists over when or by what route they arrived in the New World. Most scientists believe that the majority of ancestral Native Americans walked from northeastern Asia across the Bering land bridge during the Pleistocene Epoch. They would have moved south via an ice-free corridor that opened through Canada during a warming period. An intriguing newer theory postulates that some may have arrived from Siberia in skin boats—some settling in Alaska, most coasting around the maritime glaciers and quickly moving south to settle the more promising temperate coastal spots, then heading inland over succeeding generations.

The first **Paleo-Indians** apparently arrived 30,000 years ago, finding a land rich in mammoths, camels, large bison, mastodons, prehistoric horses and other big game. Whether the Paleo-Indians died out or were absorbed into later populations is unknown, but judging from the scant remains they left, they were anthropologically distinct from contemporary Native Americans. The oldest complete human corpse discovered in North America, the **Spirit Cave mummy** from central Nevada, was radiocarbon-dated to about 9,400 years ago and apparently has no direct descendants. The skeleton of 9,300-year-old **Kennewick Man**, found in a burial site near the Columbia River in Washington, indicates racial links nearer to southern Asian or Polynesian people than to modern Native Americans. Traces of Paleo-Indian flint projectile points have been found at Folsom and Clovis, New Mexico, and elsewhere.

The ancestors of most modern Native Americans began arriving about 15,000 years ago. Descended from northeastern Asian peoples, they also hunted big game, although larger mammals began to disappear as the climate warmed about 10,000 years ago. Succeeding generations of these **hunters and gatherers** fanned out across the Americas, adapting to specific territorial homelands.

A third migration about 9,500 years ago brought the **Athabascan** ancestors of the Navajo, Apache and peoples of the Alaskan and Canadian interior. Ancestors of the **Inuit and Aleut** people arrived in a fourth migration from Siberia about 4,500 years ago, occupying the frigid Arctic and stormy Aleutian Islands.

Hawaiians trace their ancestry to two distinct waves of Polynesian settlers who sailed northward in double-hulled canoes. The first wave arrived between AD 400 and 750, probably from the Marquesas Islands. The second migration, likely from Tahiti, arrived around 1100. These newcomers vanquished the earlier inhabitants and developed a society in which chiefs and hereditary priests held social ascendancy over large classes of farmers and fishermen.

c.30,000 BC	Paleo-Indians begin arriving in North America, probably across the Bering Land Bridge.
c.300 BC	Irrigated farming enters Arizona from Mexico.
c.AD 1200	Ancestral Puebloan cliff dwellings abandoned.

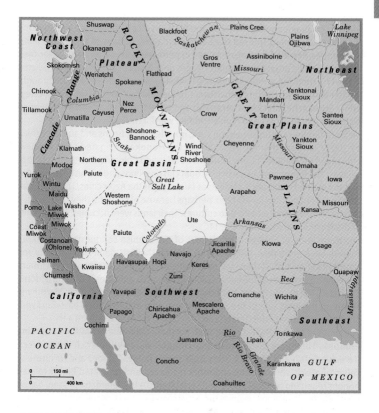

INDIAN NATIONS

When Europeans arrived at the end of the 15C, scores of nations occupied America's West. Some were migratory hunters and gatherers; others lived in fixed villages. Erroneously assuming they had landed in the East Indies, the first Europeans called Native inhabitants "Indians." Though scholars may refer to Native Americans or Amerindians, the most common term used today, even among tribal leaders, is "American Indian."

Of the 54 million people that anthropologists estimate were living in the Americas at the time of Columbus' "discovery" in 1492, about 4 million dwelled north of Mexico. At least 300 distinct languages were spoken. West of the Mississippi River, anthropologists count 56 language families, although six predominated. **Uto-Aztecan** prevailed from central Mexico into Texas; it was spoken by the Comanche, Shoshone, Paiute, and the Pueblo cultures of New Mexico. **Siouan** was the dominant language of the Great Plains and Missouri River Valley. **Algonquian** was spoken by the Blackfoot, Cheyenne and Arapaho peoples who had migrated to the northern plains from northeastern woodlands.

Salish was dominant in the Northwest coastal region. **Athabascan** was spoken in western (but not coastal) Canada and central Alaska, and by Navajo and Apache in the Southwest. **Eskimo-Aleut** was the tongue of the Inuit and Aleut people of Alaska. In California alone, there was a veritable Babel of 120 dialects (of seven separate language families).

Numerous migrations predated European contact in the late 17C. Eastern woodland farmers, including the **Mandan, Omaha, Osage, Pawnee** and **Wichita**, headed to the western prairies between 100 BC and AD 900. Later European settlement along the eastern seaboard spurred the **Lakota** and other nations to the Great Plains. Many tribes, like the Mandan, remained in permanent farming villages after their migration, while others abandoned villages once Spanish horses were introduced in the 17C, choosing a nomadic lifestyle following bison herds. Horses also brought greater leisure and a cultural renaissance to the **Lakota, Crow, Assiniboine, Cheyenne, Comanche, Blackfoot, Arapaho** and other tribes, all of whom developed elaborate religious rites and highly codified warrior rituals.

Mexican farming culture, based on corn, gourds, chiles, beans and squash spread by 300 BC into southern Arizona, where the **Hohokam** irrigated corn. Farming influenced the peoples of the southern Rockies and Colorado Plateau to settle in villages. The **Puebloans**, in particular, built cliff dwellings and sophisticated towns that maintained elaborate trade links as far distant as the Aztec cities. The **Puebloan** cities were abandoned by AD 1200, perhaps because of drought; they transformed into the modern **Hopi** and **Pueblo** cultures. Their lands were occupied by ancestors of the **Navajo** and **Apache** in the 14C.

The population of California on the eve of the Spanish conquests is estimated to have been more than 300,000. With fish and shellfish, game, roots, seeds and acorns readily available, there was never a need for farming, except among **Yuman**-speaking desert tribes of the lower Colorado River. Coastal tribes, including **Ohlone, Chumash, Yurok** and **Pomo**, traded with inland tribes such as **Miwok, Maidu** and **Yokut** on the west side of the Sierra Nevada, who in turn traded eastward with Shoshonean tribes of the Great Basin.

The tribes of the Northwest coast, from northern California to Alaska—including **Chinook, Tillamook, Skokomish** and **Tlingit**—were likewise rich in resources, particularly fish and shellfish. They built sturdy homes, canoes and furniture of cedar, hemlock, spruce, bone and other resources, and cultivated highly refined notions regarding material goods and social status. A key ceremony of song, dance, feasting and gift-giving known as the potlatch was banned by government officials in the late 19C, but has been revived today.

The inland tribes in the Columbia Basin, especially the **Nez Perce, Cayuse** and **Flathead**, migrated from the Pacific coast. They depended upon salmon runs for a major part of their diet, supplementing fish with game and plants, including the nutritious camas bulb. The arrival of the horse to this region in the 18C increased the tribes' mobility and trading contacts.

Despite the ubiquity of the American Indian tribes, new diseases brought by European contact swept the Americas and thinned native populations as much as 90 percent—perhaps the most lethal pandemic ever visited upon mankind.

1492	Christopher Columbus lands in the Western Hemisphere.

EUROPEAN INROADS

The conquest of the Aztec empire in 1521 by **Hernán Cortés** (1485-1547) enormously enriched the Spanish treasury and plunged the Spanish government into colonization of their vast new territories in the New World. Spanish exploration of North America followed rumors of gold carried back to Mexico in 1536 by **Alvar Núñez Cabeza de Vaca** (c.1490-1557).

A succession of explorers penetrated the unknown land seeking treasures in the mythical Seven Cities of Cibola—most prominently the expeditions of **Hernando de Soto** (1496-1542), who entered Oklahoma from the east in 1541, and **Francisco Vásquez de Coronado** (1510-54). Coronado marched north from Mexico in 1540, wreaking mayhem among the Pueblos, pushing as far north as the Grand Canyon and possibly as far east as Kansas, but failing to find another Aztec or Inca empire. Spain allowed its colonization of New Mexico and California to languish until **Sir Francis Drake** (c.1540-96) landed on California's north coast and claimed it for England in 1579. That sparked a northward expansion of Spanish frontiers. Throughout the 17C, expansion of Spanish settlements—and with them, the forced conversion of Indians to Roman Catholicism—progressed with checkered success throughout the Rio Grande Valley. The colonies survived despite periodic setbacks, including the devastating **Pueblo Revolt of 1680**, when Indians drove the Spanish from New Mexico for more than a decade. Spanish policy thereafter was reformed to permit native religious practices to continue, and the culture of New Mexico developed into a blend of Spanish and Pueblo, with its capital at **Santa Fe**.

The French, meanwhile, were scouring the USA West for a different treasure: fur pelts. The French seized the key to the Great Plains in the 17C by building trading posts along the Mississippi River at St. Louis and other strategic points. They called the region Louisiana after King Louis XIV. By 1682, when **René-Robert Cavalier de la Salle** (1643-87) navigated the river to its mouth and claimed the Mississippi and its tributaries for France, the vast territory stretched from Canada to the Gulf of Mexico. Separating Florida from Mexico, it prompted a Spanish frenzy to colonize Texas.

Over the next half century, French traders explored every western tributary to the Rockies, even mounting an expedition to Santa Fe in 1739. The French did not pursue a vigorous colonization of Louisiana, however, so the tribes of the Great Plains remained unaffected by their paper affiliation with the French empire. Territorial settlements developed a Creole character born of French, African slave and Native American populations. Greater numbers of American adventurers arrived after 1763, when the **Treaty of Paris**—ending the French and Indian War—extended the borders of British colonies from the Atlantic Ocean to the Mississippi River. Neglected for more than a century, Spain's claims to Alta (Upper) California were revived by fears of foreign incursions. Under **Aleksei Chirikov** (1703-48) and Dane **Vitus Bering** (1681-1741), Russians began probing Alaskan waters in 1728, sparking an influx of fur hunters and fortified colonies along that coast. English ships also investigated the Pacific: **James Cook** (1728-79) claimed British Columbia for England in 1768. Cook subsequently visited the Pacific Northwest and Hawaii in 1778, and **George Vancouver** (1757-98) mapped the Canadian coast in 1792-94.

Goaded into action, a Spanish expedition organized by Padre **Junípero Serra** (1713-84) and **Gaspar de Portolá** (c.1723-86) pushed, by land and sea, to San Diego harbor, where Serra dedicated the first of California's 21 missions on July 16, 1769. Over the next decade, a string of missions, pueblos and presidios was erected along a coastal strip that stretched from San Diego to San Francisco Bay, with a provincial capital at Monterey.

1521	Hernán Cortés defeats the Aztecs and claims Mexico for Spain.
1540-42	Francisco de Coronado marches through the Southwest in search of the "Seven Cities of Cibola."
1542	Juan Cabrillo explores the California coast.
1579	Sir Francis Drake lands in California, claiming it for England.
1609	Santa Fe is founded.
1680	Spanish colonists flee northern New Mexico after more than 400 are slaughtered in Pueblo Revolt; they return in 1692.
1682	René-Robert de la Salle sails down the Mississippi, claiming the river and its western drainage for France.

1728	Vitus Bering explores the coast of Alaska for Russia.
1762	France cedes Louisiana Territory to Spain to avoid losing it to England.
1763	Treaty of Paris extends British (American colonial) frontier west to the Mississippi River.
1768	Captain James Cook claims coastal Canada for Great Britain.
1769	Junípero Serra establishes first of 21 California coastal missions.
1776	The future San Francisco is founded at Mission Dolores.
1778	Captain Cook makes first landing in Hawaii.
1781	Los Angeles is founded.
1784	Russia establishes settlements at Kodiak and Sitka, Alaska.
1792-94	George Vancouver charts Pacific coast from San Diego to Alaska, leading to competing British and US claims to Oregon Country.
1800	Napoleonic France regains Louisiana Territory from Spain.

LOUISIANA PURCHASE

The westward expansion of the US in the late 17C and 18C—both as a collection of British colonies and as an independent republic after 1776—inexorably progressed despite warfare with Native Americans and complex political and military maneuvering among European powers in North America. The rallying cry that justified and even glorified this expansion was "**Manifest Destiny,**" the idea that the US was ordained by divine right to push its borders to the Pacific. European conflict enabled the single greatest stroke in this expansion when a shortage of funds convinced Napoleon to sell Louisiana to the US for about $15 million in 1803 to support his war against Great Britain.

Pressed as much by personal curiosity as national interest, President Thomas Jefferson selected his personal secretary, **Meriwether Lewis** (1774-1809), to head an exploratory expedition, and Lewis invited his boyhood friend, career soldier **William Clark** (1770-1838), as co-leader. Instructed to promote trade with the Indians, observe flora and fauna, map major rivers and their sources, and make records of soils, minerals and climate, the *Corps of Discovery* set course up the Missouri River on May 14, 1804, with a party of seasoned frontiersmen.

Wintering at a Mandan village in what is now North Dakota, they enlisted a French Canadian trapper, Toussaint Charbonneau, as an interpreter for their journey. Charbonneau's Shoshone wife, **Sacagawea** (c.1786-1812), unexpectedly proved a far greater asset. The presence of a native woman signaled to western tribes that this was not a war party. Sacagawea was instrumental in obtaining horses when the expedition dramatically encountered a Shoshone tribe, led by her own brother, near the Continental Divide. After a strenuous descent from the Rockies, Lewis and Clark arrived at the Pacific Ocean on November 7, 1805. They wintered at the mouth of the Columbia River and returned to St. Louis in September 1806, having lost only one man, to appendicitis.

The extraordinary success of Lewis and Clark overshadowed other government-funded forays into the West. After leading an expedition to the upper Mississippi in

Nineteenth Century Indian Territory Map

1805-06, **Zebulon Pike** (1779-1813) investigated the Colorado Front Range headwaters of the Arkansas and Red Rivers; another party, led by Major **Stephen H. Long** (1784-1864), ascended the Platte River and looped back through the high plains; Long branded the region "the Great American Desert."

Others headed west without government support, seeking adventure and profit from the burgeoning fur trade. These "mountain men" sought buffalo robes, bear and deer hides, the pelts of otter and fox, and especially beaver furs, which earned high prices in Chinese and European markets. Among them was **John Colter** (c.1774-1813), who left the eastbound Lewis and Clark party and became the first person to describe the Yellowstone country. **Jedediah Smith** (1799-1831) was a Bible-toting teetotaler who blazed trails across the Great Basin to California and north to the Columbia River. Others included **Kit Carson** (1809-68), **Jim Bridger** (1804-81), **Jim Beckwourth** (c.1800-66) and **Joe Walker** (1798-1876). Living in extreme isolation and independence, these men became thoroughly acquainted with the West, blazing the first transcontinental trails or bringing long-established Indian trails to the attention of travelers. After Mexico overthrew Spanish rule in 1821, Santa Fe began welcoming American traders. **William Becknell** (c.1790-1865) became the first American to push wagons through the plains to the New Mexico outpost, opening the **Santa Fe Trail** and earning large profits by exchanging hardware and dry goods for livestock.

The fur trade heated up on the Pacific slope, too, after New Englander **Robert Gray** (1755-1806) made a fortune on an around-the-world voyage, gathering pelts along the Northwest coast in 1789 and selling them in China for vast profits. The name of his ship, *Columbia*, was bestowed upon the Northwest's great river. As New England merchants pushed deeply into the China trade, clipper ships called at San Diego, Santa Barbara, Monterey and San Francisco Bay, resupplying and trading for tallow and cowhides. California's enviable climate and excellent harbors became common knowledge along the Eastern seaboard after **Richard Henry Dana** published his best-seller *Two Years Before the Mast* (1840).

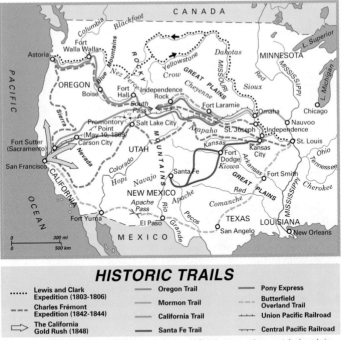

HISTORIC TRAILS

⋯⋯ Lewis and Clark Expedition (1803-1806)	▬▬▬ Oregon Trail	▬▬▬ Pony Express
- - - Charles Frémont Expedition (1842-1844)	▬▬▬ Mormon Trail	┴┴┴ Butterfield Overland Trail
⟹ The California Gold Rush (1848)	▬▬▬ California Trail	┼┼┼ Union Pacific Railroad
	▬▬▬ Santa Fe Trail	┬┬┬ Central Pacific Railroad

The boundaries shown between the United States, Mexico and Canada represent the present-day boundaries

Yankees also reaped great profits in the Pacific from hunting whales, the primary source of lamp oil in the mid 19C. One rich hunting ground was the Hawaiian Islands. Soon after Captain Cook had introduced the remote archipelago (dubbed the "Sandwich Isles") to the world, **King Kamehameha I** (c.1758-1819) unified the islands in 1795. Whaling rapidly became the economic mainstay, increasing the kingdom's reliance on foreign advisers while enabling hundreds of sturdy Hawaiian sailors to ship out. The whalers' most insidious contributions to local culture were smallpox, syphilis and other epidemics that ravaged the indigenous population, whittling their numbers from 300,000 at the time of Cook's visit to 54,000 a century later.

The **Indian Removal Act of 1830** saw the Cherokee, Chickasaw, Choctaw, Creek and Seminole nations uprooted from their homelands in the South and forced to march to the **Indian Territory**, now Oklahoma. Ironically known as the Five Civilized Tribes for their adoption of American clothing and agricultural methods, the populations were decimated by the internment and grueling march, since referred to by the Cherokee tribe as the "Trail of Tears." Moved by a delegation of Flathead Indians that arrived in St. Louis in 1831 and seeking information on Christianity, Methodist and Presbyterian missionaries set out for the isolated Oregon Country. A mission near modern Walla Walla, Washington, was built by **Marcus Whitman** (1804-47); in 1836, his wife, **Narcissa Whitman**, and her companion, **Eliza Spaulding**, became the first American women to cross the continent.

1803	US buys Louisiana Territory from France for $15 million.
1804-06	Lewis and Clark journey up the Missouri River, across the Rocky Mountains and down the Columbia River to the Pacific Ocean.
1811	Fur traders found Fort Astoria at mouth of Columbia River.

1812	Russians establish Fort Ross on northern California coast.
1818	Treaty with Great Britain establishes northern US territorial border.
1821	Mexico declares independence from Spain. Santa Fe Trail opens.
1824	US War Department creates Bureau of Indian Affairs.
1830	Indian Removal Act mandates relocation of Five Civilized Tribes from southeastern US to Indian Territory (now Oklahoma).

PIONEER MOVEMENT

The three Western destinations that most appealed to early pioneers were each claimed by a foreign nation. The promised land in the 1830s was Texas, then governed by Mexico. In the 1840s, new streams of pioneers set out for the Oregon Country, jointly (though sparsely) occupied by Britain and the US. Other pioneers set their sights on California, a neglected Mexican outpost.

Anglo-American traders and squatters had been unwelcome residents of Texas since the late 18C. Most Americans flooding into Texas had no intention whatsoever of respecting Mexican law or culture. Anglo Texans proved so assertive of their independence that political tensions had degenerated to skirmishes, and Mexico resolved to put down the rebellion. In 1836 Mexican General **Antonio López de Santa Anna** (1794-1876) took 4,000 troops to San Antonio and slaughtered a party of insurrectionists at a former mission, the Alamo. Santa Anna then marched east to San Jacinto, near modern Houston, to dispatch another small Texas army, this one led by **Sam Houston** (1793-1863). Rallying under the battle cry "Remember the Alamo!" the Texans captured Santa Anna, defeating his troops and winning their independence. The new Republic of Texas elected Sam Houston as its president. Beset by debt, Indian hostilities and conflict with a Mexico unwilling to recognize its independence, Texas was steered by Houston toward statehood in 1845.

Oregon proved a less contentious acquisition. With its salubrious climate and soil, the Oregon Country's graces were well advertised in the East. Convoys of Conestoga wagons began journeying west from Independence, Missouri, in 1842, guided by scouts familiar with a route soon known as the Oregon Trail. Stretching some 2,000mi, the **Oregon Trail** followed the Platte River across Nebraska, surmounted the Continental Divide at broad South Pass between Fort Laramie and Fort Bridger then crossed the Snake River Plain and Blue Mountains to Whitman's Walla Walla mission. A final stretch down the Columbia River brought tired travelers to the lush Willamette River Valley. In 1843 the Oregon Country petitioned Congress for protection from British claims and marauding Indians. In 1846 the US and Britain compromised on the 49th parallel as their boundary. The slaughter of Whitman and his fellow missionaries by Indians in 1847 provoked another demand for federal protection, and in 1848 the Oregon Territory was formally established.

Some parties of transcontinental migrants left the Oregon Trail for California. The Mexican residents of California, known as **Californios**, were a self-sufficient lot; they received scant attention from Mexico's government, which was content to let the landholders rule themselves. A growing population of Yankees and other foreigners were living in Monterey and other settlements, having jumped ship, adopted the Roman Catholic religion and become naturalized Mexican citizens. Many became prominent in Californio society.

Among the foreign residents was **John Augustus Sutter** (1803-80), a Swiss adventurer with vast land grants along the American River in the Sacramento Valley. Sutter entertained many travelers and immigrants at his walled fort, including US Army surveyor **John C. Frémont** (1813-90) after his exhausting 1844 winter crossing of the Sierra Nevada. Frémont's published report of his California journey became the standard guidebook for westbound travelers.

After Texas gained statehood, the resulting war with Mexico eventually brought the US the land that is today Arizona and New Mexico. A contemporaneous insurgent movement in California had declared the area an independent republic, but the rebels welcomed US help in the form of a military expedition led by General **Stephen Kearny** (1794-1848). By the end of hostilities in 1848, Texas was safely in US hands, along with the entire West all the way to Los Angeles, then a sleepy trading village, and San Diego.

1834	Mexico secularizes California missions.
1836	Texas wins independence from Mexico six weeks after slaughter at The Alamo. Whitmans establish Walla Walla mission.
1842	First settlers leave Missouri on Oregon Trail.
1845	Republic of Texas becomes US state.
1846	US acquires Oregon Territory south of 49th parallel in negotiations with Great Britain.

THE MORMONS

Even before it was relinquished by Mexico, the Great Basin had already been proclaimed the State of Deseret by a sect of pioneers who called themselves Latter-day Saints, or Mormons. The Church of Jesus Christ of Latter-day Saints was founded in 1830 in New York by **Joseph Smith** (1805-44). His zealous missionary work reaped new members, but he antagonized many others with his determined espousal of Old Testament views on polygamy and by his adherence to the unorthodox *Book of Mormon*; attributed to divine revelation, it propounded that Jesus had taught in North America after his Biblical resurrection. When the sect moved West to facilitate its missionary work, the Mormons were violently driven from Ohio to Missouri to Illinois, where Smith was murdered by an armed mob. **Brigham Young** (1801-77) assumed the role of prophet and leader.

Young led his people to the Great Salt Lake Valley in 1847. Young directed the construction of **Salt Lake City**; he returned East to bring more Mormon immigrants, encouraged others from Europe, and exhorted all to bring the tools, seeds and zeal they would need to establish a self-sufficient nation in a hard land. Thousands made the trek across the Plains and Rockies in ensuing decades, swelling the closely knit population and making the desert bloom with irrigation water from the Wasatch Mountains.

The Utah Territory was established in 1850, but friction soon developed over questions of loyalty. The institution of polygamy, and rumors of Mormon-inspired Indian uprisings, raised alarm in the East. Convinced of impending rebellion, the US government in 1857 ordered 2,500 troops to march to Utah to install a new governor to replace Young. Young portrayed the invasion as a tool of Mormon persecution. He declared martial law, mobilized a militia, recalled distant Mormon outposts, burned down Fort Bridger in Wyoming, fortified the western boundary of the Utah Territory, and even ordered Mormons to be ready to torch their own settlements. Tensions peaked when zealots slaughtered a party of non-Mormon pioneers at the Mountain

Meadow Massacre in southern Utah. But with both sides perched on the brink of disaster, common sense prevailed, and diplomats negotiated a peaceful resolution.

1847	Brigham Young leads Mormons into Great Salt Lake Valley. Whitman missionaries slain by Cayuse Indians.
1848	US wins New Mexico and California in treaty ending Mexican War. Gold discovered in California, igniting gold rush of 1849.

GOLD AND SILVER RUSHES

A few weeks before the formal peace with Mexico in 1848, flecks of gold were discovered in the sand at John Sutter's lumber mill on California's American River. The news spread like wildfire. The next year, **Forty-Niners** began pouring by land and sea into California from the eastern US, Europe, Australia, Asia, Mexico and South America. In just weeks, the port city of San Francisco grew from a sleepy village of 800 to a cosmopolitan hive of 90,000. In January 1849 alone, 61 vessels arrived at San Francisco Bay from the Eastern seaboard after sailing around stormy Cape Horn. As passengers and crews set off for the gold mines, abandoned ships rotted or were dragged ashore to serve as hotels, warehouses and offices. Meanwhile, thousands of prospectors—as well as tradesmen, money lenders, innkeepers, teamsters, preachers, gamblers, gunslingers and prostitutes—set out overland along the Oregon, California and Santa Fe trails.

Mining camps with names like Rough and Ready, Hangtown, Poker Flat and Murderers Bar sprang up in the canyons and foothills, and California's Caucasian population mushroomed from 15,000 in 1848 to almost 100,000 in 1850, when California joined the Union as the 31st state. The frenetic activity died down toward the end of the 1850s with the decline of surface gold; individual gold miners gave way to mining corporations, companies with stockholders and the capital to build and operate hard-rock, dredging and hydraulic mining operations. Thousands of fortune hunters returned home or settled into new opportunities in California, where ranching, farming, construction, and other jobs became increasingly available.

The California gold rush was the archetype of a series of mining rushes that marked the West for the next 60 years, instantly peopling remote corners with makeshift towns. Strikes in Colorado and Nevada started new stampedes just as the California rush was settling down. The Pikes Peak gold rush hit pay dirt in 1858; the nearby city of **Denver** was platted by speculators that winter, and by spring 1859 a real rush was on. New lodes were discovered higher in the Rockies; Denver's first newspaper, *The Rocky Mountain News*, began publication in April, and a US mint opened the following year. Hostile confrontations with Indians increased; reservations were established deeper into the plains, and Indians were rounded up in campaigns that degenerated into the full-blown **Indian Wars**. Numerous smaller strikes flared up throughout the West, from Arizona to Montana and South Dakota.

The 1859 discovery of Nevada's vast **Comstock Lode** of silver and gold produced a very different kind of mining rush. The difficulties of mining ore required capital investment and sophisticated engineering. Speculators from California bought up stock in the richest mines, while San Francisco merchants, farmers and transport companies earned good profits shipping supplies, food and people to the town that grew atop the mines, Virginia City. As newly minted millionaires built elegant mansions atop Nob Hill in San Francisco, Virginia City emerged as the first truly industrialized city west of the Mississippi.

1850	California enters the Union.

85

LINKING EAST AND WEST

The first overland transcontinental mail and passenger-coach service was contracted in 1857 to **John Butterfield, William G. Fargo & Associates**, who avoided the snows of the Rockies using a route from St. Louis and Memphis to El Paso, Tucson and Los Angeles. Faster service came with the **Pony Express**, which transported express mail by relays from St. Joseph, Missouri, to Sacramento, California, and by ship to San Francisco. Riding in 75mi increments, day and night, changing ponies at stations spaced every 10-15mi, a team of riders could transport the mail pouch in 10 days. The route grew shorter as telegraph lines edged across America; they joined in 1861. The West escaped the ravages of the Civil War, save for a few small skirmishes.

The US government, eager to ensure a steady flow of California gold and Comstock silver during the war, pushed for a transcontinental railroad that would link California and Nevada with the East Coast. As incentive, Congress offered land grants and subsidies to rail companies for every mile of track laid. Two companies formed to build lines from opposite ends: the **Central Pacific** eastward from California and the **Union Pacific** westward from Missouri.

Financiers **Collis P. Huntington** (1821-1900), **Mark Hopkins** (1814-78), **Charles Crocker** (1822-88) and **Leland Stanford** (1824-93)—who became known as "The Big Four"—established the Central Pacific in 1861. Construction over the most difficult sections of the Sierra's Donner Pass depended heavily upon 15,000 laborers from China, who laid the track. The Union Pacific, employing large numbers of Irish, set out across the Great Plains under chief engineer **Grenville Dodge** (1831-1916). Despite Indian resistance, the rolling terrain permitted faster progress than in the Far West. The project was known as "Hell on Wheels," both for its rambunctious crews and for the army of rascally camp followers, saloons, gambling dens and brothels that flourished in their wake. The two crews joined east and west with the **Golden Spike** at Promontory Point, Utah, on May 10, 1869.

The railroads prospered, and their boards and presidents acquired great political and economic clout. By deftly wielding their vast real-estate grants, these corporations could determine where cities and towns would be built, and which communities could prosper. The **Northern Pacific** opened the Dakota Territory and Montana to easier settlement by linking Minnesota with Portland, Oregon, in 1883, and with Seattle in 1887. The **Southern Pacific** extended a line from New Orleans to Los Angeles and San Francisco.

1858-59	Gold discovered in Colorado; Comstock Lode (silver) revealed in Nevada.
1858-61	Butterfield stagecoaches run from St. Louis to Los Angeles.
1860-61	Pony Express inaugurated.
1861-65	Civil War.
1861	First transcontinental telegraph line completed.
1866	Led by Red Cloud, Sioux eject Army from Wyoming's Fort Phil Kearny. First cattle drive on Goodnight-Loving Trail.
1867	US buys Alaska from Russia for $7.2 million.
1869	Transcontinental railroad joined in Utah. Wyoming gives women suffrage. John Wesley Powell charts Grand Canyon by boat.

THE CATTLE INDUSTRY

The Great Plains obviously were ideal for livestock. Herds of **bison** numbered perhaps 50 million prior to the arrival of Europeans. However, the buffalo were nearly wiped out in an orgy of slaughter that climaxed in the 1870s, when animals were wantonly killed from passing trains or massacred en masse for their hides. Their extermination crushed the independence of the Indians, but it also opened the ranges for cattle. Ironically, three decades later US buffalo were saved from extinction partly through the efforts of former hunters such as Buffalo Bill and Theodore Roosevelt. The **longhorn range** cattle of the Texas plains were descended from breeds brought north from Mexico in the late 17C. Most of the techniques of livestock husbandry used in 19C Texas likewise were developed from methods used in Spanish New Mexico: cattle were grazed on open ranges, gathered by roping from horseback in annual roundups, branded and driven to market in herds. Even the clothing, saddle and lingo of the Anglo cattle industry were largely adapted from the *vaqueros*.

After the Civil War, with beef in Northern markets earning 10 times as much as on the Southern plains, enterprising Texans contrived a scheme to round up wild cattle. They were driven to railheads and shipped to stockyards and meat-packing plants in Chicago, Omaha and Kansas City, thence to the Northeast. Crews of cowboys branded and drove the cattle along what soon became well-established routes, including the **Chisholm, Goodnight-Loving, Sedalia** and **Western trails**.

The drives were fraught with danger and discomfort. Rivers had to be forded; bandits, hostile Indians, wildfires, disease and extreme weather conditions took their toll. After weeks in the saddle, cowboys were ecstatic to return to some semblance of civilization. The arrival of a cattle drive in a terminal town—among them Fort Worth, Texas; Cheyenne, Wyoming; Wichita, Abilene and Dodge City, Kansas—was marked by days and nights of frantic celebration and wild roughhousing by the pleasure-starved wranglers. The excitement and ready money in cow towns attracted saloon keepers, prostitutes, gamblers and various riffraff to serve or fleece the cowboys. Gunplay was common, giving rise to a tough breed of lawmen who sometimes were hard to distinguish from hired gunslingers. Some names have become part of Western legend: **Wyatt Earp** (1848-1929), **William Barclay "Bat" Masterson** (1853-1921), **James Butler "Wild Bill" Hickok** (1837-76).

Many early Texas cattlemen—including **Jesse Chisholm** (1805-68), **John Chisum** (1824-84) and **Charles Goodnight** (1836-1929)—grew wealthy from the cattle drives, and staked out huge ranches on the plains. Soon the introduction of barbed wire in the 1870s offered a practical method of fencing large, treeless areas. Consolidation of the cattle industry on large ranches encouraged the formation of cooperative organizations to fight rustlers, look after business interests and make rules governing roundups, quarantines, branding and mavericks (unbranded stray cattle). As the industry became more regulated, it attracted well-moneyed Eastern and European investors. Powerful organizations and cattlemen sometimes tried vigilantism to hinder "nesters" (homesteaders) and small ranchers from gaining footholds. Dangerous and widespread range wars, such as New Mexico's 1878 Lincoln County War, brought notoriety to gunmen like **William "Billy the Kid" Bonney** (c.1859-81).

1872	Yellowstone is established as the first national park.
1876	Lt. Col. George Custer and his troops annihilated by Sioux and Cheyenne at Battle of the Little Bighorn.
1877	Chief Joseph and his band of Nez Perce are captured after a 1,200mi flight.
1878	"Billy the Kid" begins a short but notorious outlaw career by killing a sheriff during the Lincoln County War.

| 1883 | "Buffalo Bill" Cody launches his renowned Wild West Show. |
| 1887 | Dawes Act redistributes reservation land to individual Indians. |

THE INDIAN WARS

As ever-growing numbers of miners, cattlemen, railroad builders, soldiers and pioneers pushed across the Great Plains and Rockies, overrunning what had been designated "Indian land," the federal government sought to redraw the boundaries of native homelands. Reservations for the Cheyenne, Arapaho, Blackfoot, Sioux, Crow and other tribes were reduced in size and placed as far as possible from railways and settlements. The Army set about enforcing the tribes' removal to the reservations. As buffalo herds dwindled, and with federal troops fighting the Civil War in the East, some tribes stepped up depredations against settlements in the high plains. When one renegade band of Cheyenne sued for peace in 1864, a Colorado militia force led by Methodist minister John Chivington ambushed their camp, killing 165 to 200 men, women and children in what became known as the **Sand Creek Massacre**. Already angered by the decimation of bison herds, by countless trespasses on their hunting grounds and by broken treaties, Native Americans from Texas to Montana were convinced that they must fight to survive. The 1870s saw repeated insurrections. Among the bloodiest were the 1874-75 Red River War, staged by Comanche and Kiowa led by **Quanah Parker** (c.1845-1911); and the four-month, 1,200mi odyssey of the Nez Perce under **Chief Joseph** (c.1840-1904), who was determined not to be confined to a reservation.

The Sioux offered the most dogged resistance on the Great Plains. After the Bozeman Trail to Montana mines was cut through Sioux hunting grounds east of the Big Horn Mountains, **Red Cloud** (1822-1909) led the tribe in an 1866 campaign that forced the US Army to surrender and abandon Fort Phil Kearny. Red Cloud also secured guarantees for South Dakota's sacred Black Hills in exchange for his promise to never again go to war against the US. But when prospectors discovered gold in the Black Hills in 1874 and a full-blown gold rush ensued, the Sioux returned to war under **Crazy Horse** (c.1842-77) and **Sitting Bull** (1831-90).

Peace negotiations failed dismally. As the Sioux and their Cheyenne allies rode west toward the Big Horns, pursued by the Army, they established camp on the Little Bighorn River of Montana. When Lt. Col. **George Armstrong Custer** (1839-76) and his 7th Cavalry attacked without ascertaining the Indians' full force, he and all 225 of his troops, plus another 47 under the command of other officers, were killed. A single horse survived what became known as "Custer's Last Stand." The nation was shocked. The Indians could not exploit their resounding victory, however. With the onset of winter, they were forced to return to the reservation.

Another resilient people were the Apaches, who for centuries raided their Indian neighbors and played havoc with Spanish and Mexican settlers. Attacks continued against Americans in the 1850s and 1860s, growing more severe during the Civil War. Aided by familiar terrain and harsh climate, the Apaches—under such leaders as **Cochise** (c.1812-1874) and **Geronimo** (c.1829-1909)—for decades were able to evade Army campaigns by retreating into mountain strongholds.

In the 1880s, the messianic **Ghost Dance** religious movement swept California to the Dakotas. Originating among the Paiutes, the cult exhorted followers to dance trance-like in a circle to commune with dead ancestors. The cult promised the resurrection of ancestors and old ways, a resurgence of the buffalo and the disappearance of the whites. In 1890, when they became alarmed by dances on the Pine Ridge Reservation in South Dakota, soldiers tried to disarm the Sioux, who fled into the nearby Badlands. In an ensuing melee, soldiers opened fire and killed some 250 men, women and children. This massacre, known as the **Wounded Knee Massacre,** was the last major conflict of the Indian Wars.

White settlers also pressured the government to open for settlement some former reservation lands of Oklahoma, seized from the Indians as Civil War reparation for their support of the Confederacy. In several government-organized land runs, the first in 1889, contenders for homesteads were assembled on the edge of each new tract and released en masse at an appointed hour. Numbering as many as 100,000 when the 6-million-acre **Cherokee Outlet** was opened in 1893, emigrants fanned out at full spee

d in wagons and buggies. They overran each new territory within hours, seizing farmsteads and city lots in Oklahoma City, Norman, Guthrie and other settlements that vaulted to life overnight.

The unsettled West provided ample space for criminals and unsociable elements to hide from the law. Known for robbing coaches, trains and banks, **Jesse James** (1847-82), the four **Dalton Brothers** (b.1861-71) and the Hole-in-the-Wall Gang of **Robert "Butch Cassidy" Parker** (1866-1909?) and **Harry "Sundance Kid" Longabaugh** (1870-1909?) were among the nefarious felons. As settlements grew, however, so did demand for law and order. The frontier sheriff or marshal enforced laws against carrying firearms in towns, an unglamorous and sometimes risky task that contributed enormously to social order.

1889-93	Land rushes bring 150,000 homesteaders to Oklahoma.
1890	Wounded Knee Massacre.
1892	Sierra Club founded, with John Muir as president.

ACQUISITION OF ALASKA AND HAWAII

Russia sold its vast North American territories to the US government for $7.2 million in 1867. Secretary of State **William Seward** (1801-72) negotiated the purchase, for which he was ridiculed by a handful of politicians and newspapermen. Few settlers ventured to Alaska until 1897-98, after gold was discovered on a tributary of the Klondike River in Canada's neighboring Yukon Territory, setting off the last of the West's gold rushes. Some 100,000 stampeding prospectors poured off steamships from Seattle and San Francisco, setting off on the Chilkoot Trail. Many were unprepared for the exertion, isolation or severe climate; fewer than half arrived at the gold fields. Hardy survivors—known thereafter as Sourdoughs for the starter they used to leaven camp bread—went on to strike gold in the Yukon and Tanana River Valleys, and in far-western Alaska at Nome.

Half an ocean away, Hawaii by the mid-19C boasted one of the world's highest English literacy rates, the fruit of New England missionaries. Enormous blocks of land were bought up by Americans and other foreigners and consolidated into sugar plantations. Thousands of contract laborers from China, and later from Japan, Korea, the Philippines and Portugal, met labor demands. When Hawaiian sugar was granted duty-free access to the US market in 1874, American business interests in Honolulu began to clamor for more power in the government.

In 1887 businessmen forced King **David Kalakaua** (1836-91) to adopt a constitution that reduced him to a figurehead. An attempted palace coup to replace the weakened king with his sister, **Liliuokalani** (1838-1917), was suppressed by US Marines. When Liliuokalani became queen by succession in 1891, her efforts to create a true nation—allowing native Hawaiians to vote, for example—prompted prominent newspaperman Lorin Thurston to lead an armed overthrow of the monarchy in

1893, establishing the **Republic of Hawaii**. Calls for US annexation were answered in 1898, and Hawaii achieved territorial status in 1900.

1893	US planters depose Hawaii's Queen Liliuokalani, establishing a republic, accepted in 1898 as US territory.
1896	Utah becomes state after Mormons de-sanction polygamy.
1897	Klondike gold rush begins, drawing prospectors to Alaska; oil gusher at Bartlesville, Oklahoma, signals the start of the industry.

THE PRESERVATION MOVEMENT

The closing of the frontier brought hard recognition that the resources of the West, once seemingly boundless, were not inexhaustible. Water produced the longest and most intractable dispute; indeed, battles still rage today. The Mormons had shown that irrigation could accommodate a deficiency in rainfall and make the desert bloom. What's known as the "appropriation doctrine" was created to govern water. Whoever first captured water and put it to use had the right to it, no matter where it originated; the individual (or organization) owns the right to the water, not the water itself. This system is often explained with the now-axiomatic phrases "Use it or lose it" and "First in time, first in right." As a result, vast networks of reservoirs and canals now distribute immense amounts of water hundreds of miles from its natural paths.

The dangers of unmanaged resource exploitation were pointed out early by **John Wesley Powell** (1834-1902). A naturalist who had lost his arm as an artillery battery commander in the Civil War, Powell achieved near-legendary status by twice leading wooden-boat expeditions through the rugged drainage of the Colorado River, including the Grand Canyon, the last major unexplored region of the continental US. Sponsored by the Smithsonian Institution, Powell's first expedition descended the Green and Colorado Rivers on dories in 1869. Powell was instrumental in creating the US Geological Survey, an agency he later headed. His respect for the miracles wrought by irrigation was tempered by warnings that the public lands of the West be rationally managed to conserve water and other resources.

The federal government vastly expanded water redistribution in the 20C by sponsoring massive "reclamation" projects, constructing dams, reservoirs, canals and irrigation systems that turned California's Central Valley into the richest agricultural region in the world. Large dams built on the Columbia, Snake, Colorado, Missouri, Arkansas and other Western rivers supply electricity and channel water for public consumption, agriculture and recreation. On the Great Plains, aquifers were tapped for irrigation; coupled with the development of dry-farming techniques in the late 19C, the plains states became major producers of wheat and other grains.

Reclamation projects, however, also enabled the sprawl of vast urban tracts on arid lands. The explosive growth of Los Angeles after the capture of Owens River water in the early 20C was later followed by the runaway expansions of Las Vegas and Phoenix, beginning in the 1970s.

Beginning in the late 19C, meanwhile, large natural areas came under the protective umbrella of the US government. The paintings and photographs of **Thomas Moran** and **William Henry Jackson**, which accompanied the first detailed descriptions of the wondrous Yellowstone Country, provoked public interest and spurred Congress to create the world's first national park in 1872. Protection for California's giant sequoias and peerless Yosemite Valley followed in 1890, inspired by the writings of **John Muir** (1838-1914). The conservation movement found a friend in President **Theodore Roosevelt** (1858-1919), whose own experiences on a North Dakota ranch had brought him joy and robust health. Though a Division of Forestry had been established in the 1870s, Roosevelt quadrupled the amount of national forest land, gave a boost to the creation of national parks and national monuments in the early 20C, and created the vast federal system of wildlife refuges.

The National Park Service today manages 84 million acres (131,000sq mi) of park-lands, while another 150 million acres (234,000sq mi) are protected by the US Fish and Wildlife Service as wildlife refuges. Managed for commerce, recreation and environmental purposes are 193 million acres (301,000sq mi) of national forest and 260 million acres (406,000sq mi) of public domain under the Bureau of Land Management (BLM). These lands lie, overwhelmingly, in western states.

1900	More than 6,000 people die in Galveston hurricane.
1902	Reclamation Act diverts funds from sale of public lands to construct dams and other irrigation projects in the West.
1906	Great earthquake and fire devastate San Francisco.
1913	Los Angeles Aqueduct brings water from Owens Valley to L.A. Hollywood's first feature film, *The Squaw Man*, is released.
1916	William Boeing founds aircraft company in Seattle. National Park Service established in Washington DC.
1919	Grand Canyon National Park created.

THE WEST GROWS UP

As the percentage of women in the Western population increased, so did family life and the stability it represented. Drinking and gambling had been conspicuous features of the overwhelmingly male societies of mining settlements, lumber camps and cow towns. A scarcity of females has been cited as one reason the **women's suffrage movement** achieved its earliest successes in the Rocky Mountains, where male voters conceivably hoped enfranchisement might attract more women settlers. Wyoming Territory was the first US entity to grant women the vote, in 1869; it was followed by Utah in 1870, Colorado in 1893 and Idaho in 1896.

Government regulation and intervention transformed the West in the 20C. The Great Depression of 1929 and the 1930s coincided with one of the historically

USS Arizona Memorial, Pearl Harbor, Oahu

©iStockphoto.com/Andre Nantel

worst droughts on the Great Plains. As crops failed, winds blew away the parched topsoil and the region became known as the **Dust Bowl**. Thousands of farmers and ranchers faced bankruptcy. Foreclosures sent up to 400,000 migrant farmers, many from Oklahoma, in search of work to California (where they were labeled Okies). President **Franklin Roosevelt** (1882-1945) took revolutionary action with his New Deal, introducing programs to control erosion, regulate farm production raise agricultural prices, provide drought relief, and fund immense reclamation and irrigation projects. The **Civilian Conservation Corps** (CCC) employed thousands in public construction projects. Federal and state governments spent millions building, upgrading roads and bridges in a program that facilitated the growth of tourism throughout the West.

World War II heralded unprecedented growth and change. Burgeoning shipyards and war industries brought thousands of workers to Pacific Coast cities from other parts of the US. The Army and Navy established huge training bases and missile-testing ranges in the wide-open desert and plateau lands, while Alaska and Hawaii boomed with an influx of military personnel. The **aerospace industry** took root in southern California, Seattle and later Houston, bringing lucrative defense contracts, demands for labor, government jobs and subsidies for universities.

The booming post-war economy brought tremendous growth, especially in California, which overtook New York as the most populous state in the 1960s. Fueled by Asian and Latin American immigration, the demographic makeup of Western cities changed dramatically; Los Angeles and San Francisco became the most ethnically diverse regions of the US. Growth also brought many problems long associated with Eastern cities—scarce housing, urban blight, crime, poverty, traffic jams and pollution. Politically, the Pacific coastal areas became among the most liberal in the nation, while the Western hinterland has remained more politically conservative.

The **high-technology** revolution brought great wealth to California, major Northwest cities (at one time Seattle had 10,000 residents with at least $1 million of Microsoft stock) and other areas. It also created a trend that worries preservation-minded inland Westerners: telecommuters now may live wherever they wish, instead of being concentrated where jobs dictate. Many scenic areas, especially near public recreation lands, have become highly desirable real estate: in 2007, the median asking price for a single-family residence in Jackson Hole, Wyoming, was $2.5 million; and the Bend, OR, area grew an astounding 65 percent from 1996-2006. Ranchers find that subdividing their lands can be more profitable than agriculture. As new housing developments encroach upon diminishing wildlife habitats, they also crowd the sensibility of wide-open spaces that has always set the West apart from the Eastern US.

The new millennium has brought ever more intense battles over resource preservation, spurred by early 21C federal government proposals to expand logging and oil and gas exploration in undeveloped areas such as Grand Staircase-Escalante National Monument and the Arctic National Wildlife Refuge. Activists are starting to urge that dams be removed on Pacific Northwest rivers to help restore the region's rapidly disappearing salmon runs: the first such dam demolition took place in 2012 in Washington state, on the Elwha River. Nonetheless, there are still many places where it's customary to raise a hand in greeting when vehicles pass on country roads, a custom adapted from similar traditions on horseback a century ago. Drivers can still be forced to wait along a Western road while a cattle drive goes by. Cougars and bears have become frequent visitors to Western suburbs, and the bald eagle, America's symbol, was removed from the endangered-species list in 2007. More than a dozen Indian tribes have begun restoring buffalo herds to their ancestral grounds. And the quintessential song of the West, the yipping cries of coyote packs, rings from foothills, rangelands and ridgetops throughout the region, an open range melody that has painted the evening air for thousands of years.

1927-41	Mount Rushmore chiseled by sculptor Gutzon Borglum.
1936	Hoover Dam completed. Sun Valley resort opens.
1937	Golden Gate Bridge spans entrance to San Francisco Bay.
1941	Japanese bomb Pearl Harbor, Hawaii; US enters World War II.
1953	War hero Gen. Dwight Eisenhower, a Texas-born Kansan, succeeds Harry S Truman as US president.
1959	Alaska and Hawaii become 49th and 50th states.
1962	César Chávez organizes United Farm Workers in California.
1963	President John Kennedy is assassinated in Dallas and succeeded by Lyndon Johnson, a native Texan.
1971	Alaska Native Land Claims Settlement Act distributes $1 billion and 44 million acres of land to indigenous tribes.
1975	Bill Gates and Paul Allen establish Microsoft in Albuquerque, New Mexico; four years later, they move it to a Seattle suburb.
1980	Washington's Mount St. Helens erupts, killing 57. California governor Ronald Reagan, a former actor, is elected US president.
1989	Tanker *Exxon Valdez* spills 11 million gallons of oil into Alaska's Prince William Sound.
1995	Terrorist bombing of Oklahoma City federal building kills 168.
2000	Former Texas governor George W. Bush becomes US president, winning a second term in 2004.
2003	Austrian immigrant and actor Arnold Schwarzenegger is elected governor of California, serving through 2010.
2007	California's population passes 37 million: one in every eight Americans now lives in the Golden State.
	Devastating brush fires destroy homes in Malibu, California, before spreading south to San Diego, and even into Mexico.
2008	Hawaii-born and bred Barack Obama becomes US president, the first African-American to win the office. Obama reverses many of the Bush administration's development policies in the West.
2009	USA recession strikes hard in the West, particularly in California, Nevada and Arizona, where many homeowners face foreclosure.
2010	Seattle's Boeing Company debuts long-delayed new-technology jet, the 787.
2012	Barack Obama is reelected US president, but carries only seven of the 19 Western states.
2013	Oklahoma suffers tornado damage. Forest fires rage in California, Utah, Idaho, New Mexico and Arizona.

USA West Art and Culture

The American West fosters a wide diversity of architectural styles, arts, literature and entertainment, from the rich tribal expressions of Native Americans to the sophisticated films of Hollywood.

Taliesin West designed by Frank Lloyd Wright © Damons Point Light/Alamy

Architecture

S et in a region where, as some have observed, you can "see the bones" of the land, the West's building and housing styles are sturdy and functional and reflect the materials at hand. Native Americans utilized buffalo hides or, in the Southwest, stone and sun-baked mud (adobe) or, in the Northwest, cedar logs. Most of these elements have found more modern use in buildings that range from vacation cabins to residences to huge lodges.

EARLY DWELLINGS

Native Americans built homes to suit their environment and culture with local materials. Nomadic Plains tribes used buffalo skins spread over lean-to timber frames to build highly mobile **tepees**. Farming tribes of the Great Plains, like the Mandans and Pawnees, built permanent **earthen lodges**. Northwestern tribes erected sturdy **plank houses**, while those of the Great Basin and California lowlands preferred light summer lean-tos of thatch and brush, using more substantial materials in winter.

Most of the farming people of the Southwest built fixed houses. Ancient **cliff dwellings** and pueblos of dried mud or stone, some occupied for hundreds of years, still stand throughout the region. Raised on canyon shelves for protection from marauders, the cliff dwellings were abandoned in the late 12C. Latecomers to the Southwest, such as the Navajo, erected six-sided houses called **hogans**. The likely descendants of the cliff dwellers live today in **pueblos**. Some, like those of Taos, New Mexico, are stacked like apartment houses and are among the most remarkable buildings in America.

The Spanish built with sun-baked adobe bricks, made from wet clay and a binding material such as straw or horse hair. Structures were whitewashed and roofed with overhanging clay tiles to reduce rain damage. Adobe walls retain heat in winter and coolness in summer. Doors and windows could be carved from the sturdy walls with a minimum of effort. For their ecclesiasti-

Native American Tipi
©PhotoDisc,Inc

cal buildings, Spanish architects tried to copy structures they knew from Spain or Mexico.

Most Western settlements in the American era were initially built of wood, the cheapest and most readily available material. A prominent exception was the **sod house** of the Great Plains which, though sturdy shelter, was dark and readily abandoned when wood became available. Rudimentary **log cabins** were usually superseded by **frame houses**, while commercial establishments achieved some respectability by sporting facades of brick (often imported from the Midwest or East) or dressed stone, locally quarried. One feature of many towns was the **false front**, which served to make one-story shanties look larger and more reputable.

Ancient Puebloan Dwelling in Mesa Verde, Colorado

PhotoDisc, Inc

19C AND 20C TRENDS

Large cities looked East for architectural inspiration in the 19C, often drawing upon the Greek Revival style for banks, or a hodgepodge of styles for the mansions and row houses of residential districts. Romanticized throwbacks to the Old West have remained popular through the 20C, especially at dude ranches, resorts and national parks – a spectacular example being the **Old Faithful Inn** (1904, Robert Reamer) at Yellowstone National Park.

Widespread prosperity in the 20C enabled Westerners to experiment more. In Los Angeles, one block might boast Tudor, Norman and Mission-style houses between a Japanese garden and Swiss chalet. The 1920s and 1930s popularized whimsical structures built to resemble giant oranges, derby hats, or cartoon animals to attract customers.

TODAY'S STYLES

More thoughtful architectural fashions of the 20C included the **Mission Style**, which resurrected the arched doorways and windows, red-tile roofs and earthen walls of Spanish missions; **Art Moderne**, with streamlined contours and Art Deco detailing; and the **Prairie School**, emphasizing strong, horizontal lines and a lack of superfluous decoration. The latter, a creation of architect **Frank Lloyd Wright** (1867-1959), stressed organic architecture harmonizing with specific landscapes. Wright's most important design in the West is **Taliesin West** (1937) in Scottsdale, Arizona. With its low-profile buildings of indigenous materials, uneven rooflines and shaded entrances, Taliesin West remains a strong influence on design.

The West Coast was a stronghold for **Craftsman** style, the American adaptation of the British Arts and Crafts movement, featuring simple decorative wood trim, built-in cabinetry and porches with broad pillars. San Diego and Oakland both have notable Craftsman neighborhoods.

Contemporary Western architecture alternates between the sustainable and the sculptural, with the latter making a bigger splash in such icons as Frank Gehry's Walt Disney Concert Hall in Los Angeles; Sir Norman Foster's "donut" headquarters of Apple in Cupertino, California, scheduled for 2016; the notched, faceted and skewed facades of the Health Sciences Building at the University of Arizona (CO Architects); and Cahill Center at Caltech (Morphosis Architects). On the green side are the forested roofs of Google's new Mountain View, California, headquarters by NBBJ; and Denis Hayes' six-story Bullitt Center in Seattle, billed as the greenest commercial building in the world.

The Arts

The Western landscape is big, distinctive, vivid and compelling; and so is the art it has engendered, from the huge canvases of Albert Bierstadt and Thomas Moran to Georgia O'Keeffe's abstract landscapes, from the chants of Native Americans to Nirvana's fierce grunge rock. And the indigenous custom of storytelling finds expression in the modern art most dependent on story: film.

DECORATIVE ARTS
Native Traditions

Although US Indians created works of art, almost everything also had a utilitarian or religious purpose. Some of the finest baskets ever created were by Washoe artisans, of whom **Datsolalee**, of the late 19C, is the best known. Coastal California tribes also made baskets exceptional for their beauty and utility, some woven so tightly they could hold water. Peoples of the Northwest coast and Alaska excelled in the art of carving soapstone and walrus tusks, cedar masks and totem poles. Hawaiians created coral jewelry and finely decorated robes and helmets adorned with bird feathers.

All the tribes of the Southwest fashioned decorated pottery, although the art had slipped into a utilitarian mold by the early 20C. Potter **María Montoya Martínez** (c.1881-1980) of New Mexico's San Ildefonso Pueblo is credited with reviving the potter's art in the 1930s when she produced exquisite black-on-black ware. Southwest Indian artists also made names for themselves as painters, among them **Pablita Velarde** (1918-2006) and **Harrison Begay** (b.1917). Navajo women today weave rugs crafted in distinctive regional styles.

Spanish Influences

The Spanish decorated their missions with silver work and wood carvings, much of it made in Mexico and carried north by mule train. The Spanish probably also taught lapidary skills to the Pueblo Indians, who today produce some of the finest stone (especially turquoise) and silver jewelry in the US.

FINE ARTS
19C Painting

The American West provided an exceedingly rich canvas for artists and other chroniclers of frontier life and scenery. Early explorers often were accompanied by sketch artists, some of whom went on to become noted artists. **Karl Bodmer** (1809-93) and **George Catlin** (1796-1872) both recorded Indians and mountain men in the 1830s, while **John James Audubon** (1785-1851) made his own journey west to sketch birds and wildlife. Artist-photographer **Solomon Nuñes Carvalho** (1815-94) accompanied Frémont during a survey of the Far West. The paintings of **Thomas Moran** (1837-1926) and photographs of **William Henry Jackson** (1843-1942), part of the Hayden Expedition to Yellowstone in 1871, were crucial in swaying the public and Congress to create the first national park. **Alfred Jacob Miller** (1810-74), a Baltimore artist, made a trip west in the company of fur traders in 1837 and capitalized upon it in creating a series of paintings of great documentary value. German-born **Albert Bierstadt** (1830-1902) painted Western landscapes in a particularly Romantic style. Grittier and more lifelike are the sketches, paintings and sculptures of cowboys, Indians and other Western characters by **Frederic Remington** (1861-1909) and **Charles M. Russell** (1864-1926), both featured in many Western museums.

20C Painting

New Mexico, with its pueblos and unusual scenery, became a popular magnet for artists in the late 19C. Santa Fe, long the cultural center of the Southwest, is one of the largest art markets in the US after New York and Los Angeles; so is Scottsdale, Arizona. Taos boasted an artist colony in the very early 20C. **Georgia O'Keeffe** (1887-1986), an annual Taos visitor who later moved to the New Mexico desert, painted austere landscapes and decorated more than one famous painting with a parched cow skull against a bright Southwestern sky. The stop-action photography of **Eadweard Muybridge** (1830-1904) preceded the invention of his zoopraxiscope, a landmark in pioneering the moving-picture industry. The haunting black-and-white shots of Western landscapes, particularly Yosemite, by **Ansel Adams** (1902-84) inspired generations of photographers and conservationists. Through her poignant portraits of farm migrants and photos of vast public-works projects rising amid arid landscapes, **Dorothea Lange** (1895-1965) dramatized the tragedies and triumphs of the Depression-era West. Photographers **Edward Weston** (1886-1958) and **Imogen Cunningham** (1883-1976) were among the more influential members of a West Coast coterie known as Group f.64.

The west coast of California also exerted a strong influence on 20C painting and sculpture. Artist colonies at Carmel, La Jolla and Laguna Beach spawned the California Impressionism and Plein-Air movements, including **Franz Bischoff** (1864-1929), creating landscapes inspired by the unique light and natural features of the area. During the 1930s, abstraction, surrealism and social realism came into play. In San Francisco, **Mark Rothko** (1903-70) and **Clyfford Still** (1904-80) inspired an explosion of abstract painting by their students, who included **Robert Motherwell** (1915-91). Painters such as **Richard Diebenkorn** (1922-93) and **David Park** (1911-60) responded with a representational movement known as Bay Area Figurative. An influential art scene that has developed in southern California since the 1950s includes **David Hockney** (b.1937). Tacoma, WA, native **Dale Chihuly** (b.1941) established a blown-glass art tradition, the Pilchuck School, now famed worldwide.

MUSIC
Ceremonial Use

Native Americans employed music and dance, and still do, in all their ceremonies, both religious and social; these forms endure today at numerous annual **pow-wows**.

The Spanish, who introduced the guitar to the West, also used music for sacred and social purposes, and took pains to instruct their mission neophytes in playing instruments.

The Rocky Mountains, Lander's Peak', 1863, by Albert Bierstadt

© The Print Collector/Alamy

Pioneer Diversions

The bulk of popular music today, carried West in the folk music of pioneers and the hymns of missionaries, has roots in the British Isles. Fiddle, harmonica and banjo were the instruments of choice on wagon trains, where popular Oregon Trail tunes included "The Arkansas Traveler" and "Sweet Betsy from Pike." Accompanied by stomping feet, clapping hands and instructional dance calls, the fiddle gave life to capers, jigs and square dances at frontier gatherings, and entertained cowboys on cattle drives and soldiers in lonely barracks.

Cowboy Crooners

The archetype of contemporary Western music is a highly commercialized hybrid of cowboy songs, themselves descended from Scottish, English and Irish ballads by way of the rural South, and often incorporating elements of the Hispanic music of Mexico. The genre was popularized on radio and in film by cowboy singers like **Roy Rogers** (1912-98) and **Gene Autry** (1907-98). Influenced by well-traveled singers like **Buck Owens** (1929-2006), several of whose songs were recorded by the Beatles, cowboy music began to absorb outside elements in the 1940s, picking up the tempo, heavier rhythms and twanging guitar that characterizes popular country-and-western music today. Texans **Bob Wills** (1905-1975), the "King" of Western swing; **Ernest Tubb** (1914-1984) and **Willie Nelson** (b.1933) broadened the genre's scope, incorporating popular music elements ranging from swing to rock and blues. National radio has eroded regional distinctions, but artists such as Texas' **Don Edwards** have revived traditional Western song.

Contemporary Western

The West has made conspicuous contributions in the realm of rock music. In the early 1960s, as the Beatles emerged in England, southern California originated its own brand of lighthearted "surf" rock; its best-known ambassadors, **The Beach Boys**, sang in intricate harmony of waves, hot rods and surfer girls. Later in the decade, the social upheaval in San Francisco, culminating in 1967's "Summer of Love," drew numerous prominent singers and performers—including Texan **Janis Joplin** (1943-70) and Seattleite **Jimi Hendrix** (1942-70)—to a local scene already celebrated for its "San Francisco Sound." The music of Jim Morrison's **The Doors**, Jerry Garcia's **Grateful Dead**, Grace Slick's **Jefferson Airplane**, John Fogarty's **Credence Clearwater Revival** and other top groups was characterized by driving guitar riffs and influenced by more traditional blues. In the early 1990s, Seattle became the center of a style termed "grunge rock," with bands like Kurt Cobain's **Nirvana** and Eddie Vedder's **Pearl Jam** noted for their raw, rough-edged music.

THEATER AND FILM
Operatic Origins

Miners in the 19C were noted for their love of opera. They were so generous in supporting fine opera houses in remote towns that Eastern and European companies routinely toured San Francisco, Virginia City (Nevada), Central City (Colorado) and other thriving mining frontiers. Stage plays, running the gamut from Shakespearean excerpts to melodramas, were also popular. Among the famous actors who toured the Western mining camps were **Edwin Booth** (1833-93), **Helena Modjeska** (1840-1909) and the unconventional **Sarah Bernhardt** (1844-1923). Less exalted entertainment was offered by the scandalous exotic dancer **Lola Montez** (1818-61) and her comedic successor, **Lotta Crabtree** (1847-1924).

Today, San Francisco remains among the preeminent opera cities of the West, staging lavish productions with renowned casts. The Dallas Opera and Houston Grand Opera also are highly regarded, the latter known for its modern world premieres of John C. Adams' *Nixon in China* (1987) and *The Death of Klinghoffer* (1991). Since 1957, one of the brightest lights in the American opera scene has been the Santa Fe Opera Company, which offers outdoor summer performances. Live stage plays continue to attract tourists and local audiences in Los Angeles, San Francisco, Seattle and smaller cities like Ashland, Oregon, and Cedar City, Utah, both of which mount internationally recognized annual Shakespeare festivals.

Wild West Shows

Of all the Western-themed entertainment, nothing was more popular during the late-19C and early-20C than Buffalo Bill's Wild West Show, a commercial extravaganza.

Theater on an epic scale, the show thrilled East Coast and European audiences with dramatized excepts from **William F. "Buffalo Bill" Cody** (1846-1917) himself. Drawing on Cody's remarkable life as a Pony Express rider, bison hunter, Army scout and soldier, the show re-created famous Western battles and presented feats of sharpshooting, an Indian attack on a stagecoach, trick riding and roping, bucking broncos, bull-riding, steer wrestling and other rodeo events. Among the most famous cast members were Sitting Bull sharpshooter **Annie Oakley** (1860-1926) and Cody himself.

Spectacular live shows continue to be a hallmark of the Western stage, particularly in resort centers like Lake Tahoe, Reno and especially Las Vegas. The prototypes of Las Vegas-style performers were stand-up comedians, torch singers and chorus-line Parisian showgirls like the Folies Bergères. Shows now embrace a mind-boggling array of magician acts, circuses, water choreography, and spectacles of electronic and pyrotechnic wizardry, as well as concerts by famous singers.

Western Movies

No other medium has propounded the myth of the Old West more successfully than the **Western movie**. Like Medieval morality plays, classic Westerns depict history selectively but irresistibly, winning audiences who root for heroes and boo villains without complicating ambiguities. Larger than life, Westerns helped to establish Hollywood

as the world capital of film-making. From the first silent Westerns in the early 20C through the 1950s, Westerns' cowboy heroes were chivalrous characters; Indians were usually villains, and other ethnic minorities were rarely depicted despite the prominent roles played by Chinese, black and Hispanic people throughout the American West. Some of these Westerns were undeniably powerful. Among the most emotionally satisfying, if conventional, were *Red River* (1948), starring **John Wayne**; *High Noon* (1952), starring **Gary Cooper**; *The Searchers* (1956), also starring Wayne; and many visually exciting works by director **John Ford**, beginning with *Stagecoach* (1939), also starring Wayne. Television Westerns of the 1950s and 1960s tended to reinforce the Western myth in shows like *The Lone Ranger, Gunsmoke* and *Bonanza*.

Since the 1960s, Hollywood has produced ever-greater numbers of offbeat, thoughtful Westerns that counter earlier tradition. Protagonists are anti-heroes in *Hud* (1963), starring **Paul Newman**; *The Wild Bunch* (1969), directed by **Sam Peckinpah**; and a series of "spaghetti westerns" (including *The Good, the Bad and the Ugly*, 1967) directed by **Sergio Leone** and starring **Clint Eastwood**. Another trend reversed old roles by placing Indians as heroes and soldiers as villains, as in *Little Big Man* (1970), starring **Dustin Hoffman**, and *Dances with Wolves* (1989), starring **Kevin Costner**.

Film festivals throughout the West continue to influence the world and disseminate the medium. Among the most famous is Utah's Sundance Film Festival, created by actor-director **Robert Redford**.

LITERATURE
Frontier Facts and Fiction

Tall tales and colorful humor were popular on the frontier. Westerners were famous for telling tall tales which is why John Colter's earliest descriptions of Yellowstone's geysers, hot pools and astringent streams were thought to be lies. Humorists such as **Mark Twain** (né

Samuel Clemens, 1835-1910) and **Edgar "Bill" Nye** (1850-96) carried on the tradition of exaggeration in print, writing satire that turned on common sense and droll humor. Twain's first break came with *The Celebrated Jumping Frog of Calaveras County* (1867). *Roughing It* (1872) is considered the richest and funniest description of a dude's life in Virginia City, San Francisco, Hawaii and other parts of the Wild West.

More serious Western observations also were widely read in the East. Francis Parkman's exciting account of *The Oregon Trail* (1849) remains a standard today. John C. Frémont's government reports of his forays to the West were rewritten with dramatic flair by his wife, **Jesse Benton Frémont** (1824-1902); they were best-sellers in their day and made Frémont's guide, Kit Carson, into a great Western hero. The laconic Carson himself told his own story with less flamboyance in an autobiography not published until 1926. Other accounts embraced a wide range of views, including those of Indians (*Black Elk Speaks*, 1932) and homesteaders (the works of **Laura Ingalls Wilder**, 1867-1957).

Historians such as **Frederick Jackson Turner** (1861-1932), **Bernard De Voto** (1897-1955) and **Wallace Stegner** (1909-93) added heft and drama.

Western Genre

Sentimental stories, exemplified by the California gold-rush tales of **Bret Harte** (1836-1902), were popular throughout the 19C, but it was adventure and derring-do that gave the real impetus to a new brand of fiction, the Western. Thousands of Wild West "dime novels" were enthusiastically embraced by the public in the 1860s including several by Buffalo Bill featuring himself, and dozens more by other authors about him. The quintessential modern Western is generally considered to be Owen Wister's *The Virginian* (1902), which combined a love interest with chivalrous cowboys, treacherous Indians and a brooding bad man. Among the most enduring work is that of **Zane Grey** (1875-1939); his *Riders of the Purple Sage* appeared in

1912. The Western occasionally rose to high levels of literary complexity, as in the psychological narrative of a lynching in Walter Van Tilburg Clark's *The Ox-Bow Incident* (1940), Willa Cather's *Death Comes for the Archbishop* (1927) and Wallace Stegner's *Angle of Repose* (1971). Jack London's novel of man and dog in the Klondike gold rush, *The Call of the Wild* (1903), probably has been translated into more languages than any other novel set in the West. **Jack Kerouac's** awakening call to the Beat Generation, *On the Road* (1957), is a fictionalized account of aimless journeys through the mid-century West.

John Muir's books and articles helped arouse Eastern support for greater protection of Western lands and resources. Helen Hunt Jackson's *Century of Dishonor* (1881) helped awaken sentiment to the mistreatment of Indians, a forerunner to Dee Brown's *Bury My Heart at Wounded Knee* (1971). **Frank Norris** (1870-1902) attacked the problem of greedy railroad barons in *The Octopus* (1901). Among the defenders of the deserts' fragile beauties were **Mary Austin** (1868-1934), whose *The Land of Little Rain* exalted the Owens Valley and Mojave Desert; and the irascible **Edward Abbey** (1927-89), author of *Desert Solitaire* (1968).

Another stalwart of Western fiction is the hard-boiled detective. **Dashiell Hammett** (1894-1961) created the tone with Sam Spade in The Maltese Falcon (1930), set in San Francisco. **Raymond Chandler** (1888-1959) followed suit in *The Big Sleep* (1939) by introducing Philip Marlowe, a cynical, self-sufficient but honorable detective who guarded the mean streets of Los Angeles. **Ross McDonald's** books featuring detective Lew Archer succeeded Marlowe, painting a realistic but humane portrait of Southern California from 1949-1976. **Tony Hillerman** (1925-2008) blended Western and detective fiction in his books, which recount the adventures of Navajo policemen Joe Leaphorn and Jim Chee in the Indian lands of the Southwest.

Sports and Recreation

For exercise, entertainment, drama and fellowship, Americans love to play and watch sports. A year-round slate of professional ("pro"), collegiate and amateur competitions keeps the excitement high. College sports, especially football and basketball, attract the excited attention of fans and alumni nationwide, especially during the annual football "bowl game" series in December and January, and the "March Madness" championship basketball tournament.

POPULAR BALL GAMES

Often called the national pastime, **baseball** inspires legions of devoted fans who follow teams with religious intensity. Played on a diamond-shaped field with bases in each corner, the game tests the individual skills of batters, who try to strike a thrown ball, against pitchers and fielders, bearing some similarities to cricket. The game may appear slow-paced but can be fraught with suspense, the outcome often resting on a final confrontation between pitcher and batter. In March, when pro teams engage in their annual spring training in Arizona and Florida, seats at practice games are the hottest tickets in town. The Major League Baseball (www.mlb.com) season runs from April to October, culminating in the World Series, a best-of-seven-games matchup between the American League and National League champions.

Fast-paced **basketball** draws participants and spectators from every walk of life. In part because it requires a smaller playing area than most sports, the game is often played outdoors in crowded urban areas. Players score by throwing a ball through a suspended hoop. The 29 teams of the National Basketball Association (NBA) begin play in November, competing for a berth in the NBA Finals held in June. The 12-team Women's National Basketball Association (WNBA), founded in 1997, has inspired a new host of professional female players around the country. For information on both, visit www.nba.com.

With its unique combination of brute force and finely tuned skill, **American football** demands strength, speed and agility from players in their quest to pass, kick and run the football down a 100-yard field to the goal. The National Football League (NFL) oversees 32 teams in two conferences, the champions of which meet in late January in the annual Super Bowl, a game that draws more television viewers than any other event. The football season begins about September 1 (www.nfl.com).

OTHER PRO SPORTS

Although **ice hockey** was born in Canada, the US has adopted the game in a big way. In this breakneck sport, skated players use sticks to maneuver a hard rubber puck into a goal at either end of an ice arena. The 29-team National Hockey League (NHL) pits professional Canadian and American teams in annual competition for the coveted Stanley Cup, with finals held in June.

The US may be the world's preeminent **golf** nation, attracting golfers from around the globe to its challenging, well-manicured courses. Public and private links abound throughout much of the West, especially California, Arizona, Las Vegas and Hawaii, where the climate permits year-round play.

A yearlong slate of tournaments for men, women and senior men utilizes numerous championship courses in Arizona, California and Hawaii.

Descended from frontier horsemanship contests, **rodeo** celebrates the skills developed by generations of cowboys. Members of the Professional Rodeo Cowboys Association (PRCA) compete for millions of dollars in bronc-riding,

Rodeo Rider Roping a Calf

calf roping, steer wrestling and other events. Most dangerous is bull-riding, in which a cowboy tries to remain on the back of a rampaging bull for all of eight seconds; rodeo clowns distract the bull from goring the rider after he has been thrown.

Hugely popular pro rodeos are held in Cheyenne (Wyoming), Pendleton (Oregon), Houston, Las Vegas, Oklahoma City, Fort Worth, Denver, Reno and other cities; for schedules, visit www.prorodeo.com.

RECREATION HEAVEN

Skiing in the Colorado Rockies; **surfing** the big waves on the north shore of Oahu; whitewater **rafting** down Idaho's Salmon River; backpacking the 2,550mi Pacific Crest Trail; **mountain-biking** through Utah's slick-rock canyons; **fly-fishing** isolated lakes in Alaska's vast interior; and riding horseback through aspen-clad mountainsides: seekers of outdoor recreation and natural beauty take full advantage of the wealth of the West's mountains, forests, lakes, rivers and oceanfront, as well as urban parks and biking/running paths.

In-line skating, snowboarding and mountain biking are recent additions to the panoply of popular recreational sports. **Sky-diving** and **mountain climbing** attract increasing numbers of mainstream participants. Adventure-travel agencies design vacations around bicycling, canoeing, wildlife viewing and other themes.

Hiking, **horseback riding** and river rafting provide the best access to thousands of square miles of Western backcountry and parkland. A vast network of trails probes remote corners of the Rockies, Sierra Nevada and Cascades. Undeveloped Alaska offers plenty of true wilderness for adventurers – even for comfort-loving anglers or hunters who hire bush pilots to find the perfect lake. Throughout the West, guest ranches offer room, board and riding opportunities to "city slickers"; some even sponsor working cattle-drive vacations. The Colorado River of Utah and Arizona might be the most celebrated rafting challenge, but most Western states offer white-water to match the skill level of any rafter or kayaker.

There are plenty off quirky and offbeat adventures to be had (or to watch). The US's biggest dog mushing event, the **Iditarod**, takes place in Alaska. Other offbeat sports opportunities to play and watch in the West include **curling**, a game most popular in Canada's Prairie provinces, but practiced with relish in Seattle, Kansas City and elsewhere .

Nature

The American West conjures up vast expanses of open range, grass-waving plains, snow-topped mountain peaks, deeply scoured canyons and endless sandy beaches. Deserts and forests grace the land, some cut by grand and mighty rivers.

Colorado River on the Eastern Side of Grand Canyon National Park © National Park Service

Landscapes

The US West starts within the tier of Great Plains states west of the Mississippi—Texas, Oklahoma, Kansas, Nebraska and the Dakotas—and includes all of the continent beyond to the Pacific Ocean, as well as the isolated states of Alaska and Hawaii.

GEOLOGIC FOUNDATIONS

The easternmost part of the West is a broad swath of plains that rise gradually from the Gulf of Mexico and Mississippi Valley; the western two-thirds is a vast, corrugated expanse of mountains and plateaus interposed with canyons, valleys and basins of varying size. Although landforms have been more than two billion years in the making, the current uplift began 130 million years ago, after the Pacific Plate subducted the North American Plate. The tectonic collision brought island masses crashing into the continent and slowly raised vast uplands from what previously had been a shallow sea. Magma intruded through weakened parts of the earth's crust, welling over as volcanoes and volcanic plateaus. Faults (most aligned north-south) thrust mountain ranges sharply upward, creating abrupt escarpments; or dropped blocks of land to form grabens, typical of the Great Basin region. Streams, rushing from the rising highlands, cut deep canyons. Sediments flowing to lowlands deposited valley soils and built the Great Plains on the eastern side of the Rocky Mountains. The subduction zone where the Pacific and North American Plates meet is part of the Ring of Fire, the geologically unstable zone that circles the Pacific Ocean. The North American plate is moving southwest at almost two inches a year. In the American West, its most volatile indicators are California's earthquake-prone San Andreas Fault, the volcanic Cascade Range and Alaska's Aleutian volcanoes; a bit farther east, Yellowstone National Park is the world's largest geothermal area, lying atop what geologists call a "super-volcano."

During the early Pleistocene Epoch some 2 million years ago, alpine glaciers covered high-mountain expanses of the Rockies, Cascades, Sierra Nevada and Alaskan coastal ranges, sculpting glacial troughs, hanging valleys, cirques and other features, including Alaska's deep Pacific fjords. Enormous pluvial lakes covered thousands of square miles in the Great Basin. Cataclysmic floods periodically scoured the inland Pacific Northwest when glacial dams melted and broke. The continental ice sheets diminished the water level of the oceans, exposing a land bridge across the Bering Strait and spurring migration of animals and humans between Asia and North America.

Before about 5000 BC, cool, wet conditions prevailed in what is now the West. A drier, hotter climate subsequently began to dominate. Except for areas of high rainfall along Pacific Coast ranges and the Gulf Coast of Texas, the West today is characterized by aridity, a fact that has colored Western life in innumerable ways. An entirely new legal system called appropriation doctrine was created to manage water resources. The 100th meridian that runs through the heart of the Great Plains, marks the approximate division between traditional farming and dryland ranching. East of the meridian, annual precipitation averages more than 20in per year; west, rainfall rapidly diminishes, making agriculture impractical without irrigation. Throughout the West today, farming and urban development depend on groundwater withdrawals or massive water-transfer schemes such as the aqueduct that brings Sierra Nevada snowmelt to Los Angeles.

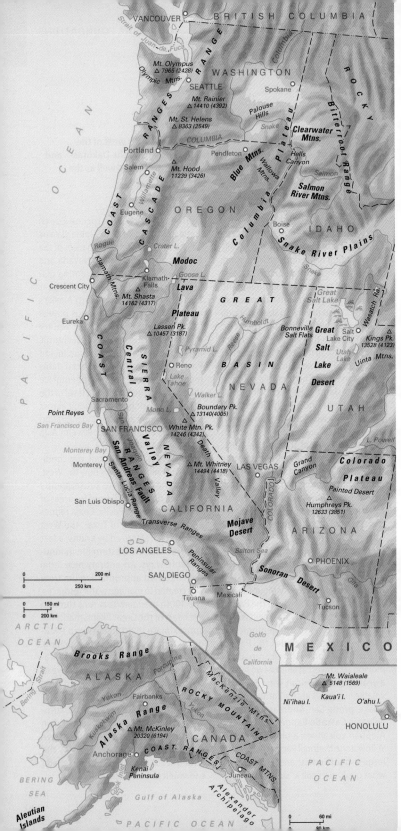

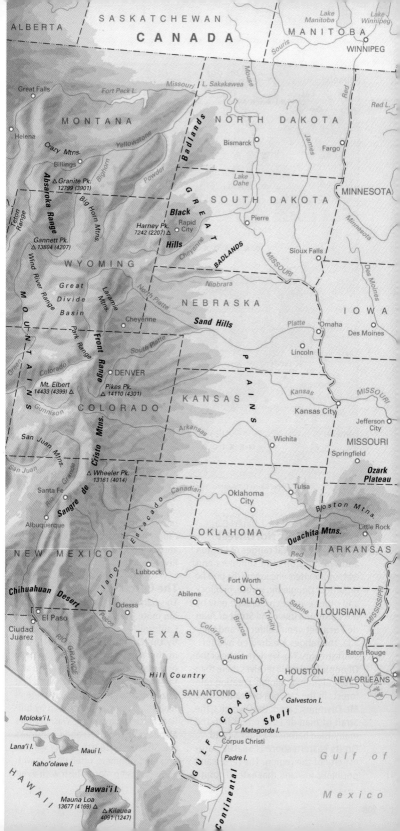

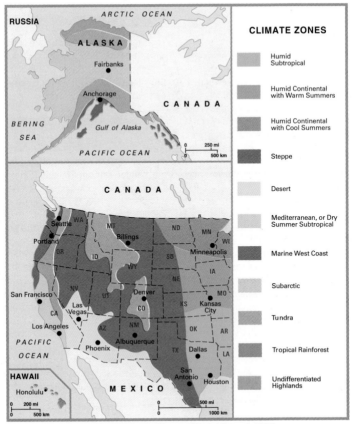

After Glenn T. Trewartha "Elements of Physical Geography," 1957.

REGIONS AND CLIMATES
Coastal Pacific Northwest

West of the **coastal ranges** of Oregon and Washington mild summers and wet, cool winters encourage the prolific growth of Douglas fir, spruce, hemlock and other evergreens. Broken only by the **Columbia River** and **Strait of Juan de Fuca** between California and Canada, the ranges are drained by short, swift streams. The western slope of the **Olympic Peninsula** receives more than 150in of annual rainfall, creating rain forests in the canyons beneath 7,965ft **Mt. Olympus**. East of the Olympics, the Strait of Juan de Fuca opens into the many-isled harbor of **Puget Sound**. On its eastern shore is Seattle, largest city of the region. The fertile and populous lowland that extends south

between the Coast Ranges and Cascades encompasses the city of Portland and, below it, the pastoral **Willamette River Valley**.

The Cascades

This barrier of volcanic peaks, stretching more than 600mi from Canada to California's **Lassen Peak**, is breached by the Columbia – the largest river in the West and a natural highway between the dry Columbia Plateau and the maritime regions to the west. Two dozen distinct peaks present a line of majestic domes, many capped by brilliant glaciers. Highest are Washington's **Mt. Rainier** (14,410ft) and California's **Mt. Shasta** (14,162ft). Snowy winters and mild summers, often doused with showers, keep slopes lush with evergreen forests, a boon to timber and recreation industries. The volcanoes are largely dormant, but scientists monitor signs of life that may escalate to explosive eruptions, as at Lassen in 1914 and **Mt. St. Helens** in 1980. Fewer than 8,000 years ago, massive Mt. Mazama exploded, leaving a gaping crater that filled with snowmelt and rain to form Oregon's **Crater Lake**.

Some hydrothermal activity remains along the lake floor, suggesting that at some point in the future Mazama may erupt again.

Lava Plateaus

Extensive lava plateaus spread eastward in the rain shadow of the Cascades at 2,000-3,000ft elevation. The **Columbia Plateau** covers most of eastern Washington and parts of Oregon and Idaho. The **Modoc Lava Plateau** covers the northeastern corner of California and part of Oregon. Farther east rise several small ranges, including the Wallowas, which form the western wall of enormous, 8,000ft-deep Hells Canyon of the Snake River. Upstream, the **Snake River Plain** of Idaho forms yet a third extensive lava plateau, tracing its origins not to the Cascades but to clusters of spatter cones and volcanoes south of the Idaho Rockies. The Columbia Plateau and Snake River Plain have proven very fertile under irrigation from the Columbia and Snake Rivers.

Coastal Northern California

The 600mi shoreline of northern and central California embraces a climate that varies from moist and mild (near Oregon) to semiarid Mediterranean. Washed by the Alaska Current, the rough, cold Pacific waters are rich in sea life but dangerous for shipping and swimming. The rugged **Coast Ranges** are breached only at the **Golden Gate,** entrance to **San Francisco Bay**. At several points, the coastal mountains yield to narrow strips of fertile lowlands – the agriculturally rich **Napa, Sonoma and Salinas Valleys**. Redwood forests grow profusely in the north and intermittently as far south as **Big Sur**. Drier

chaparral, grasses and oaks predominate inland and to the south.

The **San Andreas Fault** parallels the coastline from Point Reyes (north of San Francisco) to Point Concepcion (northwest of Los Angeles), where it cuts inland.

Coastal Southern California

Shielded from the cold waters of the Alaska Current, the southern California coast is relatively warm and hospitable. Rainfall seldom exceeds 15in per year, giving Santa Barbara, Los Angeles and San Diego an enviable Mediterranean climate, free of winter snows except in nearby mountains. The **Los Angeles Basin**, California's largest and most heavily populated coastal plain, is hemmed on the north by the **San Gabriel Mountains**. These are a part of the **Transverse Ranges** that follow the San Andreas Fault eastward from the coast, rendering southern California one of the most seismically active regions of the US. East of the basin are the lower **Santa Ana Mountains**, part of the **Peninsular Ranges** that run south through Mexico's Baja Peninsula.

Sierra Nevada

Running southeasterly almost 400mi from the Cascades, 50-80mi wide, the fault-block Sierra Nevada rises in an abrupt escarpment on the east more than 2mi above the **Owens Valley** at **Mt. Whitney (14,494ft)** – highest peak in the contiguous US. The lofty range hinders weather systems, creating a rain shadow to its east. Westward slopes descend gradually through alpine high country, evergreen forests and rugged foothills. Streams and rivers run through great canyons to feed the Central Valley, a fecund plain with the richest agricultural land in the US. Remarkable **Yosemite Valley** is the best place to see the Sierra's sculpted peaks and U-shaped glacial valleys.

Although it has prodigious winter snowfalls, providing excellent skiing, the Sierra also enjoys plenty of summer sun. **Lake Tahoe** is a year-round recreation center.

Great Basin

East of the Sierra Nevada and west of the Rocky Mountains, the sagebrush-cloaked Great Basin is a high desert of hot, dry summer days, cool nights and cold winters. It is corrugated with parallel fault-block mountain ranges, some above 13,000ft, divided by valleys known as grabens. Escarpments of 5,000-6,000ft are common; below the 11,200ft Panamint Range, **Death Valley** falls to 282ft below sea level, the lowest point in the Western Hemisphere. No streams that flow into the Great Basin drain to the sea; they evaporate or disappear into lakes or marshy sinks. Utah's **Great Salt Lake** is a remnant of prehistoric Lake Bonneville, which once covered some 20,000sq mi. For 150 years, mining towns have boomed and busted in this resource-rich, water-poor region. Except for cities at the foot of well-watered mountains – **Reno** in the west, **Salt Lake City** in the east – population density is the lowest of any region of comparable size in the contiguous US.

Colorado Plateau

The nation's highest plateau region covers 130,000sq mi of Utah, Colorado, New Mexico and Arizona at a mile above sea level. Scattered mountain ranges reach as high as 11,000ft, but the most remarkable features are the myriad canyons carved by the **Colorado River** and its tributaries – thousands of feet deep, through eons-old rock strata. More than 25 national parks and monuments – including **Grand Canyon, Zion, Bryce Canyon** and **Canyonlands** – preserve arches, eroded pinnacles, natural bridges and immense gorges in rainbow hues, all carved by wind and water. With an arid climate and a dearth of fruitful soil, the area is home to such hardy plant species as sagebrush, juniper and piñon pine. The ruins of ancient Puebloan cliff villages may still be seen at **Mesa Verde** in Colorado, Chaco Canyon in New Mexico, and at the Betatakin and **Canyon de Chelly** ruins on the Navajo Indian Reservation.

Desert Southwest

North America's largest arid region spreads east from California to Texas, containing three distinct deserts with vague transition zones. The mountainous **Mojave Desert**, which ranges into Death Valley, is home to the Joshua tree, a yucca that may grow 50ft tall. The Mojave fades into the Great Basin north of **Las Vegas** and meshes with the lower-elevation Sonoran Desert through the **Colorado Desert**, west of the Colorado River. The **Sonoran Desert**, which extends through southern Arizona and northwestern Mexico, boasts a profusion of cacti – including the giant saguaro – dependent on intense monsoon cloudbursts that bring temporary relief from summer heat. Winters are mild and sunny, luring thousands of seasonal residents to Arizona. The large **Chihuahuan Desert** of southern New Mexico, west Texas and northeastern Mexico is a high-elevation desert of parched mountain ranges, extensive grasslands, cold winters and torrid summers. The **Rio Grande** flows through its heart, scribing the huge hook of **Big Bend National Park**.

Rocky Mountains

Reaching from New Mexico to Canada, this vast mountain system comprises scores of ranges. Resort villages nestle in high valleys. A key area for timber, mining, grazing and recreation, the Rockies are crucial as a source of water. Most major rivers of the western US, including the Snake, Columbia, Yellowstone, Missouri, Colorado, Rio Grande, Arkansas and Platte, originate here, flowing to the Pacific Ocean or the Gulf of Mexico from the **Continental Divide**. The Northern Rockies are typified by the highly stratified, precipitous mountains of **Glacier National Park** in Montana, southern bulwark of the Canadian Rockies. Ranges like the Tetons rise above open plains or forested plateaus in the Middle Rockies of southern Montana and Wyoming. In the Colorado Rockies dozens of peaks pass 14,000ft. The Rockies diminish in stature in New Mexico, growing more rounded and drier.

Hayden Valley, Yellowstone National Park

© Jim Parkin/Alamy

Great Plains

Built of sediment washed eastward from the Rocky Mountains, the plains extend 1,000mi to the Mississippi. Semiarid high plains (the western third) support short grass, ideal for bison and cattle; the tapping of aquifers permits more varied farming. Some areas are so flat that one can discern the curvature of the earth's horizon, but rolling landscapes are more typical. South Dakota's **Black Hills** and **Badlands**, and the Texas **Hill Country**, enhance an otherwise open landscape. Thunderstorms and tornadoes are frequent in summer; fierce blizzards mark the winters.

Gulf Coast

Deep, rich soils extend along the Gulf of Mexico coast of Texas to Louisiana. High humidity and rainfall, and temperatures over 90°F, make summers muggy; winters are mild and snow-free. Numerous rivers, like the **Rio Grande** on the US-Mexico border, water this forested swath. Protecting most of the coast is a string of sandy barrier islands, including **Padre, Matagorda** and **Galveston Islands**, which support rich bird colonies.

Alaska

The largest US state contains more than 570,000sq mi of forests, mountains, glaciers and tundra. Bounded by the Pacific Ocean (south), Arctic Ocean (north) and Bering Strait (west), Alaska is a massive peninsula. The **Brooks Range** spans its

northern tier, dividing oil-rich tundra from interior plains.

The **Yukon River** flows through the center, bounded by the Alaska Range and North America's highest summit, 20,320ft **Mt. McKinley**. Southern coastal ranges curve west as the volcanic **Aleutian Islands** and arc east through the **Panhandle**, a fjord-strewn archipelago that shelters the Inside Passage. Although the interior is very cold and dry in winter, summer can bring high temperatures and clouds of insects that attract enormous bird migrations. The Panhandle is cool and wet year-round.

Hawaii

The world's most remote archipelago with a substantial population, Hawaii comprises 132 volcanic islands. The earliest islands surfaced as volcanoes about 5 million years ago; the most recent (the "Big Island" of Hawaii) is still growing from eruptions at Kilauea Volcano; the world's largest volcano is 13,677ft Mauna Loa. The dormant volcano of Haleakala dominates the eastern half of nearby Maui. Its tropical climate moderated by trade winds, Hawaii is diverse in weather, foliage and topography, with dramatic differences in rainfall between the wetter windward and drier leeward sides of each island. Mount Waialeale on **Kauai** receives as much as 500in of rain in a year, while the Big Island's Ka'u Desert is exceedingly arid. Fine beaches and lush foliage contribute to the islands' tourism fame.

Discovering
USA West

Bixby Creek Bridge, Big Sur, California.

California and Nevada

Civic Center cable car, San Francisco
© Peter Wrenn/Michelin

Los Angeles Area

Filling a vast coastal plain framed by towering mountains, sprawling, sun-drenched Los Angeles is the second-largest metropolitan area in the US, a collection of once-distinct cities and towns that have grown together. Its enviable climate, its role as an international entertainment center and its remarkable ethnic and cultural diversity contribute to a heady mix of sights and experiences with an ambience so casual that locals refer to their home merely by the initials: "L.A.," or the nickname "the Southland."

Highlights

1 Views from **Griffith Park** (p127)

2 A star-studded movie premier at **TCL Chinese Theatre** (p130)

3 Touring **Universal Studios** (p132)

4 Strolling **Rodeo Drive** (p132)

5 Admiring Greek antiquities at **The Getty Villa** (p134)

Los Angeles

A Sprawling Megalopolis

Greater Los Angeles spills beyond the Los Angeles Basin, a mostly flat plain that runs inland from the Pacific Ocean to the uplands. Skirting the basin to the northwest are the Santa Monica Mountains, which rise from the sea at Oxnard, 70mi northwest of downtown L.A., and create the higher elevations of Beverly Hills, Hollywood and Griffith Park.

These mountains are reminders of geological stress frequently manifested in earthquakes, and form a natural barrier for smog. Though strict laws have improved air quality in recent years, smog remains oppressive on hot summer days. Today the city of Los Angeles covers more than 467sq mi. Almost 10 times that area is embraced by L.A. County, and the metropolitan area stretches beyond county boundaries to some 34,000sq mi.

There are 88 incorporated cities within the county, many completely surrounded by the city of L.A. Both city and county are governed from Los Angeles Civic Center. Population of the city is 3.8 million, county 9.9 million and metropolitan area 18.3 million. See *Michelin Green Guide California*.

ADDRESSES

🏨 STAY

$$$$$ Hotel Bel-Air – 701 Stone Canyon Rd., Los Angeles. ☎310-472-1211. www.hotelbelair.com. 103 rooms. Ranked among the world's finest hotels, the Bel Air is secluded among 12 acres of lush gardens and waterfalls not far from Westwood. Pink, Mission-style, tile-floored bungalows harbor individually decorated lodgings including canyon-view suites. **Wolfgang Puck at Hotel Bel-Air** ($$$) serves upscale Cal-American comfort food in a sophisticated dining room that extends onto a bougainvillea-covered terrace.

$$$$$ Casa del Mar – 1910 Ocean Way, Santa Monica. ☎310-581-5533. www.hotelcasadelmar.com. 129 rooms. An opulent beach club for well-to-do Angelenos in the 20s, the Casa was neglected after its use as a military hotel in World War II. A $50 million restoration in the 1990s returned the elegant eight-story inn to its former stature. The **Catch** ($$$$) restaurant looks out on Santa Monica Bay. The eco-friendly Sea Wellness Spa opened on-site in 2009.

GETTING THERE

Five large airports handle commercial traffic. Largest is **Los Angeles International Airport (LAX)** (📞310-646-5252; www.lawa.org), 10mi southwest of downtown. Also: **Burbank-Glendale-Pasadena Airport (BUR)** (📞818-840-8840; www.burbankairport.com), 16mi north of downtown; **Long Beach Airport (LGB)** (📞562-270-2619; www.lgb.org), 22mi south of downtown; **Orange County/John Wayne Airport (SNA)** (📞949-252-5200; www.ocair.com), 35mi southeast of downtown; **Ontario International Airport (ONT)** (📞909-937-2700; www.lawa.org), 35mi east of downtown. **Rental car** branches are at all airports; call for ground transportation information. **Amtrak train**: Union Station (800 N. Alameda St.; 📞800-872-7245; www.amtrak.com). **Greyhound bus**: Downtown (E. 7th & Alameda Sts.; 📞800-231-2222; www.greyhound.com).

GETTING AROUND

Express-bus and **Metro rail service** provided by Los Angeles County Metropolitan Transit Authority (MTA) (📞213-922-6000 or 800-266-6883; www.mta.net). Fares vary depending on distance and time, from $1.25 for a basic bus fare, to $5 for an all-day Metro pass. Purchase tickets at stations. The **DASH** (Downtown Area Short Hop) shuttle system (📞213-808-2273; www.ladottransit.com) runs frequently through downtown L.A. (*25 cents*) and in other neighborhoods.
Taxi: Checker CabCo. (📞310-300-5007); Yellow Cab (📞877-733-3305).

VISITOR INFORMATION

Call the **Los Angeles Visitor Information Hotline** (📞800-228-2452; www.lacvb.com) to obtain *Essential L.A.*, a free vacation-planning guide. **Los Angeles Convention & Visitors Bureau visitor center**: (Downtown, 685 Figueroa St; 📞213-689-8822).

ACCOMMODATIONS

Hotels.com (📞800-246-8357; www.hotels.com) and Hotel Reservaton Network (📞800-715-7666; www.hoteldiscount.com) provide free reservation services. The *Essential L.A.* vacation guide (above) contains a lodging directory. Accommodations range from deluxe hotels (*more than $350/day*) to budget motels (*as little as $40/day*). Most bed-and-breakfast inns are found in residential sections of the city ($80-$200/day).

Entertainment – Consult the "Calendar" section of *The Los Angeles Times* (www.latimes.com) or the *LA Weekly* (www.laweekly.com) for a schedule of cultural events and addresses of principal theaters and concert halls. Tickets may be obtained from: **Ticketmaster** (📞213-480-3232; www.ticketmaster.com) or **Musical Chairs** (📞800-659-1702; www.musicalchairstickets.com).

$$$$$ The Ritz-Carlton Laguna Niguel – 1 Ritz-Carlton Dr., Dana Point. 📞949-240-2000. www.ritzcarlton.com. 396 rooms. South of Laguna Beach, this grand hotel perches on a hilltop above a lovely beach, and features a spa, swimming pools and tennis courts. Luxury abounds in its crystal chandeliers and rich tapestry fabrics; oceanfront rooms enjoy Pacific views. **Restaurant Raya ($$$)** offers Latin-inspired meats and tapas from a perch overlooking the ocean.

$$$$ Disney's Grand Californian Hotel & Spa – 1600 S. Disneyland Dr., Anaheim. 📞714-956-642. https://disneyland.disney.go.com. 745 rooms. Built in early-20C Craftsman style, this is one of three Disneyland Resort hotels. Together with the refurbished **Disneyland Hotel ($$$$)** and **Disney's Paradise Pier Hotel ($$$$)**, the resort has more than 2,000 rooms. **Napa Rose ($$$)** offers fine dining.
$$$$ Millennium Biltmore Hotel Los Angeles – 506 S. Grand Ave.,

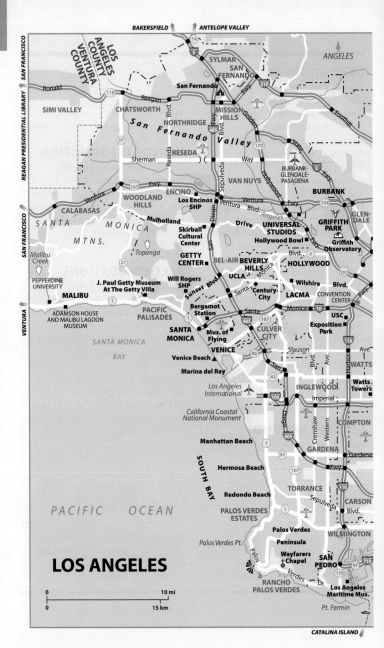

LOS ANGELES

Los Angeles. 📞213-624-1011 www.
millenniumhotels.com. 683 rooms.
Once a magnet to presidents, kings and
Hollywood celebrities, the Renaissance-
style Biltmore has maintained its
prestige through the decades. It
remains a presence on Pershing Square
in the heart of downtown. Rooms are
elegantly decorated in warm golds and
creams, and the fitness center includes a
sauna and a Roman-style pool.

$$$$ Hotel Oceana Santa Barbara –
202 W. Cabrillo Blvd., Santa Barbara.
📞805-965-4577. www.hoteloceana
santabarbara.com. 122 rooms. A 2008
renovation recast the six Spanish-style
buildings of this modern boutique hotel
in brighter colors and playful accents.

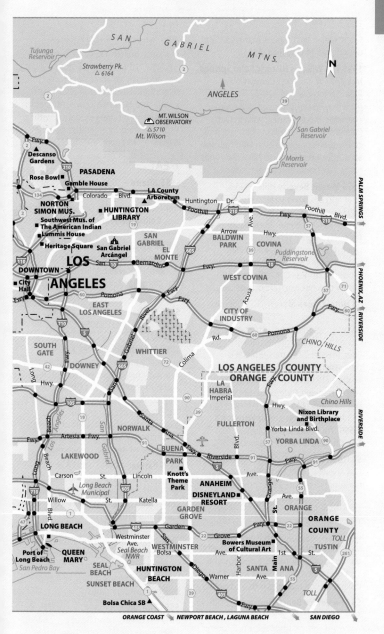

Guest rooms wrap around garden courts. Hotel Oceana also has a luxury 70-suite Santa Monica property, newly redone and renamed Oceana Beach Club Hotel.

$$$$$ Shutters – 1 Pico Blvd., Santa Monica. ☎310-458-0030. www. shuttersonthebeach.com. 198 rooms. A beachside-cottage feel (envision cabana-striped awnings and flower-covered trellises) belies the stylish service and dining behind the white-shuttered windows. Guest rooms have built-in bookcases and private balconies, and a presidential charm, thanks to a recent redo by the Obamas' White House decorator, Michael Smith.

Guests relax by the pool, in the spa, and over dinner at **One Pico ($$$$)**.

$$$$ The Willows Historic Palm Springs Inn – 412 W. Tahquitz Canyon Way, Palm Springs. ☎760-320-0771. www.thewillowspalmsprings.com. 8 rooms. A striking Mediterranean villa in Old Palm Springs, The Willows has frescoed ceilings, balconies, its own waterfall and an outdoor pool. Rooms have claw-foot tubs, slate floors and garden patios.

$$$$ Mosaic Beverly Hills – 125 S. Spalding Dr., Beverly Hills. ☎310-278-0303. www.mosaichotel.com. 49 rooms. This charming, elegant boutique property offers a serene palm-shaded pool, a cozy restaurant and a 24hr fitness center. Rooms are outfitted with modern business conveniences and comfy touches like full body pillows.

$$ Hotel Queen Mary – 1126 Queen's Hwy., Long Beach. ☎877-342-0742. www.queenmary.com. 314 rooms. Once the oceans' greatest luxury liner, this Art Deco masterpiece is permanently docked at the south end of the I-710 freeway. Its three decks of wood-paneled staterooms are quaint but romantic and memory-inducing. Its best restaurants are **Sir Winston's ($$$$)**, for Continental cuisine, and **The Chelsea ($$$)**, for seafood.

$$ Hotel Figueroa – 939 S. Figueroa St., Los Angeles. ☎213-627-8971. www.figueroahotel.com. 285 rooms. This exotic downtown hotel, dating from 1926, feels like an enclave of Morocco. The arched terra-cotta entrance leads to a lobby decked in cacti and Spanish tiles; the pool is surrounded by a lavish garden. Some rooms feature wrought-iron bed frames and reflect a vivid palette of rich oranges, reds and golds.

$$ The Venice Beach House – 15 30th Ave., Los Angeles. ☎310-823-1966. www.venicebeachhouse.com. 9 rooms. Framed by a picket fence and inviting garden, this bed-and-breakfast inn recalls the early 20C days of its beach community's founding as a Venetian-style artists' community. Some rooms have private entrances; others have cathedral ceilings or rocking chairs.

$$$$ Sunset Tower Hotel - 8358 Sunset Boulevard W., Hollywood. ☎323-654-7100. http://sunsettowerhotel.com. 74 rooms. Built in 1929 and lovingly renovated, the historic 15-story building was originally an apartment tower for celebrities like Elizabeth Taylor, Frank Sinatra and Marilyn Monroe. Art Deco meets contemporary elegance, with a spa, pet friendly amenities and the William S. Hart Park next door.

♈/EAT

$$$ JiRaffe – 502 Santa Monica Blvd., Santa Monica. ☎310-917-6671. www.jirafferestaurant.com. Dinner only. Closed Sun. **California-French.** From the airy storefront of this chic restaurant, rising star Rafael Lunetta prepares such hearty bistro-style dishes as roasted jidori chicken, almond-crusted rainbow trout and carmelized pork chop with smoked bacon and spiced apple chutney.

$$$$ Mélisse – 1104 Wilshire Blvd., Los Angeles. ☎310-395-0881. www.melisse.com. Dinner only. Closed Mon. **French.** Foodies flock here for classically prepared French dishes, from almond-crusted sole with chanterelles and butter jus to Devil's Gulch rabbit with courgettes, garlic, and olive-lamb jus. Desserts are sumptuous, but don't overlook the tableside cart of cheeses. The extensive wine list highlights California whites and French reds.

$$$$ Patina – 141 S. Grand Ave., in Walt Disney Concert Hall., Los Angeles. ☎213-972-3331. www.patinarestaurant.com. Dinner only. Closed Mon. **California-French.** Founding Chef Joachim Splichal's glitzy location is ultra-high profile; the food continues to earn acclaim. A selection of caviar leads the way to hearty, French-inflected roast fish and meat dishes, or top-price prix-fixe tasting menus.

$$$$ The Sky Room – 40 S. Locust Ave. at The Breakers, Long Beach. ☎562-983-2703. www.theskyroom.com. Dinner only. **Cal-American.** A cornerstone of Conrad Hilton's hotel empire in the 1930s and 40s, the imposing Baroque-style Breakers is now a senior residence. But its penthouse Sky Room is still lively. Where Liz Taylor and others frolicked, live bands play in Art Deco elegance. Classic cuisine includes tableside Caesar salad, rack of lamb and fresh seafood.

$$$$ Water Grill – 544 S. Grand Ave., Los Angeles. ☎213-891-0900. www. watergrill.com. No weekend lunch. **Seafood.** In downtown's vintage Pacific Mutual Building is this fine seafood restaurant. Preparations are simple and elegant. Mains include seared swordfish with braised eggplant , and Chilean sea bass with butternut squash gnocchi.

$$$ Anaheim White House – 887 S. Anaheim Blvd., Anaheim. ☎714-772-1381. www.anaheimwhitehouse.com. **Northern Italian.** This 1909 Craftsman home became a restaurant befitting a president in 1981. Veronese owner-chef Bruno Serato features fresh seafood and game dishes, including lobster ravioli, and the signature wine and horseradish-braised beef.

$$$ Hatfield's – 6703 Melrose Ave., Los Angeles, Los Angeles. ☎323-935-2977. www.hatfieldsrestaurant.com. Dinner only. **Californian.** This sophisticated dining room sports a showcase open kitchen. The small, creative menu is devoted to the rotating seasonal market that might include Tasmanian ocean trout with smoked hon-shimeji mushrooms or roasted whole quail with creamy Parmesan pearl barley.

$$$ Osteria Mozza – 6602 Melrose Ave., Los Angeles. ☎323-297-0100. osteriamozza.com. Dinner only. **Italian.** Every night a mix of chowhounds and scenesters flood this second venture by Mario Batali and Nancy Silverton. Batali's trademark rustic Italian includes homemade pastas and heartier fare. Dishes made with *burrata*, a fresh Italian cheese with an oozing cream middle, are a specialty.

$$$ Shiro – 1505 Mission St., South Pasadena. ☎626-799-4774. www. restaurantshiro.com. Dinner only. Closed Mon–Tue. **Japanese.** Sizzling whole catfish, stuffed with ginger, lightly fried and served in ponzu sauce is one reason Shiro captures a devoted clientele. All of the sauces and seafood dishes are marvelous at this friendly, off-the-beaten-track restaurant.

$$$ Spago Beverly Hills – 176 N. Cañon Dr., Beverly Hills. ☎310-385-0880. www. wolfgangpuck.com. No lunch Sun–Mon. **Contemporary.** Celebrity chef Wolfgang Puck's flagship restaurant draws Hollywood glitterati to feast on Spago classics (handmade sweet-corn agnolotti or grilled prime côte de bouef for two) and seasonal fish (wild Alaskan salmon). This super-chic restaurant with an exhibition kitchen is decorated with Italian marble and jewel-toned art glass.

$$ Bistro 45 – 45 S. Mentor Ave., Pasadena. ☎626-795-2478. www. bistro45.com. Dinner only. Closed Mon. **Californian.** Lavender and herbs scent the garden of this downtown bistro. Friendly servers deliver dishes like wild-caught calamari, Duroc pork chop with mushroom pastille, and oven fired free-range chicken with favas, mushrooms and golden beets.

$$ A.O.C. – 8700 W. 3rd St., Los Angeles. ☎310-859-9859. www.aocwinebar.com. **Mediterranean.** Tapas here include anything prepared fresh with flair. For twosomes, the best seating is at the wine bar or the charcuterie and cheese counter, where knowledgeable staff slice and cut.

$$ The Original Pantry – 877 S. Figueroa St., Los Angeles. ☎213-972-9279. www.pantrycafe.com. **American.** This downtown institution (1924) declares itself "never closed, never without a customer." White-jacketed waiters (some here for 40 years) serve such tried-and-true dishes as roast beef, fried chicken and apple pie at the cash-only eatery.

$$ Bestia – 2121 E. 7th Pl., Los Angeles. ☎213-514-5724. www.bestiala.com. Dinner only. **Italian.** Chefs Ori Menashe and Genevieve Gergi handcraft authentic regional specialties like whole grilled orate fish, wood oven-roasted Sonoma suckling pig, and squid ink spaghetti chitarra with lobster, wild fennel pollen and chili-fennel sofritto. Save room to sample some of the 60+ kinds of housemade charcuterie.

$ Il Capriccio on Vermont – 1757 N. Vermont Ave., Los Angeles. ☎323-622-5900. www.ilcapriccioonvermont. com. **Italian.** This charming trattoria in Los Feliz dishes up authentic Italian fare, from pasta to *pollo*, with fresh ingredients and in generous portions.

Los Angeles★★★

Los Angeles has the benefits and challenges of a major metropolis, though both the pros and cons are magnified by its enormous size and near-mythic reputation. The city's ethnic diversity endows it with rich cultural resources and can make a drive across town seem like a dizzying world tour. While its differences have produced clashes through the city's history, they also endow L.A. with a distinctive vitality and sense of possibilities.

▶ **Population:** 3,793,000.
🕓 **Michelin Map:** pp 118-119. Pacific Standard Time.
🔢 **Info:** ☏ 213-624-7300; www.discoverlosangeles.com; www.lacity.org
🔄 **Don't Miss:** The Getty Center; Pasadena; Griffith Observatory; the Huntington.
🕐 **Timing:** It's impossible to condense a comprehensive L.A. experience into any reasonable length of time, so focus on your personal interests: Hollywood, art, live entertainment, cultural diversity and so on.
👫 **Kids:** Universal Studios; Disneyland.

LOS ANGELES TODAY

Los Angeles' coastal setting favors it with perpetually fine weather and a beachy vibe that finds its way into the local culture. Given the city's prominent role as an entertainment, commercial and fashion capital, locals habitually find themselves on the cutting edge of national trends. Fads are born here: by the beach, at the shopping mall, in the kitchen, on camera. Angelenos take it all in their stride, with a carefree readiness to embrace (and create) the new.

A BIT OF HISTORY

Anthropologists estimate that 5,000 Gabrieleño Indians lived in this area before the first Spanish colonizing expedition in 1769. The mission town (1781) was named El Pueblo de Nuestra Señora la Reina de Los Angeles de Porciúncula, "The Town of Our Lady the Queen of the Angels by the Porciúncula (River)." By the time the dusty town was designated capital of Mexican California in 1845, it had become the commercial and social center for a region of vast cattle ranches and vineyards.

After the city passed into American hands, the advent of the railroad promoted a population boom. Images of a sun-kissed good life helped create communities like Hollywood, and by 1900 Los Angeles was home to more than 100,000. L.A.'s reputation was further enhanced by the **citrus industry**, as vast orange groves were planted to meet rising nationwide demand for the fruit. Growth, however, was severely limited by a lack of water. To meet this need, the $24.5 million **Los Angeles Aqueduct** opened in 1913, its Sierra Nevada waters coursing through 142 separate mountain tunnels. Although the controversial project ruined the livelihoods of many farmers, it enabled unprecedented growth for L.A.

The early 20C brought the fledgling motion-picture industry from New York and Chicago to Southern California, whose varied locations and consistently gentle climate encouraged outdoor filming. The studios settled in and around Hollywood. By 1920, 80 percent of the world's feature films were being produced in California, and by the mid-20C, Hollywood's film industry employed more than 20,000 people. Movie stars bought homes in the hills of Hollywood and nearby Beverly Hills. After World War II, the halcyon days of the Eisenhower era encouraged still more Americans to head west. Orange groves gave way to housing tracts. The city is still healing from devastating racial riots in 1965 and 1992, yet

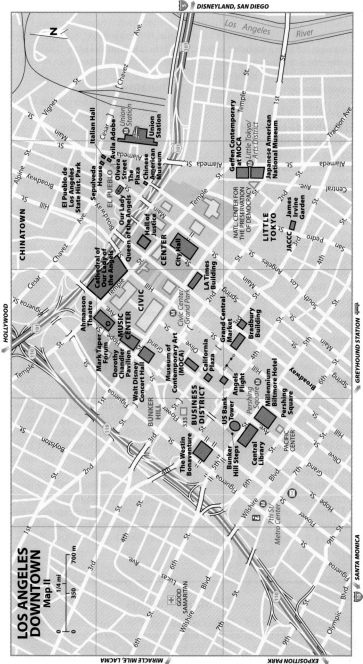

DISNEYLAND, SAN DIEGO

Los Angeles River

HOLLYWOOD

CHINATOWN

El Pueblo de Los Angeles State Hist Park

Italian Hall

Sepulveda House

Avila Adobe

Union Station

Olvera Street

EL PUEBLO

Our Lady Queen of the Angels

The Plaza

Chinese American Museum

Cathedral of Our Lady of the Angels

Hall of Justice

CENTER

City Hall

CIVIC

Ahmanson Theatre

MUSIC CENTER

Mark Taper Forum

Dorothy Chandler Pavilion

Walt Disney Concert Hall

Museum of Contemporary Art (MOCA)

Civic Center Grand Park

LA Times Building

Geffen Contemporary at MOCA

Little Tokyo/ Arts District

Japanese American National Museum

NATL CENTER FOR THE PRESERVATION OF DEMOCRACY

LITTLE TOKYO

James Irvine Garden

JACCC

California Plaza

Grand Central Market

Bradbury Building

BUNKER HILL

BUSINESS DISTRICT

333

US Bank Tower

Angels Flight

Pershing Square

Millennium Biltmore Hotel

The Westin Bonaventure

Bunker Hill Steps

Central Library

PACIFIC CENTER

Pershing Square

7th St/ Metro Center

GREYHOUND STATION

SANTA MONICA

LOS ANGELES DOWNTOWN
Map II

1/4 mi

700 m

350

0

GOOD SAMARITAN

MIRACLE MILE, LACMA

EXPOSITION PARK

the efforts of individuals and local and federal organizations are bearing fruit. Groups such as the **Los Angeles Conservancy** dedicate themselves to preserving historic architecture, from the Art Deco masterpieces of Wilshire Boulevard to residences by such architects as Frank Lloyd Wright. The city hosted the **Summer Olympic Games** in 1932 and 1984, and its unquenchable dynamism continues unabated, assisted by the repeal of a law limiting building height, which ushered in the construction of a new generation of skyscrapers.

DOWNTOWN★
El Pueblo de Los Angeles Historic Monument★

125 Paseo de la Plaza ✕⚬ ☎213-628-1274. www.ci.la.ca.us/elp.

The city's historic heart is a 44-acre cluster of early 19C buildings. The village was restored as a Mexican marketplace between 1926 and 1930. Shops and wooden stalls along brick-paved **Olvera Street★**, a pedestrian way, sell an assortment of crafts, clothing and food. A zigzag pattern in the pavement marks the path of the city's first water system (1781). The oldest house in Los Angeles, the one-story **Avila Adobe★** (E-10 Olvera St.), was built in 1818. The nearby **Sepulveda House** (W-12 Olvera St.), a two-story Victorian (1887), blends Mexican and Anglo influences.

The Plaza (Olvera St. between Main & Los Angeles Sts.) has occupied its site since 1825; on its west side is **Our Lady Queen of the Angels Catholic Church** (535 N. Main St.), built in 1822 and popularly known as Old Plaza Church.

Union Station

800 N. Alameda St. opposite El Pueblo. ☎213-683-6875.

A $13 million combined venture of the Southern Pacific, Union Pacific and Santa Fe Railroads (1939, Parkinson & Parkinson), this building gracefully blends Mission Revival, Spanish Colonial, Moorish and Art Deco styles. Union Station is known as the "Last of the Great Railway Stations" built in the US.

Chinatown

Roughly bounded by Sunset Blvd. and Alameda, Bernard & Yale Sts.

This small (15sq-block) district serves as one of two main centers for the city's residents of Chinese descent. A pagoda-style gateway (900 block of N. Broadway) marks the entrance to **Gin Ling Way**; chinoiserie-embellished buildings line this original pedestrian precinct. Herbalists, curio shops, restaurants and discount stores attract shoppers. Visit www.chinatownla.com for details of special events and festivals, such as walking tours and art nights.

Little Tokyo

Roughly bounded by E. 1st, E. 3rd, Los Angeles & Alameda Sts.

Japanese immigrants in late-19C Los Angeles congregated in the area preserved as the **Little Tokyo Historic District** (1st St. between San Pedro St. & Central Ave.). Today the **Japanese American Cultural and Community Center** (244 S. San Pedro St.; ☎213-628-2725; www.jaccc.org) and Japan America Theatre host community events. Adjacent is the **James Irvine Garden★**, an 8,500sq-ft garden designed in traditional style by Takeo Uesugi. Overlooking the garden is a brick sculpture plaza designed by L.A. native and internationally acclaimed artist **Isamu Noguchi** (1904-88).

TV Show Tapings

To attend the taping of a TV show as a member of the studio audience, visit the network's website and click on the show you are interested in. Or, you can sign up for limited same-day tickets at the individual studio. **Audiences Unlimited** (all major networks), ☎818-753-3470; www.tvtickets.com. **On Camera Audiences,** www.ocatv.com. **ABC Tickets**, http://abc.go.com. **CBS**, www.cbs.com. **NBC Audience Services**, www.nbc.com. **Fox**, www.fox.com. **Paramount**, www.paramount.com. Be sure to read the ticket's rules, as some tickets do not guarantee admittance.

Japanese American National Museum★

100 N Central Ave. ✕♿
☎213-625-0414. www.janm.org.
America's first museum dedicated to Japanese-American history occupies the former Nishi Hongwanji Buddhist Temple (1925) and a Pavilion (1998), linked by a plaza with a stone-and-water garden.

Civic Center Area

Roughly bounded by W. 1st, Hope, Temple & Los Angeles Sts.
The largest center for municipal administration in the US, this group of buildings and open plazas, planned and erected between the 1920s and the 1960s, occupies 13 blocks. The random array of structures ranges in style from the monumental **Hall of Justice Building** (1925), with its Neoclassical details (northeast corner of S. Broadway & W. Temple St.), to the contemporary structures of the Music Center.

Los Angeles City Hall★★

200 N. Spring St. ☎213-485-2121.
www.lacity.org.
City Hall's 28-story, pyramid-topped 454ft tower (1928) remains one of downtown L.A.'s most distinctive features and most widely recognized symbols. The 135ft-wide **rotunda★** reveals French limestone walls and a floor composed of 4,156 inlays cut from 46 varieties of marble. The **observation deck** 👥 in the tower (27th floor) affords sweeping **panoramas★★** of the Los Angeles Basin.

Music Center

135 N Grand Ave. ☎213-972-7211.
www.musiccenter.org.
Los Angeles' elegant hilltop mecca for the performing arts (1964, Welton Becket) includes three white marble structures occupying a seven-acre plaza. The largest and most opulent building in the complex is the 3,197-seat **Dorothy Chandler Pavilion★** (1964); this imposing composition of towering windows and columns hosts music, opera and dance productions.

Innovative dramatic works are presented at the 752-seat **Mark Taper Forum** (1967), a low, cylindrical structure framed by a reflecting pool and a detached colonnade. The rectilinear 2,071-seat **Ahmanson Theatre** (1967) hosts plays, musicals, dance concerts and individual performing artists. The $170 million, Frank Gehry-designed **Walt Disney Concert Hall** opened in 2003. Home of the L.A. Philharmonic Orchestra, the fancifully shaped stainless steel structure is acclaimed for its acoustics.

Cathedral of Our Lady of the Angels★

555 W. Temple St. ☎213-6380-5200.
www.cathedral.org.
L.A.'s $163-million cathedral, opened in 2002, fills a 5.6-acre site between the Music Center and Hall of Justice. Spanish architect José Rafael Moneo's striking design allows natural light to flood the congregational space through alabaster glass, beneath a copper roof. A 150ft campanile rises beside the cathedral.

Business District★★

Roughly bounded by Figueroa, 2nd, Spring & 9th Sts.
Anchored by Broadway and Spring Street, Los Angeles' historic business center reveals Beaux-Arts and Art Deco buildings dating primarily from 1890-1930; today it presents a lively Latino street scene. Queen of the district is the **Bradbury Building★★** (304 S. Broadway; ☎213-626-1893), a modest brick building (1893, George H. Wyman) whose marvelous five-story **atrium** was inspired by a futuristic novel of the time, Edward Bellamy's *Looking Backward*. Skylit from the rooftop by diffuse natural light, the atrium has lacy wrought-iron railings and open-cage elevators, red-oak trim and stair treads of Belgian marble. It is opposite the **Grand Central Market★** (317 S. Broadway; ☎213-624-2378, www.grandcentralsquare.com), built in 1897 and converted to a public market in 1917.

The gleaming commercial skyscrapers of Los Angeles' downtown community are focused on 5th and Grand Streets. They are climaxed by **Library Tower★** (633 W. 5th St.), among the tallest office buildings in the US west of Chicago. Soaring 1,017ft, the 73-story Italian-granite building (1992, I.M. Pei) is topped by an illuminated crown. It stands opposite the **Los Angeles Central Library★** (630 W. 5th St.; &323-228-7000; www.lapl.org/central), a striking building (1926, Bertram Goodhue) conceived as an allegory on "The Light of Learning," expressed through sculptures, murals and tilework.

Around the corner, the 11-story, 683-room **Millennium Biltmore Hotel★★** (see ADDRESSES)(1923, Schultze & Weaver) was once the largest hotel in the West. It is graced with opulent 16C Italian-style brickwork and terra-cotta, and high, hand-painted ceilings in its Rendezvous Court. Another downtown landmark is the **Westin Bonaventure★** (404 S. Figueroa St.; &213-624-1000; www.bonaventure.com), a 35-story hotel (1976, John Portman) composed of five cylindrical towers of mirrored glass.

Museum of Contemporary Art (MOCA)★★

250 S. Grand Ave. ✗&P &213-621-1710. www.moca.org.

An assemblage of geometric forms clad in red sandstone and green aluminum, this museum showcases late 20C visual art. Arata Isozaki (1986) designed an intimate, low-lying **complex★** of cubes, a cylinder and 11 pyramidal skylights above underground galleries.

Changing selections from the 6,000-piece permanent collection include pieces by Borofsky, Johns, Nevelson, Oldenburg, Pollock, Rauschenberg, Rothko and Stella.

Temporary shows are held here and at the museum's other two locations: **The Geffen Contemporary at MOCA★** (152 N. Central Ave.; &213-626-6222), a former police car warehouse complex in Little Tokyo renovated by Frank Gehry; and the **Pacific Design Center** (8687 Melrose Ave.; &213-626-6222; www.pacificdesigncenter.com).

EXPOSITION PARK AREA★★

This park (bounded by Exposition Blvd., Figueroa St., Martin Luther King Blvd. & Vermont Ave.) occupies the site of the original (1872) city fairgrounds, 3mi southwest of downtown adjacent to the **University of Southern California** campus. A 1913 civic campaign made it the setting for public museums and exhibit halls, athletic facilities and gardens, laid out in grand Beaux-Arts tradition by landscape architect Wilber D. Cook Jr. The rose garden is the location of choice for weddings and photographs of family gatherings. A $350 million facelift added greenery, promenades and new facilities.

Los Angeles Memorial Coliseum★★

3911 S. Figueroa St. ✗&P &213-747-7111. www.lacoliseum.com.

This 93,000-seat oval arena (1923, Parkinson & Parkinson) is Los Angeles' preeminent sports stadium, hosting football, soccer, rock concerts and other outdoor events. Once the world's largest arena, the Coliseum gained renown as the principal venue of the 1932 and 1984 Olympic Summer Games.

▲▲ Natural History Museum of Los Angeles County★★

900 Exposition Blvd. ✗&P &213-763-3466. www.nhm.org.

This natural-history collection of more than 35 million specimens and artifacts is among the largest in the US. The dignified Beaux-Arts structure (1913) contrasts with the skeletons of a tyrannosaur and a triceratops poised for battle that greet visitors in the main foyer. The **Halls of African and North American Mammals** display animals in natural habitats. The **Hall of Gems and Minerals★** houses more than 2,000 specimens.

Two history halls depict ancient Latin American cultures and California's peoples from 1540-1940. The **Discovery Center** offers fossils and bones to touch, and live creatures to pet. The **Insect Zoo** includes 30 terrariums and aquariums crawling with live specimens.

Native American cultures are represented by a large collection of Zuni fetish carvings.

The **Hall of Birds**★ is filled with interactive displays, including three walk-through habitats.

California ScienCenter★

700 Exposition Park Dr. ✕&🅿🔗323-724-3623. www.californiascience center.org.

The largest and oldest (1951) institution of its kind in the western US, this reconstructed complex includes an IMAX theater and numerous interactive galleries.

Exhibits in **World of Life** and **Creative World** explore the relationship between science and technology, from human cells to solar cars.

Nearby, the ScienCenter's Frank Gehry-designed **Air and Space Gallery** (1984) holds a three-story open space with stairs, landings and walkways that provide close-up looks at a century of replica aircraft, ranging from a pre-Wright Brothers glider to an A-12 Blackbird.

Ecoystems houses live animals and plants; visitors can walk through a living kelp forest or experiment on a polar ice wall.

California African American Museum★

600 State Dr. ✕&🅿🔗213-744-7432. www.caamuseum.org.

Opened in 1981, this facility focuses on the heritage of California's large African-American population, particularly the role of black people in settling the American West. Changing exhibits of artworks and artifacts, ranging from ancient West African art to modern music and art, are displayed in three galleries around a central sculpture court.

GRIFFITH PARK★★

Enter from Los Feliz Blvd., Ventura Fwy. (Rte. 134) or Golden State Fwy. (I-5). 🔗323-913-4688.

One of the largest urban parks in the US, Griffith Park straddles 4,210 acres (6.6sq mi) of the Santa Monica Mountains northwest of downtown Los Angeles. Wealthy miner Col. Griffith J. Griffith donated the land in 1882, along with money for a park observatory and the **Greek Theatre**, an open-air concert venue. A zoo, two museums and recreational facilities complement those attractions, but Griffith Park remains largely a natural oasis inhabited by deer, opossums, quail and raptors. Miles of hiking and bridle trails weave through the park.

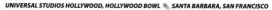

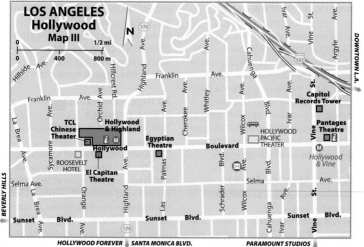

Griffith Observatory

© Photoshot/Eye Ubiquitous

👥 Griffith Observatory★★★

2800 E. Observatory Rd. ✕♿🅿 ☏213-473-0800. www.griffithobs.org.
On the south slope of 1,625ft Mount Hollywood, this Art Deco observatory (1935) is a local landmark. A 240-pound brass Foucault pendulum in the **rotunda** demonstrates the earth's rotation. Beneath an 84ft copper dome is a **planetarium. Views★★★** sweep over downtown L.A., the coast and the nearby Hollywood Sign.

👥 Museum of the American West★★

4700 Western Heritage Way. ✕♿🅿 ☏323-667-2000. www.theautry.org.
Established in 1988 by Western singer-film star Gene Autry (1907-98), the collection is presented in spacious galleries. Exhibits range from a large assembly of Colt firearms to western movie memorabilia and art. Several galleries explain the romance and lure of the West that drew settlers from the region's diverse ethnic groups.

👥 Los Angeles Zoo★★

5333 Zoo Dr. ✕♿🅿 ☏323-644-4200. www.lazoo.org.
Begun in the late 1890s by silent-film producer William Selig to provide animals for motion pictures, the zoo was donated to the city in the early 1920s. In 1966 it moved to 80 acres in northeastern Griffith Park; today it has more than 1,100 mammals, birds, amphibians and reptiles of some 250 species, including 29 endangered species.

A walkway leads to a three-acre children's zoo, then extends to trails that follow hilly terrain to visit aquatic animals, birds, and denizens of Australia, North America, Africa, Eurasia and South America. At the Gorilla Reserve, seven western lowland gorillas gambol and interact. A documentary display is devoted to the California condor, and the zoo's successful part in breeding this rare species and re-introducing it to the wild.

WILSHIRE BOULEVARD★

Wilshire Boulevard is the city's grandest thoroughfare, extending west 16mi from downtown through central Los Angeles, Beverly Hills and Westwood to Santa Monica.
The so-called **Miracle Mile** (La Brea to Fairfax Aves.) shows off some remarkable Art Deco buildings.

La Brea Tar Pits★

North side of Wilshire Blvd., west of Curson Ave.
Some 38,000 years ago, saber-tooth tigers, mammoths and giant sloths that came here to drink from pools were trapped in a thick, tar-like asphalt (*brea* in Spanish) at the surface. Since 1905, excavations have unearthed more than 100 tons of specimens—the world's largest cache of Ice Age fossils. Asphalt still bubbles through the water.

👥 Page Museum at the La Brea Tar Pits★★

5801 Wilshire Blvd. ♿🅿 ☏323-857-6300. www.tarpits.org.
Cast-fiberglass friezes of Ice Age animals top this square-sided museum. Skeletons are reconstructed from bones found at the pits—since 1906 more than one million bones of more than 231 vertebrate species have been collected. Displays create the illusion

of skeletons—of a **saber-tooth cat** and 9,000-year-old La Brea Woman—transforming into flesh and blood. In a glass-windowed **paleontology laboratory**, scientists clean and examine bones.

Los Angeles County Museum of Art (LACMA)★★★

5905 Wilshire Blvd. ✕&🄿 ✆323-857-6000. www.lacma.org.

This sprawling 20-acre complex is the nation's largest art museum west of Chicago. LACMA's holdings comprise more than 150,000 works that range from Egyptian and Asian art to contemporary works. Its **Rifkind Gallery for German Expressionism** is the largest and most comprehensive collection of its kind in the world. Other strengths include Asian art, Central and South American art, Old Masters paintings and Islamic works of art.

The **Ahmanson Building** holds much of the permanent collections: modern art from Picasso to Hans Hoffman; European art and ancient Egyptian, Mesopotamian, Iranian, Greek and Roman art, as well as Middle Ages to 19C works - and Islamic, South and Southeast Asian, Indian, Tibetan and Nepalese art

The **Hammer Building** displays **Chinese and Korean** art as well as photography. The **Art of the Americas Building** houses **American Decorative Arts** and **American Painting and Sculpture** and Art of the Ancient Americas and Latin American Art.

Open-air **sculpture gardens**, one with Rodin bronzes, the second with contemporary works by Alexander Calder and Henry Moore, flank the building. The **Pavilion for Japanese Art** (1988, Bruce Goff and Bart Prince), a curvilinear structure surrounded by Japanese gardens, highlights the Price Collection of **Shin'enkan**: some 300 scroll paintings and screens created during the Edo period (1615-1868). Also exhibited are textiles, ceramics and lacquerware. In 2008, the Broad Contemporary Art museum opened as part of the museum's 10-year Transformation expansion project. In late 2010, the single-story, glass- and stone-enclosed Resnick Pavilion opened to house special exhibits. Plans call for a new building, designed by Swiss architect Peter Zumthor, to house the permanent collection.

One block away, a 1939 Streamline Moderne edifice became **LACMA West** (Wilshire Blvd. & Fairfax Ave.) in 1998. Home to an interactive children's gallery, it is undergoing renovations to add space for exhibits of prints, drawings, textiles, and photography.

♟♟ Petersen Automotive Museum★★

6060 Wilshire Blvd. &🄿 ✆323-930-2277. www.petersen.org.

Imaginative dioramas, photographs and computer stations show how automotive evolution influenced the growth of Los Angeles, the quintessential "car town." More than 150 rare cars, trucks and motorcycles are displayed. The **Streetscape** exhibit sets classic vehicles into dioramas illustrating Los Angeles at various points in history. Exhibits detail civic decisions to build broad boulevards, and eventually freeways, in place of trolley and streetcar lines. In 2014 a dramatic redesign of the building's exterior will begin, and the collection will be upgraded and expanded.

Farmers' Market★

6333 W. Third St. at S. Fairfax Ave. ✕🄿 ✆323-933-9211. www.farmersmarketla.com.

This open-air market retains a rustic charm with more than 100 permanent businesses. Green grocers and butchers serve locals; international food and souvenir stands cater to visitors.

HOLLYWOOD★★

As much a state of mind as a geographic entity, Hollywood is the symbolic and real heart of the movie industry. Part of the city of Los Angeles, it is located 6mi northwest of downtown and 12mi east of the Pacific coast, sweeping south from the Hollywood Hills (an extension of the Santa Monica Mountains). Prohibitionist H.H. Wilcox founded the suburb in 1883, and by the turn of the 19C the quiet community of 5,000 was most notable for a lack of saloons. Incorporated in 1903, it was annexed seven years later by L.A. in anticipation of water from the Los Angeles Aqueduct and the growth that would ensue. In 1911, filmmaker David Horsely opened Hollywood's first movie studio in an abandoned roadhouse. By 1912, five large East Coast film companies and many smaller producers had relocated here. Investors in 1923 developed "Hollywoodland," a tract of elegant Mediterranean homes in the hills of Beachwood Canyon. To publicize the venture, the financiers erected what now is known as the **Hollywood Sign★**, of white sheet-metal letters 30ft wide and 50ft tall. (Located in Griffith Park, the sign is best viewed from the Griffith Observatory). Through the 1940s, Hollywood remained the center of the film industry and community, although many studios relocated to other nearby areas such as Burbank. Some landmark buildings subsequently deteriorated, but since the 1980s, energetic efforts have restored several landmarks along Hollywood and Sunset Boulevards. In mid-2013 city authorities approved controversial plans for two high-rise buildings opposite Capitol Records; the Hollywood Millennium Project would add 1 million sq ft of residential and commercial space. The Hollywood Chamber of Commerce (7018 Hollywood Blvd.; ℘323-469-8311; www.hollywoodchamber.net) has more information about Hollywood.

Hollywood Boulevard★★

Hollywood's main thoroughfare is 4.5mi long. The 1mi stretch between Gower Street and Sycamore Avenue is easily seen on foot. Grand movie palaces the **Pantages Theatre★** (6233 Hollywood Blvd.; www.hollywoodpantages.com), **Egyptian Theatre★** (6712 Hollywood Blvd.; www.americancinematheque. com) and **El Capitan Theatre★★** (6838 Hollywood Blvd.; http://elcapitan. go.com) rub shoulders with souvenir stands and theme museums. Embedded in the sidewalks of the **Walk of Fame★** (Hollywood Blvd. between Gower St. & La Brea Ave., and Vine St. between Sun-

set Blvd. & Yucca St.; ℘323-469-8311) are more than 2,400 bronze-trimmed coral-terrazzo stars, conceived in 1958 by the Hollywood Chamber of Commerce as a tribute to entertainment personalities.

The intersection of **Hollywood and Vine** was immortalized as the hub of Hollywood in the 1930s and 40s. Its landmark is the **Capitol Records Tower★** (1750 Vine St.), a 150ft-tall complex of offices and studios (1954, Welton Becket) that resembles a stack of records surmounted by a phonograph needle.

Hollywood & Highland★

Hollywood Blvd. & Highland Ave. ✕&🅿 The new locus of Hollywood is this $615 million development (2001, Ehrenkrantz, Eckstut & Kuhn) which is anchored by David Rockwell's 3,650-seat **Dolby Theatre** (℘323-308-6300, www.dolbytheatre.com), new home of the Academy Award ceremonies (March).

The **Awards Walk**, a staircase from Hollywood Boulevard, cites every "best picture" honoree since the first Oscars were doled out in 1927. Retail shops surround Babylon Court, with 33ft-high elephant statues flanking a courtyard that echoes a 1916 D.W. Griffith movie set; winding into it is a granite path of anonymous "How I Got to Hollywood" quotes.

TCL Chinese Theatre★★

6925 Hollywood Blvd. ℘323-465-4847. www.tclchinesetheatres.com.
An ornate fantasy of chinoiserie, this theater (1926, Meyer & Holler), formerly **Grauman's** Chinese Theatre but renamed in early 2013, was commissioned by showman **Sid Grauman**. Opened in 1927 for the gala premier of Cecil B. deMille's *King of Kings*, "The Chinese" is an eclectic, mansard-roofed pagoda, topped by stylized flames and flanked by white-marble dogs. The U-shaped cement forecourt features footprints and signatures of more than 180 Hollywood stars, with new ones added each year.

Sunset Boulevard★

Stretching 20mi from El Pueblo to the Pacific Ocean, this thoroughfare runs past the Latino neighborhoods of Elysian Park; the studios and street life of Hollywood; the mansions of Beverly Hills; and the upscale neighborhoods of Westwood, Bel Air, Brentwood and Pacific Palisades. Its most famous stretch is the 1.5mi **Sunset Strip★★** (Crescent Heights Blvd. to Doheny Dr.). Hugging the Santa Monica Mountains, the street transits a once-unincorporated strip (hence its nickname) between Los Angeles and Beverly Hills. It is now part of the city of **West Hollywood**, whose identity as one of L.A.'s largest gay enclaves is more evident on Santa Monica Boulevard.

Melrose Avenue★

Although it stretches 7mi from Hollywood to Beverly Hills, Melrose distills its creativity and craziness into 16 blocks between La Brea and Fairfax Avenues. Boutiques, restaurants and shops specializing in bizarre collectibles and gifts draw a swath of humanity that ranges from Versace-clad businesspeople, to pierced-and-tattooed Generation Xers, to the flamboyantly gay, to camera-toting tourists from Tokyo.

Paramount Studios★

5555 Melrose Ave. ✕ ✆323-956-8398. www.paramountstudios.com.
This complex is the only major studio left in Hollywood; daily guided tours require reservations. The wrought-iron Spanish Renaissance-style gates, surmounted by "Paramount Pictures" in script, endure as a well-known symbol just north of Melrose at Marathon Street.

Hollywood Forever

6000 Santa Monica Blvd., adjoining Paramount Studios lot. ✆323-469-6349. www.hollywoodforever.com.
The 65-acre cemetery (formerly Hollywood Memorial Park) shelters the graves of such Hollywood legends as Rudolph Valentino, Douglas Fairbanks, Tyrone Power and Cecil B. DeMille.

Hollywood Bowl★★

2301 N. Highland Ave. ✕♿🅿 ✆323-850-2000. www.hollywoodbowl.com.
Occupying a hollow surrounded by acres of greenery, this natural amphitheater is a popular concert site and summer home to the Los Angeles Philharmonic Orchestra, a Hollywood icon since 1919. A series of band shells designed by Lloyd Wright (son of Frank Lloyd Wright) replaced the original concrete stage in 1927; a 100ft white quarter-sphere was finalized in 1929. In 2004, a new acoustically improved shell was installed. Frank Sinatra, the Beatles, Igor Stravinsky and Luciano Pavarotti all performed here. Picnicing at the tables in the surrounding hills is permitted.

Hollywood Bowl

♟♟ Universal Studios Hollywood★★★

100 Universal Plaza, Universal City, 3mi northwest of Hollywood Blvd. via US-101. ✕&🅿 ✆800-864-8377. www.universalstudioshollywood.com.

Part film and TV studio, part live-entertainment complex and amusement park, 415-acre Universal Studios sprawls over a hillside above the San Fernando Valley. Silent-film producer Carl Laemmle established a studio here in 1915. In 1964 Universal began to offer tram rides to boost lunchtime revenues at its commissary; visitors were shown makeup techniques, costumes, a push-button monster and a stunt demonstration. Today, Universal Studios Hollywood is among the largest man-made tourist attractions in the US, annually welcoming close to 6 million visitors. **Universal CityWalk** is a shopping, dining and entertainment complex designed to appear as a compressed version of Los Angeles.

At Universal's **Animal Actors** stunts are performed by more than 60 trained animals. The **Special Effects Stage** offer lessons in moviemaking magic: sound, makeup and computer effects. Among film-related rides are **Jurassic Park** (an escape from dinosaurs), **Transformers: The Ride3D** and **Shrek 4-D** (join the cartoon character's world).

On the **Studio Tour★★** (*45min*), trams wind through movie sets portraying the Wild West, small-town America, New York City, Mexico, Europe and other locales. En route, they pass the Bates house built for Alfred Hitchcock's *Psycho* (1960); are attacked by the shark from Steven Spielberg's *Jaws* (1975); witness robotic racers in fast-paced street races; and endure a collapsing bridge, a flash flood and an earthquake.

BEVERLY HILLS★★

Surrounded by Los Angeles and West Hollywood, Beverly Hills (www.beverlyhills.org) is an independent 6sq-mi municipality of nearly 35,000 citizens, founded in 1907. The city's name is synonymous with wealth and elegance, qualities seen in village-like shopping streets lined with international boutiques, fashionable restaurants and luxurious mansions lining gracious, tree-shaded drives. Architect Wilbur Cook laid out the grid and landscape architects John and Frederick Law Olmsted plotted sinuous drives through the foothills. The 1912 Beverly Hills Hotel (9641 Sunset Blvd.) began to attract stars to the area; Mary Pickford and Douglas Fairbanks built the first mansion, **Pickfair** (1143 Summit Dr.), high on a hill in 1920.

Rodeo Drive★★

This renowned street is a three-block stretch of mostly two- and three-story buildings north of Wilshire Boulevard. Boutiques and clothiers, jewelers, antique dealers and art galleries cater to expensive tastes. On the northeast corner of Wilshire and Rodeo Drive, the four-story **Via Rodeo** shopping complex (1990) whimsically resembles the street of an Italian hillside town. **Anderton Court** (328 N. Rodeo Dr.), an angular complex with an open ramp that winds around a spire, was built in 1954 from a Frank Lloyd Wright design.

WESTSIDE
University of California, Los Angeles (UCLA)★

Roughly bounded by Le Conte, Hilgard & Veteran Aves. and Sunset Blvd. ✕&🅿 ✆310-825-4321. www.ucla.edu.

Lodged on a 420-acre foothills campus between Westwood Village and Bel Air, UCLA is the largest member of the University of California's 10-campus system, with nearly 40,000 students. Brick-and-stone buildings of the Lombard Romanesque style encircle **Royce Quadrangle★**. **Royce Hall** (1929) houses an 1,850-seat theater. The entrance to **Powell Library** (1928) was modeled after the Church of San Zeno in Verona.

Fowler Museum at UCLA★

✆310-825-4361, www.fowler.ucla.edu

An anthropology museum noted for its **silver collection** from England, Europe and America.

UCLA Hammer Museum★

10899 Wilshire Blvd., Westwood Village. ♿🅿ℰ310-443-7000. www.hammer. ucla.edu.

The **Armand Hammer Collection**, features paintings and drawings by Old Masters (Tintoretto, Titian, Rubens), Impressionists and Postimpressionists (Degas, Manet, Cézanne, Gauguin, Toulouse-Lautrec).

The **UCLA Grunwald Center for the Graphic Arts** is one of the top US collections of works on paper. The **Franklin D. Murphy Sculpture Garden★★** (northeast corner of campus) showcases more than 70 works by artists such as Rodin, Matisse, Miró and Moore.

The Getty Center★★★

1200 Getty Center Dr., just off I-405. ✗♿🅿ℰ310-440-7300. www.getty.edu.

Oil millionaire **Jean Paul Getty** (1892-1976) began collecting paintings in 1931. After World War II, he resided in Europe, developing his worldwide oil business while expanding his art holdings and commissioning a Malibu museum, to display them. The collections quickly outgrew the Malibu space, and the Getty Center opened in 1997.

Architect Richard Meier designed the facility, a travertine-clad complex melding six buildings on a 110-acre campus with courtyards, walkways, fountains, gardens and stunning views.

The **Central Garden** was conceived by artist Robert Irwin.

The various branches of the J. Paul Getty Trust, including research and conservation organizations, occupy several of the structures; the **J. Paul Getty Museum★★★** takes the remainder of the complex.

The museum showcases its founder's superior assemblages of French decorative arts; 17-20C European paintings, including such well-known works as Rembrandt's *St. Bartholomew* (1661) and Van Gogh's *Irises* (1889); and works on paper, encompassing drawings, illuminated manuscripts and photographs. It occupies five pavilions arranged around an open courtyard and bridged by walkways on two levels, allowing visitors to create their own routes through the collections. Paintings are on the upper floors, displayed in natural light augmented as needed by artificial illumination.

Highlights include the **illuminated manuscripts★★** from 9-18C France, 9-16C Italy and from 15-16C Belguim and the Netherlands, monumental French tapestries from the period of Louis XIV, and Impressionist canvases, including works by Renoir, Pissarro, Monet, Manet, Van Gogh, Munch and Cézanne.

Skirball Cultural Center★★

2701 N. Sepulveda Blvd., just off I-405. ✗♿🅿ℰ310-440-4500. www.skirball.org.

The West Coast's preeminent Jewish cultural center describes and interprets Judaism, and chronicles the tumultuous history of the faith from its origin to the present. **Visions and Values: Jewish Life from Antiquity to America** tells of cultural influences affecting the Jews and spread by them during migrations. The importance of the flow of time is illustrated in religious holidays; "Sacred Space" explains artistry and symbolism in temples.

👥 **Noah's Ark** is an interactive exhibit that interprets the Biblical tale for young visitors.

EXCURSIONS
Santa Monica★

⬀ 14mi west of downtown Los Angeles. ℰ800-544-5319. www.santamonica.com.

This seaside city of 88,000 is a center of entertainment and arts, replete with galleries, theaters, fashionable cafes and boutiques. Both visitors and residents throng the **Third Street Promenade★**, a pedestrian mall (3rd St. between Wilshire Blvd. & Broadway), and **Santa Monica Place** (Broadway between 2nd & 4th Sts.), a shopping center designed by Frank Gehry (1979). Jutting 1,000ft over the ocean, the wooden **Santa Monica Pier★★** 👥 (end of Colorado Ave.) has been a landmark and gathering place since the early

20C. Its 9.5-acre expanse features an antique **carousel★**, fishing docks and an amusement park evoking the carnival spirit of a festive past. The present structure consists of the Municipal Pier (1909) and Pleasure Pier (1916), the latter designed by Coney Island creator Charles I.D. Looff. Both were restored during the 1980s.

Malibu★

◗ Pacific Coast Hwy. (Rte. 1), bordering Santa Monica to the northwest.

Malibu enjoys the loveliest setting of any Los Angeles-area beachside community. An exclusive residential enclave, the **Malibu Colony**, was established here in 1928, the beachside homesites drawing many celebrities. Stars still occupy multimillion-dollar homes in the security-gated colony, while others live in luxury aeries clinging to the mountainsides.

In fall 2007, several homes and businesses were destroyed in a sweeping fire. The Malibu pier near Surfrider Beach was renovated in 2008 and is a good place to watch surfers ride the waves.

The Getty Villa★★★

◗ 17985 Pacific Coast Hwy., between Sunset & Topanga Canyon Blvds. ✘⌖🅟 ✆310-440-7300. www.getty.edu.

Sequestered in a lushly landscaped 65-acre canyon, this re-creation of a 1C BC Roman villa overlooks the Pacific. A replica of a villa in Herculaneum buried during the eruption of Mount Vesuvius in AD 79, the building was erected in 1974 and now is a showcase for Greek, Roman and Etruscan antiquities.

Venice and South Bay★

Venice Beach★★ is renowned not only for its sand but for its colorful street life —particularly along **Ocean Front Walk**, a beachside pedestrian way lined with cafes, boutiques and souvenir stalls, plus folksingers and rappers, comedic jugglers and swimsuit-clad skaters and muscle-bound weightlifters.

South along the coast is **Marina del Rey**, the world's largest artificial harbor for 10,000 private yachts and sailboats.

Pasadena★★

◗ 9mi northeast of downtown Los Angeles. ✆626-795-9311. www.pasadenacal.com.

A city of 138,500, Pasadena boasts architectural and cultural attractions worthy of a larger community. A winter resort in the 1880s (many lavish mansions survive today), its early prosperity is reflected in the Spanish Baroque and Renaissance buildings of the **Civic Center**, erected in the 1920s. In 1889, Pasadena's elite Valley Hunt Club marked New Year's Day with a parade of flower-decked coaches.

Over the years the carriages evolved into elaborate floats covered with flowers and, in 1916, the parade was coupled with a championship college football game. Today the **Rose Parade★★** and the **Rose Bowl Game** are televised across North America.

Santa Monica Farmers' Markets

Santa Monica's cuisine is very often inspired by the fresh, seasonal offerings of the city's four farmers' markets with some 9,000 food shoppers attending each week. Established in 1981, these bustling outdoor markets feature organic and exotic produce, flowers, and herbs. The Wednesday **Downtown Farmer's Market** (Third & Arizona Sts., Wed 9am–2pm, Sat 8.30am–1pm) is the most frequented by local chefs; local restaurants are found in the food tent. The **Pico Farmer's Market** (Virgina Park, Sat 8am–1pm) is fairly serious, with excellent produce. The **Main Street Farmer's Market** (2640 Main St. Sun 9.30am–1pm) has a more street-fair atmosphere, with live music, pony rides and face-painting.

Norton Simon Museum★★★

411 W. Colorado Blvd. ✕✖🅿 ✆626-449-6840. www.nortonsimon.org.

Elegantly displayed in a spare contemporary building are 1,000 works from a private art collection spanning seven centuries of European painting and sculpture and 2,000 years of Asian sculpture. Entrepreneur Norton Simon (1907-93) began collecting paintings in 1954, beginning with canvases by Gauguin, Bonnard and Pissarro. Before he died, Simon had amassed more than 11,000 pieces, with particular strengths in 14-18C European art, French Impressionist paintings, the works of Edgar Degas, and Indian and Southeast Asian sculpture; today the collection numbers more than 12,000 objects.

Immediately recognizable are Renoir, Monet and Van Gogh, as well as Degas' famous sculpture, *The Little Fourteen-Year-Old Dancer* (1878-81). Also presented are Picasso (*Woman with a Book*, 1932), Daumier, Manet, Toulouse-Lautrec, Cézanne, Matisse, Modigliani, Braque, Klee and Kandinsky. In the sculpture garden are works by 19C and 20C sculptors, most notably Auguste Rodin (studies of the *Burghers of Calais*, 1885-95), Aristide Maillol and Henry Moore.

Gamble House★★

4 Westmoreland Pl., paralleling 300 block of N. Orange Grove Blvd. ✎✎Visit by guided tour only. ✆626-793-3334. www.gamblehouse.org.

A masterpiece of the Arts and Crafts movement (1907-09, Charles and Henry Greene), this house was the winter residence of David Gamble, heir of the Procter & Gamble company.

Covered in redwood shingles, the sprawling, two-story gabled "bungalow" and its contents show a dedication to craftsmanship and integrated design. Decorative masterworks include furnishings and intricate woodwork.

Huntington Library, Art Collections and Botanical Gardens★★★

1151 Oxford Rd., San Marino, off E. California Blvd. 2.3mi southeast of downtown Pasadena ✕✖🅿 ✆626-405-2100. http://huntington.org.

The Huntington comprises one of the world's finest research libraries of rare books and manuscripts; a world-class collection of 18-19C British art, French and American works; and renowned botanical gardens. Secluded in the upscale Pasadena suburb of San Marino, it occupies the ranch of rail tycoon Henry E. Huntington (1850-1927).

The stately **Library★★** houses more than six million manuscripts, books, photographs and other works, with emphasis on British and American history, literature and art from the 11C to the present. Displays include the **Ellesmere Chaucer**, an exquisitely illustrated manuscript (c.1410) of *The Canterbury Tales*, and a **Gutenberg Bible** (c.1450), one of few vellum copies in the US. Other highlights are a **First Folio** of William Shakespeare's plays and a large edition of Audubon's *Birds of America*. The Dibner Hall of the History of Science houses an exhibit on scientific achievements over time.

The **Huntington Art Gallery★★** is housed in the Beaux-Arts-style former residence. Its **British art★★★** collection is outstanding, particularly for its 20 full-length portraits. Among them are Gainsborough's *Jonathan Buttall: "The Blue Boy"* (c.1770) and Thomas Lawrence's *Sarah Barrett Moulton: "Pinkie"* (1794). The Virginia Steele Scott Galleries feature works of **American art** ranging from the 18C to the early 20C. The Dorothy Collins Brown wing is devoted to Arts and Crafts movement architects. Covering 120 landscaped acres, the **Botanical Gardens★★** include 14,000 species. The 10-acre desert garden presents more than 5,000 types of mature cacti and succulents. The terraced **Japanese garden★** encompasses a koi pond, moon bridge, Zen rock garden and bonsai. Rose and camellia gardens each have more than 1,200 cultivars.

Other gardens display herbs, palms, Australian plants and tropical species. A new visitor center is slated to open in early 2015.

San Gabriel Arcángel Mission★

▶ 428 S. Mission Dr., San Gabriel, 7mi southeast of Pasadena via I-210, Sierra Madre Blvd. & Junipero Serra Dr. ♿🅿 ✆626-457-3035. sangabrielmissionchurch.org.

The mission was established in 1771 and moved here in 1775. The impressive **church** (1779-1805), still active, was inspired by the Moorish cathedral in Córdoba, Spain. A cemetery dates from 1778.

On the grounds are remnants of a water cistern, an aqueduct, soap and tallow vats, a kitchen and a winery.

Los Angeles County Arboretum and Botanical Garden★★

▶ 301 N. Baldwin Ave. at I-210, Arcadia, 5mi east of Pasadena. ✗♿🅿 ✆626-821-3222. www.arboretum.org.

These 127-acre grounds showcase more than 18,000 plants, including more than 1,700 species of orchids. A spring-fed lake was once a location for Hollywood films. South of the lake are historic buildings furnished in period style: reconstructed Gabrieleño wicki-ups; the rustic, three-room **Hugo Reid Adobe** (1840); and the ornately decorated **Lucky Baldwin Cottage** (1885).

Warner Bros. Studios★

▶ 4000 Warner Blvd., Burbank, off Rte. 134 (Ventura Fwy.) at Hollywood Way, 14mi west of Pasadena. ●▪Visit by guided tour (3hrs) only; ✆reservations recommended. ♿🅿 ✆818-954-8687. http://vipstudiotour.warnerbros.com

This 110-acre complex has been Warner Bros. headquarters since 1928. Today its 29 sound stages are in constant use for movies, TV programs, commercials and sound recordings. Visitors are transported via golf cart to the backlot for a no-frills walk through sets, prop rooms, and construction shops.

♟♟ NBC Studios

▶ 3000 W. Alameda Ave, Burbank, off Rte. 134 (Ventura Fwy.), 14mi west of Pasadena. ●▪Visit by guided tour (1hr) only. ♿ ✆818-840-4444.

Housing the largest color television studio in the US, this complex offers a look at simple static and videotaped displays.

Tours begin with a history of NBC, and visit studios like *The Tonight Show* with Jay Leno, and demonstrate special effects, sound, makeup, costumes and sports broadcasting.

Long Beach★

▶ 25mi south of Los Angeles. ✆562-436-3645. www.visitlongbeach.com.

Long Beach's growth began in earnest with the 1921 discovery of oil at Signal Hill. World War II brought a naval port and shipbuilding facilities; today the 2,807-acre **Port of Long Beach** ranks first in foreign-trade value and total liner-cargo tonnage among all US ports. Together with the adjacent Worldport L.A., it is the largest, busiest waterborne shipping center in the US. The sprawling city now has a population of 461,500.

♟♟ Queen Mary★★★

▶ 1126 Queens Hwy. ✗ ✆562-435-3511. www.queenmary.com.

Dominating Long Beach Harbor, this renowned passenger ship was permanently docked after 31 years in England's Cunard White Star line.

The 81,237-ton vessel is 1,019ft long. Built in Scotland between 1930-34, the *Queen Mary* made her maiden voyage in May 1936. Converted for military use during World War II, she carried more than 750,000 troops over 550,000mi, earning the nickname "Gray Ghost" for her camouflage paint and zigzag routes. The ship returned to civilian use in July 1947 and became a favorite of celebrities and socialites. By the mid-20C, air travel had eclipsed the era of the great passenger ships, and the *Queen Mary* completed the last of her 1,001 transatlantic voyages in 1967.

Visitors may explore the bridge, officers' quarters and other spaces; passenger suites and dining rooms; and the engine room, with its massive propeller box. Guided tours penetrate luxuriously furnished staterooms.

Overnight guests can stay in one of the more than 300 first-class staterooms that occupy three of the 12 decks (👌see ADDRESSES).

👥♂ Scorpion Submarine★

❍ 1126 Queens Hwy. 📞562-432-0424. www.queenmary.com.

The 3,000-ton *Scorpion*—more officially, the Soviet Foxtrot-class submarine Povodnaya Lodka B-427—is moored next to the *Queen Mary*. Nearly all of this 1972 diesel-electric sub (decommissioned in 1994) is open for tours.

👥♂ Long Beach Aquarium of the Pacific★★

❍ 100 Aquarium Way (off Shoreline Dr. south of Ocean Blvd.). ✖👌🅿 📞562-590-3100. www.aquariumofpacific.org.

The flowing wave shapes of this $117 million shoreside aquarium (1998) contain a fine marine exhibition. Its canvas is the Pacific Ocean, represented by more than 11,000 creatures—from the icy arctic waters off Russia and northern Japan, the temperate waters of the California and Mexico coasts, and the tropical islands and lagoons of the Palau archipelago in Micronesia. These three marine ecozones are divided into 19 major habitats and 32 smaller exhibits with nearly 500 species of fish, birds, marine mammals, turtles and other denizens of the Pacific.

Catalina Island★

❍ By passenger ferry from Long Beach, San Pedro or Newport Beach (45min-2hrs one way). 📞310-510-1520. www.catalinachamber.com.

Catalina's only town (of 3,600), **Avalon** is packed with pastel-colored houses and bungalows, hotels and restaurants. Autos are restricted. The stately **Wrigley Mansion** (1921), now a country inn, overlooks the town from 350ft above crescent-shaped Avalon Bay—not far from the adobe **Zane Grey Hotel** (1929), former home of the Western novelist.

From the **Pleasure Pier**, glass-bottomed boats depart to view undersea life.

The old **Casino Building★★** (1 Casino Way; 📞310-510-2000), a 140ft-tall, circular Art Deco building (1928-29) with Spanish and Moorish flourishes, dominates Avalon Bay's north end. In the 1930s and 40s, big-band legends Benny Goodman and Kay Kyser performed in its **Avalon Ballroom**. Murals adorn the box-office loggia and 1,184-seat Avalon Theatre.

The 38-acre **Wrigley Memorial and Botanical Garden** (1400 Avalon Canyon Rd., 1.3mi inland from Avalon Bay; 📞310-510-2897; www.catalinaconservancy.org) highlights Catalina's native plants. Exhibits at the nearby Santa **Catalina Island Interpretive Center** (1202 Avalon Canyon Rd.; 📞310-510-0954, parks.lacounty.gov) examine isle flora and fauna, marine ecology, geology and native history.

San Pedro

❍ Rtes. 47 & 110, 6mi west of Long Beach & 22mi south of downtown Los Angeles.

Linked to Long Beach by the **Vincent Thomas Bridge**, San Pedro's vast Worldport L.A. is one of the nation's busiest ports and the West Coast's leading passenger terminal, with major cruise lines offering vacation cruises to Baja California, the Mexican Riviera, Hawaii, Alaska, the Panama Canal and beyond. The **Los Angeles Maritime Museum** 👥♂ (Berth 84, foot of 6th St.; 📞310-548-7618, www.lamaritimemuseum.org) recounts harbor history. Housed in a novel structure (1981, Frank Gehry) designed to evoke maritime images, the **Cabrillo Marine Aquarium★** 👥♂ (3720 Stephen White Dr. off Pacific Ave.; 📞310-548-7562, www.cabrillomarineaquarium.org) offers an introduction to Southern California marine life with its innovative exploration center and exhibit hall, including a touch tank, crawl-in aquarium and mud walkthrough.

Orange County★★

Sprawling east and south of Los Angeles, Orange County's broad plain, formerly cloaked with the orange groves for which the county is named, is an exurban metropolis that extends 22mi from the 5,687ft crest of the Santa Ana Mountains to Pacific beaches. Population has more than doubled since the 1960s, especially in and around Anaheim and Santa Ana, capitals of suburban housing and shopping malls.

▶ **Population:** 3,010,000.
⚅ **Michelin Map:** 493 B10, 11 and map p 118-119. Pacific Standard Time.
▧ **Info:** ✆714-765-8888; www.anaheimoc.org.
⊚ **Don't Miss:** Disneyland Park.
⊙ **Timing:** Allow 3 days. Disneyland dwarfs California Adventure, so plan to devote twice as much time to the bigger park.

👫 DISNEYLAND® RESORT★★★

Between Katella Ave., West St., Ball Rd. & Harbor Blvd., Anaheim. ✆714-781-4565. https://disneyland.disney.go.com.

For 46 years, after it opened in 1955 as America's ultimate fantasy land, Disneyland was without peer. In 2001, after a $1.4 billion expansion, Disneyland evolved into Disneyland Resort. The original 90-acre park was joined by the 55-acre Disney's California Adventure. Linking the two is Downtown Disney.

Walter Elias Disney (1901-66) began working in animation before he headed for Hollywood at age 22. He and his brother, Roy, established a studio and scored their first big success with the 1928 debut of *Steamboat Willie*, starring a character named **Mickey Mouse** and combining animation with sound. In the early 1950s, Disney purchased a 180-acre tract of orange groves for an amusement park. The park opened in July 1955 to national fanfare.

Disneyland Park★★★

Roughly elliptical in shape, Disneyland has eight distinct sections radiating from a Central Plaza.

Tidy Victorian storefronts, horse-drawn trolleys and a double-decker omnibus accent **Main Street, USA**, an idyllic re-creation of early 20C, small-town America. Evenings bring the "**Remember... Dreams Come True**" fireworks show, featuring a Tinker Bell flyby. "The Disneyland Story Featuring Great Moments with Mr. Lincoln" is a journey through American history narrated by an Audio-Animatronics Abraham Lincoln. At the Main Street Cinema, animated black-and-white classics, including *Steamboat Willie*, are continuously screened. Passengers board the **Disneyland Railroad** here to circle the park. At the end of main street is Sleeping Beauty's Castle, a renowned icon with gold-leafed turrets and a moat.

Tomorrowland represents a look at an imagined future. "**Space Mountain**" is a roller coaster enclosed in a futuristic mountain. "**Star Tours**," conceived by *Star Wars* creator George Lucas, takes travelers to the Moon of Endor by means of special effects. The "**Astro Orbiter**" is both a 64ft-high kinetic sculpture and a spinning ride. "**Captain EO**" is a 3-D film starring Michael Jackson that was shown in the park in the 1980s and 1990s and brought back in 2010. "**Innoventions**" showcases emerging technologies in electronics and computer applications. In "Finding Nemo Submarine Voyage" yellow submarines submerge into the Tomorrowland Lagoon.

Fantasyland was Walt Disney's personal favorite. At the "**King Arthur Carrousel**," Disney movie tunes are pumped from a calliope as antique horses take their riders in continual circles. "**It's a Small World**" boats float visitors past more thn 300 Audio-Animatronics® children and animals representing nearly 100 nations, all singing a theme song promoting cultural understanding. Carnival-style rides include the "**Mad Tea Party**," a tilt-a-whirl of colorful cups and saucers. For the very young, "**Dumbo the Flying Elephant**" soars up and down in gentle circles; "**Storybook Land Canal Boats**" glide past a series of scale-model miniatures. Bigger kids prefer the "**Matterhorn Bobsleds**," which speed downhill through ice caves.

Mickey's Toontown is an exclusive residential address for Disney characters. At "**Mickey's House**," the celebrity mouse may pose for a photo. His loyal sweetheart invites friends to check on what's cooking at "**Minnie's House**." Donald Duck's boat, the "**Miss Daisy**," offers a bird's-eye view of Toontown from its bridge. A spiral staircase invites exploration of "**Chip 'n Dale's Tree House**." Other characters include princesses, Winnie the Pooh and Tinker Bell.

Frontierland offers a return to the Old West. The "**Golden Horseshoe Stage**" features musical revues. "**Big Thunder Mountain Railroad**," a runaway mine train, scales the crags and caves of a reddish mountain. Plying the "**Rivers of America**" are the "**Mark Twain Riverboat**," a Mississippi River paddle wheeler, and the "**Sailing Ship Columbia**," a three-masted windjammer. Coonskin-capped guides paddle voyagers in "**Davy Crockett's Explorer Canoes**." At night, visitors crowd the riverbank to see "**Fantasmic!**," a fiber-optic show (*22min*) with Disney animation at its pyrotechnic best.

Riders float through the swamps and bayous within "**Splash Mountain**," at the top of which awaits a 52ft flume that hurtles down a 47° slope to a drenching splash.

New Orleans Square is a re-created French Quarter. In the "**Pirates of the Caribbean**," which spurred the namesake movies, visitors float through a swamp and enter a village of buccaneers. Ghosts spook the "**Haunted Mansion**"; doom buggies travel eerily among holographic specters.

Adventureland's "**Enchanted Tiki Room**" stars fantastical tropical birds and flowers with enough charisma to inspire the audience to sing along. "**Jungle Cruise**" safari boats travel through a forest populated by mechanized crocodiles, hippos, elephants and tigers. In the "**Indiana Jones Adventure®**," transport vehicles make a harrowing journey through an archaeological site.

Disney California Adventure Park★★

This park, which opened in 2001 celebrates its home state in several themed areas. Golden State pays homage to the state's historical, agricultural and recreational treasures; Hollywood Pictures Backlot recalls the golden days of Hollywood; Paradise Pier is a beachfront amusement zone.

Golden State visitors may head for **Condor Flats**, designed as a 1940s high-desert airfield, to go "**Soarin' Over California**." This simulated ride surrounds guests in a giant projection dome and takes them on a flight around the state. There's hiking and whitewater rafting on "**Grizzly Peak**," and seafood with sourdough on Monterey's Cannery Row.

Hollywood Pictures Backlot, a two-block version of Hollywood Boulevard, includes an animation studio and live-entertainment theater. "**Muppet*Vision 3D**" showcases the lovable puppet creatures, while "**Twilight Zone Tower of Terror**" simulates a horrifying 13-storey elevator ride.

Paradise Pier is not for the faint of heart. Among the thrill rides, "**California Screamin'**" is a roller coaster that accelerates from 0 to 55mph in less than 5sec. "**Maliboomer**" is a 180ft free fall; "**Jumpin' Jellyfish**" is an underwater parachute ride. "**Toy Story Mania**" is an interactive ride introduced as part of a $1.1 billion expansion announced in 2007. The most recent additions are the 12-acre **Cars Land** inspired by the Pixar film *Cars* and featuring the Radiator Springs Racers ride; and Buena Vista Street,where visitors can board a red trolley and dine in a variety of restaurants.

Downtown Disney★

Linking the two theme parks with the hotels along a long avenue, this arcade includes a 12-theater cinema complex and dining-and-performance venues.

ADDITIONAL SIGHTS
Knott's Theme Park

8039 Beach Blvd., Buena Park, off I-5. ✖&🅿🖉714-220-5200. www.knotts.com.

In the 1920s, Walter Knott established a berry farm and roadside stand here. During the Great Depression his wife began selling chicken dinners.

In 1940 Knott constructed an Old West town to amuse hungry patrons waiting to get in. Today, Knott's features relocated or replicated historic structures, shows, and rides such as the popular Silver Bullet roller coaster. The expanded Boardwalk includes surfside gliders, which riders "pilot" 28ft above the park.

Bowers Museum of Cultural Art★★

2002 N. Main St., Santa Ana; off I-5. ✖&🅿 Closed Mon. 🖉714-567-3600. www.bowers.org.

Dedicated to indigenous fine art of the Americas, Africa and the Pacific Rim, this collection comprises more than 130,000 artworks dating from 1500 BC to the mid 20C.

Highlights include the **African collection, pre-Columbian collection** and **Native American art**. Artifacts from California's mission and rancho periods have a gallery.

Richard Nixon Library & Birthplace★

18001 Yorba Linda Blvd., Yorba Linda, 3.5mi east of Rte. 57 (Orange Fwy.). &🅿🖉714-993-5075. www.nixonfoundation.org.

Letters, papers, memorabilia and interactive exhibits commemorate the life of Richard Nixon (1913-94), 37th US president (1969-74). Nixon was born in a small farmhouse in Yorba Linda. A lawyer, he served in the US Navy in WWII. He was a US senator, and vice president before being elected US president.

Newport Beach★

Pacific Coast Hwy. (Rte. 1) & Newport Blvd. (Rte. 55). 🖉949-719-6100. www.visitnewportbeach.com.

The maritime roots of this resort and residential community of 87,000 are evident on the **Balboa Peninsula**, a large pleasure-craft anchorage. The **Balboa Pavilion★** (400 Main St.) was a popular dance hall in the 1940s. Extending east is the **Fun Zone** ♟♜ of arcades and carnival rides. Private companies operate **harbor cruises**.

The respected **Orange County Museum of Art★** (850 San Clemente Dr., Fashion Island, off Jamboree Rd.; 🖉949-759-1122; www.ocma.net) focuses on modern and contemporary work, especially 20C California art.

Laguna Beach★

Pacific Coast Hwy. (Rte. 1) & Laguna Canyon Rd. (Rte. 133). 🖉949-497-9229. www.lagunabeachinfo.org.

A magnificent sea-cliff **setting★** has attracted artists since 1903. More than 90 studios and galleries share the community of 24,500 residents. The **Laguna Art Museum★** (307 Cliff Dr.; 🖉949-494-8971; www.lagunaartmuseum.org) is a center for modern California art.

San Juan Capistrano Mission★★

26801 Ortega Hwy. (Rte. 74) & Camino Capistrano, San Juan Capistrano, off I-5. 🖉949-234-1300. www.missionsjc.com.

The seventh California mission was founded in 1776 by Padre Junípero Serra. In its **Great Stone Church** (1806) three rooms in the west wing display items from Native American, mission and rancho periods. In the east wing is the original mission chapel (1777).

Both San Juan Capistrano and the mission are famous for the swallows that return each year from winter nesting grounds in Argentina to build their mud nests on the ruins of the Great Stone Church. Their arrival each March is celebrated with a popular festival.

Palm Springs★★

Palm Springs is the most celebrated of a string of resort and retirement towns in the Coachella Valley east of Los Angeles. The area annually welcomes more than 3.5 million visitors and part-time residents, among them celebrities who come to play golf (more than 100 courses dot the valley) and browse galleries and boutiques. The town is noted for its mid-century modern architecture.

▶ **Population:** 45,000.
○ **Michelin Map:** 493 C 11. Pacific Standard Time.
Info: ℘760-770-9000; www.visitpalmsprings com.
○ **Location:** Dividing coastal LA and inland desert, San Gorgonio Pass is one of the country's windiest places, with one of America's biggest wind-power farms.
○ **Don't Miss:** The aerial tramway.
Kids: The Living Desert botanical garden and zoo

SIGHTS

Aerial Tramway★★★

Tramway Rd. west off Rte. 111, 2mi north of downtown Palm Springs. ✕&🅿
℘760-325-1391. www.pstramway.com.
Revolving, 80-passenger gondolas ascend Mt. San Jacinto on cables suspended from towers anchored n the slope. The 5,900ft climb (14min) to the 8,516ft summit crosses five biotic zones, from desert to alpine forest.

Palm Springs Art Museum★★

101 Museum Dr., 2 blocks west of N. Palm Canyon Dr. and Tahquitz Wy. ✕&
℘760-322-4800. www.psmuseum.org.
Modern and contemporary art, art glass, baskets, Mesoamerican artifacts and photography are displayed here.

Indian Canyons★

S. Palm Canyon Dr., 4mi south of downtown, off Rte. 111. 🅿 ℘760-325-3400. www.aguacaliente.org.
The Agua Caliente Band of Cahuilla Indians retains ownership of three canyons in the San Jacinto Mountains with groves of California-native **fan palms: Palm Canyon★★**, **Andreas Canyon★** (.8mi) and **Murray Canyon** (1mi). From the **Tahquitz Canyon Visitors Center★** (500 W. Mesquite Dr.; ℘760-416-7044; www.tahquitzcanyon.com), ranger-led tours depart for another canyon with rock art and a 60ft waterfall.

The Living Desert★★

Portola Ave., 1.3mi south of Rte. 111, Palm Desert, 15mi east of Palm Springs. ✕&🅿 ℘760-346-5694.
www.livingdesert.org.
This 1,200-acre botanical garden and zoo offers a survey of 1,500 plants and animals from each main subdivision of North American deserts, including the Upper Colorado Desert, the Yuman Desert and the arid Baja Peninsula.

EXCURSIONS

Joshua Tree National Park

◗ North entrance at Twentynine Palms (Rte. 62), 52mi northeast of Palm Springs & 140mi east of Los Angeles via I-10.
& ℘760-367-5500. www.nps.gov/jotr.
This 1,240sq-mi park contains two distinct deserts: the high (Mojave) and low (Colorado). The transition can be experienced in a short drive. The **Joshua tree** (*Yucca brevifolia*) is common in the cool Mojave Desert (above 3,000ft).

Rim of the World Drive★★

◗ Rte. 18 from San Bernardino to Big Bear City (40mi), 85mi northwest of Palm Springs via I-10.
The rugged San Bernardino Mountains, including 11,499ft San Gorgonio Mountain, dominate the landscape north of their namesake city. The drive links 6mi-long **Big Bear Lake★** with **Lake Arrowhead**, a summer-home colony.

Central Coast★

The Central Coast region balances a vital agricultural economy with a robust tourist industry. Natural beauty, historic Spanish roots, and a blend of cultural sophistication with casual friendliness contribute to its popularity.

♿ **Michelin Map:** 493 A, B10. Pacific Standard Time.

ℹ **Info:** ☏805-966-9222; www.santabarbaraca.com.

SIGHTS
Ventura
Pacific Coast Hwy., US-101 & Rte. 126, 62mi west of Los Angeles. ☏805-648-2075. www.ventura-usa.com.
This low-key coastal city of 110,000 grew up around San Buenaventura Mission.

San Buenaventura Mission
211 E. Main St. ☏805-643-4318. www.sanbuenaventuramission.org.

Padre Serra set his ninth mission half-way between San Diego and Carmel. Inside the structure (1809) that serves as the parish church, the reredos was made in Mexico City. A **museum** displays religious relics.

Channel Islands National Park★
Headquarters, 1901 Spinnaker Dr., Ventura. ⚠ ☏805-658-5730. www.nps.gov/chis.
This park encompasses the northern five of eight islands along the coast south of Santa Barbara: **Anacapa Island; Santa Cruz Island**, where sea lions inhabit **Painted Cave★**; **Santa Rosa Island; San Miguel Island**, which harbors a caliche forest, the calcium-carbonate castings of ancient trees; and tiny **Santa Barbara Island**, a breeding ground for elephant seals.
The visitor center is located at park headquarters. Boats depart from Ventura with Island Packers (☏805-642-1393; www.islandpackers.com), from Santa Barbara with Truth Aquatics (☏805-962-1127; www.truthaquatics.com).

Santa Barbara★★
US-101, 94mi west of Los Angeles. ☏805-966-9222. www.santabarbaraca.com.
Red-tile roofs, stucco buildings and palm-fringed beaches create a Mediterranean ambience in this coastal city of 90,000. The showpiece is the 1929 **Santa Barbara County Courthouse★★** (1100 block of Anacapa St.; ☏805-962-6464; www.sbcourts.org), a Moorish castle around a sunken garden.
The city's **waterfront★** extends from the **Santa Barbara Yacht Harbor** (W. Cabrillo Blvd.) to **Stearns Wharf★** (foot of State St.). The **Sea Center** 👥

Old Mission Santa Barbara

©iStockphoto.com/S. Greg Panosian

(211 Stearns Wharf, ✆805-962-2526; www.sbnature.org) is an aquarium; and **Shoreline Park** provides a vantage point to watch whales during the migrating season (Nov–Apr).

Santa Barbara Museum of Art★

1130 State St. ✕✆805-963-4364. www.sbmuseart.org.
Galleries showcase some 27,000 artworks, including Asian, European and American art. **Greek and Roman antiquities** include the Lansdowne Hermes (AD 2C). **French and British art, American art** and a gallery of 20C art round out the exhibits.

Old Mission Santa Barbara★★★

2201 Laguna St. 🅿✆805-682-4713. www.sbmission.org.
California's 10th mission dominates the city. Dedicated in 1786, the first church was replaced three times by larger structures. The present church (1820) serves as a parish church, research library and archive for the entire chain. The **padres' quarters** contain mission artifacts from the late 18C to early 19C. The **interior** of the church is adorned with bright motifs; the painted canvas reredos (1806) formed the basis for the detailed design scheme.

Santa Barbara Museum of Natural History★

2559 Puesta del Sol. From the mission turn right on Los Olivos St. ♿🅿
✆805-682-4711. www.sbnature.org.
Exhibits in this complex display flora, fauna, geology and ethnography of the West Coast. The **Chumash Indian Hall** contains artifacts from this tribe.

Solvang

Rte. 246 east of US-101, 34mi northwest of Santa Barbara.
Founded as a Danish farm colony in 1911, Solvang retains Danish provincial architecture at **Elverhøj Museum** (1624 Elverhoy Way; ✆805-686-1211; www.elverhoj.org), which resembles an 18C Jutland farmhouse.

© California Travel & Tourism Commission

Stearns Wharf, Santa Barbara

Santa Inés Mission★

1760 Mission Dr., Solvang. ♿🅿✆805-688-4815. www.missionsantaines.org.
Founded in 1804, Santa Inés was the final link in the chain between San Francisco and San Diego. In the museum **vestments★** date back to the 16C.

La Purísima Mission★★

2295 Purisima Rd., via Mission Gate Rd., 1.8mi off Rte. 246 near Lompoc, 53mi northwest of Santa Barbara via US-101 and Hwy. 1. 🅿✆805-733-3713. www.lapurisimamission.org.
The long, narrow **church** (1818) was built to provide access to travelers on El Camino Real (Royal Road or King's Highway), the old 600mi trail linking California's string of missions.
Step inside the **residence building★**, which housed padres' quarters, a library, office, wine cellar, guest quarters and chapel. Plants raised for food and medicine are cultivated in the **mission garden★**.

San Diego Area

This scenic, sun-kissed area of Southern California mixes relaxed residential communities with beaches, mountains and the beginnings of a vast desert. North of San Diego is upscale La Jolla, and beyond the urban area, San Diego County's 4,255sq mi encompasses towns, beaches and rural climes. An inland jumble of mountains and valleys climaxes at Anza-Borrego Desert State Park.

Highlights

1 Walking around **Old Town** (p147)

2 Meeting the **San Diego Zoo's** polar bears (p149)

3 **Surfing** (or surf-watching) (p151)

4 **Gaslamp Quarter** at dusk (p150)

5 Taking in panoramic **Font's Point** views (p155)

California's Origins

California began in San Diego. Hunter-gatherer Indians of the Kumeyaay tribe probably watched a trio of Spanish ships under Juan Rodríguez Cabrillo enter San Diego Bay in 1542 before sailing north. The next flotilla visited in 1601, but it was another century before Europeans came to stay. Jolted by English land claims from Point Reyes to Canada, Spain launched its own colonists, led by Capt. Gaspar de Portolá and Padre Junípero Serra. The pair established California's first mission and Spanish garrison at San Diego on July 16, 1769. The mission was eventually moved 6mi to the San Diego River; both church and state prospered in the remote outpost, albeit slowly. Following Mexican independence in 1821, a town, or *pueblo*, now called Old Town San Diego, grew below the garrison. The pueblo became a center for *Californios*, ranchers of Spanish and Mexican descent who owned parcels of California land. An American corvette captured San Diego during the Mexican American War in 1846. Mexican Governor Pío Pico surrendered near San Diego a year later, completing the US conquest of California.

San Diego enjoys a mild coastal climate, but east of the hills that block the daily sea breeze, temperatures may soar into triple digits in summer.

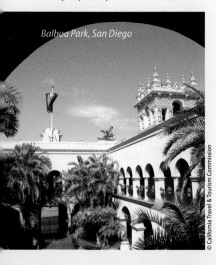

Balboa Park, San Diego

© California Travel & Tourism Commission

ADDRESSES

🛏 STAY

$$$$$ La Costa Resort and Spa – 2100 Costa del Mar Rd., Carlsbad. ☎760-438-9111. www.lacosta.com. 552 rooms. Sprawled across 450 hilltop acres along the coast north of San Diego, this utopian escape boasts two golf courses, 17 tennis courts and six pools, as well as detox wraps and shiatsu massage. La Costa is a true splurge for recharging body and mind. Special spa cuisine is a menu option at each of five restaurants, including the **Bluefire Grill ($$$$)**.

$$$$$ Rancho Valencia - 5921 Valencia Cir., Rancho Santa Fe. 858-756-1123. www.ranchovalencia.com. 49 rooms. Opened in 1989, the Relais & Châteaux property recently finished a $30 million restaurant-to-spa renovation that updated its 49 casitas to the pinnacle of Mediterranean-style luxury (the bedroom-size baths have enormous soaking tubs). The Pony Club bar and bistro is a legendary celebrity hangout, while **Veladora ($$$$)** restaurant looks like it belongs in a European castle, serving artful coastal cuisine like crispy skin dorade in saffron rouille bouillabaisse.

$$$$$ La Valencia – 1132 Prospect St. La Jolla. 858-454-0771. www.lavalencia.com. 112 rooms. On a bluff overlooking the Pacific, this landmark pastel-pink stucco palace is a statement of opulent American beachside style. Surrounded by palms, topped by Spanish tile and a domed tower, La Valencia has witnessed nearly 90 years of California sunsets. Accommodations include 15 Ocean Villas built in 2000. Of three restaurants, the **Mediterranean Room ($$$)** is the most intimate with its tables overlooking La Jolla Cove.

$$$$ Crystal Pier Hotel – 4500 Ocean Blvd., San Diego. 858-483-6983. www.crystalpier.com. 29 rooms. On a dock that juts into the ocean at Pacific Beach, a series of blue-and-white cottages provide unique over-the-water lodging. The 1927 bungalows have kitchenettes and wicker-chair furnishings, patios with umbrellas and deck furniture. Guests rent rods and fish from the pier, or close their shutters and fall asleep to the sound of rumbling surf.

$$$$ Hotel del Coronado – 1500 Orange Ave., Coronado. 619-435-6611. www.hoteldel.com. 757 rooms. This seaside gingerbread castle is a massive white Victorian of whimsical turrets and red-shingled roofs. "The Del" has hosted 16 presidents and countless celebrities since 1888. Guests stroll the resort's 26 oceanfront acres and indulge in a massive Sunday brunch in the **Crown Room ($$$)**, with its 33ft-high, rib-vaulted ceiling.

$$$$ Hotel Solamar – 435 6th Ave., San Diego. 619-819-9500. www.hotelsolamar.com. 235 rooms. Conveniently located downtown, this 10-story Kimpton property is awash in eye-catching contemporary decor, from the floating-candle chandelier in the common room to the tented sofa in the lobby. Spacious bedrooms, done in bold fabrics of deep browns and aqua blues, sport mahogany furniture; bathrooms combine shower and tub and have plenty of counter space. The rooftop terrace offers a lap pool, fire pits, a bar and good city views.

$$$ Andaz San Diego – 600 F St., San Diego. 619-849-1234. http://sandiego.andaz.hyatt.com. 159 rooms. Formerly the Ivy, the Andaz San Diego is a true urban resort. Classic 1914 architecture on the outside fuses with the latest in interior design. It's perfectly located amid the shopping, museums and nightlife of the famed Gaslamp district and just minutes from San Diego's best beaches as well as within walking distance to downtown businesses and PETCO Park. Eight minutes to San Diego Int'l Airport and a short drive to San Diego Zoo/Balboa Park.

$$ Horton Grand Hotel – 311 Island Ave., San Diego. 619-544-1886. www.hortongrand.com. 132 rooms. This historic Victorian-era hotel has been restored to its 1886 glory, when it shone above the brothels, saloons and opium dens of young San Diego's red-light district, now the Gaslamp area. Period decor, including an Austrian grand staircase, recaptures 19C charm.

EAT

$$$ Candela's – 416 Third Ave., San Diego. 619-702-4455. www.candelas-sd.com. Dinner only. **Mexican-French**. No tacos here. This East Village spot combines upscale Mexican cuisine (think Mexico City) with a dash of

French fusion and dark, European romantic decor. The menu offers new takes on seafood and flavorful steaks; the ceviche is excellent, as is the Chilean sea bass with grape cream sauce.

$$$ Croce's – 802 5th Ave., San Diego. 619-233-4355. www.croces.com. No lunch Mon–Fri. **American.** This shrine to folk-rock singer Jim Croce was opened by his wife, Ingrid, after Jim died in a 1973 plane crash. Its bars offer live music every night—including from A.J. Croce, a child when his father passed on. The walls are decorated with photos, original lyrics and guitars. Seafood specialties (seared scallops in blueberry gastrique with Sriracha roasted peanuts) and Jamaican jerk baby back ribs are fine dining choices.

$$$ George's at the Cove – 1250 Prospect St., La Jolla. 858-454-4244. www.georgesatthecove.com. **Seafood**. All three stories of this seaside showplace have views of La Jolla Cove, whether inside the formal modern dining room (dinner only) or out on the terrace, under canvas umbrellas. George's is famous for fish – including sesame crusted tombo with oyster mushrooms and leek fondue – and for its signature soup of smoked chicken, broccoli and black beans.

$$ The Prado at Balboa Park – 1549 El Prado, San Diego. 619-557-9441. www.pradobalboa.com. Closed for dinner Mon. **American**. In an exquisite garden location in the center of Balboa Park, the Prado offers lush views and varied new American fare, from paella in lobster-saffron broth to slow-roasted prime rib. The outdoor dining plaza is a delight, especially in lovely weather.

$$ Arrivederci – 3845 4th Ave., San Diego. 619-299-6282. www.arrive derciristorante. **Italian**. An easygoing, Italian-family atmosphere rules this longstanding restaurant in the Hillcrest neighborhood. The menu is stocked with traditional Italian favorites; try the meltingly rich lobster ravioli in saffron cream sauce , the amaretto chicken or any of the perfectly prepared risotti. Portions are generous, but save room for a cannoli or two.

$$ The Red Door –741 W. Washington St., San Diego. 619-295-6000. www. thereddoorsd.com. **American**. Cozy and casual, The Red Door specializes in modern comfort food: red wine braised short ribs , Duroc pork schnitzel and grilled seafood and steaks. The popular Sunday brunch features fluffy egg dishes and bottomless mimosas.

$$ Searsucker - 611 5th Ave., San Diego. 619-233-7327. www.searsucker.com. **American**. Bravo's Top Chef finalist Brian Malarkey proves that he's got chops in the kitchen, for inventive, thoughtful (and sometimes quirky) dishes like sea bass with drunken cherries and smoked almonds, or lamb tater tots. Admire the surroundings; the decor is Architectural Digest 2.0.

$ Aqui es Texcoco – 1043 Broadway, Chula Vista. 619-427-4045. http://aquiestexcoco.com. **Mexican**. *Barbacoa de borrega* (barbecued lamb) takes center stage at this unassuming spot tucked away at the end of a strip mall in Chula Vista. The service and food here win raves, from the lamb-based flautas, tacos and soups to the menu centerpiece, an assortment of lamb head meats served with fresh condiments and sides. It doesn't get any more authentic than this.

$ Goldfish Point Cafe – 1255 Coast Blvd., La Jolla. 858-459-7407. http://goldfishpointcafe.com. **American**. Perched atop the bluff overlooking La Jolla cove, this hugely popular breakfast-and-lunch eatery draws an equal mix of locals, tourists and students. Coffee, pastries and fresh-made sandwiches are good, but the prime draw is the stunning view – the tables are oriented to face the cove.

$ Corvette Diner –2965 Historic Decatur Rd. San Diego. 619-542-1476. www.cohnrestaurants.com. **American**. A disc jockey plays requests at this classic 1950s diner, as pink-and-black poodle-skirted waitresses carry burgers, fries and shakes to crowded tables. Photos of Elvis and Sinatra adorn the walls, alongside neon signs and 50s kitsch. Soda jerks mix cherry Cokes at the fountain, as cooks sling hash behind the counter.

San Diego★★★

Cosmopolitan San Diego is California's second-largest city and the eighth-largest in the US. Balboa Park's cultural institutions share the mesas and canyons north of downtown with Spanish-style mansions. San Diego Bay was the Pacific Fleet headquarters during both world wars and remains an important naval center. World-class tourist attractions, proximity to beaches and a mild climate have earned San Diego a reputation as one of the most livable cities in the nation.

▶ **Population:** 1,338,348.
Michelin Map: 493 B11. Pacific Standard Time.
Info: ✆619-236-1212; www.sandiego.org.
Parking: Parking is free at Balboa Park, but spaces fill up after 11am; use the park's free trams to get around.
Don't Miss: Balboa Park, Old Town and San Diego Zoo & Wild Animal Park.
Timing: Take a trolley to Downtown, Old Town, Balboa Park (free trams within the park) and Seaport Village; allow 4 hours for each.

OLD SAN DIEGO★★★

Sights preserving and commemorating the birth of San Diego and the beginning of the European presence in Alta California lie in the vicinity of Interstate 8 as it stretches east to west, roughly following the course of the San Diego River.

Old Town San Diego State Historic Park★★

4002 Wallace St.; exit I-5 at Old Town Ave. ✕&🅿✆619-220-5422. www.parks.ca.gov.
A broad plaza surrounded by restored adobe and wooden structures lies at the foot of Presidio Hill. Colorful shops and eateries re-create Mexican and early American periods, with demonstrations of quilting, blacksmithing, carpentry and other activities that would have taken place in the 1800s. The 1853 **Robinson-Rose House**, at the plaza's west end, is home to the Old Town San Diego Visitor Center, which has a diorama of Old San Diego. **La Casa de Machado y Silvas★** (1830-43), restored as a period restaurant, was once a boardinghouse, a brothel and a church. **La Casa de Machado y Stewart★** (1833) is an outstanding example of adobe restoration. **La Casa**

San Diego skyline and marina

© California Travel & Tourism Commission

de Estudillo★★ (1829), the largest and most impressive of the original adobes, has 13 rooms connected by a veranda; it offers a glimpse of upper-class lifestyle.

Presidio Park★

2727 Presidio Dr.; from Old Town, take Mason St. north to Jackson St.; turn left and follow signs.

The highlight of this beautifully landscaped park is the **Junípero Serra Museum** (☎619-232-6203; www.sandiegohistory.org), a stately white Mission Revival building (1929, William Templeton Johnson). Its five galleries of early San Diego history include a remarkable collection of Spanish Renaissance furniture and an exhibit interpreting the effect of colonization on local Indians.

Mission Basilica San Diego de Alcalá★★

10818 San Diego Mission Rd.; from Old Town, take I-8 east 7mi to Mission Gorge Rd. and follow signs. P ☎619-283-7319. www.missionsandiego.com.

California's first mission occupies a secluded site on the north slope of Mission Valley. Padre Junípero Serra's 1769 Presidio Hill mission was relocated here by Padre Luís Jayme in 1774. The mission was restored between 1895 and 1931 and designated a Minor Basilica by Pope Paul VI in 1976.

An original white-stucco, buttressed facade and five-bell campanario her-ald the entrance to the complex. The sparsely furnished **Casa del Padre Serra**, where the friar resided during frequent visits, is all that remains of the original monastery. The narrow 139ft-by-34ft church **interior** is restored to its 1813 appearance; early hand-carved wooden statues are in the sanctuary.

BALBOA PARK★★★

San Diego's cultural focal point is a 1,200-acre park immediately north of downtown, holding one of the most extensive collections of cultural attractions on the continent. Lawns, gardens and century-old shade trees harbor the world-renowned San Diego Zoo, as well as theaters and museum buildings created for two world fairs. The 1915 Panama-California Exposition was a city of stylized pavilions surrounding two central plazas—Plaza de Balboa and Plaza de Panama—linked by El Prado, a broad pedestrian thoroughfare. Architecture was Spanish Colonial Revival, a rich hybrid of Moorish, Baroque and Rococo ornamentation contrasting with colorful tiles and unadorned walls. The 1935 California Pacific International Exposition added new pavilions surrounding Pan-American Plaza in Art Deco, Maya-Aztec and Southwestern styles.

The **visitor center** in the House of Hospitality (1549 El Prado; ✕&P ☎619-239-0512; www.balboapark.org) offers books, maps and general information.

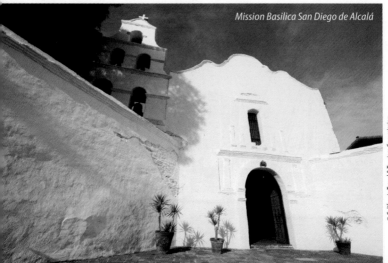

Mission Basilica San Diego de Alcalá

© California Travel & Tourism Commission

Parking is free, as are trams that run between attractions.

▲♦ San Diego Zoo★★★

2920 Zoo Dr. ✕♿🅿 ✆619-231-1515, www.sandiegozoo.org.

One of the largest and most celebrated zoological parks in the world, the San Diego Zoo occupies 100 acres of hillsides and ravines at the northern end of Balboa Park, lushly landscaped with some 6,500 botanical species. Habitats disguise moats and fences used to separate, protect and display 4,000 animals of 800 species, divided into 10 bioclimatic zones.

Guided bus tours (*35min*) orient visitors around the undulating terrain. Moving sidewalks climb steep hills to assist those who wander the network of pathways by foot. Some buses allow hop-on, hop-off access to major points of interest. The Skyfari aerial tram carries visitors to the **Polar Bear Plunge**, with live polar bears and interactive exhibits. Animal shows (*25min*) are staged in Wegeforth Bowl and Hunte Amphitheater.

Reached by the Monkey Trail, resident **gorillas** include troops of western lowland gorillas and pygmy chimpanzees. Three separate aviaries hold hundreds of species of rare birds; a fourth has hummingbirds.

Tiger Trail descends into a misty rain forest, passing crocodiles, Chinese water dragons, fishing cats, tapirs, pythons and mouse deer, ending at a Sumatran tiger habitat. In **Panda Canyon**, the Giant Panda Research Station houses four giant pandas.

▲♦ San Diego Natural History Museum★

1788 El Prado. ✕♿🅿 ✆619-232-3821. www.sdnhm.org.

A major 2001 expansion more than doubled the size of this museum, preserving the original 1933 building facade but creating a new north-facing entrance set in a four-story wall of glass. A permanent exhibit on fossils traces the 75-million-year prehistory of southern California and Baja California, from the age of dinosaurs to the Ice Ages. Another permanent exhibit explores regional water challenges through natural history specimens, live animals, photos and interactive exhibits. State-of-the-art dioramas and computer stations add to the museum's interactive nature. Other displays highlight geology and paleontology.

▲♦ Reuben H. Fleet Science Center

1875 El Prado. ✕♿🅿 ✆619-238-1233. www.rhfleet.org.

Five galleries, a dome-screen Space Theater for planetarium shows and IMAX films, and a 23-rider motion simulator for "space voyages" share this Spanish Colonial-style building.

Casa de Balboa★

1649 El Prado. ✕♿🅿

This richly ornamented structure (1914) is based on the Federal Government Palace in Queretaro, Mexico. The **Museum of San Diego History** (✆619-232-6203; www.sandiegohistory.org) looks at the city's development since 1850. The **Museum of Photographic Arts** (✆619-238-7559; www.mopa.org), presents rotating exhibits of historic and contemporary photography, including video and film.

Timken Museum of Art★★

1500 El Prado. ♿🅿 ✆619-239-5548. www.timkenmuseum.org.

Clad in Italian travertine marble, the museum (1965) displays a collection of 50 European and American paintings and tapestries, and 17 remarkable **Russian icons★★** of the 14-19C. Works by Hals, Rubens, Rembrandt, Bierstadt and Copley are among those on exhibit.

San Diego Museum of Art★

1450 El Prado. ✕♿🅿 ✆619-232-7931. www.sdmart.com.

The ornate Plateresque facade of this building (1926) was inspired by Spain's University of Salamanca. Depicted are Spanish Baroque masters; replicas of Donatello's *Saint George* and Michelangelo's *David*; and heraldry of Spain, America, California and San Diego. Highlights of the wide-ranging collection include such Medieval European art as Luca Signorelli's *Coronation of the Virgin* (1508) and El Greco's *The Penitent Saint Peter* (c.1600). Impressionism is represented in works by Monet, Degas, Matisse and Pissarro. Acclaimed 20C works include Modigliani's *Le Garçon aux Yeux Bleux* (*The Boy With Blue Eyes*) and Georgia O'Keeffe's *White Trumpet Flower* (1932). An extensive collection of contemporary art features Deborah Butterfield, Bruce Conner, David Hockney and Wayne Thiebaud.

Mingei International Museum★★

1439 El Prado. ♿ 🅿 *619-239-0003. www.mingei.org.

This museum's expansive collection holds 26,000 objects from 141 countries, with special concentrations in Asian, Mexican, African and US "art of the people." Highlights include Navajo weavings and Mexican *retablos*.

♟♟ San Diego Museum of Man★★

1350 El Prado. 🅿 *619-239-2001. www.museumofman.org.

Exhibits on human evolution (including a cast of "Lucy," among the oldest protohuman skeletons yet found), anthropology and ethnology are drawn from a collection of more than 100,000 ethnograpic items. Emphasis is placed on the cultures of Egypt and pre-Columbian Maya and Incas. The museum occupies the **California Building**, a Spanish Colonial structure (1915) with a massive Moorish-tile dome and a three-story belfry, 180ft campanile that rings on the quarter-hour.

♟♟ San Diego Aerospace Museum★★

2001 Pan American Plaza. ♿ 🅿 *619-234-8291. www.sandiegoairandspace.org. The white and blue, ring-shaped, Art Moderne structure (1935) displays six dozen vintage aircraft from biplanes to space capsules, 14,000 scale models,

and 10,000 aviation-related items. Next door the **♟♟San Diego Automotive Museum★** (2080 Pan American Plaza; ♿🅿 *619-231-2886; www.sdautomuseum.org) displays classic automobiles and motorcycles.

DOWNTOWN SAN DIEGO

Civic leaders and developers restored the Gaslamp Quarter's Victorian treasures in the 1970s and 80s, spurring further revitalization along Broadway. A waterfront redevelopment soon followed, including Seaport Village, the San Diego Convention Center and numerous luxury hotels.

Across Harbor Drive from the convention center, **PETCO Park**, the $474 million, 42,445-seat Padres baseball stadium, was completed in 2004 (☎tours available: *619-795-5000; sandiego.padres.mlb.com).

Gaslamp Quarter★

4th & 5th Aves. between Broadway & Harbor Dr. *619-233-5227. www.gaslamp.org.

Sixteen blocks of restored late 19C and early 20C Victorian buildings have become San Diego's trendiest restaurant and nightlife district. Walking tours begin from a neighborhood visitor center in the 1850 saltbox **William Heath Davis House** (410 Island Ave.).

Broadway★

Shopping and office complexes of cutting-edge architectural distinction reign here. **Horton Plaza★** (bordered by Broadway & G St., 1st & 4th Aves.; *619-239-8180) is a mall (1985, Jon Jerde) with twisting post-Modern passageways and a 50-color crazy-quilt of design styles. The **U.S. Grant Hotel★** (326 Broadway; *619-232-3121) is a stately, 11-story Italian Renaissance Revival inn (1910); its interior boasts 107 chandeliers and 150 tons of marble. **Emerald Plaza★** (402 W. Broadway) is perhaps the most memorable building (1990, C.W. Kim) on the skyline, a 30-story cluster of eight hexagonal glass office towers lit at night with emerald-green neon. The **Museum of Contem-**

La Jolla Shores

© Dreamstime.com/Alysta

CATCHING A WAVE

Although Malibu's Surfrider Beach claims to be the birthplace of surfing in California, every beach with predictable waves from La Jolla, north to Santa Barbara and beyond, has a loyal band of surfers. Most sit patiently just beyond the surf line, waiting for the next perfect wave, then paddle madly to catch the crest and ride to shore. The artistry and grace on display—as surfer after surfer skims the face of a breaking wave—is breathtaking. There may be as many surf shops as fast-food outlets along San Diego County beaches, which have bigger waves in winter but bigger crowds in summer. Most surfers wear wet suits all year to ward off the chill. Watching surfers is even more popular than surfing itself; bring a light jacket in winter, plenty of drinking water in summer, and sunblock all year. Binoculars bring the action closer.

San Diego has beaches for all kinds of surfers. Experts and pros compete for epic waves at the famous river mouth set up at Trestles. Down the coast at Old Man's, slow, easy rollers draw learners and longboard veterans. The 3mi Oceanside beachfront has gentle breaks, but is particularly known for the jetties flanking the harbor. **Swami's** in Encinitas is a prime surf spot for experienced surfers. **Black's Beach** breaks in long, organized lines year-round. Conditions at Cardiff are great for cutbacks and action in the lip. Popular and protected, **La Jolla Shores** is a safe, gentle spot to learn.

Oceanside has one of the nation's finest surfing museums: the **California Surf Museum** (312 Pier View Way; ℘760-721-6876; www.surfmuseum.org). The museum boasts a large collection of vintage boards and surf memorabilia, and honors surfing legends and history with rotating exhibits.

porary Art San Diego Downtown (1100 & 1001 Kettner Blvd., between Broadway and B St., ℘858-454-3541; www.mcasd.org) includes commissions by Richard Serra and RIchard Wright.

Waterfront★

One of the city's first modern harborside projects was **Seaport Village★** (849 West Harbor Dr. at Kettner Blvd.; ℘619-235-4014), a 14-acre shopping-and-dining complex of New England- and Mediterranean-style buildings linked by cobblestone pathways and a boardwalk. Its centerpiece is an 1890 carousel. Not far away is the huge **San Diego Convention Center** (111 W. Harbor Dr.; ℘619-525-5000), its open-air rooftop plaza surmounted by a giant white tent that resembles a futuristic sailing vessel.

♣♟ Maritime Museum of San Diego★

1492 N. Harbor Dr. ℘619-234-9153. www.sdmaritime.org.
Historic ships are the centerpieces of this floating museum. The **Star of India★★**, the oldest iron merchant ship afloat (launched from Britain's Isle of Man in 1863), circumnavigated the globe 21 times in the late 19C.
The **Berkeley** (1898), the first successful propeller-driven ferry on the Pacific coast, was built in San Francisco, and helped rescue victims of that city's 1906 earthquake. Moored alongside is the **Medea** (1904), a 140ft iron-hulled luxury steam yacht that once plied the lochs of Scotland.
Also on hand are a Soviet submarine and a replica of a British Navy frigate that was used in the movie Master and Commander.

ADDITIONAL SIGHTS
Coronado★

Take I-5 south to Rte. 75;
cross westbound toll bridge.
This affluent enclave of residences, hotels, restaurants and boutiques is serenely sheltered on a peninsula .5mi across the bay from downtown San Diego. Its landmark structure is the

Hotel del Coronado★★ (1500 Orange Ave.; ℘619-435-6611, www.hoteldel.com; ☕ see ADDRESSES), California's sole surviving Victorian seaside resort (1888).
Its white wood and red shingles, sweeping balconies and graceful spires rising beside Coronado's southern shore are immortalized in books and film.

Cabrillo National Monument★★

1800 Cabrillo Memorial Dr., Pt. Loma; from downtown San Diego, drive 7mi north on Harbor Dr., then left on Rosecrans St., right on Canon St. & left on Catalina Blvd. ♿🅿℘619-557-5450. www.nps.gov/cabr.
Located on the crest of a sandstone ridge 400ft above the sea, this park commemorates the Spanish discovery of the California coast in 1542. From the foot of a **statue** of explorer Juan Rodríguez Cabrillo, visitors may watch the passage of Navy ships, planes and submarines. A short uphill walk from the **visitor center** is the **Old Point Loma Lighthouse** (1855), one of the oldest on the coast.

♣♟ SeaWorld San Diego★★

500 SeaWorld Dr.; take I-5 to SeaWorld Dr. Exit. ✗♿🅿℘619-226-3901. http://seaworld.com.
The first (1964) of three US SeaWorlds, this Mission Bay marine park mixes education and entertainment in five live shows and 25 exhibits and aquariums. Highlight of the animal shows (25min) are those featuring **Shamu★**, a trained orca (killer whale). Other shows feature dolphins, sea lions, walruses and birds. **Dolphin Point★** invites visitors to feed bottle-nosed dolphins.
Penguin Encounter recreates icy Antarctica. **Shark Encounter** offers a close-up look at these marine predators in a coral reef setting. **Wild Arctic** hosts beluga whales, walruses and polar bears.
The revolving **Skytower** provides bird's-eye views of the park and San Diego skyline from a 265ft observation point. Shipwreck Rapids is a thrill ride along

a winding river. **Guided tours** offer a behind-the-scenes look at SeaWorld's animal-rescue, training and medical facilities.

EXCURSIONS
La Jolla★★

12mi northwest of downtown San Diego via I-5 and Ardath Road. ☎619-236-1212. www.lajollabythesea.com.

An upscale, sun-kissed suburb, La Jolla (la-HOY-ya) hugs a breathtakingly beautiful shoreline. The community is noted for posh shopping; important national research enclaves lie at its fringes. Rugged coastal beauty beckons swimmers and snorkelers to cliff-fringed **La Jolla Cove★★**, downslope from Prospect Street.

Museum of Contemporary Art, San Diego★★

700 Prospect St. ✕♿☎858-454-3541. www.mcasd.org.

San Diego's premier venue for contemporary art occupies the remodeled home of publishing baroness Ellen Browning Scripps (1916, Irving Gill). Exhibits rotate from a permanent collection of 3,000 Minimalist and Conceptual paintings, photographs, video and mixed-media pieces. A sculpture garden with native plants overlooks the Pacific.

♣♦ Birch Aquarium at Scripps★★

2300 Expedition Way, off Torrey Pines Rd. South of La Jolla Village Dr. ✕♿🅿☎858-534-3474. www.aquarium.ucsd.edu.

The contemporary Mission-style complex, atop a bluff above the Scripps Institution of Oceanography, encompasses a modern aquarium and the largest US museum of oceanography. Marine life from the Pacific Northwest, Southern California, Mexico and tropical seas is displayed in more than 60 tanks housing some 5,000 specimens representing more than 380 species. The Shark Reef exhibit houses whitetip and blacktip reef sharks, nurse sharks, epaulette sharks, and other sharks that inhabit tropical reefs. Three living tide pools provide up-close looks at starfish, sea cucumbers and hermit crabs.

Salk Institute★

10010 N. Torrey Pines Rd. ♿🅿☎858-453-4100. www.salk.edu.

This striking Louis Kahn structure (1960) features two identical six-story buildings of reinforced concrete, teak and steel, facing each other across a travertine courtyard bisected by a narrow channel of water. A scientific staff of more than 850 work here, including visiting scientists, postdoctoral fellows and graduate students.

Torrey Pines State Reserve★

N. Torrey Pines Rd., 2mi north of Genesee Ave., 1mi south of Carmel Valley Rd. 🅿 ☎858-755-2063. www.torreypine.org.

This 1,750-acre blufftop reserve was established in 1921 to preserve one of the world's rarest evergreens. Fewer than 4,000 Torrey pines (Pinus torreyana) remain from an ancient forest; they grow naturally only here and on Santa Rosa in the Channel Islands. There are 8mi of trails and guided nature walks on weekends and holidays. Groups of porpoises and whales can sometimes be seen from the beaches.

San Diego County Coast

North of La Jolla, scenic beaches and beach towns are strung like pearls along Route S21, the commercial artery that parallels Interstate 5. It passes through **Del Mar**, home of the renowned Del Mar Racetrack, and **Encinitas**, world-famous for its poinsettias, before reaching Carlsbad, a spa town, now mostly visited for its big outlet center.

♣♦ LEGOLAND California★

1 LEGO Dr., off Cannon Rd. East of I-5. ✕♿🅿☎760-918-5346. www.california.legoland.com

The first US theme park for the Danish-designed children's building blocks uses 30 million signature LEGO bricks in 5,000 models of animals, buildings and famous sights. Childhood stories are rendered along Fairy Tale Brook; life-size African beasts lurk on Safari Trek; an

LEGOLAND California

Adventurers ClubWalk penetrates the Pyramids, an Amazon rain forest and an Arctic icescape. A Legoland Waterpark and new 4D film are the most recent attractions.

👥 San Diego Zoo Safari Park★★★

15500 San Pasqual Valley Rd., Escondido, 30mi northeast of San Diego; take I-15 to Via Rancho Parkway Exit and follow signs north and east. 🍴🚻🅿️ ✆760-747-8702. www.sdzsafaripark.org.

Exotic and endangered animals find safe haven in this 2,200-acre park, formerly named San Diego Wild Animal Park. It was created as a breeding facility to ensure species survival.

Visitors enter through **Nairobi Village**, a replica Congo fishing village with exotic-bird aviaries. Animal shows demonstrate natural behaviors and abilities of birds of prey, North American animals and Asian elephants.

There are six principal biogeographical areas: East and South African savanna, North African desert, Asian plains and waterholes, and Mongolian steppe. Roaming freely are herds of giraffes, wildebeests, gazelles, oryxes and the largest collection of southern white rhinoceroses in the US. Walking exploration is encouraged in the **African Outpost** and **African Plains**. Warthogs, duikers, bonteboks, elands, giraffes, cheetahs

and vultures are among free-roaming denizens. Several smaller habitats feature success stories from zoo breeding programs, including Sumatran tigers, Przewalski's wild horses, okapi and pygmy chimpanzees.The highlight of **Condor Ridge★★** is the park's most celebrated captive breeding success, rare California condors.

The climate-controlled Hidden Jungle houses neotropical birds and tropical plants in a rainforest environment. At Lorikeet Landing, visitors feed brightly colored brush-tongued parrots. Opening in 2014 is a new Tiger Trail exhibit.

San Luis Rey de Francia Mission★★

4050 Mission Ave., San Luis Rey, 40mi north of San Diego via I-5 & Rte. 76. ♿🅿️ ✆760-757-3651. www.sanluisrey.org.

The "King of the Missions" was founded in 1798 and named for King Louis IX of France. It became one of the most successful outposts of Catholicism in California, with 2,800 neophytes in residence.

The mission housed a Franciscan monastery in the late 19C and now serves an active parish. A domed bell tower crowns the right front corner of the large cruciform mission church. Only 12 arches remain of the 32 that formerly graced a two-story cloister.

Anza–Borrego Desert★★

Inland San Diego County is a jumble of mountains and valleys that climax at Anza-Borrego Desert State Park, the largest state park in the western US. West of the mountains are the charming hamlet of Julian and the Palomar Observatory atop 6,126ft Palomar Mountain. East of the state park is the agriculturally rich Imperial Valley, with the Salton Sea at its north end.

- **Michelin Map:** 493 C, D 11. Pacific Standard Time.
- **Info:** Tourist Information ℰ760-767-4205 or ℰ619-445-4180; www.visitsandiegoeast.com.
- **Location:** Here are San Diego County's cool mountain heights around Julian, and the Mojave Desert fringes on the east side of the mountains.

SIGHTS

Anza-Borrego Desert State Park★★

80mi northeast of San Diego via Rte. 78. △&ℰ760-767-5311. www.park.ca.gov. Named for Juan Bautista de Anza, the Spanish military explorer who traversed the region in 1774, and for endemic *borregos*, or bighorn sheep, this 939sq mi preserve contains mountains, badlands, hidden palm groves and pioneer trails. Check at the **visitor center** (200 Palm Canyon Dr., Borrego Springs; &🅿 ℰ760-767-4205) for road conditions in areas accessible only by four-wheel-drive vehicle.

The **Erosion Road Auto Tour**, running east along Route S22 from Borrego Springs, traverses rolling plains below the Santa Rosa Mountains.

Ten markers describe geologic forces that shaped the landscape. At Mile 29.3, a sandy side road (four-wheel drive recommended) leads 4mi to **Font's Point** and views★★ over the Borrego Badlands.

Popular hiking trails include the 3mi **Borrego Palm Canyon Trail** (trailhead at campground 2mi north of visitor center), a moderately difficult canyon trail that ascends an alluvial fan to a hidden fan-palm oasis. Palm Canyon Creek creates a waterfall and pool.

The .5mi **Narrows Earth Loop Trail** (trailhead 12.2mi south of Borrego Springs on Rte. S3, then 4.7mi east on Rte. 78), offers an extended look at can-

Anza–Borrego Desert

Joyce Holly/Michelin.

Wildflower Season

Each year, the Anza-Borrego Desert State Park bursts into a brief riot of color, as wildflowers suddenly decorate the desert landscape. Dozens of wildflower and cacti species participate in the spectacular display, including primroses, poppies, Ocotillo, Chuparosa, lavender, bluebells, agave, desert lilies, chicory, desert sunflowers, indigo, and rock daisies.

Flowers bloom in the park between February and April, but are at their peak for a mere two weeks. The peak's timing varies each year, depending on rain, temperature and wind. Before planning a tour of the desert floor, call the park's 24-hour "Wildflower Hotline" at 760-767-4684; www.parks.ca.gov. The park also assembles a guide each year detailing which flowers can be seen in various areas of the park.

yon geology. In the southeast part of the park, **Carrizo Badlands Overlook** (mile 52.7) offers a **panorama** of giant ridges.

On the eastern edge of the park, 5.8mi south of Octolio Wells, a gravel road leads to Elephant Trees Nature Trail, named for trees whose outer trunks bear a skinlike appearance.

EXCURSIONS

Julian★

◐ 57mi northeast of San Diego via I-8 & Rte. 79. ✆760-765-1857. www.julianca.com.

At 4,200ft, this mountain village developed in the wake of the gold rush. Today is a popular weekend getaway spot known for apples, peaches, pears and 19C-style storefronts along Main Street.

To the south, the 24mi Sunrise National Scenic Byway (Rte. 51 between I-8 and Rte. 79) traverses the Cleveland National Forest, offering views to the east of Anza-Borrega Desert State Park. Northwest of Julian (8mi), the **Santa Ysabel Asistencia Mission** (23013 California 79; ✆760-765-0810) was established in 1818 as an outpost of the San Diego de Alcalá Mission.

♣♟ Palomar Observatory

◐ 🅿 Rte. S6, 55mi northeast of San Diego via I-15 & Rte. 76. ✆760-742-2119. www.astro.caltech.edu/palomar.

Located near the peak of 6,126ft Palomar Mountain, this California Institute of Technology observatory boasts the celebrated **Hale Telescope★**, with its 200in Pyrex lens that has a range surpassing 1 billion light years.

Imperial Valley★

◐ 117mi east of San Diego via I-8, Rte. 111 (north) & Rte. 78 (east).

Fields of lettuce, melons, tomatoes and other vegetables cluster around El Centro, the main town of this subsea-level valley. Its east side is part of the **Imperial Sand Dunes Recreation Area** (Rte. 78; ✆760-337-4400), whose dunes crest up to 300ft. Eighty percent of these hills, once known as the Algodones Dunes, are open to off-road vehicles (ORVs), but the Imperial Sand Dunes National Natural Landmark remains a protected area, popular with birdwatchers. Osborne Overlook, 3mi east of Gecko Road, off Rte. 78, offers the best viewpoint.

Salton Sea

◐ 168mi east of San Diego via I-8 & Rte. 86.

This sea was formed when Colorado River irrigation canals went haywire and flooded an ancient lake bed in 1905, creating an inland sea 35mi long by 15mi wide—the largest in California—but just 20ft deep. The **Sonny Bono Salton Sea National Wildlife Refuge** (Rte. 86; ✆760-348-5278) protects migratory bird habitat for more than 400 species on the marshy southern shore. The **Salton Sea State Recreation Area** (Rte. 111, ✆760-393-3052) and other north-shore areas offer swimming beaches.

Las Vegas Area

Las Vegas is one of the largest and most distinctive resort destinations in the world, a 20C boomtown based on gambling, entertainment and recreation. Boosted by a mild winter climate and an advantageous setting along busy Interstate 15 between the Los Angeles area and Salt Lake City, the once-small railroad town staked its future upon the 1931 legalization of gambling by the state of Nevada. It has developed with unprecedented extravagance. Las Vegas now ranks among the prime tourist and convention destinations on earth.

Highlights

1 Seeing the **Bellagio's** choreographed **fountain music show** (p164)
2 **The Springs Preserve** (p163)
3 Hiking **Red Rock Canyon** (p166)
4 Touring **Hoover Dam** (p168)
5 Surveying **Death Valley** from 5,475ft at Dante's View (p172)

A Desert Oasis

Such prosperity is an anomaly in North America's hottest, driest desert, the Mojave (mo-HAH-vee). Remarkable for its lofty mountains, its high plateaus and the lowest elevations in the Western Hemisphere, the Mojave reaches from western Arizona to the Sierra Nevada, fading north to the Great Basin and south into the Colorado Plateau and Sonoran Deserts. Here, Ancestral Puebloan clans established isolated farms before AD 1000, followed in the mid-19C by Mormon emigrants.

The construction of Hoover Dam on the Colorado River in the 1930s revolutionized settlement patterns in the desert by providing cheap hydroelectricity and abundant reservoir water, enabling new communities to sprout and existing towns to prosper. As it has for more than a century, water continues to fuel conflict, as Las Vegas attempts to extract new water supplies from northern Nevada and Utah.

Las Vegas Strip

© Raga Jose Fuste / age fotostock

ADDRESSES

🏨 STAY

$$$$ Bellagio – 3600 Las Vegas Blvd. S., Las Vegas, NV. ☎702-693-7111. www.bellagio.com. 3,933 rooms. One of Vegas' most sophisticated casino-hotels, this Strip property offers Northern Italian sensibility in its decor and ambience. Fountains dance amid light and music on an eight-acre lake. Chihuly glass sculpture in the lobby, a fine-art museum and botanical conservatory, and several of the city's finest restaurants plus a strict no-unaccompanied-minors policy all add to its adult appeal.

$$$$ Wynn Las Vegas – 3131 Las Vegas Blvd. S., Las Vegas, NV. ☎702-770-. www.wynnlasvegas.com. 2,359 rooms. This $2.7 billion curving bronze glass monolith at the north end of the Strip was named for its creator, Steve Wynn. With a Tom Fazio-designed golf course, designer boutiques, and a Ferrari-Maserati dealership on-site, Wynn's posh playground leaves little to be desired. At 640sqft, a Resort Room here tops the "most-spacious" list. Be sure to catch a showing of the water-based spectacle *Le Rêve*, named for a Picasso painting displayed in the hotel.

$$$$ Four Seasons Hotel Las Vegas – 3960 Las Vegas Blvd. S., Las Vegas, NV. ☎702-632-5000. www.fourseasons. com/lasvegas. 424 rooms. Occupying the 35th to 39th floors of the Mandalay Bay Resort's 43-story glass tower is this quiet, elegant retreat from glitter. The non-gaming hotel combines spacious rooms with top-end shops and an intimate spa. Every element is sublime, from poolside misting devices to filet mignon with tiger prawns in the **Charlie Palmer Steak ($$$)** restaurant.

$$$$ Furnace Creek Inn & Ranch Resort – Rte. 190, Death Valley, CA. ☎760-786-2345. www. furnacecreekresort.com. Inn has 66 rooms; ranch has 224 units (**$$**). One resort with two hotels, Furnace Creek includes a 1927 Mission-style luxury inn, set in an oasis-like palm grove, and a rambling late-19C Western ranch resort of cabins and motel-style rooms. In the complex are four restaurants, two bars, and a golf course 214ft below sea level.

$$$ Westin Lake Las Vegas – 101 Montelago Blvd., Henderson, NV. ☎702-567-6000. www.westinlakelasvegas. com. 447 rooms. This sprawling resort complex calls itself "the other Vegas." Once you look out on the lovely waters of Lake Las Vegas with the rugged peaks in the distance, you won't miss the neon and the crowds at all. The hotel offers a spa, two pools, and access to two championship golf courses as well as watersports. For the best water panorama, book a premium lake view or a grand luxury king room.

$$$ The Venetian – 3355 Las Vegas Blvd. S., Las Vegas, NV. ☎702-414-1000. www.venetian.com. 3,036 rooms. The

Red Rock Canyon

GETTING THERE

The Las Vegas airport is the **McCarran International Airport** (5757 Wayne Newton Blvd.; ☎702-261-5211; www.mccarran.com). Rental car agencies are at the airport. **Greyhound Bus**: (200 S. Main St.; ☎702-384-9568; www.greyhound.com). **Amtrak Thruway bus**: (McCarran International Airport and Greyhound Station; www.amtrak.com).

GETTING AROUND

Many hotels operate shuttles to and from the airport. Public buses ply the Strip frequently 24 hours a day; fare is $3 (www.rtcsnv.com). The **Las Vegas Monorail** (☎702-699-8299, www.lvmonorail.com) runs down the east side of the strip (behind hotels) from the MGM Grand to the Sahara Hotel.

Double-decker Deuce buses also run along the strip.

Taxis line up in front of all major hotels and casinos. Major cab companies include Desert Cab (☎702-386-9102), Yellow Cab (☎702-873-2000) and Checker Cab (☎702-873-2000).

VISITOR INFORMATION

The Visitor Center (3150 Paradise Rd; ☎877-847-4858; www. lasvegas.com) can supply a free information guide, maps and more.

ACCOMMODATIONS

Accommodation prices vary widely from budget motels to luxury hotels. The Las Vegas Visitors Center (above) is a good source for information.

Strip's first all-suite hotel boasts huge standard rooms (700sq ft) and a spa run by the renowned Canyon Ranch. Replicas of the architectural highlights of Venice, Italy, including a Grand Canal lined with shops and fine restaurants, transport guests to another world.

$$$ Mandarin Oriental, Las Vegas – 3752 Las Vegas Blvd. S., Las Vegas, NV. ☎702-590-8888. www.mandarinoriental.com/lasvegas. 392 rooms. This newly opened (2009) CityCenter oasis features gourmet dining, spa services, spacious guest rooms and a fitness center offering Pilates and yoga classes. Guests can enjoy relaxing in a poolside cabana near one of the two outdoor lap or plunge pools. The hotel is connected via skybridge to the Crystals shopping and entertainment center.

$$ Boulder Dam Hotel – 1305 Arizona St., Boulder City, NV. ☎702-293-3510. www.boulderdamhotel.com. 22 rooms. Built in 1933 to house supervisors on the Hoover Dam project, this National Historic Trust property—an air-conditioned rarity at the time—soon was welcoming European royalty and Hollywood celebrities. The Dutch Colonial-style inn was refurbished in the 1990s and reopened as a bed-and-breakfast in 2000.

❦ EAT

In addition to the suggestions below, nearly every major hotel has a casino buffet catering to visitors with big appetites and slender wallets.

$$$$ Aureole – 3950 Las Vegas Blvd. S. at the Mandalay Bay. ☎702-632-7401. www.aureolelv.com. Dinner only. **American.** Chef Charlie Palmer's high-tech restaurant boasts a four-story, glass-enclosed wine tower crawling with human "wine angels" who retrieve diners' selections from among 10,000 bottles. The top-shelf menu includes citrus-braised lobsters and fruit-wood-grilled salmon with sage ratatouille.

$$$$ Joël Robuchon – 3799 Las Vegas Blvd. S. at MGM Grand. ☎702-891-7925. www.mgmgrand.com. Dinner only. **Contemporary.** Modeled after a 1930s French salon, the striking interior is drenched in rich jewel tones, velvety banquettes and chandeliers. Nightly tasting menus are parades of culinary genius, featuring dishes such as fresh sea bass over tender baby leeks, topped with a dollop of lemongrass foam.

$$$$ Le Cirque – 3600 Las Vegas Blvd. S. at Bellagio. ☎702-693-7223. www.bellagio.com. Dinner only. Closed Mon. **French.** The colorful circus decor doesn't detract from the serious food at this top-end Strip hotel. The signature dish is honey-glazed duck; beef tenderloin comes with sauteed foie gras.

$$$$ Picasso – 3600 Las Vegas Blvd. S. at Bellagio. ☎702-693-7223. www.bellagio.com. Dinner only. Closed Tue. **Continental.** Original Picasso works hang on the walls of this eclectic yet sophisticated restaurant. Chef Julian Serrano, first Las Vegas-resident chef to win the James Beard Award as best in the Southwest, prepares outstanding French and Spanish-inspired cuisine.

$$$ Delmonico Steak House – 3355 Las Vegas Blvd. S. at The Venetian. ☎702-414-3737. www.emerils.com. **Creole-American.** Not a typical steakhouse, this spacious restaurant – with vaulted ceiling and 12ft oak doors – is an update on Chef Emeril Lagasse's New Orleans eatery. Diners relax in the piano bar after chateaubriand for two, a double-cut pork chop or blackened snapper.

The Springs Preserve

© The Springs Preserve

$$$ Piero's Restaurant – 355 Convention Center Dr. ☎702-369-2305. www.pieroscuisine.com. Dinner only. **Italian.** Locals love this old-time Vegas place with tiger-print carpeting and a lively bar crowd. Stone-crab claws and mixed-grill items are served at booths lining the walls.

$$ Bouchon – 3355 Las Vegas Blvd. S. at The Venetian. ☎702-414-6200. www.venetian.com. **French.** Cousin of Thomas Keller's original Bouchon in the Napa Valley, The Venetian's rendition shares the same menu, but is also open for breakfast. Morning dishes include quiche, *boudin blanc* and fresh-baked brioches; dinner adds standard bistro fare, from steak frites to roasted chicken to trout amandine.

$$ Canyon Ranch Cafe – 3355 Las Vegas Blvd. S. at The Venetian. ☎702-414-3633. www.venetian.com. Breakfast and lunch only. **Contemporary.** This serene bistro in the Venetian unabashedly positions itself as the antidote to Vegas excess—nutritional quality and metabolic moderation are its objectives, with dishes such as turkey wraps, chicken salad sandwich and whole wheat pancakes.

$ Hofbräuhaus – 4510 Paradise Rd. ☎702-853-2337. www.hofbrauhaus lasvegas.com. **German.** Seekers of high-spirited dining and drinking love this lively reproduction of Hofbräuhaus München, which recreates an authentic German beer hall. Waitresses clad in Bavarian garb serve beer, soft pretzels and Bavarian specialties to patrons seated on long, wooden, communal tables or in the *biergarten*, as a German band entertains.

$ Tacos el Gordo – 3049 S Las Vegas Blvd. ☎702-641-8226. **Mexican.** Crowds pour into this beloved institution on the Strip for a Vegas bargain that also offers some of the most authentic Mexican cuisine in the US. Dozens of varieties of hand-made tacos include *lengua* (tongue), *cabeza* (beef head) and tripe. Expect to stand in line 15 minutes, pay $2 per order, and depart fully sated.

Las Vegas★★★

Globally famed for its spectacular casinos, lavish resort hotels, world-class entertainment, lax social ethos and garish character, Las Vegas is without peer on the planet. The city draws 40 million annual visitors, has some 150,000 hotel rooms, and reaps almost $10 billion a year in gaming revenue. Dubbed "Lost Wages" by visitors who regularly invest their paychecks at the gaming tables, and "Sin City" in popular parlance, Vegas unabashedly revels in its no-holds-barred persona devoted to dining, drinking and 24-hour clubbing.

A BIT OF HISTORY

Meadows (vegas) at which travelers on the Old Spanish Trail made watering stops distinguished the city's humble beginnings. In 1855, Mormon pioneers established the **Mormon Fort** (500 E. Washington Ave.; ℘702-486-3511; parks.nv.gov) but abandoned it three years later to ranchers. The San Pedro, Los Angeles & Salt Lake Railroad, later the Union Pacific, planned its route through here in the early 20C, building a train yard at what became Fremont Street and auctioning off 1,200 lots in a single day in May 1905. The town became a rail-transfer point during construction of Hoover Dam, but its prosperity and future character owed far more to the legalization of gambling in 1931, and the later collapse of Havana as a nightclub mecca.

Gambling clubs grew up along Fremont Street, which acquired the sobriquet "Glitter Gulch" by virtue of the casinos' brilliant signs, many of which are now "retired" and on view at the **Neon Museum** (770 Las Vegas Blvd. N.; ℘702-229-5366; guided tours only; www. neonmuseum.org). Taking advantage of cheaper land and fewer restrictions beyond the city limits, investors in the 1940s began to build new casinos along the main highway to Los Angeles, a thoroughfare soon dubbed "The Strip."

▶ **Population:** 596,000.
⌂ **Michelin Map:** p 162 Mountain Standard Time.
▤ **Info:** ℘702-892-7575; www. lasvegas.com.
▷ **Location:** There's little need for a car in Vegas; once ensconced in one of the myriad hotels on or near "the strip," most attractions are within walking distance.
⌣ **Don't Miss:** The Strip.
▲▲ **Kids:** Several hotel outdoor shows are still family-oriented – and the rides atop the Stratosphere are guaranteed to challenge the most fearless.
⌂ **Also See:** Red Rock Canyon.

The booming gambling business attracted organized crime, and alarmed state authorities imposed stiff regulations on the industry, driving many shadier interests to sell out to corporate buyers. Among the most acquisitive was reclusive millionaire Howard Hughes, who started his Las Vegas empire by buying the Desert Inn in 1966.

Las Vegas casinos grew and prospered through the 1970s, attracting a strictly adult clientele. Part of their appeal was sophisticated entertainment by such acts as Elvis Presley, Liberace, Frank Sinatra, Sammy Davis Jr., and Dean Martin. By the 1980s, pressure to compete with new gaming venues in Atlantic City, New Jersey, and other places prompted a trend toward remarkable resorts that offer not only luxury lodgings, shows and gambling, but also amusement parks, simulation rides, gourmet dining, and trendy nightclubs. In 2009, MGM, aided by funds from Dubai, opened the 67-acre, $9.2-billion CityCenter, between the Bellagio and Monte Carlo, with three hotels, a casino and Crystals, a 500,000sq ft shopping and entertainment complex. SLS Las Vegas Hotel & Casino will open in 2014 in the former Sahara hotel (1952).

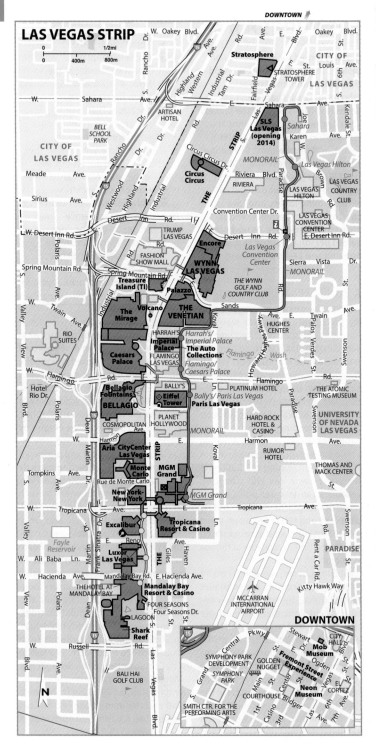

DOWNTOWN

LAS VEGAS STRIP

0 — 1/2mi
0 — 400m — 800m

W. Oakey Blvd.

CITY OF
LAS VEGAS

Stratosphere

STRATOSPHERE
TOWER

CITY OF
LAS VEGAS

**SLS
Las Vegas
(opening
2014)**

MONORAIL

Las Vegas Hilton

**Circus
Circus**

Riviera Blvd.

RIVIERA

LAS VEGAS
HILTON

LAS VEGAS
COUNTRY
CLUB

BELL
SCHOOL
PARK

Convention Center Dr.

LAS VEGAS
CONVENTION
CENTER

CITY OF
LAS VEGAS

ARTISAN
HOTEL

TRUMP
LAS VEGAS

FASHION
SHOW MALL

Encore

**WYNN
LAS VEGAS**

*Las Vegas
Convention
Center*

Sierra Vista Dr.

E. Desert Inn Rd.

MONORAIL

THE WYNN
GOLF AND
COUNTRY CLUB

RIO
SUITES

**Treasure
Island (TI)**

The Mirage

Palazzo

Volcano

**THE
VENETIAN**

HARRAH'S
IMPERIAL
PALACE

HUGHES
CENTER

**Imperial
Palace**

*Harrah's/
Imperial Palace*

**The Auto
Collections**

*Flamingo
Wash*

**Caesars
Palace**

FLAMINGO
LAS VEGAS

*Flamingo/
Caesars Palace*

Flamingo

PLATINUM HOTEL

THE ATOMIC
TESTING MUSEUM

Hotel
Rio Dr.

**Bellagio
Fountains**

BELLAGIO

BALLY'S

**Eiffel
Tower**

*Bally's/
Paris Las Vegas*

Paris Las Vegas

COSMOPOLITAN

PLANET
HOLLYWOOD

MONORAIL

HARD ROCK
HOTEL &
CASINO

UNIVERSITY
OF NEVADA
LAS VEGAS

**Aria
CityCenter
Las Vegas**

**Monte
Carlo**

**MGM
Grand**

RUMOR
HOTEL

THOMAS AND
MACK CENTER

**New York-
New York**

MGM Grand

Excalibur

**Tropicana
Resort & Casino**

PARADISE

*Fayle
Reservoir*

**Luxor
Las Vegas**

THE STRIP

MCCARRAN
INTERNATIONAL
AIRPORT

Kitty Hawk Way

W. Hacienda

**THEHOTEL AT
MANDALAY BAY**

**Mandalay Bay
Resort & Casino**

FOUR SEASONS
Four Seasons Dr.

LAGOON

**Shark
Reef**

DOWNTOWN

BALI HAI
GOLF CLUB

SYMPHONY PARK
DEVELOPMENT

SYMPHONY
PARK

GOLDEN
NUGGET

**Fremont
Street
Experience**

**Mob
Museum**

CITY
HALL

EL
CORTEZ

**Neon
Museum**

COURTHOUSE

SMITH CTR. FOR THE
PERFORMING ARTS

N

SIGHTS
Fremont Street Experience★★

Fremont St. between Main St. & Las Vegas Blvd. www.vegasexperience.com. Suspended 90ft over downtown, a barrel-arched canopy jolts to life several times nightly.

The illuminated extravaganza of flashing, rolling images is generated by more than 12 million LED lights and synchronized to music from a 550,000-watt sound system. Created by a consortium of 10 casinos, the attraction was designed to rejuvenate tourism along five blocks that were the first focus of Vegas' gaming industryhome of the Lady Luck, the Golden Nugget and Benny Binion's **Horseshoe Club**. Illuminated marquees and neon signs were so colossal and flashy that the street was universally known as Glitter Gulch. A 60ft-tall talking cowboy, **Vegas Vic★★**, has been an icon since 1951.

The Mob Museum★

300 E. Stewart Ave. ℘702-229-2734. http://themobmuseum.org.

One of Vegas' popular new (2012) sights occupies, ironically, a stately former 1933-vintage courthouse at the north end of downtown. Its three floors of exhibits focus heavily on organized crime figures such as Lucky Luciano, Bugsy Siegel and Mickey Cohen, all instrumental in the city's mid-20C growth boom. Visitors may line up the sights of a submachine gun, vicariously take part in the Estes Kefauver racketeering hearings, and ponder the way Hollywood glorified the gangster life.

The Strip★★★

2000-4000 blocks of Las Vegas Blvd. S. This 4.5mi stretch of exurban highway – extending from the Stratosphere in the north to Mandalay Bay Resort in the south – embraces Las Vegas' greatest concentration of resorts and casinos, and its most sensational architecture and street-side displays.

When casinos first boomed on Fremont Street, The Strip was a stretch of vacant highway. In 1941, seeking to avoid taxes and restrictions on buildings within city limits, Thomas Hull chose a lonely site to build El Rancho Vegas. Later that year, Guy McAfee—who coined the reference to "The Strip"—opened The Last Frontier. In 1946, Benjamin "Bugsy" Siegel's Flamingo Hotel became only the third Strip resort, but its upscale tone set it apart from downtown casinos. By the 1960s, scores of flashy new casinos and resorts were displacing the downtown venues as visitor favorites. The Strip today is undisputedly a prime locus of world tourism.

Most of the largest US hotels occupy sites along the Strip and its intersecting blocks. The enormous scale of these properties has been ameliorated with a growing network of elevated walkways between selected casinos.

Public buses ply the Strip with high frequency, 24 hours, from the airport to downtown; a one-way fare is $3 (www.rtcsnv.com). The $650 million Las Vegas Monorail (℘702-699-8299; www.lvmonorail.com) runs down the east side of The Strip (behind hotels) from the MGM Grand to the Sahara Hotel. Expansion plans are in the works to extend the Monorail to the McCarran International Airport. A recent (2009) CityCenter tram runs between the CityCenter, Monte Carlo and Bellagio. Innumerable cabs, limousines, sightseeing buses and other conveyances also work the area, as most tourists do not rent cars.

EXCURSIONS
The Springs Preserve★★

◗ 333 S. Valley View Blvd. between US 95 and Alta Dr. ⚠&♿P ℘702-822-7700. www.springspreserve.org.

Opened in 2007 as the city's first nod to its desert history, this 180-acre park occupies the site of the original springs that were the birthplace of Las Vegas. The **Origen Experience** is a three-gallery museum that depicts the human history of the area. The **Desert Living Center★★** promotes respect for the region's sensitive environment; outside, four trails (1.8mi) lead through gardens that display native Mojave vegetation and ways residents can wisely

CASINOS ON THE STRIP

These casino-hotels, presented from north to south, are listed as attractions only. Ratings reflect degree of tourism interest, not lodging recommendation.

Stratosphere★ – 2000 Las Vegas Blvd. S. ✆702-380-7777. www.stratospherehotel.com. This 1,149ft tower is capped by an observation deck with tremendous **views★★** and thrilling rides. **Insanity, The Ride** spins riders over the tower's edge; the **Big Shot** free falls with a force four times that of gravity.

Circus Circus★ – 2880 Las Vegas Blvd. S. ✆702-734-0410. www.circuscircus.com. Famed for the live trapeze artists and tightrope walkers beneath the "Big Top" of its main casino, this circus-themed casino entertains younger guests with roller coasters, water rides and laser tag in the 5-acre **Adventuredome**.

Wynn Las Vegas★ – 3131 Las Vegas Blvd. ✆702-770-7000. www.wynnlasvegas.com. When the sun goes down, the secluded Lake of Dreams dazzles visitors with a multimedia show. *Le Rêve* is an aquatic production with aerial acrobatics. Encore, a companion property, is even more deluxe.

Treasure Island at the Mirage★★ – 3300 Las Vegas Blvd. S. ✆702-894-7111. www.treasureisland.com. Outside, the Sirens of TI clash with pirates keeping with a buccaneer theme. Cirque du Soleil's **Mystère★** plays within.

The Mirage★★ – 3400 Las Vegas Blvd. S. ✆702-791-7111. www.mirage.com. South Seas flair is bolstered by a tropical "island" embellished by lagoons, waterfalls, an aquarium, a fireball-spewing **volcano★**, dolphin pools and a zoo enclosure with white tigers and other exotic animals. Cirque de Soleil's LOVE interprets The Beatles music.

The Venetian★★★ – 3355 Las Vegas Blvd. S. ✆702-414-1000. www.venetian.com. An engaging imitation of Venice, Italy, the resort features architectural replicas of the **Doge's Palace, St. Mark's Square,** and **Rialto Bridge**. Gondoliers glide along the **Grand Canal★**, lined by a faux-15C street of shops. **Madame Tussaud's★** portrays celebrities in wax. Shows include the Priscilla Queen of the Desert.

Caesars Palace★★ – 3570 Las Vegas Blvd. S. ✆702-731-7110. www.caesarspalace.com. Imperial Rome influences this vast complex adorned with majestic fountains and marble statues and famed for boxing extravaganzas. The **Forum Shops★★**, a sumptuous mall in the form of a splendid Roman street, has a sky-like ceiling that simulates the passing days and nights. Rod Stewart, Shania Twain and Celine Dion perform regularly at hotel venues.

Bellagio★★★ – 3600 Las Vegas Blvd. S. ✆702-693-7111. www.bellagio.com. A lake with twice-hourly **light and fountain shows★★** graces the front of this opulent complex, designed to recall a village on Italy's Lake Como. From the **Conservatory and Botanical Gardens★** visitors enter the **Bellagio Gallery of Fine Art★★**, with rotating exhibits such as an Andy Warhol retrospective. Cirque du Soleil's acrobats, synchronized swimmers and divers perform in water-themed O.

Paris Las Vegas★★ – 3655 Las Vegas Blvd. S. ✆702-946-7000. www. parislasvegas.com. Towering over scaled-down likenesses of the **Arc de**

Paris Las Vegas at night

© Caesars Entertainment

Triomphe and the **Champs-Elysées** is a 50-story **Eiffel Tower★★** replica, ascended via glass elevators. The casino setting is old cobblestone Paris streets; **Jersey Boys** is the resident show.

Aria – 3730 Las Vegas Blvd. 📞702-590-7111. www.arialasvegas.com. In the heart of the CityCenter complex (2009), Aria boasts striking architecture and sustainable design. Cirque du Soleil offers an acrobatically-oriented show, **Zarkana**. Just outside Aria is the 500,000sq ft **Crystals** shopping and entertainment center.

Monte Carlo Resort & Casino★ – 3770 Las Vegas Blvd. S. 📞702-730-7777. www.montecarlo.com. Patterned after Monaco's Palais du Casino, this elegant hotel cultivates adult patronage and has a pub with more than 50 selections of beer. Blue Man Group is the resident entertainment.

New York-New York★★ – 3790 Las Vegas Blvd. S. 📞702-740-6969. www.nynyhotelcasino.com. This building simulates the Manhattan skyline with 12 skyscrapers, including a 45-story version of the **Empire State Building**. The street-level facade is a tableaux of other structures, including a 300ft-long **Brooklyn Bridge★** and a 150ft-tall **Statue of Liberty★★**. A roller coaster takes a 144ft plunge at 67mph.

MGM Grand★ – 3799 Las Vegas Blvd. S. 📞702-891-1111. www.mgmgrand.com. Flagship property of one of Vegas' largest chains, this venerable hotel offers entertainment ranging from martial arts to comedy to magic. Magician David Copperfield is the resident performer in the **Hollywood Theater**. Shows include Cirque du Soliel's Kà and MGM Grand's CSI the Experience.

Tropicana Resort & Casino – 3801 Las Vegas Blvd. S. 📞888-826-8767. www.troplv.com. The Tropicana is noted for the 4,000sq-ft **stained-glass ceiling** that curves over the main casino floor, and for its lavish pool complex.

Excalibur★ – 3850 Las Vegas Blvd. S. 📞702-597-7777. www.excalibur.com. This castle-based complex bristles with ramparts and battlements; Merlin wages battle against a dragon, and the shopping mall is a Medieval village with wandering minstrels. **Tournament of Kings** features jousting and fireworks.

Luxor★★ – 3900 Las Vegas Blvd. S. 📞702-262-4000. www.luxor.com. A 10-story sphinx stands before a 36-story pyramid, clad in 13 acres of bronze-tinted glass. "Inclinators" climb to hotel rooms via a shaft angled at 39 degrees. **Titanic: The Artifact Exhibition** displays items from the ill-fated ship.

Mandalay Bay Resort & Casino★ – 3950 Las Vegas Blvd. S. 📞702-632-7777. www.mandalaybay.com. A tropical water theme lends elegance to this resort with an 11-acre Lagoon, including an artificial wave pool and beach. In **Shark Reef★★** sharks, crocodiles, moray eels and venomous lionfish glide through a replicated sunken temple.

landscape their yards. Visitors can take an up-close look at a living bat cave, witness a live flash flood and enjoy an outdoor cooking demonstration in the gardens. The springs themselves stopped flowing in 1962. Also on the preserve's campus is the (2011) **Nevada State Museum Las Vegas★**, a compact compendium of exhibits devoted to the human history of the state, from Paiute Indians to California Trail pioneers through gold and silver prospectors to the entertainers who helped make Vegas famous (✆702-486-5205; http://museums.nevadaculture.org).

Red Rock Canyon National Conservation Area★★

W. Charleston Blvd. (Rte. 159), 17mi west of Las Vegas. ⚠️♿🅿️✆702-515-5350. www.nv.blm.gov/redrockcanyon.

A stunning escarpment of banded white, red and gray rock, 20mi long and 3,000ft high, represents the western extent of the Navajo Sandstone Formation prevalent in the Colorado Plateau. It was formed 180 million years ago of sand dunes cemented and tinted by water acting on iron oxide and calcium carbonate.

With more than 30mi of trails, a **visitor center★** and many boulders and sheer walls popular among rock climbers, the 300sq-mi Red Rock **Canyon National Conservation Area★★** preserves the northern end of the formation. Among highlights along a 13mi loop road are the old **Sandstone Quarry★★**, where blocks of red-and-white rock were mined from 1905 to 1912, and the adjacent Calico Hills. Hikers explore ancient petroglyphs at **Willow Spring** or escape desert heat via the **Ice Box Canyon Trail★** (*2.5mi round-trip*) into a steep, narrow canyon.

The more recent history of the canyon is preserved at the 528-acre **Spring Mountain Ranch State Park★** (Rte. 159, Blue Diamond; ✆702-875-4141; http://parks.nv.gov/smr.htm), dating from 1876. The ranch was once owned by German actress Vera Krupp and purchased in 1967 by reclusive financier Howard Hughes. A re-created ghost town called **Old Nevada★** (Rte. 159, Bonnie Springs; ✆702-875-4191; www.bonniesprings.com) has transformed another pioneer ranch. A saloon, restaurant, wax museum, church and other buildings along the dusty main street serve as backdrops for mock shootouts and melodramas.

Spring Mountains National Recreation Area★

Rtes. 156, 157 & 158, 35mi northwest of Las Vegas. ⚠️♿🅿️✆775-331-6444. www.fs.usda.gov/htnf.

A biologically unique oasis surrounded by the Mojave Desert, Mount Charleston (11,918ft) and other peaks of this 494sq-mi Toiyabe National Forest preserve are home to many species found nowhere else, including Palmer's chipmunks. The Spring Mountains are a haven for deer, elk, mountain lions, wild horses and bighorn sheep. Skiers throng to **Las Vegas Ski and Snowboard Resort** (Rte. 156) each winter, while mild summer temperatures draw motorists to enjoy seven developed campgrounds (and several campsites in undeveloped areas) and the **Mount Charleston Resort** (2275 Kyle Canyon Rd., Las Vegas; ✆702-872-5500; www.mtcharlestonresort.com). Linking the Kyle and Lee Canyons, the 9mi **Deer Creek Road** (Rte. 158) offers access to **Desert View Trail** (.1mi), where views north into the Nevada Test Site range once attracted crowds to witness atomic-bomb tests in 1952-62.

Desert National Wildlife Range★

Mormon Well Rd., 23mi north of Las Vegas off US-95. ⚠️✆702-515-5450. www.fws.gov/desertcomplex.

The largest US wildlife sanctuary outside of Alaska protects 2,200sq mi of mountainous habitat favored by desert bighorn sheep, Nevada's state mammal. Travel is restricted to designated roads, and no all-terrain vehicles are permitted. Information and maps are available from the **Corn Creek Field Station**, a historic oasis that has been an Indian camp, stagecoach stop and ranch.

Lake Mead Area★

North America's largest reservoir is a deep-blue desert lake along the Nevada-Arizona border. Created in 1936 on the Colorado River with construction of the Hoover Dam, one of the world's tallest dams, Lake Mead has become a recreational showpiece, bringing waterskiing, boating, fishing and other water sports to an arid land.

⌚ **Michelin Map:** 493 D 9, 10.
Mountain Standard Time.
🛈 **Info:** ℘702-293-8990;
www.nps.gov/lame.
✪ **Don't Miss:** Hoover Dam.
👪 **Kids:** Lake Mead.

A BIT OF HISTORY

The region's history goes back far before the 20C. Colonies of Ancestral Puebloans farmed the fertile valley of the Muddy River, near Overton, as early as AD 800. Their Paiute successors were working the bottomlands when Mormon settlers arrived in the mid 19C.

SIGHTS

Clark County Museum★

1830 S. Boulder Hwy., Henderson, 15mi southeast of Las Vegas. ♿🅿℘702-455-7955. www.clarkcountynv.gov.
This large, pueblo-style exhibit hall highlights southern Nevada history with dioramas of Pleistocene animals, an ancient pueblo, Colorado River steamboating, mining and gambling. Outside, on **Heritage Street★★**, are such relocated buildings as a c.1900 desert mining settlement and the 1931 Boulder City rail depot.

Boulder City★

US-93, 25mi southeast of Las Vegas.
℘702-892-0711.
www.visitbouldercity.com.
Tidy and green, Boulder City is one of only two gambling-free communities in Nevada (the other is Panaca). Constructed in 1931 for 8,000 dam workers, it was the first US city built according to Community Planning Movement principles, integrating social planning into physical design. Saco Reink DeBoer designed greenbelts, schools, parks and separate zones for residential, business, government and industrial uses.
The city now has 15,000 residents; its national historic district encourages pedestrian use with shady arcades

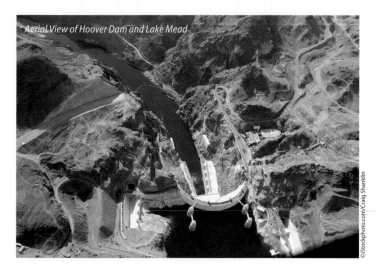
Aerial View of Hoover Dam and Lake Mead

©iStockphoto.com/Craig Shanklin

and Southwest Art Deco architecture, although the prominent 1933 **Boulder Dam Hotel★** (1305 Arizona St.; ℘702-293-3510; www.boulderdamhotel.com) strays from the plan with its Colonial Revival facade.

The two-story hotel also houses the **Hoover Dam Museum★** (℘702-294-1988, www.bcmha.org), where exhibits and a film provide background on the physical hardships and social conditions prevailing during the Depression-era construction project.

Hoover Dam★★★

US-93, 31mi southeast of Las Vegas.
♿🅿℘702-494-2517. www.usbr.gov/lc/hooverdam.

Stretched like a gargantuan wall across the 800ft-deep Black Canyon of the Colorado River, Hoover Dam is an intensely dramatic monument to civil engineering. Designed, built and operated by the federal Bureau of Reclamation for flood control and to provide water for irrigation, municipal use, electricity and recreation, it was the world's largest hydroelectric dam from its completion in 1936 until 1949. Rising 726.4ft from a 660ft-thick base to a 45ft-wide crest, capable of producing nearly 50 million kilowatts from 17 massive generators, Hoover Dam was the primary catalyst behind the population and economic boom of Arizona and Nevada.

Conceived to control devastating floods on the lower Colorado, the dam was first planned for Boulder Canyon, upstream from the present site. Four tunnels were bored through canyon walls to divert the river; after two cofferdams were built, the construction area was pumped dry and excavated to bedrock. The first concrete was poured in June 1933, the last in 1935, two years ahead of schedule. The dam began operation in October 1936. The project (including Boulder City) was under budget at a cost of $165 million, but 96 construction workers died on the job.

Note that all vehicles approaching the dam are subject to search. A multi-story parking garage on the Nevada side of the dam (RVs must park on the Arizona side) also holds a **visitor center★**, from which there are sensational **views★★** down the front of the dam and Black Canyon. Multimedia presentations focus on the construction; an upstairs gallery includes a dynamic desert **flash-flood demonstration★**. Two guided tours are offered: a shorter Power Plant tour and the more comprehensive **Hoover Dam Tour★★★**.

A striking new (2010) bridge spans the canyon 900 feet above the river, downstream of the dam, offering a bypass for traffic that once was forced to drive across Hoover dam.

Lake Mead National Recreation Area★

US-93 & Rte. 166, beginning 27mi east of Las Vegas. ⛺🍴♿🅿℘702-293-8990. www.nps.gov/lame.

Embracing two vast reservoirs on the Colorado River, this 2,350sq-mi desert preserve was created in 1936. Although 67mi-long **Lake Mohave**, impounded by Davis Dam in 1950, subsequently became an integral part of the park, the centerpiece remains **Lake Mead**.

With six large, full-service marinas on Lake Mead, and two on Lake Mohave, the recreation area offers superlative opportunities for boating, fishing, water skiing and houseboating. Miles of remote inlets and coves provide privacy. **Sightseeing cruises** of short duration depart from Lake Mead Marina near Boulder Beach, on the lake's western shore. **River-rafting** day trips from below Hoover Dam to Willow Beach are also popular.

The information source is the **Alan Bible Visitor Center★★** (Lakeshore Scenic Dr. at Rte. 93, 2mi west of Hoover Dam; ℘702-293-8990), with many interactive exhibits on the geology and natural history of one of the world's most extreme areas on earth, the Mojave Desert. The **Northshore Scenic Drive** (Rte. 167) offers the most impressive desert views on the Nevada shore, including ruddy-colored sandstone formations around the Redstone Picnic Area, where the gentle **Redstone Trail★** (.5mi loop) explores the petrified sand dunes.

©Gwen Cannon/Michelin

London Bridge, Lake Havasu City

Valley of Fire State Park★★

Rte. 169, 55mi northeast of Las Vegas.
♪702-397-2088. parks.nv.gov/vf.htm.
Nevada's oldest state park preserves 35,000 acres of desert scenery, including a half-mile-thick layer of Aztec Sandstone Formation, dyed reddish or leached white by chemical erosion and shaped by wind into arches, fins, knobs, domes, ridges and other odd shapes. From the **visitor center★★**, a 7mi spur road leads to the **White Domes Area★★**, a landscape of multihued monuments and smooth, wind-carved sandstone. The intriguing **Petroglyph Canyon Trail★★** (*.8mi round-trip*) traverses a narrow canyon to **Mouse's Tank★★**, a natural, water-filled basin where a renegade Paiute hid out in 1897. On the west end of the park, a steep metal stairway climbs up to **Atlatl Rock★**, named for a rare petroglyph of an atlatl, a weapon that predates the bow and arrow.

Lost City Museum of Archaeology★

1721 S. Rte. 169, south of Overton, 63mi northeast of Las Vegas. ♿🅿♪702-397-2193. museums.nevadaculture.org.
This flat-roofed adobe was built in 1935 to preserve archaeological discoveries. On its hilltop site is a reconstructed Ancestral Puebloan house built atop a genuine **pueblo foundation★**.

Laughlin

Rte. 163, 21mi east of US-95, 96mi south of Las Vegas. ♪702-298-2214. laughlinchamber.com.
In contrast to Las Vegas, where casinos are loath to divert gamblers' attention from the tables, casinos here often sport big picture windows on the river.

EXCURSION
Lake Havasu City

▶ Rte. 95, 19mi south of I-40, 154mi south of Las Vegas. Visitor center at 422 English Village (near the bridge). ♪928-855-5655. www.golakehavasu.com.
Spreading over the Arizona bank of Lake Havasu, a reservoir created by the Parker Dam in 1938, this resort and retirement town of 56,000 is celebrated as the site of the rebuilt **London Bridge★**, bought for $2.5 million from the City of London and erected at a cost of a further $7 million.
Longer cruises of the lake are available (check with the visitor center), but for a short, inexpensive crossing (*30min*), board the ferry at the English Village for the Havasu Landing Resort Casino; once on the California side, disembark and wait at the dock about 5min for the ferry to board for the return voyage (unless you want to stay and visit the casino).

Death Valley National Park★★★

At nearly 5,300sq mi, this sun-blasted expanse of mountain, canyon and playa is the largest national park in the contiguous US. Confronting visitors with vast, silent and stark landscapes unobscured by vegetation or human intrusion, Death Valley is a veritable textbook on geology. The enormous basin—130mi long, 5mi to 25mi wide—formed as a block of the earth's crust sagged and sank between mountain ranges, creating an astounding difference in elevations. Altitudes range from 11,049ft at Telescope Peak to 282ft below sea level near Badwater. Mountains are flanked by alluvial fans, delta-like deposits built up as debris washes out of canyons during flash floods. It is a land of extremes, both in temperature and natural beauty. The floral blooms in spring provide a striking contrast to the stark landscape.

- **Michelin Map:** p 171 Pacific Standard Time.
- **Info:** ☏760-786-3200; www.nps.gov/deva.
- **Location:** From the bottom of Death Valley to the top of Telescope Peak, a view common in the valley, is more than twice the depth of Grand Canyon.
- **Don't Miss:** Zabriskie Point and Dante's View.
- **Timing:** An overnight stay in Death Valley, either at one of its famous lodges or in a campground, is a lifetime memory–in the cool season. It's best to visit between late autumn and early spring, as the relentless summer sun heats the valley to some of the highest temperatures on earth. The 134°F recorded at Furnace Creek has been exceeded only in the Sahara Desert.

A BIT OF HISTORY

For centuries, the Panamint Shoshone made hunting and gathering forays into the valley during cooler months. Death Valley proved a formidable obstacle to 19C western migration, acquiring its name after a party was stranded for weeks in 1849. Prospectors combed surrounding mountains In the late 19C and early 20C, striking pockets of gold and other metals, sparking short-lived mining booms and leaving a heritage of abandoned settlements. Commercial exploitation of borax brought 20-mule-team wagons to haul the white mineral to a distant railhead. Organized tourism followed after railroad magnates built the Furnace Creek Inn in 1927.

SIGHTS

Park services and lodgings are concentrated at Furnace Creek, Stovepipe Wells and Panamint Springs. Visitors gather information at the **visitor centers at Furnace Creek** (Rte. 190; ☏760 -786-3200) and **Scotty's Castle** (Rte. 267; ☏760-786-2392).

Furnace Creek

Rtes. 190 & 178, 121mi northwest of Las Vegas.

Death Valley's main concentration of lodging and other facilities clusters around an oasis of date palms. **Furnace Creek Ranch** (☏760-786-2345; www.furnacecreekresort.com) occupies the site of the 1874 Greenland Ranch. The **Inn at Furnace Creek** (☏760-786-2345), built in 1927, is the park's premier hotel. The **Borax Museum**★★ here occupies the oldest house in Death Valley.

Badwater Road★

Rte. 178 south of Furnace Creek.
The paved road to Badwater (*36mi round-trip*) traverses a spectacularly bleak, sunken salt pan that sprawls

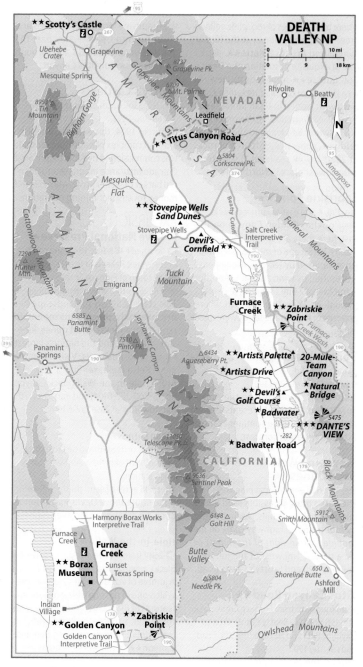

DEATH VALLEY NP

westward to the escarpment of the 11,200ft Panamint Range. From a small parking area west of the road (*2.5mi from Furnace Creek*), a gently climbing trail (*2mi round-trip*) winds through the badlands of **Golden Canyon★★**, cut by flash floods through tilted deposits of an ancient alluvial fan. **Artist's Drive★** (*10mi from Furnace Creek*) winds through the Amargosa Range's steep foothills, where brilliant hues of red, pink, yellow, green and purple climax at the highly mineralized **Artist's Palette**★★. A picture of exquisite desolation, the **Devil's Golf Course**★★ surrounds its viewing area (*12mi from Furnace Creek, then 1.3mi west*) with jagged low salt pinnacles. A short hike (*.8mi round-trip from trailhead off Badwater Rd.*) leads to the **Natural Bridge**★, a massive, 35ft arch of rock. At 282ft below sea level, **Badwater**★ is the lowest place in North America.

Zabriskie Point★★

Rte. 190, 4.5mi east of Furnace Creek.
Overlooking Golden Canyon on the east, here there are splendid views of a bizarre landscape of multicolored badlands, uplifted by tectonic movements and eroded by wind and rain. Another 1.2mi east, a 2.9mi scenic drive detours through **20-Mule-Team Canyon**, where deposits of high-grade borax were once mined.

Dante's View★★★

Dante's View Rd., 24mi southeast of Furnace Creek via Rte. 190.
From a 5,475ft perch atop the Amargosa Range, this point presents a stunning **view**★★★ of the continent's most extreme elevation contrast.

Stovepipe Wells Sand Dunes★★

Rte. 190, 6mi east of Stovepipe Wells.
The park's most accessible sand dunes pile up in billowing hills, reached either by foot from the highway (*park on the shoulder within sight of the dunes*) or via a turnoff 1mi west of the junction of Route 190 and Scotty's Castle Road.

Titus Canyon Road★★

98mi roundtrip from Furnace Creek. Take Rte. 190 north to Beatty Cutoff, then to Daylight Pass and Nevada Rte. 374. Road ends at Rte. 190.
Among the most memorable drives in the park, this one-lane dirt road traverses a landscape of layered cliffs, peaks of tilted and twisted sediments, and remnants of great volcanic eruptions. From a high point of 5,250ft in the Grapevine Mountains, it winds and squeezes into Death Valley past the ghost town of **Leadfield** and through the **narrows**★★ of Titus Canyon.

Scotty's Castle★

Rte. 267, 53mi north of Furnace Creek.
℘760-786-2392.
Begun in 1924, this eclectic, Spanish-Moorish complex of house and grounds was commissioned by Albert Johnson, a Chicago insurance magnate and financial backer of Walter Scott, who solicited money for suspect mining operations.

EXCURSION

Mojave National Preserve★

❯ South of I-15 & Rte. 164, 53mi south of Las Vegas; Baker is at Rte. 127 & I-15, 113mi south of Furnace Creek.
℘760-252-6100. www.nps.gov/moja.
This stark, 2,500sq-mi landscape has dry lake beds, precipitous mountain ranges, lava mesas, sand dunes, limestone caverns, and the nation's largest forest of Joshua trees. Visitor centers are in Kelso (Kelbaker Rd.; ℘760-252-6108), Hole-in-the-Wall (Black Canyon Rd.; ℘760-252-6104) and Barstow (2701 Barstow Rd.; ℘760-252-6100).

Kelso Dunes★

❯ Access on foot from a dirt road that turns off Kelbaker Rd., 7.4mi south of Kelso Station.
These 45 acres of sand dunes, billowing up to 600ft above Devils Playground's floor, are among the Mojave's highest.

Hole-in-the-Wall★★

❯ 26mi from I-40 via the paved Essex & Black Canyon Rds. ℘760-928-2572.
A jumble of volcanic cliffs, Hole-in-the-Wall is one of the more bizarre geologic features of Black Canyon. From the visitor center, a footpath (*2mi round-trip*) leads down narrow, twisting **Banshee Canyon**★★ to the steepest areas.

Mitchell Caverns★

❯ 16mi north of I-40 via Essex Rd. ℘760-928-2586. www.mitchell-caverns.com.
Six ancient limestone caverns were formed by percolating groundwater.

San Francisco Area

From the redwood forests to the towering cliffs of Big Sur, Northern California possesses unequalled natural beauty. The cosmopolitan city of San Francisco and its surrounding Bay Area form the hub of a region that embraces the Wine Country of the Napa and Sonoma Valleys, the charming and historic Monterey Peninsula, the remote coves and beaches of the rocky Pacific coast, historical mission settlements and the deep forest solitude of the Redwood Empire.
◔ For in-depth coverage, see the *Michelin Green Guide San Francisco*.

Highlights

1 Riding a cable car to **Fisherman's Wharf** (p184)
2 **Alcatraz'** cellhouse (p185)
3 Watching the fog around the **Golden Gate Bridge** (p186)
4 **Napa Valley** winetasting (p190)
5 Big Sur's **Hearst Castle** (p198)

Earthquake Country

The rugged mountains that run the length of California's northern coast once formed part of the Pacific Ocean floor. Some 25 million years ago, the tectonic collision of the Pacific and North American plates formed the Coast Ranges. The San Andreas Fault, running parallel to this continental collision zone, is the largest of many earthquake faults that periodically shake the region. Northern California's natural resources supported a dense native population. Spanish soldiers, building mission settlements in the 18C, decimated it trying to colonize the land. The mission society ended with Mexican secularization of the missions in 1834. After the US seized California in 1846, and especially with the gold rush of 1849, immigrants flooded into the state, shifting economic and political power from the Spanish capital of Monterey to the San Francisco Bay Area.
Development of the North Coast accelerated as redwood forests were harvested for timber to build San Francisco.

ADDRESSES

🏨 STAY

$$$$$ Meadowood – 900 Meadowood Ln., St. Helena. ✆707-531-4788 or. www.meadowood.com. 85 rooms. Words don't do justice to this world-class resort just off Napa's Silverado Trail. Meadowood offers exquisite grounds and rustic cottages that dot a cool, wooded grove. Service is top-flight. The resort offers golf, tennis, croquet, swimming pools, a full-service spa and the Restaurant at **Meadowood ($$$$)**, offering regional cuisine.

$$$$$ Post Ranch Inn – 47900 Hwy 1, Big Sur. ✆831-667-2200. www.post ranchinn.com. 40 rooms. Vast, stunning views of the Pacific Ocean at Pfeiffer Point extend from the inn's steel-roofed redwood cottages. Guests may recline under skylights or in front of wood-burning fireplaces in their minimalist, eco-friendly rooms, or walk the 98-acre ranch through oak and madrone forest. At night, there are stargazing classes or dips in the warm-water, infinity-edge basking pool. **Sierra Mar ($$$$)** offers exquisite eclectic global dining in a glass walled room atop the cliffs.

GETTING THERE

The Bay Area has three major airports: **San Francisco International Airport (SFO)** (☎650-821-8211; www.flysfo.com), 11mi south of downtown; **Oakland International Airport (OAK)** (☎510-563-3300; www.oaklandairport.com), 22mi southeast of San Francisco; and **San Jose International Airport (SJC)** (☎408-392-3600; www.flysanjose.com), 42mi south of San Francisco. From SFO and Oakland, taxi to downtown is about $45. **Amtrak train**: 5885 Horton St., Emeryville (☎800-872-7245; www.amtrak.com). **Greyhound bus**: 200 Folsom St. (☎415-495-1569; www.greyhound.com).

GETTING AROUND

Routes and fares on all Bay Area transportation are available from Bay Area Traveler Information (☎511; http://511.org). Most public transportation is operated by the San Francisco Muncipal Railway (**Muni**). Lines operate daily 5:30am–12:30am; a limited number of routes operate 24hrs/day. Fare for buses and streetcars is $2.00; transfers within 90min are free; exact fare required.

Cable cars: operate daily 6am–12:30am; fare $5. Purchase tickets on-board or at the visitor center. Muni Passports are good for 1 ($13), 3 ($20) or 7 ($26) days. BART (Bay Area Rapid Transit), the region's expansive light-rail system, is convenient for trips to Berkeley and Oakland (☎415-989-2278; www.bart.gov) and to the San Francisco and Oakland airports.

Taxi: DeSota Cab (☎877-691-2170), Yellow Cab (☎415-282-3737), Luxor Cab (☎415-282-4141). Blue and Gold Fleet ferries (☎415-773-1188; www.blueandgoldfleet.com) depart from Fisherman's Wharf and the Ferry Building to Sausalito, Tiburon, Angel Island and Oakland. **Train**: The Caltrain (☎800-660-4287; www.caltrain.com) runs between San Francisco and San Jose.

VISITOR INFORMATION

City visitor center at Hallidie Plaza (900 Market St.; ☎415-391-2000; www.sanfrancisco.travel). City Pass offers discounted admission to several attractions, as well as a 7-day MUNI pass (www.citypass.com). Visitors bureaus for Berkeley (☎510-549-7040; www.visitberkeley.com), Marin County (☎415-925-2060; www.visitmarin.org), Napa Valley (☎707-251-5895; www.visitnapavalley.com), Sonoma (☎707-552-5800; www.sonomacounty.com) and Monterey (☎877-666-8373; www.seemonterey.com) supply maps and information.

ACCOMMODATIONS

San Francisco Lodging Guide (www.onlyinsanfrancisco.org) from the San Francisco Convention & Visitors Bureau. Reservation services: San Francisco Reservations (☎877-243-8072; www.hotelres.com); Quikbook (☎800-789-9887; www.quikbook.com). Bed & Breakfast San Francisco (☎800-452-8249; www.bbsf.com).

ENTERTAINMENT

Consult the arts and entertainment sections of local newspapers like the daily *San Francisco Chronicle* (www.sfgate.com) or the weekly *SF Weekly* or *San Francisco Bay Guardian* (www.sfweekly.com; www.sfbg.com) for listings of current events, theaters and concert halls, or call San Francisco's Cultural Events Hotline (☎415-391-2000; www.onlyinsanfrancisco.org). Or refer to the California Travel and Tourism Commission's events calendar (☎916-444-4429; www.visitcalifornia.com). Obtain event tickets from Tickets.com (www.tickets.com) or Tix Bay Area, a Ticketmaster outlet, which offers full and half-price tickets for selected events on the day of the show (☎415-433-7827; www.tixbayarea.org).

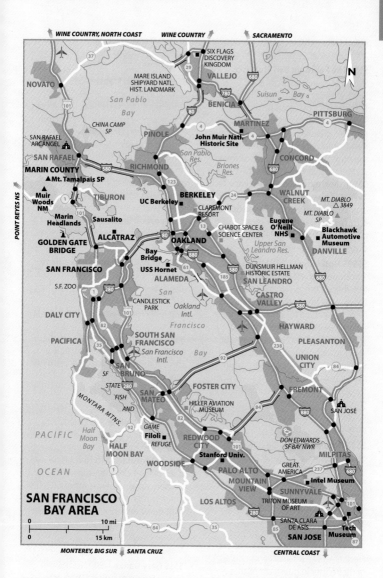

SAN FRANCISCO BAY AREA

| 0 | 10 mi |
| 0 | 15 km |

$$$$$ Taj Campton Place Hotel – 340 Stockton St., San Francisco. 415-781-5555. www.tajhotels.com. 110 rooms. An intimate hotel, once popular with the white-gloved "carriage trade" set, the Campton Place is the epitome of fine service. Elegant contemporary decor (maplewood armoires, limestone bathrooms) teams up with Mediterranean-inspired **Campton Place Restaurant ($$$$)** to provide a rarefied experience in a discreet location just off Union Square.

$$$$ The Claremont – 41 Tunnel Rd., Berkeley. 510-843-3000. www. claremontresort.com. 279 rooms. Sprawling across the Berkeley-Oakland hills a mere 30min drive from downtown San Francisco, the blazing white, castle-like Claremont offers activities for all. There's a tranquil spa, a fitness center, a tennis club, three pools and a kids' camp. Room décor, especially in the new wing, reflects a casual West Coast elegance. **Meritage ($$$$)** impresses with Cal-Med signatures like ahi a la plancha with sweet chili hummus, toasted almonds, preserved orange and mint salsa.

$$$$ The Fairmont San Francisco – 950 Mason St., San Francisco. ℰ415-772-5000. www.fairmont.com. 591 rooms. This famous hotel atop Nob Hill survived the 1906 earthquake and saw the 1945 creation of the United Nations. Handsomely appointed rooms are in the original building and a 1961 tower with extensive views across the city. An $85 million renovation was completed in 2001. The hotel has three restaurants, including the delightful **Tonga Room & Hurricane Bar ($$$)** for exotic Asian cuisine and authentic Mai Tais around a tropical indoor pool.

$$$$$ Hotel Bijou – 111 Mason St., San Francisco. ℰ415-771-1200. www.hotelbijou.com. 65 rooms. Located a block away from cable-car stops, the Art Deco-style Bijou recalls a 1920s movie palace; on its walls hang photos of San Francisco's old movie houses. Bright, jewel-toned guest rooms are named for films shot in the city, many of which are screened nightly in the small lobby theater. Rates include a complimentary continental breakfast and nightly movies in Le Petite Theater with free popcorn.

$$$$ Hotel Monaco – 501 Geary St., San Francisco. ℰ415-292-0100. www.monaco-sf.com. 201 rooms. This Theater District boutique hotel, a 1910 Beaux-Arts classic, offers the warmth and comfort of home, including a no-fee, all-size pet friendly policy. Baroque-plaster fireplaces and sumptuous striped armchairs invite lobby conversation; French Art Nouveau accents and silk fabrics glitter in guest rooms that were completely redesigned for a modern-European flair in 2013. Downstairs, the stunning **Grand Café ($$$)** offers French bistro-style lunch and dinner.

$$$$ Inn Above Tide – 30 El Portal, Sausalito. ℰ415-332-9535. www.innabovetide.com. 29 rooms. Guest rooms at this inn, built upon the water, boast picture windows that frame spectacular views (binoculars provided). Decorated in a serene palette of whites and tans, rooms feature waterside decks; many have fireplaces. Rates include room-service continental breakfast and sunset wine-and-cheese reception; options include in-room spa treatments.

$$$$ Westin St. Francis – 335 Powell St., San Francisco. ℰ415-397-7000. www.westinstfrancis.com. 1,195 rooms. The most visible hotel in the city from its location facing Union Square, Westin's flagship hostelry is a Renaissance- and Baroque-revival structure built in 1904. An historic charm pervades rooms in this main building; more contemporary rooms with city views occupy a 32-story tower built in 1972. Michael Mina's on-site **Bourbon Steak ($$$$)** impresses with real Wagyu streak and premium seafood.

$ 24 Henry Guesthouse and Village House – 24 Henry St., San Francisco. ℰ415-864-5686. www.24henry.com. A largely gay and lesbian clientele frequents these two bed-and-breakfast inns in classic Victorian houses a few blocks from one another in the heart of the Castro. Rates include a complimentary breakfast served in the spacious parlor.

⍾ EAT

$$$$ Chez Panisse – 1517 Shattuck Ave., Berkeley. ℰ510-548-5525. www.chezpanisse.com. Dinner only. Closed Sun. **California**. California cuisine was born here under the watchful eye of culinary doyenne Alice Waters. Organic greens and heirloom vegetables pair with free-range poultry and carefully selected meats to create memorable prix-fixe meals that change nightly. Make reservations a month in advance.

$$$$ Gary Danko – 800 North Point St.,San Francisco. ℰ415-749-2060. www.garydanko.com. Dinner only. **Continental**. Elegant but understated decor allows chef-owner Danko's culinary creations to take center stage at his restaurant near Fisherman's Wharf. Five-course tasting menus might offer crispy farm egg with grits and Royal Trumpet mushrooms, seared filet of beef with cumin potatoes and Swiss chard, and a chocolate praline parfait.

$$$$ Jardinière – 300 Grove St., San Francisco. ℰ415-861-5555. www.jardiniere.com. Dinner only. **California**

French. Bubbles sparkle on the domed ceiling of the Champagne Rotunda in this elegant two-story restaurant, favored for pre- or post-theater dining. Menus are updated daily, but chef-owner Traci Des Jardins may start diners with house-made charcuterie or a French green bean salad in gizzard vinaigrette, then present herb-crusted loin, shoulder and belly of lamb with Nicoise olives, followed by buffalo milk, Marcona almond and chocolate parfait.

$$$$ Le Papillon - 410 Saratoga Ave., San Jose. ✆408.296.3730. www. le papillon.com. **French**. Lunch Fri only. The tech boom fueled this fine-dining oasis, but it's chef Scott Cooper's inventive cooking that keeps it by reservation only. A la carte dishes are excellent, but the prix fixe and tasting menus make deciding much easier. Seasonal options include quail with steelcut oatmeal in Madeira reduction, salsify soup with duck royale and truffle, or sturgeon Wellington. The wine list features 500+ labels.

$$$ A 16 – 2355 Chestnut St., San Francisco. ✆415-771-2216. www. a16sf.com. No lunch Sat–Tue. **Italian.** The name refers to the highway linking Naples with Canosa in Puglia, Italy. The menu follows the course, too, at this always-packed shrine to Slow Food. Featured are homemade pasta, house-made charcuterie, and perfect authentic Neapolitan pizza alongside one of the city's best Italian wine lists.

$$$ Café de la Presse – 352 Grant Ave., San Francisco. ✆415-398-2680. www. cafedelapresse.com. **French**. Casual brasserie meals are served at this cafe and international newsstand near Chinatown. Menus du jour may feature French onion soup, Boeuf Bourguignon and duck confit over French green lentils. The espresso bar, with its many pastries, is popular with locals.

$$$ Mustard's Grill – 7399 St. Helena Hwy., Yountville. ✆707-944-2424. www.mustardsgrill.com. **American**. A long-standing Napa Valley favorite, this casual ranch-style restaurant draws winemakers and industry VIPs for its top-notch wine list and fresh American regional cuisine, with nods to Continental and Asian fare. Some come just for the sublimely thin and crispy onion rings served with house-made tomato-apple ketchup.

$$$ Nepenthe – 48501 Hwy. 1, Big Sur. ✆831-667-2345. www.nepenthebigsur. com. **American**. Greek mythology describes nepenthe as a potion used to obliterate pain and sorrow. And, indeed, the spectacular views from Nepenthe's terraces, 800ft above the Pacific and 31mi south of Carmel, inspire pure joy. Built of redwood and adobe in 1949, the restaurant offers a basic menu of chicken, steaks and seafood. Regulars love the Ambrosia burger: ground steak on a French roll.

$$ Fior d'Italia – 2237 Mason St., San Francisco. ✆415-986-1886. www.fior. com. **Northern Italian**. Billing itself as America's oldest Italian restaurant, this institution opened in 1886 but has moved six times since then, most recently in 2005. Cuisine remains tradition-bound: calamari, gnocchi, osso buco and cioppino.

$$ The Slanted Door – 1 Ferry Building, San Francisco. ✆415-861-8032. www. slanteddoor.com. **Vietnamese**. This trendy cafe in the bustling Ferry Building offers fresh, Viet-inspired cuisine and expansive bay views. Crowds arrive early for grapefruit and jicama salad; spring rolls stuffed with pork, shrimp, and mint; or Dungeness crab with cellophane noodles.

$ Dottie's True Blue Café – 28 Sixth St., San Francisco. ✆415-885-2767. www.dotties.biz. Breakfast and lunch only. Closed Tue–Wed. **American**. A kitschy nook, Dottie's is an edge-of-the-Tenderloin oasis. Its menu offers generous portions of whole-wheat and raspberry-cornmeal pancakes, eggs with black-bean cakes and smoked chicken and apple sausage.

$ Zarzuela – 2000 Hyde St. ✆415-346-0800, San Francisco. Dinner only. Closed Sun. **Spanish**. Flamenco guitar accents paellas served on hand-painted plates at this friendly, always-packed Russian Hill place. Dishes include poached octopus and zarzuela, a seafood stew from the Catalan coast of northeast Spain. You can bring your own wine and pay corkage.

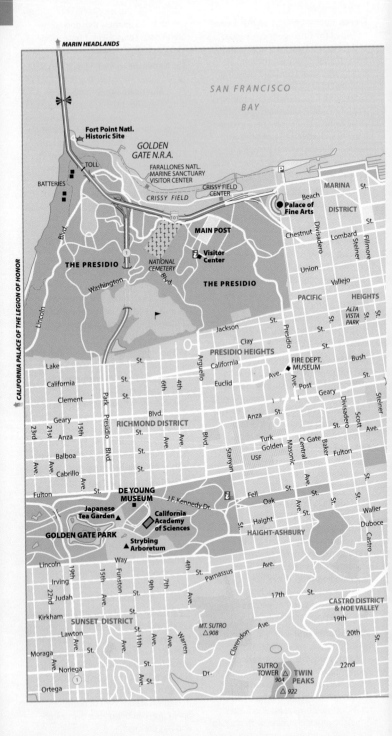

MARIN HEADLANDS

SAN FRANCISCO BAY

Fort Point Natl. Historic Site

GOLDEN GATE N.R.A.

TOLL

BATTERIES

FARALLONES NATL. MARINE SANCTUARY VISITOR CENTER

CRISSY FIELD CENTER

CRISSY FIELD

MARINA St.

Beach

Palace of Fine Arts

MARINA DISTRICT

Divisadero

Chestnut

Lombard

Steiner

Fillmore

St.

MAIN POST

Union

Vallejo

THE PRESIDIO

Blvd.

NATIONAL CEMETERY

Visitor Center

THE PRESIDIO

PACIFIC HEIGHTS

ALTA VISTA PARK

St.

Washington

Blvd.

Presidio

Jackson

Clay

PRESIDIO HEIGHTS

St.

Bush

Lincoln

Lake

St.

California

Euclid

FIRE DEPT. MUSEUM

Ave.

Post

Geary

Steiner

California

6th

4th

St.

St.

Divisadero

Scott

St.

Clement

St.

Anza

St.

St.

Ave.

Geary

Park

Presidio

Blvd.

RICHMOND DISTRICT

Ave.

Blvd.

Turk

Golden

Masonic

Central

Gate

Baker

Fulton

23rd

21st

15th

St.

St.

Stanyan

USF

Anza

Balboa

St.

Cabrillo

Ave.

Fulton

St.

DE YOUNG MUSEUM

J.F. Kennedy Dr.

Fell

Oak

Ave.

St.

Waller

Duboce

Japanese Tea Garden

California Academy of Sciences

Haight

HAIGHT-ASHBURY

Castro

GOLDEN GATE PARK

Strybing Arboretum

Lincoln

19th

Way

4th

St.

Parnassus

Ave.

Irving

15th

Funston

9th

7th

St.

17th

St.

CASTRO DISTRICT & NOE VALLEY

22nd

Judah

Ave.

19th

Kirkham

St.

MT. SUTRO △ 908

Lawton

11th

Ave.

St.

Ave.

Warren

Clarendon

Ave.

20th

St.

Moraga

Ave.

St.

SUTRO TOWER 904

Noriega

1

TWIN PEAKS △ 922

Ortega

Dr.

CALIFORNIA PALACE OF THE LEGION OF HONOR

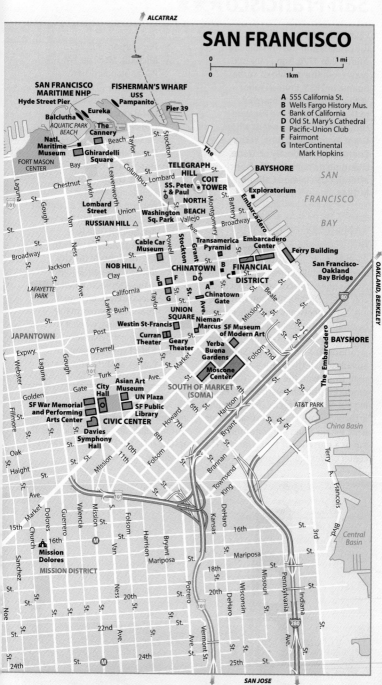

SAN FRANCISCO

0   1 mi
0   1km

A   555 California St.
B   Wells Fargo History Mus.
C   Bank of California
D   Old St. Mary's Cathedral
E   Pacific-Union Club
F   Fairmont
G   InterContinental Mark Hopkins

ALCATRAZ

SAN FRANCISCO MARITIME NHP
Hyde Street Pier
Balclutha
Eureka
AQUATIC PARK BEACH
The Cannery
Natl. Maritime Museum
Ghirardelli Square
FORT MASON CENTER

FISHERMAN'S WHARF
USS Pampanito
Pier 39

Beach
Taylor St.
Stockton St.
The

BAYSHORE
Exploratorium

SAN FRANCISCO BAY

TELEGRAPH HILL
COIT TOWER
SS. Peter & Paul
NORTH BEACH
Washington Sq. Park

Chestnut
Lombard
Columbus
Leavenworth
Larkin
Hyde
Union
Vallejo
Broadway
Montgomery
Battery
Embarcadero

Lombard Street
RUSSIAN HILL △

Cable Car Museum
Transamerica Pyramid
Embarcadero Center
Ferry Building

San Francisco-Oakland Bay Bridge
OAKLAND, BERKELEY

NOB HILL △
CHINATOWN
FINANCIAL DISTRICT

Broadway
Jackson
Clay
California
Bush
Post
O'Farrell

Van Ness
Gough
Franklin
Larkin
Leavenworth
Taylor
Powell
Stockton
Grant
Ave.
Kearny
Montgomery
Sansome
Battery
Front
Davis
Beale
1st
Mission
2nd

Chinatown Gate
E F
G D
A
B C
UNION SQUARE
Nieman-Marcus
Westin St-Francis
Curran Theater
Geary Theater

JAPANTOWN
Webster
Fillmore
Laguna
Gough
Turk
Gate
Golden

Expwy.
Ave.
Market St.

SF Museum of Modern Art
Yerba Buena Gardens
Moscone Center

BAYSHORE
The Embarcadero

City Hall
Asian Art Museum
UN Plaza
SF Public Library
SF War Memorial and Performing Arts Center
CIVIC CENTER
Davies Symphony Hall

SOUTH OF MARKET (SOMA)

Howard
6th
7th
8th
Folsom
10th
11th
Mission
Harrison
Bryant
Brannan
Townsend
King
DeHaro
Kansas
4th
3rd

AT&T PARK
China Basin

Oak St.
Haight
Ave.

Central Basin

15th
Church
Dolores
Guerrero
Valencia
Mission St.
Folsom
Harrison
Bryant
Potrero
20th
22nd
24th
Sanchez
Noe

16th
Mission Dolores
MISSION DISTRICT
16th
Mariposa
18th
20th
25th
24th

Wisconsin
Missouri
Pennsylvania
Indiana
Vermont St.
DeHaro
Terry A. Francois Blvd.

SAN JOSE

San Francisco★★★

Founded as Mission Dolores (by priests) and the Presidio (by soldiers) in 1776, San Francisco grew from the pueblo of Yerba Buena. In 1835, English sailor William Richardson, married to the daughter of the Presidio comandante, set up a tent where Grant Avenue now runs. Yerba Buena grew modestly on trade, changing its name to San Francisco after the US claimed California in 1846.

SAN FRANCISCO TODAY

Ethnically diverse, well-educated, open-minded, tech-savvy, food-loving, and environmentally conscious, San Francisco is one of the country's most desirable cities. Despite the high cost of living, San Franciscans enjoy life in their beautiful, cosmopolitan city.

From high-tech professionals to service-industry workers, residents take advantage of their city's attractions right along with the visitors, gathering produce at the farmers' markets, hanging out in North Beach cafes, shopping in Union Square, jogging in Golden Gate Park, biking along the waterfront, taking in a museum or two. The city is a center of West Coast fashion and a culi-nary mecca as well; San Franciscans dine out regularly and closely monitor the restaurant scene (&consult the *Michelin Guide San Francisco*).

▶ **Population:** 805,235.
Michelin Map: pp 178-179. Pacific Standard Time.
Info: &415-391-2000; www.sanfrancisco.travel.
Location: At the northern end of the San Francisco Peninsula between the Pacific Ocean and San Francisco Bay.
Don't Miss: Golden Gate Bridge; Lombard Street; sourdough bread at Fisherman's Wharf; a cable car ride; SF Museum of Modern Art; Golden Gate Park.
Timing: Allow a week to see the sights of the city. Visit Golden Gate Bridge in the afternoon, when it is less likely to be fogged in, and Chinatown in the early evening, when it is at its most dynamic.
Kids: Exploratorium; Cable Car Museum.

Golden Gate Bridge

© Rick Dole/Michelin

A BIT OF HISTORY

The discovery of Sierra gold in 1848 put San Francisco in the fast lane toward the future. The village exploded into a boomtown serving 90,000 transients. New buildings rose daily (and burned with alarming frequency). Another burst of fortune came with the discovery in 1859 of a vein of Nevada silver known as the Comstock Lode. Its investors' profits flooded San Francisco with fabulous wealth. Ostentatious and high-living new millionaires funded a wide range of civic improvements and construction – factories, offices, theaters, wharves, hotels, ferries and the famous cable cars. The city's famous liberal openness derives from those early days of progressivism.

With a population of some 300,000 at the turn of the 19C, San Francisco was the largest American city west of the Mississippi River. An earthquake and fire in 1906 destroyed the city center, leaving 250,000 people homeless and 674 dead or missing. The plucky city reconstructed with phenomenal speed, riding its progressive momentum through the first half of the 20C with epic civil-engineering projects that included two of the largest bridges in the world. In the mid-19C, San Francisco's Financial District was dubbed the "Wall Street of the West." Servicemen returning from World War II, massive immigration, liberalizing attitudes and other factors led to the city becoming a center of liberal activism.

DOWNTOWN
Union Square

Roughly bounded by Sutter, Taylor, Kearny & O'Farrell Sts.

San Francisco's prestigious urban shopping district faces 2.6-acre **Union Square Park**★ with Saks Fifth Avenue, Macy's and Nordstrom. **Neiman-Marcus** has a **rotunda**★ topped by an art-glass dome. The **Westin St. Francis Hotel**★★ (335 Powell St.; &415-397-7000; see ADDRESSES), west of the square, is a Renaissance and Baroque Revival landmark finished in 1904 and rebuilt after 1906.

An active theater district fans out to the west, embracing the historic **Geary Theater**★ (415 Geary St.; &415-749-2228; www.act-sf.org), home of the American Conservatory Theater, and the **Curran Theatre**★ (445 Geary St.; &415-551-2000, www.shnsf.com).

Financial District★★

Bounded by Market, Kearny & Jackson Sts. and The Embarcadero.

Though tourism is the backbone of the city's economy, it is also the home of numerous international financial institutions. The commodities-trading and corporate-business center is concentrated in a triangular district around California and Montgomery Streets. The building at **555 California St.** is the former headquarters of Bank of America, which financed much of the development of San Francisco.

Wells Fargo Bank recalls its Old West roots at the **Wells Fargo History Museum**★ (420 Montgomery St.; &415-396-2619; www.wellsfargohistory.com). The city's grandest bank edifice is the Neoclassical **Bank of California**★★ (400 California St.).

San Francisco's tallest building, the 48-story **Transamerica Pyramid**★★ (600 Montgomery St.; www.thepyramidcenter.com), rises 853ft from street level to the tip of its 212ft hollow lantern; built in 1972, the slender pyramid is a symbol of the city. **Embarcadero Center**★ (bounded by Sacramento, Battery & Clay Sts. & the Embarcadero; www.embarcaderocenter.com), a series of four slablike office towers (1967-72), incorporates a three-level, open-air shopping center.

Chinatown★★★

Bounded by Montgomery, California & Powell Sts. and Broadway.
www.sanfranciscochinatown.com.

A teeming fusion of Cantonese market town and Main Street USA, Chinatown spreads along the lower slope of Nob Hill. With 30,000 residents in its 24-block core, it is one of the most densely populated neighborhoods in North America.

The main thoroughfare, **Grant Avenue★★**, starts with a flourish at **Chinatown Gate** on Bush Street and runs eight blocks north to Broadway. Exotic ambience is provided by distinctive architectural chinoiserie: painted balconies, curved-tile rooflines and red, green and yellow color schemes. Shops selling souvenirs, jewelry, artwork, furniture, cameras and electronics share the street with tourist restaurants, hardware stores, banks, poultry and fish markets, herbalists' shops, tea stores and cafes that cater to local residents.

Old St. Mary's Cathedral★ (660 California St. at Grant Ave.; ☎415-288-3800; www.oldsaintmarys.org), dedicated in 1854, was built of brick and iron shipped from New England, laid upon a foundation of granite quarried in China. **Portsmouth Square★** (between Clay & Washington Sts., one-half block below Grant Ave.), the original plaza of Yerba Buena, is now a social gathering point for Chinatown residents.

A less commercialized neighborhood of markets surrounds **Stockton Street★**, a block uphill from Grant, and a maze of narrow alleys between. **Waverly Place★** is noted for its temples and brilliantly decorated balconies. The 1852 **Tin How Temple** (125 Waverly Pl., 4th floor; ☎415-421-3628) is Chinatown's oldest. The story of the Chinese experience in the American West is depicted at the new museum of the **Chinese Historical Society of America Museum** (965 Clay St.; ☎415-391-1188; www.chsa.org). Located in a former YWCA building with pagoda-like towers, designed by Julia Morgan (1932), it has six galleries and a learning center.

North Beach★★

Columbus Ave. and adjacent streets from Pacific Ave. to Bay St. www.northbeachchamber.com.

The erstwhile heart of the Italian community, North Beach, inspires dawdling at coffeehouses by day and restaurants by night. The Beat Generation – "beatniks" – flocked here in the 1950s seeking relaxed Mediterranean attitudes along with the cheap food and drink of family-run trattorias, bars and cafes. A traditional Latin flavor persists at **Washington Square Park★**, backed by the twin spires of **SS Peter and Paul Church★** (666 Filbert St.; ☎415-421-0809; www.sspeterpaulsf.org), known as the Italian Cathedral.

On the east side of North Beach, 274ft **Telegraph Hill★** is capped by fluted-concrete **Coit Tower★★★ ▲▲** (☎415-362-0808), which rises an additional 212ft to an observation deck offering fine city **views★★**. Built in 1934, during the Great Depression, the tower has a lobby decorated with **murals★★** painted by 26 local artists as part of the Public Works of Art Project. Bluntly critical of social and political conditions, the murals sparked heated controversy.

Russian Hill★

Roughly bounded by Columbus Ave., Bay & Polk Sts., Broadway & Mason St.
From Hyde Street, north of Lombard Street, visitors gaze north to extensive **views★★★**. Turning east, **Lombard Street★★★** undulates down to Leavenworth Street; the brick-lined one-block stretch, flanked by flower gardens, is nicknamed "The Crookedest Street in the World." The eight switchbacks were built in 1922, taming the hillside's gradient of 27 percent to a manageable 16 percent.

Nob Hill★★

Roughly bounded by Broadway and Stockton, Bush & Polk Sts.
Nob Hill achieved its reputation as an abode of the rich in the late 1860s. Construction of a cable-car line in 1873 made the hilltop more accessible and, by the 1880s, the residents included railroad potentates and silver barons. With the exception of James Flood's mansion, now the exclusive **Pacific-Union Club★** (1000 California St.; ☎415-775-1234), all original mansions were destroyed in the 1906 earthquake and fire.

The opulent, historic **Fairmont Hotel★★** (950 Mason St.; ☎415-772-5000; www.fairmont.com) is famed for its views and glamorous lobby. The **InterContinental Mark Hopkins** (999 California St.; ☎415-

392-3434; www.intercontinental.com) offers views★★★ from its swank bar, the **Top of the Mark.**

The most dynamic sight on Nob Hill is the **Cable Car Museum**★★ 👥👤 (1201 Mason St.; ☎415-474-1887; www.cablecarmuseum.org) that doubles as the powerhouse for the clanging cars of San Francisco's steep hills, gripping a moving cable that loops continuously through a slot in the city streets. From the balcony of the museum, visitors may gaze upon the humming engines and whirling sheaves that drive the cable.

Civic Center★

Bounded by Market St., Van Ness & Golden Gate Aves.

San Francisco's governmental center comprises one of the nation's finest groupings of Beaux-Arts-style buildings—a result of city leaders who subscribed to the City Beautiful Movement. Buildings are arranged along a central axis running three blocks west from Market and Leavenworth Streets to City Hall. At the eastern head of this pedestrian mall, **United Nations Plaza★** commemorates the founding of the UN at Civic Center in 1945. After passing the **San Francisco Public Library★** (100 Larkin St.; ☎415-557-4400; http://sfpl.org), the axis opens up to the Civic Center Plaza, foreground for the imposing dome of **City Hall★★** (facing Polk St.). Rising to 307ft above a massive, four-story colonnaded building, the black and gold dome is 13ft taller than that of the US Capitol building in Washington, DC. Inside, a grand staircase ascends to a 181ft open rotunda.

On the west side of City Hall, the **San Francisco War Memorial and Performing Arts Center★★** (401 Van Ness Ave. between McAllister & Grove Sts.; ☎415-621-6600; sfwmpac.org) comprises the War Memorial Opera House and the Veterans Building, site of a theater and art gallery. Immediately south is **Davies Symphony Hall** (Grove St. & Van Ness Ave.; www.sfsymphony.org), home of the renowned San Francisco Symphony. East of city hall, San Francisco's **Asian**

Art Museum★★★ (200 Larkin St.; ☎415-581-3500; www.asianart.org) opened in 2003. French architect Gae Aulenti converted the former Main Library, a 1917 Beaux-Arts building. The museum features the finest collection of Asian art in the US, spanning 6,000 years and including Chinese ceramics and bronzes, Japanese screens and scroll paintings, Korean stoneware and Indian sacred sculptures.

SOUTHERN NEIGHBORHOODS

Mission Dolores★

16th & Dolores Sts. ☎415-621-8203. www.missiondolores.org.

Officially named Misión San Francisco de Asís, the city's oldest extant structure dates from 1791. The 4ft-thick adobe walls of the sturdy **chapel**★★ are covered with stucco and roofed by a beamed ceiling painted with Ohlone Indian designs. The marked graves of Catholic pioneers adorn the chapel and **cemetery★**, where thousands of Ohlone neophytes lie in unmarked plots. Today "The Mission" is a bustling and ultra-hip neighborhood marked by the new and trendy within the neighborhood's deep Hispanic roots. A recent restaurant boom has made it a destination for both haute cuisine and excellent, cheap burritos

Yerba Buena Gardens★★

Bounded by Mission, Howard, 3rd & 4th Sts.

Uniting an outdoor garden with cinemas, galleries, playgrounds, museums and the **Moscone Convention Center**, Yerba Buena Gardens is the city's most ambitious recent entertainment and cultural complex. At the 5.5-acre **Esplanade**, visitors relax on grassy terraces and visit a memorial to Dr. Martin Luther King Jr., curtained by an exhilarating waterfall. Adjacent are the theaters, gallery and forum of the **Yerba Buena Center for the Arts★** (3rd & Mission Sts.; ☎415-978-2787; www.ybca.org) and **Rooftop at Yerba Buena Gardens**★★ 👥👤 (750 Folsom St.; ☎415-777-3727; www.yerbabuenagardens.com), a children's complex with a high-tech studio-theater and year-round ice-skating rink. From May to October, more than 200 free artistic, cultural and community programs take place in the grounds. The four-story **Metreon** 👥 (4th & Mission Sts.; ☎415-369-6000) houses 15 cinemas and a 600-seat IMAX theater.

San Francisco Museum of Modern Art★★

151 3rd St. ☎415-357-4000.
www.sfmoma.org.

This premier showcase for contemporary art occupies an innovative building (1995, Mario Botta) opposite Yerba Buena Gardens. The **atrium★★** resembles an urban piazza, sheathed in bright woods and polished granite. A grand staircase rises through the building's heart, culminating in a narrow steel **catwalk★** five stories above the rotunda floor. Permanent holdings include 1,200 paintings, 500 sculptures, 9,000 photographs and 3,000 works on paper, representing major artists and schools of Europe and the Americas. Major works include Henri Matisse's *Femme au Chapeau* (1905), Deigo Rivera's *The Flower Carrier* (1935) and Jackson Pollock's *Guardian's of the Secret* (1943).

BAYSHORE
The Embarcadero★

Along San Francisco Bay from China Basin to Fisherman's Wharf.

Fisherman's Wharf, Pier 39

© California Travel & Tourism Commission

The warehouses of the waterfront have either been torn down or converted into offices, shops and restaurants. Crossing the bay are the towers, two-tiered roadway and twin suspension spans of the western part of **San Francisco–Oakland Bay Bridge★★**. Joining the eastern cantilever section at Yerba Buena Island, the 5.2mi bridge is one of the world's longest high-level steel bridges. When opened in 1936, it ended the bay ferries and their terminus, the 1898 **Ferry Building★★** (foot of Market St.). The 253ft clock tower was the city's only high-rise undamaged by the 1906 quake; it has been converted to a shopping, dining and office complex. Formerly housed in the Palace of Fine Arts, the **Exploratorium★★** 👥 (Embarcadero at Green St.; ☎415-528-4444; www.exploratorium.edu) now occupies a striking new building (2013) on Pier 15. This state-of-the-art science museum features 150 new displays among a total of 600 exhibits on physics, electricity, life sciences, thermodynamics, weather and other subjects. Make reservations ahead of time for the Tactile Dome, a spectacular sensory experience.

👥 Fisherman's Wharf★★★

North of Bay St. between The Embarcadero & Van Ness Ave.
www.fishermanswharf.org.

The Wharf draws throngs to its colorful docks, carnival amusements and multitudinous seafood eateries. Although fishermen still bring in their catch during early-morning hours, tourism now dominates. Most popular of the diversions is **Pier 39★** 👥, a marketplace of shops, restaurants, aquarium and theater; it is famed for the pod of California sea lions that slumber off its west side (many of which disappeared in late 2009).

Pier 45 visitors may tour the World War II submarine **USS Pampanito★★** 👥 (☎415-775-1943), one of several ships at the **San Francisco Maritime National Historic Park** (Beach St. at Polk St.; ☎415-447-5000; www.nps.gov/safr). Other ships moored at the **Hyde Street Pier★★** 👥, include the three-

Exploratorium, with fog bridge

© Esther Kutnick/Exploratorium

masted, steel-hulled square-rigger, **Balclutha**★★, and the 1890 passenger and car ferry, **Eureka**★.

Don't miss the **Musée Mécanique** (Pier 45; ℘415-346-2000; www.museemecanique.org), with its collection of antique pinball games, fortune-telling machines, and other novelties of yesteryear.

Fisherman's Wharf, the terminus for **bay cruises**★ (Pier 39, ℘415-773-1188; www.blueandgoldfleet.com) and ferry excursions to Marin County (Pier 39 1/2), Alcatraz and Angel Island, lures shoppers in search of souvenirs. T-shirts and knickknacks dominate the shops of **Jefferson Street**, while a more eclectic array fills the refurbished warehouses at **The Cannery at Del Monte Square**★★ (2801 Leavenworth St.) and the old chocolate factory of **Ghirardelli Square**★▲▲ (Larkin, Beach, Polk & North Point Sts.).

Boudin at the Wharf (160 Jefferson St., ℘415-928-1849; www.boudinbakery.com) is a shrine to sourdough bread, including a restaurant, demonstration bakery and museum.

▲▲ Alcatraz★★★

Ferry departs from Pier 33.; 55 Francisco St.; ℘415-981-7625. www.alcatrazcruises.com.

Known as "The Rock," this barren 12-acre island began as an army fortress and prison in 1850. It became famous as a maximum-security penitentiary for "desperate and irredeemable criminals" after being transferred to the US Department of Justice in 1933. Among its notorious inmates were Al Capone, George "Machine Gun" Kelly and Robert Stroud, the "Birdman of Alcatraz." Worsening conditions prompted the government to close the prison.

Today the island is open to tourists who watch an **orientation video** and take a self-guided audio tour of the bleak **cellhouse**★★, the recreation yard, the cafeteria and control center. While most of the island's buildings have been reduced to ruins, the forbidding cellhouse is intact enough to provide a chilling glimpse into the bleak life of prisoners here. A 3hr evening tour offers a darker view of prison life. A haunting view of the city skyline contributes to the sense of isolation. Strong winds often buffet the island, and paths can be steep and rough. Wear protective clothing and comfortable shoes.

Palace of Fine Arts★★

Baker & Beach Sts.

The sole remaining structure from the celebrated Panama-Pacific International Exposition of 1915, the Palace was designed by Bernard Maybeck as a fanciful Roman ruin. The wood-and-plaster building was spared demolition by admiring citizens and rebuilt in concrete.

The Presidio★★

West of Lyon St. & south of the Golden Gate Bridge. ☎415-561-4323. www.nps.gov/prsf.

This 1,480-acre former military reservation is now part of the Golden Gate National Recreation Area. Established in 1776, it remained an army base through most of the US eras, though an angry shot was never fired. A brick barracks on the historic **Main Post★★** has been converted to a **visitor center** (Moraga Ave.). Built in 1861 to guard the Golden Gate from Confederate attack during the Civil War, **Fort Point National Historic Site★** (end of Marine Dr.; ☎415-556-1693; www.nps.gov/fopo) sits beneath the Golden Gate Bridge, work on which keeps the fort closed Mon–Thu.

♣♣ Golden Gate Bridge★★★

US-101 north of the Presidio. ☎415-921-5858. www.goldengatebridge.org.

As much a symbol of the US to the Pacific Rim as the Statue of Liberty is across the Atlantic, this graceful Art Deco suspension bridge spans the channel via twin 746ft towers and an intricate tracery of cables that support a 1.6mi roadway. Despite treacherous tidal surges, strong winds, bone-chilling fogs and the deaths of 10 workers in a scaffolding collapse, the bridge opened in 1937 to great fanfare. More than 112,000 vehicles cross it daily. Astounding **views★★** of the city, the Marin Headlands and the vertiginous 220ft drop to the surface of San Francisco Bay are reserved for pedestrians and bicyclists. For a stroll across the east sidewalk, wear a jacket to ward off stiff winds. Visiting the bridge at sunset is particularly spectacular.

ADDITIONAL SIGHTS
Legion of Honor★★

Legion of Honor Dr. & El Camino del Mar, Lincoln Park. ☎415-750-3600. legionofhonor.famsf.org/

This stately edifice (1924) is a replica of Paris' Palais de la Légion d'Honneur. A glass pyramid added to the outdoor Court of Honor in the 1990s serves as a skylight while paying homage to I.M. Pei's larger pyramid at the Louvre in Paris. Permanent holdings include Medieval stained glass, tapestries, Rodin sculptures, and paintings from the early Italian Renaissance through the French Impressionist period.

Golden Gate Park★★★

Stanyan St. to Ocean Beach, between Fulton St. & Lincoln Way. ☎415-831-2700. www.sfgov.org.

With 1,017 acres of meadows and gardens, the largest cultivated urban park in the US stretches 3mi from Haight-Ashbury to the Pacific. The enchantingly natural, yet entirely artificial, scenery of lakes and woods accomodates 27mi of footpaths and 7.5mi of horse trails. **Strybing Arboretum★★** (Martin Luther King Jr. Dr.; ☎415-661-1316; www.sfbotanicalgarden.org) covers 70 acres of rolling terrain with 6,000 species of plants from all over the world. The **Japanese Tea Garden★★ ♣♣** (west of Music Concourse; ☎415-752-4227; www.japaneseteagardensf.com) harbors a delightful maze of winding paths, ornamental koi ponds and bonsai.

California Academy of Sciences★★

55 Music Concourse Drive. ☎415-379-8000. www.calacademy.org.

The oldest scientific institution in the West, the venerable academy aims to explore, explain and celebrate the natural world. An aquarium, planetarium, natural history museum, and four-story rain forest are housed in a recently completed (2008) building with a living roof.

de Young Museum★★

50 Hagiwara Tea Garden Dr. ☎415-750-3600. deyoung.famsf.org/

Swiss architects Herzog & de Meuron designed this three-story structure (2005) of recycled redwood, eucalyptus and copper. The de Young is noted for its **American Collection**, including works by Bierstadt, Eakins, Sargent, Homer, Diebenkorn, O'Keeffe, Hopper and Wood. Other collections include African, Oceanic and pre-Columbian American art.

East Bay★

Directly across the bay from San Francisco, Oakland and Berkeley nestle on the flanks of steeply wooded hills. The San Francisco-Oakland Bay Bridge (1936) ushered in a new era for Oakland, and in 2013 its newly completed eastern span was unveiled. Berkeley is a dynamic city famous for its University of California branch, with an endless appetite for political activism, energetic intellectualism and cultural diversity.

- ◷ **Michelin Map:** p 175. Pacific Standard Time.
- 🛈 **Info:** ℘510-839-9000; www.oaklandcvb.com; ℘510-549-7040; www.visitberkeley.com.
- ◉ **Don't Miss:** UC Berkeley Oakland Museum.
- 👪 **Kids:** *USS Hornet;* The Campanile.

OAKLAND

The East Bay city boasts gleaming waterfront and civic center districts, an exceptional museum, and ambitiously restored mid-19C to 20C residential and commercial buildings. Completed in 2013, the 2.2mi self-anchored-suspension bridge—the new eastern span of the San Francisco-Oakland Bay Bridge—is the widest in the world and features a single 525ft tower.

👪 Oakland Museum of California★★

1000 Oak St., Oakland. ℘510-318-8400. www.museumca.org.

California's nature history is the focus of this sprawling museum located in the heart of Oakland adjacent to lovely **Lake Merritt**. The vast collection features the art spanning California's history, contemporary exhibits, and a newly-renovated Natural Sciences wing.

New Art and History Galleries, opened in 2010, present the multilayered story of California and its people in a dynamic way, with chronological and theme-based displays, oral histories and interactive digital exhibits. The Gallery of Natural Sciences focuses on major representative California habitats.

City Hall

1 Frank Ogawa Plaza. ♿ ℘510-444-2489. The present-day center of downtown Oakland was ordained by city planners to be the dynamic intersection where Broadway, San Pablo Avenue and 14th Street converged. Since the opening of City Center in the 1980s, the focus of business has shifted one block south. A vaulting symbol of the city's progressive spirit, when it was completed in 1914 (Palmer, Hornbostel & Jones), City Hall's 18-story shaft rises from a three-story Beaux Arts podium, capped by a Baroque-style clock tower.

Inside, an elegant staircase leads from the lobby to a third-floor council chamber.

Ronald Y. Dellums Federal Building

Between 12th, 14th, CLay & Jefferson Sts. This monumental, twin-towered structure is the largest building in Alameda County. Completed in 1993, the limestone-clad towers are linked by a 75ft glass rotunda that serves as a lobby. A marble-and-granite map of the Bay Area spreads across the rotunda floor.

Old Oakland★

Bounded by Broadway and 7th, 10th & Washington Sts. ℘510-745-7100. www.oldoakland.org.

This restored historic district formed the heart of downtown Oakland during the 1870s. Today it remains an extraordinary grouping of 19C commercial buildings. The shops, hotels and restaurants were built between 1868 and 1880 for the throngs of travelers passing through the Central Pacific passenger depot at 7th and Broadway (terminus of the first transcontinental railroad). The sturdy, two- and three-story structures were restored in the 1980s, now splendid showcases of Victorian craftsmanship. The **Housewives' Market** (9th & Washington Sts.; open year-round) shelters an ethnically diverse emporium of food counters, produce and fish markets, butcher shops and other stalls.

BERKELEY

A dynamic college town, Berkeley is remarkable for its academic prowess, political awareness and vibrant artistic and culinary communities.

University of California★

Roughly bounded by Bancroft Way, Oxford St. & Hearst Ave., Berkeley. ✆510-642-5215. www.berkeley.edu. John Galen Howard designed the 178-acre "Cal" campus (now 36,000 students strong) with Neoclassical buildings of white granite walls and red-tile roofs. At the north end of **Sproul Plaza★** (Bancroft Way & Telegraph Ave.), a lively gathering place, **Sather Gate** (1910) marks the campus' ceremonial entrance.

Designed to recall a Roman temple, **Doe Library★** ovesees part of the university's more than 10 million bound volumes. Adjacent **Bancroft**

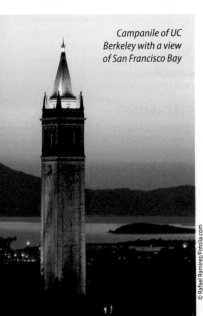

Campanile of UC Berkeley with a view of San Francisco Bay

© Rafael Ramirez/Fotolia.com

Library (✆510-642-3781; http://bancroft.berkeley.edu) stores rare books and the largest collection of Mark Twain's manuscripts and papers. The 307ft Sather Tower, known as **The Campanile★★** 👥 (✆510-642-5215; http://visitors.berkeley.edu/camp/), offers **views★★** of the surrounding campus from the eighth floor.

EXCURSIONS

👥 USS Hornet★★

◗ Pier 3, Alameda. ✆510-521-8448. www.uss-hornet.org.
This Essex-class aircraft carrier, 849ft-long, served in the Pacific, destroying enemy craft without once sustaining a hit. In 1969 the Hornet retrieved the *Apollo 11* after splashdown from the first manned lunar landing. **Hangar Deck** exhibits highlight this mission.

Blackhawk Auto Museum★★

◗ 3750 Blackhawk Plaza Circle, Danville. ✆925-736-2277.
www.blackhawkmuseum.org.
The collection includes rare Duesenbergs and European custom coaches.

Eugene O'Neill National Historic Site★★

◗ Shuttles from Railroad Ave. & Church St., Danville. ✆925-838-0249. www.nps.gove/euon. Visit by reservation only.
This modest **Tao House** was home to Nobel-prize-winning playwright **Eugene O'Neill** (1888-1953) from 1937 to 1944. He wrote five plays here, including *Long Day's Journey into Night*.

John Muir National Historic Site★

◗ Rte. 4, Martinez. ✆925-228-8860. www.nps.gov/jomu.
This Italianate frame residence was home to conservationist John Muir (1838-1914) from 1890 until his death. He wrote books on the second floor, his "scribble den." His writings led to the creation of Yosemite National Park.

Marin County ★★

Roughly divided by a mountainous spine into an eastern corridor of upscale suburbs and bayside towns, and a far larger western portion of dairy farms, rural villages and extensive parklands, Marin County is conveniently situated for day trips at the north end of the Golden Gate Bridge.

- **Michelin Map:** p 175. Pacific Standard Time.
- **Info:** ℰ415-925-2060 or www.visitmarin.org.
- **Don't Miss:** Muir Woods.
- **Timing:** Cross the Golden Gate northbound before noon; return in the late afternoon or late evening.

SIGHTS
Marin Headlands ★★

Alexander Ave. exit from northbound US-101; turn left, then right onto Barry Rd. ℰ415-331-1540. www.nps.gov/goga. These windswept coastal cliffs and hills anchor the northern end of the Golden Gate. Of strategic importance, the area was long owned by the US Army and thus was spared commercial development. Today, part of Golden Gate National Recreation Area, the headlands are reached by **Conzelman Road**, which offers **views ★★★** of San Francisco and the Golden Gate. The road passes abandoned military installations and ends near **Point Bonita Lighthouse ★**. The **Marin Headlands Visitor Center ★** mounts exhibits on the natural and human history of the headlands.

Sausalito ★

4mi north of San Francisco via US-101. ℰ415-331-7262. www.sausalito.org. Developed as a resort in the 1870s, Sausalito has winding streets, attractive hillside neighborhoods and fine views. Visitors arrive on weekends to window-shop and relax in restaurants along **Bridgeway Boulevard ★**, the waterfront commercial district. The docklands of **Marinship** (1mi north on Bridgeway), a shipbuilding center during World War II, now shelters a houseboat community. The **Bay Model Visitor Center ★** (2100 Bridgeway Blvd.; ℰ415-332-3871; www.spn.usace.army.mil/bmvc) holds a two-acre hydraulic scale model of the San Francisco Bay and Delta. The US Army Corps of Engineers uses it to study the effects of dredging, shoreline development and other ecological projects.

Muir Woods National Monument ★★★

Muir Woods Rd., 19mi north of San Francisco. ℰ415-388-2596. www.nps.gov/muwo. Picnicking, camping and pets are not permitted.

Named for conservationist John Muir, this tranquil, 560-acre plot of virgin forest is the largest grove of coast redwoods near San Francisco. The world's tallest trees, the coastal redwoods (Sequoia sempervirens) can attain heights equal to that of a 36-story building.

Saved from the ax first by the relative inaccessibility of the rugged canyon, the woods became a national monument in 1908 when William Kent donated 295 acres of Redwood Canyon to the federal government in 1907.

The park contains 6mi of trails that wind along Redwood and Fern Creeks, and up the slopes of Mount Tamalpais. The level, paved **Main Trail** (1mi) loops from the visitor center through giants more than 1,000 years old in **Bohemian Grove**, site of the park's tallest tree, measuring 253ft (tree is unmarked).

Mount Tamalpais State Park ★★

3801 Panoramic Hwy., 20mi north of San Francisco. ℰ415-388-2070. www.parks.ca.gov. The serpentine ascent of the 2,572ft east peak of Mount Tamalpais (tam-ul-PIE-us), or "Mount Tam," is rewarded with sweeping **views**★★ of San Francisco, its bay and the Pacific Ocean. Hundreds of miles of trails lace the mountain's flanks, leading to reservoirs, remote cascades and the Pacific shore.

♟♟ Point Reyes National Seashore★★

Bear Valley Rd. off Hwy. 1 at Olema, 40mi north of San Francisco. ℘415-464-5100. www.nps.gov/pore.

This 102sq-mi park embraces white sand beaches, rocky headlands, salt marshes, lush forests and abundant wildlife. The cape is located where the Pacific and North American Plates meet along an active San Andreas rift zone. The **Bear Valley Visitor Center**★ (west of Hwy. 1 intersection) contains exhibits on local ecology and history. Hikers on the adjacent **Earthquake Trail**★ (*.6mi*) can see a fence line shifted 16ft by the 1906 earthquake. A 22mi drive from the visitor center is **Point Reyes Lighthouse**★★, clinging to a rocky shelf on a 600ft precipice. It offers sweeping **views**★★ of the Farallon Islands and magnificent winter whale migrations.

Wine Country★★

Within a two-hour drive north from San Francisco, Napa and Sonoma Counties thrive on the abundant sunshine, occasional fogs and fertile soil that produce grapes for some of North America's finest wines. Visitors flock here, drawn by the temperate climate, acclaimed wineries, gourmet restaurants, and luxurious estate inns and villas, many with spas.

A BIT OF HISTORY

Hungarian immigrant Agoston Haraszthy (1812-69) planted the first commercial vineyards and founded the **Buena Vista Winery**★★ (18000 Old Winery Rd., Sonoma; ℘707-938-126; www.buenavistawinery.com) in 1857. Other vintners followed Haraszthy's lead, expanding the acreage under cultivation, experimenting with new varietals and production methods. The industry recovered from a plague of phylloxera that devastated vineyards in the late 19C, but a heavier blow fell when Prohibition (1919-33) curtailed production of alcoholic beverages. Not until the early 1970s did the wine industry recover completely.

- ⌚ **Michelin Map:** 493 A 8. Pacific Standard Time.
- ℹ **Info:** ℘707-522-5800; www.sonomacounty.com; ℘707-226-7459; www.napavalley.org.
- ◔ **Don't Miss:** St. Helena; Calistoga.
- ⌚ **Timing:** Driving Napa Valley's main road, Hwy. 29, often entails sitting in traffic May–November. The Silverado Trail, the road on the east side of the valley, may be less crowded.
- ♟♟ **Kids:** Charles M. Schulz Museum.

NAPA VALLEY★★

Cradled between two elongated mountain ranges, this world-renowned valley harbors some of California's most prestigious wineries, which cluster thickly along Route 29, and dot the more tranquil Silverado Trail to the east.

Napa

Rtes. 29 & 121. ℘707-226-7459.

A charming city of 78,000 on the banks of the river of the same name, Napa boasts scores of elegant Victorian residences from the late 19C, when riverboat captains and bankers helped turn the town into a regional center.

di Rosa Preserve★★

5200 Carneros Hwy. (Rte. 121). 🅿 ☏707-226-5991. www.dirosaart.org.
René di Rosa's personal store of late 20C Bay Area art comprises one of the largest collections of regional art in the US. Nearly 2,000 works by some 800 artists are presented on his 217-acre estate. Many are displayed on the walls of a c.1870 stone winery, surrounded by vineyards and 150yr-old olive trees; others are sculptures that line a lakeshore.

St. Helena★

Rte. 29. ☏707-963-4456.
www.sthelena.com.
A base for exploring Napa Valley, this town of 6,000 boasts fine restaurants along a picturesque main street. The **Robert Louis Stevenson Silverado Museum★** (1490 Library Ln.; ☏707-963-3757; www.silveradomuseum.org) is devoted to the life and works of the Scottish author whose Napa Valley honeymoon in 1880 is described in *The Silverado Squatters*.
The **Culinary Institute of America at Greystone** (2555 Main St.; ☏707-967-1100; www.ciachef.edu), West Coast branch of the premier culinary institution in the US, occupies a massive stone building (1889).

Calistoga★

Rtes. 29 & 128. ☏707-942-2803.
www.ci.calistoga.ca.us.
Founded in 1859, this resort town of 5,000 is famed for hot-spring spas. Tourists "take the waters," enjoy mud baths or ride hot-air balloons. Privately owned **Old Faithful Geyser★** (Tubbs Ln.; ☏707-942-6463; www.oldfaithfulgeyser.com) spews superheated water 60ft in the air about every 40min.

SONOMA VALLEY★★

Agriculturally and topographically more diverse than Napa Valley, Sonoma Valley is anchored by the historic town of Sonoma, and dominates southern Sonoma

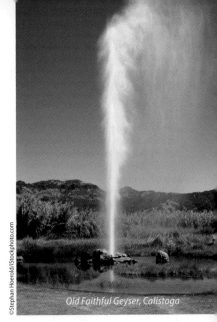

©Stephan Hoerold/iStockphoto.com

Old Faithful Geyser, Calistoga

county, where vineyards and wineries rub shoulders with orchards and fields.

Sonoma★★

Rte. 12. ☏707-996-1090.
www.sonomavalley.com.
The Wine Country's most historically significant town, now with 10,000 residents, Sonoma is built around the largest Mexican-era plaza in California. On June 14, 1846, the eight-acre public square was the scene of the **Bear Flag Revolt**, when American settlers raised a flag emblazoned with a bear, proclaiming California an independent republic; it became a US possession a month later. Around the plaza stands a venerable array of buildings under the auspices of **Sonoma State Historic Park★★** (☏707-935-6832; www.sonomaparks.org). They include **San Francisco Solano Mission★** (1823), California's northernmost and final mission; **Sonoma Barracks★**, (1841), built for Mexican troops; the **Toscano Hotel**, a general store in the 1850s; and the 1840 **Blue Wing Inn**, a two-story adobe saloon and hotel. Also managed by the park is **Lachryma Montis★** (north end of 3rd St. W.; ☏707-938-9559), retirement home of Mariano Vallejo (1807-90), founder of the pueblo of Sonoma, and now a state historic landmark.

Jack London State Historic Park★★

2400 London Ranch Rd., Glen Ellen. ✆707-938-5216. www.jacklondonpark.com.

Sprawling among peaceful hills, 80-acre Beauty Ranch was the Sonoma Valley home of writer Jack London (1876-1916) in his later life. London planned Wolf House, a four-story mansion of hewn red boulders and redwood logs; it burned just a few days before he and his wife, Charmian, were to move in. Charmian later resided at the **House of Happy Walls★**, now a museum furnished with memorabilia and furniture custom-made for Wolf House. A wooded trail leads to the Londons' hilltop graves and the impressive ruins of **Wolf House★**.

UPPER SONOMA–RUSSIAN RIVER REGION★

This region of northern Sonoma County comprises three principal wine areas: the Russian River Valley, following the meandering Russian River through Guerneville; the narrow 12mi-long Dry Creek Valley; and the pastoral Alexander Valley, hemmed by majestic mountain ridges.

Vineyard in Napa Valley

© Peter Wrenn/Michelin

Santa Rosa

US-101 & Rte. 12. ✆707-577-8674. www.visitsantarosa.com.

This city of 170,000 is the seat of Sonoma County. Its historic district dates from 1870, and today hosts an attractive group of offices, boutiques, restaurants and inns; a visitor center occupies the former train depot.

Horticulturalist Luther Burbank (1849-1926) lived most of his adult life in Santa Rosa; **Burbank Home & Gardens★** (Sonoma & Santa Rosa Aves.; ✆707-524-5445;www.lutherburbank.org) preserves his residence and workshop. Other native sons include collector Robert Ripley (1893-1949) of Believe It or Not! fame.

👪 Charles M. Schulz Museum and Research Center★

1 Snoopy Lane, off Steele & Hardies Lanes. ♿🅿✆707-579-4452. schulzmuseum.org.

For nearly 50 years, until his death in early 2000, Santa Rosa resident Charles Schulz illustrated the world's most popular comic strip, *Peanuts*. This museum celebrates his cartoon characters.

Healdsburg★

Founded in 1857 by Harmon Heald, a migrant farmer-turned-merchant, tranquil Healdsburg (HEELDS-burg) sits at the confluences of the Alexander, Dry Creek and Russin River valleys. Several excellent restaurants and inns make it an ideal starting point for forays into these areas. At the heart of this town is **Plaza Park** (Healdsburg Ave. and Plaza, Center & Matheson Sts.), scene of civic festivals and events.

Lake Sonoma★

11 mi north of Healdsburg by Dry Creek Rd. 🏊🚴🛶⛺🅿✆707-433-9483. www.parks.sonoma.net.

Nestled in Northern Sonoma County's coastal foothills, this elongated lake was created in 1983 when the Warm Springs Dam was constructed. It is now a popular recreation area.

North Coast★★

The first Europeans to colonize this coast were Russians who established themselves at Fort Ross, in 1812. The fort was abandoned in the 1830s. Gold was discovered on the Klamath and Smith Rivers in 1848; after the mid 19C, logging dominated the economy. Sawmills and port facilities sprang up in the coastal towns of Mendocino, Arcata, Eureka and Crescent City. Since 1918, acres of old-growth redwoods have been preserved in state and federal parks.

SIGHTS

Fort Ross State Historic Park★★

Hwy. 1, 97mi north of San Francisco. ☎707-847-3286. www.parks.ca.gov. Open Fri–Sun.

Built on a grassy promontory above a sheltered cove, Fort Ross reigned as Russia's easternmost outpost for nearly three decades after its founding in 1812. Abandoned in the mid-1830s and deeded to the State of California in 1906, it has been partially restored with an Orthodox **chapel, officials' quarters** and two **blockhouses**.

Mendocino★★

Hwy. 1, 72mi north of Fort Ross. ☎707-961-6300. www.mendocinocoast.com.
Seated on a foggy headland where the Big River meets the Pacific, this picturesque Victorian village appears little changed from its heyday as a lumber town in the late 19C. Favoring New England-style architecture, it has a "skyline" of clapboard houses with steep gabled roofs, wooden water towers, a Gothic Revival-style **Presbyterian church** (1868) and the false-fronted **Mendocino Hotel** (1878). Mendocino's prosperity declined in the 1920s; in the 1960s artists discovered the idyllic setting. Hollywood directors have shot numerous films here.

Enveloping the town, **Mendocino Headlands State Park★★** (☎707-937-

- ᠖ **Michelin Map:** 493 A 6, 7, 8. Pacific Standard Time.
- ᠍ **Info:** ☎800-346-3482; www.redwoods.info; www.northcoastca.com.
- ᗑ **Location:** From the Golden Gate, **Hwy. 1★★** follows the coast north for 205mi, mostly via well-paved, two-lane roads. In Humboldt County it meets US-101, known as the Redwood Highway.
- ☺ **Don't Miss:** Humboldt Redwoods State Park.
- ᗒ **Timing:** It takes 7hrs to drive straight through to Eureka from San Francisco.
- ᨀ **Kids:** The drive-through tree along US 101.

Fort Ross State Historic Park
© John Anderson/MICHELIN

5804; www.parks.ca.gov) preserves marvelous **views★★** of fissure-riddled rocks and sea caves. Mendocino County is noted for its wine production and microbreweries.

Humboldt Redwoods State Park★★

South entrance on US-101, 6mi north of Garberville. ☎707-946-1811. Humboldtredwoods.org.
Established along the Eel River in 1921, this 80sq mi park contains a spectacu-

lar reserve of coast redwoods easily seen along the 29mi **Avenue of the Giants★★★**, which runs parallel to US-101. A nature trail through **Founder's Grove★★** begins at the Founder's Tree, once considered the world's tallest (364ft before the top 17ft broke off). The world's largest remaining virgin stand of redwoods is the 16sq mi **Rockefeller Forest★★★**. Hiking trails probe the sublime depths of these venerable groves 🚶.

Eureka★

US-101. ℘707-443-5097.
www.ci.eureka.ca.gov
The largest Pacific coastal community in the US north of San Francisco, this town of 25,000 grew as a shipping hub for minerals and lumber in the mid to late 19C. Buildings in its 10-block waterfront **historic district** (2nd & 3rd Sts. between E & M Sts.) include the ornate Victorian **Carson Mansion★★** (2nd & M Sts.), a three-story redwood mansion built in 1886 for a lumber magnate.

Redwood National and State Parks★★

Mainly along US-101 between Orick & Crescent City. ℘707-464-6101.
www.nps.gov/redw.
With majestic redwood groves and 33mi of beaches, this 165sq-mi expanse joins three venerable state parks—**Prairie Creek Redwoods** (℘707-465-7347), **Del Norte Coast Redwoods** (℘707-465-2146) and **Jedediah Smith Redwoods** (℘707-458-3018)—within the jurisdiction of Redwood National Park.

The parks are cooperatively managed and casually linked by a network of highways and roads, few of them designed for sightseeing. There are two visitor centers: the **Redwood Information Center** (US-101, 1mi south of Orick; ℘707-464-6101) and the **Park Headquarters** (1111 2nd St., Crescent City; ℘707-464-6101).

Highlights include the **Lady Bird Johnson Grove★★** and **Tall Trees Grove★**, both in the Redwood Creek watershed. The latter contains a 367.8ft-high **tree★**, known as the Libbey Tree. Discovered by a National Geographic Society scientist in 1963, it was at that time believed to be the world's tallest, although taller trees have been found since.

The Newton B. Drury Scenic Parkway passes through **Prairie Creek Meadows** with its herds of grazing Roosevelt elk, and **Fern Canyon★**, a narrow ravine walled with lush ferns.

South Bay★

San Jose, California's third-largest city and center of the US high-tech industry, sprawls around the southern end of San Francisco Bay. Founded as a farming pueblo in 1777, the city was state capital for several months in 1849.
Electronics factories began to replace orchards in the mid 20C. By the late 1960s, San Jose began to define itself as the "capital of Silicon Valley." Such computer giants as IBM, Apple and Hewlett Packard developed facilities in the city and its environs.

- **Michelin Map:** p175. Pacific Standard Time.
- **Info:** ℘408-295-9600; www.sanjose.org.
- **Don't Miss:** Filoli.
- **Kids:** Tech Museum.

SIGHTS
Filoli★★

86 Cañada Rd., Woodside, 13mi north of Palo Alto. ℘650-364-8300.
www.filoli.org.
This 700-acre estate was built in 1916 for Empire Mine owner William Bourne

(1857-1936). The modified Georgian Revival **mansion★★**, designed by Willis Polk, is furnished with 17-18C Irish and English furniture. Bruce Porter and Isabella Wood designed the 16-acre **gardens★★★** in Italian and French style.

Stanford University★★

Main Quadrangle on Serra St., Palo Alto. &650-723-2300. www.stanford.edu.

Railroad magnate Leland Stanford (1824-93) and his wife, Jane, established this private institution in memory of their late son. Now it is a leading academic and research center (nearly 16,000 students). The campus —a creation of architect Charles Allerton Coolidge and landscape architect Frederick Law Olmsted—is noted for Romanesque buildings shaded by bay, eucalyptus and palm trees.

The historic heart of campus is the **Main Quadrangle★**, a cloistered courtyard bordered by colonnaded buildings. Its **Memorial Church★★**, built in 1903 by Jane Stanford, is famed for its Byzantine-style mosaics, stained glass and 7,777-pipe organ.

Hoover Tower★ (&650-723-2053), a 285ft landmark campanile with a 35-bell carillon, offers views over campus from its observation deck.

Iris & B. Gerald Cantor Center for Visual Arts★ (Lomita Dr. & Museum Way; &650-723-4177; http://museum.stanford.edu) houses 20,000 pieces of ancient to contemporary sculpture, paintings and crafts. The adjacent **Rodin Sculpture Garden★** contains 20 large-scale bronze casts by sculptor Auguste Rodin.

Intel Museum★★

2200 Mission College Blvd., Santa Clara. &408-765-5050. www.intel.com/museum.

As the world's largest semiconductor company, the Intel Corporation invented (in 1968) the technology that put computer memory on tiny silicon chips.

Exhibits here in the company headquarters walk visitors through the principles of transistor technology.

🏛👤 The Tech Museum of Innovation★★

201 S. Market St., San Jose. &408-294-8324. www.thetech.org.

This interactive exhibition of cutting-edge technology is housed in a domed, mango-colored building. The Tech entertains all ages, but mainly courts young people with playful exhibits in such fields as space exploration, microelectronics and robotics.

San Jose Museum of Art★

110 S. Market St., San Jose. &408-271-6840. www.sjmusart.org.

This facility concentrates on art of the 20C and 21C, displaying works by emerging West Coast artists and internationally celebrated figures such as Ed Ruscha, Joan Brown and Tino Rodriguez. Highlights include three unusual chandeliers by Dale Chihuly.

Rosicrucian Egyptian Museum★

1660 Park Ave., San Jose. &408-947-3636. www.egyptianmuseum.org.

Set amid a complex of Egyptian and Moorish-style buildings in Rosicrucian Park, this treasury is modeled after the Temple of Amon at Karnak. The 5,000 pieces include pottery, jewelry, glass, mummies, sarcophagi, painted coffins and a full-scale reproduction of a **Middle Kingdom Rock Tomb★**.

🏛👤 Winchester Mystery House

525 S. Winchester Blvd., San Jose. &408-247-2101. www.winchestermysteryhouse.com.

This rambling, 160-room mansion is the legacy of Winchester heir Sarah Winchester. Hoping to appease ghosts of people killed with Winchester rifles, she compulsively added rooms, secret passages, and doors and stairways that go nowhere. The immense house has 47 fireplaces and is known for its collection of Tiffany and European **art glass**.

The **Historic Firearms Museum** on the grounds displays an international assemblage of pistols and rifles.

Monterey and Big Sur★★★

At the southern end of Monterey Bay, 115 south of San Francisco, California's longtime Spanish-Mexican capital of Monterey retains its historic adobe charm. A few miles south lies the picturesque village of Carmel. The spectacular Big Sur coastline weaves its magic with silent redwood canyons and along granite ridges that plunge steeply into the Pacific surf.

- ♿ **Michelin Map:** 493 A 9. Pacific Standard Time.
- 🛈 **Info:** ☎831-657-6400; www.seemonterey.com.
- ◗ **Location:** Monterey is 115mi south of San Francisco; Big Sur begins south of Carmel and runs roughly 90mi south.
- ◉ **Don't Miss:** Hearst Castle.
- ◷ **Timing:** Reserve tickets for Hearst Castle weeks in advance. Monterey is worth a full day; driving to San Luis Obispo takes 3–4hrs.
- 👥 **Kids:** Monterey Bay Aquarium.

A BIT OF HISTORY

Sebastián Vizcaíno sailed into Monterey Bay in 1602, his enthusiastic response to the harbor enhanced by the lack of anchorages along the Big Sur coastline. Not until 1770 did Spain found the presidio, chapel and pueblo that became its California capital. Padre Junípero Serra subsequently moved his mission a few miles south to Carmel, away from the influence of Monterey.

On July 7, 1846, a few weeks after the Bear Flag Revolt in Sonoma, the US officially seized California at Monterey. But after Sierra gold was discovered in 1848, Monterey's political and economic preeminence gave way to San Francisco. In the 1880s, Chinese and Italian fishermen discovered the wealth of Monterey Bay and built a port and cannery town of national significance, until harvests were depleted in the 1950s.

In its heyday, industry was focused at Cannery Row, a raucous industrial strip described by author John Steinbeck as "a poem, a stink, a grating noise."

Tourism is now the mainstay of the economy of Monterey, a city of 29,000; Cannery Row has been reborn with shops, restaurants and an aquarium. The bay is *the* place on the West Coast to see playful sea otters in the wild.

Carmel, which developed as an artists' community near the old mission in the early 20C, is a genteel resort town. It is a perfect complement to historic Monterey and rugged Big Sur, whose primeval beauties extend 90mi down the California coast to the imposing hilltop estate known as Hearst Castle.

SIGHTS

Monterey State Historic Park★★

Headquarters at Pacific House, Custom House Plaza. ☎831-649-7118. www.parks.ca.gov.

Monterey's compact central district is ideally explored on the **Path of History Walking Tour★**, a 2mi route blazed by bronze discs embedded in sidewalks, and described in maps and pamphlets available at an information center at **Pacific House**. This two-story adobe, built in 1847 to house US troops, also contains a history museum.

Fisherman's Wharf is lined with shops and cafes. Adjacent is broad **Custom House Plaza★★**. At Stanton Center, a theater presents a film outlining Monterey history. The **Maritime Museum of Monterey★** (☎831-372-2608; museumofmonterey.org) exhibits model ships, navigational devices and nautical paraphernalia from 300 years of seafaring. The adobe **Custom House★** served port authorities from 1827 to 1867.

The two-story **Larkin House★★** (Calle Principal & Pearl St.), built in 1834, melded New England architecture— high ceilings, a hipped roof and central hallway—with the local adobe motif, giving rise to the Monterey Colonial style of architecture. The **Cooper-Molera Complex★★** (Pearl St. at Munras Ave. & Polk St.) features a large home whose separate wings—an adobe section and a two-story Victorian—contrast Hispanic and Anglo cultures.

Monterey Bay Aquarium★★

West end of Cannery Row. ℘831-648-4800. www.montereybayaquarium.org.
Built out over the water in a revamped cannery building, this modern, two-level aquarium presents the rich marine life of Monterey Bay – focal point of the **Monterey Bay National Marine Sanctuary**, North America's largest offshore natural preserve. With more than 35,000 live animals and plants of over 550 species, the aquarium represents the full range of Monterey Bay habitats, from coastal wetlands and tide pools to deep sea.

The west wing houses the touch pools, playful sea otters and a 28ft-high **kelp forest★** tank of the Ocean's Edge gallery. It also contains the Monterey Bay Habitats, the last of which focuses on animals from the deep reefs, the sandy seafloor, the shale reefs and the wharf. Habitats in the east wing showcase dwellers of the open ocean in the **Open Sea★** gallery, highlighted by an enormous **ocean tank★★**, where sea turtles, sharks, barracudas and other species swim.

17-Mile Drive★★

Access via the Carmel Gate (N. San Antonio Ave. off Ocean Ave.) or the Pacific Grove Gate (Sunset Dr., Pacific Grove). Entry fee at gatehouse. ℘831-624-6669.
Celebrated for exquisite coastline views, this private toll road winds through exclusive estates and the 8,000-acre Del Monte Forest. Turnouts offer spectacular vistas, including **Lone Cypress**, a classic landmark of the Monterey Peninsula. Golfers from around the world play the renowned links at Pebble Beach and Spyglass Hill.

Carmel★★

Hwy. 1, 5mi south of Monterey. ℘831-624-2522. www.carmelcalifornia.org.
A delightful square mile of carefully tended cottages beneath a canopy of pine, oak and cypress, Carmel began to attract artists and writers in the very early 20C. While strict ordinances preserve residential charm, a painstakingly quaint commercial district of upscale boutiques, galleries, inns and restaurants nestles around Ocean, 6th and 7th Avenues (between Junipero Ave. & Monte Verde St.). Steep Ocean Avenue meets the turquoise waters of Carmel Bay at **Carmel City Beach★★**, a wide sweep of white sand bounded on the south by rocky Point Lobos and on the north by the clifftop greens of the Pebble Beach Golf Club.

San Carlos Borromeo de Carmelo Mission★★★

Rio Rd. & Lasuen Dr. ℘831-624-1271. www.carmelmission.org.
Headquarters of the mission chain in its expansive early years, the Carmel Mission resonates with the vision of Padre Junípero Serra, whose remains are interred in the sanctuary. Founded in 1771 when Serra moved his neophytes from Monterey, this mission prospered under his care and that of his successor, Padre Fermín Lasuén, who rebuilt the original adobe chapel with sandstone in 1782. Restored in 1931, the chapel preserves original 18C paintings and a statue of the Virgin Our Lady of Bethlehem that Serra brought from Mexico in 1769.

Tor House★★

Ocean View Ave. off Scenic Rd., ℘831-624-1813. www.torhouse.org.
Overlooking Carmel Bay, this enchanting stone complex embodies the spirit of its builder, poet Robinson Jeffers (1887-1962), who settled in Carmel in 1914. Guided tours offer a peek at the rooms, including the whimsical Hawk Tower, with Jeffers' desk and chair.

Point Lobos State Reserve★★

Hwy. 1, 3.5mi south of Carmel. ☎831-624-4909. www.pointlobos.org

This small but dramatic peninsula defines the southern end of Carmel Bay. Early Spanish explorers named the site *Punta de Los Lobos Marinos* ("point of the sea wolves") because of the barking of resident sea lions. Deeded to the state in 1933, the site comprises 1,250 acres including 750 submerged acres of the first US underwater reserve.

Big Sur★★★

Hwy. 1 between Carmel and San Simeon. ☎831-667-2100. www.bigsurcalifornia.org.

This rugged coastline, extending 90mi south from Carmel, is celebrated for its wild beauty. A precipitous coastal wall, plunging 4,000ft to the sea, thwarted settlement by the Spanish, who called it *El Pais Grande del Sur* : "the Big Country to the South." Mid-19C homesteaders trickled into narrow valleys to ranch and log redwoods. Completion of the highway in 1937 opened the area to visitors. Traveling south from Carmel, the concrete-arch **Bixby Creek Bridge**, built in 1932, is one of the 10 highest single-span bridges in the world. **Point Sur State Historic Park** preserves an 1889 stone lighthouse built 272ft above the surf on a volcanic rock connected to the mainland by a sandbar. Near the **village of Big Sur** (23mi south of Carmel), in the forested Big Sur River valley, **Andrew Molera State Park** and **Pfeiffer Big Sur State Park★** offer coastal vistas and access. Four miles south, the venerable **Nepenthe★** bar and restaurant boasts sweeping **views★★★** from its cliffside terraces 800ft above the ocean.

Hearst Castle★★★

Rte. 1, 98mi south of Monterey. Visit by reservation only. ☎800-444-4445. www.hearstcastle.org.

Overlooking the Pacific Ocean from atop a Santa Lucia Mountain crest, this 127-acre estate and the opulent mansion crowning it embody the flamboyance of William Randolph Hearst. It was eclectically designed and lavishly embellished with the newsman's world-class collection of Mediterranean art. Hearst's father, George, purchased this ranch in 1865. In 1919, William hired architect Julia Morgan to create a "bungalow" that over 28 years grew from a modest residence to "The Enchanted Hill." Morgan designed a Mediterranean Revival-style main house, **Casa Grande**, and three guest houses. From twin Spanish Colonial towers with arabesque grillwork and Belgian carillon bells, to Etruscan colonnades that complement the Greco-Roman temple facade of the **Neptune Pool★**, and gold-inlaid Venetian glass tiles of the indoor **Roman Pool★**, the design emerged as a mélange that defies categorization. The 65,000sq-ft main house contains 115 rooms, including 38 bedrooms, 41 bathrooms, two libraries, a billiards room, a beauty salon and a theater. All feature Hearst's art holdings, including silver, 16C tapestries, terra-cotta sculpture and ancient Greek vases.

EXCURSIONS

National Steinbeck Center★★

◗ 1 S Main St., Salinas, 17mi east of Monterey. ☎831-796-3833 www.steinbeck.org.

Exhibits, written excerpts and film clips depict themes and settings of John Steinbeck's writings. Born in Salinas, **John Steinbeck** (1902-68) grew up amid the communities and characters that animate his stories and novels, including *Tortilla Flat* (1935), *The Grapes of Wrath* (1939), *Cannery Row* (1945) and *East of Eden* (1952). He won Pulitzer and Nobel prizes for his sympathetic depiction of local brothels, labor organizers and ne'er-do-wells.

Pinnacles National Monument★

◗ Rte. 146, 22mi south of Salinas. ☎831-389-4485. www.nps.gov/pinn.

The ridgetop rock formations of this 37sq mi park are the remnants of a volcano formed 23 million years ago. **Juniper Canyon Trail★** (*2.4mi round-trip*) climbs steeply into the Pinnacles.

Sierra Nevada

The mountains along California's eastern and northern boundaries historically have been both barriers and magnets. The bulwark of the Sierra Nevada marches 400mi from Tehachapi Pass, southeast of Bakersfield, to the Cascade Range near Lassen Peak, walling off the fertile Central Valley from the Great Basin. From Lassen north to Mt. Shasta and beyond, the generally lower, though similarly rugged, the Cascade Range is punctuated with tall, isolated volcanic peaks. It was the gold in these mountains that inspired the massive influx of prospectors to California during the Gold Rush of 1849.

Highlights

1   A **Lake Tahoe** driving tour (p202)

2   Time traveling to mining **ghost towns** and **Old Sacramento** (p205)

3   Majestic **sequoias** (p207)

4   Climbing **Half Dome** (p210)

5   Bubbling mudpots in **Lassen Volcanic National Park** (p215)

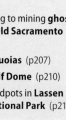

Nature Untamed

Mining heritage remains strong in the mountains and foothills, but the Sierra now is better known for its recreational opportunities. Some of the nation's largest and most sublime national parks, wilderness areas and outdoor resorts abound throughout these ranges, preserving landscapes of extraordinary character, where evidence of human life is rare. Here are the giant forests of Sequoia National Park, the deep canyons and jagged peaks of Kings Canyon, the polished walls and glistening waterfalls of Yosemite. Here, too, are Mt. Shasta's soaring white dome and the deep blue waters of Lake Tahoe, as well as remnants of a recent volcanic past that still smolder at Lassen Peak. West of the Sierra sprawls the Central Valley, created by silt carried in rivers from the mountains over the millennia.

The state capital of Sacramento is here. To the east, in the rain shadow of the great ranges, lies a high desert of stark mountains and deep valleys. The Great Basin, highly mineralized with ores that spawned their own repeated gold and silver rushes, has left a colorful legacy that epitomizes Nevada.

ADDRESSES

☎ STAY

$$$$$ The Ahwahnee Hotel – Yosemite Village, Yosemite National Park. ℘801-559-4884. www.yosemitepark.com. 123 rooms. This towering timber-and-stone hotel has hosted famous guests from Winston Churchill to Charlie Chaplin since opening in 1927 and still maintains its historic charm while the rooms were renovated in 2011 to more modern standards. Nature lovers sit around a granite fireplace and conjure the spirit of John Muir. American cuisine is served at the **Ahwahnee Dining Room** (**$$$**). The **Yosemite Lodge** (**$$$**), **Curry Village** (**$$**), the **Wawona Hotel** (**$$$**) and the **High Sierra Camps** (**$**) provide a range of in-park lodging options.

$$$$ Wuksachi Village and Lodge – Rte. 198, Sequoia National Park. ℘559-565-4070. www.visitsequoia.com. 102 rooms. At the heart of a park village near Giant Forest, Wuksachi Lodge has its rooms in three beautiful cedar-and-stone buildings. Native granite, oak and hickory furnishings blend with the great

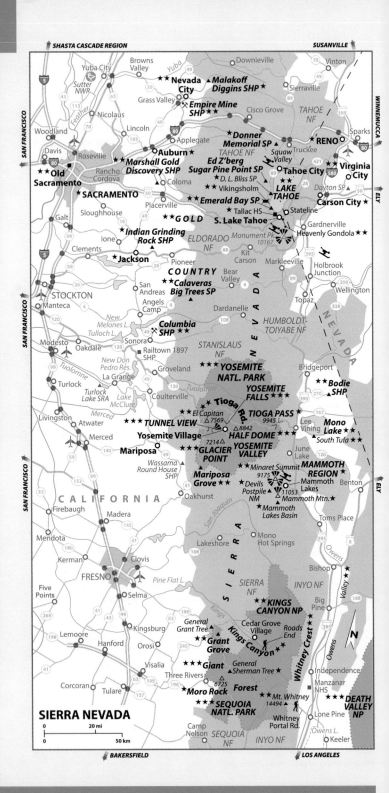

WINNEMUCCA

Browns Valley
Downieville
Vinton
Yuba City
Sierraville
★★ Nevada ★ Malakoff
City ★ Diggins SHP ★
Grass Valley
Cisco Grove
TAHOE NF
★★ Empire Mine
SHP ★★
Nicolaus
Lincoln
Applegate
★★ Donner
Memorial SP ★
TAHOE NF
Squaw Valley
RENO
Sparks
Truckee
Woodland
★ Auburn ★
Rancho Cordova
Roseville
★★ Marshall Gold
Discovery SHP ★
Davis
★ Old
Sacramento
Coloma
★ SACRAMENTO
Placerville
Galt
★★ GOLD
Sloughhouse
★ Indian Grinding
Rock SHP
ELDORADO NF
Monument Pk
10167
Clements
Ione
Pioneer
★ Jackson
COUNTRY
★★ Calaveras
Big Trees SP
San Andreas
STOCKTON
Angels Camp
Dardanelle
★ Columbia
SHP ★★
Sonora
STANISLAUS NF
Railtown 1897 SHP
Groveland
★★★ YOSEMITE
NATL. PARK
YOSEMITE
FALLS ★★★
★★ Tioga
★★★ TUNNEL VIEW
El Capitan
7569
HALF DOME ★★★
Yosemite Village
7214
YOSEMITE
VALLEY
★★★ GLACIER
POINT
★★ Mariposa
Grove ★★
Mariposa
Wassama
Round House
SHP
Oakhurst
CALIFORNIA
Firebaugh
Madera
Mendota
Clovis
FRESNO
Five Points
Selma
SIERRA
Kingsburg
Orosi
General
Grant Tree
★★ Grant
Grove
Visalia
General
★ Sherman Tree ★
Three Rivers
6725
★ Moro Rock
★★★ SEQUOIA
NATL. PARK
SIERRA NEVADA
Camp Nelson
SEQUOIA NF

Emerald Bay, Lake Tahoe

trees outside. The **Peaks** restaurant ($$$) offers Italian and American cuisines.

$$$ The Shore House – 7170 North Lake Blvd., Tahoe Vista. ☏530-546-7270. www.shorehouselaketahoe.com. 9 rooms. Each room at this bed-and-breakfast has a private entrance that overlooks private gardens and a sandy beach on Lake Tahoe's north shore. The Moon Room has a Tahoe sky painted on the ceiling; the Tree House is framed by ponderosa pines.

$$ Riverboat Delta King – 1000 Front St., Sacramento. ☏916-444-5464. www.deltaking.com. 44 rooms. During Prohibition, this "floating pleasure palace" ran from Sacramento to San Francisco. Today the red paddlewheeler remains in one place, on the Sacramento River in Old Town. Guests stroll on the promenade deck, listen to Dixieland jazz and dine in the **Pilothouse Restaurant ($$)**. Cabins are cozy, with solid oak and polished brass.

♈/ EAT

$$$$ Erna's Elderberry House – Rte. 41, Oakhurst. ☏559-683-6800. www.elderberryhouse.com. Dinner and Sun brunch only. **Contemporary**. Just 20min south of Yosemite Park, this country manor offers three French-provincial dining rooms and Sierra views. Prix-fixe menus of simple, natural ingredients change daily, perhaps including Savoy spinach soup with crisp prosciutto, enoki and preserved lemon salad , Kern Farm autumn lettuces with strawberry cloud and poppy yogurt, or beer braised boneless short rib in marrow crust. Elderberry bushes surround the estate, which embraces a luxurious inn, the **Château du Sureau ($$$$$)**.

$$ Louis' Basque Corner – 301 E. Fourth St., Reno. ☏775-323-7203. www.louisbasquecorner.com. **Basque**. Many Basques came to the US from their European homeland in the late 19C, lodging in family boardinghouses. The tradition lives on at Louis', where unacquainted diners share large tables. All-inclusive meals include soup, salad, beans, potatoes and hearty entrées like chicken Basquaise or oxtails bourguignon.

$$$ Sunnyside Restaurant – 1850 W. Lake Blvd., Tahoe City. ☏530-583-7200. www.sunnysidetahoe.com. **American**. Diners moor their boats at the Sunnyside Marina on Lake Tahoe before dining oon fine steakhouse fare, from ribeye with smoked tomato butter or alderwood smoked trout , to Sunnyside's special crispy zucchini sticks. Fresh seafood and salads are also on the menu. The building doubles as a comfortable mountain lodge, with views of the surrounding High Sierra.

$ Peg's Glorified Ham 'n' Eggs – 420 S. Sierra St., Reno. ☏775-329-2600. http://eatatpegs.com. Breakfast and lunch only. **American**. Lines usually stretch down the sidewalk at this beloved family-owned institution, where bustling servers plop down enormous plates of New York steak and eggs smothered in onions and mushrooms, giant crab cake Caesar salads, juicy jalapeno Jack burgers, and overstuffed salmon tacos. (Also at 6300 Mae Anne Ave., Reno; ☏775-624-2700.)

Lake Tahoe★★

Encircled by a ring of lofty ridges and peaks, this deep blue lake straddles the California–Nevada border at an elevation of 6,225ft. Measuring 22mi long and 12mi wide, it is the most popular resort area in the Sierra, despite its cold waters (68˚F in summer).

- **Michelin Map:** Opposite. Pacific Standard Time.
- **Info:** ✆775-588-5900; www.bluelaketahoe.com.
- **Location:** Lake Tahoe straddles two states; the California-Nevada line bisects the lake.
- **Don't Miss:** Squaw Valley Cable Car.

A BIT OF HISTORY

The lake was formed in a basin created by tectonic faulting 24 million years ago. Later, the Washoe people summered here. It was rapidly claimed and developed after the 1859 discovery of the Comstock Lode, when its broad surface was used by steamboats that transported timber to shore up the mines. Subsequent developers recognized the lake's rare beauty, staking shoreline claims for early resorts and summerhouses. The federal government set aside most of the hinterlands as national forest in the late 19C; some lakeside properties became California state parks in the 20C. But most of the lakefront remains privately owned.

🚗 DRIVING TOUR

▶ Drive north on Rte. 89 from South Lake Tahoe. 👣See map opposite.

South Lake Tahoe

A small city of motels, shops and restaurants serves vacationers who flock for summer recreation, winter skiing and casino entertainment in the adjacent Nevada community of Stateline. Highways encircle the lake, linking ski resorts and smaller, rustic settlements geared for summer visits. Excellent hiking includes the 150mi **Tahoe Rim Trail**, encircling the lake near the ridgeline. The cable car at **Squaw Valley** (✆530-583-6985; www.squaw.com) offers splendid views from the 8,200ft-elevation sundeck at **High Camp★**. Skiing and snowboarding provide winter sport at Squaw Valley; an ice-skating rink, swimming pool, restaurants and spa are open year-round. A splendid view of Lake Tahoe rewards riders who ascend the 10,167ft Monument Peak on the **Heavenly Gondola★★** (✆530-586-7000; www.skiheavenly.com).

North of South Lake Tahoe, Rte. 89 crosses a high narrow ridge. Inspiration Viewpoint offers a striking **view★** of Emerald Bay.

Emerald Bay State Park★★

Emerald Bay Rd. (Rte. 89), 8mi northwest of South Lake Tahoe CA. △ ✆530-541-3030. www.parks.ca.gov.

Embracing a glacier-carved fjord, this park provides majestic alpine views, hiking trails and guided tours of a strikingly eccentric mansion, **Vikingsholm★★** (1929; www.vikingsholm.org), designed to resemble an AD 9C Nordic castle.

The 5.3mi Rubicon Trail leads to **Eagle Falls** and **D.L. Bliss State Park★**.

Ed Z'berg-Sugar Pine Point State Park★

10mi south of Tahoe City. ✆530-525-7982. www.parks.ca.gov.

Encompassing part of the General Creek watershed west of the lake, this park houses the **Hellman-Ehrman Mansion★** (1903), built for San Francisco financier Isaias W. Hellman and open for guided tours.

Tahoe City

Visitor center at 560 N. Lake Tahoe Blvd. One of the oldest settlements on the lake, this town serves as a northern gateway to the area's many attractions.

▶ Continue on Rte. 89 past junction of Rtes. 89 and 28.

Donner Memorial State Park★

Off I-80 at Rte. 89, 2.3mi west of downtown Truckee CA.
⛺ 🅿 ✆530-582-7892.
www.parks.ca.gov.
Commemorating the Donner Party disaster of 1846-47, the centerpiece of this ironically peaceful park on Donner Lake is a bronze statue of a family in the desperate straits of starvation.
Caught by early snows, while attempting to cross the 7,239ft Donner Pass, the party of 87 emigrants erected makeshift cabins and settled in to await rescue as a smaller party set out for help. Before their rescuers returned in mid-February, the survivors were forced to cannibalize their dead; only 47 survived the ordeal. Their story is related in exhibits and film at the park's **Emigrant Trail Museum★★**.

▶ Return to the junction of Rtes. 89 and 28. Drive north on Rte. 28.

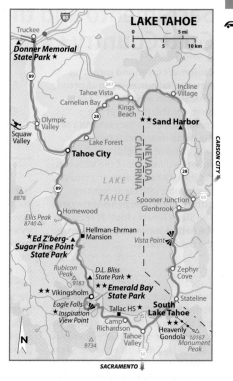

Sand Harbor★★

3mi south of Incline Village on Rte. 28
Picnic facilities, rounded granite outcrops and a sandy beach fringe a sheltered cove where the shallow water tends to be warmer than in other parts of the lake. South at Vista Point, **views★** extend across the lake to the western side.

Lake Tahoe Trails

The Taylor Creek Visitor Center (3mi north of South Lake Tahoe on the lake side of Hwy 89; ⛺♿🅿 ✆530-543-2674; www.fs.fed.us/r5/ltbmu; May–Oct) is the starting point for four self-guided trails. Several trails approach the lakeshore, though only the hardiest swimmers brave its frigid waters. The Rainbow Trail (.5mi) follows the fringe of an aspen-ringed meadow to the **Stream Profile Center★**, where subterranean plate-glass windows provide a fish's-eye view of life in a Sierra brook. This walk is most sensational in October, when spawning kokanee salmon fill Taylor Creek with thousands of flaming-red fish.

The trail to **Tallac Historic Site★** (✆530-541-5227; www.tahoeheritage.org/tallac-historic-site) leads to the remains of a fashionable 19C resort hotel and casino built by mining speculator Lucky Baldwin. Other private estates farther east from Baldwin's are now likewise owned by the Forest Service, which maintains the **Pope-Tevis Estate** (1899) and **Valhalla** mansion (1924), and opens the **Baldwin-McGonagle House★** (1921) in summer as a museum.

Sacramento and the Gold Country★★

California's green and sprawling state capital possesses an appealing all-American gentility and a rich heritage. This flat site at the confluence of the Sacramento and American rivers was urbanized with a grid of straight, tree-lined streets reminiscent of the Midwest. Yet the city has an aura of a modern metropolis, with contemporary attractions to complement the past. The Sierra Nevada foothill region to the east of Sacramento is known as the Gold Country.

- ◔ **Michelin Map:** p 200. Pacific Standard Time.
- **Info:** ℘916-808-7777; www.discovergold.org.
- **Don't Miss:** Calaveras Big Trees State Park.
- **Kids:** Columbia State Park.

A BIT OF HISTORY

The city was founded during the Gold Rush at the confluence of the American and Sacramento Rivers, a port of disembarkation for steamboat passengers. The site lay 2mi west of Sutter's Fort, a spacious rancho founded on a Mexican land grant by Swiss adventurer **John Sutter** in 1839. Ironically, the stampede sparked by his own workman's discovery of gold ultimately cost Sutter both his property and his mercantile advantages. Despite terrible floods and fires, Sacramento's waterfront commercial district thrived as a vital link between trans-Sierra roads and Sacramento River shipping. A protective levee and new brick buildings brought prosperity and stability, prompting California to relocate its capital here in 1854. The city's destiny as a transportation hub was boosted when the Central Pacific line was leveraged eastward across the Sierra Nevada, completing the first transcontinental rail link in 1869.

Today, sitting astride two major interstate highways, Sacramento, with a population of 467,000, remains a primary agricultural distribution center in addition to its role as state capital.

SACRAMENTO★

California State Capitol★★

10th St. between L & N Sts. ✕&℘916-324-0333. www.capitolmuseum.ca.gov. Surrounded by Capitol Park, a 40-acre rectangle of stately trees and lawn, and crowned by a 210ft Neoclassical dome, the 1860 capitol rises grandly at the head of the Capitol Mall. When the legislature is in session, visitors may observe the Senate and Assembly at work from third-floor balcony seats; both chambers are decorated to appear c.1900.

California Museum★

1020 O St. &P℘916-653-7524. www.californiamuseum.org. Through multimedia exhibits, this sleek treasury of archival documents, artifacts and newsreels attempts to illuminate the qualities of geography, history, politics and population that make California unique. The California Hall of Fame honors icons from John Wayne to

California State Railroad Museum

© California Travel & Tourism Commissiona

Steve Jobs. The Constitution Wall is a 140ft long 95ft tall artwork with words taken from the 1879 State Constitution sculpted in to its surface.

👤👤 Old Sacramento★★

I to L Sts., between Sacramento River & I-5. Self-guided walking tour brochure at visitor center (1002 Second St.). ✕♿🅿📞916-442-7644. www.oldsacramento.com

Sacramento's original downtown holds the nation's largest assemblage of Gold Rush-era buildings. Springing up in the early 1850s beside Sutter's *embarcadero*, the brick and wood buildings, fronted by covered wooden sidewalks, now house a collection of souvenir shops, museums and eateries. Permanently docked as a floating hotel along the waterfront levee, the *Delta King* is a sternwheeler that once shuttled passengers from here to San Francisco. Historic addresses include **B.F. Hastings & Co. Building** (2nd & J Sts.), western terminus of the Pony Express; today it houses gold-rush paraphernalia in a snug **Wells Fargo History Museum** (📞916-440-4263; www.wellsfargohistory.com).

The high point is the **California State Railroad Museum★★ 👤👤** (125 I St.; 📞916-445-7387; www.csrmf.org), where 21 meticulously restored locomotives, a railway post office, a sleeping car, a luxurious private car and other stock illustrate the impact of local and trans-Sierra railroading. Mining and agricultural history and pioneer domestic life are dynamically illustrated in exhibits in the **Discovery Museum Gold Rush History Center★ 👤👤** (101 I St.; 📞916-575-3942; www.thediscovery.org).

👤👤 Sutter's Fort State Historic Park★★

2701 L St. 🅿📞916-445-4422. www.parks.ca.gov.

Founded in 1839 as headquarters of a 76sq mi land grant known as New Helvetia, Sutter's Fort welcomed early pioneers and explorers with legendary hospitality. John Sutter's prosperity was in sharp decline by the 1850s, however. The state acquired the abandoned and dilapidated fort in 1890, renovating and furnishing it. Visitors may explore the living quarters, bakery, and blacksmith's, and other work rooms.

GOLD COUNTRY★★

The foothills region east of Sacramento counted nearly 90,000 miners at the peak of the Gold Rush in 1852; some 106 million troy ounces of gold were extracted before "gold fever" subsided in 1867. While many settlements were quickly depopulated, others developed into commercial centers that today depend more on ranching, tourism and timber production than on mining. Route 49 links the principal communities from Sierra City to Mariposa.

Nevada City★★

With scores of handsome Victorian houses on its forested hills above Deer Creek, this picturesque town of 3,000 has long been known as the graceful "Queen City" of the northern mines. Elegant shops and restaurants in the colorful commercial district today cater to overnight visitors.

👤👤 Empire Mine State Historic Park★★

10791 E. Empire St. , off Rte. 49; 5mi south of Nevada City, near Grass Valley. 🅿📞530-273-8522. www.empiremine.org.

California's largest and richest mine boasts 367mi of tunnels that produced 5.8 million troy ounces of gold in a century of operation (1856-1956). Visitors may tour the home and gardens of mine owner William Bourn, Jr., learn about the gold-mining process and mining equipment, and descend 30ft to gaze down the main winze, or diagonal shaft, extending 10,000ft to a depth of nearly a mile.

Malakoff Diggins State Historic Park★

27mi northeast of Nevada City. Take Rte. 49 north 11mi; turn on Tyler Foote Crossing Rd., left on Cruzon Grade Rd.

and follow signs. ⚠ 🅿 ℘530-265-2740. www.parks.ca.gov.

California's largest hydraulic mining pit is a lurid example of the disastrous effects on hillsides wrought by miners armed with high-pressure streams of water. The gaping gulch of the Malakoff Pit was eroded from 1855 until 1884, when hydraulic mining was banned by the state because it caused such destructive silting and flooding of downstream farmlands. Gold Rush-era buildings survive in the pleasant, tree-shaded village of North Bloomfield, site of the park visitor center. The spectacular Yuba River flows through the park and is a haven for swimmers, campers, and hikers.

Auburn★

The Gold Country's largest town, with nearly 13,000 people, Auburn is a rail and highway junction with a charming 19C Old Town and an informative **Gold Country Museum** (1273 High St.; ℘530-823-4533).

Marshall Gold Discovery State Historic Park★★

Rte. 49, 8mi northwest of Placerville. 🅿 ℘530-622-3470. www.parks.ca.gov. This park preserves two-thirds of the village of Coloma, built where James Marshall discovered gold on January 28, 1848. A reconstructed sawmill and visitor center commemorate the events that touched off the California Gold Rush.

Jackson★

Founded in 1849, Jackson today displays handsome 19C Main Street architecture and is home to several antiques stores. It is also the departure point for guided tours to local Black Chasm underground cave. The **National Hotel** (1863) claims to be the oldest continually operating hotel in the state.

A historic brick house (1859) atop a small knoll overlooking downtown has been home to the **Amador County Museum★** (closed indefinitely; 225 Church St.; ℘209-223-6386) with its gold-rush artifacts.

🏃🧍 Indian Grinding Rock State Historic Park★

14881 Pine Grove Volcano Rd., 12mi east of Jackson via Rte. 88. ⚠ ♿ 🅿 ℘209-296-7488. www.parks.ca.gov.

Pitting a flat limestone outcrop are hundreds of mortar holes once used by native Miwok Indians to grind acorns into meal. Re-created Miwok bark dwellings and a ceremonial roundhouse stand near a small regional museum.

Calaveras Big Trees State Park★★

Rte. 4, 24mi east of Angel's Camp. ⚠ 🅿 ℘209-795-2334. www.parks.ca.gov.

The first grove of giant sequoias to be developed for tourism was discovered in 1852 by a bear hunter. Visitors see giants along the well-groomed, self-guided nature trail (1mi) through the **North Grove**. Fewer hike the more remote trail (4.7mi round-trip) to the **South Grove**, although it leads to the park's largest specimens.

🏃🧍 Columbia State Historic Park★★

Rte. 49, 4mi north of Sonora. ✗ 🅿 ℘209-588-9128. www.parks.ca.gov.

Founded in 1850, the boomtown of Columbia survived several fires and a lengthy decline before the state acquired it in 1945. Cars are banned from downtown, where costumed park employees re-create daily life in 1850-70 at shops and businesses. Visitors may pan for gold or tour an operating hard-rock tunnel, the **Hidden Treasure Mine★** (℘209-532-9693; www.hidden-treasuregoldmine.com).

Mariposa

A gateway to Yosemite National Park, Mariposa hosts the 🏃🧍 **California State Mining and Mineral Museum★★** (Mariposa County Fairgrounds; ℘209-742-7625; www.parks.ca.gov), with displays on mining history. The 20,000-specimen collection offers eye-catching exhibits of California gold, a working model of the 1904 Union Iron Works stamp mill, and a walk-through model of a Gold Country mine.

Sequoia and Kings Canyon National Parks★★

The world's largest stands of giant sequoia trees are found in these impressive twin parks which, together with adjacent national forest, preserve the second-largest roadless area in the continental US.

> 🕐 **Michelin Map:** p 200. Pacific Standard Time.
>
> 🛈 **Info:** ℘559-565-3341; www.nps.gov/seki; www.visitsequoia.com.
>
> 👁 **Don't Miss:** The Giant Forest.

A BIT OF HISTORY

This land is a rugged terrain of plunging canyons, deep forests, and wildlife and mountain crests soaring above 14,000ft. Formed in 1890 to protect uncut sequoia groves, Sequoia National Park was soon tripled in size when Congress established General Grant National Park to protect Grant Grove. In 1940, the new Kings Canyon National Park absorbed Grant Grove. Among many superlative features are the General Sherman Tree, earth's largest single tree; Kings Canyon, one of the deepest canyons in the US; and Mt. Whitney, highest peak in the continental US.

No road crosses the Sierra here. Visitor facilities lie on the parks' western edge, separated from the east boundary by a broad wilderness open only to hikers and packers. (The eastern slope is accessible by trail from roadheads near the Owens Valley (🕐 p 211). Most visitors arrive by the General's Highway (Rtes. 198 and 180), a fine, two-lane loop road that links the Central Valley cities of Fresno and Visalia.

Lodging is available in Sequoia at Wuksachi Village (℘866-807-3598), or at Grant Grove (℘559-335-5500) and Cedar Grove villages (℘559-565-0100) in Kings Canyon.

In Sequoia Park, a shuttle bus carries visitors between Wuksachi Village, Lodgepole, the Giant Forest Museum, Moro Rock and Crescent Meadow roughly every half hour on summer days.

Winter brings heavy snows to the parks, but the General's Highway is kept plowed.

SEQUOIA NATIONAL PARK★★
Giant Forest★★★

30mi southeast of Big Stump entrance, 16mi northeast of Ash Mountain entrance. 🅿

Containing 8,000 mature sequoias, the sprawling Giant Forest is one of the largest of 75 sequoia groves in the Sierra; only the remote Redwood Mountain Grove in the Grant Grove section of Kings Canyon is larger. The largest single tree on earth—the **General Sherman Tree★**—grows near the forest's northern end, adjacent to General's Highway. With a circumference of 102.6ft and a height of 275ft, it forms a conspicuous starting point for several trails that fan out into the Giant Forest. The **Congress Trail** (2mi) loops through some of the forest's largest and most spectacularly homogeneous stands of *Sequoiadendron giganteum*, including the House and Senate groups.

Crescent Meadow

Described by John Muir as the "Gem of the Sierra," this curving glade—lush with wildflowers and fenced by giant sequoias—lies on the southern edge of the Giant Forest.

A .8mi trail winds through meadow and woods to **Tharpe's Log**, a cabin made in the 60ft-hollow of a single log. The 8ft open end was closed off in the 1860s with a chimney, door and window, by a cattleman.

Kings Canyon National Park, Kern Valley

©National Park Service

Moro Rock★

South of Giant Forest via Crescent Meadow Road. 🅿

An ingenious trail (*.5mi round-trip*) climbs some 400 steps to the top of this sheer-faced dome, providing fine **views★★** 4,000ft down the Kaweah River Canyon, west to the Central Valley, and 12mi east to the jagged wall of the Great Western Divide. Built in 1931, the stairway was added to the National Register of Historic Places in 1978 in recognition of its harmonious integration with natural rock clefts.

KINGS CANYON NATIONAL PARK★
Grant Grove★★

1mi west of Grant Grove Village.

A short loop trail (*.5mi*) passes among several noteworthy giants, including the **General Grant Tree**, officially named the "Nation's Christmas Tree" in 1926. The world's third-largest sequoia, this massive specimen is the broadest, with a circumference of 107.6ft

The Pacific Crest Trail passes through the park close to the eastern border of the Kern Valley, part of a continuous 2,640mi footpath from Canada all the way to Mexico.

Panoramic Point★

2.mi northeast of Grant Grove Village; follow road to cabins, then turn right.

A trail (*.5mi round-trip*) leads up to this overlook, offering **views** of the austere, 14,000ft Sierra peaks and Lake Hume. From the overlook, the **Park Ridge Trail** (*4.7mi round-trip*) offers vistas of the high country and Central Valley.

Kings Canyon★★

North and east of Grant Grove Villlage

Rte. 180 winds 30mi to Cedar Grove, hugging the South Fork of the Kings River canyon walls. From rim to base, the gorge measures 4,000ft to 8000ft deep, making it one of the continent's deepest canyons.

In the lower canyon is Boyden cave, a marble cavern hung with luminous cave formations (✆ 888-965-8243; www.kingscanyoneering.com; Apr-Nov).

From Boyden Cave, Rte. 180 follows the South Fork to **Cedar Grove Village**, a cluster of park facilities and a small visitor center and picnic tables nestled below peaks that loom more than 3,000ft above. Most popular of many canyon-floor trails is **Roads End** (*5mi beyond Cedar Grove*), where lush Zumwalt Meadows lies 3,500ft beneath North Dome, on the north wall, and Grand Sentinel, on the south. The Mist Falls Trail (*8mi*) follows the Kings River in a moderate ascent to **Mist Falls★**, where the river falls down a sheer granite face. ❄Winter snows can close this highway November to May.

Yosemite National Park★★★

Sheer-walled Yosemite Valley stands center stage at this sprawling national park that encompasses 1,170sq mi of pristine forests, giant sequoia groves, alpine lakes, wildlife, and awe-inspiring peaks. Ice Age glaciers grinding down the Merced River canyon scooped out Yosemite's distinctive U-shaped trough, 7mi long and 4,000ft deep, sculpting massive rocks and polishing cliffs where waterfalls now plummet.

- **Michelin Map:** p 200. Pacific Standard Time.
- **Info:** ☎209-372-0200 or www.nps.gov/yose
- **Parking:** The main day-use lot at Valley Village is huge; arrive early, leave your car and use the park's excellent shuttle bus system.
- **Don't Miss:** Yosemite Falls, El Capitan.
- **Kids:** Tunnel Tree.
- **Also See:** The Awahnee Hotel; Tuolumne Meadows.

A BIT OF HISTORY

The native Ahwahneechee people surrendered Yosemite to European and American pioneers in 1851; just 13 years later, the federal government set aside Yosemite Valley and the Wawona Grove as a natural preserve. The effusive writings of naturalist John Muir prompted Congress in 1890 to preserve the surrounding region as Yosemite National Park. Today, millions of annual visitors come to hike, fish, camp, ski and enjoy the magnificent scenery.

Though it constitutes less than six percent of the park's land area, Yosemite Valley remains the principal attraction. Lodging, dining facilities, shops and other amenities are found at rustic Camp Curry, motel-style Yosemite Lodge and at the magnificent hotel **Ahwahnee★★** (*see ADDRESSES; ☎801-559-4884; www.yosemitepark. com/lodging.aspx). Visitors may tour the east end of the valley on a free shuttle bus. Outside the valley, a more modest array of park facilities exists at Tuolumne Meadows, White Wolf and Wawona in summer, and at Badger Pass Ski Resort in winter.

YOSEMITE VALLEY
Yosemite Village

The administrative and commercial center of the park includes a post office, the **Ansel Adams Gallery** (☎209-372-

Half Dome, Yosemite National Park

© John Anderson/Michelin

4413; www.anseladams.com) and a Wilderness Office where hikers obtain backcountry permits. Staffed by rangers, the **visitor center** presents exhibits on geology and natural history. The **Yosemite Museum** houses a collection of native artifacts, changing art exhibits and a snug library. Behind the museum, the reconstructed Ahwahneechee Village displays bark dwellings.

Yosemite Falls★★★
Plunging 2,425ft in three stages down the valley's north wall, the highest waterfall in North America appears spectacularly as a billowing plume on windy spring days. It may dry up by late summer. From parking lots near Yosemite Lodge, a short path (*.2mi*) leads to the base of the **lower fall★★** (320ft). The strenuous Yosemite Falls Trail (*7mi round-trip*) switchbacks up the north wall, passing above the middle cascade (675ft) to a ledge near the lip of the **upper fall★** (1,430ft).

Happy Isles★
At the mouth of the Merced River Canyon, small islands split the roaring cataract into smaller channels. A picnic spot, at 4,050ft elevation, Happy Isles is the start of the **John Muir Trail**. The short, steep jaunt to **Vernal Fall Bridge★★** (*.7mi*) is popular; from here, the Mist Trail climbs to the brink of 317ft **Vernal Fall★★** (*1.5mi*). Ambitious hikers may proceed to the top of 594ft **Nevada Fall** (*3mi*). A farther trail continues to the summit of **Half Dome★★★** (*8.2mi*), a massive rock that rises 4,800 vertical feet (to 8,842ft elevation) at the eastern head of the valley. Not for the weak of limb, the final climb ascends a 45-degree granite slab with the aid of an exposed cable ladder.

Tunnel View★★★
From this s viewpoint at the east end of the Wawona Tunnel, visitors gaze eastward into Yosemite Valley. Its portals are framed on the south by **Cathedral Rocks** and on the north by the 3,593ft face of **El Capitan★★★**, the world's largest unbroken cliff. **Bridalveil Fall★**

hangs in the foreground, as do ephemeral Ribbon and Silver Strand Falls in early spring. The distinctive, sheer face of Half Dome peers round the shoulder of Glacier Point from the eastern end.

EXCURSIONS
Glacier Point★★★
▶ 30mi south and east from Yosemite Village; 0.2mi from parking area. ✕&. Road may be closed Nov–late May.
Jutting 3,000ft above the valley floor, this majestic cliff-top perch offers an unforgettable view of Yosemite Valley. To the northwest, Yosemite Falls hang at full length; to the east are Vernal and Nevada Falls, while Half Dome looms in the foreground.

Mariposa Grove★★
▶ 34mi south of Yosemite Village. ✕&. Tours by foot (loop trips 1mi–7mi) or 1hr tram tour.
The largest of the park's three groves of giant sequoias spreads over 250 acres of a steep hillside. Most massive is the **Grizzly Giant**, an 1,800-year-old specimen with a base circumference of 96ft and a pronounced lean of 17 degrees. The adjacent ♣♣ **California Tunnel Tree** was bored in 1895 to allow coaches to pass through it.

Tioga Road★★
▶ 62mi one-way north and east from Yosemite Village to Tioga Pass. Last 45mi (past Crane Flat) closed Nov–late May.
Rte 120 snakes 14mi in forests, then opens to broad high-country views **Olmsted Point★** provides striking vistas down Tenaya Canyon to Half Dome and Clouds Rest (9,926ft). Passing subalpine **Tenaya Lake**, the park's largest natural body of water, the road enters **Tuolumne Meadows★★**, an alpine grassland at 8,600ft elevation. The heart of the high country, Tuolumne Meadows has rustic lodging, dining, a visitor center and access to backcountry trails. A short trail climbs to the glacier-polished summit of 9,450ft **Lembert Dome★** (*3mi round-trip*). Beyond 9,945ft **Tioga Pass★**, Route 120 descends 13mi to the US-395 junction near Mono Lake.

Eastern Sierra ★

The eastern escarpment of the Sierra Nevada rises abruptly from the sagebrush flats of the Great Basin sere by virtue of the rain shadow cast by the Sierra crest. Running parallel, US-395 is among the most spectacular highways in the US, with continuous views of towering granite peaks and awesome volcanic scenery, including numerous natural hot springs. Side roads probe narrow canyons to lakes and trailheads in rugged alpine regions. The highway peaks in broad, deep Owens Valley.

♿ **Michelin Map:** p 200. Pacific Standard Time.

ℹ️ **Info:** ☎760-934-2712; www.visitmammoth.com.

👁 **Don't Miss:** Owens Valley; Mono Lake; Devils Postpile.

SIGHTS

Bodie State Historic Park ★★

Rte. 270 east from US-395; final 3mi unpaved. Road may close in winter ☎760-647-6445. www.parks.ca.gov.

This stark ghost town rambles along dirt streets in the sagebrush hills of the high desert. Although the 1859 gold discovery brought a rush of prospectors, not until 1874 did corporate investment shape Bodie into a mining city of 10,000 people. The town's bad reputation put the "bad man from Bodie" into Western lore. Population dwindled when mining waned in 1882; the town was eventually abandoned. The state acquired it in 1962, maintaining it in a state of "arrested decay" with no restoration. The **Miners Union Hall** functions as a museum and visitor center.

Mono Lake ★★

Remnant of a prehistoric lake five times larger than its present 60sq mi, Mono Lake is three times saltier than the ocean and 80 times more alkaline. Dubbed "the Dead Sea of California" by Mark Twain, Mono, in fact, supports a wealth of brine shrimp and alkali flies that attract migratory birds and waterfowl. The native Paiutes valued the flies, eating the shelled pupae and traded them to the Yokuts; the Yokut word mono, meaning "fly eaters," was attached to the lake itself.

The **US Forest Service Visitor Center** (north end of Lee Vining, off US-395; ☎760-647-6323) offers information on the region's history. The lake is famed as an example of the way urbanization influences distant spots: Mono Lake's level dropped dramatically when Los Angeles ran the valley's water south in an aqueduct. The grotesque limestone spires of **South Tufa ★★** (6mi south of Lee Vining on US-395, then 4.5mi east on Rte. 120 to gravel access road) formed between AD 1100 and 1900 as calcium deposits from submerged springs combined with lake-water carbonates.

Tufa on Mono Lake

©iStockphoto.com/Henning Semat

Mammoth Region★

A 19C mining town transformed into a four-season resort community, **Mammoth Lakes** (www.ci.mammoth-lakes.ca.us) lies beneath the 11,053ft dormant volcano of **Mammoth Mountain★**. Camping, fishing and hiking in **Mammoth Lakes Basin★** and the surrounding high country dominate the snow-free season (May–Oct). Winter brings skiers; the thaw attracts mountain bikers; and, year-round, a gondola climbing the summit offers magnificent views. Summer trams take hikers over panoramic **Minaret Summit★★** to **Devils Postpile National Monument★** (Rte. 203; ✆ 760-934-2289; www.nps.gov/depo). An easy trail (*.4mi*) leads to the monument's namesake, a 60ft wall of six- to eight-sided basalt columns at the face of a 100,000-year-old lava flow.

Ancient Bristlecone Pine Forest★★

23mi east of Big Pine (US-395) off Rte. 168. ✆ 760-873-2400; www.fs.usda.gov/inyo.

Here atop the White Mountains are earth's oldest living single creatures, 4,000-year-old bristlecone pines. Trails lead through the ancient groves; the new (2012) Schulman Visitor Center explains the pines' astounding longevity in this harsh environment.

Whitney Crest★★

The 60mi stretch of the **Owens Valley★★** from Bishop to Lone Pine, bounded by the Sierra Nevada and White-Inyo Range, is among North America's most dramatic valleys. At Lone Pine, the valley floor is two vertical miles below the 14,494ft summit of **Mt. Whitney★★**, the highest point in the contiguous US. The view of the jagged Whitney crest is from **Alabama Hills★★**, west of Lone Pine. **Eastern Sierra Interagency Visitor Center** (US-395, 1mi south of Lone Pine; ✆ 760-876-6222) provides maps. The steep, winding, well-paved **Whitney Portal Road** climbs to a lovely mountain canyon (8,360ft), trailhead for the rugged **Mt. Whitney Trail** (21.4mi round-trip; permit required. ✆ 760-873-2483).

Reno Area★

Straddling the Truckee River where the Sierra Nevada meets the Great Basin, Reno has a reputation as a center for outdoor recreation, especially given its proximity to Lake Tahoe. With a population of more than 227,000, the city enjoys a broad-based economy as the banking center, transportation hub and entertainment dynamo of northern Nevada. although casino gaming is its foremost draw.

A BIT OF HISTORY

The city was founded around a toll bridge in the 1860s and named for a Civil War general. It achieved an economic boost when Central Pacific rail construction crews passed through in 1868, and grew as a distribution center

   Michelin Map: p 200. Pacific Standard Time.

   Info: ✆ 800-367-7366; www.visitrenotahoe.com.

   Don't Miss: Virginia City.

   Kids: Virginia & Truckee R.R.

after the transcontinental line was completed in 1869. The prosperity of nearby Virginia City in the 1870s, and later mining rushes to Tonopah and Goldfield, bolstered its role. Reno became a county seat in 1870 and home of the University of Nevada in 1886.

Although gambling and other vices had always thrived in Reno, casino gaming underwent a revolution when Raymond "Pappy" Smith opened **Harold's Club** on Virginia Street in 1935 and began courting a "respectable" clientele through widespread advertising. With this new image, gambling trips to Reno became a weekend pastime of Californians. They increased in popularity after William Harrah opened **Harrah's** in 1946; by the 1950s, new casinos filled the downtown area with pulsating neon lights, establishing Reno as the supreme gaming destination of Nevada. In the 1960s, the Las Vegas Strip took over that reputation; by the 1980s, Las Vegas had also surpassed Reno in population. The Reno area nevertheless experienced unprecedented growth at the end of the 20C.

RENO★
North Virginia Street★★
Between I-80 & the Truckee River.
✕&⊞.
This seven-block "Strip" contains Reno's greatest concentration of gambling casinos, flamboyantly celebrated in the **Reno Arch★** (Virginia & Commercial Sts.), which proclaims Reno "The Biggest Little City in the World." Rectangular city blocks compel casinos, many of them linked by sky bridges, to conform to regular architectural footprints. Conventional, high-rise facades rely on extravagant **lighting displays★** and open shopfronts to attract pedestrians to their slot machines and gaming tables. Harrah's, Fitzgerald's, the Cal-Neva, the Eldorado and other casinos established before the 1990s likewise abstain from the fantastic themes that pervade many casino-hotels of the Las Vegas Strip. The most notable exception is the **Silver Legacy Casino Resort** (407 N. Virginia St.; ✆775-325-7401; www.silverlegacyreno.com), which features a light show beneath a central dome. The casino strip ends at the Truckee River, where wooded promenades trace the banks of the cold mountain stream through downtown Reno.

National Automobile Museum★★
10 Lake St. S. &⊞✆775-333-9300. www.automuseum.org.
More than 200 antique, classic and custom automobiles constituting the **Harrah Collection** are displayed in imaginative period settings. Visitors watch a high-tech multimedia history of the auto industry, then stroll among indoor "streets" lined by vintage autos and facades that represent the turn of the 19C, the 1930s, the 1950s and contemporary times. Exceptional displays include an 1892 steam-driven Philion carriage, the 1907 Thomas Flyer that won the New York-to-Paris Automobile Race in 170 days, Al Jolson's 1933 Cadillac V-16, and the 1949 Mercury driven by James Dean in *Rebel Without a Cause*.

W.M. Keck Museum★
1664 N. Virginia St., Mackay School of Mines, University of Nevada. &✆775-784-4528. www.mines.unr.edu/museum. The Mackay School of Mines (1908), north of UN's tree-lined quadrant, is a preeminent school of mining engineering. Specimens of Nevada minerals and fossils line the walls of its Keck Museum, illustrating Nevada's role as a leader in this field. The silver collection recalls the role of John Mackay (1831-1902) as one of the Comstock "Bonanza Kings."

EXCURSIONS
Carson City★
❍ 30mi south of Reno on US-395. ✆775-687-7410. www.visitcarsoncity.com.
Founded in 1858, the city was named for the Carson River, itself named by adventurer John C. Frémont for scout Kit Carson. The town became the Nevada territorial capital, then the state capital in 1864, acquiring a US Mint. Today it has a population of 55,000.
The **Kit Carson Trail** winds past the 1895 home of Washoe basket-weaver Datsolalee, the 1909 Governor's Mansion and a house built in 1864 by Orion Clemens. Clemens, the only secretary of the Nevada Territory, accompanied his brother Samuel ("Mark Twain") Clemens from Missouri in a journey described by the author in *Roughing It*.
Capped by a silvery cupola, the 1871 sandstone **Nevada State Capitol** (Carson Ave.; ✆800-638-2321; http://museums.nevadaculture.org) still houses the offices of the governor and other officials; the Senate and Assembly now

meet in the Nevada State Legislature (1970) across the adjacent plaza.

Nevada State Museum★★

◉ 600 N. Carson St. ✆775-687-4810. museums.nevadaculture.org.

Housed in the 1869 Carson City Mint, this institution provides an overview of Nevada's flora, fauna, geology and human history. The state's mining heritage gallery surveys the process that produced more than 56 million coins from Nevada gold and silver in 1870-1895; workers on occasion still strike medallions on **Coin Press No. 1**. Natural-history galleries display mounted Great Basin animals. The **Changing Earth** exhibit features a walk-through exhibit of Devonian Nevada, 35 to 40 million years ago, when these precincts were on the ocean floor.The Marjorie Russell Clothing and Textile Research Center (by appointment only ✆775-687-6173) is devoted to fashion history.

Virginia City★★

◉ 14mi northeast of Carson City, 23mi southeast of Reno, on Rte. 341. ✆775-847-7500. www.visitvirginiacitynv.com.

Preserved as a National Historic Landmark, this bustling old mining town on the steep slopes of Mount Davidson ranks among the most fascinating in the West. Virginia City is built on steep terraces, its downtown concentrated along C Street. Few buildings predate

a devastating 1875 fire, but about half were built before 1890.

Linked by uneven wooden sidewalks with overhanging roofs and porches, four densely packed blocks of wood and brick buildings are occupied by stores, restaurants, saloons and several private collections of curios optimistically labeled "museums."

Among the historic sites is the office of the *Territorial Enterprise*, where young Mark Twain worked in the 1860s. Even children are free to enter the colorful saloons on C Street, the **Best and Belcher Mine**★ (✆775-847-0757) behind the Ponderosa Saloon, and the **Chollar Mine**★ (✆775-847-0155) on the south edge of town.

Among old mansions seasonally open for tours are **The Castle** (B Street; ✆775-847-0275) and the **Mackay Mansion** (D Street; ✆775-847-0173; www.uniquitiesmackaymansion.com). Built in 1875, **Pipers Opera House**★ (B & Union Sts.; ✆775-847-0433; www.nps.gov/nr/travel/nevada) still offers dramas where Jenny Lind and Edwin Booth once performed. One of the city's better historical collections occupies the four-story, 1876 **Fourth Ward School**★ (✆775-847-0975). The ♁♁ **Virginia & Truckee Railroad** (✆775-847-0380; www.virginiatruckee.com), built to transport silver to Carson City, and Tahoe Basin timber to shore up Virginia City's mines, still offers rides from its F Street station.

Shasta–Cascade Region★

At the northern end of the Sierra Nevada, the mountains meet the Cascade, Trinity and Klamath ranges in an arc of peaks at the head of the Sacramento Valley, the agricultural center of Redding at its hub.

A BIT OF HISTORY

Dominating the landscape for hundreds of miles around is the volcanic cone of Mt. Shasta (14,162ft), an enchanting symbol of this highly volcanic region.

- ◉ **Michelin Map:** 493 A, B6, 7. Pacific Standard Time.
- ℹ **Info:** ✆530-225-4100; www.visitredding.com
- ◉ **Don't Miss:** Lassen Volcanic National Park.
- ♁♁ **Kids:** Shasta Lake.
- ◉ **Also See:** Turtle Bay Park and Sundial Bridge.

Lassen Peak (10,457ft) erupted violently in 1914-17; today it forms the nucleus of a serene, though still smoldering, national park. Three large man-made lakes are in the Whiskeytown–Shasta-Trinity National Recreation Areas (http://www.fs.usda.gov/stnf/). Beyond the Cascades, the Modoc Lava Plateau covers 26,000sq mi of California's north-eastern corner, a desert upland noted for lava tubes and stark, craggy scenery.

SIGHTS

Turtle Bay Exploration Park★

1355 Arboretum Dr., Redding.Hwy. 44 one mile west of Interstate 5 Exit 678. öjō t530-243-8850. www.turtlebay.org. The highlight of the 300-acre park is the 700ft-long **Sundial Bridge★★**, a graceful pedestrian span (2004) over the Sacramento River designed by Santiago Calatrava. The botanical gardens show off 20 acres of "Mediterranean-climate" gardens divided into sections geographically. The McConnell Arboretum features a butterfly conservatory.

Lassen Volcanic National Park★★

47mi east of Redding via Rte. 44.
&530-595-4480. www.nps.gov/lavo.
Lassen Peak erupted May 30, 1914, the first of 298 eruptions over several years. Congress established the 106,000-acre park in 1916, allowing visitors to witness the spectacular effects of volcanism. The scenic Park Road (Rte. 89) makes a winding 30mi arc around Lassen Peak. From **Manzanita Lake Visitor Center** (Loomis Museum; &530-595-6121), the road passes through the **Devastated Area**, blasted at the height of Lassen's 1915 eruptions, though now recovering with new forests of aspen and pine. At the road's closest approach to Lassen Peak, at 8,500ft, a strenuous trail (5mi) begins climbing to the summit. The highlight of current volcanic activity is **Bumpass Hell★★**. Accessible only by a 3mi round-trip hike from the roadhead, its sulfuric fumaroles, boiling springs and bubbling mudpots are seen safely from a boardwalk.

McArthur-Burney Falls Memorial State Park★

65mi northeast of Redding via Rtes. 229 & 89. ⚠♿🅿 &916-335-2777. www.parks.ca.gov.
Highlight of this popular park is **Burney Falls★★**, where the combined flows of Burney Creek and an underground stream tumble over a 129ft cliff of basalt. Springs in the face of the cliff engorge the falls with ribbons of water, so that the flow is visibly greater at the bottom than the top.

Lava Beds National Monument★★

170mi northeast of Redding via Rtes. 299, 139 & 10. &530-667-8100. www.nps.gov/labe.
This remote stretch of the Modoc Lava Plateau contains more than 300 lava tubes. Several penetrate as far as 150ft below the earth's surface, others extend horizontally for thousands of feet. Notable are the Crystal Ice and Fern caves, accessible only by reserved, tours. Rangers provide flashlights, hard hats, and maps for exploring tubes along **Cave Loop Road** and farther afield.
In 1872, 53 Modoc warriors and their families held off the US Army for five months at a natural fortress now called **Captain Jack's Stronghold★★**. The Modoc leader, Kientpoos (known to settlers as Captain Jack), opted to fight rather than endure exile on a reservation. Outnumbered, the Modocs used the crags and caves for hiding and ambushes. Captain Jack finally led the Modocs out after fatally shooting an Army general in peace negotiations. He was later captured and hanged; the remainder of the tribe was exiled to Oklahoma.

Mount Shasta★

Visible for miles in northern California, this glacier-clad, 14,162ft volcano is second in height only to Mt. Rainier in Washington. Hikes start from the **Everitt Memorial Highway**, a scenic route that ascends through Shasta-Trinity National Forest. The quaint town of Mt. Shasta sits at the mountain's base along I-5.

Southwest and Canyons

Downtown Phoenix
© Gwen Cannon/Michelin

3rd St. 300 E

Grand Canyon Region

Nearly 2 billion years old, 277mi long and averaging 10mi wide and 1mi deep, the Grand Canyon is superlative. No other place has so much of the earth's geological history on display.

Highlights

1 Epic **East Rim Drive** (p224)

2 Walking out over the canyon on a **glass-floor bridge** (p225)

3 Sedona's **red-rock "vortices"** (p228)

4 Lovely **Oak Creek Canyon** (p228)

A Canyon to Dwarf All Others

Most visitor services are centered on the canyon's South Rim. One may also explore the less commercialized North Rim and, beyond that, the largely undeveloped Arizona Strip just south of the Utah border. The drive from South Rim to North Rim takes 4hrs; many visitors opt for a shorter hop to Williams (60mi south), terminus for the Grand Canyon Railway. Northwest of Williams via old Route 66— the historic,

pre-interstate highway that linked Chicago with Los Angeles —lie the Native American reservation lands of the Havasupai and Hualapai tribes.

Some 80mi southeast of the South Rim is cool, high-country Flagstaff, the region's biggest city. Nearby are the San Francisco Peaks, rising to 12,633ft at Humphreys Peak. The 30mi drive south from Flagstaff to the famed red-rock scenery of Sedona, descending through the forests and Oak Creek Canyon, is brief but captivating. Sedona has lured artists for a century. Northeast of Sedona, occupying nearly

Grand Canyon NP

AZ

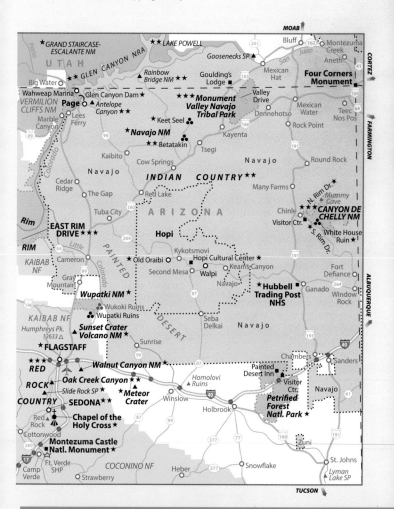

one-sixth of the state of Arizona, are the Navajo and Hopi Indian reservations. The Navajo is the largest US Indian reservation; within it are revered locales such as Canyon de Chelly and Monument Valley, plus ancient Indian ruins. Just south of the reservation are the Petrified Forest, and the Painted Desert, a subdued, pastel-colored expanse.

ADDRESSES

🏨 STAY

$$$$ L'Auberge de Sedona – 301 L'Auberge Ln., Sedona, AZ. ☎928-282-1661. www.lauberge.com.87 rooms and cottages. The main lodge's stone columns blend into Sedona's buttes and spires, while the cottages have a Country-French feel. Eleven acres of botanical gardens are joined to the well-reputed, creekside **L'Auberge Restaurant ($$$)**.

$$$$Enchantment Resort – 525 Boynton Canyon Rd., Sedona, AZ. ☎928-282-2900. www.enchantmentresort.com. 218 rooms. Low-profile, adobe-style casitas, with beehive fireplaces and private balconies, are nestled amid Boynton Canyon's red rocks. Tennis, golf and swimming are possible, and the spa offers earth-clay wraps. The **Yavapai Restaurant ($$$)** features 180-degree views.

$$$ El Tovar Hotel – 1 Main St., Grand Canyon, AZ. ☎928-638-2631. www.grandcanyonlodges.com. 78 rooms. Native stone and heavy pine logs create an old-European-hunting-lodge atmosphere, and the views are out of this world. Dining room highlights include fresh Atlantic salmon.

$$ La Posada – 303 E. 2nd St., Winslow, AZ. ☎928-289-4366. www.laposada.org. 54 rooms. Fred Harvey used his Santa Fe Railroad to civilize the West with silverware and china, and La Posada was his last (1930) and most elegant hotel. Designed as a Spanish hacienda, it was a favorite retreat for Hollywood stars. Closed for 40 years; it reopened in 1997, and is a magical oasis in which to stay and relax.

$$ Hotel Monte Vista – 100 N. San Francisco St., Flagstaff, AZ. ☎928-779-6971. www.hotelmontevista.com. 50 rooms. Guest rooms at this four-story remnant of the Roaring Twenties are named after famous folks who stayed here: Teddy Roosevelt, Humphrey Bogart, Clark Gable and Carole Lombard.

🍴 EAT

$$$ Cottage Place – 126 W. Cottage Ave., Flagstaff, AZ. ☎928-774-8431. www.cottageplace.com. Dinner only. Closed Mon–Tue. **Continental**. This beautiful 1909 bungalow home brings a touch of Europe to Northern Arizona, from herb stuffed mushrooms and escargots to parmesan encrusted scallops and spinach and goat cheese strudel.

$$$ The Heartline Cafe – 1610 W. US-89A, Sedona, AZ. ☎928-282-0785. www.heartlinecafe.com. **Regional**. This eclectic but acclaimed restaurant serves sesame-crusted Ahi tuna, roasted layered vegetables in tomato sauce and pistachio-crusted chicken.

$$$ René at Tlaquepaque – Rte. 179 at Oak Creek, Sedona, AZ. ☎928-282-9225. www.rene-sedona.com. **Continental**. René is famed for its baked French onion soup and its signature rack of lamb, carved tableside. Other favorites are Dover sole and eggplant roulade in this stylish, expansive space.

$$ Criollo Latin Kitchen – 16 N. San Francisco St., Flagstaff, AZ. ☎928-774-0541. www.criollolatinkitchen.com. **Latin American**. Always abuzz with conversation, this intimate eatery in downtown Flagstaff ensconces diners in a hip urban setting of brick walls and colorful wall paintings; all of its pine is locally harvested ponderosa. Incorporating numerous ingredients from Arizona farms, entrées reflect a meld of Spanish-Latin flavors. Try the almond tostada with goat cheese and black-bean spread, the signature paella with saffron-infused Calasparra rice, or the catfish tacos with jalapeno glaze.

Grand Canyon National Park★★★

If any single landscape feature symbolizes the United States in the minds of world travelers, it is Arizona's Grand Canyon.

GEOLOGICAL NOTES

Waters from seven western states—Arizona, Utah, New Mexico, Colorado and Wyoming, plus Nevada and California below the Grand Canyon—drain into the mighty Colorado River, 1,450mi long from its source in Colorado's Rocky Mountains to Mexico's Gulf of California.

This is not the world's deepest canyon. In North America alone, there are deeper chasms in Mexico (Copper Canyon), California (Kings Canyon) and the Pacific Northwest (Hells Canyon). Older rocks may be found in northern Canada and elsewhere. But the Grand Canyon of the Colorado River is known throughout the world for its spectacular landscape and its special, almost mystical characteristics.

At dawn and dusk, the low-angle sun highlights the vividly colored canyon walls. Bands of green, blue, purple, pink, red, orange, gold, yellow and white define a succession of exposed ancient rock layers. It is one of the most extreme cases of erosion anywhere, and a site where visitors feel humbled by the relentless sculpting power of nature.

- **Michelin Map:** pp 218-219. Mountain Standard Time.
- **Info:** ℘928-638-7888; www.nps.gov/grca.
- **Location:** Just 10 miles as the crow flies, the South Rim and North Rim are more than 200 road miles apart.
- **Parking:** The lots at Grand Canyon Village on the South Rim fill up early on summer days.
- **Don't Miss:** It's worth the walk to one of the less-crowded viewpoints to quietly experience the sense of infinity the canyon engenders.
- **Timing:** Perhaps the best way to visit the Grand Canyon is to drive to the South Rim early (arriving by 8 am), then get on the road to the North Rim before noon for an overnight stay there.
- **Kids:** Grand Canyon Railway.
- **Also See:** North Rim's Bright Angel Point.

A BIT OF HISTORY

The Grand Canyon has been inhabited for at least 4,000 years, as evidenced by artifacts of the Desert Archaic culture,

Grand Canyon National Park

© iStockphoto.com/Ryan Morgan

found in niches in the canyon walls. By AD 500, the Ancestral Puebloan culture was established. About 2,000 sites, including petroglyph sites, have been found within park boundaries; most impressive is Tusayan Pueblo (c.1185) on the South Rim. These ancestors of the modern Hopi left the canyon by the late 13C, to be replaced by the forebears of the Hualapai and Havasupai, who today inhabit the western canyon.

The earliest European visit was by Francisco Vásquez de Coronado's gold-hungry 1540 expedition. In 1869 a one-armed Civil War veteran named **John Wesley Powell** led an expedition of nine men in small wooden boats down the canyon. Six men survived the journey through uncharted rapids, including Powell, who was at times lashed by ropes to his boat for safety. Two years later, the fearless Powell led a second expedition. Late 19C mining efforts in the canyon generally failed, but they opened the doors for a tourism industry. The first rim-top hotels were little more than mining camps. Guided mule trips took visitors to the canyon floor.

Not until 1919 was it set aside as a park. Much credit goes to the **Fred Harvey Company**, which built railroad hotels and restaurants throughout the Southwest. Tourism began in earnest with the 1905 completion of the El Tovar Hotel, the most elegant in the West. Designer Mary Colter conceived many of the Harvey buildings, including the canyon-floor Phantom Ranch (1922), and the Bright Angel Lodge (1935). Most were staffed by "Harvey Girls," well-dressed and educated young women, usually from the East; the "Girls" are gone, but the lodges continue to serve visitors.

In its first year as a national park, 44,000 people visited the Grand Canyon.

Today, about 5 million tourists enter the park each year. Their impact on the environment has led the National Park Service to contemplate dramatic action to protect the Canyon for future generations, and to establish a model that is being adopted at other US national parks.

Shuttle buses, operating along the South Rim and out to West Rim Drive, attempt to ease traffic congestion.

SIGHTS
👤👤 South Rim★★★

Most visitor activities in Grand Canyon National Park are focused along a 35mi strand of paved road that extends from the East Rim Entrance Station (29mi west of US-89 at Cameron) to Hermits Rest.

Grand Canyon Village
⛺✕👤♿🅿.

Site of park headquarters, the main visitor center and the lion's share of historic hotels, restaurants and tourist facilities within the park, this community links East Rim and West Rim drives with Williams (60mi south via Rte. 64) and Flagstaff (80mi southeast via US-180).

The **Grand Canyon Village Historical District**★ comprises nine buildings, including the El Tovar Hotel, Hopi House, Bright Angel Lodge and Lookout Studio. Trains still arrive at the **Santa Fe Railway Station** (1909, Francis Wilson). Perched on the rim, west of the Bright Angel Lodge, the **Kolb Brothers Studio** (1904) is now a bookstore and gallery. The two brothers photographed tourists descending by mule into the canyon, processed the film at Indian Garden, 4.5mi (by trail) and 4,000ft below the rim, and one would run back uphill to sell the photos to returning visitors. A mile east of the visitor center, the **Yavapai Observation Station** acts as a sort of geology museum. Exhibits focus on the Grand Canyon's fossil record; 👣 guided geology walks depart several times daily. The **Rim Trail** (*9.4mi*) extends gently west from here to Hermits Rest, its first 2.7mi (to Maricopa Point) are paved and highly accessible.

West Rim Drive (Hermit Road)★★

Between March and November, only free shuttle buses ply this 7mi road west from Grand Canyon Village. The drive passes **viewpoints★★★** at Maricopa Point, the John Wesley Powell Memorial, Hopi Point, Mohave Point and Pima

GEOLOGIC LAYERS OF THE GRAND CANYON

Kaibab Formation

Toroweap Formation

Coconino Sandstone

Hermit Shale

Supai Group

Redwall Limestone

Temple Butte Formation
Muav Limestone

Bright Angel Shale

Tapeats Sandstone

Precambrian Rocks of
the Inner Gorge

Frank Sierra/National Park Service

HOW THE GRAND CANYON WAS FORMED

In the earth's infancy, the area now defined by the Grand Canyon was covered by shallow coastal waters and accented by active volcanoes. Over millions of years, layers of marine sediment and lava built to depths thousands of feet thick. About 1.7 billion years ago, heat and pressure from within the earth buckled the sedimentary layers into mountains 5-6mi high, changing their composition to a metamorphic rock called Vishnu schist. Molten intrusions in the mountains' core cooled and hardened into pink granite. Then erosion took over, reducing the mountains to mere vestiges over millions of years.

The process repeated itself: another shallow sea covering the land, more layers of sediment 12,000ft thick were laid down. A new mountain range formed; erosion again assaulted the peaks so thoroughly that only ridges remained and, in many places, the ancient Vishnu schist was laid bare.

The horizontal layers above the schist, to 3,500ft below the modern canyon rim, were formed over 300 million years as oceans advanced across the Southwest, perhaps as many as seven times, and each time regressed. The environment was alternately marsh and desert, subject to rapid erosion. The era coincided with the age of dinosaurs and concluded about 65 million years ago with the end of the Cretaceous period. Then the Colorado River began to cut the canyon, gouging through rock and carrying debris away to sea. As erosion thinned the layer of rock above the earth's core, lava spewed to the surface. The most recent volcanic activity was in the 11C, at Sunset Crater, southeast of the park.

Point before ending at **Hermits Rest★**, named for a 19C prospector, loner Louis Boucher.

East Rim Drive★★★

The 24mi road from Grand Canyon Village to the East Rim Entrance Station passes numerous dizzying viewpoints, including Yaki, Grandview, Moran and Lipan Points. A small pueblo ruin marks the **Tusayan Ruin and Museum★**, 20mi east of the village. Displays trace the pre-13C culture of Ancestral Puebloans in the Grand Canyon region.

The **Desert View Watchtower★**, 22mi from Grand Canyon Village, may be the most photographed structure in the park. Modeled after an ancient Pueblo lookout, the three-story building is dominated by a circular 70ft tower that commands expansive **views★★★** of the convoluted canyon and Colorado River far below. The pastel Painted Desert appears on the far eastern horizon.

Canyon Floor Trails★

From Grand Canyon Village, the depth of the Grand Canyon—South Rim to canyon floor—is about 5,000ft. The distance on foot, via any of several steep and narrow trails, is 7mi to 10mi. Most popular is the **Bright Angel Trail**, originating at Bright Angel Lodge in Grand Canyon Village. The trail descends 4,460ft in 9mi to the Colorado River at Phantom Ranch, which lodges adventurers in cabins or dormitories. The trail is recommended only for exceptionally fit individuals. Hikers are strongly advised not to try hiking to the river and back to the rim in a single day. An option for descending to the canyon floor is by commercial **trail ride** on the back of a mule: one day down, one day back (reservations, booked well in advance: ☎888-297-2757; www.grandcanyon-lodges.com).

Several companies offer guided rafting trips in a range of distances and vessel sizes. Advance bookings are essential.

North Rim★★

Open mid-May–mid-Oct, weather permitting. △✕♿🅿.

The drive from Grand Canyon Village (South Rim) to Grand Canyon Lodge on the North Rim (Rte. 64 east to Cameron, US-89 north to Marble Canyon, US-89A west to Jacob Lake, then Rte. 67 south) leads to a part of the park far less developed than the South Rim. At 7,700-8,800ft above sea level, it is about 1,200ft higher than the South Rim; and it is several degrees cooler, with mid-summer temperatures averaging in the high-70s rather than mid-80s. To many

North Rim, Grand Canyon

©Leslie Forsberg/Michelin

visitors, the North Rim offers a connoisseur's experience of the Grand Canyon. The North Rim visitor center, adjacent to the Grand Canyon Lodge, is a good place to get one's bearings. A paved .5mi trail leads from here to Bright Angel Point, with glorious **views★★★** of the canyon. Also visible is the strenuous **North Kaibab Trail** (*14.2mi*), which descends 5,840ft to Phantom Ranch. Day hikers should not venture beyond Roaring Springs (4.7mi each way), water source for the entire Grand Canyon National Park. Full- and half-day mule trips are available from the North Rim, but do not descend all the way to the river.

The **Cape Royal Road★** extends 23mi from the Grand Canyon Lodge southeast across the Walhalla Plateau to Vista Encantadora and Cape Royal, with a spur route to Point Imperial, the highest point on the canyon rim at 8,803ft.

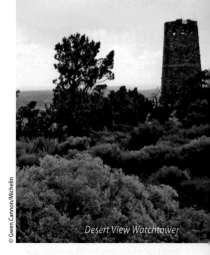
© Gwen Cannon/Michelin
Desert View Watchtower

Grand Canyon Railway★

233 N. Grand Canyon Blvd., Williams, 65mi south of Grand Canyon Village. ✕&🅿 ✆303-843-8724. www.thetrain.com.

The Atchison-Topeka-Santa Fe Railroad operated between Williams and the canyon from 1901 to 1968; service was re-established in 1989. Today the restored Grand Canyon Railway runs daily trips from the 1908 Williams Depot. The 65mi one-way trip takes 2hrs 15min, and is enlivened by strolling musicians and the antics of Wild West characters on board. Passengers can spot elk, mule deer, prairie dogs and bald eagles, other among creatures. It is a worthy alternative to driving and parking at the crowded South Rim.

Havasupai Indian Reservation

From I-40 at Seligman, 44mi west of Williams, drive 34mi northwest on Rte. 66, then 65mi north on Tribal Road 18 to Hualapai Hilltop. Supai is another 8mi by foot or mule. ⚠✕✆928-448-2121. www.havasupai-nsn.gov

The village of **Supai**, site of the Havasupai tribal center, lies at the bottom of the canyon, where the Havasupai have lived at least since the 16C. Several hundred tribal members continue to farm the fertile bottomlands and provide tourism services. Accessible only by foot, mule or helicopter, **Supai** has a small tourist lodge, a restaurant, several shops, a campground and a post office. Visitors can see the farms and livestock areas kept along Havasu Creek by the Havasupai, and hike to nearby distinctive turquoise-colored **waterfalls★★** pouring out of steep cliffs.

Hualapai Indian Reservation

From I-40 at Seligman (44mi west of Williams), drive 41mi northwest on Rte. 66 to Peach Springs. ⚠✕✆928-769-2216. http://hualapai.nsn.gov

The Hualapai control a 108mi-long portion of the South Rim, beginning about 50mi west of Grand Canyon Village. Here is the sensational **Grand Canyon Skywalk★★** (at Grand Canyon West; ✆928-769-2636, www.grandcanyon-west.com), a semicircular, cantilevered glass "bridge" that extends out 70ft over a side arm of the main canyon. The complex includes demonstration villages of the region's Native Americans, plus craft booths and food vendors.

Tribe members also operate bus tours and one- or two-day rafting trips on the Colorado River from Diamond Creek to Pearce Ferry. A permit, available in Peach Springs, is required for private car travel off Route 66.

Flagstaff–Sedona Area★★

Towering red-rock spires and buttes and history-rich Native American sites have long attracted visitors and new residents to these north-central Arizona towns. Flagstaff, established as a logging and livestock-ranching center, grew as a transportation hub—first for the railroad in 1882, later for auto travelers on historic Route 66. Today it is home to 67,500 people. Sedona, 30mi south, renowned for its wind- and water-sculpted scenery, is a magnet for artists, tourists and retirees. The cities are linked by spring-fed Oak Creek Canyon, a magnificent gorge that ranges from 800-2,000ft in depth and descends 2,500ft down the southern escarpment of the vast Colorado Plateau.

- ⓒ **Michelin Map:** pp 218-219. Mountain Standard Time.
- **Info:** ℘928-774-9541; www.flagstaffarizona.org; ℘928-282-7722; www.sedonachamber.com.
- **Don't Miss:** Oak Creek Canyon.
- **Kids:** Slide Rock State Park.

A BIT OF HISTORY

Redwall Limestone, the first stratum of sedimentary rock exposed in the red-rock formations, began to form 330 million years ago when seawater blanketed the area. The basaltic lava that caps the walls of Oak Creek Canyon was the result of volcanic activity 9-15 million years ago.

Hunter-gatherer groups of Paleo-Indians probably occupied the region as early as 6,000 years ago. Over the centuries, various tribes, including the Hohokam and Sinagua, thrived here. In modern times, the Yavapai and Tonto Apaches made this area their home. Flagstaff traces its history to 1876, when New England immigrants attached a US flag to the top of a tall, trimmed pine tree to honor their nation on Independence Day. That original flagstaff became a trail marker for westbound travelers. The opening in 1899 of the Arizona Teacher's College (now Northern Arizona University) cemented the town's future.

In the 1950s and 60s, Flagstaff was a key stop on historic Route 66, the "Mother

Oak Creek Canyon

© Gwen Cannon/Michelin

Road" that ran 2,000mi from Chicago to Los Angeles in the days before the interstate highway system.

A strip of neon motels, mom-and-pop cafes and "last-chance-for-gas" truck stops recalls that era.

Settlers trickled into Oak Creek Canyon after the first homesteader set up housekeeping in 1876, but by 1900 there were only about 15 families in the area. Sedona evolved after World War II into a destination that is part resort town, part artist colony and part retirement center. Today the town accommodates some 10,000 permanent residents and attracts about 2-4 million tourists each year.

SIGHTS
Flagstaff★
I-40 & US-89. ⚠✖♿🅿

This city is the commercial hub for a huge and sparsely populated area. Within the boundaries of Coconino County are Sedona, the Grand Canyon, Glen Canyon Dam, the western third of the Navajo Indian Reservation and three national monuments—Wupatki, Sunset Crater and Walnut Canyon.

From a visitor center in the 1926 Tudor Revival **railway station** (1 E. Rte. 66 at Leroux St.; ☎928-774-9541), ●self-guided walking tours take in Flagstaff's downtown **historic district**, whose highlights include the 1887 Hotel Weatherford (23 N. Leroux St.). On the **Northern Arizona University** campus (S. San Francisco St., south of Butler Ave.; ☎928-523-9011; www.nau.edu), eight buildings, erected between 1894 and 1926, are listed on the National Register of Historic Places. The 13,000sq ft **Riordan Mansion** (409 W. Riordan Rd.; visit by guided tour only; ☎928-779-4395; www.azparks.gov), 1904 home of two timber-baron brothers, features log siding, volcanic stone arches and Craftsman-style furniture.

👥 Lowell Observatory★
1400 W. Mars Hill Rd. ♿🅿 ☎928-233-3212. www.lowell.edu.

Astronomer Percival Lowell established this facility in 1894, 1mi west of downtown Flagstaff. Here in 1930, Clyde Tombaugh discovered Pluto by photographing sections of the night sky at six-day intervals and looking for movements in the minuscule dots of light. Lowell's 24in Alvan Clark refracting telescope is on display and in use during frequent nighttime sky-viewing sessions.

👥 Museum of Northern Arizona★
3101 N. Fort Valley Rd. (US-180 N.). ♿🅿 ☎928-774-5213. www.musnaz.org.

Well-considered exhibits provide an overview of southwestern Native American cultures, both ancient and modern, as well as an introduction to the geology, archaeology, anthropology and arts of northern Arizona.

Wupatki National Monument★
Sunset Crater-Wupatki Rd., east of US-89, 33mi northeast of Flagstaff. ♿🅿 ☎928-679-2349. www.nps.gov/wupa.

Hundreds of Pueblo-style masonry ruins are spread across this vast volcanic plain, remains of a Sinagua farming community that lived here 800 years ago. The highlight of the 55sq-mi preserve is the **Wupatki Pueblo**, accessible from an overlook or a paved (.5mi round-trip) trail. The extraordinary site includes a 100-room pueblo, ball court and amphitheater.

Sunset Crater Volcano National Monument★
Sunset Crater-Wupatki Rd., east of US-89, 14mi northeast of Flagstaff. ♿🅿 ☎928-714-0565. www.nps.gov/sucr.

A 1,000ft-high cinder cone, which erupted in 1064, is surrounded by 3,040 acres of black lava flows and cinders, out of which sprouts an improbable pine forest. A 1mi loop trail skirts the base of the volcano. You cannot climb Sunset Crater itself, but trails access smaller, nearby cinder cones.

Walnut Canyon National Monument★
Walnut Canyon Rd., 3mi south of I-40, 7.5mi east of Flagstaff. ♿🅿 ☎928-526-3367. www.nps.gov/waca.

A set of Sinagua cliff dwellings, occupied from the early 12C to mid 13C, are built into the 400ft-high walls of Walnut Creek canyon. Most ruins are well below the canyon rim, nestled in alcoves in the overhanging rock. The **Island Trail** (*1mi round trip*) requires high-altitude fitness, but visitors who descend 185ft (via 240 steps) see two dozen ancient dwellings.

Meteor Crater★

Meteor Crater Rd., 6mi south of I-40, 35mi east of Flagstaff. ✕&🅿 𝒫928-289-2362. www.meteorcrater.com.
The best-preserved meteor impact site on earth was created 50,000 years ago. A relatively small meteorite, 150ft in diameter, left a hole 570ft deep and nearly 1mi across when it crashed into the earth. Trails provide access to the crater rim; guided tours are available several times a day. The **Discovery Center** has interactive displays on meteors and the threat of collisions with earth; an **American Astronaut Wall of Fame** honors space pioneers who trained in the crater's virtual moonscape.

Oak Creek Canyon★★

Take US-89A south 14mi from Flagstaff to Oak Creek Vista to begin scenic drive.
⊕The two-lane highway is often crowded with traffic; passing other vehicles may be difficult or dangerous. Oak Creek began cutting its gorge into a fault line about 1 million years ago. Today, a 13mi scenic drive plunges more than 2,000ft through a steep-walled, 1,200ft-deep canyon, about a mile wide. The main descent begins at **Oak Creek Vista★★** (elevation 6,400ft) with a dramatic 2mi series of switchbacks. Stunning views down the gorge encompass forests of ponderosa pine and fir trees crowning the Mogollon Rim.
The creek pours over tiers of smooth sandstone at **Slide Rock State Park★** ♣♨ (8mi north of Sedona; 𝒫928-282-3034; www.azparks.gov), a hugely popular swimming hole on hot summer days. Just outside Sedona, the road skirts the banks of sparkling Oak Creek (elevation 4,500ft), where ash, cottonwood, sycamore, willow and walnut thrive.

Sedona★★

US-89A & Rte. 179. ⚠✕&🅿 𝒫928-282-7722. http://visitsedona.com.
This small city, its economy based upon tourism and the arts, owes its mystique to the variety of striking red buttes and spires that surround it. It is located in the heart of **Red Rock Country★★★**, bounded by Oak Creek and Sycamore Canyons, the Mogollon Rim and Verde Valley. The region takes its name from rust color exposed in three mid-level sandstone strata deposited between 270 million and 300 million years ago. Maps of the Sedona area identify such landmarks as Cathedral Rock, Bell Rock and Boynton Canyon.
In the 1980s, some of these sites were identified as "vortices," where energy emanates from the earth. Sedona's red rocks have become a beacon for the New Age, attracting visitors seeking spiritual enlightenment. (*Vortex tours are offered; contact the Sedona Metaphysical Spiritual Association, www. sedonaspiritual.com.*)
To experience Red Rock Country up close, you'll need sturdy hiking boots or a four-wheel-drive vehicle.
Several companies provide off-road **Jeep tours** to viewpoints, vortices, wildflower meadows and Sinagua ruins. Sedona's original commercial core is called not "downtown" but **Uptown**. Just north of the "Y" intersection on US-89A, shops and galleries in Old West-style structures offer Native American crafts to New Age items.

Tlaquepaque Arts & Crafts Village

366 Rte. 179 (at the bridge). 𝒫928-282-4838. www.tlaq.com.
This utterly charming shopping complex is modeled after the village of San Pedro de Tlaquepaque in Guadalajara, Mexico. Narrow passageways, fountains and tiled plazas planted with bright flowers and shaded by venerable sycamore trees envelop 45-plus shops.

Chapel of the Holy Cross★

End of Chapel Rd. off Rte. 179, 3 mi south of uptown Sedona. &🅿 𝒫928-282-4069. www.chapeloftheholycross.com.

This awe-inspiring contemporary Roman Catholic chapel was completed in 1956 (Anshen & Allen), the brainchild of local artist and rancher Marguerite Brunswig Staude.

Characterized by its cruciform shape, the concrete aggregate-and-glass chapel rises from the base of a red-rock butte and overlooks the valley floor some 200ft below.

Tuzigoot National Monument★

Tuzigoot Rd. off Historic 89A (Main St.), Clarkdale; 23mi southwest of Sedona via US-89A to Cottonwood. ♿🅿✆928-634-5564. www.nps.gov/tuzi.

Tlaquepaque Arts & Crafts Village

Occupied from 1000 to 1400, this ancient Sinagua pueblo tops a ridge 120ft above the Verde River. At its height in the late 1300s, Tuzigoot (Apache for "crooked water") was home to about 225 people, who farmed the fertile valley and lived in 110 rooms, including both ground-floor accommodations and rooms located in two- and three-story structures.

Limestone and sandstone boulders, bound together with mud mortar, formed the pueblo's walls.

Modern visitors, following a gently sloping .25mi trail, may enter several rooms to glimpse how the Sinaguans lived. Artifacts in the visitor center help interpret cultural practices.

Jerome★

US-89A, 29mi southwest of Sedona. ✗♿🅿✆928-634-2900. www.jeromechamber.com.

Clinging precariously to the slope of Cleopatra Hill, 2,000ft above the adjacent plain, Jerome began as a rough-and-tumble mining camp in 1876. One of the world's richest veins of copper ore – more than $4 billion worth was extracted– had the community flourishing by the early 20C. In the late 1920s, the population stood at 15,000, but then Jerome went into a steady decline until the last mine closed in 1953. During the 1960s and 70s, Jerome became a haven for artists and others seeking solidarity in the counterculture. Today,

figurative art and handicrafts such as jewelry making thrive, and the town is home to 444 residents, 300 historic structures and a handful of artisans' galleries along its winding streets. Maps and information about local merchants and tourist attractions are available at the visitor information center, which is located in a small "gypsy" wagon on Hull Avenue.

Exhibits at **Jerome State Historic Park★** (Douglas Rd.; ✆928-634-5381, www.azparks.gov) in a 1916 adobe mansion built for mine owner "Rawhide Jimmy" Douglas, explore town history.

Montezuma Castle National Monument★

Montezuma Castle Rd., Camp Verde, 1mi east of I-17 Exit 289. ♿🅿✆928-567-3322. www.nps.gov/moca.

Impossibly tucked into a natural limestone alcove 50-100ft above the floor of Beaver Creek, Montezuma Castle was part of a larger early 12C Sinaguan community. The five-story, 20-room "castle" was misnamed by Europeans, who presumed it had been constructed for 16C Aztec emperor Montezuma.

The dwelling's location safeguarded its occupants from the elements and supplied natural insulation against heat and cold. It was one of the first sites of historical and cultural significance protected by President Theodore Roosevelt's 1906 Antiquities Act.

Indian Country★★

The largest of all Native American enclaves, the Navajo Indian Reservation covers more than 26,000sq mi of mountains, forests, buttes, mesas and other wide-open desert spaces whose imagery is so often associated with the Southwest. The reservation cloaks mainly northeastern Arizona, though small portions of it extend into southeastern Utah and northwestern New Mexico.

- ⏱ **Michelin Map:** pp 218-219. Mountain Standard Time.
- ▮ **Info:** ☎928-871-6436; www.discovernavajo.com, www.vistihopi.com.
- ▶ **Location:** The Hopi and Navajo nations are sovereign entities with their own laws and customs: be sure to observe these, such as the alcohol ban on reservation lands.
- ⊛ **Don't Miss:** Monument Valley.

A BIT OF HISTORY

Most tribal land is open range. The Navajo—descended from Athabaskan hunter-gatherers, who migrated around 1600 to the Four Corners area after the disappearance of the earlier Ancestral Puebloan and Sinagua cultures—have raised sheep on isolated homesteads for centuries. The wool produces the distinctive Navajo rug and blanket weavings renowned around the world. After the Mexican War gave the US control of the Southwest, Navajo raids induced the Army to invade tribal lands. In 1863-64, troops razed the earth, destroying homes and crops, killing people and livestock.

The 8,500 survivors were marched nearly 300mi to a reserve in eastern New Mexico, a tragic ordeal etched firmly in Navajo memory as the "Long Walk." The Army's plan to turn nomadic herdsmen into sedentary farmers failed, and in 1868, the Navajo were allowed to return to their own land with enough sheep to start anew.

About 200,000 Navajo live on the reservation today; 100,00 reside elsewhere. Many who remain continue to ranch tribal lands and speak the Navajo language, a complex tongue used during World War II as an unbreakable code against the Japanese.

It is common on the reservation to see contemporary homes with satellite dishes and new cars. Alongside these often stands at least one hogan, a traditional round log-and-adobe structure.

Surrounded by the Navajo Reservation is the 2,500sq mi **Hopi Indian Reservation**, home to 7,000 descendants of the Ancestral Puebloan peoples. Arizona's only Pueblo tribe (most are in New Mexico), the Hopi live in 12 villages, most on a trio of 6,000ft mesas. Masters of dryland farming, the Hopi have lived here since the 11C, and remain perhaps the most traditional of Native American tribes. Their spirituality is reflected in their carvings of colorful kachinas, benevolent cloud dwellers supplicated for rain, good crops and a harmonious life. (Hopi means "people of peace.")

Both the Navajo and the Hopi are sovereign entities within Arizona and the United States. Tourists are welcome within these two nations; however, *alcohol is strictly prohibited–do not bring any on tribal land.* Because nearly all reservation land is part of traditional use area, off-road travel requires a permit (☎928-734-2401). Other tribal customs govern conduct on both Navajo and Hopi lands—for instance, scattering cremation remains offends Navajo custom. Please consult and observe codes of conduct throughout this region.

Note that, while Arizona does not observe Daylight Savings Time, both the Hopi and Navajo do, so from mid-March through early November, the rest of Arizona is an hour later than the two Indian nations.

SIGHTS

Navajo National Monument★

Rte. 564, 10mi north of US-160, 21mi
west of Kayenta. ⚠ 🅿 𝒫928-672-2700.
www.nps.gov/nava.

Two of the finest Ancestral Puebloan
ruins are located here at 7,300ft in lit-
tle-visited Tsegi Canyon. The 135 rooms
Betatakin★★ ("ledge house"), late 13C
home of a community of 100, nestle
into a huge, south-facing alcove in a
sandstone cliff. **Keet Seel★** ("remains
of square houses"), occupied about AD
950 to 1300, was larger (160 rooms),
home to perhaps 150 people.

From a visitor center and museum, a
steep trail (.5mi) leads to a spectacular
overlook of Betatakin, across a narrow
canyon. The only way to visit the ruins
up close is on a ranger-led hike (🐾5mi
round-trip). Keet Seel, an overnight trek,
is an arduous 8.5mi each way (☺60-day
advance reservations recommended).

Monument Valley★★★

Tribal Rd. 42, 4mi east of US-163, 24mi
north of Kayenta. ⚠✕♿🅿𝒫435-727-
5874. www.navajonationparks.org.

To many, Monument Valley represents
the essence of the American Southwest
conveyed in movies and commercials.
The distinctive landscape covers 150sq
mi on both sides of the Arizona-Utah
border. Massive sandstone monoliths
rise up to 1,000ft from a relatively flat
desert floor.

The most authentic experience of the
landscape can be found at **Monument
Valley Navajo Tribal Park★** (entrance on
US-163). The unpaved, 17mi **scenic road**
(for high-clearance or four-wheel-drive
vehicles only) loops through the park
and past many of its most prominent
features, including The Mittens, Camel
Butte, The Thumb and the Totem Pole.
Other monoliths like Sentinel Mesa, Castle Butte and The King on His Throne are
easily viewed from the visitor center.
Guided Jeep and horseback tours reach
parts of Monument Valley that are off-
limits to private vehicles, including several Navajo homesteads and isolated
petroglyphs.

The new (2008) Navajo-owned **View
Hotel** is a red-toned, 95-room facility. A
campground, picnic facilities and small
visitor center also greet visitors.

At **Goulding's Lodge** (Goulding's Rd.,
2mi west of US-163 in Utah; 𝒫435-727-
3231; www.gouldings.com), a small
museum surveys the film history of
the area.

Four Corners Monument
Tribal Park

1mi north of US-160, 11.5mi northeast
of Teec Nos Pos. 🅿 http://navajonation
parks.org

The point at which Arizona, New
Mexico, Colorado and Utah converge
is covered by a cement slab bearing
each state seal. It is the only point in
the US where the boundaries of four
states intersect.

Canyon de Chelly National
Monument★★★

Tribal Rds. 7 & 64, 3mi east of US-191 at
Chinle. ⚠✕♿🅿𝒫928-674-5500.
www.nps.gov/cach.

This 130sq-mi park holds two scenic
canyon networks framed by sheer cliff
walls. In the fertile canyon bottoms lie
at least nine major ruins dating from
AD 350 to 1300. The Navajo Nation and
the National Park Service jointly manage the park.

The reddish cliffs rise just 30ft above
the Chinle Wash at the meeting of
the canyons—26mi-long Canyon de
Chelly (SHAY) to the south, 25mi-long
Canyon del Muerto to the north. Miles
upstream, they climb as high as 1,000ft
above canyon floors that are often covered in water.

Perhaps better than any other site,
Canyon de Chelly reveals the historical range of Southwest Indian culture.
Archaeologists have unearthed evidence of the earliest Archaic Indians
and ensuing Basketmakers. After the
Ancestral Puebloans (11-13C) disappeared about 1350, their Hopi descendants moved in during the 14-15C. Navajo
have been farming here since the 17C.
From the **visitor center** (Tribal Rds. 7 &
64), two paved roads follow the canyon

rims and can be driven by anyone; each drive takes about 2hrs. Except for the **White House Trail**, entry into the canyon itself is restricted to those traveling with authorized Navajo guides. Tours by Jeep, horseback or foot, guided by Navajo locals, provide an in-depth understanding of the canyon's cultural and natural history.

The 16mi **South Rim Drive★** (Tribal Rd. 7) is more traveled. From its White House Overlook, the steep White House Trail (*1.3mi*) descends 600ft to the multistory **White House Ruin★**, an Ancestral Puebloan site and the only ruin that may be visited (on foot) without an official guide. The 15mi **North Rim Drive★** (Tribal Rd. 64) overlooks such sites as Antelope House, named for late 7C paintings found near a Basketmaker pit house, and Mummy Cave, continuously occupied by various cultures for 1,000 years.

Hubbell Trading Post National Historic Site★

Rte. 264, 1mi west of Ganado. ♿ 🅿
📞928-755-3475. www.nps.gov/hutr.
The oldest continuously operating trading post on the Navajo Reservation was established in 1878 by John Lorenzo Hubbell. He provided his Navajo clientele with items they couldn't make, such as sugar and coffee, and matches, nails and shovels, in exchange for rugs and blankets, silverwork and jewelry.
Visitors today can buy Navaho rugs, baskets, pottery and other crafts, as well as a few groceries. Navajo and Hopi interpreters staff the **interpretive center** and explain traditional lifestyles.

Hopi Reservation

Rte. 264 between Tuba City & Ganado, 70mi northeast of Flagstaff. ⛺ ✕ ♿ 🅿
📞928-734-2441. www.visithopi.com
Occupying an "island" surrounded by the Navajo Nation, the Hopi Reservation is home to 7,000 Hopi and Tewa people, who live in villages on or near three sheer-walled mesas. **Old Oraibi★**, on the more westerly Third Mesa (*50mi east of Tuba City*), was first occupied about

1100 and is presumed to be the oldest continuously inhabited village in the US. A good place for visitors to get their bearings is the modern **Hopi Cultural Center★** at Second Mesa (Rte. 264; 📞928-734-2401; www.hopiculturalcenter.com). The museum (attached to a 30-room inn) has excellent exhibits on Hopi history and lifestyle, and tribal artisans market their distinctive silver jewelry and wood carvings, including kachinas. A second lodging is the Moenkopi **Legacy Inn & Suites at Kayenta** (1 Legacy Lane; experiencehopi.com), just outside Tuba City.

Highly traditional, the Hopi welcome visitors, but no photography, recording or even sketching may be done in the villages. Ceremonial **dances,** always of spiritual significance, may be open to visitors (inquire locally); they are announced only a week in advance, in accordance with ritual practices.

EXCURSION
Petrified Forest National Park★

▶ I-40 Exit 311, 26mi east of Holbrook.
✕ ♿ 🅿 📞928-524-6228. www.nps.gov/pefo. Removal of specimens is illegal.
An immense concentration of petrified wood and fossils, more than 225 million years old, is spread over the striated, pastel-hued badlands of the **Painted Desert★**.

The main park road runs 28mi between I-40 and US-180, an easy detour from the interstate. At its north end, the **Painted Desert Visitor Center** offers a 20min film and exhibits. Two miles up the road is the **Painted Desert Inn** (1924), a national historical landmark. The structure was originally a trading post, then an inn; it's now a museum and gift shop. **Overlooks** on the southbound road pass 13C Ancestral Puebloan ruins and a landscape strewn with colorful petrified logs.

The terrain is like a moonscape, with pastel bands of pink, yellow and golden sands, blue-and-gray badlands and bleak hills in stark streaks of black and white. Short hikes access off-road areas.

Canyonlands

As far as the eye can see in southern Utah's Canyonlands region, undeveloped land extends in undulating contours and sharp angles, its vivid colors bent in whimsical and raw shapes. Earth, water and sky hold sway here.

Highlights

1. Towering monoliths in **Zion National Park** (p237)
2. **Bryce Canyon's** rocks (p238)
3. Boating to **Rainbow Bridge** (p242)
4. Natural stone arches in **Arches National Park** (p244)
5. Canyonlands **moutainbiking** (p246)

Nature on an Epic Scale

Located mainly in Utah, most of this land is owned by the federal government, and much is protected for public recreational use. Canyonlands National Park is split into three areas by the confluence of the Colorado and Green rivers, its colorful rock strata witness to billions of years of geologic history. Arches National Park is a landscape of wind- and water-sculpted rocks, formed into freestanding arches and natural bridges spanning hundreds of feet. Capitol Reef National Park's central feature is a 100mi-long rock form known as Water-pocket Fold.

Bryce Canyon National Park features dizzying, multicolored rock spires and hoo-doos. The canyons of Zion National Park are surrounded by cliffs as high as 3,000ft. At Natural Bridges National Monument, three mammoth stone spans are set in a network of narrow canyons.

Both the Navajo and Paiute peoples consider Rainbow Bridge National Monument a sacred place; it is reached via boat on Lake Powell, created in the 1960s when Glen Canyon Dam was built on the Colorado River. Grand Staircase-Escalante National Monument adjoins Glen Canyon.

Cities are few and far. Serving as gateways to the parklands are St. George, Utah, on the west side, and Page, Arizona, near Glen Canyon Dam. St. George is the earliest Mormon colony in southern Utah. Cedar City

Delicate Arch, Arches National Park

© National Park Service

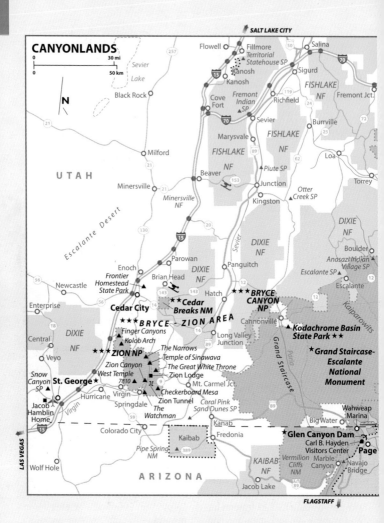

CANYONLANDS

hosts an annual Shakespearean festival. Moab is of national renown to river rafters and mountain bikers as an outdoor recreation center.

ADDRESSES

STAY

$$$$$ Green Valley Spa and Hotel –1871 W. Canyon View Dr., St. George, UT. ☏435-237-1068. www. greenvalleyspa.com. 45 rooms. Frequently lauded as one of the top destination spa resorts in the country, Green Valley Spa offers tennis instruction, over 50 massage and alternative medicine treatments, hiking and rock-climbing, yoga and fitness classes, and a variety of all-inclusive wellness and weight-loss packages, all amid a beautiful backdrop of Southern Utah's red-rock canyons. Rooms feature fireplaces, six-foot jetted tubs, private patios and goose-down comforters. Hotel dining focuses on healthy eating.
$$$$ Sorrel River Ranch – Rte. 128, mile 17, Moab, UT. ☏435-259-4642. www. sorrelriver.com. 12 rooms. Located 17mi from Moab, this luxury resort and spa attracts guests seeking peaceful isolation. Rooms feature wood floors and rustic furnishings, as well as private decks and picture windows with views of the Colorado River, red-rock

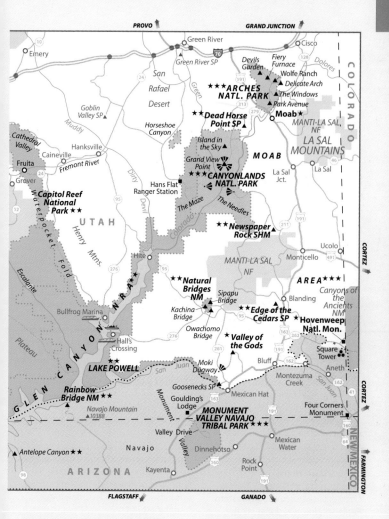

cliffs and mountain buttes. The **River Grill Restaurant ($$$)** offers seasonal American fare, from local bison to produce grown on the ranch.

$$$ Boulder Mountain Lodge – Rte. 12 near Burr Trail Jct., Boulder, UT. ☎435-335-7460. www.boulder-utah. com. 20 rooms. This sandstone-and-timber building complex, surrounding a lake and bird sanctuary, still seems undiscovered. **Hell's Backbone Grill ($$)** uses ingredients from its own farm.

$$$ Sunflower Hill – 185 N. 300 East, Moab, UT. ☎435-259-2974. www. sunflowerhill.com. 12 rooms. Wooded pathways, and flower gardens provide a quiet retreat from nearby downtown Moab. Guests relax on wicker chairs

on the covered porch, or collapse into antique iron beds. Breakfast is included and there's an outdoor pool.

$$ Bryce Canyon National Park Lodge – Bryce Canyon National Park, UT. ☎435-834-8700. www.brycecanyonforever. com. 110 rooms. Open Apr–Oct. A shingled roof, stone piers and green shutters reflect the restoration of this 1930s National Historic Landmark to its former rustic elegance. Its porch overlooks Bryce's famed pinnacles.

$$ Desert Pearl Inn – 707 Zion Park Blvd. (Rte. 9), Springdale, UT. ☎435-772-8888. www.desertpearl.com. 61 rooms. Nestled along the Virgin River at the gateway to Zion Canyon, this lodge is built of fir and redwood from an old railroad trestle. Balconies and terraces give every room a river or cliff view.

$$ Lake Powell Resort – 100 Lakeshore Dr., Page, AZ. ℘928-645-2433. www.lakepowell.com. 350 rooms. Overlooking the Wahweap Marina at the west (and most accessible) end of Lake Powell, this full-service hotel is a great place from which to launch lake tours or houseboating (**$$$$$**) excursions.

$ Valley of the Gods B&B– East of Rte. 261, 9mi north of Mexican Hat, UT. ℘970-749-1164. www.zippitydodah.com/vog. 4 rooms. This solar- and wind-powered stone ranch house is located in a mini-Monument Valley north of the San Juan River. Visitors enjoy Red Rock country from the front porch; rooms have rock walls and wood stoves.

℣ EAT

$$$ Painted Pony – 2 W. St. George Blvd.,St. George, UT. ℘435- 634-1700. www.painted-pony.com. **American**. Local art hangs on the walls and white linens cover the tables in this cozy spot. Located on the second floor of the Tower Building, the dining room overlooks Ancestor Square. The menu, offers entrées like bacon-wrapped duck with apple stuffing and pan-roasted rack of New Zealand lamb paired with an apple-fennel slaw and a mint sauce.

$$ Buck's Grill House – 1393 N. Hwy. 191, Moab, UT. ℘435-259-5201. www.bucksgrillhouse.com. **Southwestern**. Regionally inspired dishes fills the menu, from slow-cooked elk stew with root vegetables, and duck tamales with adobo and dried apricot salsa to lamb shepherd's pie. Outdoor patio.

$$ Cafe Diablo – 599 W. Main St., Torrey, UT. ℘435-425-3070. www.cafe diablo.net. **Southwestern**. Local trout gets a pumpkin-seed crust, lamb is paired with casamiento and pasilla verde sauce, turkey is simmered in guajillo mole cream. Chef Gary Pankow's chipotle-fired ribs heat up diners' tongues.

$$ Oscar's Cafe – 948 Zion Park Blvd., Springdale, UT. ℘435-772-3232. www.cafeoscars.com. **Mexican/American**. After the end of a long day of hiking in Zion National Park, head to Oscar's cozy dining room or outside patio to refuel on echiladas verdes, giant salads, sandwiches with sweet potato fries, or any of numerous vegetarian or vegan options of regular menu items.

$$ Rusty's Ranch House – 2275 E. Hwy. 14, Cedar City, UT. ℘435-586-3839. www.rustysranchhouse.com. **American**. High up in the canyon, Rusty's offers friendly service in a rustic setting. Steaks and barbecue are the specialty, but the menu includes plenty of seafood and pasta options as well.

$ Slackers – 635 Elm St., Page, AZ. ℘928-645-5267. www.slackersquality grub.com. **American**. A Page staple, Slackers is a local standby when burger cravings strike. Choose from burgers (including a green chile burger with pepperjack cheese and a bacon cheeseburger), hot and cold subs and salads.

$ Slick Rock Cafe – 5 N. Main St., Moab, UT. ℘435-259-8004. www.slickrockcafe.com. **Southwestern**. This hip spot, with murals and petroglyph replicas on walls, is a hangout for mountain bikers and river rafters. Diners munch on platters of nachos and spicy buffalo wings at tables facing Main Street activity, or dine inside on burgers, club sandwiches, and an old-fashioned pot roast.

$ Whiptail Grill – 445 Zion Park Blvd., Springdale, UT. ℘435-772-0283. **Mexican**. Located in an old gas station, this popular locals' haunt is close to Zion National Park. Diners enjoy excellent views of the canyon walls while choosing from a menu that mixes Mexican (fish tacos with grape salsa, chile rellenos and chipotle chicken enchilladas) and American standards (burgers, flank steaks and wraps).

Bryce–Zion Area★★★

Considered by some the most appealing area in all of Utah, this region contains three national parks (Zion, Bryce Canyon and Capitol Reef), two national monuments (Grand Staircase-Escalante and Cedar Breaks), stunning state parks and national forests, accented by an annual dose of Shakespeare in Cedar City.

◔ **Michelin Map:** p 234. Mountain Standard Time.
▯ **Info:** ✆435-634-5747; www.utahstgeorge.com.
◉ **Don't Miss:** Zion and Bryce Canyon National Parks.

SIGHTS

St. George★

I-15 Exit 8. ✕♿▯ ✆435-634-5747. www.utahstgeorge.com.
Mormons sent south from Salt Lake City settled St. George during the Civil War. Today the city of 75,000 is one of Utah's fastest-growing communities.

The red-sandstone 1876 **Mormon Tabernacle** (Main & Tabernacle Sts.; ✆435-628-4072; www.lds.org/locations) is open to visitors (the nearby St. George Temple is not). **Brigham Young's Winter Home** (67 W. 200 North; ✆435-673-5181) was built in 1873 by the Mormon leader. The **Jacob Hamblin Home** (Santa Clara Blvd. & Hamblin Dr., 3mi west of St. George; ✆435-673-5181) was the homestead of the first Mormon missionary, who gained a reputation for social skills with previously hostile Indians, converting many to Mormonism. **Snow Canyon State Park** (Rte. 18, Santa Clara, 10mi northwest of St. George; ✆435-628-2255, stateparks.utah.gov) has eroded red-and-white sandstone formations, some coated with layers of lava.

Zion National Park★★★

Rte. 9, Springdale, 42mi east of St. George & 23mi west of US-89. ⛺✕♿▯ ✆435-772-3256. www.nps.gov/zion.
Surrounding a 2,500ft-deep sandstone canyon decorated with waterfalls and damp hanging gardens, Zion is one of the oldest (1919) national parks. More than 65mi of hiking trails lead into its backcountry wilderness. Non-hikers can go on horseback or join shuttle-bus tours of the valley (Apr–Oct).

The massive sandstone features began forming 225 million years ago, when the park was an ancient sea floor. Later, it was a river delta and a lake bottom, and was covered in ash by volcanic eruptions. Shellfish flourished here; dinosaurs walked here. Around 170 million years ago, huge deposits of wind-blown sand left the region covered in dunes. Over time, the sand hardened into the 2,000ft-thick compacted sandstone that is now Zion's major geologic feature.

Over the last 15 million years, a short span of geological time, the forces of the Virgin River began carving Zion Canyon. Even today, the river continues its carving: A million tons of rocky sediment are washed out of **Zion Canyon** yearly.

Zion Canyon—8mi long, .5mi wide and .5 mi deep—begins at the park's south entrance off Route 9. **Zion Scenic Canyon Drive** runs 8mi to the **Temple of Sinawava**, a natural sandstone amphitheater. (Apr–Oct the road is closed to private vehicles beyond historic **Zion Lodge**, 1mi from Route 9.) From the Temple, a paved 1mi trail follows the Virgin River to **The Narrows**, barely 20ft wide in the river bottom, squeezed between rock walls rising 2,000ft.

Other sandstone monoliths include **The Watchman**, rising 2,555ft above the canyon floor; and the massive 7,810ft **West Temple**, standing more than 4,100ft above the river road. **The Great White Throne** is a prominent monolith that rises majestically 2,400ft behind a red-rock saddle. An attraction of a different sort is **Weeping Rock**, a cool rock niche carved over millennia by seeping water. Fertile hanging gardens thrive in the damp confines of its grotto.

The **Kolob** area of Zion Park—accessible only by road from I-15 Exit 40, 20mi south of Cedar City—features a 5mi scenic drive along the Hurricane Fault, where twisted layers of exposed rock may be seen. Kolob's **Finger Canyons** extend southeast toward the main park area and are favored by backcountry hikers. A strenuous 7mi hike from Lee Pass, on La Verkin Creek, leads to **Kolob Arch**, one of the world's largest stone spans at 310ft across.

Route 9 east from Springdale to US-89, through 5,607ft-long **Zion Tunnel**, features six switchbacks; the tunnel was blasted out between 1927 and 1930. At the east end is **Checkerboard Mesa**, horizontal and vertical lines etched into the sandstone by geological fractures eroded by rain and snow.

Cedar City

Rtes. 14 & 56 at I-15 Exit 59. 51 miles northeast of St. George & 252mi southwest of Salt Lake City. ⚠✕♿🅿 𝒸435-586-5124. www.scenicsouthern utah.com.

Known for its **Utah Shakespeare Festival★** (late Jun–early Oct; 𝒸435-586-7878; www.bard.org), this town

of 29,000 was the site of the first iron foundry west of the Mississippi River. At **Frontier Homestead State Park** (Rte. 91; 𝒸435-586-9290; http://stateparks. utah.gov), formerly the Iron Mission State Park, the old foundry (1851-58) has been converted into a museum of farm machinery.

Cedar Breaks National Monument★★

Rte. 14, 23mi east of Cedar City & 3mi south of Brian Head. ⚠♿🅿 𝒸435-586-0787. www.nps.gov/cebr. Facilities open late May–mid Oct.

A 3mi-wide sandstone amphitheater is rimmed by bristlecone pines, some of the oldest living plants on earth. Cedar Breaks' heavily eroded features are sculpted to a depth of 2,500ft below the 10,000ft rim in a series of rugged, narrow walls, fins, pinnacles, spires and arches that resemble Bryce Canyon. Mormon settlers misnamed the site for trees in the canyon bottom—they were junipers, not cedars.

In winter Cedar Breaks road is impassable. But that makes it more appealing to cross-country skiers, who easily ascend the unplowed road from **Brian Head Resort** (Rte. 143; 𝒸435-677-2035; www.brianhead.com), just 3mi north. Brian Head is southern Utah's largest ski area, with eight lifts and 65 runs; its base elevation of 9,600ft is the state's highest.

Bryce Canyon National Park★★★

Bryce Canyon, 24mi southeast of Panguitch & 77mi east of Cedar City. ⚠✕♿🅿 𝒸435-834-5322. www.nps.gov/brca.

This 56sq mi park contains an array of rock spires, pinnacles, arches and hoodoos tinted in a palette of rich shades, considered by some to be the most brightly colored rocks on earth. Red, yellow and brown shades derive from iron content; purple and lavender rocks contain more manganese. The odd rocks rise from the floor of a series of vast horseshoe-shaped natural amphitheaters.

Cedar Breaks National Monument

NPS/Lee Rademaker

Silent City Formation, Bryce Canyon National Park

The sculpted rocks began forming during the Cretaceous Period, around the time dinosaurs disappeared and flowering plants appeared. Deposits of sand and minerals, uplifts forced out of the earth, and erosional effects of rain and running water combined with snowfall, freezing and thawing to gradually remove billions of tons of rocks from the amphitheater rim. Eventually this debris was washed away by the Paria River, a tributary of the Colorado. Southern Paiute Indians lived around Bryce Canyon for hundreds of years prior to white settlement in the late 1800s. Native Americans called this place "red rocks standing like men in a bowl-shaped canyon." Americans shortened it to Bryce Canyon after rancher Ebenezer Bryce, who grazed livestock in the canyon bottoms in 1875 and called it "one hell of a place to lose a cow." President Warren Harding declared the area a national monument in 1923; it became a national park in 1928.

An 18mi (one-way) scenic drive leads along the pine-clad rim top to popular views and trailheads leading down into the maze-like amphitheaters. Rim spots such as Sunrise, Sunset, Rainbow and Inspiration Points, all around 8,000ft elevation, afford differing views of the crenellated and sculpted rocks.

Hiking into Bryce Canyon provides a very different perspective of the rock forms. The park has more than 50mi of trails for hiking and horseback riding. Winter visitors, for whom the park may be virtually empty, cross-country ski on park roads or borrow snowshoes (gratis) from the Bryce Canyon Visitor Center for ranger-guided tours.

Grand Staircase-Escalante National Monument★

Access from Rte. 12 between Cannonville & Boulder or US-89 west of Page. ⚠ ♿ 🅿
🕿435-826-5600 (Escalante visitor center) or 435-644-1300 (Kanab visitor center). www.ut.blm.gov/monument.

This national monument (1997) occupies 1.9 million acres of southern Utah wilderness west of the Waterpocket Fold and north of Lake Powell. This area was one of the last regions in the continental US to be mapped.

High, rugged and remote, it rises 4,500ft above the Colorado River and Lake Powell, and is considered a geological sampler, containing a huge variety of sedimentary rock formations. It has also been the subject of much political controversy over cattle grazing and proposals to drill for oil within the monument. The **Grand Staircase** – mammoth cliffs and miles-long ledges formed into natural steps of colored rock strata – dominates its western third. Stretching across the distant horizon for a distance of more than 100mi is layer upon layer of rock comprising the Pink, Gray, White, Vermilion and Chocolate Cliffs.

The area also includes the **Escalante River**, which flows from Boulder Mountain to Lake Powell in Glen Canyon National Recreation Area. The Escalante has carved deep canyons and gorges into an immense puzzle of sandstone mazes and slot canyons that offer extensive opportunities for self-sufficient and well-prepared backpackers and hikers. There are no services within the large and remote backcountry that comprises this park. Services are available only in the adjacent communities of Boulder, Escalante, Cannonville and Kanab.

Kodachrome Basin State Park★★

9mi south of Cannonville off Rte. 12. ✆435-679-8562. http://stateparks.utah.gov.

The primary characteristic of this park is the concentration of numerous tall sandstone chimneys—sand pipes—that rise from the desert floor. The spires appear white or gray in midday light. In low-angle sun of early morning or late afternoon, they begin to glow in unexpected shades of crimson, mauve and burnished orange. The National Geographic Society explored and photographed the area for a story that appeared in the September 1949 issue of their magazine, using a new brand of Kodak film, from which the area got its name.

Capitol Reef National Park★★

Rte. 24, 11mi east of Torrey. ⚠ ♿ 🅿 ✆435-425-3791. www.nps.gov/care.

This park displays an amalgam of rocks of numerous varieties and colors—great slabs of white, pink, gold, purple, orange and red rocks combined into immense, vividly colored 1,000ft-tall cliffs, stone arches and natural bridges. Primarily a backcountry park, it features miles of unpaved driving roads as well as hiking, biking and Jeep trails leading toward remote wilderness.

A visitor center is located in the heart of the park, 9mi east of the junction of Routes 12 and 24.

The park was named by 19C Mormon pioneers, whose travels across Utah were impeded by a huge, convoluted, eroded rock uplift known as the **Waterpocket Fold**. Stretching 100mi to Lake Powell, it blocked travel as a coral reef would a ship. This "reef" is crowned by white domed rock that reminded pioneers of the US Capitol in Washington DC. Waterpocket Fold itself is named for its eroded rock basins, also called pockets or tanks, that can hold thousands of gallons of water after a rainfall.

The fold is a classic monocline, thrusting the earth's crust upward, with one extremely steep side, in an area otherwise characterized by flat layers of horizontal rocks. The fold is 50 million to 70 million years old and the result of movement along an ancient fault line. Around AD 700, the Fremont culture established farming communities in the area, drawn by the water reserves of the rock pockets, and by the **Fremont River**, which also attracted abundant game and nourished wild foods. Their residency lasted 600 years. Fremont cultural history is told in petroglyphs (rock carvings) and painted pictograph panels throughout the park.

In the 1880s, Mormon pioneers established farms and orchards along the Fremont River at **Fruita**, in the vicinity of today's park visitor center. Their descendants raised cattle and fruit here until 1969, two years before Congress declared Capitol Reef a national park. The orchards are still maintained, and visitors may pick fruit in season.

A 10mi (one-way) scenic drive from the visitor center leads to overlooks of remote canyon country, slick-rock terrain, arches and spires. Turnouts offer views of such geological features as Capitol Dome, Chimney Rock, Egyptian Temple and The Goosenecks.

A short, moderately strenuous hike leads to Hickman Bridge, a natural stone bridge. A short, steep path climbs to the Golden Throne and Capitol Gorge.

Glen Canyon Area★★

Environmentalists still lament damming the Colorado River to form Lake Powell in 1963. Glen Canyon, they say, was even more beautiful than its southerly neighbor, the Grand Canyon, though not as deep. But most visitors acclaim the 186mi-long lake, whose 1,960mi shoreline is longer than California's entire Pacific coast.

NATURE'S PRECARIOUS DOMAIN

Lake Powell is the centerpiece of an area characterized by a relative lack of human intrusion throughout history. In places such as the remote Valley of the Gods or Natural Bridges National Monument, nature holds sway, not people. Even Rainbow Bridge National Monument—revered by the Navajo, whose reservation lands surround it, and visited by hundreds of tourists traveling by Lake Powell tour boats daily—retains its natural grandeur, arcing in a great curve over lake-lapped desert beaches. In other places, however, man has produced obvious changes. The town of Page, Arizona, the primary gateway to Lake Powell, didn't exist before the Glen Canyon Dam was built. The dam, considered an engineering marvel, was constructed between 1956 and 1966 to store water for development of the desert Southwest. Nearby, the Four Corners Power Generating Station's tall stacks protrude into clear-blue sky.

SIGHTS

Glen Canyon National Recreation Area★★

US-89 at Page, AZ; Rte. 276 at Bullfrog Marina & Hall's Crossing, 158mi southwest of Moab, UT; Rte. 95 at Hite UT, 155mi southwest of Moab. ⚠✕♿🅿 ✆928-608-6200. www.nps.gov/glca.

This vast area extends from Canyonlands National Park southwest to

- ♿ **Michelin Map:** p 235. Mountain Standard Time.
- 🛈 **Info:** ✆888-261-7243; http://visitpagearizona.com.
- ▶ **Location:** The gateway city Page is in Arizona, but Lake Powell is mainly in Utah.
- 🕷 **Don't Miss:** Rainbow Bridge.

Grand Canyon National Park, covering more than 1,900sq mi. **Lake Powell★★**, its centerpiece, is a huge recreational playground, whose watery fingers reach into sandy coves, inlets and slot canyons, between towering red-rock cliffs to depths of 500ft. The waters, which took 17 years to fill to a surface elevation of 3,700ft above sea level, provide opportunities for houseboating, power boating, fishing and water skiing. On the lake are four marinas and several campgrounds.

Lake Powell occupies only one-eighth of the parkland's acreage. The surrounding lands, with their myriad inlets and coves, are fascinating as well. Side canyons protect ancient ruins and a full array of natural stone features, including arches and bridges, pinnacles, fins, towers and stone chimneys known as sand pipes. Extensive backcountry hiking, biking and Jeep trails may be found throughout. Food, water and gasoline services, however, are generally available only in small communities on the periphery of the national recreation area.

Page

US-89, 157mi east of St. George UT & 135mi northeast of Grand Canyon Village AZ. ✕♿🅿 ✆888-261-7243. http://visitpagearizona.com.

Established during construction of the Glen Canyon Dam in 1956, this Arizona town, at the northwest corner of the Navajo Indian Reservation, grew as the lake behind the dam began filling with water in 1963. The national recreation area has its headquarters here.

Sipapu Bridge, Natural Bridges National Monumentt

The **John Wesley Powell Museum & Visitor Information Center★** (6 N. Lake Powell Blvd.; ✆928-645-9496; www.powellmuseum.org) features artifacts from exploration of the region about 140 years ago. The museum describes the exploits of Major Powell, a one-armed Civil War veteran who first charted the waters of the Colorado River in a wooden boat in 1869. At **Navajo Village** (Coppermine Rd. & Hwy. 98; ✆928-660-0304, www.navajovillage.com), a traditional dinner is prepared and crafts, songs and dances are demonstrated.

Tours of **Antelope Canyon★★** (5mi east of Page off Rte. 98) may be booked through the Powell Museum. Here, on the Navajo Reservation, is one of the swirling, narrow slot canyons often seen in photographs of the Southwest. Rain and wind have sculpted the porous sandstone into a slender crevice, 130ft deep and only 3ft wide in places. Tours must be taken with a licensed guide and a fee is payable in addition to the general admission charge.

Glen Canyon Dam★

US-89, 2mi northwest of Page. ✆928-608-6404. www.nps.gov/glca.
The dam produces more than 1.3 million kilowatts of electricity, serving Utah, Colorado, Wyoming, Arizona and New Mexico. With all eight of its generators operating, 15 million gallons of water pass through the dam each minute. The **Carl B. Hayden Visitor Center** (US-89; ✆928-608-6404) provides free tours of the dam.

Rainbow Bridge National Monument★★

✆520-608-6200. www.nps.gov/rabr.
Rainbow Bridge stands 290ft above the waters of Lake Powell, beside an inlet just inside the Utah border with Arizona. Higher than the US Capitol, it spans 275ft, nearly the length of a football field. Called Nonnezoshi ("rainbow turned to stone") by the Navajo, who believe that passing beneath Rainbow Bridge without offering special prayers will bring misfortune. To respect these beliefs, the Park Service asks visitors to refrain from walking under the bridge. Boat tours depart daily from **Wahweap Marina**, north of the Glen Canyon Dam, and cover the 50mi to Rainbow Bridge. Hikers may reach the bridge by a 14mi trail around Navajo Mountain from Tribal Road 16 (85mi east of Page). Permission must first be obtained from the **Navajo Nation Parks and Recreation Department** (✆928-871-6647; navajonationparks.org).

Natural Bridges National Monument★★

Rte. 275 off Rte. 95, 42mi west of Blanding UT. ⚠♿🅿 ✆435-692-1234. www.nps.gov/nabr.
This remote parkland contains the eroded stone networks of Armstrong and White Canyons. Over centuries, erosion created three natural stone bridges

that are among the largest in the world. The three bridges may be seen from overlooks along a 9mi paved park road. Short hiking trails lead to each site, and an 8.5mi trail links all three bridges. The bridges were given Hopi Indian names. **Sipapu Bridge** is the longest (268ft) and highest (220ft); it is thought to be the second-largest natural bridge in the world. **Kachina Bridge** is 204ft long, 210ft high and 93ft thick.

Owachomo Bridge is the oldest and smallest of the park's natural bridges; it spans 180ft in length, but is only 9ft thick in spots and barely 27ft wide. Owachomo is considered a late-stage natural bridge.

Valley of the Gods★

Rte. 261, 10mi north of Mexican Hat UT & 35mi south of Natural Bridges National Monument. **P**.

Similar, though smaller in scale, to its southerly neighbor, Monument Valley, Valley of the Gods is far less crowded.

A rough 17mi dirt road passes through the valley. A four-wheel-drive vehicle is recommended, with plenty of gas for the car and water for its passengers. Hardy bike riders particularly enjoy the Valley of the Gods loop for its isolation and lack of motor traffic. There are no services whatsoever. The best view of Valley of the Gods is from the **Moki Dugway** (Rte. 261), where it descends in 1,000ft of steep switchbacks from Cedar Mesa to the valley floor.

Just past Valley of the Gods, a side road leads 3mi to **Goosenecks State Park** (Rte. 316; ℘435-678-2238; http://stateparks.utah.gov), a clifftop aerie offering a view of the meandering San Juan, 500-1,000ft below.

Moab Area★★★

A town of 5,000 residents that serves as gateway to the Arches and Canyonlands National Park areas, Moab is surrounded by breathtaking scenery of carved rock and powerful flowing water. It is the staging area for a wide range of outdoor activities, particularly rafting on the Colorado River and "slick rock" mountain biking. Many expedition outfitters and guided-tour operators are based in Moab, which offers more lodging and dining options than other southeastern Utah communities. The smaller towns of Monticello, Blanding and Bluff have a limited number of services.

- ⏱ **Michelin Map:** p 235. Mountain Standard Time.
- ℹ **Info:** ℘435-259-8825; www.discovermoab.com.
- ⚑ **Don't Miss:** Arches and Canyonlands National Parks.

SIGHTS
Moab★
US-191, 244mi southeast of Salt Lake City. ⛰✕**P**℘435-259-8825. www.discovermoab.com.

A 1950s uranium boomtown, Moab is the center of an adventure travel indus-

try built around two national parks—Arches and Canyonland—and state parks; and adjacent public lands straddling the Colorado and Green Rivers. Moab was settled in 1855 by Mormon colonists dispatched from Salt Lake City by Brigham Young.

In subsequent decades, the eroded deserts near Moab have been a hideout for such outlaws as Butch Cassidy, a dock for a Colorado River boat company, and a setting for novels by Zane Grey.

Today mountain biking, golf, river rafting, kayaking, hiking and Jeep driving are pursued by residents and visitors alike. Winter attracts cross-country skiers to the La Sal Mountains, that rise east of Moab to more than 13,000ft.

The town's **Museum of Moab** (118 E. Center St.; ☎435-259-7985; www.moabmuseum.org) displays artifacts of ancient Indians and exhibits on Moab's role in the uranium boom. The Nature Conservancy's **Scott M. Matheson Wetlands Preserve** (Kane Creek Blvd.; ☎435-259-4629; www.nature.org) protects a riparian slough rich in bird and plant life.

Arches National Park★★★

Off US-191, 5mi northwest of Moab.
△ & 🅿 ☎435-719-2299.
www.nps.gov/arch.

The greatest concentration of natural stone arches - more than 2000- in the US is found in this rugged 120sq-mi park's serpentine network of multi-colored canyons, distinguished by enormous, narrow rock fins, slender spires and improbably balanced rocks. Arches' unique terrain represents the effects of 150 million years of erosion on 5,000 vertical feet of rock, revealing a porous layer of 300ft-thick Entrada Sandstone, out of which today's arches were formed.

Created as a national monument in 1929, Arches was upgraded to a national park in 1971. Previously, only Native Americans had lingered long in this daunting landscape. One rare settlement was established in the late 19C by Civil War veteran John Wesley Wolfe and his son Fred, who raised cattle for 20 years at **Wolfe Ranch**; the ruins of their log cabin and corrals remain today. Many geological attractions may be seen from the park's 18mi (one-way) main road. Short hikes from the roadway offer more intimate perspectives on some of the most dramatic features. Two miles from the visitor center is **Park Avenue**, a tapering red-rock canyon resembling a city skyline. Seven miles farther a paved spur road leads 3mi to **The Windows** section. Short trails lead to major features, including the North and South Windows and Double and Turret Arches.

Returning to the main road, another spur road (2.5mi farther) leads to Wolfe Ranch and the viewpoint for **Delicate Arch**, perhaps the park's most recognizable feature. A steep hike (1.5mi) from Wolfe Ranch leads to the base of the 46ft-high, 35ft-wide arch, which frames the La Sal Mountains in the eastern distance.

At the end of the main road, the **Devils Garden** area contains numerous arches,

Edward Abbey

Author Edward Abbey (1927-89) gained fame in the late 20C as a champion of the pristine desert environment. A park ranger at the Arches in the 1950s, he immortalized his experiences in a book called *Desert Solitaire* (1968), now considered a classic of the ecology movement. Abbey, who called himself "a man with the bark still on," wrote of the seasonal changes in the then-largely deserted park. Living alone in a small, isolated trailer, he found time to note and describe subtleties in the rock formations as well as the interplay of weather conditions, plant and animal life and humans' place in it all.

The cynical Abbey considered humans insignificant but careless and short-sighted creatures. He felt man lacked the good sense to preserve the wilderness areas where primitive human urges could be expressed harmlessly.

Other books by the gruff philosopher include the nonfiction *The Journey Home* (1977), *Abbey's Road* (1979) and *Down the River* (1982). His best-known novels are *The Monkey Wrench Gang* (1975), a humorous but insightful look at environmental terrorism, and *The Brave Cowboy* (1956), made into a 1962 movie (starring Kirk Douglas) called *Lonely Are the Brave*. Other novels include *Good News* (1980), *The Fool's Progress* (1988) and *Hayduke Lives!* (1990).

including Skyline Arch and Landscape Arch—one of the world's longest, spanning 290ft although it is only 10ft thick in one spot. A mostly level trail (2mi one-way) reaches the Garden's highlights.

The **Fiery Furnace** area contains a jumble of rock fins, towers, pinnacles and twisting canyons.

🐾 It is so confusing to navigate that visitors are encouraged to walk only with a park ranger as a guide (Mar–Oct only).

Canyonlands National Park★★★

Island in the Sky District, Rte. 313, 35mi southwest of Moab via US-191. The Needles District, Rte. 211, 87mi south of Moab via US-191. The Maze District, Rec. Rd. 633, 136mi southwest of Moab via US-191, I-70, Rte. 24 & Lower San Rafael Rd. △🅿 𝒫435-719-2313. www.nps.gov/cany.

The deep canyons of the Colorado and Green Rivers divide Utah's largest national park into three main sections, reached via different routes.

Canyonlands contains 527sq mi of deep canyons, characterized by sheer cliffs, outstanding mesas and all other varieties of bizarrely shaped hoodoos, balanced rocks, spires, fins and arches. Below Moab, the Green River flows into the Colorado, which proceeds through the strong rapids of Cataract Canyon and empties into Lake Powell. The rivers are separated by the **Island in the Sky** District, a gigantic level mesa reached via a spur road that turns south off US-191 about 9mi north of Moab. At its tip, 3,000ft above the confluence, is **Grand View Point**, with panoramic views of 100mi of tiered canyons, changing colors in dramatic red, orange and pink layer-cake slices in the low-angle light of the late-afternoon or early-morning.

The Needles District, with its massive city-size formation of vertical standing rocks, is reached from a westbound turnoff 39mi south of Moab. The Needles is separated from Island in the Sky by more than 100 road miles, although their respective paved roads end just 10mi apart, the Colorado flowing between.

The road entrance to **The Maze** District is hours from the rest of the park. From Route 24, 90mi west of Moab via I-70 at the town of Green River, drivers must navigate the dirt Lower San Rafael Road another 46mi southeast to **Hans Flat Ranger Station**. Although most high-clearance vehicles can travel it with ease, the road may nonetheless be impassable in wet weather. Considered one of the most remote locations in the continental US, the 30sq mi Maze District contains a severely convoluted canyon network, in which innumerable rock fins, towers and mesas are found. Ancient Indian pictographs, depicting ghostly characters twice human size, are seen in the Great Gallery at **Horseshoe Canyon** (Lower San Rafael Rd., 30mi north of Hans Flat). These primitive paintings may be as old as 2,000 years. The dark grotto is reached via a steep 2mi hike down Barrier Creek Canyon.

Dead Horse Point State Park★★

Rte. 313, 32mi southwest of Moab via US-191. △♿🅿 𝒫435-259-2614. http://stateparks.utah.gov.

This park, en route to Island in the Sky, was named for a herd of wild horses once corralled and left to die on this isolated point 2,000ft above the Colorado River. The sunset views from this point, light tracing across the multi-hued sandstone canyons and cliffs, are among the most dramatic in all the Canyonlands.

Newspaper Rock State Historical Monument★★

Rte. 211, 51mi south of Moab via US-191. This small roadside park, 12mi west of US-191 on the route to The Needles District, contains a rock wall with hundreds of Indian pictographs and etched petroglyph carvings.

Portrayed in or on the stone wall is nearly every figure found in ancient Indian art throughout the Southwest:

Mountain Biking

The diverse terrain and moderate desert climate of the Canyonlands make this region irresistible to mountain bikers. Two-wheel adventurers can be found from the river-carved red-rock canyons to the heights of 13,000ft mountains, in between tackling Moab's challenging, world-famous slick rock hills.

The **Slickrock Bike Trail** is probably the best-known trail of its type anywhere. It stretches over 10 technically demanding miles on undulating slickrock, a form of eroded sandstone that takes on graceful curved shapes and swirls, becoming dangerously slippery when wet. Riders follow a track, indicated by dotted white lines painted on red rocks, that hugs cliff faces and potentially lethal drop-offs.

Other biking trails with international reputations include the 100mi **White Rim Trail** (also suitable for 4WDs) through Canyonlands National Park, and the shorter, off-road Hurrah Pass Trail and Poison Spider Trail. The paved roads through Arches National Park are likewise popular with bikers, although off-road biking is prohibited in Arches.

One of the most demanding bike trails anywhere, the **Kokopelli Trail**, begins at the Slickrock Trail and covers 142mi from Moab to Grand Junction, Colorado. Along the way, the multi-day route traces the route of the Colorado River, passing from the desert canyon country of Utah into the pine-and-aspen forests of neighboring Colorado.

Each year, Moab is host to several of the biggest mountain-biking events anywhere, luring riders from around the world. Numerous bicycle shops in Moab provide full retail and rental services, and link riders with specialized tour operators for group biking adventures.

the hunchbacked flute player Kokopelli, hunters with bows and arrows, horses and wild animals.

Archaeologists believe the site was a message board for ancient people.

Edge of the Cedars State Park★★

660 W. 400 North, Blanding, 74mi south of Moab. ♿🅿️☎435-678-2238. http://stateparks.utah.gov.
The small and very well done museum within this park contains the remains of a pre-Columbian Ancestral Puebloan village, occupied from AD 700-1200. There is also a fine collection of Indian artifacts including pottery and weavings. A picnic area is available.

Hovenweep National Monument★

Square Tower Ruins, Hovenweep Rd. (County Rd. G), 31mi east of US-191 south of Moab, UT. ⛺🅿️☎970-562-4282. www.nps.gov/hove.
Founded in 1923 to preserve six Ancestral Puebloan villages, Hovenweep includes the unusual **Square Tower** Ruins, where a small visitor center offers exhibits. The unique square, oval, circular and D-shaped towers provided residents, as recently as 800 years ago, extensive views of their surroundings.

Phoenix–Tucson Area

To some, southern Arizona's Sonoran Desert is brutal. Its average annual rainfall is less than 10in and temperatures often exceed 100°F. Saguaro cactus, some 40ft tall, mark this land as an alien climate for most visitors. But others find heaven here. A brief, sudden thunderstorm can cause the desert to erupt in color—the ocotillo's flaming orange, the palo verde's yellow, the prickly pear's peach, the saguaro's dazzling ivory. And Phoenix, sixth-largest city in the US, has more major golf and spa resorts than anywhere else between Florida and Southern California.

Highlights

1 See hundreds of **Hopi kachina dolls** at the Heard Museum (p252)

2 Tour Frank Lloyd Wright's **Taliesin West** (p254)

3 Dodge hummingbirds at the **Desert Museum** (p259)

4 Hike among **giant saguaros** (p259)

A Land of Rugged Beauty

Thousands of years ago, this land of stark beauty was home to Tohono O'odham and Hohokam Indians, who built an elaborate canal system for irrigating fields of squash, beans and corn. In the 16C, Spaniards tramped through the mountains searching for gold, and though they found no riches, the conquistadors paved the way for priests and soldiers who established missions and walled forts called presidios.

Most of this rugged region didn't become US territory until the 1853 Gadsden Purchase. Soon after, folks came to mine or ranch. The most prosperous early communities in the Arizona Territory were in the far southeast. The copper town of Bisbee had opera, money and Victorian architecture. Tombstone's silver mine was prolific, its citizens wealthy, its restaurants "the best between New Orleans and San Francisco." Today the sunshine and heat of the Sonoran Desert are the chief draws in one of the fastest-growing regions in the US.

ADDRESSES

🏨 STAY

$$$$$ Hyatt Regency Scottsdale Resort and Spa at Gainey Ranch – 7500 E. Doubletree Ranch Rd., Scottsdale. ☏480-444-1234. www.scottsdale.hyatt.com. 493 rooms. A "water playground," with 10 swimming pools, a three-story waterslide and a sand beach, is at the heart of this desert resort that also boasts a luxury spa. **Alto Ristorante E Bar** ($$$) features seasonal Italian fare; dinner includes a Venetian gondola ride.

$$$$$ Royal Palms Resort and Spa – 5200 E. Camelback Rd., Phoenix. ☏602-840-3610. www.royalpalmshotel.com. 119 rooms. An intimate and secluded resort at the foot of Camelback Mountain, Royal Palms was built in Spanish Colonial style in 1929 as the gracious winter retreat for a New York City financier. The original mansion houses highly regarded **T. Cook's** ($$$$), serving Mediterranean-style cuisine.

$$$$$ Canyon Ranch – 8600 E. Rockcliff Rd., Tucson. ☏520-749-9000. www.canyonranch.com. 110 rooms. This high-profile spa opened in 1979 to

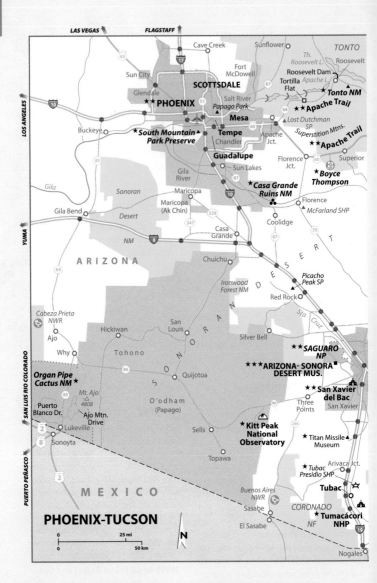

PHOENIX-TUCSON

help inaugurate the notion of long, European-style restorative retreats. Stucco casitas are scattered amid 150 acres of desert landscape in the Santa Catalina foothills.

$$$$ The Boulders – 34631 N. Tom Darlington Dr. (off Rte. 74), Carefree. ☎480-488-9009. www.theboulders. com. 223 rooms. The red boulders are just part of the allure of this world-class resort, a mecca for spa, golf and tennis lovers just northeast of Phoenix. Finest of seven restaurants is the

Palo Verde ($$$), featuring delicious Mediterranean fare.

$$$$ Westward Look Resort – 245 E. Ina Rd., Tucson. ☎520-297-1151. www. westwardlook.com. 241 rooms. An artful cross between a guest ranch and a leisure resort, the comfy casitas here line a ridge beneath the Santa Catalina Mountains. A lavish exercise center complements a pool, an extensive trail system and lovely landscaped grounds.

$$$$ Arizona Inn – 2200 E. Elm St., Tucson. ☎520-325-1541. www.arizona

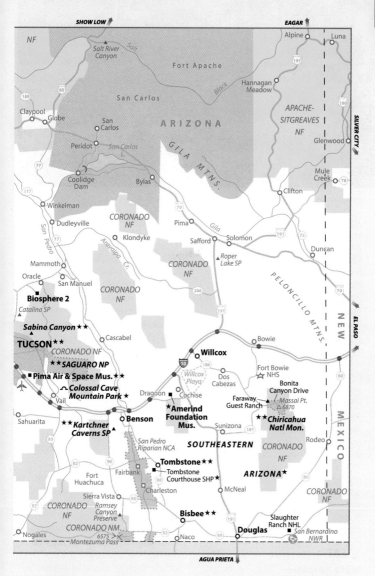

NF

Alpine

Luna

Salt River
Canyon

Fort Apache

191

Hannagan
Meadow

180

APACHE-
SITGREAVES
NF

185

60

Claypool

Globe

San Carlos

ARIZONA

Glenwood

Peridot

San Carlos L.

Mule
Creek

78

77

Coolidge
Dam

Bylas

GILA MTNS.

Clifton

177

Winkelman

CORONADO
NF

70

Gila

Pima

Duncan

75

191

San Pedro

Dudleyville

77

Klondyke

Safford

Solomon

Mammoth

Aravaipa Cr.

CORONADO
NF

Roper
Lake SP

P E L O N C I L L O   M T N S.

70

Oracle

San Manuel

CORONADO
NF

266

80

Biosphere 2
Catalina SP

Sabino Canyon ★★

Cascabel

191

Bowie

TUCSON ★★
CORONADO NF

Willcox

Fort Bowie
NHS

★★ **SAGUARO NP**

10

186

Willcox
Playa

Dos
Cabezas

Bonita
Canyon Drive

Massai Pt.
6870

N E W

■ **Pima Air & Space Mus.** ★★

∩ **Colossal Cave
Mountain Park** ★

Dragoon

Cochise

Faraway
Guest Ranch

Vail

★ **Amerind
Foundation
Mus.**

★★ **Chiricahua
Natl Mon.**

M E X I C O

Sahuarita

Benson

Sunizona

181

Rodeo

★★ **Kartchner
Caverns SP**

San Pedro
Riparian NCA

SOUTHEASTERN

CORONADO
NF

83

82

90

Tombstone ★★

ARIZONA ★

80

Fort
Huachuca

Fairbank

Tombstone
Courthouse SHP ★

Sierra Vista

Charleston

McNeal

CORONADO
NF

92

CORONADO
NF

Ramsey
Canyon
Preserve

90

Bisbee ★★

191

Slaughter
Ranch NHL

CORONADO NM
6575
Montezuma Pass

Nogales

92

Naco

80

Douglas

■ San Bernardino
NWR

inn.com. 95 rooms. Little has changed since Franklin Roosevelt came to "rough it" in the 1930s at this hacienda-style hotel. Velvet lawns surround pink casitas with sunny patios; the pool is graced by flower-edged walkways. The handsome **Main Dining Room ($$$)** features creative American and Southwest cuisine.

$$$$ Hermosa Inn – 5532 N. Palo Cristi Rd., Paradise Valley. ℘602-955-8614. www.hermosainn.com. 34 rooms. Cowboy artist Lon Megargee built this

1930s hacienda as a home and studio. Casitas spread over six acres of prickly pear and barrel cactus. Aged chaps on walls create a ranch feel. The original house is now Lon's at the **Hermosa ($$$)**, a fine-dining restaurant.

$$$$ Rancho de la Osa – Sasabe. ℘520-823-4257. www.ranchodelaosa.com. 18 rooms. Nestled near the Boboquivari Mountains, this 300-year-old Spanish hacienda was established as a guest ranch in 1924 and has hosted guests from Hollywood stars Tom Mix and

Sonoran Desert, Organ Pipe Cactus National Monument

John Wayne to US presidents Franklin Roosevelt and Lyndon Johnson. Modern adobe casitas are furnished with Mexican antiques and wood-burning fireplaces. Aside from horseback riding, hiking and swimming, birdwatching is popular: 300 bird species visit the area.

$$ Copper Queen Hotel – 11 Howell Ave.,Bisbee. ☎520-432-2216. www.copperqueen.com. 53 rooms. Built in 1902 as the hub of a copper-mining metropolis, this landmark property still rivets visitors' attention. Completely renovated, all rooms have modern amenities and period furnishings.

$$ Hotel San Carlos – 202 N. Central Ave., Phoenix. ☎602-253-4121. www.hotelsancarlos.com.128 rooms. A yellow-brick downtown classic since 1928, the San Carlos is an historic anomaly in a region of spa resorts and golf haciendas. Chandeliers and period wallpaper give an Old World ambience. Rooms and bathrooms are compact. The rooftop pool is a modern amenity.

ⴹ EAT

$$$ La Hacienda – 7575 E. Princess Dr. at The Fairmont Scottsdale, Scottsdale. ☎480-585-4848. www.fairmont.com/scottsdale/. Dinner only. **Mexican**. La Hacienda offers new takes on traditional Mexican recipes. Crab enchiladas meld Dungeness crab, Oaxaca cheese and tomatillo corn sauce; slow-cooked pork shoulder comes with chicharon, avocado salsa and sweet corn-habanero slaw.

$$$ DOWNTOWN Kitchen+Cocktails – 135 S. 6th Ave., Tucson. ☎520-623-7700. downtownkitchen.com. Dinner only.

American Fusion. Founded by Janos Wilder, arguably the best-loved chef in Southern Arizona, this restaurant features an open dining room with exposed brick walls and outdoor seating. The emphasis is on fresh ingredients and unexpected flavor combinations, with a menu ever in flux.

$$$ Old Town Tortilla Factory – 6910 E. Main St., Scottsdale. ☎480-945-4567. www.oldtowntortillafactory.com. Dinner only. **Southwestern**. Fresh tortillas, made daily in two dozen flavors, are the basis for a creative gourmet menu. In rich wood decor beneath cathedral ceilings, servers present pork chops with an Ancho-raspberry sauce, grilled Mahi Mahi tacos and filet mignon with a chipotle mushroom demi glaze.

$$$ Café Roka – 35 Main St., Bisbee. ☎520-432-5153. www.caferoka.com. Closed Sun– Wed. Dinner only. **American Fusion**. Owner-chef Rod Kass serves meals that combine elements of Italian, Mediterranean and Californian cuisines. The four-course dinners include soup, salad, sorbet and entrée. The menu changes seasonally, but the roasted half-duck has been a mainstay since the restaurant opened.

$$ Cafe Poca Cosa – 110 E. Pennington St., Tucson. ☎520-622-6400. www.cafepocasatucson.com. Closed Sun–Mon. **Mexican**. Housed in a sleek setting, with polished metal and pomegranate walls, Tucson's premier Mexican restaurant features imaginative food from all over Mexico and the Southwest with a menu that changes twice daily.

Phoenix★★

Located in the heart of the Sonoran Desert, greater Phoenix is known as the Valley of the Sun, with the hottest climate of any major city in the US. This desert oasis stretches across more than 2,000sq mi and takes in Scottsdale, Tempe, Mesa and other communities surrounding the relatively young urban center of Phoenix. Main streets are laid parallel in 1mi-by-1mi grids, making orientation and navigation simple.

A BIT OF HISTORY

A mid-1860s hay camp built atop a Hohokam site was dubbed "Phoenix," intimating that a new city might rise from ancient ruins just as the mythical bird rose from its ashes. A town site was laid out in 1870. By the end of that decade the village was a supply center for central Arizona mines and ranches; by 1899 it was territorial capital. Its transition from frontier town was assured in 1911, one year before Arizona became the 48th US state, when the Salado (Salt) River was dammed 60mi east of Phoenix. Roosevelt Dam and Theodore Roosevelt Lake fostered growth.
The Southern Pacific arrived in 1926. Chewing-gum magnate William Wrigley Jr., industrialist Cornelius Vanderbilt Jr. and architect Frank Lloyd Wright established second homes in the area, beginning a boom that continues today.

DOWNTOWN

The city hub is Patriots Square, flanked by Washington and Jefferson Streets, and on its east by Central Avenue. A $1 billion revitalization has made **Civic Plaza** a major cultural center, home to **Phoenix Symphony Hall** (75 N. 2nd St.; ✆602-262-6225; www.phoenixconventioncenter.com/venues/symphony-hall) and the **Herberger Theater** (222 E. Monroe St.; ✆602-252-8497; www.herbergertheater.org). **Heritage and Science Park** (between N. 5th, N. 7th, E. Washington & E. Monroe Sts; ✆602-262-5071; www.phoenix.gov/parks/parks/heritagepk) houses the Arizona Science Center.

Just north, the **Arizona Center** (400 E. Van Buren St. between N. 3rd & N. 5th Sts.; ✆602-271-4000; www.arizona-center.com) is a shopping complex with fountains and sunken gardens.

A few blocks west is the **Orpheum Theatre** (203 W. Adams St.; ✆602-262-6225; www.phoenix.gov/conventioncenter/orpheum), built in the Spanish Colonial Revival style, opened in 1929, and recently restored.

The **Comerica Theatre** (400 W. Washington St. at N. 4th Ave.; ✆602-379-2800) is a 5,000 seat performing-arts facility.

▶ **Population:** 1,488,750.
Michelin Map: pp 248-249. Mountain Standard Time.
Info: ✆602-254-6500; www.visitphoenix.com.
▶ **Location:** Although I-10 is an east-west highway, it heads almost straight south out of central Phoenix to Tucson. Expressways encircle the metro area, but the broad boulevards are still often the best way to cover ground.
P **Parking:** There is adequate parking at virtually all Phoenix-area attractions. Walking distances May–October in the hot sun is not a good idea.
Don't Miss: The Heard Museum is one of the best facilities devoted to native peoples of North America.
Timing: Allow 2 days to visit Phoenix. Plan your outdoor activities for before 1 pm, except November–March.
Kids: Arizona Science Center; the Phoenix Zoo.
Also See: Scottsdale's galleries for superb Western arts and crafts.

Heritage Square

115 N. 6th St. between E. Monroe & E.Washington, N. 5th & N. 7th Sts. ✕🚹 🅿 ✆602-262-5071. www.phoenix.gov/parks/parks/heritagepk

Of the Phoenix townsite homes, built 1895–1923, the 1895 **Rosson House** (113 N. 6th St.; ✆602-262-5070; www.rossonhousemuseum.org) is the oldest. **Stevens House** (602 E Adams St.; ✆602-253-9337) has a doll and toy museum.

♟♟ Arizona Science Center★

600 E. Washington St. ✕🚹🅿 ✆602-716-2000. www.azscience.org.

This concrete monolith (1997, Antoine Predock) has 300 hands-on exhibits, a 5-story IMAX theater and a cutting-edge planetarium. **My Digital World** explores how digital communications work. The latest permanent exhibit, **W.O.N.D.E.R. Center**, surveys the human and animal brain.

Chase Field★

401 E. Jefferson St. ✕🚹🅿 ✆602-462-6500. www.azchasefield.com.

This air-conditioned, natural-grass baseball stadium has a retractable roof and a centerfield swimming pool where home runs make a big splash.

"The Bob," as locals know it, is home to the Arizona Diamondbacks.

Arizona Capitol Museum

1700 W. Washington St. 🚹 ✆602-926-3620. www.azlibrary.gov/museum/.

The Territorial Capitol when it was built in 1901, this tuff-and-granite structure became state capitol in 1912. Displays include artifacts from the USS Arizona, sunk at Pearl Harbor in 1941.

The Heard Museum★★★

2301 N. Central Ave. 🚹🅿 ✆602-252-8840. www.heard.org.

Devoted to Native American culture and art, this museum contains almost 40,000 works of art. Arches, colonnades and courtyards are hallmarks of Spanish Colonial architecture. The story of its 1929 founding is told in the **Sandra Day O'Connor Gallery**. **Home: Native People in the Southwest** displays some 2,000 treasures from the collections. Showcased in rotating exhibits are hundreds of hand-carved Hopi **Katsina dolls★★**. **Remembering Our Indian School Days★★** depicts the boarding schools American Indian children were forced to attend.

Kachina dolls

A Hopi kachina (*kat-SEE-na*), also spelled Katsina, made by a well-known carver can fetch $10,000, although the average price ranges from $500 up. Originally carved by Hopi men and given to their female children to ensure fertility, these dolls (*tihu* to the Hopi) represent the spirits who intercede with the gods in the growing season. Children are given kachinas not as toys but to inspire spiritual values. Hopi religion forbids certain dolls to be produced for anyone outside the tribe. But many other figures, such as Mud Head Clown and Morning Kachina, are found in museums and shops around the state. No kachina is considered authentic unless it is carved from the root of a cottonwood tree, is anatomically correct and bears the artist's signature.

© iStockphoto.com/CW Lawrence

Musical Instrument Museum★★★

4725 E. Mayo Blvd. 📞480-478-6000. www.mim.org.

Opened in 2010, this fascinating museum boasts a collection of some 15,000 musical instruments from around the world. Both familiar and little-known instruments in the light-filled 200,000sq ft building are grouped over two floors by seven regions of the world and exhibited with **native costumes** and cultural artifacts. Visitors don headsets as they tour to listen to audio recordings; video monitors are stationed throughout to show the instruments actually being played. Among the many highlights are an 18C viola, an adufe from Spain, a Kenyan lyre, West African drums called djembes and John Lennon's upright piano.

Phoenix Art Museum★★

1625 N. Central Ave. ✕👤🅿 📞602-257-1222. www.phxart.org.

An **orientation theater** introduces the 17,000-work collection, which includes a reproduction of Gilbert Stuart's 1796 portrait, George Washington, pictured on the $1 bill. Featured are American art of the 19C–20C, Western Americana, European art, and Latin American art by Rivera, Tamayo, Orozco and Kahlo.

PAPAGO SALADO

Southeast Phoenix, between Scottsdale and Tempe north of the Salt (Salado) River, is dominated by the vast 1,200-acre Papago Park. 16C Spanish explorers, who at Pueblo Grande found remains of a Hohokam civilization, labeled these vanished desert farmers papago, or "bean eaters." They left a complex system of aqueducts among the buttes.

Desert Botanical Garden★★

1201 N. Galvin Pkwy., Papago Park. ✕👤🅿 📞480-941-1225. www.dbg.org.

With more than 20,000 desert plants, this arid-lands arboretum has won awards for environmental education. Trails snake past cacti and succulents, regional plants and animals. Displays include Indian and Hispanic residents' use of native plants.

👥 Phoenix Zoo★

455 N. Galvin Pkwy., Papago Park. ✕👤🅿 📞602-273-1341. www.phoenixzoo.org.

A motorized **Safari Train** runs through the four habitats where 1,300 animals reside. The **Forest of Uco** simulates a Colombian rain forest. The **Arizona Trail** visits a desert home for coyotes, Mexican wolves and other Southwest wildlife. White rhinos, Sumatran tigers, South American spectacled bears and a breeding colony of Arabian oryxes are among 150 endangered animals.

👥 Hall of Flame Fire Museum

6101 E. Van Buren St., Papago Park. 👤🅿 📞602-275-3473. www.hallofflame.org.

Retired firefighters share tales of their profession as visitors operate alarms and see fully restored fire engines dating back to 1725.

Pueblo Grande Museum and Archaeological Park

4619 E. Washington St. 👤🅿 📞602-495-0901. www.pueblogrande.com.

In the 14C, 1,000 people lived at this Hohokam site beside the head gate of the canal system. Storage rooms, cemeteries and ball courts are discernible at this National Historic Landmark.

SCOTTSDALE

Founded as a farm village in 1888, **Scottsdale** (📞480-421-1004; www.scottsdalecvb.com) is full of resorts, golf courses and shopping districts. In this city of 217,000 there are more than 100 art galleries. The city is known as well for its museums and art festivals.

Downtown Scottsdale

Between Camelback Rd., 2nd St., 68th Ave. & Civic Center Blvd. ✕👤🅿 📞480-947-6423. www.downtownscottsdale.com.

For almost 40 years, galleries in this district (Main St., Marshall Way & Fifth Ave) have scheduled new exhibits and artist appearances to coincide with **Scottsdale ArtWalk** (Thu nights; free trolley shuttles).

Among the city's famed **shopping centers★★** are glitzy **Scottsdale Fashion Square** (Camelback & Scottsdale Rds.; ✆480-941-2140; www.fashion-square.com); **The Borgata** (6166 N. Scottsdale Rd.; ✆602-953-6538; www.borgata.com); **Kierland Commons** (15205 N. Kierland Blvd.; ✆480-348-1577; www.kierlandcommons.com) and the **Summit at Scottsdale** (Asher Hills & Scottsdale Rd., summitatscotts-dale.com), home to the **Heard Museum North Scottsdale** (✆480-488-9817).

Old Town Scottsdale★
Scottsdale & Indian School Rds. ✕🖪🄿
A faux strip of the 19C West, Old Town has wooden sidewalks, hitching rails, and rustic storefronts. Its pink ice-cream parlor, the **Sugar Bowl** (4005 N. Scottsdale Rd.; ✆480-946-0051; www.sugarbowlscottsdale.com), has been an institution since 1958.

Neighboring **Scottsdale Civic Center Mall** includes the **Scottsdale Museum of Contemporary Art★** (7374 E. 2nd St.; ✆480-874-4666; www.smoca.org), the **Scottsdale Center for the Performing Arts** (7380 E. 2nd St.; ✆480-994-2787; www.scottsdaleperformingarts.org) and the **Scottsdale Historical Museum** (7333 E. Scottsdale Mall; ✆480-945-4499; www.scottsdalemuseum.com).

Other area attractions perpetuate the Old West theme. **Rawhide Western Town** 🄿🄸 (5700 West North Loop Rd., Chandler; ✆480-502-5600; www.rawhide.com) recreates an 1880s community with stagecoach rides, mock gunfights and burro rides for kids.

Cosanti
6433 Doubletree Ranch Rd., Scottsdale 🖪🄿 ✆480-948-6145. www.arcosanti.org/cosanti.

Italian architect Paolo Soleri defines "arcology" as the integration of architecture and ecology in new urban habitats. A prototype an hour's drive north is **Arcosanti** (off I-17 Exit 263, Cordes Junc-tion; ✆928-632-7135, www.arcosanti.org) with large solar greenhouses to create an alternative urban experience.

Taliesin West★★
12621 Frank Lloyd Wright Blvd., via Taliesin Dr. off Cactus Rd. ✎👁Visit by guided tour only. 🖪🄿 ✆480-860-2700. www.franklloydwright.org.

Frank Lloyd Wright built this complex of low-lying buildings by gathering desert stone and sand from washes. Taliesin West served as his winter home, from 1937 until his death in 1959, and is now the headquarters of the Frank Lloyd Wright Foundation.

ADDITIONAL SIGHTS
South Mountain Park Preserve★
10919 S. Central Ave. 🖪🄿 ✆602-262-7393. www.phoenix.gov/parks.

This municipal park offers city views from Dobbins Lookout and trails for hiking, biking and riding. At its foot is **Mystery Castle** 🄸🄿 (800 E. Mineral Rd., end of S. 7th St.; ✆602-268-1581), an 8,000sq-ft manse hand-built in 1930-45 of everything from desert rocks to Bing Crosby's golf club (✎👁tours available).

Tempe
US-60 & Loop 202. ✆866-914-1052. www.tempetourism.com. ✕🖪🄿

Founded in 1871 on the Salt River, this city of 166,842 is home to Arizona State University. The Tempe (tem-PEE) historical district extends along Mill Avenue. On the fringe of Papago Park, the Arizona Historical Society's **Museum at Papago Park** (1300 N. College Ave.; ✆480-929-9499; www.arizonahistori-calsociety.org) focuses on Arizona's 20–21C history.

East of Mill Avenue, **Arizona State University** (✕🖪🄿 ✆480-965-2100. www.asu.edu) boasts **ASU Gammage Auditorium★** (Apache Blvd. & Mill Ave.; ✆480-965-3434; www.asugammage.com), Frank Lloyd Wright's last major nonresidential design (1959). Antoine Predock's 1989 **J. Russell and Bonita Nelson Fine Arts Center★** (10th St. &

Mill Ave.) is a collision of boxes and triangles that resembles a Hopi pueblo.

Mesa

US-60 & Rte. 87, 15mi east of Phoenix.
✕&🅿️ 𝒫480-827-4700.
www.visitmesa.com.
Mesa was founded by Mormon pioneers in 1878. Their **Arizona Temple** (525 E. Main St.; 𝒫480-833-1211) remains a landmark. The **Arizona Museum of Natural History** (53 N. Macdonald St.; 𝒫480-644-2230, www.azcama.com) spotlights the region's natural past. At Falcon Field (Greenfield & McKellips Rds.), the **Commemorative Air Force Aviation Museum - Arizona Wing** (2017 N. Greenfield Rd.; 𝒫480-924-1940; www.azcaf.org) has vintage aircraft.

EXCURSIONS
Apache Trail★★
▶ Rte. 88 & US-60. △✕&🅿️
This 164mi loop includes a 78mi stretch of Route 88 between Apache Junction and Globe that crosses over the **Superstition Mountains**, skirts **Weaver's Needle Lookout** and passes three major lakes created by **Roosevelt Dam**. The 25mi from **Tortilla Flat**, a ghost town of six residents, to Roosevelt is a narrow, winding gravel road.

Tonto National Monument★
▶ Rte. 88, 4mi east of Roosevelt Dam.
🅿️𝒫928-467-2241. www.nps.gov/tont.
This preserve holds the remains of 13C Salado Indian cliff dwellings. A .5mi trail climbs to the 20-room Lower Dwelling where the Salado lived. ⌚Upper Dwellings tours need reservations (Nov-Apr).

Boyce Thompson Arboretum★
▶ 37615 Rte. 60, Superior. &🅿️𝒫520-689-2723. arboretum.ag.arizona.edu.
Mining magnate William Boyce Thompson turned this site beneath Picketpost Mountain into a 300-acre public park in the 1920s. The 1.5mi main trail takes in vegetation that attract birds a year-round. An interpretive center with two greenhouses are on-site.

Casa Grande Ruins National Monument★
▶ 1100 Ruins Dr., Rte. 87, Coolidge.
52mi southeast of Phoenix; take Rte. 387 at I-10 Exit 185 and follow signs. &🅿️
𝒫520-723-3172. www.nps.gov/cagr.
Along the Gila River, this four-story, 60ft-long structure was among the last constructions of the 12C Hohokam. Built of sand, clay and limestone mud, it became the first US archaeological preserve in 1892. South along the interstate is **Picacho Peak State Park** (I-10 Exit 219), a solitary 1,500ft-high landmark.

©National Park Service

Casa Grande Ruins National Monument

Tucson★★

Unlike Phoenix, which has conquered the desert with massive irrigation projects, Tucson (pronounced Two-sahn) embraces dry land. With little or no agriculture, the city has come to consider green lawns a waste of time and water. Most residents focus on enjoying the sunshine (350 days a year) and high Sonoran Desert. Five mountain ranges surround this city that sprawls across 500sq mi and includes the University of Arizona.

A BIT OF HISTORY

Tucson's night skies have inspired astronomers, professional and amateur, to set up telescopes. City regulations restrict outdoor lighting at night to preserve the starscape. The first star-gazers, the Hohokam, left petroglyphs, ball courts and pit houses that may be seen in parks, canyons and excavations around the city. Pima and Tohono O'odham tribes later took up residence. The name "Tucson" was not applied until 1694, when Spanish missionaries had trouble pronouncing stjukshon, an Indian word that means "spring at the foot of a black mountain." The city was founded in 1775 by Irishman Hugo O'Connor, a mercenary serving in the Spanish army. The walled **Presidio San Agustín del Tucson** was built under his direction; a reconstruction can be found in the El Presidio Historic District. Tucson became part of newly independent Mexico in 1821, then was transferred to the US with the Gadsden Purchase in 1853. It became capital of the Arizona Territory in 1867. The seat of government later moved north to Phoenix, but Tucson is well established as a cultural center. Its modern streetcar line is scheduled to begin regular service in mid-2014, from the university campus to the west side of downtown.

▶ **Population:** 520,116.

◐ **Michelin Map:** pp 248-249. Mountain Standard Time.

▤ **Info:** ☏520-624-1817; www.visittucson.org.

◖ **Location:** The Santa Catalina Mountains form the northern boundary of the Tucson metro area. Streets run north–south or east–west, except in the historic district, downtown.

☻ **Don't Miss:** Tucson's Arizona-Sonora Desert Museum.

◕ **Timing:** Allow 1 day. Tucson's mild months are November–March; the rest of the year, plan to visit outdoor desert sights before 1pm, and mountain or indoor attractions in the afternoon.

♟♟ **Kids:** The hummingbird exhibit at the Desert Museum and Pima Air & Space Museum.

DOWNTOWN AREA

Tucson's downtown core is condensed within a few square blocks east of Interstate 10. Some old adobes and Spanish Colonial edifices remain. A walking tour takes in the 1896 **St. Augustine Cathedral** (192 S. Stone Ave.; ☏520-623-6351; www.augustinecathedral.org). At the original presidio site, Tucson's government complex includes the **Pima County Court House** (Church Ave. between Alameda & Pennington Sts.) with its tiled Spanish-style dome. El Presidio Historic District preserves 19C and early-20C homes and shops, including **La Casa Cordova** (140 N Main Ave.), perhaps Tucson's oldest (c.1850) surviving building. A recent (2007) reconstruction of the **1775 Presidio★** (Church & Washington Sts.; ☏520-837-8119; www.tucsonpresidiotrust.org) recalls life in the fort.

Tucson Museum of Art & Historic Block★

140 N. Main Ave. ✕&🅿 ℘520-624-2333. www.tucsonmuseumofart.org.

This contemporary museum showcases avant-garde art and photography in a series of descending galleries, plus fine 19–20C American and international works (Chuck Close, Jasper Johns, Marsden Hartley, Max Weber). The museum boasts a sculpture garden and a gallery of Western art.

Old Town Artisans

201 N. Court Ave. ✕&🅿 ℘520-623-6024. www.oldtownartisans.com.

This restored 1850s adobe in El Presidio holds shops selling Latin American folk art and Native American tribal art. There is a Spanish-style courtyard and patio planted with regional plants, and a cantina that has live entertainment featuring local musicians, as well as food and drinks.

University of Arizona★

Between Euclid & Campbell Aves., 6th & Elm Sts. ✕&🅿 ℘520-621-2211. www.arizona.edu.

More than 40,000 students attend this 391-acre top research institution 1mi northeast of downtown.

West of campus, **Fourth Avenue's** (University Blvd. to 9th St.) features eccentric shops, unusual restaurants and colorful murals. Sun Link, a light rail system scheduled to go into service in 2014 (www.tucsonstreetcar.com), runs through the Fourth Avenue shopping district, connecting the university main campus to downtown Tucson.

Arizona State Museum★

1013 E. University Blvd. at Park Ave. &🅿 ℘520-621-6302.
www.statemuseum.arizona.edu.

This anthropology museum specializes in cultures of the Southwest and Mexico. In the north building, the **Paths of Life★★** exhibit interprets origins, history and modern lifestyles of 10 desert cultures. **The Pottery Project** exhibit features some of the museum's 20,000 whole vessels, the world's largest and most comprehensive collection of Southwest American Indian pottery.

UA Museum of Art★

1031 N. Olive Rd.; E. 2nd St. & Speedway Blvd. &🅿 ℘520-621-7567.
http://artmuseum.arizona.edu.

Paintings by Rembrandt, Picasso and Rothko, and Jacques Lipchitz sculptures, highlight a 5,000-piece collection dating from the 14C to contemporary times. Also displayed is the 26-panel *Retablo de la Cathedral de la Ciudad Rodrigo* by 15C Spanish painters Fernando Gallego and Maestro Bartolomé, perhaps the finest late Gothic Spanish painting in the US.

Center for Creative Photography★★

1030 N. Olive Rd. between E. 2nd St. & Speedway Blvd. &℘520-621-7968.
www.creativephotography.org.

Founded in 1975 by Ansel Adams and University of Arizona President John Schaefer, the center celebrates 20C photography as an art form, and retains the archives of more than 60 photographers, including Ansel Adams, Edward Weston, Garry Winogrand and Harry Callahan. Changing exhibits draw also from the work of other photographers.

👥 Flandrau Science Center and Planetarium★

1601 E. University Blvd. at Cherry Ave., east side of campus. &℘520-621-4515. www.flandrau.org.

Interactive exhibits deal with mirrors, vacuums, holograms, kinetics and other basic physics. An observatory offers stargazing through a 16in telescope.

Arizona Historical Society Museum Tucson★

949 E. 2nd St., across Park Ave. from UA campus. &🅿 ℘520-628-5774.
www.arizonahistoricalsociety.org.

Exhibits include a stagecoach that was used on the Tombstone-Fairbank route, military gear and uniforms, and Spanish silverwork. Personal items used by Wyatt Earp and Geronimo are also on display.

4th Avenue

University Blvd. south to 9th St. and 4th Ave. underpass. www.fourthavenue.org.
As the major thoroughfare connecting the university and its surrounding neighborhoods to downtown, this avenue serves as the city's melting pot. Shops and restaurants sit side-by-side in an eclectic mix, reflecting what is left of Tucson's hippie culture along with thriving cowpunk, Goth and information-age sensibilities. On warm weekend evenings when the sidewalks fill up with locals, especially college students, a carnival-like atmosphere prevails.

NORTH SIDE

Tucson Botanical Gardens

2150 N. Alvernon Way, south of Grant Rd. ♿🅿️ ℘520-326-9686. www.tucsonbotanical.org.
This 5.5acre urban oasis holds gardens with cacti, wildflowers and Native American crops. A xeriscape garden demonstrates landscaping in an arid climate.

Sabino Canyon★★

5900 N. Sabino Canyon Rd. at Sunrise Dr. ♿🅿️ ℘520-749-1900. www.sabinocanyon.com.
Once visited by mammoths and soldiers, who rode from Fort Lowell to swim, this canyon in the foothills of the Santa Catalina Mountains was "civilized" in the 1930s. Flash floods here in 2005 demonstrated the power of summer thunderstorms. Resident wildlife include javelina, white-tailed deer, snakes, road runners and tarantulas. Closed to automobile traffic, the canyon may be accessed on foot, bicycle, or by trams operated by Sabino Canyon Tours (℘520-749-2861; www.sabinocanyon.com). Evening tours to see canyon flora and fauna at night are available in the spring and autumn.

WEST SIDE

Overlooking downtown is **"A" Mountain** (Sentinel Peak Rd., off Congress St.), so nicknamed for a big "A" whitewashed on the side of Sentinel Peak in 1915 by fans of the university football team. **Views★★** are excellent from atop the peak. Much of west Tucson is embraced within **Tucson Mountain Park** (Gates Pass & Kinney Rds.), 27sq mi of mountain and mesa lands that encompass one of the world's most magnificent saguaro forests.

👥 Old Tucson Studios★

201 S. Kinney Rd. ✖♿🅿️ ℘520-883-0100. www.oldtucson.com.
Hollywood in the desert, this 1880s Western town has been the location for more than 350 movies and TV shows since it was built in 1939 by Columbia Pictures as the set for *Arizona*, starring William Holden. John Wayne (Rio Lobo, 1966; *McClintock*, 1962) did several films here; Clint Eastwood (*The Outlaw Josey Wales*, 1976) and Paul Newman (*Hombre*, 1966) were among other stars who filmed here.

The Giant Saguaro

The giant saguaro is found only in the highly specialized Sonoran Desert climate. The largest species of cactus in the US grows slowly: after three years, a young saguaro is barely half an inch high. It will be 50 before it flowers and 75 before it sprouts its first arm. An individual saguaro produces some 40 million seeds, but generally only one develops into a mature plant. For germination, heavy summer rains must fall; of those that sprout, only one percent survive. It's illegal to damage saguaros or remove them from the desert, living or dead, without a permit. But poaching has long been a problem. Investigators for the Arizona Department of Agriculture, sometimes called "Cactus Cops," patrol the desert in search of violators. The ultimate revenge was exacted years ago on a Phoenix man who began blasting a saguaro with a 16-gauge shotgun. A spiny 4ft arm fell off the cactus, crushing the vandal.

The dusty frontier town was turned into an entertainment park in 1959, but has continued to operate as a film set. Visitors can saunter by jails, saloons and dance halls.

Town Hall is a museum of film history; there are stunt shows, stagecoach rides, gunfights, theaters, and a thrilling **Iron Door Mine Ride**.

🐾👤 Arizona-Sonora Desert Museum★★★

2021 N. Kinney Rd. ✆520-883-2702. www.desertmuseum.org.

A combination zoo and botanical park with natural-history exhibits, this is also one of the world's leading institutions devoted to the study and appreciation of deserts. The "museum" is best seen by walking 2mi of trails through 21 acres of desert.

More than 230 animal and 1,300 plant species, all indigenous to the Sonoran Desert, include ocelots and coatimundi in a red-rock canyon, mountain lions and Mexican wolves in a mountain woodland, bighorn sheep climbing rock ledges, and javelina rooting among prickly pears. Visitors come nose to snout with Gila monsters, prairie dogs and red-tailed hawks.

An artificial limestone cave with stalagmites and stalactites contains an **Earth Sciences★** display. In the **Hummingbird Aviary★★**, native hummingbirds buzz by.

The new (2013) Warden Aquarium illustrates the vital role rivers like the Colorado play in the Sonoran Desert.

Saguaro National Park★★

⚠️♿🅿️ ✆520-733-5100. www.nps.gov/sagu.

The giant saguaro, iconic symbol of the Southwest, grows only in the Sonoran Desert of Arizona and northern Mexico. This park protects thriving communities of the cacti, which can grow to 50ft in height, 8 tons in weight and 200 years in age. Saguaros anchor diverse communities of animals and smaller plants. The park has two units. In the 37sq mi **Tucson Mountain District** (2700 N. Kinney Rd.; ✆520-733-5158), saguaros are thicker and younger. Beginning from the Red Hills Visitor Center, 1mi north of the Desert Museum, trails and the **Bajada Loop Drive** (*9mi*) offer views of cacti on mountain slopes. Starting 3.5mi north of the visitor center, the **Valley View Overlook Trail** (*.8mi*) offers views of Avra Valley and Picacho Peak.

The 103sq mi eastern unit of the park, the **Rincon Mountain District** (3693 S. Old Spanish Trail; ✆520-733-5153), is on the east side of Tucson, 15mi from downtown. The **Cactus Forest Drive** (*8mi*) loops from the visitor center through a saguaro forest; 128mi of hiking and horse trails climb over 7,000ft ridges into a woodland shared by scrub oak and ponderosa pine.

Mercado San Agustinos

West of downtown business district.
This new 15,000sq ft public market features a bakery, restaurant, gift shop, and a farmer's market every Thu year-round. Live music is sometimes performed.

Shops along 4th Avenue

©Joyce Holly/Michelin

SOUTH SIDE

Mission San Xavier del Bac★★

1950 W. San Xavier Rd. ♿🅿 📞520-294-2624. www.sanxaviermission.org.

San Xavier del Bac was founded in 1692 by Father Eusebio Kino, though the Catholic mission wasn't finished until 1797. With bricks, stone and limestone mortar, Tohono O'odham Indians created an exquisite white-domed building of Mexican Renaissance, Moorish and Byzantine styles.

The walls and ceilings of the sanctuary, entered through mesquite-wood doors, are beautifully painted in historical frescoes. Throughout are statues and carvings. Small handmade objects with ribbons, *milagros*, are left by people seeking a miracle or giving thanks for one already granted.

👥 Pima Air and Space Museum★★

6000 E. Valencia Rd. at I-10 Exit 267. ♿🅿 📞520-574-0462. www.pimaair.org.

This museum boasts a full replica of the Wright Brothers' 1903 Flyer and the SR-71 Blackbird, capable of speeds over 2,000mph. Visitors see more than 275 military, private and commercial aircraft and spacecraft, including the Air Force One used by President Kennedy. Tours visit the **Aerospace Maintenance and Regeneration Center** (AMARC) on Davis-Monthan Air Force Base, where retired aircraft are stored. The **Challenger Learning Center** enrolls kids in space "missions."

Pima operates the **Titan Missile Museum★** (1580 W. Duval Mine Rd., Sahuarita, at I-19 Exit 69, 25mi south of Tucson; 📞520-625-7736; www.titanmissilemuseum.org), a chilling reminder of the Cold War. For two decades, the US kept 54 nuclear warhead missiles ready to be launched at a moment's notice from various sites. All except this one were dismantled in the mid 1980s.

EXCURSIONS

👥 Colossal Cave Mountain Park★

⏵ 16721 E. Old Spanish Trail, 6mi north of I-10 Exit 279, Vail. 📞520-647-7275. www.colossalcave.com.

🗣Tours of this large, dry cave follow a .5mi route planned by the Civilian Conservation Corps in the mid 1930s. It serves as the home or way station to bat species found in Arizona.

Biosphere 2

⏵ 32540 S. Biosphere Rd., near Oracle, 40mi north of Tucson. 📞520-838-6200. www.b2science.org.

The spaceship-like facility in which researchers lived for two years is now managed by the University of Arizona. 🗣Guided tours take in parts of the self-sustaining lab that gained world attention in 1991-93; most of the facility is devoted to environmental research.

👥 Kitt Peak National Observatory★

⏵ Rte. 86, Tohono O'odham Reservation, 56mi southwest of Tucson. ♿🅿📞520-318-8726. www.noao.edu/kpno.

Atop 6,875ft Kitt Peak, this observatory houses the world's largest collection of optical telescopes, funded by the National Science Foundation and managed by a consortium of universities. 🗣Tours (1hr) canvass an array of observatories up to 18 stories tall. The nightly observing program offers visitors glimpses of planets and distant galaxies through 16in and 20in telescopes (🖉reservations recommended).

Organ Pipe Cactus National Monument★

⏵ Rte. 85, 140mi west of Tucson via Rte. 86. ⛺♿🅿📞520-387-6849. www.nps.gov/orpi.

This 516sq mi preserve on the Mexican border is the only place in the US to see wild organ pipe cacti, cousins of the saguaro. Gravel-surfaced **Ajo Mountain Drive** (*21mi*) winds along the foothills of the 4,800ft Ajo Range. **Puerto Blanco Drive** (*5mi*) provides access to the Pinkley Peak Picnic Area.

Southeastern Arizona★

Southeast Arizona is a landscape rife with Old West history. Here the Apache Indians—led by Cochise and later, the warrior, Geronimo— battled the US Cavalry to a standstill. Here Wyatt Earp and Doc Holliday got into a disagreement with the Clanton Gang at the O.K. Corral. Today, with rugged mountains, desert vistas and superb bird-watching, this former frontier land bordering Mexico complements its colorful past with some of the most impressive scenery in the Southwest.

- **Michelin Map:** pp 248-249. Mountain Standard Time.
- **Info:** &520-432-9215. www.explorecochise.com; www.visittucson.org.
- **Location:** South of Tucson, with higher elevation and cooler temperatures.
- **Don't Miss:** Kartchner Caverns.

SIGHTS

Tubac

I-19 Exit 34, 45mi south of Tucson. ✗ P &520-398-2704. www.tubacaz.com. Tubac was the first European settlement in Arizona. **Tubac Presidio State Historic Park★** (Presidio Dr. & Burreul St.; &520-398-2252; www.azstateparks. com) recounts the 260-year history of the fortress. Tubac's economy centers on 100 shops, **artists' studios** and galleries that line the half-dozen streets of the historic village.

Tumacácori National Historical Park★

I-19 Exit 29, 50mi south of Tucson. ♿P &520-398-2341. www.nps.gov/tuma. Construction of Tumacácori's Franciscan mission began in 1800. Self-guided tours take in the sanctuary, cemetery and convent. Guided tours are available.

Tombstone★★

US-80 between Benson & Bisbee, 67mi southeast of Tucson via I-10 Exit 303. ✗♿P &520-457-3929. www.tombstone.org. "The Town Too Tough to Die" transports visitors back to 1881, when Marshal Wyatt Earp, his brothers and Doc Holliday vanquished the cattle-rustling Clanton Gang in the legendary "Gun-

fight at the O.K. Corral." Buildings still stand from the halcyon mining years of 1877-85. Wooden sidewalks line **Allen Street★★**. Horse-drawn stagecoaches offer tours, shops sell Western souvenirs and saloons like the Crystal Palace Saloon are open for business. Gunslingers, gamblers and dance-hall hostesses wander the town of 1,570. Gunfights are reenacted daily at the original **O.K. Corral** (Allen St. between 3rd & 4th Sts.; &520-457-3456, www.ok-corral.com). Other sights to see are the 1881 **Bird Cage Theatre** (6th & Allen Sts.; &520-457-3421); the **Rose Tree Inn** (4th & Toughnut Sts.; &520-457-3326); and **Tombstone Courthouse State Historic Park★** (219 E. Toughnut St.; &520-457-3311; www.azparks.gov/parks/toco).

Bisbee★★

US-80 & Rte. 92, 96mi southeast of Tucson. ⚠✗♿P &520-432-5421. www.bisbeearizona.com. This historic mining town, its buildings clinging precariously to the sides of Tombstone Canyon, was the largest settlement between St. Louis and San Francisco when ore was discovered in 1880. The Copper Queen Mine closed in 1975, after $2 billion in copper, gold, lead, silver and zinc had been taken. Today a number of Bisbee's 5,500 people operate galleries, shops and coffeehouses within the late 19C and early 20C buildings of Italianate Victorian architecture. The **Bisbee Mining and Historical Museum** (5 Copper Queen Plaza; &520-432-7071; www.bisbee-museum.org) once served as the mining company's office. The **Copper Queen Hotel** (11 Howell Ave.; ℘520-432-2216; www.copperqueen.com) has been the town's informal focal point since 1902. **Queen Mine Tours★★** (US-80 to Historic Old Bisbee Exit; ℘520-432-2071; www.queenminetour.com) are guided by retired miners. This 1hr 15min tour of the now-inactive mine descends 1,500 ft underground, where the temperature is a constant 47°F. A nearby overlook offers dramatic views of the **Lavender Pit** open-pit mine.

Douglas

US-80 & US-191, 119 miles southeast of Tucson. ✕&🅿 ℘520-364-2478. www.visitdouglas.com.

This old copper town of 17,000 bordering Agua Prieta, Mexico, has 335 buildings on the National Historic Register. The 1907 **Gadsden Hotel** (1046 G Ave.; ℘520-364-4481; www.hotelgadsden. com) has a neo-Renaissance lobby with a marble staircase and a 42ft stained-glass mural. The 300-acre **Slaughter Ranch** (Geronimo Trail), 16mi east, has an adobe ranch house, ice house, wash house, granary and commissary. The **Grand Theatre** opened in 1919, with Ginger Rogers and Anna Pavlova being two of the stars who have graced its stage.

Benson

I-10 Exits 302-306, 45mi east of Tucson. ⚠✕&🅿 ℘520-586-4293. www.bensonvisitorcenter.com.

Founded in 1880 on the Southern Pacific line, Benson grew as a copper-smelting center. The **Benson Railroad Historic District** (E. 3rd St.) preserves late 19C buildings.

Kartchner Caverns State Park★★

Rte. 90, 9 mi south of Benson. &🅿 ℘520-586-4100. www.azstateparks. com/parks/kaca. ☛Visit by guided tour only; reservations strongly recommended (℘520-586-2283).

This huge "wet" limestone cave in the Whetstone Mountains was discovered in 1974 but kept secret until 1988.

Unveiled to the public in late 1999, the stunning cave, home to 2,000 bats, is actively dripping stalactites and growing stalagmites. Visitors enter via the **Discovery Center**, with exhibits and videos on cave geology; natural history and spelunking. Two separate tours are available; one includes one of the largest known (21ft-by-3in) soda straws, and a 58ft column called Kubla Khan. The entire cave may rival New Mexico's Carlsbad Caverns in size.

Amerind Foundation Museum★

1mi east of I-10 Exit 318, Dragoon, 16mi east of Benson. 🅿 ℘520-586-3666. www.amerind.org.

A nonprofit archaeology institute, Amerind is devoted to studying native cultures from Alaska to Patagonia. Exhibits include beadwork, costumes, pottery, basketry, ritual masks, weapons, children's toys and clothing, and cover everything from Cree snowshoe-making tools to the finest 19C Navajo weavings. Its Spanish Colonial Revival buildings (1931-59, H.M. Starkweather) blend dramatically with the boulders of Texas Canyon.

Chiricahua National Monument★★

Rte. 186, 37mi southeast of Willcox. ⚠🅿 ℘520-824-3560. www.nps.gov/chir.

Chiricahua Apaches called this the "Land of the Standing-up Rocks," a name befitting the fantastic wilderness of sculptured columns, spires, grottoes and balanced rocks that climaxes this preserve. The region became a national monument in 1924 after promotion by the Swedish-immigrant owners of the **Faraway Guest Ranch**, now a historic property open for guided tours.

From the entrance, **Bonita Canyon Drive** rises 8mi, past a small visitor center, to Massai Point at 6,870ft atop the Chiricahua Range. Hiking trails extend to such unusual rock formations as Duck on a Rock and Totem Pole. Believed to have been formed 27 million years ago by volcanic eruption, the Chiricahuas harbor numerous rare birds.

El Paso Area

Separated from the Lone Star State's other population hubs by 500mi of high desert, this bilingual city is geographically and culturally far nearer to Albuquerque and Tucson—and indeed, to Ciudad Juárez, Mexico—than to Houston or Dallas. It's even in a different time zone than other Texas cities.

El Paso

TX

Highlights

1 **El Paso's Museum of Art** (p266)

2 Peer into a **107in telescope** (p269)

3 Hike **Big Bend** National Park (p269)

4 Drive through the largest area of **white gypsum sand dunes** (p274)

5 **Carlsbad Caverns** cave tour (p275)

A Different Texas

Some 75 percent of the El Paso area's nearly 800,000 people are of Spanish heritage. Native American cultures of the Southwest, particularly the Pueblo tribe known as the Tigua, had a major impact on the region's development, as did white Americans, including railroad builders and soldiers.

The Rio Grande River divides New Mexico and sculpts the international boundary between Texas and Mexico. The most dramatic scenery is 300mi southeast of El Paso in the isolated canyons of Big Bend National Park. Much of this unique wilderness belongs to wild animals but nearby are human habitation sites considered among the oldest in North America.

Other national parks and monuments are within an easy day's drive east or north of El Paso, most of them in southern New Mexico. Best known is Carlsbad Caverns National Park, one of the world's largest underground labyrinths. Other attractions range from the ancient—such as the centuries-old Puebloan cliff dwellings and pueblos—to the futuristic. The area claims the world's best-documented crash of a supposed UFO (unidentified flying object) as well as the wasteland that witnessed the world's first atomic bomb test.

Prickly Pear Cactus Bloom, Big Bend National Park

©iStockphoto.com/Eric Foltz

ADDRESSES

🛏 STAY

$$$ Camino Real El Paso – 101 S. El Paso St., El Paso, TX. ✆915-534-3050. www.caminorealelpaso.com. 350 rooms. At 17 stories, this historic landmark overlooks three states in two nations. Decked in brass, cherry and marble, the lobby is topped by a Tiffany glass dome of mosaic leaves and blue sky. The ambience of **The Dome ($$)** restaurant takes fine dining back to the turn of the 19C.

$$$ Gage Hotel – 102 US-90 W., Marathon, TX. ✆432-386-4205. www.gagehotel.com. 39 rooms. This adobe-style inn, built in 1927 and renovated in 1978, is an ideal place to pause en route to Big Bend. Some rooms have fireplaces; all boast historic artifacts. The **12 Gage Restaurant ($$)**, entered off a rustic patio, features local beef and game augmented by produce from the hotel's own garden.

$$$ The Lodge – 601 Corona Pl., Cloudcroft, NM. ✆800-395-6343. www.thelodgeresort.com. 59 rooms. At 9,200ft elevation, The Lodge was built in 1899 as a retreat for overheated Texans. Paddle fans and gently clanging radiators remain. Guests perch on the copper-domed observatory for views that stretch 150mi, and dine on steaks and Southwestern cuisine at **Rebecca's Restaurant ($$)**.

$$ Chisos Mountains Lodge – Big Bend National Park, Basin Rural Station, TX. ✆432-477-2292. www.chisosmountainslodge.com. 72 rooms. The only hotel in Big Bend National Park, this relaxed lodge high in the Chisos Mountains offers beautiful views and convenient proximity to trail heads. Standard rooms are basic; five stand-alone stone cottages have patios. The restaurant serves three meals a day.

$$ Hotel Limpia – Fort Davis. ✆432-426-3237. www.hotellimpia.com. 31 rooms. The original hotel opened in 1884 in the Davis Mountains of southwest Texas in mile-high Fort Davis. After Fort Davis was abandoned in the late 1800s, the town declined and the hotel became a private residence in the 1890s. The present hotel was built in 1912. Restored, with period furnishings and with free Wi-Fi, it's a peaceful and comfortable hideaway with a courtyard garden, glassed-in verandah, and porches with rocking chairs.

$$ Inn of the Mountain Gods – 287 Carrizo Canyon Rd., Mescalero, NM. ✆800-545-9011 www.innofthemountaingods.com. 273 rooms. Overlooking a scenic lake and golf course just outside of Ruidoso, this Apache-owned mountain resort and 38,000sq ft casino offers a pool, a fitness center and five restaurants and bars. Skiing, hunting, fishing and horseback riding are all available.

White Sands National Monument

$ Gardner Hotel – 311 E. Franklin Ave., El Paso, TX. $915-532-3661. www. gardnerhotel.com. 40 rooms. Well established when gangster John Dillinger slept here in the 1930s, this three-story brick hotel is neat, tidy and the region's best bargain. Rooms still have original antique furniture, with cable TV and telephones added. Located just a mile from the Mexican border, the Gardner includes the 10-dorm-room **El Paso International Hostel ($)**.

¥/ EAT

$$$ Double Eagle – 308 Calle de Guadalupe, Las Cruces, NM. $575-523-6700. www.double-eagle-mesilla. com. **Southwestern**. Built in the early 19C on Old Mesilla's historic Plaza, this National Historic Register building was a private residence until 1972. It remains a repository of fascinating antiques, from the cast-iron entry gates to imperial French crystal chandeliers. Menu highlights include tournedos Maximillian. The Double Eagle also claims the world's largest green chile cheeseburger, measuring 12in.

$$$ Pelican's – 130 Shadow Mountain Dr., El Paso, TX. $985-581-1392. www.pelicanselpaso.com. **American**. Pelican's turns out surprisingly good seafood, from seared ahi tuna to crab cakes to lobster (the trick: the fresh catch is delivered bi-weekly). Steaks are the other Pelican specialty, including peppered New York strip and charbroiled ribeye.

$$ Flying "J" Ranch – Rte. 48, Alto, NM. $575-336-4330. www.flyingjranch.com. **American**. A foot-stompin' night of gunfights, pony rides, gold panning and cowboy fixin's near Ruidoso, this chuck-wagon supper of beef, beans and biscuits recalls what cowboys once ate trailside. Guests explore an Old West village until the dinner bell rings, then are serenaded by a western band and its champion yodeler.

$$ Starlight Theatre – Rte. 170, Terlingua, TX. $432-371-3400. www. thestarlighttheatre.com. Dinner only. **American**. In the 1940s, the old Chisos Mining Company's Adobe Deco theater drew movie fans from far and wide.

El Capitan at Guadalupe Mountains National Park

© Dreamstime.com/Michael Thompson

It's been given a new life as a dinner theater where live music and stage shows accompany provender such as wild boar and venison sausage, Terlingua chili, grilled quail and chicken-fried antelope.

$ The Famous Burro – US-90 & Ave. D, Marathon, TX. $432-386-4100. www. famousburro.com. Dinner only. Closed Mon–Tue. **American**. Locals and tourists feel equally at home in this quaint, low-key spot. The menu is short, but every dish is prepared well, from a butter-battered mushrooms to a wide selection of burgers.

$ L&J Cafe – 3622 E. Missouri Ave., El Paso, TX. $915-566-8418. **Mexican**. A hole-in-the-wall El Paso institution that is more than 80 years old, L&J Cafe is a friendly melting pot of locals and visitors, all chowing down on generous portions of green chile chicken enchiladas and ground beef tacos.

$ Nopalito – 310 S. Mesquite St., Las Cruces, NM. $574-524-0003. **Regional**. A longtime Las Cruces staple, family-owned Nopalito serves up New Mexican fare in an open, comfortable dining room with adobe mission-style decor. The chile-centric menu has all the expected offerings, from chiles rellenos to enchiladas to chicken flautas.

El Paso★

Located in Texas' westernmost corner, El Paso is linked to adjacent Ciudad Juárez, Mexico, just across the Rio Grande. International trade keeps the border busy in both directions. El Paso is a manufacturing center, active in the production of cotton clothing. The El Paso Museum of Art is the vanguard of downtown revitalization in the 14-block Union Plaza cultural and entertainment district.

- **Population:** 614,000.
- **Michelin Map:** 492 G, H 12. Mountain Standard Time.
- **Info:** ℘915-534-0600; www.visitelpaso.com.
- **Don't Miss:** Museum of Art.

A BIT OF HISTORY

El Paso originally was home to Manso Suma Indians. The region was claimed for Spain in 1598 by Juan de Oñate, who named it El Paso del Rio del Norte. Six decades later, priests arrived to establish a series of missions on the Juárez side of the Rio Grande. In 1680, the Pueblo Indians in northern New Mexico drove out Spanish settlers, who fled to the El Paso region with Christianized Indians known as Tiguas and Piros. They founded Ysleta and Socorro, and together with Franciscan padres built the first Texas missions.

In the mid 19C, the US Army constructed Fort Bliss for defense of the city and surrounding areas; it is now a major contributor to the city's economy. El Paso was incorporated in 1873; it became a boomtown a decade later with the arrival of the railroad. Throughout the late 19C, the city had a Wild West reputation, with gunfights and a renegade atmosphere. The fairly new (2007, Joe Gomez and Cesar Duran) **El Paso Museum of History** (510 N. Santa Fe St.; ℘915-351-3588; www.elpasotexas.gov/history) celebrates the area's distinctive, multicultural past. The city is emerging as the US-Mexico border's most centralized hub, with Ciudad Juárez students crossing each day to attend schools in El Paso.

Rising behind the city are the Franklin Mountains, southernmost tip of the Rockies. This warm, dry region is part of the Chihuahuan Desert; altitudes range from 3,800ft in the city to 7,200ft in the mountains.

SIGHTS

El Paso Museum of Art★★

1 Arts Festival Plaza at Santa Fe & Main Sts. ℘915-532-1707. www.elpasoartmuseum.org.

This spacious two-level museum includes a reference library, auditorium and the Arts Festival Plaza, which features a reflecting pool, waterfall and performance areas.

The **Works on Paper Collection** showcases drawings and prints from the 16–20C, including Cézanne, Degas, Picasso, Goya and Rivera. The **American Collection** (late 18C–mid 20C) has works by Frederic Remington and post-Depression Figurative painter Moses Soyer. The **Samuel Kress Collection** highlights 13–18C European paintings and sculpture, including pieces by Canaletto and Van Dyck. The **Spanish Viceroyal Collection** features 17–19C artists and includes Mexican folk retablos. Pieces created in the American Southwest and Mexico since 1945 are the emphasis of the **Contemporary Collection**.

El Paso Holocaust Museum and Study Center★

715 N. Oregon. ♿ P ℘915-351-0048. www.elpasoholocaustmuseum.org.

Memorializing the Holocaust's 6 million victims and its survivors, this museum's bone-chilling exhibits include a three-quarter-scale model of a railroad used to carry victims to concentration camps. The Garden of the Righteous commemorates Gentiles who risked their lives to assist Jews during the war.

Chamizal National Memorial★

800 S. San Marcial St. ♿🅿
𝓟915-532-7273. www.nps.gov/cham.
Located near the Bridge of the Americas, this memorial to peaceful US–Mexico relations recalls the 1963 resolution of a century-old border dispute caused by the Rio Grande shifting course. Three galleries include the **Los Paisanos Gallery** exhibits art from several countries. The park's 500-seat indoor theater offers evening performances by *ballet folklórico* troupes or modern dancers.

Mission Trail★

1 Civic Center Plaza, I-10 Zaragoza Exit, 4mi southeast of downtown. ♿🅿
𝓟915-534-0630.
www.visitelpasomissiontrail.com.
South of El Paso along the Rio Grande are three 17C missions that once lured settlers as farming and ranching centers. Northernmost is **Mission Ysleta** (131 S. Zaragoza Rd. at S. Old Pueblo Dr.; 𝓟915-859-9848; http://ysletamission. org), built for Spanish and Tigua refugees from the Pueblo Revolt in 1680. Floods destroyed the original mission; this one dates from 1851. Descendants of those Tiguas still use the mission for religious services. Their **Tigua Cultural Center★** (305 Ya Ya Lane; 𝓟915-859-7700) has a museum and gift shops.
Mission Socorro★ (338 S. Nevares Rd., 2.6mi south of Mission Ysleta; 𝓟915-859-7718; www.nps.gov/nr/travel/tx/tx1.htm) also was built for refugees and rebuilt after a 19C flood. An example of Spanish Mission architecture, the mission features roof beams hand-sculpted by Piro Indians.
Also still in use, the gilded **Presidio Chapel of San Elizario★** (Socorro Rd., 6mi south of Mission Socorro; 𝓟915-851-1682; www.nps.gov/nr//travel/tx/tx4.htm) combines Southwestern attributes with European characteristics.

Franklin Mountains State Park★

1331 McKelligon Canyon Rd. (I-10 to Canutillo Exit, Loop 375 east 4mi to entrance). ⚠𝓟915-566-6441.
www.tpwd.state.tx.us.
The largest urban wilderness park in the US spans 37sq mi of Chihuahuan Desert, from El Paso to the New Mexico state line. Along with desert plants such as sotol and ocotillo, the park is home to mule deer, birds and mountain lions.

Fort Bliss

Fred Wilson Rd. east of US-54. t915-568-2121. www.bliss.army.mil.
This fort was established in 1848 to protect the region from Indian attack. During the Civil War, it was headquarters for the Confederate forces of the Southwest, and later was a post for troops charged with capturing Apache chief **Geronimo**. At the Robert E. Lee entrance gate stands the **Buffalo Soldier Monument**. Feared and respected, the African-American Buffalo Soldiers patrolled the Western frontier during the late 19C. The **Fort Bliss Museum** (Bldg. 5051; 𝓟915-568-5412), in a replica of a c.1857 adobe fort, recalls the post's history. Today Fort Bliss is a US Army Air Defense Center.

EXCURSION
Guadalupe Mountains National Park★★

⊳ US-62/180, 110mi east of El Paso. ⚠🅿
𝓟915-828-3251. www.nps.gov/gumo.
The highest mountains in Texas peak at 8,749ft at Guadalupe Peak. Part of the most extensive Permian limestone fossil reef in the world, this terrain ranges from lowland desert to high-country conifer forest. Mescalero Apaches hunted here in the early 16C. The Pine Springs' **Headquarters Visitor Center** focuses on the ecology and geology of the mountains. There are other exhibits at **Historic Frijole Ranch**. Of the 80mi of trails, the most popular are those to El Capitan limestone formation and to **McKittrick Canyon**, where maple, walnut, ash, oak and Texas madrone trees show off their colors in fall.

Big Bend Area★★

Much of this rugged and sparsely populated region is preserved within sprawling Big Bend National Park, located where the Rio Grande turns sharply from southeast to northeast. More than 100mi is edged by the Rio Grande's swirling waters, which have carved the Santa Elena, Mariscal and Boquillas Canyons. Cut deep into the Chisos Mountains, these limestone chasms at first appear barren. But closer inspection reveals them—and the surrounding Chihuahuan Desert—to be rich with animal and plant life.

- ⏱ **Michelin Map:** 492 H, I 13, 14. Central Standard Time.
- **Info:** www.visitbigbend.com.
- **Location:** Summer is not Big Bend's best visiting season because of the area's extreme heat.
- **Don't Miss:** Big Bend.
- 👥 **Kids:** McDonald Observatory.

A BIT OF HISTORY

Man has lived in the Big Bend area at least 8,000 years. Ancient residents—who relied upon bison, and later agriculture, for sustenance—left pictographs and petroglyphs on canyon walls. By 1535, when the first Spanish arrived, the region was a seasonal home to the nomadic Chisos Indians. They were displaced by Mescalero Apaches and finally by Comanches, who moved through the area, making raids on Mexico, into the late 19C.

After the Mexican War, US forts, including Fort Davis, gave security to modern settlement. Early 20C mining brought prospectors. In the 1930s, the state of Texas began to acquire and preserve land in the Big Bend area, consolidating it as Texas Canyons State Park. The state deeded the land to the US government in 1944 and the site became Big Bend National Park.

🚗 DRIVING TOUR

4 days, 581mi one-way.

▶ From El Paso, take I-10 east 157mi to Kent, then Rte. 118 south 37mi.

👥 McDonald Observatory★★

Rte. 118, 16mi northwest of Fort Davis. 🅿 ✆432-426-3640. www.mcdonaldobservatory.org.
Located far from city lights, this University of Texas facility is one of the world's best astronomy research centers. Visitors join tours of the 107in Harlan J.

Balanced Rock, Big Bend National Park

©iStockphoto.com/Eric Foltz

Smith Telescope and the Hobby-Eberly Telescope. Public viewings (☺by reservation) and family-oriented "star parties" are scheduled year-round.

▶ Continue 16mi southeast on Rte. 118.

Fort Davis National Historic Site★★

Main St. (Rtes. 17 & 118), Fort Davis. ♿🅿 ℘432-426-3224. www.nps.gov/foda.
Fort Davis is one of the best surviving examples of a frontier post. Built in 1854 to protect the El Paso-San Antonio road from Indian attack, it was abandoned during the Civil War; troops found mainly ruins when they returned to rebuild in 1867. Fort Davis' role as a bulwark for mail and wagon-train routes continued until 1891. Today costumed docents staff some of the buildings. Historical exhibits are at the fort museum, in a reconstructed barracks. The fort anchors the community of Fort Davis, home to about 1,050.

▶ Follow Rte. 118 south 103mi through Alpine to Study Butte, at west entrance to Big Bend National Park.

Big Bend National Park★★★

Rte. 118 south of Alpine or US-385 south of Marathon; Panther Junction is 320mi southeast of El Paso. ⛺✗♿🅿 ℘432-477-2251. www.nps.gov/bibe.
Big Bend spans 1,252sq mi of spectacular canyons, lush bottomlands, sprawling desert and mountain woodlands on the north side of the Rio Grande. Ranging across more than 6,000ft of elevation, it boasts a wealth of animal and plant life. Big Bend has more than 450 species of migratory and resident birds. Bats, rodents and other small mammals are nocturnal; javelina and deer are often seen, mountain lions rarely. Reptiles thrive in the extreme climate. Torrential thunderstorms may follow droughts. Temperatures approach 120°F in summer but may drop below 10°F in winter. The area has a remarkable geological history, and a long and fascinating chronology of human habitation.

Geologic History

The oldest rocks, nearly 300 million years old, were deposited as sediment on an ancient ocean floor. Marine fossils in Persimmon Gap predate dinosaurs, that wandered a swampy Cretaceous landscape 100 million to 65 million years ago. Among them was the largest flying creature ever known, a pterodactyl with a 51ft wingspread. Volcanism and tectonic buckling between 42 million and 26 million years ago created the Chisos Mountains, which top out at 7,835ft Emory Peak. The park's canyons were carved over the past 3 million years during the ice ages.

Human History

Ten thousand archaeological sites tell of hunters who ventured into the area 11,000 years ago pursuing giant bison and woolly mammoths. Artifacts found

Judge Roy Bean

From behind the bar of his saloon, Judge Roy Bean served up frontier justice with beer and whiskey, leaving a legacy of fact and fiction. A silver spike driven at Dead Man's Gulch, near Langtry, linked the final section of Southern Pacific track between New Orleans and San Francisco in 1882. With the railroad came an influx of rowdy construction crews and their attendant evils – stealing, gambling and prostitution. With no law enforcement office within 100mi, shopkeeper Roy Bean was named Justice of the Peace. Bean chose his jurors from among saloon customers. He presided over trials with a six-shooter at one hand and his single book of law at the other. His favorite punishment was to exile offenders into the desert without food, water, weapons or money. Bean died in 1903.

in caves and rock shelters indicate that these Paleo-Indians had adopted a nomadic lifestyle by 6000 BC. Ruins of pueblo villages in the Rio Grande floodplain document a culture well established by AD 500. Later, Big Bend was a sanctuary for Apaches driven south by warlike Comanches in the 17C.

Survey parties explored Big Bend by riverboat and camel in the late 1850s. Ranching and mining achieved minor success. A small factory at **Glenn Spring** produced wax from the candelilla, a perennial desert plant, until Mexican bandits destroyed the community in 1916. The US Army then began an aerial border patrol in an attempt to capture the infamous Pancho Villa.

Visit

Park headquarters and the main visitor center are at **Panther Junction** (US-385 & Rio Grande Village Rd.) in the heart of Big Bend. Other visitor centers— at **Persimmon Gap** (US-385 at north entrance), **Chisos Basin** (Basin Rd.) and **Rio Grande Village** (Rio Grande Village Rd.)—also provide information on archaeology and ecotourism activities. Campgrounds and rustic lodges can be found at various locations.

Hikers can choose from 200mi of trails in the park, ranging from easy to strenuous. Naturalists guide walks year-round. Outfitters based outside the park offer Rio Grande float trips through rugged canyons.

▶ From Panther Junction, 25mi east of Study Butte, take US-385 north 69mi to Marathon. Turn east on US-90 for 115 mi to Langtry.

Judge Roy Bean Visitor Center★
.5mi south of US-90 on Loop 25, Langtry. ♿🅿 ✆432-291-3340.
The story of the Wild West's most famous frontier judge is told in dioramas and exhibits. Adjacent stands **The Jersey Lilly**, the restored saloon and courtroom used by Judge Bean in the 1880s.

▶ Continue east on US-90 for 18mi.

Seminole Canyon State Park★★
US-90, 133mi east of Marathon. ⚠♿🅿 ✆432-292-4464. www.tpwd.state.tx.us.
On the limestone walls of this park are pictographs drawn by ancient peoples 4,000 years ago. Symbols represent animals, hunters and supernatural shamans. Archaeologists believe the early residents of Seminole Canyon were hunter-gatherers, living on plants such as sotol, prickly pear and lechugilla. Ranger-led tours take visitors to the **Fate Bell Shelter**, which displays the oldest rock art in the region.

▶ Continue east on US-90 for 27mi.

👤👤 Amistad National Recreation Area★★
US-90 between Langtry and Del Rio, 160mi east of Marathon. ⚠🅿 ✆830-775-7491. www.nps.gov/amis.
Surrounding Lake Amistad on the US-Mexico border, this recreation area is popular for water sports. The 85mi-long lake is formed by a dam built in 1969 below the confluence of the Pecos and Devils Rivers with the Rio Grande. Amistad, the Spanish word for "friendship," was a joint US-Mexico project. Much of the lake is lined with limestone canyons, some containing caves with prehistoric pictographs. There are more than 250 sites within 100sq mi.

▶ Driving tour concludes in Del Rio, 41mi farther east.

Southern New Mexico ★

Southern New Mexico is a cultural crossroads. Here the Hispanic culture of Mexico meshes with the Native American culture of the American Southwest, its glaze of "Anglo" society layered on top. Extending north of El Paso 150mi, from the Texas and Mexico borders through numerous fertile valleys and basins amid mountainous areas, this expansive region contains many natural and historical attractions.

♿ **Michelin Map:** 493 G, H 11, 12. Mountain Standard Time.
ℹ **Info:** ℘505-827-7336; www.newmexico.org.
🚫 **Don't Miss:** Carlsbad Caverns.
👫 **Kids:** Space History Museum.

A BIT OF HISTORY

Millions of years ago, this was the floor of an inland sea. When the waters receded, a rich store of fossils was left. Carlsbad Caverns, one of the world's most complex cave systems, began forming within this fossil reef 250 million years ago. Relative newcomers, Ancestral Puebloan and Mogollon Indians established a foothold only 8,000 years ago. Their legacy remains in the ruins of cliff dwellings and pueblo communities.

Ranching, farming and mining have supported the regional economy since the first Spanish missions were built in the 17C. In the late 19C, Las Cruces grew from a mining-supply center to the largest city in the area.

On July 16, 1945, the first atomic bomb was exploded at the Trinity Site near White Sands. Two years later, some folks contend, an interplanetary spacecraft crash-landed near Roswell, its alien crew put under lock and key by the US Army. Meanwhile, the world's most powerful radio telescopes send signals toward unseen civilizations, and the Space Center in Alamogordo is a tribute to aerospace fact.

🚗 DRIVING TOUR

5 days, 969mi round-trip.

▷ Tour begins and ends in El Paso. Take I-10 north 42mi to Las Cruces.

Las Cruces

I-10, I-25 & US-70. ✕ ♿ 🅿 ℘575-541-2444. www.lascrucescvb.org.

This city of 101,000 occupies the fertile Mesilla Valley between the Rio Grande and the Organ Mountains. Juan de Oñate founded the village of La Mesilla in 1598 while searching for gold. Las Cruces was founded in 1849 on the east bank of the Rio Grande, US

Gila Cliff Dwellings National Monumentt

© National Park Service

territory after the Mexican War; it was named for "the crosses" that marked primitive graves of travelers. In 1854, La Mesilla became part of the US in the Gadsden Purchase.

Built in 1851 and reconstructed in 1906, San Albino Church towers over **Old Mesilla Plaza★** (Rte. 28, 4mi southwest of downtown Las Cruces). Cafes, galleries and antique shops occupy its 19C buildings. In the Masonic cemetery is the grave of Sheriff Pat Garrett, who tracked and shot down Billy the Kid after the outlaw fled La Mesilla jail while awaiting execution. The Mesilla Valley is a leading producer of chiles, pecans and cotton. Farm and factory tours can be arranged.

Fort Selden State Monument

Between I-25, exit 19, & Rte. 185, 15mi north of Las Cruces. ♿🅿 ☎575-526-8911. www.nmmonuments.org.

This adobe fort, built in 1865 and abandoned in 1891, was home to the Buffalo Soldiers, the famed African-American cavalry that shielded settlers from Indians. And it was the boyhood home of Gen. Douglas MacArthur, the World War II hero whose father was stationed here. A visitor center displays photos.

▷ Take I-10 west 59mi to Deming, then US-180 north 53mi to Silver City.

Silver City

Rte. 90 & US-180. ✗♿🅿 ☎575-538-3785. www.silvercity.org.

In the foothills of the Piños Altos Range, this town of 10,000 was founded as a mining community in the 1870s. Its downtown historic district features mansard-roofed Victorian homes and cast-iron commercial buildings. The 1881 H.B. Ailman House is home to the **Silver City Museum** (312 W. Broadway; ☎505-538-5921; www.silvercitymuseum.org). Silver City is surrounded by the 3.3-million-acre Gila National Forest, whose Gila Wilderness Area was the first designated by the US Congress in 1924.

Gila Cliff Dwellings National Monument★

Rte. 15, 44mi north of Silver City. ♿🅿 ☎575-536-9461. www.nps.gov/gicl.

The cliffside stone-and-masonry homes of a 13C Mogollon agricultural village are preserved within this park, a narrow, winding, 2hr drive from Silver City. In a side canyon above the West Fork of the Gila River, a half-dozen shallow caves contain 42 mostly intact rooms, believed to have housed as many as 50 people. A **trail** (*3mi round trip*) climbs 175ft to the dwellings, offering a rare glimpse of a prehistoric culture. The Mogollon were fine builders. Stones were anchored by clay mortar, roof beams cut with stone adzes and shaped by fire. The people hunted and grew corn, squash and beans in the Gila flood plain's rich soil.

▷ Turn northwest on US-180 along the scenic Mogollon Rim for 93mi, then east on Rte. 12 for 74mi to Datil, at junction of US-60.

Very Large Array★

VLA Access Rd. west of Rte. 52 & south of US-60, 9mi east of Datil and 50mi west of Socorro. 🅿 ☎575-835-7302. www.vla.nrao.edu.

Astronomers use this powerful radio telescope on the Plains of San Augustin to research the nature of the universe. Composed of scores of dish-shaped metal mirrors, each 82ft in diameter, extending across the Plains of San Agustin in a trio of miles-long arms, the facility gathers radio signals from the Milky Way galaxy and beyond. At the **visitor center**, guests may view a slide show and displays on radio astronomy, then take a self-guided tour.

▷ Continue east 61mi on US-60 to Socorro; then north 26mi on I-25 to Bernardo; then east 39mi on US-60 to Mountainair.

Billy the Kid and Smokey Bear

Tributes to two American legends stand 12mi apart on US-380 north of Ruidoso. **Lincoln State Monument** (36mi northeast of Ruidoso; www.nmmonuments. org) preserves a 19C village that recalls the life of Billy the Kid. **Smokey Bear Historical Park** ♣♦ (118 Smokey Bear Blvd., Capitan, 24mi north of Ruidoso; www.smokeybearpark.com) honors a national symbol.

Billy the Kid – Born of Irish immigrants, Henry McCarty (1859?-81), alias William Bonney, moved to New Mexico with his widowed mother after the Civil War. Orphaned in 1873, he worked as a cowboy in Arizona; he was pursued for thefts and one killing as he fled back to New Mexico in 1877. A range war in Lincoln County climaxed in 1878 with a 5-day gun battle in which Billy killed a sheriff and deputy. While awaiting execution, he overpowered a guard and as he escaped, killed two more deputies and made his way to Fort Sumner.hFort Sumnerf. On the night of 14 July 1881, Sheriff Pat Garrett tracked down Bonney and shot him through the heart. More than two dozen movies have purported to tell his tale, about which historians still disagree.

Smokey Bear – The real-life Smokey Bear emerged from the devastation of a Lincoln National Forest fire in 1950. Although badly burned, the rescued black-bear cub was nursed back to health and adopted by the US Forest Service. Smokey became the living symbol of a campaign, started during World War II, to prevent fires caused by careless humans. His cartoon image had captured American hearts via print media by the time the real cub was introduced. Smokey lived in the National Zoo in Washington DC until his death in 1976. He was returned to New Mexico and buried in Smokey Bear Historical Park. Smokey's message – "Only you can prevent forest fires" – has become part of American popular culture.

Salinas Pueblo Missions National Monument★

Headquarters on US-60, one block west of Rte. 55, Mountainair. ♿🅿 ☏505-847-2585. www.nps.gov/sapu.

Stone ruins are all that remain of the pueblos of the Salinas Valley, inhabited by descendants of Ancestral Puebloan and Mogollon peoples in the 13–17C. Conflicts with Apaches, as well as a severe drought and famine, led to their abandonment during the 1670s. The **visitor center** in Mountainair has exhibits.

The **Abó Ruins** (9mi west on US-60 & .5mi north on Rte. 513) include an unexcavated pueblo and ruins of Misión de San Gregorio de Abó. The **Quarai Ruins★** (8mi north on Rte. 55, then 1mi west) include walls of Misión de Nuestra Señora de la Purisima Concepción de Cuarac, most complete of the Salinas chapels.

The **Gran Quivira Ruins★** (25mi south on Rte. 55) have a small museum, excavations of the San Isidro Convent and ruins of the Misión de San Buenaventura.

▶ From Mountainair, drive east 12mi on US-60 to Willard; southeast 38mi on Rte. 42 to Corona; then south 47mi on US-54 to Carrizozo.

Trinity Site

Range Rd. 7 in the White Sands Missile Range, 21mi south of US-380, 54mi west of Carrizozo.

At this location in the Jordana del Muerto desert, the world's first atomic bomb was exploded on July 16, 1945. It is closed to the public, except the first Saturday in April and October.

▶ Continue south 57mi on US-54 to Alamogordo.

Alamogordo

US-54 & 70. ✕♿🅿 ☏575-437-6120. www.alamogordo.com.

The "Rocket City" was a mere desert oasis until World War II. Flanked on the north by lava fields, on the south by white sand dunes and on the east by the 1.1-million-acre Lincoln National Forest, this community has grown into a boomtown of 36,000 people. Holloman Air Force Base, home to the Stealth F-117A aircraft, and the White Sands Missile Range administer hundreds of square miles of uninhabited land to train bombing crews and research rockets.

👥 New Mexico Museum of Space History★★

Rte. 2001 via Indian Wells Rd. & Scenic Dr., off US-54. ♿🅿 ☎575-437-2840. www.nmspacemuseum.org.

A five-story, gold-colored cube at the foot of the Sacramento Mountains, this complex salutes man's exploration of space through exhibits on history, science and technology.

Displays in the **Space Museum★★** range from examples of Robert Goddard's early experiments in rocketry and the capsule flown in 1961 by the first astrochimp to futuristic models of space stations. The **International Space Hall of Fame** honors space pioneers. **John P. Stapp Air and Space Park★**, named for the man who rode the Sonic Wind 1 rocket sled at 632mph, exhibits full-size spacecraft. The **Astronaut Memorial Garden★** honors the seven men and women who lost their lives in the 1986 Challenger space-shuttle disaster.

👥 White Sands National Monument★★

US-70, 15mi southwest of Alamogordo. ♿🅿 ☎575-479-6124. www.nps.gov/whsa.

The world's greatest expanse of white gypsum sand dunes, this mountain-ringed northern edge of the Chihuahuan Desert is preserved as a delicate ecological system. Nearly half the sands are contained within this 240sq mi site in the Tularosa Basin, inhabited only by a few hardy plant species, a few small birds and other animals (some of which have evolved a white camouflage).

The visitor center has displays on the ever-moving dunes, driven by a relentless southwesterly wind; they can be seen on an 8mi (one-way) drive through the park. The **Alkali Flat Trail** (4.6mi) is designed for backcountry hikers; the **Interdune Boardwalk** (♿.25mi) has interpretive exhibits on dune ecology.

▶ From Alamogordo, return 3mi up US-54, then east 16mi on US-82.

Cloudcroft

US-82. ✗♿🅿 ☎575-682-2733. www.cloudcroft.net.

Located at 8,663ft, about twice the elevation of Alamogordo, this mountain village of 750 offers hiking and mountain biking in summer, skiing in winter. **The Lodge at Cloudcroft** (1 Corona Pl.; ☎800-395-6343; www.thelodgeresort. com) is a Victorian gem built in 1898 for rail workers. The **National Solar Observatory** (Rte. 6563, 17mi south of Cloudcroft; ☎575-434-7000; www. nso.edu) is located atop 9,255ft Sacramento Peak; tours begin at the **Sunspot Astronomy and Visitor Center** (Sunspot Scenic Byway).

▶ Take Rte. 244 east and north 29mi to US-70 in the Mescalero Apache Indian Reservation, then east 12mi on US-70 to Ruidoso.

Ruidoso

US-70 & Rte. 37. ⛺✗♿🅿 ☎575-257-7395. www.ruidosonow.com.

A resort town of 9,000 on a Sacramento Mountain stream, Ruidoso (pronounced rue-uh-DOH-so) is famous for horse racing. The season runs mid May to Labor Day with the All-American Futurity at **Ruidoso Downs** racetrack (US-70, 4mi east of Ruidoso).

Ruidoso is on the northern edge of the 723sq mi Mescalero Apache Indian Reservation, highlighted by the luxurious Inn of the **Mountain Gods** resort (287 Carrizo Canyon Rd.; ☎505-464-7777; www.innofthemountaingods.com). The tribe also owns southern New Mexico's largest winter resort, **Ski Apache** (Forest Rd. 532; ☎575-464-3600; www.

skiapache.com), which has a gondola and eight chairlifts on a flank of 12,003ft Sierra Blanca. in the summer, the resort is open for hiking its trails.

👥 Hubbard Museum of the American West★★

841 US-70 West, Ruidoso Downs. ♿🅿 𝒫575-378-4142. www.hubbardmuseum.org.

More than 10,000 historical and cultural items chronicle the relationship between horse and man. Firearms, farm tools, wagons and carriages are on display, along with an art collection that includes works by Russell and Remington. At the entrance is an equine monument by Ruidoso sculptor Dave McGary.

Spencer Theater for the Performing Arts★

Airport Rd. 220, Alto, 5mi north of Ruidoso. ♿🅿 𝒫575-336-4800. www.spencertheater.com.

Designed to echo the surrounding Capitan and Sacramento Mountains with white limestone and steep angles, this 514-seat theater (1997, Antoine Predock) also showcases the glass art of Dale Chihuly.

▶ Continue east 71mi on US-70 to Roswell.

Roswell

US-70, 285 & 380. ✖♿🅿 𝒫575-623-5695. www.roswellnm.org.

This city of 49,000 was once known merely for its ranching economy and esteemed military school. Then the "Roswell Incident" occurred. In 1947, a "flying saucer" or unidentified flying object (UFO) allegedly crashed in a field 20mi northwest. The incident was reported by local media but quickly hushed up by the US Army.

The **International UFO Museum & Research Center★ 👥** (114 N. Main St.; 𝒫575-625-9495; www.roswellufomuseum.com) features exhibits both on the Roswell Incident and cover-up, and on UFO sightings around the world. At the **Roswell Museum and Art Center** (11th & Main Sts.; 𝒫 575-624-6744; www.roswellmuseum.org), the highlights are the Robert H. Goddard Planetarium and the workshop of Goddard, father of modern rocketry. The art collection showcases works by Peter Hurd, Henriette Wyeth and Georgia O'Keeffe; the Rogers Aston Collection features Western history.

▶ From Roswell, drive south 76mi on US-285 to Carlsbad. Turn southwest on US-62/180 for 16mi to Whites City, at entrance to Carlsbad Caverns National Park.

👥 Carlsbad Caverns National Park★★★

Off US-62, 23mi southwest of Carlsbad. ✖♿🅿 𝒫575-785-2232. www.nps.gov/cave.

One of the largest cave systems in the world, the labyrinth of Carlsbad Caverns takes in 88 known caves, including Lechuguilla Cave, at 1,604ft the deepest limestone cavern in the US.

The caverns were discovered in the early 1900s. Cowboy Jim White saw a cloud of dark smoke, rising on the horizon near dusk, that turned out to be thousands of Mexican free-tailed bats. (Bats still cling to the roof of the cave entrance before beginning their nightly insect-hunting.) White descended on a rope ladder to the cave floor, where he was stunned by the formations: soda straws and ice-cream cones, strings of pearls and miniature castles. By 1923 the caves were part of the national park system, and were designated a World Heritage Site in 1995.

Perpetually 56 degrees, the damp caves can be entered through their natural entrance or by elevator. Tour highlights include beautiful formations as the Temple of the Sun and the Frozen Waterfall, as well as the Green Lake Room, the uppermost of the "Scenic Rooms", which contains a deep, malachite-coloured pool, as well as The Big Room, more than 350,000 sq ft in size.

▶ Continue west on US-180, 35mi to Guadalupe Mountains National Park and another 110mi to El Paso.

Santa Fe Area

New Mexico is a cultural mélange of ancient and modern Indian and Spanish, American pioneer and high-technology influences. The chosen home of artists and authors such as Georgia O'Keeffe and D.H. Lawrence offers stark adobe architecture in brilliant contrast to strikingly blue skies, towering mountains and precipitous gorges.

Highlights

1 **Gallery-hop** down Canyon Rd. (p284)

2 Hear **Santa Fe Opera arias** (p285)

3 Take home **holy soil** (p286)

4 Ride the world's longest **jig-back aerial tram** (p289)

5 Rewind time at **Taos Pueblo** (p290)

Santa Fe

NM

"Land of Enchantment"

Though not its largest city, the state capital of Santa Fe is New Mexico's cultural and tourism hub. The former Spanish capital, founded in 1609, is home to outstanding museums, galleries, restaurants and summer opera.

New Mexico is isolated by extreme geography. The Rocky Mountains begin here, dividing the Great Plains from the southern desert. Santa Fe is an hour's drive north of modern Albuquerque, an hour's drive south of the rustic mountain art town of Taos. East is the historic Santa Fe Trail town of Las Vegas. West is the domain of the Navajo, Zuni and Jicarilla Apache tribes, where Gallup and Farmington are the largest towns. A thousand years ago, Ancestral Puebloan civilization spawned a sophisticated trade network. Ruins of their culture can be seen at such far-flung sites as Bandelier, Pecos and Aztec Ruins National Monuments and Chaco Culture National Historical Park. Spanish explorer Francisco Vasquéz de Coronado and his expedition searched for gold from the legendary Seven Cities of Cibola in 1540.

New Mexico entered the modern era in the 1940s, when scientists working in Los Alamos, near Santa Fe, created the atomic bombs that ended World War II and changed the world forever.

Mission of San Miguel de Santa Fe

©iStockphoto.com/Lillis photography

ADDRESSES

🛏 STAY

$$$$ The Bishop's Lodge – 1297 Bishop's Lodge Rd., Santa Fe. ☎505-983-6377. www.bishopslodge.com. 111 lodge rooms, 15 villas. Built in 1851 as the retreat of the first bishop of Santa Fe, this resort lies hidden in a valley

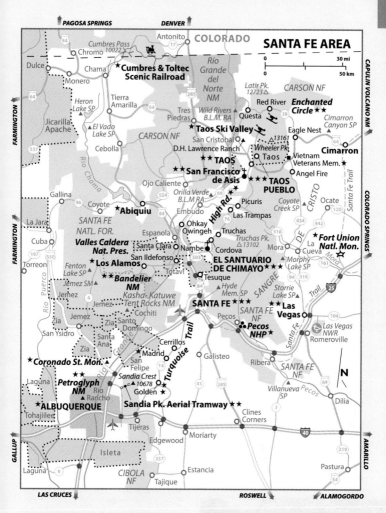

SANTA FE AREA

PAGOSA SPRINGS • DENVER

COLORADO

Cumbres Pass 10022 Chromo • Antonito 17

Dulce • Chama

★ Cumbres & Toltec Scenic Railroad

Monero

Río Grande del Norte NM

Latir Pk. 12723△ Red River • **Enchanted Circle** ★★

CARSON NF

Tierra Amarilla

Heron Lake SP

Wild Rivers B.L.M. RA • Questa 38 Eagle Nest

Cimarron Canyon SP

Jicarilla Apache

★ El Vado Lake SP

Tres Piedras

★ **Taos Ski Valley**

CARSON NF

San Cristobal

★ **Cimarron**

Cebolla

D.H. Lawrence Ranch

△13161 Wheeler Pk.

Vietnam Veterans Mem. ★

Gallina

Río Chama

Ojo Caliente

★★ **TAOS**

Taos

Coyote

★★ **San Francisco de Asis**

★★★ **TAOS PUEBLO**

Angel Fire

La Jara

Orilla Verde B.L.M. RA 68

Picuris

Coyote Creek SP

Ocate

★ **Abiquiu**

Embudo

Las Trampas

High Rd.

SANTA FE NATL. FOR.

Cuba

Ohkay Owingeh

Truchas

Truchas Pk. △ 13102

Ocate 120

La Jara

Espanola

76

Torreon

Valles Caldera Nat. Pres.

Santa Clara

Nambe

Cordova

Mora

La Cueva

Fenton Lake SP

San Ildefonso

503

EL SANTUARIO DE CHIMAYO ★★★

Morphy Lake SP

★ **Fort Union Natl. Mon.** ☆

Los Alamos

Totavi

Tesuque

★★ **Bandelier NM**

Kasha-Katuwe Tent Rocks NM

Hyde Mem. SP

Storrie Lake SP

Jemez SM

Cochiti

SANTA FE ★★★

SANTA FE NF

★★ **Las Vegas**

Jemez

Zia

Santo Domingo

Pecos

★★ **Pecos NHP** ★

Las Vegas NWR

Romeroville

San Ysidro

Zia Santa Ana

Cerrillos

Galisteo

Ribera

SANTA FE NF

★ **Coronado St. Mon.**

★★ Madrid

San Felipe

Turquoise Trail

Villanueva SP

Dilia

★★ **Petroglyph NM**

Sandia Crest △10678

Golden ★

Clines Corners

★ **ALBUQUERQUE**

Rio Rancho

Sandia Pk. Aerial Tramway ★★

Tijeras

Isleta

Edgewood

Moriarty

40

Laguna

6

CIBOLA NF

Estancia

Tajique

Pastura

54

N

LAS CRUCES • ROSWELL • ALAMOGORDO

3.5mi north of downtown. The bishop's chapel and garden are at the heart of 450 acres of piñon-juniper forest harboring guest villas. Horseback riding and tennis are popular. **Las Fuentes** (**$$$**) offers fine Western cuisine.

$$$$ Rosewood Inn of the Anasazi – 113 Washington Ave., Santa Fe, NM. ☎505-988-3030. www.innoftheanasazi. com. 58 rooms. With traditional beamed ceilings of peeled log and sculpted stairways, the inn's design is a rich blend of Southwestern cultures. Indian baskets and cacti adorn a lobby with a warm fireplace. The **Anasazi Restaurant** (**$$$**) focuses on regional cuisine, including grilled elk, New Mexico lamb and duck enchiladas.

$$$ Hotel Santa Fe – 1501 Paseo de Peralta, Santa Fe, NM. ☎505-243-2300. www.hotelsantafe.com. 163 rooms. The only Native American-owned hotel in Santa Fe is characterized by Puebloan artwork and a traditional terrace design. The three-story building features ceremonial dance performances and storytellers who immerse guests in Picuris culture. The restaurant **Amaya** (**$$**) focuses on indigenous cuisine, such as bison tenderloin and roasted poblano chile.

$$$ Hotel Albuquerque – 800 Rio Grande Blvd., Albuquerque. ☎505-843-6300. www.hotelabq.com. 188 rooms. This hotel's historic mid-century tower rises over Old Town and includes spacious grounds, an Olympic-size pool and every modern element in its refurbished rooms, but holds numerous traditional touches such as extensive tilework, wrought-iron chandeliers and dark vigas (wood beams). It's one among a New Mexico-owned boutique lodging chain, Heritage Hotels & Resorts, that includes lovely, distinctive properties in Santa Fe, Las Cruces and Taos; visit www.hhandr.com.

$$ Andaluz – 125 2nd St. NW, Albuquerque, NM. &505-242-9090. www.hotelandaluz.com. 107 rooms. A $30 million renovation has transformed the historic La Posada de Albuquerque, which was New Mexico's tallest building when Conrad Hilton opened it in 1939 on the site of a livery stable. Arches, balconies and tiles reflect Moroccan and Spanish colonial influences, and **Lucia** restaurant serves Mediterranean-inspired cuisine.

$$ El Rey Inn – 1862 Cerrillos Rd., Santa Fe, NM. &505-982-1931. www. elreyinnsantafe.com. 86 rooms. Best of the Cerrillos Road motels south of the Plaza, El Rey ("the King") succeeds with its Spanish Colonial architecture and carefully tended grounds. Built in the 1930s, renovated and well maintained, the motel boasts a Southwestern decor of hand-painted tiles and hand-crafted furnishings. Fountains and sculptures adorn the garden areas.

Hotel Santa Fe

© Gwen Cannon/Michelin

$$ The Historic Taos Inn – 125 Paseo del Pueblo Norte, Taos, NM. &505-758-2233. www.taosinn.com. 44 rooms. Beginning in 1895, Dr. T. Paul Martin, Taos County's first physician, rented many small adobes in this complex to artists and writers. Rooms showcase kiva fireplaces and bedspreads loomed by Indian weavers. **Doc Martin's ($$)** restaurant, once his waiting room, serves chiles rellenos, trout, elk and New Mexico lamb.

$$ The Hotel Blue – 717 Central Ave. NW, Albuquerque, NM. &505-924-2400. www.thehotelblue.com. 135 rooms. An Art Deco-style "chic boutique" hotel wedged between downtown and Old Town on Route 66, the Blue brings a Route 66 sensibility into the 21C. Rooms are simple, but display modern frills.

$ The El Rancho Hotel – 1000 E. Rte. 66, Gallup, NM. &505-863-9311. www.elranchohotel.com. 102 rooms. Katharine Hepburn, Errol Flynn, Spencer Tracy and even Ronald Reagan made their homes-away-from home at this Navajoland inn while filming in the 1940s and 50s. Built in 1937 by R.E. Griffith, brother of movie pioneer D.W., the hotel is now a National Historic Site. Brick and stone with huge wooden beams, it is decorated in Old West style, with dozens of autographed movie-star photos on its walls.

⑂ EAT

$$$ Geronimo – 724 Canyon Rd., Santa Fe. &575-982-1500. www. geronimorestaurant.com. Dinner only. **Regional**. Southwest tradition and 21C innovation merge in this Territorial-style adobe, built in 1748 by Spanish farmer Geronimo Lopez. In the sophisticated and romantic space, chef Eric DiStefano prepares meals such as New Mexico lamb with chile-mint sauce, and elk tenderloin with apple-wood smoked bacon.

$$$ La Boca – 72 W. Marcy St., Santa Fe. &505-982-3433. www.labocasf.com. **Spanish**. Lively and popular, this downtown tapas restaurant focuses on flavorful, creative small plates, such as cured tuna with fried quail eggs, or smoky grilled artichokes with orange zest.

Cathedral Basilica of St. Francis of Assisi, Santa Fe

$$$ La Casa Sena – 125 E. Palace Ave., Santa Fe. ☎505-988-9232. www.lacasasena.com. **Regional**. An early Santa Fe merchant, Don Juan Sena was as prolific in love as he was in business. He built his hacienda, now Sena Plaza, in the 1830s, and expanded it to 33 rooms to house his wife and 23 children. Today the central patio welcomes overflow diners from the fine restaurant, which serves hearty dishes such as green chile hanger steak. Casual diners at adjacent **La Cantina ($$)** are entertained by musical performances ranging from Broadway to the Beatles.

$$$ Rancho de Chimayo – County Rd. 98, south of Chimayo. ☎505-984-2100. www.ranchodechimayo.com. **Regional**. Housed in a restored territorial ranch house, this northern New Mexico institution serves classic specialties such as carne adovada and chiles rellenos. The signature dish is a carne asada composed of a New York steak topped with chile verde.

$$ The Artichoke Cafe – 424 Central Ave. SE, Albuquerque. ☎505-243-0200. www.artichokecafe.com. **Contemporary American**. A charming bistro in a historic neighborhood east of downtown, this bright, artsy corner draws lunchtime diners with its sandwiches, salads and pasta entrées. Dinner may begin with a steamed artichoke (with three dipping sauces); main courses include pan-seared duck breast with kim chee fried rice, daily

seafood specials and beef tenderloin with bacon-butter sauce.

$$ Maria's New Mexican Kitchen – 555 W. Cordova Rd., Santa Fe. ☎505-983-7929. www.marias-santafe.com. **Mexican**. Strolling mariachi troubadours serenade diners as cooks craft handmade tortillas on an open grill. Servers carry platters of burritos, tacos and blue-corn enchiladas with Spanish rice. A Santa Fe institution of 50 years, Maria's offers more than 100 varieties of margaritas.

$$ Orlando's – 1114 Don Juan Valdez Ln. at Paseo del Pueblo Norte, Taos. ☎505-751-1450. www.orlandostaos.com. **Mexican**. Orlando's mom still makes the sopaipillas and other sweets – how's that for a local family restaurant? Voted best Mexican food in Taos County since 2005, Orlando's offers a variety of Mexican beers, as well as a kids' menu. Cozy, casual and festive, especially on the crowded patio, Orlando's has won Taoseños' hearts with its chile-smothered enchiladas and burritos, carne adovado and fish tacos.

$ 66 Diner – 1405 Central Ave. NE, Albuquerque. ☎575-247-1421. www.66diner.com. **American**. A tribute to the days when Route 66 was the "Mother Road," this white, Art Deco-style diner serves all the meals you'd expect, from burgers to liver and onions. Service comes with a bubble-gum smile.

Santa Fe★★★

Home to Puebloan Indians for more than 1,000 years, Santa Fe was a Spanish territorial capital at the beginning of the 17C, an American frontier city in the 19C, a state capital and center for high-tech research in the mid 20C. Today it has coalesced into a world-renowned center for the arts, cuisine and shopping, its diverse elements and heritage maintaining their unique characters. Distinctive adobe and Territorial-style architecture (required by municipal law) spreads across the foothills of the Sangre de Cristo Mountains. Art galleries and shops surround the historic Plaza and wind down Canyon Road, once a trail leading to the Pecos Indian pueblos. Visitors make special trips for the summer Santa Fe Opera and impressive Indian Markets.

A BIT OF HISTORY

Colonists from Spain, including missionaries, founded the first territorial capital in the Española Valley, north of Santa Fe, in 1598. Eleven years later, Don Pedro de Peralta established Santa Fe as the Spanish seat of power. By 1610,

▶ **Population:** 72,000.

🌡 **Michelin Map:** p281.
Mountain Standard Time.

🔋 **Info:** ✆505-955-6200;
www.santafe.org.

◉ **Location:** Nearly all Santa Fe's visitor attractions are within a square-mile area in the center of the city.

🅿 **Parking:** Summer poses parking challenges near the Plaza; several outlying fee lots run shuttles to downtown. There is also a fair amount of on-street parking up Canyon Road.

◈ **Don't Miss:** The Georgia O'Keeffe Museum.

◕ **Timing:** Staying at one of the hotels downtown vastly eases getting around in central Santa Fe – but be sure to save one night for a performance at the Santa Fe Opera.

🧒 **Kids:** Museum of International Folk Art.

🌡 **Also See:** Bandelier National Monument. El Santuario de Chimayo.

the Plaza and Palace of the Governors had been constructed; the city would become the oldest seat of government in the US. That same year, the Mission Church of San Miguel was built. By 1617, 14,000 Indians had been converted to Roman Catholicism.

With the opening of the Santa Fe Trail in 1821, US westward expansion led adventurous Americans from Missouri to the trade hub of Santa Fe, though many continued to California. Briefly occupied by the Confederacy during the Civil War, Santa Fe rebounded strongly. It was attracting artists as early as 1878-81, when Territorial Governor Lew Wallace scribed his novel, *Ben Hur*.

Since 1909, the "Palace" has been run as a history museum by the Museum of New Mexico, which also operates four other museums: the New Mexico

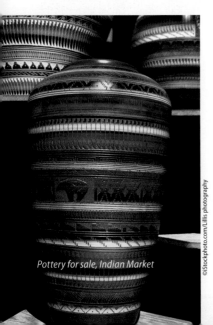

Pottery for sale, Indian Market

©iStockphoto.com/Lillis photography

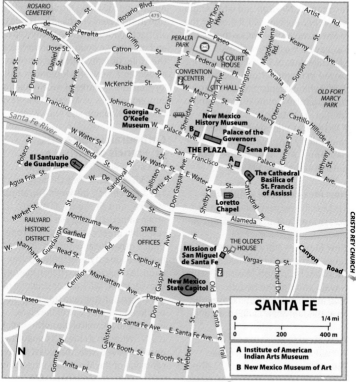

SANTA FE

0		1/4 mi
0	200	400 m

A Institute of American
Indian Arts Museum

B New Mexico Museum of Art

MUSEUM HILL

Museum of Art, near the Palace of the
Governors; the Museum of Indian Arts
and Culture and Museum of International Folk Art, both 2mi southeast on
the beautiful Museum Plaza (*Camino
Lejo*); and the Governor's Gallery in the
State Capitol building.

SIGHTS
The Plaza★★
Flanked by Palace Ave., Old Santa Fe
Trail, San Francisco St. & Lincoln Ave.
✕ﻪ🅿 www.santafe.org.
Faced on its north by the Palace of the
Governors, this National Historic Land-
mark was the original center of Santa
Fe, the focus of a Pueblo Indian revolt
in 1680, and recapture of the city by the
Spanish in 1692-93.
Later, it was the end of the Santa Fe
Trail for 19C American travelers heading
west. It remains the heart of downtown
Santa Fe today.

Strict laws today protect historic adobe
and Territorial-style architecture; these
buildings are home to shops, galleries,
restaurants and hotels. All downtown
structures must abide by a building
code that limits their choice of color to
"42 shades of brown." Many of Santa
Fe's finest shops are located on or near
the Plaza; it is hard to top **Montez** (125
E. Palace Ave.; 𝄞505-982-1828) for traditional Spanish Colonial art. Summer
brings popular arts and craft festivals
to the Plaza; a fall highlight is the lively
Fiestas de Santa Fe, while *farolitos* (can-
dle lanterns) light the streets at Christmas time.

Palace of the Governors★★
105 W. Palace Ave., north side of Plaza.
✕ﻪ🅿 𝄞505-476-5100. www.palaceof
thegovernors.org.
This low, flat-roofed hacienda was
the original home and seat of power

281

for Spanish, Mexican and later, Anglo governors. Built in 1610, it is one of the oldest occupied buildings in the US, and has been a museum since 1909. Some of a collection of 17,000 objects is displayed in rooms surrounding a courtyard. Exhibits depict Santa Fe history, from Spanish Colonial to the Anglo frontier era to today.

A letterpress print shop operates next to a gallery displaying historic hide paintings. Artisans sell their wares outside at the Indian Market.

New Mexico History Museum★

113 Lincoln Ave., next to the Palace of the Governors. ♿ ℘505-476-5200. www.nmhistorymuseum.org.

New Mexico's story from prehistoric times to the present—including contributions by Spanish, Mexican, Pueblo, Navajo and Apache peoples—is told with multimedia and interactive exhibits at this fairly new (2009) museum.

New Mexico Museum of Art★

107 W. Palace Ave., adjacent to the Palace of the Governors. ♿℘505-476-5072. www.nmartmuseum.org.

In a 1917 Pueblo Revival-style building a block northwest of the Plaza, the museum harbors a collection of 20,000 pieces. Contemporary and historic New Mexican works, among them many of the Taos Society and Cinco Pintores, are presented in rotating exhibits. Collections include works by O'Keeffe, Eliot Porter and extensive holdings of historic photography.

Georgia O'Keeffe Museum★★★

217 Johnson St., three blocks northwest of Plaza. ✕♿ ℘505-946-1000. www.okeeffemuseum.org.

Assembled here is the largest collection of paintings, pastels, watercolors and sculptures by Georgia O'Keeffe (1887-1986). The famed artist was fascinated by the textures created by light and color in the landscape of New Mexico, her adopted home from 1949 until her death.

Among the 130 works displayed are her signature flowers and bleached bones, abstracts, nudes, landscapes, cityscapes and still lifes. An 8min video introduces the collection. In 2001, the museum added an American Modernism gallery, featuring works of such O'Keeffe contemporaries as Marsden Hartley, Willem de Kooning and Andy Warhol.

Cathedral Basilica of St. Francis of Assisi★★

131 Cathedral Pl., one block east of Plaza. ♿ ℘505-982-5619. www.cbsfa.org.

The first church between Durango, Mexico, and St. Louis, Missouri, to attain cathedral status was intended to resemble great cathedrals of Europe. Unlike other local churches, it is not built in adobe style. Archbishop Jean-Baptiste Lamy recruited Italian masons to assist in the 1869-86 construction of the French Romanesque structure, that overlooks the east side of the Plaza.

In a niche in the wall of the north chapel is a 17C wooden statue, "La Conquistadora," believed to be the oldest representation of the Madonna in the US. It was brought to Santa Fe in 1624.

Museum of Contemporary Native Arts★★

108 Cathedral Pl., opposite St. Francis Cathedral. ♿ ℘505-983-8900. www.iaia.edu.

The Institute of American Indian Arts has trained literally hundreds of Native artists from Barrow, Alaska to the Rio Grande. It is the home of the National Collection of Contemporary Native American Art, a provocative compilation of works illustrating the dynamic nature of modern Native art. Some 7,000 works—paintings, sculptures, ceramics, jewelry, costumes, graphics and photographs—express contemporary Native themes, while incorporating traditional lifestyles.

Loretto Chapel★★

207 Old Santa Fe Trail, two blocks south of Plaza. ♿℘505-982-0092. www.lorettochapel.com.

Taos Pueblo

©iStockphoto.com/Natalia Bratslavsky

THE EIGHT NORTHERN PUEBLOS

Eight independent pueblos are known for their handmade arts and crafts and preservation of traditional lifestyles. The public is generally welcome to view special feast days, including traditional Indian dances, annually at some pueblos.

For information on all 19 pueblos in New Mexico: ℘866-855-7902; www.indianpueblo.org;

Tesuque Pueblo – US 84/285, 7mi north of Santa Fe; ℘505-983-2667. Listed on the National Register of Historic Places, Tesuque has adobe structures dating from AD 1250. A popular flea market is held adjacent to the Santa Fe Opera; the Camel Rock Casino is about 3mi farther north.

Pojoaque Pueblo – US-84/285, 12mi north of Santa Fe; ℘505-455-2278. The **Poeh Cultural Center and Museum** (℘505-455-3334) depicts tribal history and culture. Nearby are the Pojoaque (po-WAH-kay) Pueblo Visitor Information Center, with a shop offering crafts by Native American artisans, and the Cities of Gold casino-hotel.

Nambé Pueblo – 1mi east of Rte. 503, 18mi north of Santa Fe; ℘505-455-2036. Inhabited since 1300, this village is known for its stone sculptures, black-and-red micaceous pottery, textiles and beadwork. Several ancient ruins may be found near the Nambé Falls Lake and Recreation Area.

San Ildefonso Pueblo – Off Rte. 502, 24mi northwest of Santa Fe; ℘505-455-2273. The village was the home of famed potter María Martínez, whose family continues to produce her trademark black-on-black matté pottery, as well as other black, red and polychrome pottery sold by individual artisans.

Santa Clara Pueblo – Rte. 30, 2mi south of Española; ℘505-753-7330. Descended from ancestral cliff dwellers, villagers are known for their weaving, black pottery and beadwork. Several structures dating from AD 1250–1577 are found at the **Puye Cliff Dwellings** (7mi west). A tribal permit is required to reach the site by descending staircases and ladders from a 7,000ft mesa top.

Ohkay Owingeh (San Juan Pueblo) – US-84/285 to Rte. 68, 5mi north of Española; ℘505-852-4400. The largest Tewa-speaking pueblo has more than 2,000 members. The village, whose architecture ranges from French Gothic to traditional Pueblo style, operates the large Ohkay Casino and the **O'ke Oweenge Arts and Crafts Cooperative** (℘505-852-4400).

Picuris Pueblo – 2mi north of Rte. 75, 33mi south of Taos; ℘505-587-2519. Visitors need a permit to visit the restored San Lorenzo Mission and nearby pueblo ruins, including a 700-year-old kiva. Picuris was first known as pikuria, or "those who paint"; works are on display in the Tribal Museum.

Taos Pueblo – 2mi north of Taos Plaza; ℘575-758-1028. www.taospueblo.com. The oldest and best-known northern New Mexico pueblo is described in the Taos chapter (⊚p290).

Modeled after the Sainte-Chapelle church in Paris and dedicated in 1878, this chapel is noted for its famous spiral staircase. Leading to the choir loft, this staircase makes two complete 360-degree turns with no nails or other visible support. Legend claims it was built by a mysterious carpenter who appeared astride a donkey, in answer to the prayers of the Sisters of Loretto.

El Santuario de Guadalupe

100 Guadalupe St. at Agua Fria St. ℘505-983-8868.

The church dates from 1776 and is the oldest US shrine to the Virgin of Guadalupe, patroness of Mexico. It now operates as a museum and performing-arts center. A famous oil painting, *Our Lady of Guadalupe*, signed by José de Alzíbar in 1783, can be viewed inside.

Mission of San Miguel de Santa Fe★

401 Old Santa Fe Trail at E. De Vargas St. ℘505-983-3974.

Established in 1610, this old church was rebuilt a century later and has since been oft-remodeled. A Mexican sculpture of its patron saint, St. Michael, dating from the 17C, highlights a fine collection of Hispanic religious art.

New Mexico State Capitol★

Paseo de Peralta & Old Santa Fe Trail. &🅿℘505-986-4589. www.nmlegis.gov/lcs/

The only round capitol building in the US was built in 1966 in the shape of a Pueblo zia, or Circle of Life. It symbolizes the four directions, four winds, four seasons and four sacred obligations. Some 6.5 acres of gardens surround the building. Within is the **Governor's Gallery**, a fine contemporary art collection (www.nmcapitolart.org) that dominates the spacious lobby, hallways to the Senate and House galleries, and upper floors.

Canyon Road★

Santa Fe's greatest concentration of fine-art galleries—more than 100—may be found along narrow Canyon Road, interspersed with several fine restaurants 1-2mi southeast of the Plaza. Near the road's west end, the Pueblo-style **Gerald Peters Gallery** (1011 Paseo de Peralta; ℘505-954-5700; www.gpgallery.com) may be the city's largest private gallery. East, beyond the galleries, the **Cristo Rey Church** (1120 Canyon Rd. at Camino Cabra; ℘505-983-8528) is an imposing adobe edifice built in 1940. A massive stone reredos, or altar screen, dating from 1761, was taken from St. Francis cathedral.

👥 Randall Davey Audubon Center

End of Upper Canyon Rd., 2mi east of Camino Cabra. 🅿℘505-983-4609. http://nm.audubon.org.

This surprising 135-acre wildlife refuge abuts the Nature Conservancy's Santa Fe Canyon Preserve.

👥 Museum of Indian Arts and Culture★★

710 Camino Lejo. &🅿℘505-476-1250. www.miaclab.org.

A multimedia exhibit, **Here, Now and Always★★**, highlights the cultural history and lifestyles of New Mexico's Pueblo, Navajo and Apache tribes and features items from a collection of 75,000 artifacts, including basketry, jewelry, textiles and rugs. The **Buchsbaum Gallery of Southwestern Pottery★** demonstrates traditions and innovations; other galleries have rotating exhibits devoted to Native American arts.

👥 Museum of International Folk Art★★

706 Camino Lejo. &🅿℘505-476-1200. www.internationalfolkart.org.

Traditional arts from over 100 countries on six continents represent the largest folk collection in the world—more than 135,000 objects. They include historical and contemporary religious art, folk art, traditional costumes and textiles, silver and gold work, and children's toys and dolls. Miniature dioramas in the Girard Wing depict world lifestyles. In the basement, Lloyd's Treasure Chest is devoted to new exhibits.

Museum of Spanish Colonial Art★

750 Camino Lejo. &🅿️ ✆505-982-2226.
www.spanishcolonial.org.
This remarkable 3,000-piece collection spans the centuries since Spain first colonized the American Southwest in the late 16C. *Santeros, retablos*, textiles, tinwork, ceramics and furniture are presented in a former ambassador's residence on Museum Hill.
The museum produces an annual Spanish market each summer, with art, live music and dance.

Wheelwright Museum of the American Indian★

704 Camino Lejo. &🅿️ ✆505-982-4636.
www.wheelwright.org.
This small museum is built in the eight-sided shape of a Navajo **hogan**, its door facing east toward the rising sun. Founded in 1937 by a Boston scholar and a Navajo medicine man to preserve ritual beliefs and practices, the museum focuses on living arts in exhibits.

Old Santa Fe Trail Building

1100 Old Santa Fe Trail. &🅿️
✆505-988-6888.
The Intermountain Support Office of the National Park Service is a masterpiece of Pueblo Revival architecture and one of the largest adobe office buildings in the US. Built in 1937-39 (Cecil J. Doty) by the Civilian Conservation Corps, it is now a National Historic Landmark.

Shidoni★

1508 Bishop's Lodge Rd., Tesuque, 5mi north of the Plaza. &🅿️ ✆505-988-8001.
www.shidoni.com.
Established in 1971 in the rural Tesuque (te-soo-key) Valley, the Shidoni foundry is internationally acclaimed for its lost-wax casting process. Visitors may linger amid eight acres of sculpture gardens, visit gallery exhibits by 140 sculptors, or take a self-guided tour of the foundry, where molten bronze is poured into molds (on Saturdays).

Santa Fe Opera★★

US-84 & 285, 7mi north of Plaza.
&🅿️ ✆505-986-5900.
www.santafeopera.org.
Works by European composers such as Tchaikovsky, Rossini, Mozart and Richard Strauss follow on the heels of 20C American premieres at this hilltop amphitheater. The renowned opera company was established in 1957. Famed conductors and performers guest-star during a nine-week, 35-performance season, which extends from late June to late August. Year-round tours let visitors appreciate the 2,128-seat theater's soaring curves.

EXCURSIONS

Los Alamos★

◗ Rte. 502, 35mi northwest of Santa Fe.
✕&🅿️ ✆505-662-8105.
www.visit.losalamos.com.
Founded in 1942 as a top-secret community devoted to the creation of atomic weapons, this town of 18,000 perches atop a series of isolated finger canyons lined by the eponymous cottonwoods *(alamos)*. It is home to the **Los Alamos National Laboratory**, which employs 10,700 in scientific research for national security and economic strength.

Bradbury Science Museum★★

◗ 1350 Central Ave., Los Alamos.
&🅿️ ✆505-667-4444.
www.lanl.gov/museum.
This high-tech museum focuses on the historic development of the atomic bomb. More than three dozen hands-on displays educate visitors on current technology and science development at Los Alamos National Laboratory, including biomedical and energy research.

Bandelier National Monument★★

◗ Rte. 4, 15mi south of Los Alamos.
⚠&🅿️ ✆505-672-3861.
www.nps.gov/band.
This 50sq mi park preserves cliff dwellings and other sites occupied by Ancestral Puebloans for 500 years starting in AD 1050.

From a visitor center and museum, a 1.2mi paved trail along Frijoles Creek leads to the main, partially reconstructed ruins. Wooden ladders allow visitors to climb 140ft to a ceremonial kiva.

Abiquiu★

US-84, 47mi northwest of Santa Fe.

A village that provided scenic inspiration for her work, Abiquiu was home to artist Georgia O'Keeffe for nearly 40 years. Managed by the O'Keeffe Museum, her home and studio can be visited by reservation (505-685-4539), normally required months in advance.

El Santuario de Chimayo★★★

◉ Rte. 76, Chimayo, 25mi north of Santa Fe. ♿🅿 505-351-9961. www.elsantuariodechimayo.us.

A National Historic Landmark, this Spanish adobe church is the most important pilgrimage site in the Southwest.

Many enter the anteroom beside the altar to take home soil that is believed to be holy and hold miraculous healing powers. Leg braces, crutches and canes discarded by believers provide testimony. The chapel contains five sacred reredos and a number of religious carvings.

High Road to Taos★★

◉ Rte. 76 east from Chimayo to Rte. 518 near Vadito.

Traditional 19C lifestyles persist in a string of villages along this intriguing and mountainous 25mi route. Beginning in the weaving and chile center of Chimayo, it extends through the woodcarving village of **Cordova**, where crafts are often sold from roadside stalls. The farming hamlet of **Truchas**—where Robert Redford filmed his 1987 movie, *The Milagro Beanfield War*—sits atop a mesa beneath snow-capped 13,102ft Truchas Peak, the state's second-highest elevation. In the village of **Las Trampas**, founded in 1751, the San José de Gracia Church is an oft-photographed Spanish Colonial adobe structure listed on the National Register of Historic Places.

Pecos National Historical Park★

◉ Rte. 63, 4mi north of I-25 Exit 307, 27mi east of Santa Fe. ♿🅿 505-757-7200. www.nps.gov/peco.

In 1540, Spanish explorer Francisco Vázquez de Coronado (1510-1554) wrote that Pecos Pueblo was "feared through the land." Within 300 years, however, the 17 survivors of an original tribe of 2,000 had abandoned their home. This site preserves the ruins of the 14C village and a 1625 mission church.

Las Vegas★★

◉ I-25 Exit 345, 66mi east of Santa Fe. ✕♿🅿 505-425-8631. www.lasvegasnm.org.

With 900 buildings listed on the National Historic Register, a classic plaza and no pretensions, Las Vegas—no relation whatsoever to its Nevada namesake—epitomizes old New Mexico.

The friendly charm of this city of 14,500 may be discovered in nine historic districts. The campus of New Mexico Highlands University (1893) links downtown, a relic of the Route 66 era, and the Old Town Plaza Park district, surrounded by impressive 19C adobe buildings. Elsewhere, structures represent Victorian styles.

Numerous westerns have been filmed in and around the city, from *Easy Rider* (1969) to the Coen Brothers' *No Country for Old Men* (2007).

Fort Union National Monument★

◉ Rte. 161 off I-25 Exit 366, 28mi northeast of Las Vegas. ♿🅿 505-425-8025. www.nps.gov/foun.

Established in 1851, Fort Union was a base for military operations on the Santa Fe Trail and a launching point for campaigns against the Jicarilla Apaches, Utes, Kiowas and Comanches. After a railroad replaced the trail in 1879, Fort Union's role decreased, and it was abandoned in 1891. Today's visitors tour its sprawling brick-and-adobe remains and a small museum.

Albuquerque★

By far New Mexico's largest city, Albuquerque is an intriguing mix of old and new, of 14C Indian pueblos, 18C Spanish village and 21C high-technology center. Its architecture is liberally sprinkled with reminders of the city's mid-20C fling as a prime stop on cross-country Route 66.

▶ **Population:** 555,000.
ⓒ **Michelin Map:** p 277. Mountain Standard Time.
🏢 **Info:** ℘505-842-9918; www.itsatrip.org.
ⓢ **Don't Miss:** Sandia Peak Tram; Indian Pueblo Center.
👥 **Kids:** Rattlesnake Museum.
ⓒ **Also See:** Rio Grande Nature Center.

A BIT OF HISTORY

Paleo-Indian artifacts ascribed to Sandia Man, discovered in the mountains overlooking Albuquerque, have been dated from 25,000 years ago. Ancestral Puebloan farmlands, longtime homes of stationary tribes, are still inhabited pueblo communities. Spanish colonists established a villa on the Old Chihuahua Trail in 1706 and named it after the regional governor, the Duke of Albuquerque. Anglos arrived in force in the 1880s when the Santa Fe Railroad bypassed a costly mountain crossing at Santa Fe and came through this site instead. Sleepy Albuquerque was transformed into a rail boomtown, later to become a high-tech hub on the coattails of Los Alamos. Today this sprawling metropolis of 840,000 residents (city pop. 555,000) counts the University of New Mexico, Intel and Sandia National Labratory among its neighbors.

Pueblo Revival architecture, neon-lit cafes and motor courts speckle its cultural corridors, especially Central Avenue east and west of downtown. The restored 1927 **KiMo Theatre** (423 Central Ave. NW; ℘505-768-3522) may be the finest example of the Pueblo Deco style of building that fused Art Deco with Native American motifs.

Balloon Festival

More than 10 percent of hot-air balloons in the US are registered in Albuquerque. Mornings are generally windless, and on weekend dawns many of the colorful aircraft may be seen floating above the 100sq mi of the city. In October, the city's **Balloon Fiesta** is the world's largest gathering of hot-air balloons.

SIGHTS

Old Town★★

Central Ave. NW north to Mountain Rd. NW & Rio Grande Blvd. NW east to 19th St. NW. ✕♿🅿 www.albuquerque oldtown.com.

Some 150 shops and galleries face hidden gardens and cobbled walkways around a quiet, tree-shaded 18C plaza. The modern city has grown from this traditional central core. Today, restored adobes share the plaza with Pueblo Revival architecture, some structures painted in bold colors that suggest an adobe-Deco hybrid.

The **Church of San Felipe de Neri★** was built on the west side of the plaza in 1706; reconstructed on the north side in 1793, it has been in continuous use since. Pueblo and Navajo artisans display wares at the small **Indian market** along San Felipe Street, in front of the c.1706 Casa Armijo.

Old Town walking tours begin 11am most days from The Albuquerque Museum (below). Nearby, the **American International Rattlesnake Museum★** (202 San Felipe St. NW; ℘505-242-6569, www.rattlesnakes.com) endeavors to erase misconceptions about, and heighten appreciation for, this iconic desert denizen.

Albuquerque Museum of Art and History★★

2000 Mountain Rd. NW. ♿🅿 ℘505-243-7255. www.cabq.gov/museum.

The evolution of the Rio Grande valley, from pre-Columbian tribes through Coronado to the present, is chronicled in the fine **Four Centuries**★★ exhibit at this Old Town museum.

An extensive collection of Spanish colonial artifacts includes religious tapestries, maps, coins, arms and armor. Galleries of contemporary art highlight works by New Mexico artists.

New Mexico Museum of Natural History and Science★★

1801 Mountain Rd. NW. ✗❤️🅿️ ☎505-841-2800. www.nmnaturalhistory.org.

Four blocks north and east of the Old Town plaza, this lively museum offers a ramble through geologic time, from the formation of the universe to modern times. Interactive exhibits place visitors in the middle of a "live volcano" and an "Ice Age" cave. Fossil displays describe the paleontology, zoology and botany of the region from a time when dinosaurs were local residents; a sea coast exhibit reveals ocean shores. Other features include the giant-screen DynaTheater and a planetarium.

Indian Pueblo Cultural Center★★

2401 12th St. NW, 1 block north of I-40. ✗❤️🅿️ ☎505-843-7270. www.indianpueblo.org.

The arts of New Mexico's 19 Pueblo communities are exhibited at this important nonprofit center a mile from Old Town. Modeled after 9C Pueblo Bonito in Chaco Culture National Historical Park, this center is the one place to get an overview of cultures as presented by the Indians themselves, not interpreted by Anglos.

The **Indian Pueblo Cultural Museum**★★ exhibits ancient artifacts and contemporary weavings, jewelry, pottery and paintings—each piece individually chosen for display by tribal members—that trace the development of Pueblo cultures. Pottery designs are unique to each pueblo.

Traditional dancers perform weekends on an outdoor stage, and artisans demonstrate various crafts.

National Hispanic Cultural Center★

1701 4th St. SW. ✗❤️🅿️ ☎505-246-2261. www.nhccnm.org.

Rising south of downtown like a miniature Maya pyramid, this impressive complex combines a visual-arts museum with a library, genealogy center, restaurant, meeting areas, performing-arts center and other facilities. Museum rotating exhibits focus on Hispanic art and culture, from 18C–19C *retablos* to contemporary works.

Rio Grande Zoo★

903 10th St. SW. ✗❤️🅿️ ☎505-768-2000. www.cabq.gov/biopark/zoo.

Sixty-four acres of riverside cottonwood forest are home to more than 1,000 animals. The zoo includes a New Mexico prairie ecosystem, a habitat for endangered species of the Southwest. and underwater viewing areas on polar bears and sea lions. Two narrow-gauge trains link the sights, including Tingley Beach, popular for its fishing lakes.

Albuquerque Aquarium & Rio Grande Botanic Garden

2601 Central Ave. NW. ✗❤️🅿️ ☎505-768-2000. www.cabq.gov/biopark.

A 9min film on the Rio Grande biosystem introduces the aquarium, which focuses on Gulf of Mexico habitats. Highlighting the botanic garden are twin climate-controlled conservatories, the aromatic **Mediterranean Conservatory**★ and the sere Desert Conservatory, as well as a heritage farm, Japanese garden and children's fantasy garden.

Rio Grande Nature Center★

2901 Candelaria Rd. NW. ✗❤️🅿️ ☎505-344-7240. www.rgnc.org.

Ensconced in 270 acres of cottonwood bosque and riparian wetlands, this state park serves an environmental education function. The **Riverwalk Trail** (*1mi*) and the **Bosque Loop Trail** (*.8mi*) depart from a visitor center whose displays focus on the ecology and geology of the Rio Grande basin.

♟♟ Petroglyph National Monument★★

4735 Unser Blvd. NW, 3mi north of I-40 & 4mi west of Old Town. ♿️🅿️ ☎505-899-0205. www.nps.gov/petr.

More than 20,000 petroglyphs, scratched or chipped into basalt along a 17mi lava escarpment beneath five ancient volcanoes, chronicle the lives of countless Native American generations. Paved trails run through **Boca Negra Canyon**, 2.5mi north of the **visitor center** (Unser Blvd. & Western Trail Rd.).

University of New Mexico

Yale Blvd. NE at Central Ave. ✕♿️🅿️ ☎505-277-5813. www.unm.edu.

About 35,000 students attend the main campus, 2mi east of Old Town. Though founded in 1889, most of UNM's Pueblo Revival-style buildings were designed in the 1930s-40s. Its museums include the (1932) **Maxwell Museum of Anthropology★** (Redondo Dr. at Ash St. NE; ☎505-277-4405; http://maxwellmuseum.unm.edu), the **Meteorite Museum** (☎505-277-2747), and the **Geology Museum** (☎505-277-4204), with specimens typical of the New Mexico region.

National Museum of Nuclear Science & History★★

601 Eubank. Blvd. ♿️🅿️ ☎505-245-2137. www.nuclearmuseum,org.

Exhibits trace the development of atomic energy and weaponry, from the origins of atomic theory to modern advances in nuclear medicine. Visitors learn the basics of radiation and the history of the X-ray, and walk through a re-created fallout shelter from the Cold War era of the 1950s to 80s.

♟♟ Sandia Peak Aerial Tramway★★

10 Tramway Loop NE, 6mi east of I-25 via Tramway Blvd. at the Sandia Casino. ✕♿️🅿️ ☎505-856-7325. www.sandiapeak.com.

The world's longest jig-back aerial tramway covers 2.7mi from the northeastern city limits to 10,678ft **Sandia Crest**. Climbing from urban desert to alpine terrain in just 15min, the tram affords panoramic views of 11,000sq mi, across the entire Albuquerque area and other parts of northern New Mexico. Sandia Crest (☎505-243-0605) also can be reached by a 35mi drive from Albuquerque (east 16mi on I-40, north 6mi to Sandia Park on Rte. 14, then northwest 13mi on Rte. 536).

EXCURSIONS
Turquoise Trail★★

❯ Rte. 14, Tijeras (16mi east of Albuquerque at I-40 Exit 175) to Santa Fe. ☎505-281-5233. www.turquoisetrail.org.

This 52mi back road avoids I-25 and runs along the scenic eastern edge of the Sandia Mountains, which show a forested side not apparent from the desert-like west slope.

At Cedar Crest (4mi north of I-40), the **Museum of Archaeology and Material Culture** (22 Calvary Rd.; ☎505-281-2005) has a fine collection on early Native Americans, including Sandia Man, one of North America's earliest fossil-man discoveries. **Sandia Park** (2mi north of Cedar Crest), the turnoff for Sandia Crest, has its **Tinkertown Museum★** (Rte. 536; ☎505-281-5233; www.tinkertown.com), a 22-room folk-art tribute to Ross Ward's life work creating hand-carved, animated dioramas. Turquoise, gold, silver, lead and coal were once mined in great quantities in **Golden** (15mi north of Sandia Park), **Madrid★** (11mi north of Golden) and **Cerrillos** (3mi north of Madrid). When the last coal mines closed in the mid-1950s, the communities declined until rediscovered by artists and craftspeople. Madrid, largest of the three hamlets, invites visitors to descend into the **Old Coal Mine Museum** (☎505-438-3708).

Coronado State Monument★

❯ Rte. 44, Bernalillo, 1mi west of I-25 Exit 242. ☎505-867-5351. www.nmmonuments.org.

The ruins of the Kuaua Pueblo, built about 1325 on the west bank of the Rio Grande, are preserved here.

Taos★★

Taos Pueblo has been continuously inhabited for at least 1,000 years. The rustic, Spanish colonial town of Taos is perhaps 300 years old. Built around a cozy plaza that remains the heart of the modern town, it is today a center for the arts, much smaller than Santa Fe but equally alluring to aficionados of Southwest art.

A BIT OF HISTORY

Taos found its niche in the world of art in 1915 when Joseph Sharp, Ernest Blumenschein, Bert Phillips and friends founded the **Taos Society of Artists**. They focused world attention on the unique light in northern New Mexico; its reputation laid a foundation for today's prolific, tricultural art community.

Taos sits on a plateau between the Rio Grande and the Sangre de Cristo Range. Eleven miles northwest of Taos on US-64, the three-span, continuous-truss Rio Grande Gorge Bridge, 1,200ft long, crosses the river at a height of 650ft above it.

SIGHTS

Taos Pueblo★★★

2mi north of Taos Plaza via Camino del Pueblo. ℰ575-758-1028. www.taospueblo.com.

The oldest and best-known New Mexico pueblo has been designated a World Heritage Site, of enduring value to mankind, by UNESCO. A visit is a step back in time. The pueblo contains a multistory mud-and-straw adobe structure with ladders leading to upper floors. Some 150 residents live here year-round without running water or electricity. About 1,100 other pueblo members live in modern homes, but sell mica-flecked pottery, silver and turquoise jewelry, moccasins and drums from homes on the pueblo's ground floor. Guided tours by pueblo residents immeasurably enhance the visitor's understanding of this special ancient community.

▶ **Population:** 5,600.
⊙ **Michelin Map:** p 277. Mountain Standard Time.
▯ **Info:** ℰ575-751-8800; www.taoschamber.com.
⊚ **Don't Miss:** Taos Pueblo.

Ruins of the **Mission San Geronimo de Taos★** lie near the pueblo entrance. The pueblo's **Taos Mountain Casino** (Camino del Pueblo; ℰ575-737-0777) offers gaming, dining and shopping.

Fechin House and Studio★

227 Paseo del Pueblo Norte. ▯ℰ575-758-2690. www.taosartmuseum.org.
Before he moved to Taos in 1927, Nikolai Fechin (1881-1955) had secured a reputation in his native Russia and in New York as a renaissance man. His paintings, sculptures and drawings are on display inside this Russian-style home.

⚌ Kit Carson Home and Museum★★

113 Kit Carson Rd., 1 block east of Taos Plaza. ℰ575-758-4945. www.kitcarsonhomeandmuseum.com
Carson, a famous frontier scout and Indian agent (1809-68), lived in this 1825 house from 1843 until his death. The museum, in a part of the original house, illustrates Carson's career and frontier life of that era through displays of guns, clothing, saddles, furniture and period equipment used by mountain men and Indians.

Around the corner from the Carson home, the **Mabel Dodge Luhan House** (240 Morada Ln.; ℰ575-751-9686; www.mabeldodgeluhan.com), home to Mabel Dodge, darling of the counterculture and patron of the arts, is now an inn and retreat center.

Ernest L. Blumenschein Home & Museum★

222 Ledoux St., 2 blocks south and west of Taos Plaza. ▯ℰ575-758-0505. www.taoshistoricmuseums.com.

Here are works by painter Blumenschein (1874-1960) and the Taos Society of Artists. A few steps east, the **R.C. Gorman Gallery** (210 Ledoux St.; ✆575-758-3250; www.rcgormangallery.com), houses pieces by the renowned Native American painter and sculptor.

Harwood Museum of Art★★

238 Ledoux St. ♿🅿 ✆575-758-9826. www.harwoodmuseum.org.
Works by 20C Taos artists and noted American modernists (Marsden Hartley, Richard Diebenkorn) are displayed at this museum, a fixture since 1923. The Hispanic folk-art collection includes 80 19C retablos.

Hacienda de los Martinez★★

Ranchitos Rd., 2mi west of Taos.
🅿 ✆575-758-0505.
www.taoshistoricmuseums.com.
One of the few Spanish Colonial "great houses" open to the public, the fortress-like hacienda was built in 1804 by merchant Don Antonio Severino Martinez. Its windowless adobe walls rise above the west bank of the Rio Pueblo de Taos. Twenty-one spartan rooms are built around two courtyards

Millicent Rogers Museum★★

1504 Millicent Rogers Rd., 4mi north of Taos Plaza. ♿🅿 ✆575-758-2462. www.millicentrogers.org.
Founded by Standard Oil heiress Millicent Rogers (1902-53), this museum exhibits her silver and turquoise Indian jewelry, Navajo and Rio Grande weavings. Additional collections include Hispanic religious and domestic arts, and crafts from all over New Mexico, including San Ildefonso pottery, Zuni kachina dolls, basketry and textiles.

Taos Ski Valley★

Taos Ski Valley Rd. (Rte. 150), 19mi north of Taos Plaza. 🅿 ✆866-968-7386. www.skitaos.org. www.taosskivalley.com.
One of the continent's most challenging ski mountains, Taos Ski Valley has 12 lifts serving terrain that crests at 11,819ft. The village has restaurants and shops.

San Francisco de Asis Church★★

Rte. 68, 4mi south of Taos Plaza.
✆575-758-2754.
The exterior of this heavily buttressed adobe church is probably the most painted and photographed in New Mexico. Georgia O'Keeffe and Ansel Adams are among artists who have immortalized its stark, 120ft-long form. The two-story church was built between 1710 and 1755; its few doors and windows are not visible from the highway. In the chapel are images of saints, a large Christ figure and *reredos* dating to the church's founding.

EXCURSION
Enchanted Circle★★

❯ Rtes. 522 & 38 and US-64, north and east of Taos. ✖🅿 www.enchanted circle.org.
This 85mi US Forest Service Scenic Byway circles 13,161ft **Wheeler Peak**, New Mexico's highest point, and connects Taos with several small resort towns.
The town of **Questa** (Rte. 522, 24mi north of Taos; ✆505-613-2852) is a starting point for white-water trips on the upper Rio Grande. **Red River** (Rte. 38, 12mi east of Questa; ✆575-754-2366; www.redrivernewmex.com) and **Eagle Nest** (US-64 & Rte. 38, 17mi east of Red River; ✆505-377-2486; www.eaglenest.org), both 19C gold-mining towns, are bases for outdoor excursions into pine forests shadowed by Wheeler Peak, from skiing at **Red River Ski Area** (✆575-754-2223; www.redriverskiarea.com) to fishing at Eagle Nest Lake.
Angel Fire (Rte. 434, just south of US-64; ✆575-377-6353; www.angelfirechamber.org), a tiny village in the Moreno Valley of the Sangre de Cristo Range, is a year-round ski and golf resort. The **Vietnam Veterans Memorial★** (US-64, Angel Fire; ♿🅿 ✆575-377-6900; www.vietnamveteransmemorial.org), a father's tribute to his son, is a white curved structure perched on a serene hillside, offering broad views of the Moreno Valley and the Sangre de Cristo.

Gallup–Farmington Area★

Gallup is a gateway to the Navajo and Zuni reservations and a center for Indian arts and crafts. Dances are regularly presented, and fine trading posts invite shoppers and browsers. The lucrative native-art market has created many local millionaires among Gallup's 22,000 residents. Farther north, Farmington serves as the gateway to several of the world's unique and ancient Indian ruins, as well as mountain and desert recreational sites. A business hub for the Four Corners region, the city of 46,000 anchors the northeastern corner of the 250,000sq mi Navajo Indian Reservation.

- **Michelin Map:** inside cover. Mountain Standard Time
- **Info:** ℘505-722-2228; www.thegallupchamber.com; ℘505-326-7602; www.farmingtonnm.org; www.indiancountrynm.org.
- **Location:** The local landmark is Mount Taylor, halfway between Albuquerque and Gallup. At 11,301ft it's the tallest thing for hundreds of miles, and sacred to the Navajo.
- **Don't Miss:** Acoma Pueblo; Chaco Culture National Historical Park
- **Timing:** Don't be fooled by the relative proximity of Chaco to Farmington: a trip to Chaco takes a full day.
- **Kids:** Cumbres & Toltec RR.

GALLUP AREA

Gallup★

US-666 at I-40 Exit 20, 139mi west of Albuquerque. ✕&🅿℘505-722-2228. www.thegallupchamber.com.

Gallup is filled with trading posts, Indian shops and galleries along its fabled Route 66 corridor and in its 12-block historic district. For almost 90 years, the **Inter-Tribal Indian Ceremonial**★★ (℘505-863-3896; www.theceremonial.com) has been held at **Red Rock State Park** (Rte. 66 at I-40 Exit 26, 4mi east of Gallup; ℘505-722-3839). Members of 30 tribes engage in parades, dances and rodeo events in one of the largest tribal gatherings (Aug).

Zuni Indian Reservation★

Rte. 53, 37mi south of Gallup via Rte. 602. △✕&🅿℘505-782-7000. www.zunitourism.com.

The arts and ambience of an ancient Pueblo community are very much alive in modern Zuni, largest (with 10,000 residents and 259sq mi of land) of New Mexico's pueblos. A mural at the **Pueblo of Zuni Visitor Information Center**★ (1222 Rte. 53; ℘505-782-7238) depicts the Zuni origin story. The detailed work of silversmiths, carvers and potters is seen at **A:shiwi A:wan Museum & Heritage Center**★★ (1220 Rte. 53; ℘505-782-4403; www.ashiwi.org). Two dozen kachina murals in **Our Lady of Guadalupe Mission**★ (1629) depict a spiritual life blending tribal and Catholic traditions.

El Morro National Monument★★

Rte. 53 near Ramah, 54mi southeast of Gallup. △&🅿℘505-783-4226. www.nps.gov/elmo.

For 1,000 years, names and messages have been carved into a 200ft sandstone monolith. **Inscription Rock** is in a narrow catchment basin, the only water source for many miles. Pueblo Indians, Spanish explorers and frontier travelers camped here, leaving petroglyphs (AD 1000-1400) and other inscriptions.

El Malpais National Monument and Conservation Area★

Rte. 53, 23mi south of I-40 at Grants. 🅿 ℘505-783-4774. www.blm.gov/nm.

A landscape whose name is Spanish for "The Badlands," this park attracts hardy hikers and outdoors lovers. Forty different volcanoes produced a vast lava field; part of it is only 2,000 years old.

♿♿ New Mexico Mining Museum★★

100 N. Iron Ave., Grants, 61mi east of Gallup and 72mi west of Albuquerque. ♿ P 📞505-287-4802. www.grants.org. Beneath the office of Grants' city visitor center, accessed via elevator through a small mining museum, is a replica of a uranium mine.

Acoma Pueblo★

Rte. 23, 12.5mi southwest of I-40 Exit 108, 30mi southeast of Grants and 64mi west of Albuquerque. P 📞800-747-0181. www.acomaskysity.org
Native Americans say the clifftop Sky City★★★ has been inhabited "since the beginning of time." Archaeologists verify that this 70-acre, Medieval-looking, walled adobe village—perched atop a sheer mesa, 367ft above the valley floor—has been lived in at least since the 11C. Between 1629 and 1640, Spanish priests built the San Esteban del Rey Mission★★, now a National Historic Landmark. Photography restrictions are in force in Sky City. The tribe also operates the Sky City Casino (I-40 Exit 102; 📞505-552-6123).

FARMINGTON AREA

Aztec Ruins National Monument★

84 Ruins Rd., north of US-550, Aztec. ♿ P 📞505-334-6174. www.nps.gov/azru.
Parts of a 500-room Ancestral Puebloan pueblo from AD 1100-1300 remain at this site. In its heart is an immense reconstruction of a great kiva, a round chamber believed to have been used for ceremonies and other gatherings. A short video at the visitor center reveals the pre-Columbian history of the region.

Salmon Ruins★

US-64, 11mi east of Farmington & 2mi west of Bloomfield. ♿ P 📞505-632-2013. www.salmonruins.com.
Excavation has partially exposed this 150-room Ancestral Puebloan site on the San Juan River. Originally settled by Chacoans in AD 1088-1130, it was added to about AD 1185, before being abandoned around AD 1250.

Chaco Culture National Historical Park★★★

Rte. 57, Nageezi, 73mi south of Farmington via US-64 & US-550. ⚠ P 📞505-786-7014. www.nps.gov/chcu.
One of the foremost cultural and historical areas in the US, Chaco Canyon was a major center of Ancestral Puebloan culture from AD 850-1250. This hub of ceremony, trade and government for the prehistoric Four Corners area was a city of thousands whose trade network extended into Mexico. There are 13 major excavated archaeological sites in Chaco Canyon, and hundreds of smaller sites.
Pueblo Bonito (c.AD 850-1200) was the largest "great house"—four stories high, with 600 rooms and 40 kivas. Adjacent to it, Chetro Ketl (c.AD 1020-1200) contained 500 rooms and an elevated earthen plaza. Pueblo del Arroyo (280 rooms) and Kin Kletso (100 rooms) were built in the late 11C and early 12C. Situated in an isolated desert canyon, Chaco is reachable only by gravel roads. The preferred 21mi route is from the north, via County Road 7900 off US-550, 3mi southeast of Nageezi. Roads may become impassable during heavy rains.

♿♿ Cumbres & Toltec Scenic Railroad★

US-85 & Rte. 17, Chama, 110mi east of Farmington via US-64. ✕ ♿ P 📞575-756-2151. www.cumbrestoltec.com.
The longest remaining example of the original Denver & Rio Grande narrow-gauge line covers 64mi of spectacular scenery between Chama, New Mexico, and Antonito, Colorado, over trestles and through tunnels in the San Juan Mountains above the Los Piños River.

Rockies

Rocky Mountain
National Park, Colorado
©Matt Inden/Miles/CTO

Denver and the Colorado Rockies

Nicknamed the "Mile High City" because its elevation is exactly 5,280ft (1mi) above sea level, Denver is a growing metropolis of more than 2.7 million people. As the largest urban center within a 550mi radius—between Phoenix and Chicago, Dallas and Seattle —it is the capital of the Rocky Mountain region, its only possible competition being Salt Lake City. Climaxed by 53 peaks of 14,000ft elevation or higher, the Rocky Mountains dominate the western half of the state of Colorado. Many of North America's most famous ski resorts are found here, along with fascinating pieces of mining and railroad heritage.

Highlights

1 Historic preservation in Denver's **Larimer Square** (p303)

2 Native American art at **Denver Art Museum** (p306)

3 Sky-high sand at **Great Sand Dunes** (p313)

4 **Black Canyon's** chasm (p323)

5 Peaks along the **Million Dollar Highway** (p325)

A Mountain Mecca

The capital of Colorado, Denver nestles near the foothills of the Rockies on a high plain that originally was Arapaho and Cheyenne Indian land. To the east rise a few low hills, then Great Plains stretch almost 1,000mi to the Mississippi River.

The main towns north and south of Denver abut the Front Range, as the eastern edge of the Rockies is called. Little more than an hour's drive south, Colorado Springs sprawls at the base of immense Pikes Peak, its 14,110ft summit a landmark to westbound pioneers. The burgeoning city is home to the US Air Force Academy, the high-altitude US Olympic Training Center and numerous geological and architectural attractions. Just northeast of Denver

© Matt Inden/Weaver Multimedia Group/CTO

Resident herd of elk in Rocky Mountain National Park

is Rocky Mountain National Park. Two hours north of Denver lies Cheyenne, the small Wyoming state capital that clings to its Wild West heritage. Cheyenne is quiet except 10 days in late July and early August when it hosts Cheyenne Frontier Days, the world's largest outdoor rodeo.

ADDRESSES

🏨 STAY

DENVER AREA

$$$$$ The Broadmoor – 1 Lake Ave., Colorado Springs, CO. ☎719-623-5112. www.broadmoor.com. 754 rooms. At first a casino, by 1918 it was a grand resort nestled against the Rocky Mountain foothills. Today, it displays the same pink-stucco facade and curved marble staircase. A world-class spa, 9 restaurants, 3 golf courses and 3 swimming pools add to its charms.

$$$$ The Brown Palace Hotel – 321 17th St., Denver, CO. ☎303-297-3111. www.brownpalace.com. 241 rooms. When entrepreneurs seeking gold flocked west in 1892, they stayed at this distinguished inn. Presidents still shake hands in the grand atrium, its seven tiers of balconies lined in Mexican onyx and crowned by a stained-glass dome. Afternoon tea is served there daily, and in the formal **Palace Arms ($$$)**, patrons dine among European battle flags on the likes of Colorado rabbit or Rosen Ranch lamb. There's an on-site spa.

$$$ Hotel Boulderado – 2115 13th St., Boulder, CO. ☎303-442-4344. http://.boulderado.com. 160 rooms. A bright lobby, with a canopied ceiling of stained glass and mosaic tile, recalls an era of Victorian elegance intertwined with Boulder history for nearly a century. But **Q's Restaurant ($$)** serves the most contemporary of cuisine.

$$$ Cheyenne Mountain Resort – 3225 Broadmoor Valley Rd., Colorado Springs, CO. ☎719-538-4000. www.cheyennemountain.com. 316 rooms. Denver families often escape for the weekend to this nouveau-rustic resort, on 217 acres at the foot of Cheyenne Mountain. There's golf, tennis, mountain biking, five swimming pools, a 35-acre lake for canoeing and fly fishing, and three dining venues.

$$$ Hotel Monaco – 1717 Champa St., Denver, CO. ☎303-296-1717. www.monaco-denver.com. 189 rooms. In the heart of Denver, the Kimpton Group renovated two historic buildings, one of them a 1937 Art Moderne edifice, to create this boutique property. A 23ft hand-painted ceiling highlights the main lobby; guest rooms are furnished in whimsical luxury. The excellent **Panzano ($$)** restaurant offers Northern Italian cuisine.

$$$ The Oxford Hotel – 1600 17th St., Denver, CO. ☎303-628-5400. www.theoxfordhotel.com. 80 rooms. French and English antiques adorn rooms at Denver's oldest grand hotel. The redbrick exterior is classic; careful restorations have revealed false ceilings and silver chandeliers previously coated in paint. Built in 1891, it is on the National Register of Historic Places.

$$$ Warwick Denver – 1776 Grant St., Denver, CO. ☎303-861-2000. www.warwickdenver.com. 216 rooms. This elegant midsize hotel has undergone extensive renovation, with data-ports and tasteful new furnishings. An atrium, fitness center, rooftop pool and restaurant add to the first-class image.

$$ The Cliff House at Pikes Peak – 306 Cañon Ave., Manitou Springs, CO. ☎719-785-1000. http://.thecliffhouse.com. 54rooms. Built in 1873 as a hot-springs resort, The Cliff House was abandoned for years until it reopened in 1999 after a $10 million renovation. The redesign retained the manse's Victorian ambience, from guest rooms to wide verandah and open gardens, but added 21C frills and a fine restaurant.

CHEYENNE

$$ Nagle Warren Mansion B&B – 222 E. 17th St., Cheyenne, WY. ☎307-637-3333. www.naglewarrenmansion.com. 12 rooms. Built in 1888, this three-story mansion retains original features such as parquet floors, carved leather ceilings and a marble fireplace. Rooms are individually decorated and have their own bathroom. A bountiful breakfast is included in the rate.

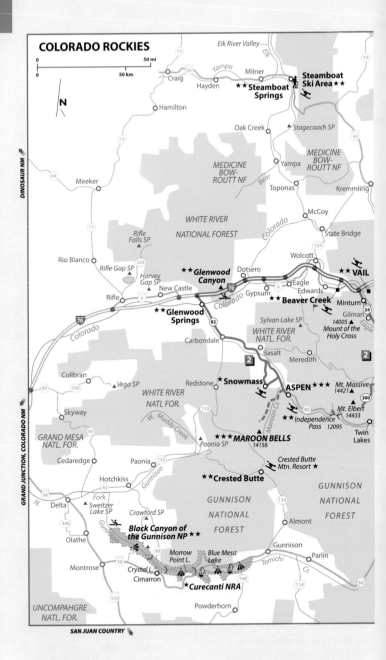

COLORADO ROCKIES

$$$$$ The Home Ranch – 54880 County Rd. 129, Clark, CO, 19mi north of Steamboat Springs. ☎970-879-1780.www. homeranch.com. 6 rooms, 8 cabins. Here is the best in Western hospitality: 100 horses, fly fishing, elegant private cabins with wood-burning stoves and lofts, gourmet meals with the likes of stuffed quail or Alaskan halibut. The minimum summer stay is one week; nightly rates are available in winter, when the ranch becomes a cross-country skiing mecca.

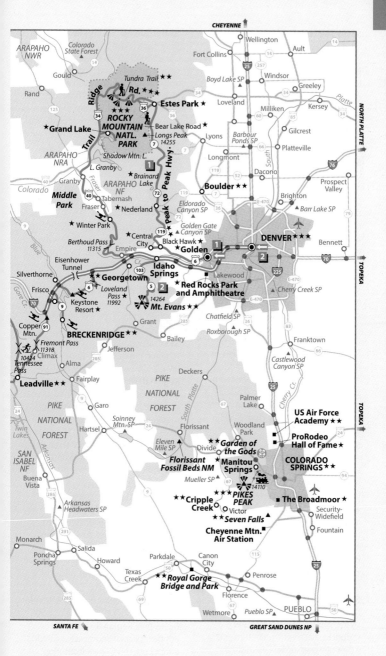

$$$$$ Hotel Jerome – 330 E. Main St., Aspen, CO. ✆970-920-1000. http://. hoteljerome.aubergeresorts.com. 94 rooms. Over a century ago, the rich mining crowd bellied up to the hotel bar to celebrate silver strikes. Aspen's elite still frequent the same three-floor redbrick landmark. Recently renovated, the hotel sports luxurious rooms with cashmere curtains, leather furnishings, Western accents and local art. In the bright and airy **Prospect Restaurant ($$$)**, small as well as large plates are available.

$$$$$ The Lodge at Vail – 174 E. Gore Creek Dr., Vail, CO. ☎970-429-5044. www.lodgeatvail.com. 165 rooms. Tyrol meets Rockies in an opulent mix 30 yards from Vail's chairlifts. Wide stairs lead to rooms of polished woods, high-backed leather chairs and private balconies. Enjoy aged prime beef at **Elway's ($$$)** and breakfast in **Cucina Rustica ($$)**. Two pools, six hot tubs and a spa.

$$$$ Sonnenalp Resort – 20 Vail Rd., Vail, CO. ☎970-476-5656. www.sonnenalp.com. 127 rooms. The only North American outpost of a famed Bavarian lodging, the Sonnenalp is composed mainly of large suites that offer the firelit ambience of an Alpine lodge, with wood beams in stucco ceilings and comfortable sofas. Guests enjoy a spa, pool and oxygen bar.

$$$ New Sheridan Hotel – 231 W. Colorado Ave., Telluride, CO. ☎970-728-4351. www.newsheridan.com. 26 rooms. Had you visited a century ago, the New Sheridan would indeed have been "new." Today, the fully restored inn, in the heart of town, embodies modern elegance. Rooms are appointed with settees and bathrobes; some feature photos of early Telluride. A historic bar and the gourmet **Chop House ($$$)** restaurant lure locals.

$$$$ The Stanley Hotel – 333 Wonderview Ave., Estes Park, CO. ☎970-586-3371. www.stanleyhotel.com. 100 rooms. ⊠ Ailing F.O. Stanley came to this valley for alpine air in 1903, and never left. His white-pillared Georgian hotel reputedly inspired guest Stephen King to write his novel The Shining. Double fireplaces and staircases still grace the lobby, and Palladian windows provide spectacular views. At the adjacent 40-room Lodge, breakfast is included in the rate.

$$$ Strater Hotel – 699 Main Ave., Durango, CO. ☎970-247-4431. http://strater.com. 93 rooms. The Strater is a redbrick palace with white trim and a hint of the Wild West. Furnished with a fabulous collection of Victorian walnut antiques, the historic hotel is embellished with brass rails and brocaded settees. Some rooms boast four-poster beds and ornate wallpaper.

$$ Hot Sulphur Springs Resort – 5609 County Road 20, Hot Sulphur Springs, CO. ☎970-725-3306. www.hotsulphur springs.com. 17 rooms. Rooms are cozy and comfortable and filled with rustic pine furniture, but that's not what brings guests to this historic lodge. Seven natural springs bring unfiltered hot mineral water to the resort's assemblage of 21 soaking pools and baths and a swimming pool (summer only).

⚟ EAT

DENVER AREA

$$$ Buckhorn Exchange – 1000 Osage St., Denver, CO ☎303-534-9505. www.buckhorn.com. **Regional.** Like Theodore Roosevelt and his contemporaries, diners at Denver's oldest restaurant can try elk, pheasant and rattlesnake in the company of more than 500 animal trophies and 125 guns at this historic (1893) eatery.

$$$ Craftwood Inn – 404 El Paso Blvd., Manitou Springs, CO. ☎719-685-9000. www.craftwood.com. Dinner only. **Regional.** This Tudor-style restaurant of beamed ceilings and stained-glass windows, once a coppersmith shop, began serving food in 1940. Views of Pikes Peak are spectacular. The cuisine is robust Colorado: wild boar tenderloin, ostrich filet, grilled red deer and pheasant.

$$$ Denver ChopHouse – 1735 19th St. Denver. ☎303-296-0800. www.denverchophouse.com. **Steakhouse.** A classic Western steakhouse located in the LoDo neighborhood, this popular, high-style spot serves only natural beef. Standouts are tenderloin tips pan-braised with mushrooms, and a 19oz Delmonico steak.

$$$ The Fort – 19192 Highway 8, Morrison, CO. ☎303-697-4771. www.thefort.com. Dinner only. **Regional.** Housed in an adobe replica of Southeast Colorado's Bent's Fort, this Denver institution perches amid the area's famed red-rock terrain. The Fort is known for its traditional High Plains repasts of elk, quail, the inimitable Rocky Mountain oysters, and a dozen dishes featuring buffalo. The outdoor patio has a splendid view of the Front Range.

$$$ John's Restaurant – 2328 Pearl St., Boulder, CO. 303-444-5232. www.johns restaurantboulder.com. Dinner only. Closed Sun and Mon. **Contemporary**. Only 30 to 40 people a night are served in this quaint home, but they are rewarded with the brother-sister chef-owners' seasonal choices that range from Colorado lamb to seared duck breast. Try the apple cheesecake for dessert.

$$$ Restaurant Kevin Taylor – 1106 14th St., Denver, CO. 303-820-2600. www.ktrg.net. Dinner only. Closed Sun. **American**. Showcase for the culinary talents of this Denver-born chef, his Hotel Teatro eatery offers fine dining amid contemporary decor. French foie gras, Colorado beef tenderloin, and white chocolate panna cotta make a marvelous meal.

$$ Rio Grande – 1525 Blake St., Denver. 303-623-5432. www.riograndemexican. com. **Mexican**. Flagship of a small chain born in Fort Collins, CO, this LoDo cafe serves mainstream, expertly prepared High Plains-style Mexican food. Green chile soup uses roasted New Mexico peppers; blue corn enchiladas add spinach and squash for a vegetarian dish; and huevos rancheros comes, as traditional, as a dinner entree.

$$ Wynkoop Brewing Company – 1634 18th St., Denver, CO. 303-297-2700. www.wynkoop.com. **American**. The oldest brewpub in Denver is housed in an 1899 warehouse downtown. The second floor holds a billiards room with 22 pool tables and the basement features a theater for impro-comedy shows. Pub fare includes queso dip, fish and chips, shepherd's pie and signature Rail Yard Ale.

COLORADO ROCKIES

$$$$ Krabloonik – 4250 Divide Rd., Snowmass Village. 970-923-3953. www. krabloonik.com. Closed May–mid-Dec. **Contemporary**. Combining fine dining with a large dog-sledding kennel, Krabloonik may be one of a kind. By winter day, dog teams pull sledders on tours of the Maroon Bells Wilderness. Afterward, diners relax and enjoy a menu of wild-mushroom soup as well as beef, fish or home-smoked game.

$$$$ Mirabelle at Beaver Creek – 55 Village Rd., Avon. 970-949-7728. www.mirabelle1.com. Dinner only. **Contemporary**. Daniel Joly, who lives with his family above this restaurant in an 1898 farmhouse, is a master chef from Belgium working in the US. Impeccable service matches the French-influenced cuisine, highlighted by such dishes as Colorado rack of lamb elk, and Dover sole.

$$$ Hearthstone Restaurant – 130 S. Ridge St., Breckenridge. 970-453-1148. www.hearthstonerestaurant.biz. Dinner only. **Regional**. A late 19C Victorian house, one block off Main Ave., is the setting for this friendly restaurant. Upper-story windows offer views of nearby mountains. Generous portions of wild game, steaks and seafood are the fare, washed down with wine from an award-winning wine list.

$$$ Sweet Basil – 193 E. Gore Creek Dr., Vail. 970-476-0125. https://sweetbasilvail. com. **Contemporary**. The menu changes seasonally, but this bistro is always packed from wall to wall. Dishes include rainbow trout with black-truffle butter, hangar steak with potato garlic hash, and a vegan dish. The main-floor wine bar is popular.

$$ Buffalo Restaurant & Bar– 1617 Miner St., Idaho Springs. 303-567-2729. http:// buffalorestaurant.com. **American**. Open for more than 100 years, this popular historic saloon was serving buffalo long before it became fashionable. Today bison finds its way into burgers, meatloaf, stew and plates of ribeye, short ribs, fajitas, pasta and more.

$$ The Palace Restaurant – 505 Main Ave., Durango. 970-247-2018. http://. palacedurango.com. **American**. Housed in a historic Beaux Arts hotel, this eatery is both a fine-dining restaurant and a tavern whose menu ranges from steak and frites to chicken and dumpling.

$ Mr. Happy's – 125 E. Main St., Cortez. 970-565-9869. http://mrhappysbbg. wordpress.com. **American**. This popular bakery, bar and grill serves up breakfast, lunch and dinner. Wraps, burgers and sandwiches share the menu with steaks, fish and chips and homemade meatloaf.

Denver★★★

The capital of Colorado, nicknamed the "Queen City of the Plains," is usually associated in the public mind not with plains but with the snowcapped peaks of the Rockies that backdrop the city. Those mountains make possible the area's ever burgeoning growth; native water supplies proved inadequate decades ago, and Denver and its suburbs rely on a massive scheme of dams, tunnels and canals that bring water across the Continental Divide.

DENVER TODAY

Denver has become a services and high-tech center, with telecommunications and computer industries contributing significantly to the economy. With thousands of state, local and federal employees, Denver claims the second-highest percentage of government workers after Washington, DC. The city is an important cultural center with museums, theaters and concert venues, and is one of only a handful of US cities with franchises in all four major-league sports: football, baseball, basketball and ice hockey. The annual National Western Stock Show (www.nationalwestern.com), one of the largest events of its kind, ties Western tradition to modern times.

▶ **Population:** 634,000.

⏱ **Michelin Map:** pp 298-299. Mountain Standard Time.

ℹ **Info:** ℘303-892-1112; www.denver.org.

▶ **Location:** Like most Western cities, the Denver area's streets are laid out in an east–west/north–south grid; streets run north–south, avenues east–west (except downtown). You can't lose track of compass directions – the Rockies are always in sight directly west.

🅿 **Parking:** Parking near downtown can be scarce on weekdays, but there are ample reasonably priced lots near the Denver Art Museum, and west of Larimer Square toward the South Platte River.

🏛 **Don't Miss:** The Denver Art Museum.

🕐 **Timing:** Plan to visit the Art Museum, state capitol and other Civic Center attractions in the morning; then hop on the free 16th Street Mall bus to reach Larimer Square, Confluence Park, the aquarium and Elitch Gardens.

👥 **Kids:** The Downtown Aquarium; Elitch Gardens.

History Colorado Center

© Gwen Cannon/Michelin

GETTING THERE
Denver International Airport

(DEN) (℘303-342-2000; www.flydenver.com) one of the major hubs in the US, is 23mi northeast of downtown. Rental car and shuttle service counters are in the main terminal. Ground transportation is on baggage-claim level. **RTD SkyRide** (℘303-299-6000; www.rtd-denver.com), **SuperShuttle** (℘303-370-1300; www.supershuttle.com) and **Green Ride** (℘888-472-6656; www.greenrideco.com) run buses and vans to downtown and surrounding areas. **Amtrak train**: Union Station (1701 Wynkoop St.; ℘800-872-7245; www.amtrak.com). **Greyhound and regional buses**: Main terminal (20th & Curtis Sts.; ℘800-231-2222; www.greyhound.com).

GETTING AROUND

The Regional Transportation District (RTD) operates local and regional buses and a light rail line that runs through downtown (℘303-299-6000; www.rtd-denver.com). Coupons and tokens are available at Market Street and Civic Center stations and some grocery stores. **Taxi**: Freedom Cab (℘303-444-4444), Metro Taxi (℘303-333-3333), Yellow Cab (℘303-777-7777).

VISITOR INFORMATION

The **Denver Convention & Visitors Bureau** (1555 California St., Suite 300, Denver CO 80202; ℘303-892-1112; www.denver.org) operates two visitor information centers: Denver International Airport main terminal, and downtown at the 16th Street Mall (16th and California St). The free Official Visitors Guide contains detailed information on accommodations, area events and attractions, and dining (available online from the Denver CVB or at the visitor centers and hotels).

ACCOMMODATIONS

See ADDRESSES p297 or contact the Denver Convention & Visitors Bureau (above) for area lodging and reservations.

A BIT OF HISTORY

Denver City was formed in 1860 by the merger of two gold-rush settlements. Despite a population laden with outlaws, prospectors and shysters, the frontier town survived the pioneer era as capital of the Colorado Territory. Denver's prosperity was pegged to silver. Between the mid 1870s and mid 1890s, strikes in Leadville and Aspen turned miners into millionaires. Successful silver production required banks to underpin the enterprises, and trains to connect the mountain towns with Denver and the East.

By 1890 Denver was a fashionable city of 106,000 with fine hotels, stores and theaters. Electric lights were installed in 1883; the first streetcars were introduced in 1888.Today, Denver remains a crossroads. Interstates 70 and 25 cross in Denver, and the 1995 opening of Denver International Airport, a key air hub, assured the city's importance.

DOWNTOWN DENVER★
LoDo★★

Between Larimer & Wynkoop Sts., 20th St. & Speer Blvd. ✕ 🅿 ℘303-628-5428. www.lodo.org.

Ardent preservationists fought for the renovation of 17 neglected c.1870-90 buildings. Their efforts culminated in 1973 in **Larimer Square★★** (1400 block of Larimer St.; ℘303-534-2367; www.larimersquare.com), a pedestrian-friendly block. The restoration movement boomed in the 1990s as 19C buildings and warehouses were revitalized into restaurants, clubs, galleries, shops, and upper-story apartments. The 1995 opening of **Coors Field** ♟♟ (2001 Blake St.; ℘303-292-0200; http://.colorado.rockies.mlb.com), a major-league base-

The Tattered Cover bookstore

ball stadium designed in traditonal style, climaxed the transformation. Larimer Square anchors the southern end of the 26-block historic district. The 1895 **Union Station** (1701 Wynkoop St.) remains a Beaux-Arts landmark on its northern fringe; it is under renovation to reopen in mid-2014 as retail space with restaurants, shops and a 110-room hotel. Across the street from the depot, the **Wynkoop Brewing Company** (1634 18th St.; ℘303-297-2700; www.wynkoop.com) is Denver's original microbrewery and one of America's first in 1988; there now are a half-dozen small brewing companies in the area. **The Tattered Cover★** (1628 16th St.; ℘303-436-1070; www.tatteredcover.

com) is one of the country's best book-stores, housed in a historic multi-story building, with reading areas and a cafe.

16th Street Mall★

16th St. between Market St. & Broadway. ✖&🅿.

Extending southeast from the bus terminal to Civic Center Park, the tree-lined Mall is flanked by office towers, street-level cafes and shops, and 11 fountains. Horse-drawn carriages and free shuttle buses are the only permitted vehicles. Highlights include the 1910 **D & F Tower★** (at Arapahoe St.), a 325ft replica of the campanile of St. Mark's Basilica in Venice; and the 1891 **Kittredge Building** (at Glenarm Pl.), a Romanesque Revival structure. The **Paramount Theatre** (1621 Glenarm Pl.; ℘303-623-0106; www.paramountdenver.com), built in 1929, has one of two operating dual-console pipe organs in the US. The $100 million **Denver Pavilions** (between Welton St. & Glenarm Pl.; ✖&🅿℘303-260-6000; www.denverpavilions.com) is downtown Denver's newest shopping-dining-entertainment complex.

Brown Palace Hotel★

321 17th St. at Tremont Pl. & Broadway. ✖&🅿℘303-297-3111. www.brownpalace.com.

Five US presidents and the Beatles have stayed at "The Brown," Denver's nine-story Italian Renaissance landmark (1892, Frank Edbrooke) made of red granite and sandstone. Stone

Entertainment

Consult the Friday and Sunday editions or the online versions of the *Denver Post* (www.denverpost.com) and the weekly *Westword* (www.westword.com), published Thursdays, for listings of current events, theaters and concert halls. Favorite **venues**: Denver Center for the Performing Arts (℘303-893-4100; www.denvercenter.org), Paramount Theatre (℘303-623-0106; www.denverparamount.com), and especially scenic outdoor Red Rocks Amphitheatre (℘720-865-2494; http://redrocksonline.com).

Denver Center for the Performing Arts

medallions depicting Rocky Mountain animals are set between the seventh-story windows. An elegant afternoon tea is served in the lobby beneath a vast atrium nine stories above.

CIVIC CENTER★★

Some of Denver's most important public buildings surround **Civic Center Park★** (between Broadway & Bannock St., W. Colfax & 14th Aves.), at the southeast edge of downtown. The grand space, sweeping westward from the capitol steps, was designed in 1904 by landscape architect Frederick Law Olmsted Jr. and Chicago city planner E.H. Bennett.

Dominating the west side is the Neo-classical **City and County Building** (1932), Denver's city hall. The slim central clock tower chimes every half hour.

Colorado State Capitol★★

200 E. Colfax Ave. (east side of Civic Center Park facing Lincoln St.) ♿ ℘303-866-2604. www.colorado.gov.

The hilltop capitol (1886, Elijah Myers) houses the General Assembly and offices of the governor. Constructed over 22 years in the shape of a Greek cross, the building is a smaller version of the US Capitol, and is built of a rare stone called Colorado rose onyx. Its gold-leaf dome is a gleaming 272ft-high landmark; workers reapply the leaf every 30 years, most recently in 2012. From the third-floor rotunda, 93 steps climb to the dome for a commanding **view★★** of the surrounding city. Two different steps leading to the building are marked as exactly a mile high.

Molly Brown House★

1340 Pennsylvania St., 3 blocks east of the capitol. ℘303-832-4092. www.molly brown.org.

Made famous by a Broadway musical and a 1964 movie, the "unsinkable" Molly Brown experienced new fame after the 1998 movie *Titanic*. In 1912, having raised two children and separated from her wealthy miner husband, Brown boarded the ill-fated *Titanic*. As the liner was sinking, and later aboard the rescue ship, she tried to bring order to chaos. She subsequently ran for US Congress three times—twice before women gained the right to vote.

Guided tours of the 7,700sq ft sandstone house (1889) offer a glimpse into Denver's Gilded Age through the prism of this remarkable woman.

🧍‍♀️ History Colorado Center★

1200 Broadway. ♿ ℘303-447-8679. www. historycolorado.org.

This spacious, new building (2011) houses exhibits about Colorado's history. Visitors can, among other activities, gaze at a floor map of the state, enter a simulated mine complete with a bouncing mine elevator, and learn the history of skiing in Colorado. Especially fun for kids are a simulated ski jump and

Denver Art Museum

a dynamite blasting game. The A–Z exhibit uses each letter of the alphabet to describe an aspect of the city.

Denver Art Museum★★★

100 W. 14th Ave. Pkwy. ✗♿🅿 ✆720-865-5000. www.denverartmuseum.org. This exceptional museum spans two buildings. The twin-towered modern fortress looming over Civic Center Park (North Building, Gio Ponti, 1971) holds exhibits on seven vertically stacked, 10,000sq-ft gallery floors. The newer **Hamilton Building★★** (Daniel Libeskind, 2006), designed to resemble a blossoming flower of titanium, granite and glass, reflects the architect's impression of the landscape as he flew over Denver.

The museum's centerpiece,the superb 17,000-item **American Indian Collection★★★** (2nd and 3rd floors) includes four house posts by famed carver Doug Cranmer; a Salish spirit figure and an Iroquois war club, both from the mid-1850s; Plains Indian horse trappings from the 19C; and a priceless California tribal feather blanket.

Maya, Aztec and Inca pieces contrast dramatically with European aesthetic in the **Pre-Columbian and Spanish Colonial★★** collections (4th floor), that culminate in a roomful of more modern Southwestern pieces.

European and American Art★ is organized thematically:landscapes in one area, portraits in another. **Western American Art★★** (Hamilton Building) includes a casting of *The Cheyenne* (1901) by famed sculptor and painter Frederic Remington.

Denver Public Library★★

10 W. 14th Ave. Pkwy. ♿ ✆720-865-1111. http://denverlibrary.org. A striking Postmodern structure (1995, Michael Graves & Brian Klipp), this $64 million building boasts 6 public floors and 47 miles of shelves.

Seventy panels by artist Edward Ruscha adorn its main hall and atriums. The acclaimed **Western History Collection** includes important early maps, documents and photographs; a $20 million

art collection features work by Bierstadt and Moran.

👤👥 US Mint★

W. Colfax Ave. & Cherokee St. (east of Civic Center Park). 🗣Visit by guided tour only; reservations required ♿ ✆303-405-4761. www.usmint.gov. One of four in the country, this mint can produce 50 million coins a day and tends one-fourth of America's gold reserves—shipped from San Francisco in 1934 because Denver is not as vulnerable to earthquakes.

The five-story, granite-and-marble building (1906, James Knox Taylor) was modeled after the Medici Riccardi Palace in Florence, Italy.

Displays of coins and currency, mint equipment and historic photos line visitors' galleries. Free tours (*online reservations advised*) offer views of the stamping and counting rooms.

WEST OF DOWNTOWN

Neglected for decades, the area along the South Platte River, west of downtown, today shows off fairly new attractions such as the **Pepsi Center** (www.pepsicenter.com) basketball and ice-hockey arena, built in 1999.

Football palace **Sports Authority Field at Mile High Stadium** (2001) (www.denverbroncos.com) incorporates the Colorado Sports Hall of Fame, which exalts such stars as quarterback John Elway.

Confluence Park★ (www.denver.org), where Cherry Creek and the South Platte River converge, is a place to cool off on hot days, with recreation trails and plazas bordering what was once an urban wasteland. Kayakers frequent the rapids here.

👤👥 Elitch Gardens★

2000 Elitch Cir. off Speer Blvd. (I-25 Exit 212A). Open May–Oct. ✗♿🅿 ✆303-595-4386. www.elitchgardens.com. One of the oldest amusement parks in the US, Elitch Gardens was established in 1890 in northwest Denver. in 1995 it moved to this riverside site. Thrill rides, a Ferris wheel and a water park (*late May-early Sept*) are among its draws.

👥 Downtown Aquarium★

700 Water St. at 23rd Ave. (I-25 Exit 211). ✗👤📁 ✆303-561-4450.
www.aquariumrestaurants.com.
This aquarium has 10 exhibit areas featuring some 500 species in desert, tropical, marine and other simulated environments. A stingray touch tank, mermaid show and restaurant add to family fun.

CITY PARK★★

This grand space (1881) was modeled after the urban parks of Boston, New York, London and Paris. From the east end, which occupies 314 acres (between Colorado Blvd and York St., 17th & 26th Aves.), visitors get a **view**★★ of the Denver skyline and the mountains.

👥 Denver Museum of Nature and Science★★

2001 Colorado Blvd., City Park. ✗👤📁 ✆303-370-6000. www.dmns.org.
This four-level museum is one of the largest in the US, with a collection of 1.4 million items.
The heralded gem display in **Coors Mineral Hall**★★★ showcases a gold nugget weighing 8 pounds found in Colorado in 1887. A 3.5-billion-year time line in **Prehistoric Journey**★★ depicts the history of life on earth. **Dioramas**★ present flora and fauna of the Rocky Mountains, South America, Africa and the world. Other exhibits examine North American Indian and ancient Egyptian cultures.

👥 Denver Zoo★

23rd Ave. between Colorado Blvd. & York St., City Park. ✗👤📁 ✆720-337-1400. www.denverzoo.org.
Some 3,500 animals are at home in this 80-acre zoo, laid out around a 1.5mi loop. Visitors may tour the grounds aboard the Pioneer Train, powered by natural gas. **Tropical Discovery**★★ is a rain-forest habitat under a glass pyramid. **Primate Panorama**★ houses nocturnal lemurs, Asian orangutans and endangered African lowland gorillas.

ADDITIONAL SIGHTS
Denver Botanic Gardens★

1007 York St. (4 blocks south of E. Colfax Ave.). ✗👤📁 ✆720-865-3500.
www.botanicgardens.org.
With 42 themed areas, these gardens are a tranquil oasis. The **Boettcher Memorial Conservatory**★★ shelters tropical plants in a humid environment.

Cherry Creek Shopping Center

1st Ave. between Steele St. & University Blvd. ✆303-388-3900; www.shopcherry creek.com. ✗👤📁
This indoor mall lies north of Cherry Creek Park. The adjacent streets of **Cherry Creek North** (1st to 3rd Aves.; ✆303-394-2903; www.cherrycreeknorth.com) are lined with boutiques, cafes, galleries and spas.

EXCURSIONS
Golden

▷ 15mi west of downtown Denver via I-70 (to Rte. 58) or US-6 (to 19th St.). ✗👤📁 ✆303-279-3113. www.cityofgolden.net.
Golden lost the state capital to Denver by one vote; its population is almost 20,000.
Walking tours take in the 1867 **Astor House Museum** (822 12th St.; ✆303-278-3557), the **Golden History Center** (923 10th St.; ✆303-278-3557), and the **Rocky Mountain Quilt Museum**★ (1213 Washington Ave.; ✆303-277-0377; https://rmqm.org), which exhibits a pioneer craft that's a true folk art.

Coors Brewery★

▷ 13th & Ford Sts. ✆ by guided tour only. 👤📁 ✆303-277-2337.
www.millercoors.com.
The world's largest brewing complex is one of Colorado's more popular attractions. It was founded in 1873 by immigrant brewer Adolph Coors. Tours follow the 16-week beer-making process through malting, brewing and packaging.

👥 Colorado Railroad Museum★

▷ 17155 W. 44th Ave. 📁 ✆303-279-4591.
www.coloradorailroadmuseum.org.

The largest rail museum in the Rocky Mountains displays more than 100 examples of trains that helped settle the frontier West. Train rides and a general store also engage visitors

Buffalo Bill Museum and Grave

○ 987-1/2 Lookout Mountain Rd. (I-70 Exit 256, 5mi west of Golden). ✕&🅿 𝒫303-526-0744. http://buffalobill.org.
The inimitable "Buffalo Bill" Cody, a Western icon and key figure in saving buffalo from extinction, died while visiting his sister in Denver in 1917 and was buried atop Lookout Mountain. The gravesite, a simple stone plot near the museum, affords a 180-degree view★ of the Front Range.

Red Rocks Park and Amphitheatre★

○ 18300 W. Alameda Pkwy., Morrison (via Rte. 26 off I-70 or Morrison Rd. off Rte. 470). ✕&🅿𝒫720-865-2494. http://redrocksonline.com.
The 9,450-seat outdoor amphitheater is a natural bowl sculpted between two 300ft sandstone outcroppings. Major concert events are staged here. The 640-acre park has hiking and biking trails.

Mount Evans★

○ Hwy. 103 from Idaho Springs to Echo Lake; then Hwy. 5, 14 mi to summit. 𝒫303-567-3000. www.fs.usda.gov.
This paved scenic highway, managed by the US Forest Service, tops out at 14,130ft. On the way up, the **Dos Chappell Nature Center** focuses on the bristlecone pine forest outside. It's a short walk to the summit, home to mountain goats and bighorn sheep, and 360-degree views★★ of the Front Range and Continental Divide. An early morning visit might be rewarded with sightings of marmots, bighorn sheep and goats.

▲▲ Boulder★★

○ 29mi northwest of Denver via US-36. ⚠✕&🅿 𝒫303-442-2911. www.bouldercoloradousa.com.
This city of 102,500 nestles against uplifted red-rock ridges called The Flatirons. Founded in 1859, Boulder boomed after Colorado founded its first state university here in 1876. Modern Boulder is largely defined by limits on residential construction it adopted in 1977, and by the 84sq mi greenbelt that surrounds it. University of Colorado's 25,000 students lend a youthful flavor. In September 2013, Boulder and nearby communities experienced heavy flooding from torrential rains that left a wide path of destruction. Recovery efforts are ongoing, but many businesses have since reopened.

Pearl Street Mall★ (11th to 15th Sts.) is a pedestrian zone of shops, galleries and sidewalk cafes; landmark buildings are the 1933 Art Deco **Boulder County Courthouse** (13th & Pearl Sts.) and the 1909 Italianate **Hotel Boulderado★** (2115 13th St. at Spruce St.; 𝒫303-442-4344; www.boulderado.com; &see ADDRESSES).

Boulder Creek Path★ ▲▲ runs creekside for 16mi through the heart of the city. The glass architecture of the **Boulder Public Library★** (1001 Arapahoe Ave.; 𝒫303-441-3100; http://boulderlibrary.org) straddles the creek near downtown. Facing a block of farmers' markets, the **Boulder Dushanbe Teahouse★★** (1770 13th St.; 𝒫303-442-4993; www.boulderteahouse.com) is a remarkable structure made of polychrome tiles, handcrafted by Tajikistani artisans in 1998 and reassembled here. It's a popular place for lunch and afternoon tea. The interior is memorable.

Just outside the city, **Celestial Seasonings** (www.celestialseasonings.com) offers popular teas from its tea packaging plant.

University of Colorado★

◯ Broadway to 28th St. & University Ave. to Baseline Rd. ✕&🅿 ℰ303-492-1411. www.colorado.edu.

Two hundred buildings are spread over this 600-acre campus. **Old Main** (1877), the university's first structure, is a turreted brick Victorian building, but most buildings are pink sandstone with red-tile roofs – the legacy of Charles Klauder's 1917 plan inspired by the hill towns of Tuscany. Visitors are welcome at the **University of Colorado Museum of Natural History** (Henderson Bldg., 15th St. & Broadway; ℰ303-492-6892; www.cumuseum.colorado.edu) and **Fiske Planetarium and Science Center** (Regent Dr. at Kittredge Loop Dr.; ℰ303-492-5002; www.fiskecolorado.edu).

Chautauqua Park

◯ Baseline Rd. & 9th St. Vehicle entrance at 6th St. ✕&🅿 ℰ303-442-3282. http://chatauqua.com.

The late 19C Chautauqua movement encouraged retreats to nurture body, mind and spirit. This park opened in 1898 with tent lodgings and two buildings that still stand—the **Auditorium** (site of the Colorado Music Festival) and **Dining Room** (now a restaurant). Trails ascend into meadows beneath The Flatirons and the 33,000-acre **Boulder Mountain Parks★** (ℰ303-413-7200; www.bouldercolorado.gov). Those who don't hike **Flagstaff Mountain★** can drive a twisting byway from Baseline Road to numerous scenic overlooks.

National Center for Atmospheric Research★

◯ 1850 Table Mesa Dr. ✕&🅿 ℰ303-497-1000. http://ncar.ucar.edu. The stunning Mesa Laboratory (1966, I.M. Pei) is set against the Flatirons and inspired by ancient Southwest cliff dwellings.

Guided 1hr tours include hands-on displays illustrating such topics as atmospheric phenomen, robotic meteorological instruments and aviation hazards. Art exhibitions change monthly.

Colorado Springs★★

Nestled at 6,035ft at the base of soaring Pikes Peak, Colorado Springs enjoys one of the most beautiful settings of any North American city. Bracketed by two US military centers—the Air Force Academy to the north, and the Army's Fort Carson south—the city has a decidedly military air.

A BIT OF HISTORY

Civil War Gen. William Jackson Palmer, builder of the Denver & Rio Grande Railroad, founded the city in 1871 on a rail link to the mining towns of Cripple Creek and Victor. He called it "Springs" to attract Easterners accustomed to

▸ **Population:** 380,307.
◔ **Michelin Map:** pp 298-299. Mountain Standard Time.
🛈 **Info:** ℰ719-635-7506; www.visitcos.com.
⊘ **Don't Miss:** Pikes Peak; Garden of the Gods.
👥 **Kids:** US Olympic Complex.

fashionable health resorts. Spencer Penrose, who made a fortune in gold and copper, built the Pikes Peak Auto Highway and developed The Broadmoor as a world-class resort. During the Cold War, "The Springs" established itself as the hub of US military air defense. Many defense contractors are based in the city, which is also a home for numerous fundamentalist Christian organizations.

Downtown reflects the vision of its founders in broad avenues and fine old buildings. Early years are documented at the **Colorado Springs Pioneers Museum** (215 S. Tejon St.; ℘719-385-5990; www.springsgov.com) in the 1903 courthouse. The **Colorado Springs Fine Arts Center★** (30 W. Dale St.; ℘719-634-5581; www.csfineartscenter.org) has paintings by O'Keeffe, Russell and Audubon in a 1936 Art-Deco landmark.

SIGHTS
Old Colorado City★
W. Colorado Ave. & cross streets from S. 24th to S. 27th Sts. ✕♿🅿 ℘719-577-4112. http://shopoldcoloradocity.com.

Before Colorado Springs there was El Dorado, settled in 1859 and soon renamed Colorado City. It became part of Colorado Springs in 1917. Housed in an 1890 church, the **Old Colorado City History Center** (1 S. 24th St.; ℘719-636-1225; www.occhs.org) exhibits historic photographs, documents and memorabilia.

Colorado Avenue is lined with restaurants, artists' studios and Western collectibles galleries in restored buildings. **Van Briggle Art Pottery** (1024 S. Tejon St.; ℘719-633-7729; www.vanbriggle.com) is a century-old facility whose works have been displayed at the Louvre and New York's Metropolitan Museum of Art.

The Broadmoor★
1 Lake Ave; west end of Lake Ave. via I-25 Exit 138. ✕♿🅿 ℘719-623-5112. www.broadmoor.com.

Born in 1891 as a small casino at the foot of Cheyenne Mountain, The Broadmoor was reincarnated when Spencer Penrose bought the 40-acre site (and 400 adjoining acres) in 1916 and turned it into a world-class resort. European artisans created ornate frescoes, tile work and marble fixtures in the pink-stucco, Italianate hotel.

Today three golf courses, tennis courts, swimming pools, riding stables, nine restaurants and lounges, a conference center and spa make up the 754-room complex. Penrose's widow built the **Carriage House Museum** in 1947 for antique vehicles.

♙♙ World Figure Skating Museum and Hall of Fame
20 1st St.; ℘719-635-5200; www.worldskatingmuseum.org.

Situated one block north of The Broadmoor, this museum offers ice-skating memories from the 17C to the present.

♙♙ Cheyenne Mountain Zoo★
4250 Cheyenne Mountain Zoo Rd. From The Broadmoor, at the traffic circle take 1st exit for Lake Ave., at 2nd traffic circle take 2nd exit to Mesa Ave., continue to Park Ave., then to El Pomar Rd., which becomes Cheyenne Mt. Zoo Rd. ✕♿🅿 ℘719-633-9925. www.cmzoo.org.

Built in 1926 by Spencer Penrose on a forested hillside to house exotic animals he had received as gifts from around the world, the zoo was deeded to Colorado Springs in 1938. Its large habitats are home to some 800 animals of 200-plus species. Unveiled in 2013, Encounter Africa houses African elephants, lions, meerkats and black rhinos.

Will Rogers Shrine of the Sun★
℘719-578-5367. www.cmzoo.org.

To reach the shrine, motorists drive up a 1.5mi winding road from the zoo entrance (see above) to a plateau 2,000ft above Colorado Springs. The 100ft granite tower was built as a Penrose family tomb, but was rededicated to philosopher-humorist Rogers when he died in a 1935 plane crash. Tower landings are photo galleries of Rogers' life: a 94-step climb reveals a **view★★** eastward.

Seven Falls★★
West end of Cheyenne Blvd.; off Mesa Dr. via Lake Ave. from The Broadmoor. ✕♿🅿 ℘719-632-0765. www.sevenfalls.com.

A road threads through the Pillars of Hercules, a slot in South Cheyenne Canyon, and terminates at this 181ft series of waterfalls. Eagle's Nest, accessed by elevator or 185 steep steps, overlooks the falls. Another staircase (224 steps) ascends beside the falls to the start of the **Inspiration Point Trail** (*0.5mi*).

👥 US Olympic Complex★★

1750 Boulder St. at Union Blvd. ♿🅿 ☎719-632-5551. www.uteamusa.org.

One of three national training centers in the US for amateur athletes, this complex was built in 1978 on the grounds of a former Air Force base. The visitor center (1 Olympic Plaza) houses the US Olympic Hall of Fame. Free 1hr tours take visitors down the Olympic Path to watch gymnasts and swimmers hone their skills; the Aquatic Center and a state-of-the-art sports-medicine clinic are of particular interest.

More than 500 coaches and athletes, in a dozen sports, live and train here.

👥 ProRodeo Hall of Fame and Museum of the American Cowboy★

101 ProRodeo Dr.; at Rockrimmon Blvd. off I-25 Exit 148. ♿🅿 ☎719-528-4764. www.prorodeohalloffame.com.

Multimedia presentations trace the lifestyle of rodeo, from its 19C origins to the present. The hall of fame honors highly skilled cowboys, clowns, showmen and behind-the-scenes personnel with plaques or bronze statues. Other displays highlight cowboy gear and garb, saddles, ropes and personal souvenirs. New members are inducted annually. Cowboys are recognized for their skills in bronco riding, tie-down roping, steer wrestling and other events. Even animals have been inducted.

US Air Force Academy★★

Academy Dr. West off I-25 at Exit 156 B (North Gate Blvd.); 14mi north of downtown. ⛺✕♿🅿 ☎719-333-2025. www.usafa.af.mil.

This is the only US service academy in the West. A self-guided auto tour includes a B-52 display and scenic overlooks. The highlight is the **Cadet Chapel★★★** (1963, Skidmore, Owings & Merrill), designed by Walter Netsch. Topped by 17 aluminum spires, each 150ft high, this soaring cathedral comprises individual Protestant, Catholic, Jewish and interfaith chapels.

At 11:35am each weekday, the academy's 4,000 cadets march smartly to lunch across the square beside the chapel. The nearby **Barry Goldwater Visitor Center★** (2346 Academy Dr.; ☎719-333-2025) explains cadet life in interactive displays.

Garden of the Gods★★

Garden Dr. (north of US-24) or Gateway Rd. (west of 30th St.). ✕♿🅿 ☎719-634-6666. http://gardenofgods.com.

Red-rock formations within this 1,400-acre geological wonder soar up to 300ft. Paved roads offer easy access to the best-known formations: Balanced Rock, Cathedral Spires, Kissing Camels, Three Graces and Tower of Babel. ♿Most are better seen on foot, bicycle or horseback on trails of .5mi to 3mi in length.

Cadet Chapel, US Air Force Academy

© Gwen Cannon/Michelin

Guided walks depart from the **visitor center** on the east side of the park (1805 N. 30th St.), which offers a natural-history display and brief multimedia show. Just south at the **Rock Ledge Ranch Historic Site** (Gateway Rd. & 30th St.; 𝒫719-578-6777; www.rockledge-ranch.com), costumed docents portray life on an 1860s homestead, an 1880s ranch and an early 20C estate. The 1901 Garden of the **Gods Trading Post** (324 Beckers Ln.; 𝒫719-685-9045), a Pueblo-style structure, can be found on the park's south side.

Pikes Peak★★★

✕♿🅿 𝒫719-385-7325.
www.springsgov.com.

At 14,110ft, Pikes Peak is not the highest mountain in the US, nor even Colorado. But it is arguably the most imposing high peak, probably the most famous, definitely the most accessible. Named in 1806 by Army Lieutenant Zebulon Pike, who declared the mountain "unconquerable," it has proven anything but. A railway mounted its flank in 1891. Spencer Penrose built a motor road in 1916 and bought the railway in 1925.

Visitors today ascend to the **Summit House** cafe and gift shop via railway, car or foot. The peak is often cold and windy, and snow may fall at any time. But when skies are clear, unrivaled **views★★★** extend west into the snow-capped Rockies, east across the plains, north to Denver and south to the Sangre de Cristo range.

The **Pikes Peak Cog Railway★★★** 👥 (515 Ruxton Ave., Manitou Springs; 𝒫719-685-5401, http://cograilway.com) remains a great excursion. Small black coal-fired steam locomotives, tilted to keep the boilers level, originally pushed trains up the mountain's eastern side. Now diesel-electric models do so (Mar–Dec; 3hr round-trip includes 30min at summit). From its depot, the train climbs more than 6,500ft in a series of steep grades with constantly changing views. Marmots and bighorn sheep cavort among the rocks.

At the peak's broad summit, the cog railway meets the **Pikes Peak Highway★★** (𝒫719-385-7325), a meandering 19mi toll road. It begins at Cascade (15mi west of Colorado Springs on US-24); after 7mi, at the **Crystal Reservoir Visitor Center**, pavement is replaced by gravel. **Challenge Unlimited** (𝒫719-633-6399) offers a 20mi ride down the Barr Trail in a guided convoy of mountain bikes with good brakes (May–Oct).

Manitou Springs★

4mi west of Colorado Springs on US-24 bypass. ⛺♿🅿 𝒫719-685-5089. http://manitousprings.org.

Indians and mountain men long knew of the restorative waters that bubbled from the ground northeast of Pikes Peak. A spa and hotels were established in the 1890s. Today galleries and inns occupy charming, if aging, structures; open-air street trolleys (free) make 1hr summer circuits of downtown. **Miramont Castle★** (9 Capitol Hill Ave.; 𝒫719-685-1011; www.miramontcastle.org), the 1895 sandstone mansion of a wealthy French priest, combines nine design styles in its 30 rooms.

👥 Cave of the Winds★

US-24 Bypass, 2mi west of Manitou Springs. ✕🅿 𝒫719-685-5444. http://caveofthewinds.com.

After two boys discovered a cavern entrance in 1880, Manitou resident George Snider broke through to a chamber—200ft long and 50ft high—that

Storefronts in Manitou Springs

© Photo by J.C. Leacock/CTO

now is the centerpiece of a commercial cave still owned by the Snider family. Guides on the **Discovery Tour** (*45min*) explain limestone cave formation to visitors walking a well-lit concrete path. Participants in the **Lantern Tour** (*90min*) follow a guide in 1880s garb.

👤👤 Manitou Cliff Dwellings Museum

US-24 Bypass, just above Manitou Springs. ✖🅿 ☎719-685-5242. www.cliffdwellingsmuseum.com.
The 40 rooms and towers in Phantom Cliff Canyon were dismantled by archaeologists in the Four Corners area in the 19C and reconstructed here to re-create a 12-13C Ancient Pueblo culture.

EXCURSIONS
Cripple Creek★★

❍ 45mi west of Colorado Springs via US-24 to Divide, then Rte. 67 south. △✖ ♿🅿 ☎877-858-4653. www.cripple-creek.co.us.
When gold was discovered on the east flank of Pikes Peak in 1890, this town at 9,396ft elevation became the world's greatest gold camp. Within 10 years its population reached 25,000. Neighboring **Victor**, 6mi south, had 18,000 residents. Mining continued until 1961, by which time more than $800 million worth of ore had been taken.
Today a different kind of gold flows: limited-stakes gambling was legalized in 1991 and Cripple Creek (albeit with only 1,200 citizens today) has been revitalized. The **Cripple Creek & Victor Narrow Gauge Railroad★** (east end of Bennett Ave.; ☎719-689-2640; www.cripplecreekrailroad.com), a 15-ton steam locomotive, pulls the train on a 4mi journey past abandoned mines to the ghost town of Anaconda (open late May–early Oct). The depot houses the **Cripple Creek District Museum** (☎719-689-2634; http://cripplecreek-museum.com). At the **Mollie Kathleen Gold Mine★★** (1mi north on Rte. 67; ☎719-689-2466; www.goldminetours.com), visitors descend 1,000ft into a hard-rock mine, where veteran miners demonstrate the mining process.

Florissant Fossil Beds National Monument

❍ 35mi west of Colorado Springs via US-24. ♿🅿 ☎719-748-3253. www.nps.gov/flfo.
More than 50,000 fossils—one of the most extensive records of the Oligocene epoch, 35 million years ago—have been removed from the shale bed of ancient Lake Florissant. Among them are 14,000 species of insects. Nature trails pass petrified sequoia stumps through habitat for a variety of mammals including bears, mountain lions, porcupines and a small herd of elk.

👤👤 Royal Gorge Bridge and Park★★

❍ Off US-50, 8mi west of Cañon City & 43mi southwest of Colorado Springs. ✖♿🅿 ☎719-275-7507. www.royalgorgebridge.com.
This landmark suspension bridge that sits 1,053ft above the Arkansas River and is more than a quarter-mile long, opened in 1929. An incline railway (1931) plunges from the rim; an aerial tramway (1969) spans the gorge. In 1999 the **Royal Gorge Route★★** began operating passenger trains on a 19C route through the river's gorge. Trains depart from **Cañon City's Santa Fe Depot** (401 Water St.; ☎719-276-4000; www.royalgorgeroute.com).

👤👤 Great Sand Dunes National Park and Preserve★★

❍ Rte. 150, 164mi southwest of Colorado Springs via I-25 & US-160. △♿🅿 ☎719-378-6399. www.nps.gov/grsa.
North America's tallest sand dunes, nearly 750ft high, are spread across 39sq mi directly beneath the Sangre de Cristo Mountains in a corner of the San Luis Valley. Formed by winds over thousands of years, the dunes are bordered by a snowmelt mountain stream that creates, for visiting families, one of the world's biggest sandboxes. Surrounding hills hold scented forests of piñon pine.

Cheyenne★

Wyoming's capital and largest city was founded in 1867 as a construction camp for rail workers just 10mi north of the Colorado border. With the train came thousands of immigrants: some real-estate speculators and confidence men, but many honest merchants, tradesmen, and cowboys who worked the surrounding grasslands. Local citizens formed vigilante committees to rid the town of outlaws. Cheyenne then settled into frontier comfort with streets of handsome mansions and a thriving social scene. When Wyoming joined the Union in 1890, Cheyenne was chosen capital. Its place in Western lore was sealed when gunslinger Tom Horn was hanged here in 1903, one of the West's last outlaws.

▶ **Population:** 59,500.
◔ **Michelin Map:** 493 H 7, 8. Mountain Standard Time.
🛈 **Info:** ℘307-778-3133; http://cheyenne.org.
☺ **Don't Miss:** Cheyenne Frontier Days Old West Museum.
👥 **Kids:** Wyoming Territorial Park.

Union Pacific Depot (121 W. 15th St.; ℘307-632-3905; www.cheyennedepot-museum.org), now a museum devoted to the city's railroad history.

SIGHTS
Wyoming State Capitol★
24th St. & Capitol Ave. ♿🅿 ℘307-777-7220. http://wyoming.gov.
Tours weekdays.
As statehouses go, this gray sandstone building (1890) is modest, but with such elegant fittings as a 24-carat gold-leaf dome and interior woodwork of maple and cherry. The stained-glass dome ceiling was imported from England. The third-floor Legislative Conference Room features a half-ton Tiffany chandelier and a 22ft mural by Mike Kopriva that depicts Wyoming history.

👥 Wyoming State Museum
2301 Central Ave. ♿🅿 ℘307-777-7022. http://wyomuseum.state.wy.us.
Sharing two floors of the Barrett Building, just southeast of the capitol, 10

VISIT
Cheyenne Frontier Days
℘307-778-7222. www.cfdrodeo.com
The world's largest outdoor rodeo, parade and carnival, the "Daddy of 'em All" was first held in 1897. It consumes all of southeastern Wyoming in late July and draws 300,000 spectators from throughout the High Plains and Rocky Mountains for rodeo events, concerts, rides and a fair. At other times, even in winter when the legislature is in session, Cheyenne remains serene.
🚶 Walking tours and trolley tours of the historic district begin at the 1886

The World of Rodeo

Throughout much of the West, rodeo is as popular as baseball or football. Like their 19C forebears who originated the sport, cowboys vie to see who is the best rider, roper or 'dogger. The best athletes, members of the Professional Rodeo Cowboys Association, are superstars who earn hundreds of thousands of dollars. A typical rodeo has six events: bull riding, saddle- and bareback-bronc riding, steer wrestling, team and individual roping, plus women's barrel racing. Scoring is based on style and difficulty in the first three events; stronger, temperamental animals earn their riders more points. Riders must stay on at least 8 seconds to receive a score. Skill and courage are critical, but the luck of the draw plays a part. In wrestling, roping and racing, speed and agility are paramount.

galleries depict Wyoming's human and natural history. Exhibits focus on dinosaurs; Shoshone and Arapaho culture; gold, uranium and coal mining; jade prospecting; and cowboy traditions.

Warren ICBM and Heritage Museum

7405 Barnes Loop, Francis. E. Warren Air Force Base. 🅿️ 𝒫307-773-2980. www.warrenmuseum.com.

Warren was the most powerful US missile base in the Cold War and remains the Intercontinental Ballistic Missile (ICBM) command center. The museum focuses on the history of the ICBMs and the lives of missile crews.

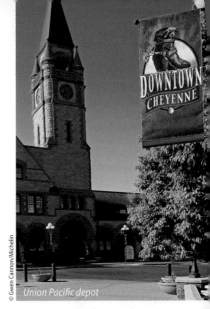

© Gwen Cannon/Michelin

Union Pacific depot

🔸🔹 Cheyenne Frontier Days Old West Museum★

4610 N. Carey Ave. Frontier Park. ♿🅿️ 𝒫307-778-7290. www.oldwestmuseum.org.

This year-round tribute to the event's history is housed in the Frontier Days headquarters. Pioneer artifacts, cowboy gear, Western art, antique carriages and wagons tell the tale.

EXCURSIONS

Laramie

❍ 46mi west of Cheyenne via I-80 or Rte. 210. 𝒫307-745-7339. www.laramie.org.

Established, as Cheyenne was, as a railroad town, Laramie took a different path with the founding in 1886 of the University of Wyoming. Today, nearly half of the town's 30,800 residents are students, faculty or staff.

University of Wyoming

❍ Ivinson Ave. & 9th St. ✗♿🅿️ 𝒫307-766-1121. www.uwyo.edu.

A standout on the campus quad is the **Geological Museum** (S.H. Knight Bldg., 505 S. Thirs St.; 𝒫307-766-2646), notable for a full-size copper tyrannosaur outside. Exhibits range from uranium to core samples from oil drilling. The **University of Wyoming Art Museum**'s (2111 Willett Dr.; 𝒫307-766-6622) 8,000-piece collection focuses on American art, including works by Bierstadt, Hopper and Moran; it shares Antoine

Predock's futuristic Centennial Complex with the **American Heritage Center**, an archival research facility.

🔸🔹 Wyoming Territorial Prison State Historic Site★

❍ 975 Snowy Range Rd. at I-80. ✗♿🅿️ 𝒫307-745-3733. www.wyomingterritorialpark.com.

Commemorating Old West heritage, this living-history park includes Wyoming's original Territorial Prison (1872-1901). Tours visit the cell that held Butch Cassidy, who served 18 months for horse-stealing. 19C costumed staff perform crafts and trades in buildings moved from other parts of Wyoming.

Fort Laramie National Historic Site★★

❍ 113mi north of Cheyenne via I-25, US-26 & Rte. 160. ♿🅿️ 𝒫307-837-2221. www.nps.gov/fola.

Built by fur traders near the North Platte River in 1834, this key Oregon Trail fort was garrisoned by the Army in 1849. Major campaigns against hostile Indian tribes were launched from this bastion until it closed in 1890. Half of its 22 buildings have been restored and furnished to their 19C appearance. The 1884 commissary holds a visitor center and museum with artifact displays and historic photos.

High Rockies★★★

Spread across more than 20,000sq mi, crossed by highways that climb high passes and dive into valleys, this lofty zone offers travelers scenic views around almost every turn. It rewards intrepid sojourners with rich flora and fauna, evocative mining heritage, and unsurpassed recreational opportunities.

A BIT OF HISTORY

The Utes were dominant from the 17C to mid 19C; Arapaho and Cheyenne also hunted in these mountains. After the US acquired the territory, Zebulon Pike explored rivers and valleys in 1806-07, Major Stephen Long ventured up the South Platte and Arkansas valleys in 1820, and John C. Frémont visited northern Colorado in 1842. It wasn't until the Civil War era that the promise of mineral wealth attracted permanent residents.

The war had a sobering effect on the gold rush that began in 1859, but silver created another flurry of prospecting. The mountains were considered so formidable that the transcontinental railroad was routed through neighboring Wyoming in 1869. Narrow-gauge railroads began serving mining camps in the 1870s. When resources were

- **Michelin Map:** pp298-299. Mountain Standard Time.
- **Info:** ℰ800-265-6723, www.colorado.com.
- **Location:** The Front Range applies to the easternmost flank of the Rockies, which embrace Pikes Peak, Mount Evans and Longs Peak. West of the Continental Divide, the region is called the Western Slope.
- **Don't Miss:** Trail Ridge Road in Rocky Mountain National Park.
- **Kids:** Glenwood Caverns and Hot Springs Pool.

exhausted, some settlements faded into ghost towns; others persisted. Central City, Georgetown, Breckenridge, Leadville, Aspen, Crested Butte and Telluride are survivors.

Hiking, golf and whitewater rafting are popular summer activities. In winter, skiing turns the Rockies into America's leading recreational playground (visit www.coloradoski.com).

🚗 DRIVING TOURS

ROCKY MOUNTAIN NATIONAL PARK★★★

2–3 days, 205mi round-trip.

▷ From Golden, west of Denver, drive 13mi west on US-6 through Clear Creek Canyon to Rte. 119, then 5mi south.

Black Hawk and Central City

Rtes. 119 & 279. ✕⚹🅿 ℰ303-582-5251.
Spawned by 1859 gold strikes, these once-forlorn foothills towns, a mile apart, are booming again, thanks to limited-stakes gambling, legalized in 1991, in some 50 casinos. The original

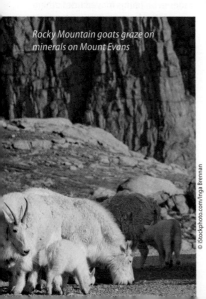

Rocky Mountain goats graze on minerals on Mount Evans

©iStockphoto.com/Inga Brennan

excavation at Gregory Gulch marks the entrance to Central City, a few steep streets with narrow sidewalks. Brick masonry in the wake of a devastating 1874 fire resulted in sturdy Victorian buildings that still stand. Among them is the 1878 **Central City Opera★** (124 Eureka St.), whose six-week summer season (𝒫 303-292-6500; www.centralcityopera.org) was launched by silent-screen star Lillian Gish in 1932.

▷ Return to Rte. 119 & continue north 65mi on the Peak to Peak Highway.

Peak to Peak Highway★★
Rtes. 119, 72 & 7. △✕

This scenic route winds through pine woods that periodically open up to tantalizing mountain views. In the small, lively, former mining-supply town of **Nederland★**, (𝒫303-258-3936; www.nederlandchamber.org), Route 119 branches east toward Boulder. Proceed north on Route 72. After 14mi, look for a left turn to **Brainard Lake★**, surrounded by the soaring snow-cloaked summits of the Indian Peaks Wilderness.

▷ Return to Route 72, continue north 9mi and turn left on Route 7 to Estes Park.

Estes Park★
US-34, US-36 & Rte. 7. △✕占 🅿 𝒫970-577-9900. www.estesparkcvb.com.
Estes Park nestles at the east edge of Rocky Mountain National Park. An **aerial tramway★** (420 E. Riverside Dr.; 𝒫970-586-3675; www.estestram.com) climbs 8,900ft Prospect Mountain in summer, with fine views of adjacent summits.
Just outside town, the white facade of the **Stanley Hotel** (www.stanleyhotel.com; ⚲see ADDRESSES) distinguishes the 1909 historic landmark.

▷ Take US-36 west from the south side of Estes Park to the main national park entrance station and the Beaver Meadows Visitor Center.

Rocky Mountain National Park★★★
US-34 & US-36. △占🅿𝒫970-586-1206. www.nps.gov/romo.
This magnificent landscape boasts craggy mountains, glaciated valleys, perpetual snowfields, small lakes and vast alpine tundra that covers one-third of its 415sq mi. It features more than 100 mountains of 11,000ft or higher, reaching its apex at 14,255ft **Longs Peak**, whose distinctive flat-topped summit dominates the park's southeast corner. The mountains northwest of the peak are known as the Never-Summer Range, an alpine fastness where snow is indeed common any month of the year.
The **Beaver Meadows Visitor Center** has park maps and information on ranger-led tours and lectures. From here, 10mi **Bear Lake Road★** runs south, providing access to trailheads.

Trail Ridge Road★★★
US-34, 50mi from Estes Park to Grand Lake. △占🅿 Open late May–Oct, depending upon weather conditions.
The highest continuous paved highway in North America ascends rapidly from coniferous and aspen forests to treeless tundra at 12,183ft, offering outstanding mountain panoramas. Viewing areas include **Many Parks Curve★★** and **Forest Canyon Overlook★★**. The **Tundra Trail at Rock Cut★★** (.5mi), an interpretive path with signs describing the geology, botany and wildlife of this harsh environment, is short and gentle, though at this elevation it may be exhausting for flatlanders. After passing its high point, the road curves downhill past **Gore Range Overlook★** and **Alpine Visitor Center**, crossing the Continental Divide at 10,758ft Milner Pass. It's important to heed signs asking visitors to stay off the extremely delicate alpine tundra.

Grand Lake★
Rte. 278 off US-34. △✕占🅿𝒫970-627-3402. http://grandlakechamber.com.
This small town at the west entrance to the park boasts Old West-style log buildings and boardwalks. It is named

for its large glacial lake (1.2mi long, 1mi wide, 400ft deep), fed by the Colorado River. Below Grand Lake, the river is dammed twice to form **Shadow Mountain Lake** and large **Lake Granby**.

▶ Continue south 15mi on US-34 from Grand Lake to Granby. Turn left (southeasterly) on US-40 and proceed 46mi to I-70 at Empire.

Middle Park

Fraser River Valley, US-40 south of Granby. ⚠️✕♿🅿️ 🖉970-726-4221. www.playwinterpark.com.

Cattle graze in this broad valley whose mountain-sheathed location renders it one of the coldest places in the continental US. **Cozens Ranch Museum★** (US-40 south of Fraser; 🖉970-726-5488; www.visitgrandcounty.com) displays pioneer and Ute artifacts in an 1870s ranch house, stagecoach stop and post office. **Winter Park★** (US-40; 🖉970-726-4221) is known for mountain biking and winter skiing on two mountains. The route crosses the Continental Divide at 11,315ft **Berthoud Pass**.

▶ Return 29mi via I-70 & US-6 to Golden.

DENVER–VAIL–ASPEN★★

3 days, 276mi one-way.

Interstate 70 is Colorado's principal east-west thoroughfare. Between Denver and Glenwood Springs, it is one of America's most scenic highways. For early settlers here, wealth came from gold, silver and other minerals. Today's gold is white at ski areas, green at golf courses.

▶ From Denver, drive west 32mi on I-70.

Idaho Springs

I-70 Exit 241. ⚠️✕♿🅿️ 🖉303-567-4660. http://clearcreekcounty.org.

Nineteenth-century commercial buildings line the main street of this old mining town of just under 2,000 citizens. Try a buffalo burger at the historic Buffalo Restaurant & Bar (1617 Miner St.; ♿see ADDRESSES). The 1913 **Argo Gold Mine & Mill** (2350 Riverside Dr.; 🖉303-567-2421; www.historicargotours.com) is an ore-processing mill open for self-guided tours and panning for gold. At the **Phoenix Gold Mine★** (right on Stanley Rd., left on Trail Creek Rd.; 🖉303-567-0422; www.phoenixmine.com), a retired miner leads an underground tour.

▶ Return to I-70 & continue 14mi west.

Georgetown★★

I-70 Exit 228. ⚠️✕♿🅿️ 🖉303-569-2555. www.georgetowncolorado.com.

The old town center of Georgetown, which enjoyed its silver-fueled heyday in the 1880s, is immaculately preserved. Now a museum, the **Hotel de Paris★** (409 6th St.; 🖉303-569-2311; http://hoteldeparismuseum.org) was built in 1875 by a French immigrant. The 1879 **Hamill House★** (305 Argentine St.; 🖉303-569-2840) reveals the luxury in which a silver baron lived. Tickets for a 1hr summer outing on the **Georgetown Loop Railroad★★** (Silver Plume Depot; 🖉888-456-6777; http://georgetownlooprr.com) are available at the historic train depot.

The 4.5mi of track between Georgetown and Silver Plume, another 19C mining town, feature a 360-degree loop on a bridge high over Clear Creek.

▶ Continue 23mi west on I-70.

The highway climbs steadily to the **Eisenhower Tunnel**, bored under the Continental Divide at 10,700ft. North America's highest road tunnel enables vehicles to avoid 11,992ft **Loveland Pass★**.

Take Exit 216 and follow US-6 for views of mountains, valleys, lingering snow-fields and (at 13,050ft) the **Arapahoe Basin Ski Area** (🖉970-468-0718; www.arapahoebasin.com), which stays open later than any other Rocky Mountain resort (until Jul 4). The highway passes modern **Keystone Resort★** (🖉970-

496-2316; www.keystoneresort.com), en route back to its junction with I-70 at **Silverthorne**, noted for its outlet stores.

▶ Continue 5mi west on I-70 to Exit 203. Turn south and take Rte. 9 for 9mi.

On the left, **Dillon Reservoir** is cradled by mountains. Route 9 passes quaint **Frisco** and follows the Blue River. The Tenmile Range—mountains numbered (north to south) "Peak 1" through "Peak 10"—forms the western backdrop.

Breckenridge★★

Rte. 9, 87mi west of Denver. ⚠✕⬧🅿
𝒫970-453-2918. www.gobreck.com.
A resort town of 3,400 residents, Breckenridge was founded in 1859 by gold miners. The **Country Boy Mine★** 👤👤 (542 French Gulch Rd.; 𝒫970-453-4405; http://countryboymine.com) offers tours and gold panning in French Creek. Main Street is lined with restaurants and shops, most housed in Old West-style buildings. The **Summit Historical Society** (𝒫970-468-2207; www.summithistorical.org) offers walking tours and mining-district tours. Historic sites include the **Barney Ford House** (Washington & Main Sts.), owned by a freed slave who became a 19C business. **Father Dyer United Methodist Church** (Wellington & Briar Rose Sts.; 𝒫970-453-2250) is dedicated to a preacher who carried mail and God's word to remote mining camps.
A bike path along the Blue River becomes a cross-country skiing avenue in winter. Ski lifts serve downhill terrain that spreads across three mountains: Peaks 8, 9 and 10, with off-piste skiing on Peak 7.

▶ Return to I-70 and continue west 6mi to Exit 195. Take Rte. 91 south 24mi to Leadville.

Exiting the interstate at **Copper Mountain Resort★** (Rte. 91 at I-70 Exit 195; 𝒫866-841-2481; www.coppercolorado.com), Route 91 cuts across 11,318ft **Fremont Pass** and passes the open pit of the defunct American Climax Moly-

bendum Mine before descending into Leadville.

Leadville★★

US-24 & Rte. 91, 103mi west of Denver.
⚠✕♿🅿𝒫719-486-3900.
www.leadvilleusa.com.
Situated at 10,152ft, Leadville was once Colorado's silver capital; in 1880, population soared to 24,000. Today the population is 2,700. But the main street is still flanked by fine Victorian commercial buildings.
Tickets for a multimedia show about the town's history are available at the **Leadville Visitor Center** (809 Harrison Ave.; 𝒫719-486-3900). The nearby **National Mining Hall of Fame and Museum★★** (120 W. 9th St.; 𝒫719-486-1229; http://mininghalloffame.org) features a walk-through replica of a hard-rock mine. The **Tabor Opera House★** (308 Harrison Ave.; 𝒫719-486-4809; www.taboroperahouse.net) was built in 1879. Remnants of millionaire Horace Tabor's **Matchless Mine** (E. 7th St., 1mi east of downtown; 𝒫719-486-1239; www.matchlessmine.com) can also be visited. About 5mi west of town, the **Leadville National Fish Hatchery★** (Rte. 300) was built in 1889; tanks hold millions of trout for release into Colorado's streams. Behind the hatchery, hiking trails begin at the foot of 14,421ft **Mount Massive**. Immediately south rises the state's highest crest, 14,433ft **Mount Elbert**. Beginning 13mi south of Leadville, Route 82, linking US-24 with I-70 at Glenwood Springs, crosses 12,095ft **Independence Pass★★** and offers incredible views from numerous hairpin turns. Snow normally closes the 38mi stretch from **Twin Lakes** (6mi west of US-24) to Aspen from mid-October to Memorial Day.

▶ From Leadville, take US-24 north 33mi to I-70.

The site of **Camp Hale**, a World War II training base for the 10th Mountain Division, a ski-and-mountaineering contingent, lies near 10,424ft **Tennessee Pass**. Descending the pass, US-24 follows the Eagle River through a valley below 14,005ft **Mount of the Holy Cross**, so-named for its distinctive, intersecting, perpetually snow-packed gullies in the shape of a cross. US-24 meets I-70 near **Minturn**, a former rail town now a Vail suburb.

◐ Backtrack east 5mi on I-70 to Vail.

Vail★★

98mi west of Denver. ⚠✕🚻♿🅿 ✆970-477-4029. http://visitvailvalley.com.
One of North America's premier mountain resorts, Vail was founded in 1963 by veterans of the World War II 10th Mountain Division. Vail Village boasts pedestrian-only streets and chalet-style buildings with fashionable shops and restaurants.
Colorado Ski & Snowboard Museum★ (231 S. Frontage Rd.; ✆970-476-1876; www.skimuseum.net) documents the state's skiing and snowboarding heritage and commemorates the skiing soldiers, who trained at Camp Hale.
Vail Nature Center★ 🚹🚺 (601 Vail Valley Dr.; ✆970-479-2291; http://vailrec.com) offers naturalist tours and guided hikes or ski trips year-round. The **Betty Ford Alpine Gardens★★** (530 S. Frontage Rd.; ✆970-476-0103; http://bettyfordalpinegardens.org), established by the former First Lady, shows off 1,500 varieties of annuals and perennials.
The town of 5,300 sits at the foot of **Vail Mountain★★★** (www.vail.com), the largest single-mountain ski area in the US—with a 3,360ft vertical drop.
Adventure Ridge★ 🚹🚺 is the site of outdoor winter sports. In summer, the new Gondola One (Vail Village) and Eagle Bahn Gondola (Lionshead Base) ascend for outstanding views.

◐ Drive 10mi west from Vail on I-70.

Beaver Creek★★

From I-70 Exit 167 at Avon, take Village Rd. 3mi south. ✕♿🅿 ✆970-496-4900. www.beavercreek.com.
This exclusive ski-and-golf resort community was created by the operators of the Vail resort in 1980. Ski terrain, which

has hosted world-championship downhill races, connects two developments, Arrowhead and Bachelor Gulch. The **Vilar Performing Arts Center★** (✆970-845-8497; https://vilarpac.org) stages classical and popular performances.

◐ Continue 50mi west on I-70.

Glenwood Canyon★★

I-70 between Exits 133 & 116.
Colorado's geological history is written on the sedimentary walls of this spectacular 18mi gorge. The oldest rock was formed 570 million years ago in the Precambrian era. The youngest rock, up to 1,500ft above the river, is iron-rich sandstone. This portion of I-70, completed in 1992, was cantilevered from granite walls and routed through short tunnels to minimize damage to the landscape. A paved biking and jogging trail runs the entire length of Glenwood Canyon. Exits access raft-launch areas and **Hanging Lake Trail★★**, which ascends 1,000ft in 1mi to an exquisite lake.

Glenwood Springs★★

Rte. 82 at I-70 Exit 116, 158mi west of Denver. ⚠✕♿🅿 ✆970-945-6589. www.glenwoodchamber.com.
This town of 9,600 is situated where the Roaring Fork meets the Colorado River below Glenwood Canyon.
Hot Springs Pool★★ 🚹🚺 (401 N. River St.; ✆970-945-6571, www.hotspringspool.com) claims to be the world's largest naturally spring-fed hot pool. Hourly tours visit lit portions of **Glenwood Caverns and Historic Fairy Caves★★** 🚹🚺 (5100 Two Rivers Plaza Rd.; ✆970-945-4228; www.glenwoodcaverns.com), high above Glenwood Canyon.

◐ Take Rte. 82 southeast 42mi to Aspen and conclusion of driving tour.

Aspen★★★

200mi southwest of Denver. ⚠✕♿🅿 ✆970-925-1940. www.aspenchamber.org.
Synonymous with glamour, Aspen boasts ski terrain that ranks among the finest in North America, as four separate

resort mountains rise within 12mi of one another. High-season guests and part-time residents include many celebrities. The Aspen Skiing Company and Aspen Institute for Humanistic Studies, both founded in the late 1940s, revived a rundown silver-mining town. Aspen's evolution into a world-class resort (and town of 6,700) became a model for other Rockies' communities.

Known for chic boutiques and fashionable restaurants, historic downtown focuses on a pedestrian mall. Jerome B. Wheeler, president of Macy's department store in New York, came to Aspen during its boom years and in 1888 and 1889 built three enduring landmarks. Elaborate **Wheeler Opera House★★** (320 E. Hyman Ave.; ✆970-920-5770; www.wheeleroperahouse.com) hosts films and live entertainment. The **Hotel Jerome★** (330 Main St.; ✆970-920-1000; ♿ see ADDRESSES) has been restored and luxuriously renovated.

The **Wheeler-Stallard House★** (620 W. Bleeker St.; ✆970-925-3721; www.aspenhistorysociety.com), a Victorian showplace, is a museum of the Aspen Historical Society.

The **Aspen Art Museum★** (590 N. Mill St.; ✆970-925-805; http://aspenartmuseum.org) offers exhibits of various works, many by local artists; it will move to a newly constructed building (E. Hyman Ave. & S. Spring St.) in mid-2014.

The **Aspen Center for Environmental Studies** (100 Puppy Smith St.; ✆970-925-5756; www.aspennature.org) is set on Hallam Lake, maintained as a wildlife sanctuary. The **Aspen Music Festival and School★★★** (225 Music School Rd.; ✆970-925-3254; www.aspenmusicfestival.com) presents summer concerts that often feature world-renowned musicians.

Aspen Mountain★★
✕🅿 ✆970-923-1227.
www.aspensnowmass.com.
Aspen's original ski mountain rises directly behind town, its slopes luring some of the world's best skiers.

The **Silver Queen Gondola★★** operates in summer for sightseeing; views from its 11,212ft summit take in wilderness areas. Northwest of town are two more resorts, **Aspen Highlands** (Maroon Creek Rd. via Rte. 82) and novice-oriented **Buttermilk Mountain** (Rte. 82).

Snowmass★
Brush Creek Rd. via Rte. 82, 12mi northwest of Aspen. ✕♿🅿 ✆970-923-1227. www.aspensnowmass.com.
Created in 1967, Snowmass has the most varied terrain of the four mountains. **Krabloonik Kennels★★** 🏂🏂 (Divide Rd. off Brush Creek Rd.; ✆970-923-3953; www.krabloonik.com) operates dog-sled rides in winter. The **Anderson Ranch Art Center★** (5263 Owl Creek Rd.;

Maroon Bells

©Matt Inden/Weaver Multimedia Group/CTO

☎970-923-3181; www.andersonranch.org) offers highly regarded workshops.

Maroon Bells★★★

13mi southwest of Aspen in the Maroon Bells-Snowmass Wilderness. ⚠️&🅿️ Colorado's most oft-photographed view is particularly inspiring across the still waters of **Maroon Lake★★**.

Summers and weekends, private vehicles are prohibited from 10mi Maroon Creek Road, so shuttle buses make the trip from Rubey Park Transit Center (Durant Ave. between S. Galena & S. Mill Sts.). In winter, **T-Lazy-7 Ranch** 🎿 (Maroon Creek Rd.; ☎970-925-4614, www.tlazy7.com) operates sleigh rides.

ADDITIONAL SIGHTS
Steamboat Springs★★

US-40, 74mi north of I-70 Exit 157, 19mi west of Vail. ⚠️✕&🅿️ ☎970-879-0880. http://steamboat-chamber.com.

A true Western town (pop. 12,000) in the Yampa River Valley, Steamboat has preserved its ranch heritage. **F.M. Light & Sons★** (830 Lincoln Ave.; ☎970-879-1822; http://fmlight.com) has sold Western clothing from the same location since 1905. The **Eleanor Bliss Center for the Arts** (1001 13th St.; ☎970-879-9008), in a renovated 1908 rail depot, offers exhibits and performances.

The **Tread of Pioneers Museum** (800 Oak St.; ☎970-879-2214; www.tread-ofpioneers.org) showcases artifacts in a 1908 Queen Anne-style home.

The paved **Yampa River Trail★** is the core of a trail system bordering downtown. Shuttles take bathers up miles of backroads to **Strawberry Park Hot Springs** (☎970-879-0342; www.strawberryhotsprings.com), where clothes are optional after dark. Fabled for its ultra-light snowfall dubbed "champagne powder," **Steamboat Ski Area★★** (US-40, 3mi south of downtown; ☎970-879-6111; www.steamboat.com) has 18 lifts and a 3,668ft vertical drop.

Its **Gondola★** runs in summer for sightseeing, and **Howelsen Hill★** (☎970-879-8499) has a historic ski-jumping facility.

Crested Butte★★

Rte. 135, 28mi north of US-50 at Gunnison, 66mi west of Salida. ⚠️✕&🅿️ ☎970-349-6438. www.cbchamber.com. This entire former mining town of 1,500 is a National Historic District, its false-front Victorian buildings conveying an Old West flavor. Adjacent **Crested Butte Mountain Resort★** (Rte. 135, 2mi north of Crested Butte; ☎970-349-2222; www.skicb.com) has off-piste terrain that is challenging enough to host extreme skiing competitions; in summer, these wildflower-cloaked slopes offer some of Colorado's best mountain-biking trails.

Shops in Crested Butte

©Matt Inden/Weaver Multimedia Group/CTO

Western Slope★

The only major city in this vast semi-desert is Grand Junction, whose nearly 60,000 people live near the confluence of the Gunnison and Colorado rivers. These rivers—and, to a lesser extent, the Yampa and White farther north—provide lifeblood for ranching, and agriculture that embraces peaches, apples, pears and wine grapes. Front Range (Denver) residents often drive west for a weekend to bring home boxes of fresh fruit. For a list of orchards selling produce from July to October, access www.visitgrandjunction.com.

SIGHTS

Cross Orchards Historic Site★

3073 F Rd., Grand Junction. ℘970-434-9814 or 970-242-0971. www.visitgrandjunction.com.
The remnants of an early 20C farm, once one of the state's largest orchards, are preserved here. Costumed staff demonstrate trades such as blacksmithing, and the original bunkhouse and packing shed can be toured. Seasonal events include hayrides, cider-pressing and other activities.

Colorado National Monument★★

Off Rte. 340, via I-70 Exit 19 at Fruita, 12mi west of Grand Junction. △ P ℘970-858-3617. www.nps.gov/colm.
Embracing canyons, rock spires and habitat for bighorn sheep and golden eagles, this 32sq mi wilderness rises more than 2,000ft above the Colorado River, along the northern rim of the Upcompahgre Plateau.
Rim Rock Drive★★★ (23mi) weaves past such red-rock formations as the Kissing Couple, Devils Kitchen and Window Rock, many composed of 1.7-billion-year-old sandstone, among the oldest rocks on earth. The visitor center sits near the Saddlehorn Campground.

☼ **Michelin Map:** 493 G 8, 9 and map pp 298-299. Mountain Standard Time.
❚ **Info:** ℘970-244-1480, www.coloradowest.org.
▲▲ **Kids:** Cross Orchards Farm in Grand Junction.

Dinosaur National Monument★★

31mi north of US-40 at Dinosaur, 108mi north of Grand Junction. △ P ℘970-374-3000. www.nps.gov/dino.
A scenic drive to **Harpers Corner** climaxes with a 1.5mi hike to a viewpoint over the confluence of the Yampa and Green rivers at **Echo Park**.
To see dinosaur fossils, visitors must travel west 20mi on US-40 to Jensen, Utah, then north 7mi on Rte. 149 to the **Quarry Visitor Center**, from which shuttle buses depart (summer) for the **Dinosaur Exhibit Hall**.

Black Canyon of the Gunnison National Park★★

Rte. 347, 5mi north of US-50, 8mi east of Montrose & 58mi west of Gunnison. △ P ℘970-641-2337. www.nps.gov/blca.
Neither the deepest nor narrowest canyon in the West, this chasm combines both aspects for its dramatic appear-

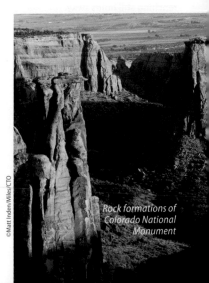

Rock formations of Colorado National Monument

©Matt Inden/Miles/CTO

ance. The westward-flowing Gunnison River has scoured a virtually impenetrable 53mi-long, 2,700ft-deep, 1,000ft-wide path through Precambrian gneiss and schist. A 7mi road along the south rim offers 12 scenic **overlooks**★★. Incredibly enough, a rail line once penetrated this chasm.

Built to carry crops and mine ore, the narrow-gauge track from Gunnison to Montrose was abandoned in 1949; a short section of track, several cars and Locomotive #278 are on display at **Cimarron** (21mi east of Montrose on Hwy. 50; www.nps.gov/cure).

Curecanti National Recreation Area★

US-50 between Montrose & Gunnison. ⚠ 🅿 ℘970-641-2337. www.nps.gov/cure.

Three consecutive reservoirs on the Gunnison River are the heart of this recreational heaven for watersports lovers. Farthest upstream is **Blue Mesa Lake**, Colorado's biggest lake and the largest kokanee salmon fishery in the state. Below Blue Mesa are **Morrow Point Lake**, locked into the upper Black Canyon, and **Crystal Lake**. Ranger-led pontoon **boat tours** depart twice daily in summer from Morrow Point into the upper reaches of Black Canyon (reservations required).

San Juan Country★★

Colorado's southwestern corner is a largely mountainous area dominated by the sharply angled slopes and precipices of the San Juan Mountains. The Rockies' youngest range includes more than 2 million acres of national forests, parks and designated wilderness areas laced with scenic rivers and lakes. Fourteen lofty peaks surpass 14,000ft; at lower elevations, ranching still holds sway.

A BIT OF HISTORY

Historic 19C mining towns characterize human settlement in the high San Juans. But long before white settlement, Ancestral Puebloans were present. Between AD 600 and 1300, they built numerous cities amid the piñon-and-sage mesas feathering off the San Juans. Abandoned seven centuries ago, the foremost cliff-dwelling sites in the world are contained within Mesa Verde National Park.

Much later, pioneers seeking gold and silver discovered the San Juans. In 1880 a railroad—a portion of which survives

⚭ **Michelin Map:** 493 F, G 9, 10. Mountain Standard Time.

🗓 **Info:** ℘800-933-4340 or www.swcolotravel.org.

today as the Durango & Silverton Narrow Gauge Railroad—was built to haul ore and supplies. The Million Dollar Highway was blasted through the mountains to link far-flung sites with service towns like Durango and Cortez; mine wealth built their Victorian main streets.

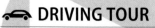

🚗 DRIVING TOUR

2–3 days, 290mi.

Durango★

US-160 & US-550. ℘970-247-3500. www.durango.org.

This Animas River town of 17,000 was founded in 1880 when the Denver and Rio Grande Railroad built a rail line to alpine mines near remote Silverton. The **Durango & Silverton Narrow Gauge Railroad**★★★ 👥 (479 Main Ave.; ℘970-247-2733; www.durangotrain.com) still employs coal-fired steam locomotive engines to pull restored narrow-gauge cars 45 slow miles through the wilderness. The train depot anchors the **Main Avenue National Historic District★** (Main Ave., 5th-12th Sts.), where the star attraction is the **Strater Hotel★** (699 Main Ave.; ✆970-247-4431; http://strater.com; ♿see ADDRESSES), a four-story brick Victorian featuring the Diamond Belle Saloon, a bar with a honky-tonk pianist and garter-clad waitresses.

▶ Drive north 50mi from Durango on US-550.

Silverton★

US-550 & Rte. 110. △✕♿🅿 ✆970-387-5654. http://silvertoncolorado.com.

A boom town in the 1880s, Silverton relies largely on rail tourists on layover here, who have time to explore the 50-or-so Victorian buildings of the historic district (between 10th, 15th, Mineral & Snowden Sts.).
North of town, US-550 courses through country pocked by abandoned mines along the **Million Dollar Highway★**. Sheer drops plunge from the shoulders of this roadway to jagged rocks hundreds of feet below.

▶ Continue north 25mi from Silverton on US-550.

Ouray★

73mi north of Durango.
△✕♿🅿 ✆970-325-4746.
http://ouraycolorado.com.

The seven-block **Main Street Historic District** of this "Switzerland of America," founded by miners in 1876, lies in a dramatic canyon. Visitors can see steam rising from the **Ouray Hot Springs Pool** (US-550, north end of Ouray; ✆970-325-7073), its gallons of thermal water as hot as 106°F. South of town, in Uncompahgre Gorge, 285ft **Box Cañon Falls** (mid-May–late Oct; Rte. 261, ✆970-325-7080) becomes Ouray Ice Park (www.ourayicepark.com) in winter. In summer, Ouray is a center for Jeep excursions.

▶ Drive north 10mi from Ouray on US-550; at Ridgway, turn west (left) on Rte. 162; after 23mi, turn east (left) on Rte. 145 and continue 17mi to Telluride.

Telluride★★

125mi north of Durango. △✕🅿 ✆888-605-2578. www.visittelluride.com.

The 1878 **National Historic District**, nestled in a steep-sided glacial box canyon, is linked with ultra-modern **Mountain Village** by a state-of-the-art gondola. Rich veins of silver and gold made Telluride a boisterous, Wild West town. Its affluence was not lost on Butch Cassidy, who in 1889 launched his outlaw career by robbing the Bank of Telluride. Nine years later, American politician William Jennings Bryan delivered his famous "Cross of Gold" speech (defending the falling gold standard) from the steps of the **New Sheridan Hotel** (231 W. Colorado Ave.; ✆970-728-4351; www.newsheridan.com; ♿see ADDRESSES). At the east end of Telluride's box canyon is Colorado's longest free-flowing waterfall, 365ft **Bridal Veil Falls★**. **Telluride Ski Resort★★** (✆970-728-6900; http://tellurideskiresort.com) is one of the Rockies' most acclaimed and challenging. Its 3,522ft vertical drop (climaxing at 12,266ft) is accessible from downtown or Mountain Village.

▶ Drive south 65mi from Telluride on Rte. 145.

Dolores

Rtes. 145 & 184, 45mi west of Durango. △✕♿🅿✆970-882-4018. http://doloreschamber.com.

This small town has a historic train station and **Galloping Goose** (Rte. 145; ✆970-882-7082), a hybrid train/bus contraption that once simultaneously carried passengers and removed snow from the railroad tracks.
Three miles west the **Anasazi Heritage Center★★** (Rte. 184; ✆970-882-5600; www.co.blm.gov/ahc) is a museum depicting Ancestral Puebloan culture throughout the Four Corners region. It serves as the visitor center for **Canyons**

Where the Past Is Still Present

In some parts of the West, especially the Southwest, Great Basin and Canyonlands, it's easy for visitors to come upon evidence of past inhabitants—pottery shards, arrowheads, shaped pieces of flint, shell and obsidian. These objects are not nifty souvenirs, they are legally protected pieces of history and should (and must) be left where they are. "Pot-hunting" is prohibited under federal law, and authorities in 2009 broke up a major Four Corners theft ring devoted to scavenging antiquities from public land for sale to "collectors." Penalties are severe, both legally and ethically. Not only are public lands not meant to provide visitors "collectibles," archaeologists are still working to understand the long and fascinating story of humanity's arrival in North America, and even tiny artifacts can hold important clues. Please, help keep history alive—not stolen.

of the Ancients National Monument (County Rd. CC, 28mi northwest of Cortez; www.co.blm.gov/canm) a largely undeveloped expanse of canyonlands.

▷ Continue south 12mi from Dolores on Rte. 145.

Cortez

US-160, US-666 & Rte. 145, 46mi west of Durango. ⛺✕🅿 ℘970-565-3402. www.cityofcortez.com.

An agricultural town of 8,400, Cortez features an historic district that stretches along Main Street.

The **Ute Mountain Tribal Park★★** (12mi southwest via US-160; ℘970-565-3751; http://utemountainute.com; ☎visit by guided tour only) contains excavated cliff dwellings, petroglyphs and thousands of pottery shards. Tours depart from the tribe's **Visitor Center and Museum** (US 160 and 491).

Less than an hour's drive away, the **Four Corners Monument** (US-160, 38mi southwest of Cortez) is the only place where four US states intersect: Colorado, New Mexico, Arizona and Utah.

▷ Take US-160 east 10mi from Cortez; turn south into Mesa Verde National Park.

Mesa Verde National Park★★★

US-160, Mancos. ⛺✕🅿 ℘970-529-4465. www.nps.gov/meve.

The first US national park to preserve the works of man (as opposed to nature), Mesa Verde was created by Congress on September 29, 1906. Today this World Heritage Site attracts 500,000 annual visitors, mostly in summer, when they can walk through five major cliff dwellings and additional mesa-top structures displaying primitive construction methods used by Ancestral Puebloans between AD 750 and 1300. A newly constructed visitor center was opened in late 2012 at the park entrance.

The 21mi drive from the park entrance to the **Chapin Mesa Archeological Museum★** winds around the mesa, offering spectacular views of four states. Adjacent is **Spruce Tree House★★★**, a major cliff dwelling and the only one open year-round.

Nearby, the 6mi **Mesa Top Loop Road** is also open year-round. Overlooks provide views of **Square Tower House★★**, the **Twin Trees★** site and **Sun Temple★**. In warmer weather, guided tours are offered to spectacular sites built into overhanging cliffs at **Cliff Palace★★** and **Balcony House★★**.

▷ Continue east 36mi on US-160 to return to Durango.

Salt Lake City Area

Set between the Wasatch Mountains and the saline expanse of the Great Salt Lake and Desert, Salt Lake City was founded in the 1840s by persecuted religious refugees from the east. It grew as the world capital of the Church of Jesus Christ of Latter-day Saints (Mormons), a distinction that still dominates social, cultural and political life in the region. Salt Lake City is a thriving modern city, firmly rooted in its heritage and a leading center of the high-technology and biomedical industries.

Highlights

1 Mankind's family tree at the **Family History Library** (p331)

2 An inland sea at **Great Salt Lake State Park** (p334)

3 Bobsled ride at **Utah Olympic Park** (p335)

4 Railroad history at the **Golden Spike** (p337)

5 **Garden of dinosaurs** in Vernal (p338)

The City and the Lake

The Great Salt Lake itself, less than 15mi west of the city, spreads across 2,500sq mi when filled to capacity, but nowhere is it deeper than 42ft. The inland sea is a remnant of ancient Lake Bonneville, eight times larger. Twice as salty as any ocean, it draws water and dissolved minerals from mountain streams, and has no outlet and little aquatic life.

More than 1 million people live today in Salt Lake County. Many more live a short drive south in Provo and north in Ogden, for a metropolitan population of nearly 2.4 million. Within an hour's drive of these three urban hubs are 10 downhill and six cross-country ski resorts – an unparalleled concentration that helped earn Salt Lake the honor of hosting the 2002 Winter Olympic Games. Many of the competitions were held around Park City, a mining town high in the Wasatch Range 30mi east of Salt Lake City. Not only is this sophisticated resort center surrounded by three world-class ski areas, it is home to the renowned annual Sundance Film Festival.

ADDRESSES

🏨 STAY

$$$$$ Stein Eriksen Lodge – 7700 Stein Way, Deer Valley Resort, Park City. ✆435-649-3700. www.steinlodge. com. 180 rooms. Skiers pay top dollar to experience the alpine decor, prime service and mid-mountain ski-in, ski-out privileges of "The Stein," named for Norway's 1952 Olympic champion. **The Glitretind** ($$$) restaurant serves contemporary cuisine year-round.

$$$$ The Grand America Hotel – 555 S. Main St., Salt Lake City. ✆801-258-6000. www.grandamerica.com. 775 rooms. Earl Holding, whose hotel and resort empire extends to Idaho's Sun Valley Resort, spared no expense in creating his crown jewel before the 2002 Winter Olympics. A 24-story, white-granite hotel with central gardens and a boutique sensibility, the Grand America has French cherry-wood furniture, English wool carpets, Italian glass chandeliers and marble that carries into guest rooms.

$$$ Alta Lodge – Rte. 210, Alta. ☏801-742-3500. www.altalodge.com. 57 rooms. Beds are narrow, and there are no TVs, but that's part of the charm. Opened in the late 1930s by the Denver & Rio Grande Railroad, the lodge is an institution for the skier's skier. Unpretentious regulars come for family-style dining and floor-to-ceiling windows looking out to the Wasatch Mountain peaks.

$$$ Goldener Hirsch Inn – 7570 Royal St. E. (Stewart St.), Park City. ☏435-649-7770. www.goldenerhirschinn.com. 20 rooms. Situated mid-mountain in the Silver Lake area of the world-renowned Deer Valley Resort in Park City, this Austrian Alps-style ski lodge has hand-painted imported Austrian furniture. Frette linens, plush down comforters and luxury bathroom amenities boost the ambience. Most of the suites have private balconies and wood-burning fireplaces. Located at 8,000ft, with ski-in/ski-out and indoor/outdoor hot tub.

$$$ Hotel Monaco – 15 W. 200 South, Salt Lake City. ☏801-595-0000. www.monaco-saltlakecity.com. 225 rooms. Salt Lake's preeminent boutique hotel, the Monaco occupies a restored 15-story Deco-era bank building. Eclectic decor extends from the lobby to guest rooms, where pets are welcomed. Chef Nathan Powers presides over the kitchen at **Bambara** (**$$$**), one of the city's best restaurants.

$$$ Peery Hotel – 110 W. 300 South, Salt Lake City. ☏801-521-4300. www.peeryhotel.com. 73 rooms. A classic grand staircase is the centerpiece of the recently renovated and smoke-free Peery, built in 1910 in Prairie Style with classical Revival motifs. European ambience extends from the expansive lobby to extensive use of padded leather and walnut in the rooms.

$$ Homestead Resort – 700 N. Homestead Dr., Midway. ☏435-654-1102. www.homesteadresort.com. 152 rooms. A Swiss farmer discovered mineral "hot pots" over a century ago in the Heber Valley, 20mi southeast of Park City; buggy-loads of visitors convinced him to create a resort. Lodgings range from cottages and condos; decor is Southwestern or New England. Guests may snorkel year-round or ride in a horse-drawn sleigh.

$$ Old Town Guesthouse – 1011 Empire Ave. Park City. ☏435-649-2642. www.oldtownguesthouse.com. 4 rooms. A short walk to Park City slopes, this small lodging can help you organize guided backcountry ski trips, as well as hiking, fly-fishing, and snowshoeing excursions. Expect massive mountain breakfasts, in-room towel robes, a hot tub, movie library and afternoon snacks. Each of the four rooms has its own bathroom, but two rooms must share a large shower room.

Temple Square and Salt Lake Temple

© Visit Salt Lake

Salt Lake valley looking southeast

© Visit Salt Lake/Adam Barker

℘ EAT

$$ Chimayo – 368 Main St., Park City. ℘435-649-6222. www.chimayo restaurant.com. Dinner only. **Southwestern**. In a handsome Spanish Colonial-style room with heavy-oak decor, regional dishes arrive with a French touch. Examples are skewers of elk marinated in coffee, and buffalo flank steak with wild mushrooms sauteed in port.

$$$ Log Haven Restaurant – 6451 E. Canyon Rd., 4mi east of S. Wasatch Blvd., Salt Lake City. ℘801-272-8255. www. log-haven.com. Dinner only. **American**. Built in 1920 of Oregon logs hauled by horse-drawn wagon, this forest cabin nestles at the base of the Wasatch Range. Walls glow with rustic warmth, and the food is gourmet: seared buffalo steak, and Utah-grown steelhead trout pan-fried with soba noodles.

$$ Market Street Grill – 48 W. Market St., Salt Lake City. ℘801-322-4668. www.marketstreetgrill.com. **Seafood**. More fresh shellfish (300 pounds daily) are shucked at the Grill and adjoining Oyster Bar than anywhere else in Utah. The noisy restaurant seats as many as 250 diners under mock palm trees in the 1906 New York Building. Fresh fish is flown in daily: ahi from Hawaii, halibut from Alaska, sea bass from Chile.

$$$ Snake Creek Grill – 650 W. 100 South, Heber City. ℘435-654-2133. www.snakecreekgrill.com. Dinner only. Closed Mon–Tue. **Contemporary**. Park City locals say the town's best restaurant is miles away in Heber Old Town, an abandoned railroad village. Chef-owner Barbara Hill prepares hangar steak with wild mushroom sauce, bison burgers, and white-corn crusted trout. Antiques and funky collectibles on a wood-plank floor create a homey roadhouse ambience.

$$$ 350 Main – 350 Main St., Park City. ℘435-649-3140. www.350main. com. **Contemporary**. South Carolina native chef Carl Fiessinger's eclectic menu ranges from Southern to South American—fried chicken, quinoa, smoked pork belly and lobster-and-grits exemplify the wide culinary range. A central fireplace at its heart, this restaurant occupies an old saloon in the 1910 Golden Rule Building.

$ Red Iguana – 736 W North Temple St., Salt Lake City. ℘801-322-1489. **Mexican**. Mexican regional cuisine is the Cardenas family's long-time specialty at this iconic Salt Lake eatery: *carne asada Tampiqueña, pollo a la Moreliana*—and *Lago Salado* enchiladas, combining potatoes, chorizo and enchilada sauce.

$ Rio Grande Café – 270 S. Rio Grande St. (244 West), Salt Lake City. ℘801-364-3302. **Mexican**. Old timers at this diner in the old rail depot claim the establishment is haunted by an eerie but harmless ghost, the "Purple Lady." The menu features tacos, burritos, blue-corn enchiladas and chile-verde tamales.

Salt Lake City★★

Historic Temple Square, with its concentration of buildings tied to Mormon religion and history, is the central attraction of Salt Lake City, certainly worthy of several hours' exploration by anyone with a desire to understand this modern world religion. Other sights include museums and especially, scenic attractions.

SALT LAKE CITY TODAY

Long thought of only as the capital of the Mormon faith, Salt Lake City gained a different image following the 2002 Winter Olympics. With mountains and desert at every side, it's a recreation capital, home of a leading outdoor recreation industry show. It's also, because of the Mormon Family Search Center (http://familysearch.org), now fashioning itself the "Genealogy Capital of the World."

A BIT OF HISTORY

Salt Lake City was founded in 1847 by Mormon pioneers led by **Brigham Young**. A late frost, a drought and a plague of crickets nearly destroyed their harvest until seagulls descended upon the insects and enabled the settlers to survive that winter.

Ownership of the Salt Lake Valley transferred from Mexico to the US in 1848, and in 1850 the Utah Territory was formed, with Brigham Young as its first governor. To the Mormons, their home was the State of Deseret. A deseret honeybee is acknowledged in *The Book of Mormon* for its industriousness; bee-like hard work and a sense of community, coupled with extensive irrigation, enabled the Mormons to succeed.

Utah's isolation ended in 1869 with the completion of the first transcontinental railroad. Through World War I, copper, silver, gold and lead mines opened in Utah canyons. Mine owners built luxuri-

▶ **Population:** 189,000.

Michelin Map: 493 E, F 7, 8. Mountain Standard Time.

Info: ☏801-534-4900 or www.visitsaltlake.com. Visitor Center in the Convention Center (90 S. West Temple St.; ☏801-534-4900).

Location: Because of the strong influence of the Mormon church, few sights (except natural ones) are open Sundays. Call ahead to check. The distinctive Mormon city-grid plan persists in Salt Lake City. Long blocks of broad streets radiate in 10-acre squares from Temple Square. Addresses and street names, confusing to visitors, reveal their direction from the hub. Thus 201 E. 300 South Street is two blocks east and three blocks south of Temple Square; 201 S. 300 East Street is two blocks south and three east of the square.

Parking: There's no parking at Temple Square, and the two hours available from metered spots on nearby streets aren't adequate. Use parking garages.

Don't Miss: Temple Square.

Kids: Tracy Aviary.

ous manors in the city, in stark contrast to modest Mormon homes.

Largely because of early Mormon adherence to polygamy, Congress was slow to grant statehood to Utah. Only after the church withdrew its sanction of multiple-spouse marriages was Utah admitted to the union (in 1896, as the 45th state). Polygamous cults persist in southern Utah and northern Arizona, though officials have been cracking down on the practice.

SIGHTS
Historic Temple Square★★★

50 W. South Temple St. (between North, South & West Temple Sts. & Main St.). ♿ ✆801-240-1706.
www.visittemplesquare.com.

This landscaped 10-acre plot is the hub of downtown and the heart of the Mormon faith. Here are the six-spired temple, the silver-domed tabernacle, the Assembly Hall and several statues and monuments.

Utah State Capitol building

Young Latter-day Saint missionaries from the world over conduct ☛free tours★★ and discuss their faith in 30 languages. Only baptized Mormons may enter the **Salt Lake Temple★** (or any other temple), but audiovisual presentations in the **North and South Visitor Centers** show its highlights. The red-sandstone foundation was laid in 1853-55. The structure has granite walls 9ft thick at ground level, 6ft thick at top, and a statue of the angel Moroni, cast in copper (by sculptor Cyrus E. Dallin) trumpeting from a 210ft spire.

The **Salt Lake Tabernacle★** took just three years to construct; it opened in 1867. Seating 6,000 people, it contains an 11,623-pipe, 32ft-tall **organ★★** that accompanies the world-famous **Mormon Tabernacle Choir**. Weekly broadcast choir performances and rehearsals are free. Organ recitals are held daily. The semi-Gothic **Assembly Hall★** (1880) is a miniature cathedral that now hosts free concerts and lectures. The **Miracle of the Gulls Monument** (1913, Mahonri Young), honors the seagulls that saved the first pioneers' crop. The **Nauvoo Temple Bell**, a 782-pound bronze bell, rings hourly on the square.

Outside the southeast corner of Temple Square is the **Brigham Young Monument** (1897). Opposite Temple Square to the west are the following two important facilities.

Museum of Church History and Art★★

45 N. West Temple St. ♿
✆801-240-3310. history.lds.org.
This well-presented museum is an essential stop for visitors seeking to understand The Church of Jesus Christ of Latter-day Saints. Interpretive exhibits tell the history of the religion. There are galleries of 19-20C Mormon and American Indian art and portraits of historic church leaders.

Family History Library★

35 N. West Temple St. ♿ ✆801-240-2331. www.familysearch.org.
The world's largest collection of genealogical materials offers free public access for research. Church staff are available to assist.

Established in 1894, this is the hub of more than 3,400 Family History Centers in 65 countries and territories. An introduction is offered at the Family Search Center (👆see Joseph Smith Memoial Building below).

Church Office Building

50 E. North Temple St. ✆801-240-1000. www.lds.org.
This 26-story building holds the administrative offices of the church. From the top-floor observation deck, there are **views★★** of the greater Salt Lake area.

Joseph Smith Memorial Building★

15 E. South Temple St. ✗♿🅿
✆801-539-3130. www.templesquare hospitality.com.
The former Hotel Utah (1911), restored in 1987, reopened as a community center. "Legacy", a 53min film telling the saga of the pioneers, is shown in the Legacy Theater. The **Family Search Center** (✆801-240-4085; www.lds.org/

The Great Basin

Utah's Great Salt Lake marks the northeastern edge of the US Great Basin, a 200,000sq mi interior region between the Rocky Mountains and Sierra Nevada from which no water flows to the sea. It is marked by hundreds of small mountain ranges, such as Utah's Wasatch, that collect snow in winter and spill it into valleys below as snowmelt. Half of Utah, part of southern Oregon and almost all of Nevada are within the Great Basin. Contained within it is North America's fourth major desert, whose signature plant is the sagebrush and animal, the pronghorn antelope.

locations) introduces visitors to genealogical research by means of computer access.

The Beehive House★

67 E. South Temple St. ✕ ♿ 𝄞801-240-2671. www.lds.org/locations.
The official home, from 1854 to 1877, of Brigham Young and his large family (16 wives bore him 57 children, not all of whom lived to adulthood), this restored National Historic Landmark is filled with period furnishings. ✦▸Guided tours take in family rooms, several bedrooms, the kitchen and office.
Young's gravesite is a block east of here in the tiny **Mormon Pioneer Memorial Cemetery** (140 E. First Ave.).

Salt Palace Convention Center

100 S. West Temple St. ♿ 𝄞 𝄞385-468-2222. www.saltpalace.com.
This large building includes the **Visitor Information Center** (90 S. West Temple St.; 𝄞801-534-4900). Across from Temple Square is the 1993 **Maurice Abravanel Concert Hall** (123 W. South Temple St.; 𝄞801-355-2787; www.arttix.org), home of the Utah Symphony Orchestra. The **Energy Solutions Arena** (301 W. South Temple St.; 𝄞801-325-2500) is home to professional basketball's Utah Jazz.
The Gateway (18 N. Rio Grande St.; 𝄞801-456-2000) is an elegant shopping complex. Near the city center, **Galivan Center** (239 S. Main St.; 𝄞801-535-6110) has a seasonal ice-skating rink and summer concerts.

Farther east, **Trolley Square** (600 South & 700 East Sts.; 𝄞801-521-9877) is a shopping center listed on the National Register of Historic Places.

Utah State Capitol★★

North end of State St. ♿ 𝄞 𝄞801-538-1800. www.utahstatecapitol.utah.gov.
Completed in 1915 (Richard Kletting), this Renaissance Revival-style building was patterned after the US Capitol. The interior of the dome, 165ft above the foyer, is adorned with seagulls and historic murals. ✦▸Guided tours are offered on weekdays.

Pioneer Memorial Museum

300 N. Main St. ♿ 𝄞 𝄞801-532-6479. www.dupinternational.org.
Located opposite the State Capitol to the west, this collection of pioneer artifacts—on four floors and in an adjacent carriage house—includes sacred and sectarian items, especially from 1847 to 1869.

University of Utah★

Presidents Circle & University St., 2mi east of downtown via 200 South. ✕♿𝄞 𝄞801-581-7200. www.utah.edu.
Founded in 1850 as the University of Deseret, this 1,494-acre campus serving 31,000 students today is Utah's oldest university. Opening and closing ceremonies of the 2002 Olympic Winter Games were held at its Rice-Eccles Stadium.

Natural History Museum of Utah/Rio Tinto Center★★

301 Wakara Way. ✕♿🅿 ☏801-581-4303. http://nhmu.utah.edu.
Sheathed in Utah copper designed to mimic local sandstone, powered largely by solar PV cells on the roof, tucked into the Wasatch foothills in terraces, this stunning new museum building (2012) features extensive galleries devoted to the human and natural history of Utah. Highlights include priceless Paiute beadwork, Navajo basketry and dinosaur models. Guided tours explain the building's sustainability features.

Utah Museum of Fine Arts★

410 Campus Center Dr. (1725 East).
✕♿🅿 ☏801-581-7332.
http://umfa.utah.edu.
This five-story building is home to a permanent collection of 17,000 objects that features paintings and decorative arts from all over the world.

Red Butte Garden★

300 Wakara Way off Foothill Dr.
♿🅿 ☏801-585-0556.
www.redbuttegarden.org.
Spread across a semi-arid hillside above the university, next to the new natural history museum, these gardens preserve wildflowers, shrubs and trees (1,500 species), and cultivated gardens.

♿👤 This Is the Place Heritage Park★

2601 Sunnyside Ave. east of Foothill Dr.
♿🅿 ☏801-582-1847.
www.thisistheplace.org.
It is said that as Brigham Young and his party crested the Wasatch Range in 1847, Young gazed upon the Salt Lake Valley and said, "This is the place." On the centennial of that occasion, **This Is The Place Monument** was erected to honor the passage from Illinois on the 1,300mi Mormon Pioneer National Historic Trail. Mormon pioneer lifestyle (c.1847-69) is re-enacted in the **Heritage Village★★** in summer. In three dozen reconstructed buildings, villagers demonstrate domestic crafts and skills; a Native American village includes tipis.

♿👤 Utah's Hogle Zoo

2600 Sunnyside Ave. east of Foothill Dr.
✕♿🅿 ☏801-582-1631.
www.hoglezoo.org.
More than 1,000 animals, both exotic and regional, are displayed at this community zoo. Children are delighted by a working scale-model railroad.

♿👤 Tracy Aviary★

Liberty Park, 589 E. 1300 South St. ♿🅿
☏801-596-8500. www.tracyaviary.org.
Established in 1938, this is one of the oldest public bird parks in the US. Some 500 birds of 150 species, including exotics and 21 threatened or endangered species, live here.

EXCURSIONS

Big Cottonwood Canyon★

⊙ Rte. 190, extending 15mi east from I-215 Exit 6. ⚠✕♿🅿
Old mining claims and impressive scenery mark this canyon that extends into the Wasatch Range from southeast Salt Lake City.
Two popular ski areas, both rising above 10,000ft, are at its end. Powder-rich **Solitude** (28mi from downtown; ☏801-534-1400; www.skisolitude.com) is just 2mi from family-oriented **Brighton** (30mi from downtown; ☏801-532-4731; www.brightonresort.com).

Little Cottonwood Canyon★

⊙ Rte. 210, extending 14mi south & east from I-215 Exit 6. ⚠✕♿🅿
The primary lure of this gorge, shorter and narrower than Big Cottonwood, is its two vaunted resorts. Nearest to Salt Lake City is **Snowbird★** (25mi from downtown; ☏801-933-2222; www.snowbird.com), whose 11,000ft summit and 3,240ft vertical surpass all other Wasatch resorts. A 125-passenger aerial tramway climbs from base to summit in 8min and provides a contemporary European-style ambience. **Alta★★** (27mi from downtown; ☏801-359-1078; www.alta.com) opened in 1938 as the second (after Idaho's Sun Valley) destination ski resort in the western US. Famed for relaxed, old-fashioned atmosphere and deep powder snow

Kennecott's Bingham Canyon Mine

© David R. Frazier Photolibrary, Inc. / Alamy

(over 500in per year), Alta steadfastly refuses to install high-capacity or high-speed lifts or to permit snowboarding, and daily lift rates are lower than other top resorts. In the village library, the **Alta Historical Society** (℘801-742-3522; www.altahistory.org) maintains a permanent exhibit on Alta's silver-mining boom days of 1864-78.

Kennecott's Bingham Canyon Mine★★

❍ 4.5mi southwest of the intersection of Rtes. 48 & 111 near Copperton, and 29mi from downtown Salt Lake City via Rte. 48, west off I-15 Exit 301. ♿📖 ℘801-204-2005. www.kennecott.com.

The largest copper mine on earth is more than 2.8mi in diameter and nearly 4,000ft deep—almost twice the height of the world's tallest buildings. Since mining operations began in 1903, 6 billion tons of earth have been removed from what was once a mountain. The Bingham Canyon Mine has yielded more wealth than the California, Comstock and Klondike rushes combined: 18 million tons (30 billion pounds) of copper, 700 million pounds of molybdenum, 175 million ounces of silver and 20 million ounces of gold.

The best panoramas of the largest man-made excavation in the world (which could be seen by space shuttle astronauts as they passed over the US) are from an outside observation area.

👥 Great Salt Lake State Marina★★

❍ I-80 Exit 104, 17mi west of Salt Lake City. ℘801-250-1898. http://stateparks.utah.gov.

A marina and beach provide access to the largest US lake west of the Mississippi River. Only the Dead Sea has a higher salt content. Brine shrimp harvested in the Great Salt Lake are sold in Asia as food for tropical fish. Water-birds of all varieties thrive here—more than 257 species inhabit the shores and island.

👥 Bonneville Salt Flats★

❍ I-80, Wendover, NV, 120mi west of Salt Lake City.

The remnant of a time when Great Salt Lake was part of the much-bigger Lake Bonneville, this world-famed landscape is unlike any other in North America.

The 30,000-acre flats lie beneath 11,000-foot mountain peaks; the crust is composed of gypsum and ordinary salt, and can be 5ft thick near the center. Arid as they may seem, the flats flood each winter, helping maintain the perfectly level surface.

Interpretive tours are available from Intermountain Guide Service in Wendover (℘877-882-4386; www.intermountainguidenevada.com).

Northern Utah★

A startling backdrop to the Salt Lake area, the Wasatch Mountains rise like a 7,000ft wall east of the metropolis, 150mi from Logan south to Nephi, climbing above 1,000ft in elevation. Once an obstacle to exploration, they were pierced by silver miners in the late 19C. Today the range is a leading source of white gold—the downy powder into which winter-sports lovers cast skis and snowboards. Utah's vehicle license plates even declare: "The Greatest Snow on Earth." Park City, largest of the resort communities and a mere 35mi east of Salt Lake City, was the hub of most mountain activities during the 2002 Olympic Winter Games.

- ⌖ **Michelin Map:** 493 E, F 8. Mountain Standard Time.
- 🛈 **Info:** ℘800-200-1160; www.utah.com.
- ⌾ **Don't Miss:** Park City's Main Street.
- ♟♙ **Kids:** Utah Olympic Park.

SIGHTS

Park City★★

Rte. 224, 5mi south of I-80 Exit 145.
△✕♿🅿 ℘435-649-6100.
www.parkcityinfo.com.

A rich mining district in the late 19C, producing more than $400 million in silver, Park City was founded in 1872. In its heyday, nearly 10,000 residents supported theaters, dance halls, saloons and brothels. An 1898 fire destroyed three-quarters of the city; the surviving 19C structures now are part of the **Main Street National Historic District★★**, which entices visitors with galleries, boutiques and restaurants. Walking tours begin from the **Park City Museum** (528 Main St.; ℘435-649-7457; www.parkcityhistory.org), in the territorial jailhouse.

Park City established itself as a year-round resort in the 1960s. Modern growth has it approaching its halcyon size. Three major ski areas are a short shuttle-bus run from Main Street; one, family-oriented **Park City Mountain Resort★** (Lowell Ave.; ℘435-649-8111; www.pcski.com), is merely steps away. Celebrity-conscious **Deer Valley Resort★** (Deer Valley Dr.; ℘435-649-1000; www.deervalley.com) is more chic. Flush with new development is **The Canyons★** (The Canyons Dr.; ℘435-649-5400; www.thecanyons.com), 3mi north off Route 224. Among them, the three similarly sized resorts offer 9,290ft of vertical (at least 3,000ft each) served by 44 lifts.

Near The Canyons, the **Utah Olympic Park★** (♟♙ Bear Hollow Dr. off Rte. 224; ℘435-658-4200; http://utaholympiclegacy.com) is a training facility for US national teams; it has six jumping hills of 18m–120m, four ramps for freestyle aerial jumps and a 1,335m (4,331ft) bobsled/luge track. The public may watch athletes perform, take a bobsled ride or ride the world's steepest zip-line.

The arts calendar is highlighted by the **Sundance Film Festival★★** (℘435-658-3456; www. sundance.org/festival) in January. The world's best independent filmmakers premiere new works at this Robert Redford-produced event, held in Park City (not at Redford's eponymous ski area) since 1986.

Heber Valley Historic Railroad★

450 S. 600 West St., Heber City, 18mi southeast of Park City. 🅿 ℘435-654-5601. www.hebervalleyrr.org.

Restored vintage coaches and a 1907 steam locomotive take passengers on an excursion around Deer Creek Reservoir to Vivian Park in Provo Canyon.

Sundance Resort

Rte. 92, Sundance, 15mi north of Provo via US-189. ✕♿🅿 ℘801-223-6000. www.sundanceresort.com.

Purchased in 1969 by actor-director Robert Redford and named for the Utah-born character he played in *Butch Cassidy and the Sundance Kid*, this enclave is devoted to recreation and environment. In winter a modest ski area serves a flank of 11,750ft Mount Timpanogos. In summer, Sundance is a hiking and riding center with outdoor musical theater.

Timpanogos Cave National Monument★

Rte. 92, American Fork, 9mi east of I-15 Exit 287. ✗ ▣ ✆801-756-5239. www. nps.gov/tica. **Advance ticket purchase recommended on weekends.**

Three limestone caverns, linked by man-made tunnels, are located on the northern slope of Mount Timpanogos. Reached by a steep 1.5mi, 1,065ft uphill hike from the canyon-floor visitor center, the caves hold impressive features that are still in formation: dripstone, helictites, stalagmites and stalactites.

♠♣ North American Museum of Ancient Life

Thanksgiving Point Resort, 3003 N. Thanksgiving Way, Lehi (I-15 Exit 287). ✗♿▣✆801-768-2300. www.thanksgivingpoint.com.
Sixty full dinosaur skeletons, interactive displays and a giant-screen theater are integral to this educational facility. The museum is part of a theme village and residential community with botanical gardens, a children's farm, performing-arts venues and a golf course.

Provo

US-89 & US-189 at I-15 Exit 268. ⚠✗♿▣ ✆801-851-2100. www.utahvalley.com.
The third-largest city in Utah, with 116,000 people, Provo nestles midway down the eastern shore of large fresh-water Utah Lake.
Besides Brigham Young University, the city boasts the gold-spired **Provo Mormon Temple** (N. Temple Dr. off N. 900 East), on a hill above the university, and the **Utah County Courthouse** (Center St. & University Ave.), built in the 1920s of limestone.

Utah Skiing

Utah's ski industry advertises its reliable, light powder as the "Greatest Snow on Earth," but it could also fashion it the most convenient snow on earth. Within an hour's drive of the Salt Lake City airport lie 11 major ski resorts, a combination of concentration and proximity likely matched nowhere else. Many visitors simply get a hotel room in the city and sample the various resorts day to day, depending on weather, snow conditions and preference. The average yearly snowfall in the Wasatch Range east of the city ranges from 300 to 600 inches (25 to 50 feet) and snow bases often surpass 60 inches by January. The region's desert climate and atmospheric characteristics mean the snow is justifiably famed for its light, powdery quality: Climatologists have studied the way in which winds, moisture and elevation combine to create feathery snowflakes in Utah's mountains. Among other things, westerly storms pick up moisture from Great Salt Lake and drive it up to the Wasatch alpine through the canyons east of Salt Lake City.

Another distinction marks Utah skiing—two of the region's biggest resorts, Alta and Deer Valley, ban snowboarders. Only one other area in all of North America is for skiers only, and several resorts that had once barred snowboarders have now abandoned the prohibition. Alta and Deer Valley both are committed to maintaining their skier-only status, and with 11 resorts clustered so close together, there is plenty of room for 'boarders in Utah. And more than enough snow. Visit www.skiutah.com for information on both skiing and snowboarding on Utah powder.

Brigham Young University★

Campus Dr. off E. 1230 North. ✗⛷♿🅿
✆801-422-4636. www.byu.edu.
Established in 1877 by Brigham Young, this 638-acre educational center of Mormonism is one of the largest private universities in the US. The **Museum of Art** (✆801-422-8287) features 19C American and European works and a collection of musical instruments. The **Museum of Paleontology★** (✆801-422-3680) boasts an outstanding research collection of Jurassic dinosaurs. The **Monte L. Bean Life Science Museum** (✆801-422-3680) explores natural history, with a new facility scheduled to open in 2014. The **Museum of Peoples and Cultures** (✆801-422-0020) focuses on Southwest Indian, Mexican and Maya artifacts.

Springville Museum of Art★

126 E. 400 South, Springville, 6mi south of Provo. 🅿✆801-489-2727. www.smofa.org.
Perhaps the best collection of Utah art and artists, this small museum, housed in a Hispano-Morrocan style building, has 29 exhibition galleries presenting works by painters, sculptors and printmakers since 1862. Soviet Socialist Realism and American art are also represented.

♟♂ Antelope Island State Park★

Rte. 127; 7.5mi west of I-15 Exit 335 via Rte. 108; 40mi northwest of Salt Lake City. ⛰✗⛷♿🅿✆801-773-2941. http://stateparks.utah.gov.
A long causeway crosses the shallow flats of the Great Salt Lake to this 28,000-acre wildlife refuge, largest island in the lake.
Besides pronghorn antelope, the island is home to mule deer, bighorn sheep, coyotes, bobcats, upland game birds, waterfowl, and 500 bison descended from a late 19C herd.
From a visitor center (4528 W. 1700 South, Syracuse), guests can hike, bike or ride horses on 40mi of trails.

♟♂ Hill Aerospace Museum

7961 Wardleigh Rd., Hill Air Force Base. ♿🅿✆801-777-6818. www.hill.af.mil.
One of the largest collections of vintage aircraft and ordnance in the US includes 90 bombers, cargo planes, helicopters, missiles, bombs and other weapons.

Ogden

US-89 east of I-15 Exit 344. ✗⛷♿🅿
✆866-867-8824. www.visitogden.com.
Established as a railroad town named Fort Buenaventura, Ogden—with 85,000 residents—echoes its past in restored buildings along its historic **25th Street**. In the former depot, the **Utah State Railroad Museum** (2501 Wall Ave.; ✆801-393-9890, www.theunion-station.org) has exhibits and a model-railroad room. The **Salomon Center★** (383 23rd St.; www.salomoncenter.com) offers a climbing wall, bowling, gyms, and a wind tunnel where visitors can fly.

Ogden River Scenic Byway★

Rte. 39 east from Ogden to Huntsville.
This 62mi route follows Ogden River Canyon upriver past Pineview Reservoir and across the crest of the Wasatch Range. Leaving Ogden, it skirts the **George S. Eccles Dinosaur Park** ♟♂ (1544 E. Park Blvd.; ✆801-393-3466; www.dinosaurpark.org), whose 98 replicas are depicted in a realistic outdoor setting. **Snowbasin Resort** (Rte. 226, Huntsville; ✆801-620-1000; www.snowbasin.com) is 17mi east of Ogden.

EXCURSION
Golden Spike National Historic Site★

▶ 32mi west of I-15 Exit 368, Brigham City, via Rtes. 13 & 83. ✆435-471-2209. www.nps.gov/gosp.
This site recalls the completion of the transcontinental railroad with the driving of a symbolic "golden spike" connecting Central Pacific and Union Pacific lines on May 10, 1869.
Working replicas of the two **steam locomotives** that first met here are on display May to October. Costumed reenactments of the original ceremony are staged Saturdays in summer.

Green River Country

Largely isolated from population centers and major highways, northeastern Utah has developed in relative seclusion on either side of the lofty Uinta Mountains and along the Green River and its tributaries. Its principal interest to tourists today revolves around water sports, especially river rafting, and its deposits of dinosaur bones, among the richest on earth. Backpackers and mountain climbers strive for the summits of 13,528ft Kings Peak, Utah's highest, and a raft of other 12,000ft-plus pinnacles in the Uinta, the largest east-west mountain range in the Rockies. Sprawling through the heart of the region, the Uinta and Ouray Indian Reservation is the second-largest reservation in the US, home to 1,600 members of four related tribes.

SIGHTS
Price
US-6 & 191 and Rte. 10, 118mi southeast of Salt Lake City. △✕☎435-636-3701. www.castlecountry.com.

This late-19C coal town is still a center for coal mining nearby. The **Utah State University Eastern Prehistoric Museum** ▲▲ (155 E. Main St.; ☎435-613-5060; usueastern.edu) displays several full-size dinosaur skeletons and 12C Fremont Indian figurines of unbaked clay. Curators provide self-guiding tour information to the **Cleveland-Lloyd Dinosaur Quarry**★ (BLM 216 Rd., 11mi east of Cleveland & 30mi southeast of Price via Rtes. 10 & 155; ☎435-636-3600; www.blm.gov/ut), where the bones of at least 70 species of prehistoric animals have been unearthed. **Nine Mile Canyon Road**★ (60mi from Wellington, US-6/191, to Myton, US-40/191), a backcountry route beginning 7mi east of Price, leads to a 40mi canyon with hundreds of ancient Indian petroglyphs.

⌚ **Michelin Map:** 493 F 7. Mountain Standard Time.

ℹ **Info:** ☎800-200-1160; www.utah.com.

▶ **Location:** The Uinta Mountain range runs east–west.

▲▲ **Kids:** Dinosaur Garden at State Park Museum.

Vernal
US-40 & 191, 176mi east of Salt Lake City. ☎435-789-6932. www.dinoland.com.

Western gateway to **Dinosaur National Monument**★★ and southern gateway to Flaming Gorge National Recreation Area (below), Vernal is in an area of much geological and paleontological interest. **Natural History State Park's** ▲▲ (235 E. Main St.; ☎435-789-3799; www.stateparks.utah.gov) Utah Field House illustrates the prehistory of the region. The **State Park Museum**★ (496 E. Main St., ☎435-789-3799) guides visitors through geologic epochs represented by local fossil finds; outside, a **dinosaur garden** holds 20-ft models of Tyrannosaurus rex and 16 other prehistoric denizens of the area. Events, such as lectures and walks, take place throughout the year.

Flaming Gorge National Recreation Area★
US-191 & Rte. 44, 43mi north of Vernal. ☎435-789-1181. www.fs.fed.us/r4.

Straddling the Utah-Wyoming border, this recreation area surrounds a 91mi-long reservoir that backs up through canyons carved through the Uinta Mountains by the Green River. The **Red Canyon Visitor Center and Overlook**★★ (Rte. 44; ☎435-676-2676) offers a bird's-eye view of the reservoir, in summer, from 1,400ft above Red Canyon.

Guided tours of a 502ft concrete-arch dam are provided at the **Flaming Gorge Dam Visitor Center** (US-191, Dutch John; ☎435-885-3135; www.usbr.gov).

Yellowstone Region

The world's first national park, Yellowstone National Park was established by the US Congress in 1872. Much of the park sits astride an ancient collapsed volcanic caldera, 28mi wide and 47mi long. Within the borders of this 3,472sq mi World Heritage Site (roughly the size of the eastern state of Connecticut) can be found the largest free-roaming wildlife population in the lower 48 states; the world's greatest concentration of thermal features and its largest petrified forest.

Yellowstone NP

Highlights

1 Bison in **Hayden Valley** (p345)
2 Teton scenery on **Jenny Lake Scenic Drive** (p350)
3 Magnificent wapiti at the **National Elk Refuge** (p351)
4 Condors at the **Birds of Prey Center** (p359)
5 Surreal landscape at **Craters of the Moon** (p359)

America's First National Park

One of the pleasures of a visit to Yellowstone is that it is so accessible. More than 370mi of paved road weave a course through the park, introducing Old Faithful and its surrounding geysers, the travertine terraces of Mammoth Hot Springs and the spectacular chasm of the Grand Canyon of the Yellowstone. Majestic elk, bison, moose and other large animals range widely through this realm of steamy beauty, often visiting campgrounds and lodges, and wandering close to main roads.
Immediately south of Yellowstone is Grand Teton National Park, enclosing a dramatic mountain range that rises high above the Snake River and a series of pristine lakes created by glacial moraines. East of Yellowstone is Cody, founded by William F. "Buffalo Bill" Cody himself in the late 19C.
The Snake River Valley runs west from Yellowstone through southern Idaho, and here, too, are a plethora of worthy stops, including the classic resort facilities of Sun Valley and the roof-of-the-world scenery of Sawtooth National Recreation Area.

ADDRESSES

🛏 STAY

The many famous hotels and lodges inside Yellowstone park, such as Old Faithful Inn and the Lake Yellowstone Hotel, as well as a half-dozen others, are operated by park concessioner Xanterra Parks & Resorts. Reservations at all are highly advisable months in advance; call ☎866-439-7375 or visit www. yellowstonenationalparklodges.com.

$$$$$ Amangani – 1535 North East Butte Rd., Jackson, WY. ☎307-734-7333. www.amanresorts.com. 40 suites. Often rated the best hotel in North America, this outpost of Asia's deluxe Aman chain perches atop a ridge facing the Tetons. Room decor is an imposing mix of native stone and wood, the famous pool overlooks the valley, and the nonpareil service is flawless,

$$$$$ Jenny Lake Lodge – Grand Teton National Park, Moran, WY. ☎307-733-4647. www.gtlc.com. Closed Oct–late May. 37 rooms. Secluded log cabins surround the main lodge, where guests gather in front of a stone fireplace or relax in rockers on the porch. Visitors to this former dude ranch are unburdened by phones, radios or TVs as they repose beneath country-quilt bedspreads. A

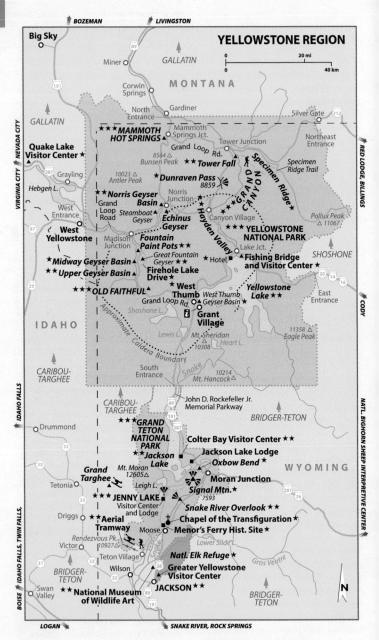

formal five-course meal is included in the rate.

Also in Grand Teton National Park are the **Jackson Lake Lodge** (**$$$**) and **Colter Bay Village** (**$$**).

$$$$ Spring Creek Ranch – 1800 Spirit Dance Rd., Jackson, WY. ✆307-733-8833. www.springcreekranch.com.

125 rooms. Views of the Teton Range are spectacular from this sprawling 1,000-acre ranch-resort atop East Gros Ventre Butte in the heart of Jackson Hole. Horseback riding, tennis and the gourmet **Granary** (**$$$**) restaurant tempt guests, whose lodgings come with pine furniture and stone fireplaces.

$$$$ Sun Valley Lodge – 1 Sun Valley Rd., Sun Valley, ID. ☎208-622-2001. www.sunvalley.com. 148 rooms. The Union Pacific Railroad opened this majestic hotel in 1936, enabling East Coast society to "rough it" in style alongside Hollywood stars. The oak-paneled lodge still attracts well-heeled visitors to ski and golf. **The Lodge Dining Room ($$$)** serves jazz and regional cuisine, while **Gretchen's ($$)** caters to families. Sun Valley Resort has a total of 510 rooms among the lodge, Tyrolean-style **Sun Valley Inn ($$$)** and condo units.

$$$$ Rainbow Ranch Lodge – 42950 Gallatin Rd., Gallatin Gateway, MT. ☎406-995-4132. www.rainbowranch bigsky.com. 21 rooms. Originally a frontier cattle ranch, then a roadhouse for early Yellowstone visitors, Rainbow Ranch has evolved into a newly spiffy, deluxe retreat in the Gallatin River Valley. Many of its elegant log-lodge rooms and suites are furnished with handmade lodgepole pine beds. Activities range from hiking and fishing to mountain biking.

$$$ The Wort Hotel – 50 N. Glenwood St., Jackson, WY. ☎307-733-2067. www. worthotel.com. 59 rooms. Earth tones and Southwestern flourishes embellish the background of wood and leather at this heritage property in the heart of downtown. The Swiss-style hotel, opened in 1941, is famous for its Silver Dollar Bar, an S-curve embedded with 2,032 uncirculated 1921 silver dollars.

$$ The Irma Hotel – 1192 Sheridan Ave., Cody, WY. ☎307-587-4221. www. irmahotel.com. 40 rooms. Cody's founder and namesake, Buffalo Bill, built this basic Victorian, full of tales and personalities, and named it for his daughter in 1902. The cherry-wood bar was a present from Queen Victoria. Mock gunfights are staged in the street outside each summer evening.

$$ Voss Inn – 319 S. Willson St., Bozeman, MT. ☎406-587-0982. www.bozeman-vossinn.com. 6 rooms. An English perennial garden and Victorian rose garden surround this charming 1883 bed-and-breakfast mansion, situated between downtown Bozeman and Montana State University.

©iStockphoto.com/ Steve Geer

Old Faithful

All rooms have private baths, and are furnished with antiques.

$ The Hostel – 3315 Village Drive, Teton Village, WY. ☎307-733-3415. www. thehostel.us. 54 rooms. "Low end" by ski-resort standards, this bunkhouse—12mi from Jackson at the foot of Rendezvous Peak—has a sense of style. Though rooms are basic, all have one king or four bunk beds, and private baths. There's a fireplace in the guest lounge, a laundry and a game room.

⑂ EAT

$$$ Gun Barrel Steak & Game House – 862 W. Broadway, Jackson, WY. ☎307-733-3287. www.gunbarrel.com. **Regional**. This warehouse once was a wildlife museum, but now the game is saved for the plate. Velvet elk with sun-dried tomatoes and three different cuts of bison head a menu heavy on steaks and game. Double Barrel home brew tempts bar patrons.

$$$ Lake Hotel Dining Room – Yellowstone National Park, WY. ☎307-344-7311. www.yellowstone nationalparklodges.com. Closed early Oct–mid May. **Creative American**. The park's oldest inn may offer its best dining experience. Beyond the sunroom of the bright, wicker-furnished 1891 hotel is the spacious dining room. Hungry park explorers enjoy breakfast buffets, creative lunches (blackened salmon wrap, Montrachet spinach salad) and gourmet steak-and-seafood dinners. After a meal, a stroll along the Yellowstone Lake is in order.

Yellowstone National Park★★★

The earth is a living force in Yellowstone, its dynamic natural features laid bare. Set aside primarily for its geological features—the brilliant, multicolored hot pools and lively geysers, and the dramatic Grand Canyon of the Yellowstone—the park serves as a haven for wildlife, a role of equal importance. This vast wilderness is one of the last remaining strongholds of the grizzly bear; in recent years it has gained additional attention with the reintroduction of wolves into its ecosystem. While visitors can count on Old Faithful to erupt regularly, their chance encounters with the park's large mammals are most endearing—and enduring.

- **Michelin Map:** p 340. Mountain Standard Time.
- **Info:** ℰ 307-344-7381; www.nps.gov/yell.
- **Location:** Though Yellowstone remains a remote part of the West, scheduled air service reaches Jackson, Idaho Falls, Billings and Bozeman, all within a few hours' drive of the park.
- **Parking:** The most important parking consideration in Yellowstone is where not to park: not in the roadway, as so many hapless tourists do during the "gawker blocks" that form when animals are near the road. Please pull to the side!
- **Don't Miss:** Hayden Valley, Grand Canyon of the Yellowstone.
- **Timing:** A sketchy Yellowstone visit is possible in one day, starting on the west side at Old Faithful before crowds arrive, then circling around to the east. But an entire week can also be devoted to the park, with hikes and side trips.
- **Kids:** Fountain Paint Pots.

GEOLOGICAL NOTES

Located on a high plateau bisected by the Continental Divide and bounded to the north, east and south by mountains, Yellowstone occupies the northwest corner of the state of Wyoming, with small portions spilling over into adjacent Montana and Idaho. Five highways (from west, north, northeast, east and south) provide access to its main Grand Loop Road, which dissects the forested landscape in a large figure eight between the principal scenic attractions. Yellowstone boasts more than 10,000 thermal features, the result of a rare, migrating hot spot in the earth's crust that originated near the southern border of Oregon and Idaho, 300mi to the southwest, about 17 million years ago.

The lava flows of the Snake River Plain trace the "movement" of this hot spot as the continental plate slides southwesterly above the source of heat, a stationary magma plume only 1-3mi beneath the earth's surface. The Yellowstone Caldera was created 600,000 years ago by a volcanic blast dwarfing that of Mount St. Helens in 1980.

A BIT OF HISTORY

Nomadic tribes hunted here for thousands of years, but few, chiefly Shoshone bands called "Sheep eaters," lived in the Yellowstone basin, out of respect for spirits they believed spoke through the rumblings of the earth. They named the canyon Mi-tse-a-da-zi, "Rock Yellow River." The first white man to explore the area was probably John Colter, who left the Lewis and Clark party in 1806 to spend several months trapping. His descriptions of Yellowstone's wonders fell on deaf ears back East, where they were considered just tall tales.

Grand Canyon of the Yellowstone

©iStockphoto.com/Aimin Tang

Generations and rumors came and went before the 1870 Washburn-Langford-Doane party braved the wilds to finally separate fiction from fact. Stunned to discover the awesome truth, this party convinced the US Geological Survey to investigate.

In June 1871, Survey director Ferdinand Hayden explored Yellowstone with 34 men, including painter Thomas Moran and photographer William Henry Jackson; in 1872, armed with Hayden's 500-page report and Moran's and Jackson's visuals, Congress proclaimed this the world's first national park.

Tourists weren't far behind, especially when a rail link from Livingston, Montana, to Gardiner eased access. The park's early civilian administrators couldn't handle the poaching and vandalism, so the US Army took over. From 1886 to 1918, 400 soldiers were stationed at Mammoth Hot Springs, enforcing park regulations and guarding scenic attractions.

Massive fires burned almost 800,000 acres in 1988, but the forest is recovering from the conflagration naturally. Today the Yellowstone Association (✆406-848-2400; www.yellowstoneassociation.org) offers naturalist-led hikes and other activities in Yellowstone's fascinating backcountry. The Park Service offers a full range of activities as well.

SIGHTS

Park roads are generally open to motor vehicles May–Oct, and for over-snow vehicles mid-Dec–Mar. Snow may fall at any park elevation any time of year. The following attractions are best seen by driving Yellowstone's 172mi **Grand Loop Road** in a clockwise direction around the park, beginning and ending at any of the five park entrances. The greatest traffic comes through the West Entrance in West Yellowstone, Montana, gateway for this tour.

Afire with Controversy

Just as the earth beneath the surface of Yellowstone Lake seethes, public policy controversies embroil Yellowstone National Park management. Area ranchers believe that wolves (reintroduced in 1995) and bison leaving the park hunt lambs and calves, or carry disease, and should be shot. And environmental activists want to shut down the wintertime snowmobile tours that roar into the park, as they produce both noise and air pollution. These controversies have boiled for years, and continue unabated.

Norris Geyser Basin★★

Left (west) off the Grand Loop Road at Norris Junction, 14mi north of Madison Junction, then .25mi to parking 🅿.

The oldest and hottest thermal area in the park is also its most dynamic. The major geysers are in **Back Basin★**, where thermal features are scattered among trees. **Steamboat Geyser** is the world's tallest active geyser. Its rare major eruptions (it is dormant for years at a time) can reach heights of 400ft. **Echinus Geyser**, the largest acid-water geyser, used to erupt every 40-80min- but in recent times can sometimes go for months without activity.

Just north of the Norris Basin, on the east side of the Grand Loop Road, the **Museum of the National Park Ranger** hosts exhibits on the ranger profession, in a historic early-20C army outpost.

Mammoth Hot Springs★★★

North Entrance & Grand Loop Rds. ♿🅿.

Change, constant throughout Yellowstone, is most obvious at Mammoth. Each day, two tons of travertine are deposited by the relatively cool (170ºF) hot springs. The water mixes with carbon dioxide to form carbonic acid, which dissolves underlying limestone to produce the travertine, similar to that found in limestone caves. As this solution reaches the surface, it cools rapidly and releases carbon dioxide, leaving behind deposits of calcium carbonate. Brilliant color is added to this three-dimensional "canvas" by algae and tiny living bacteria.

Elevated boardwalks climb and descend the ornate flows of the Main Terrace and the **Minerva Springs★★★**. Impressive from a distance, this formation is truly remarkable when viewed up close, where the elaborate collection of minute cascades and multicolored terraces resemble a still photo of a waterfall.

The most visibly active feature is **Opal Terrace★★**, which sprang to life in 1926 after years of dormancy. Popular with elk, which recline here like living sculptures, it is growing rapidly. A couple of hundred yards north, the distinctive **Liberty Cap★** juts from the earth like a massive Christmas tree. This extinct hot-spring cone was named for its resemblance to the hats worn by colonial patriots.

Perched on a hillside with multicolored terraces above, Mammoth is the park's command post. Headquarters are located in the complex's historic buildings. The green lawns and orderly appearance recall Mammoth's early history as an army post. Mammoth's red-roofed buildings, many of stone, were built as part of Fort Yellowstone in the 1890s and early 1900s. Today they shelter administration, staff housing and the **Albright Visitor Center★★** (📞307-344-2263). The center's exhibits trace the human and natural history of the park, highlighting Thomas Moran paintings and William Henry Jackson photographs from the 1871 Hayden expedition.

The facility also serves as the primary Yellowstone information center and backcountry permit office.

The most interesting aspect of the 1937 **Mammoth Hot Springs Hotel** (📞307-344-7311, www.yellowstonenational-parklodges.com) is a US map, assembled on a wall like a large puzzle, the states carefully cut from 15 different woods of nine countries.

Specimen Ridge★

Access by trail 2.5mi east of Tower Junction, 19mi east of Mammoth Hot Springs. 🅿.

This 8,442ft crest and 40sq mi of surrounding uplands constitute the largest petrified forest in the world. Remnants of more than 100 different plants, including redwoods similar to those of California, are found here. Ash and mudflows buried the trees 50 million years ago; erosion reversed the process.

Tower Fall★★

2mi south of Tower Junction. 🅿.

This impressive waterfall squeezes between namesake stone "towers" and plunges 132ft to join the Grand Canyon of the Yellowstone at its narrowest point. A steep **trail** (.5mi) descends 300ft to the base of the fall.

Geysers

Geysers are created by constrictions in the subterranean plumbing of a hot spring. Steam bubbles, like commuters at rush hour, create immense pressure as they force their way through the water above them, erupting with even more superheated water and steam from the depths.

About 300 of the world's geysers (about two-thirds of the global total) are located in Yellowstone. "So numerous are they and varied," wrote naturalist John Muir, "nature seems to have gathered them from all over the world as specimens of her rarest fountains to show in one place what she can do."

The dramatic **gorge★★** is best viewed from a turnout at **Calcite Springs**, from which basaltic columns may be seen rimming the 500ft bluffs beneath which the river flows.

Dunraven Pass★

14mi south of Tower Junction. High point of the Grand Loop Road, 8,859ft. Dunraven Pass offers the park's best perspective on the contours of the ancient Yellowstone Caldera, along with spectacular **views★★** of the Absaroka and Beartooth ranges to the east. Looming over the pass is 10,243ft **Mount Washburn**.

Grand Canyon of the Yellowstone★★★

Canyon Village, 19mi south of Tower Junction. △&🅿.
After Old Faithful, this magnificent canyon is probably the park's best-known feature, roughly 20mi long, 800-1,200ft deep and 1,500-4,000ft wide. The brilliant color of its rhyolite rock is due to iron compounds "cooked" by hydrothermal activity. Weathering oxidation of the iron produced the yellow, orange, red and brown colors. At the end of the last Ice Age, scientists believe ice dams formed at the mouth of Yellowstone Lake. When breached, they released tremendous amounts of water, carving the canyon.

The one-way loop **Inspiration Point Road** visits several canyon viewpoints. **Lookout Point** offers a classic view of the 308ft **Lower Fall★★**—most impressive in spring, when 63,500gal of water cross its crest each second. A little far-ther west, a trail leads to the brink of the 109ft **Upper Fall★**, where a railing is all that separates viewers from the surging water. Upstream, a 2.5mi spur road crosses the Yellowstone River to the South Rim. **Artist's Point★★** offers perhaps the best views of the canyon and Lower Fall.

Hayden Valley★★

5–10mi south of Canyon Village. 🅿.
A placid contrast to the dramatic canyon, this lush valley of meadow and marsh is the best place to observe wildlife. Hayden Valley is home to large herds of bison, plus moose and elk, and in spring is a good place to catch a glimpse of grizzly bears. Coming across even a portion of the bison herd is as close as one can come to viewing life in the West before European settlement. Bears are often seen in spring and early summer, when they feed on newborn bison and elk calves.

In summer, traffic backs up for miles when bison decide to cross the road. Turnouts, situated in key positions for viewing, may be occupied by a ranger with a spotting scope happily shared with visitors.

Fishing Bridge

East Entrance & Grand Loop Rds. 🅿.
Until 1973, fishermen stood shoulder-to-shoulder here, angling for abundant cutthroat trout. Fishing was terminated to protect fish spawning and to allow grizzly bears to forage unmolested. **Fishing Bridge Visitor Center★** (✆307-242-2450) has fine exhibits of the birds of the national park.

Travertine formation at Mammoth Hot Springs

© Gwen Cannon/Michelin

Yellowstone Lake★★

⚠️ ♿ 🅿️.

At 7,733ft altitude, the largest natural high-elevation lake in North America has 136sq mi of surface area, 110mi of shoreline and depths of nearly 400ft. Although the surface is frozen half the year, lake-bottom vents produce water as hot as 252°F. The Yellowstone River flows into the lake from the southeast, and exits at Fishing Bridge through the Grand Canyon of the Yellowstone, continuing 671mi to its confluence with the Missouri River. It is the longest river still undammed in the lower 48 states.

The stately, three-story **Lake Yellowstone Hotel★** (1.5mi south of Fishing Bridge; ✆307-344-7311, www.yellowstonenationalparklodges.com) faces eastward on the lakeshore. Yellow clapboard with white trim, it was built in 1891; the exterior received its first major facelift in 1903 when architect Robert Reamer added Ionic columns and 15 false balconies; it was extensively renovated in 2013.

At **Bridge Bay** (3mi south of Fishing Bridge), a marina offers 90min boat tours and supplies anglers.

West Thumb★

♿ 🅿️.

This small collapsed caldera within the big Yellowstone Caldera includes the **West Thumb Geyser Basin★** on its western shore. It extends beneath Yellowstone Lake where hot springs and even underwater geysers mix their boiling contents with the frigid lake water. A boardwalk winds through the shoreline thermal features, among which are 53ft-deep, cobalt-blue **Abyss Pool★**, and **Fishing Cone Geyser★**.

Grant Village

2mi south of West Thumb. ♿ 🅿️.

Named to honor US President Ulysses S. Grant, who signed the legislation that created Yellowstone in 1872, this full-service park community includes the **Grant Village Visitor Center★** (✆307-242-2650). Exhibits and a 20min film explain the natural benefits of wild fires, such as the conflagration that engulfed the park in 1988.

👥 Old Faithful★★★

18mi northwest of West Thumb & 16mi south of Madison Junction. ♿ 🅿️.

The world's most famous geyser has been spouting with uncanny regularity since it was discovered by the Washburn-Langford-Doane party in 1870. Averaging 135ft in height when it erupts, sometimes reaching 180ft, Old Faithful puts on a show approximately every 65- to 91min. Eruptions last 90sec to 5min and spew between 3,700gal and 8,400gal of boiling water (call ✆307-545-2751 for real-time eruption predictions or check at the Old Faithful Visitor Education Center).

A semicircular boardwalk with benches surrounds the geyser. During the high season of July and August, thousands of people wait patiently for an eruption, then scurry to other activities, creating a phenomenon locals refer to as a "gush rush." Restaurants fill immediately after an eruption and clear out just before.

The village flanking Old Faithful is the park's most commercial, with massive parking lots and numerous buildings facing the geyser. Chief among them is **Old Faithful Inn★★** (✆307-344-7311; www.yellowstonenationalparklodges. com), likely the world's largest log building. This National Historic Landmark was designed by Robert Reamer and constructed in 1903-04. It is the definitive structure of "parkitecture"—seven stories high, its massive lobby featuring whole log columns, a stone fireplace and tortured lodgepole-pine railings. **Old Faithful Lodge** (✆307-344-7311; www.yellowstonenationalparklodges. com), another large log-and-stone building, was completed in 1928; it functions as a gathering place, and accommodations are provided in surrounding cabins.

The large plate-glass windows of the **Old Faithful Visitor Education Center** (✆307-344-7381) enable visitors to watch Old Faithful erupt without leaving the building.

Upper Geyser Basin★★
&.🅿.

Surrounding Old Faithful is the world's largest concentration of geysers. Among the better known are **Grand Geyser★**, which unleashes a 200ft fountain every 7-15hrs; **Riverside Geyser★**, whose stream spurts up to 80ft over the Firehole River at 5-6hr intervals; and **Castle Geyser★**, which explodes to 90ft twice daily from an ancient 12ft cone. Because no organism can survive in water 161°F or warmer (at this altitude), the Upper Geyser Basin's hottest pools typically reflect the color of the sky. The best-known spring, **Morning Glory Pool★★**, is not as blue as it once was, however: Its hot-water vent has been clogged by coins and other objects thrown into the pool by park visitors, leading to a gradual cooling.

Midway Geyser Basin★
6mi north of Old Faithful. 🅿.

Mist from the wide **Excelsior Geyser** envelops visitors who cross the footbridge and climb past a multicolored bank of the Firehole River. Runoff from acidic **Grand Prismatic Spring★★** has created terraced algae mats, often decorated with hoof prints from bison. Wooden walkways allow visitors to closely approach the waters. At 370ft across and 120ft deep, rainbow colored Grand Prismatic is the second-largest hot spring in the world.

Firehole Lake Drive★
8mi north of Old Faithful. 🅿.

A quiet 3mi, one-way circuit east of the Grand Loop Road, this route winds past **Great Fountain Geyser★★**, the White Dome and Pink Cone geysers, and **Firehole Lake**, with runoff in every direction. Between Great Fountain's 45-60min eruptions at intervals of 8-12hrs, the still water of its broad, circular pool mirrors the sky in myriad terraces. Firehole Lake's thermal waters flow through the forest here, giving trees a skeletal appearance of stark white stockings and gray trunks. The absorption of sinter (dissolved minerals) kills the trees but acts as a preservative, delaying their decay.

🏊 Fountain Paint Pots★★
9mi north of Old Faithful. &.🅿.

Visitors may view all four types of Yellowstone thermal features on a short tour of this area. A boardwalk leads past colorful bacterial and algae mats, hot pools and the namesake bubbling "paint pots." Adults, as well as children, revel in the implied messiness, oozing and rotten-egg stench of the spring's hydrogen sulfide gas. The perpetually active **Clepsydra Geyser★** is especially scenic in winter, when bison wander in front of its plume of steam.

Grand Teton National Park★★★

The Teton Range rises dramatically above a broad valley near the headwaters of the Snake River, immediately south of Yellowstone National Park. Cresting atop 13,770ft Grand Teton, the Tetons, which extend about 40mi from south to north, are the highlight of the park—485sq mi of rugged peaks, alpine lakes, streams, marshland and sage-and-aspen plains.

- ♿ **Michelin Map:** p 340. Mountain Standard Time.
- 🚹 **Info:** ☎307-739-3300; www.nps.gov/grte.
- ▶ **Location:** Except for experienced wilderness travelers, the Tetons themselves are experienced through vistas from highways that parallel the range on the east and west sides.
- 🅿 **Parking:** As in Yellowstone, please don't park in the roadway to watch wildlife.

GEOLOGICAL NOTES

The Tetons are the result of a continuing cycle of mountain building and erosion. Geologic youngsters at 5 to 9 million years, they are still growing along a north-south fault line.

As the valley floor—once a flat layer of sediment left by an ancient inland sea—has subsided, the blocks of rock that form the Tetons have risen, tilting westward. Erosion has shaved soft sandstone from the caps of the peaks, gradually filling the valley several miles deep with sediment.

The high peaks attract significant precipitation, especially as snow in winter. As snowfall rates exceed melting, glaciers form, chiseling singular peaks like the Grand Teton. Twelve active glaciers—most retreating, as with other North American glaciers—surround lie on several of the peaks, especially the Grand Teton and 12,605ft **Mount Moran**. Glacial debris, deposited at the base of the mountains, has formed lateral and terminal moraines that act as natural dams, capturing melt-water to form lakes.

A BIT OF HISTORY

Known to Native Americans as *Teewinot*, "many pinnacles," the Tetons' modern name came from early-19C French trappers, who saw them as *Les Trois Tétons*,

Laurance S. Rockefeller Preserve

© Gwen Cannon/Michelin

"the three breasts," as they approached from the west.

Although Native Americans used Jackson Hole as a summer hunting ground for thousands of years, few chose to endure the harsh winters. Hardy cattle ranchers were gradually supplanted by tourism following the establishment of Yellowstone Park in 1872.

Grand Teton's transition to national park was not smooth. Early settlers proved as stubborn as the winter weather when it came to turning the land over to federal jurisdiction. Fearing development, philanthropist John D. Rockefeller Jr. secretly bought up ranchland and deeded it to the government. The original 1929 park boundaries expanded to their present margins in 1950. The **John D. Rockefeller Jr. Memorial Parkway**, a corridor linking Grand Teton and Yellowstone parks, was created in 1972. The Laurance S. Rockefeller Preserve Center explains the philanthropic family's vision for preservation of the area (4mi south of Moose, WY, on Moose-Wilson Rd.).

SIGHTS

Park headquarters are adjacent to the **Craig Thomas Discovery & Visitor Center** (in Moose, Teton Park Rd., 0.5mi west of Teton Junction & 12mi north of Jackson, WY; 307-739-3399), at the southern end of the park. A driving tour from here is best done in a counterclockwise direction, heading northeast along the Snake River to Jackson Lake, returning south at the foot of the mountain range. The center was structured with eco-friendliness in mind, incorporating recycled glass tiles and high efficiency cooling and electrical systems. Though the park is open year-round, only the Thomas Center is open in winter.

Snake River Overlook★★

US-26/89/191, 8mi north of Moose Junction. ♿ P.

Immortalized by photographer Ansel Adams, this is the most popular vista point in the park. Adams created a definitive black-and-white image of the

ragged Tetons with the silvery Snake River in the foreground.

Oxbow Bend★

US-89/191/287, 4mi northwest of Moran Junction. ♿ P.

The Snake River almost doubles back on itself at this bulbous elbow. This is one of the most dependable spots in the park to spy moose, which often feed in the shallows.

Jackson Lake★★

△✕♿ P.

The largest of seven natural morainal lakes in the park, 438ft-deep Jackson Lake—16mi long and 8mi wide—was enlarged by a succession of dams at its Snake River outlet that raised the lake 39ft. **Boat tours** (*90min*) are offered daily in summer.

Jackson Lake Lodge

US-89/191/287, 6mi northwest of Moran Junction. △✕♿ P. 307-543-3100. www.gtlc.com.

Designed by Gilbert Stanley Underwood, architect of the Ahwahnee Hotel in California's Yosemite National Park, this concrete, steel and glass structure was built above the beaver ponds of Willow Flats. The lobby features massive, 60ft-tall picture windows framing a classic view of the Tetons.

👥 Colter Bay Visitor Center★★

1mi west of US-89/191/287, 11mi northwest of Moran Junction. △✕♿ P 307-739-3594. Open summer only.

Newly renovated in 2012, the center offers a splendid view of Mount Moran, and displays 35 items from the famous Vernon Indian Arts collection—beadwork, weaponry, moccasins, shields and pipes—widely considered one of the best in the US.

Signal Mountain★

Off Teton Park Rd., 16mi north of Moose Junction & 5mi south of Jackson Lake Lodge. ♿ P.

Rising above lakefront resort **Signal Mountain Lodge** (Teton Park Rd.;

Grand Teton Mountains, near Jackson

📞 307-543-2831) on the east side of Jackson Lake, 7,593ft Signal Mountain provides great **views**★★ of the Tetons and Jackson Hole. The **Signal Mountain Summit Road** is a narrow, winding, 5mi, 800ft climb with few turnouts.

Jenny Lake Scenic Drive★★★

Off Teton Park Rd., beginning 11.5mi north of Moose Junction. ♿🅿.
This 4mi loop weaves along the eastern shore of gem-like **Jenny Lake**★★★ before reconnecting with Teton Park Road. En route are numerous impressive views of the high Tetons.

From the **Cathedral Group Turnout**★, the peaks crowd together like church steeples.

Little **String Lake** ties Jenny Lake to more northerly **Leigh Lake**. Beyond here, the two-way road becomes a narrow, one-way southerly drive. A cluster of 37 log cabins surrounds **Jenny Lake Lodge** (📞307-733-4647, www.gtlc. com), the park's premier accommodation.

From the **Jenny Lake Overlook**★★, lake waters reflect the Tetons rising abruptly from the water's edge. The **Jenny Lake Visitor Center** at South Jenny Lake has a set of geology exhibits.

Menor's Ferry Historic Site★

Teton Park Rd., 1.5mi north of Moose Junction. ♿🅿.
An interpretive trail (.5mi) leads to a replica of a flat-bottomed ferry that Bill Menor operated from 1894 to 1927. Interpreters reenact the Snake River crossing in summer. Menor's white log cabin is decorated as the country store he also ran from the home.

Chapel of the Transfiguration★

0.5mi east of Teton Park Rd., 1.5mi north of Moose Junction. ♿🅿.
The window behind the altar of this rustic little chapel, built in 1925, frames the Tetons. Services are offered summer Sundays.

Moose-Wilson Road★

Craig Thomas Visitor Center to Rte. 22 (1.6mi east of Wilson). ♿🅿.
This scenic drive to the small community of Wilson, at the base of Teton Pass, skirts groves of aspens and a network of willow-clogged beaver ponds. Moose are often spotted from **Sawmill Ponds Overlook**. The road—all but about 2mi of it paved—accesses several popular trailheads, especially to emerald **Phelps Lake** (*2mi*).

Jackson ★★

The resort town of Jackson sits at 6,350ft altitude near the south end of the 45mi-long valley known as Jackson Hole, between the Tetons and the Gros Ventre Mountains. The town's economy has shifted from cattle ranching in favor of tourism and outdoor recreation; it is now a year-round paradise both for wildlife and the wild life. River rafting, fishing, hiking, horseback riding and mountain climbing are among its offerings, and in winter, Jackson is one of the finest ski destinations in the world. Three ski areas, famed for light and ample powder snow, are a short drive away; the **Jackson Hole Mountain Resort★★** (Rte. 390, Teton Village, 12mi west of Jackson; ℰ307-733-2292; www.jacksonhole.com) **has the greatest vertical (4,139ft) of any US ski area, and a 100-passenger tram that whisks skiers (and summer visitors) to the top.**

JACKSON TODAY

Jackson is crowded with fine restaurants, high-end Western-wear boutiques and fine-art galleries, and its proliferation of modern resort developments has attracted many wealthy part-time residents. But it has retained a firm grip on its Western heritage.
Town Square (Broadway & Cache Dr.) is the hub of this community of 9.400. An arch of elk antlers frames each of its four corners—a tiny fraction of what is collected each winter on the National Elk Refuge. Prior to 1957, the antlers were offered as souvenirs. Today they are auctioned by Boy Scouts in mid May during Elkfest (www.elkfest.org). Of the $100,000 typically raised, 80 percent goes to augment the elk-feeding program at the refuge.
On summer nights at Town Square, actors re-create a stagecoach robbery and **♟♟ Jackson Hole Shootout**—even though no such incident ever took place in Jackson.

- ◉ **Michelin Map:** p 340. Mountain Standard Time.
- ▤ **Info:** ℰ307-733-3316; www.jacksonholechamber.com.
- ◍ **Don't Miss:** National Museum of Wildlife Art.
- ◉ **Also See:** Teton Village Aerial Tram.

Facing the Square is the **Million Dollar Cowboy Bar** (25 N. Cache St.; ℰ307-733-2207; www.milliondollarcowboybar.com), with saddles for stools and silver dollars inlaid into its bar.

SIGHTS

Jackson Hole and Greater Yellowstone Visitor Center

532 N. Cache St. ♿ ℙ ℰ307-733-9212. www.fs.fed.us/jhgyvc.
This contemporary sod-roofed building, an interagency visitor center, features a platform with spotting scopes for viewing the adjacent elk refuge and marsh, and interpretive exhibits on fire management and wildlife migration.

National Elk Refuge ★

Elk Refuge Rd. off E. Broadway. ℰ307-733-9212. www.fws.gov/nationalelkrefuge.
Between 7,000 and 9,000 elk spend their winters in this 24,700-acre refuge after migrating from higher elevations in the national parks and Bridger-Teton National Forest. The refuge was established after cattle ranching and development disrupted normal migration patterns.
♟♟ **Sled tours★★** (45min) are offered daily in winter. Draft horses pull sleighs to herds, where most animals graze sedately—although bull elk may joust with their immense racks. The refuge also provides winter range for bison, bighorn sheep, coyotes, deer, wolves and, occasionally, pronghorn antelope and mountain lions. Tickets are sold by the National Museum of Wildlife Art (below).

Each spring, local Boy Scouts patrol the refuge to gather the antlers shed by bull elk the previous fall, which are sold at a famous auction.

👥 National Museum of Wildlife Art★★

2820 Rungius Rd., off US-89, 2.5mi north of Jackson. ✕&🅿 𝒫307-733-5771. www.wildlifeart.org.

Tucked into a hillside overlooking the National Elk Refuge, this sandstone complex (1994) resembles Ancestral Puebloan ruins, and is the most extensive facility of its kind in North America. Covering five centuries, the expansive collection of more than 5,000 works includes John J. Audubon, Robert Bateman, Albert Bierstadt, George Catlin, John Clymer and Charles M. Russell. The **American Bison Collection★** features 18C to 20C works exploring man's relationship with buffalo. Also featured is the largest body of work in the US by wildlife artist Carl Rungius (1869-1959).

Teton Village Aerial Tramway★★

Rte. 390, Teton Village. &🅿 𝒫307-733-2292. www.jacksonhole.com.

A gondola whisks sightseers skyward on a brisk ride, climbing over 4,000ft in 12min to the 10,450ft ridge of Rendezvous Peak at the Jackson Hole Ski Area. Spread to the east is Jackson Hole, bisected by the Snake River.

Many hikers descend Rendezvous Peak on foot via the steep 10mi **Granite Canyon Trail** through Grand Teton National Park, which has campgrounds open from May to September.

EXCURSIONS

Grand Targhee Resort

⬦ 3300 E. Ski Hill Rd., Alta, 5mi east of Driggs, Idaho, & 32mi northwest of Jackson via Rtes. 22 & 33. ✕🅿 𝒫307-353-2300. www.grandtarghee.com.

Nearly 40ft of light, dry snow falls on the "back side" of the Teton Range each winter, making this a mecca for powder hounds. In summer, music festivals and ecology classes complement outdoor recreation and scenic chairlift rides.

National Bighorn Sheep Interpretive Center★★

⬦ 907 W. Ramshorn St., Dubois, 85mi east of Jackson via US-26/287. &🅿 𝒫307-455-3429. www.bighorn.org.

Visitors here may "manage" a herd of wild sheep, balancing reproduction rates, expected mortality and forage requirements with management techniques including hunting, culling the herd and non-intervention.

Nearby **Whiskey Mountain** is home to the largest wintering herd of Rocky Mountain bighorn sheep in the US, with more than 1,000 animals.

Stagecoach rides in Jackson

© Gwen Cannon/Michelin

Cody★★

William F. "Buffalo Bill" Cody
founded this town as his own in
1896, two decades after he first
scouted the region. Cody envisioned
a place where the Old and New
West could meet; this site, 50mi
east of Yellowstone National Park,
was ideal. Cody poured the profits
from his popular Wild West Show
into the town's growth. By 1901, rail
service was established; by 1905,
construction was under way on the
ambitious Shoshone (now Buffalo
Bill) Dam.

- ⓘ **Michelin Map:** 493 G 6.
  Mountain Standard Time.
- **Info:** ✆307-587-2777;
  www.codychamber.org.
- **Don't Miss:** Buffalo Bill
  Historical Center.
- **Kids:** Cody Nite Rodeo.
- **Also See:** Hot Springs
  State Park.

CODY TODAY

Tourism remains the major industry of
the town, whose population now stands
at 9,600. Yellowstone-bound guests still
drive the economy.

The **Cody Country Chamber of Commerce** (836 Sheridan Ave.; ✆307-587-2777) has information on walking tours
of the historic town, including **The Irma**
(1192 Sheridan Ave.; ✆307-587-4221;
www.irmahotel.com). This 1902 hotel,
built by Buffalo Bill and named for his
youngest daughter, features an ornate
cherry backbar hand-crafted in France
and shipped to Cody as a gift from
Queen Victoria of England.

The summer-long **Cody Nite Rodeo★**
(W. Yellowstone Hwy.; ✆307-587-5155; www.codynightrodeo.com)
is a lively introduction to the sport of
rodeo. Contestants vie in bronco and
bull riding, calf roping, bulldogging
and barrel racing; a highlight is the calf
scramble, in which children pursue a
calf with a yellow ribbon tied to its tail.

SIGHTS

Buffalo Bill Center of the West★★★

720 Sheridan Ave. ✆307-587-4771. www.bbhc.org.

Four internationally acclaimed galleries and a research library, occupying
three levels of this fan-shaped complex, explore aspects of the history of
the American West.

Also on the site is the boyhood home of
William F. "Buffalo Bill" Cody, shipped by
train from Iowa in 1933.

The **Whitney Western Art Museum★★**
presents a broad spectrum of paintings
and sculpture, including oils by Catlin,
Bierstadt and Russell, and bronzes by
Remington. The wing is named for
sculptor Gertrude V. Whitney, whose
dynamic *The Scout*, north of the complex, depicts a mounted William F. Cody.

The **Buffalo Bill Museum★★** chronicles
the storied life of "Buffalo Bill," man and
myth. Much of the collection focuses on
his Wild West Show and its relationship
to public perception of the West. Displays include firearms, clothing, silver-studded saddles, and film gathered
from Cody's private and public lives.

The **Plains Indian Museum★★** interprets the cultural history and artistry
of the Arapaho, Blackfoot, Cheyenne,
Comanche, Crow, Gros Ventre, Kiowa,
Pawnee, Shoshone and Sioux, incorporating modern oral tradition with historical and contemporary artifacts. The
new (2013) **Paul Dyck Plains Indian Buffalo Culture Gallery** presents a world-class collection of 80 pieces depicting
the long Native American association
with bison.

The **Cody Firearms Museum★**, which
traces the evolution of guns, is the
world's most comprehensive collection
of post-16C American and European
firearms—nearly 4,000 in all.

Exhibits in the **Draper Museum of Natural History★★** focus on the greater Yellowstone ecosystem and the relationship
between man and the natural world.

Old Trail Town★

1831 DeMaris Dr. off W. Yellowstone Hwy. Open mid May–mid Sept. 🅿
☎307-587-5302. http://oldtrailtown.org. More than 100 wagons and 25 buildings dated 1879-1901, moved from a 150mi radius, are arranged with memorabilia of the Wyoming frontier on the original surveyed site for Cody City.

EXCURSIONS

Bighorn Canyon National Recreation Area★★

◐ Via Rte. 37 northeast of Lovell. Visitor center on US-14A, Lovell, 48mi northeast of Cody. △✕&🅿 ☎406-666-2412. www.nps.gov/bica.

Bighorn Lake, a 60mi-long reservoir created by Montana's 525ft-high Yellowtail Dam, is wedged between 1,000ft cliffs. Flanking the recreation area on its west is the expansive **Pryor Mountain Wild Horse Range**, with 100 to 200 wild horses.

▲▲ Hot Springs State Park★

◐ US-20 & Park St., Thermopolis, 83mi southeast of Cody. △✕&🅿 ☎307-864-2176. http://wyoparks.state.wy.us.

Shoshone and Arapaho Indians sold these springs to Wyoming in 1896 with the stipulation that they remain free for public use.

Today 8,000 gallons of 135°F water flow daily from Monument Hill, piped through the center of two 20ft travertine terraces.

The free Wyoming State Bathhouse sits between two commercial facilities at the foot of the springs.

Montana Gateways★

Although less than eight percent of Yellowstone National Park is in Montana, three of its five entrances are in the "Big Sky" state. The West Yellowstone entrance is the busiest, capturing one-third of park visitors. Mammoth Hot Springs lies near Gardiner, at the north entrance. The magnificent northeastern-approach road climbs nearly to 11,000ft at Beartooth Pass.

- 🕑 **Michelin Map:** 493 F, G 5. Mountain Standard Time.
- ⃗ **Info:** ☎406-556-8680; www.yellowstonecountry.net.
- ⊚ **Don't Miss:** Beartooth Highway.
- ▲▲ **Kids:** Grizzly Discovery Center.

SIGHTS

West Yellowstone

US-20 & 287. △✕&🅿 ☎406-646-7701. destinationyellowstone.com.

The Union Pacific Railroad built a spur line to the park's border in 1907. Today this town has 1,200 year-round residents; in winter, it is a center for snowmobile touring, with hundreds of miles of groomed trails.

In the former Union Pacific Depot – designed in "park rustic" style by Gilbert Stanley Underwood—the **Yellowstone Historic Center Museum** (30 Yellowstone Ave.; ☎406-646-1100; www.yellowstonehistoriccenter.org) offers wildlife dioramas and a highly regarded display of Indian beadwork and quillwork.

▲▲ Grizzly & Wolf Discovery Center★★

201 S. Canyon St. &🅿 ☎406-646-7001. www.grizzlydiscoveryctr.org.

The habitats and lives of grizzly bears and gray wolves are the focus of this educational facility. Two packs totaling seven wolvesinhabit fenced enclosures. Nearby, nine grizzlies enjoy their own enclosure with two ponds and a flowing stream. An interpreter discusses behavior, from eating habits to intelligence and mating.

Quake Lake Visitor Center★

US-287, 25mi northwest of West Yellowstone. ✆406-823-6961. www.fs.usda.gov.

Just before midnight on August 17, 1959, a magnitude-7.5 earthquake triggered a landslide that buried 19 people at a Madison River campground and destroyed miles of highway. Soon the Madison was backing up behind a natural-earth dam, as cracks developed in the manmade dam at Hebgen Lake. The story of the tragedy, and of how a secondary disaster was averted, is told at this Forest Service visitor center. It is perched on a hillside overlooking the slide scar and natural dam; a quickly engineered spillway; and **Quake Lake**, 190ft deep and 6mi long.

Virginia City and Nevada City★★

Rte. 278, 84mi northwest of West Yellowstone. ⛺✕🅿 ✆406-843-5555. www.virginiacity.com.

These sister villages, 1.5mi apart in Alder Gulch, feature Wild West architecture embellished with vigilante legends. Both prospered during an 1863 gold rush; Virginia City survived to become the capital of the Montana Territory, while Nevada City became a ghost town.

Today **Nevada City★★** is a restored mining camp with more than 90 period buildings—some originals, some reconstructions, some moved from other sites. **Virginia City★★** is a living museum, the entire town listed on the National Register of Historic Places. The Main Street boardwalk is fringed with storefronts that display 19C wares.

Three Forks Area★

I-90, 28mi west of Bozeman. ⛺✕🅿.

Lewis and Clark named the three rivers that merge to form the Missouri—the Madison, Jefferson and Gallatin—for statesmen of their day.

The area's rich resources drew many Plains Indian nations, who accessed salt deposits and pursued nearby bison herds. **Missouri Headwaters State Park★** (Rte. 286, 5mi north of Three Forks; ✆406-285-3610; http://stateparks.mt.gov) marks the start of North America's longest river system, the Missouri–Mississippi.

👪 **Lewis and Clark Caverns State Park★★** (Rte. 2, 19mi west of Three Forks; ✆406-287-3541; http:// state parks.mt.gov) boasts 3-million-year-old stalactites and stalagmites as well as a colony of bats.

Bozeman★

Rte. 84 at I-90 Exit 309, 92mi north of West Yellowstone. ✕♿🅿 ✆406-586-5421; www.bozemanchamber.com.

Home to **Montana State University**, this town of 38,700 was named for wagonmaster John Bozeman. A railroad spur to West Yellowstone was completed in the early 20C.

Today, restaurants, bookshops, galleries and boutiques occupy the historic brick buildings on either side of Main Street, and nearby **Willson Avenue★** is lined with beautiful c.1900 homes.

👪 Museum of the Rockies★★

600 W. Kagy Blvd. ♿🅿 ✆406-994-2251. www.museumoftherockies.org.

Exhibits in this outstanding museum trace the geologic history of the Rockies. The **Siebel Dinosaur Complex★★**, showcases the prominent role played by Montana and Wyoming in modern paleontology, and displays one of the world's largest collections of dinosaur fossils. Moving models of the great lizards are popular with children.

The Taylor Planetarium features star and laser shows.

Outside, the Tinsley Homestead is the venue for living history demonstrations depicting an early Gallatin Valley farm.

Big Sky

Rte. 64, 3mi west of US-191, 45mi south of Bozeman & 47mi north of West Yellowstone. ⛺✕♿🅿 ✆406-995-5001; www.bigskyresort.com.

Developed by TV newsman Chet Hunt-ley (1911-1974), Big Sky is a summer-win-ter resort with 16 lifts that access 5,000 acres of ski terrain in winter. In summer, there is golf, horseback riding, biking and fishing; gondola rides go part way up 11,150ft Lone Peak and take in wide-ranging views.

Livingston

US-89 at I-90 Exit 332, 60mi north of Mammoth Hot Springs. △✕&🅿
𝒫406-222-0850; www.livingston-chamber.com.

Founded in 1882 by the Northern Pacific, Livingston was the point at which rail tourists boarded a spur line to Yellowstone National Park's north entrance. The town of 7,000 has pre-served 436 buildings from its heyday.

Red Lodge★

US-212, 115mi east of Mammoth Hot Springs. ✕&🅿 𝒫406-855-4796.
www.redlodge.com.

Red Lodge began as a coal town. After the mines died, tourism and skiing brought new life to the community of 2,400. Main Street is lined with brick buildings, most constructed around the turn of the 19C. Oldest is the 1893 **Pollard Hotel** (2 N. Broadway; 𝒫406-446-0001; www.thepollard.net), a National Historic Register site.

Beartooth Highway★★

US-212 from Red Lodge to Cooke City.
Open May–Oct depending on snow.
Former CBS correspondent Charles Kuralt called this 67mi route "the most beautiful road in America." Precipitous switchbacks climb from Red Lodge, ascending nearly 4,000ft in 5mi.
Views★★★ are spectacular from an overlook at 10,947ft **Beartooth Pass**; an interpretive trail is frequented as often by mountain goats as by humans. The broad summit plateau is carpeted with wildflowers in summer.

Billings

US-87 at I-90 Exit 450. ✕&🅿
𝒫406-245-4111. www.visitbillings.com.
Montana's largest city (107,000 people) spreads across a floodplain of the Yel-lowstone River. Its most compelling sight is the **Moss Mansion★** (914 Divi-sion St.; 𝒫406-256-5100; www.moss-mansion.com), a 1903 banker's home built by Henry Janeway Hardenbergh, architect of New York's Waldorf-Astoria Hotel. A castle-like 1901 Romanesque library houses the **Western Heritage Center** (2282 Montana Ave.; 𝒫406-256-6809; www.ywhc.org), a history museum. The **Yellowstone Art Museum** (401 N. 27th St.; 𝒫406-256-6804; www.artmuseum.org), built around the old county jail, features contemporary High Plains and Western art.

Snake River Valley★

Rising in Wyoming and flowing through Yellowstone and Grand Teton National Parks, the Snake River arcs across southern Idaho, carving deep canyons and nourishing rich agricultural lands. A series of dams have turned this high lava plain into productive land, supporting cities and towns of moderate size.

- 🕐 **Michelin Map:** 493 D, E, F 6.
  Mountain Standard Time.
- 🛈 **Info:** 𝒫208-334-2470;
  www.visitidaho.org.
- 📍 **Location:** In Idaho, the Snake River follows I-15 south to I-86, then parallels I-84 west through Twin Falls.
- 👁 **Don't Miss:** World Center for Birds of Prey.
- 👥 **Kids:** Bruneau Dunes State Park.

GEOLOGICAL NOTES

Once an inland sea that drained westward as the land mass uplifted, the region was covered by lava that oozed through faults to cloak the rich marine silt. To the south, great Lake Bonneville, 340mi long and 140mi wide, covered much of modern Utah and eastern Nevada. When the lake breached a volcanic plug 15,000 years ago, a flood of Biblical proportion raged for eight weeks at a volume three times that of the modern Amazon River, sweeping millions of tons of rocks and debris and carving the magnificent Snake River and Hells Canyons.

SIGHTS
Idaho Falls

US-20 & 26 at I-15 Exit 118, 90mi west of Jackson. ✕&🅿 ☏208-523-1010. www.idahofallschamber.com.

This agricultural center is the gateway to the **Idaho National Laboratory** (www.inl.gov). Spread across 890sq mi of lava rock are scores of nuclear reactors, the largest concentration on earth. Experimental Breeder Reactor 1 was the first in the US, having operated 1951-64; free tours of the facility, known as **EBR-I★** (Van Buren Blvd., Atomic City, 48mi west of Idaho Falls; ☏208-526-0050) are offered summers.

Nearby, in Pocatello, the new (2010) **Museum of Clean★**, brainchild of janitorial services magnate Don Aslett, is devoted to everything clean—sanitation, hygiene, health, lifestyle (711 S 2nd Ave.; ☏ 208-236-6906; www.museumofclean.com).

Twin Falls★

US-93, 6mi south of I-84 Exit 173, 110mi west of Pocatello. ✕&🅿☏208-733-9458. www.twinfallschamber.com.

This town of 74,000 boasts the **Herrett Center for Arts & Science★** (315 Falls Ave. W., College of Southern Idaho; ☏ 208-733-9554; http://herrett.csi.edu), whose anthropology collection, emphasizing Native American cultures, is highly regarded. Interstate 84 travelers enter Twin Falls via the 1500ft-long

Perrine Bridge, a truss arch span 486ft above the **Snake River Canyon**.

The main attraction here is **Shoshone Falls★★** (3300 East Rd., 5mi east of Twin Falls via Falls Ave.; ☏ 208-733-3974). Nicknamed "the Niagara of the West," these 212ft falls are 52ft higher than the eastern US cataract.

In spring, before upriver irrigation diversions steal much of the thunder, this is an impressive sight, a 1,000ft-wide wall of water that drops into its own cloud of mist.

Thousand Springs Scenic Route★★

US-30 between Buhl (18mi west of Twin Falls) and Bliss (I-84 Exit 141). &🅿☏208-837-9131. www.hagermanvalleychamber.com.

The **Thousand Springs★★** seep or gush from the opposite (north) wall of the Snake River canyon, an outflow from the Lost Rivers that disappear into the porous Snake River Plain, emerging through gaps or fractures in the rock. Numerous **fish hatcheries** and trout farms in the valley take advantage of the pristine water. Perched on a bluff on the southwest side of the Snake is **Hagerman Fossil Beds National Monument★** (W. 2700 South Rd.; visitor center at 221 N. State St., Hagerman; ☏208-933-4100; www.nps.gov/hafo). The richest trove of Pliocene fossils in North America, the beds were first excavated in the 1930s when Smithsonian Institution scientists unearthed a zebra-like horse extinct for more than 3 million years. There are overlooks and trails but no on-site facilities.

♟♟ Bruneau Dunes State Park★

Rte. 78, 18mi south of Mountain Home at I-84 Exit 95. ⚠&🅿☏208-366-7919. http://parksandrecreation.idaho.gov.

These 470ft sand dunes occupy a 600-acre depression in an ancient bend of the Snake. Hiking trails climb the stationary dunes, composed mainly of quartz and feldspar particles. A small observatory attracts weekend stargazers.

Boise★★

US-20/26/30 at I-84 Exit 53, 120mi northwest of Twin Falls. ✕&⏏
🕾 208-344-7777. www.boise.org.

The Boise (BOY-see) River lends a unique character to this city of 212,000, Idaho's capital and its commercial and cultural center. High-tech office workers on their lunch hours wade into the stream and cast flies for trout, as Boise State University students drift by on rafts and inner tubes within sight of the Neoclassical **Idaho State Capitol★** (700 W. Jefferson St.; 🕾 208-332-1000). Built of native sandstone in 1905-20, and patterned after the US Capitol in Washington DC, the capitol is the beneficiary of the modern world's first urban geothermal heating system. Since 1892, 700,000gal of 172°F water have been pumped daily from an aquifer adjacent to the **Warm Springs Historic District**. Four hundred private residences and eight government buildings are so heated.

Activity downtown centers on **Grove Plaza** (8th Ave. & Grove St.), a broad pedestrian space. Nearby, the **Basque Museum and Cultural Center** (611 Grove St.; 🕾 208-343-2671; www.basquemuseum.com) reflects the fact that Boise is the largest Basque community outside the group's native Spain and France.

The **Boise River Greenbelt★★**, a mostly paved 25mi network of walking and biking paths, links a series of riverside parks through the heart of the city. Nearest to downtown, **Julia Davis Park** (Julia Davis Dr. & Capitol Blvd.) is home to the **Idaho State Historical Museum** ▲▲ (610 Julia Davis Dr.; 🕾 208-334-2120, www.idahohistory.net), **The Boise Art Museum** (670 Julia Davis Dr.; 🕾 208-345-8330; www.boiseartmuseum.org) and the hands-on **Discovery Center of Idaho** ▲▲ (131 W. Myrtle St.; 🕾 208-343-9895; www.scidaho.org). Also in the park is **Zoo Boise** ▲▲ (355 N. Julia Davis Dr.; 🕾 208-384-4260, www.zooboise.com). East of the park is the **Morrison Knudsen Nature Center★** ▲▲ (600 S. Walnut St.; 🕾 208-334-2225; http://fishandgame.idaho.gov), which re-creates the life cycle of a mountain stream.

Two miles east, the **Old Idaho State Penitentiary★** (2445 Old Penitentiary Rd., off Warm Springs Blvd.; 🕾 208-334-2844; www.idahohistory.net) is one of only four US territorial prisons still in existence. The fortress-like sandstone edifice was built by convict labor in 1870 and used until 1973.

▲▲ World Center for Birds of Prey★★★

5668 W. Flying Hawk Lane off S. Cole Rd., 6mi south of Boise via I-84 Exit 50.
&⏏ 🕾 208-362-8687.
www.peregrinefund.org.

The **Peregrine Fund** was established in 1970 to save the once-endangered peregrine falcon from extinction, and this center has now become one of the world's leading institutions devoted to raptors. The fund has turned its captive-breeding efforts to populations of other threatened birds, including the California condor, the South American harpy eagle and the aplomado falcon of the southwestern US. Video cameras and one-way mirrors enable guests to view incubation chambers and birds without disturbing them.

A **California condors enclosure**, new in 2010, allows visitors to watch a pair of these rare birds in a natural setting, the only such facility outside California. Nearby, the world's highest concentration of raptors nest on bluffs overlooking the Snake River.

Peregrine Falcon

©iStockphoto.com/ Andrew Howe

The 755sq mi **Morley Nelson Snake River Birds of Prey National Conservation Area**★★ is accessed via Swan Falls Road (3mi west of Kuna and 23mi south of Boise via I-84 Exit 44; ℘208-384-3300; www.blm.gov/id). Best times to visit are late spring, when the young have hatched, and early autumn, when birds congregate to migrate south.

Hells Canyon National Recreation Area★★

See description p 485.

Sun Valley★★

Rte. 75, 83mi north of Twin Falls & 151mi east of Boise. △✕点₽ ℘208-726-3423. www.visitsunvalley.com.

The Wood River Valley was a sleepy backwoods until the 1870s, when the discovery of gold, silver and lead transformed it into a bustling mining district. Sheep ranching later drove the economy, the former tent town of **Ketchum** becoming the second-largest export center in the world. Later, W. Averell Harriman, chief executive of the Union Pacific Railroad, purchased a 4,000-acre ranch and began building a European-style winter resort. When the **Sun Valley Lodge**★★ (1 Sun Valley Rd., Sun Valley; ℘208-622-4111; www.sunvalley.com) opened in 1936, it attracted a Hollywood clientele and set the tone for what then was known as North America's finest ski area, complete with the first chair lift (patterned after a maritime banana hoist).

With a new gondola (2009) and 18 lifts on two mountains—including 9,150ft **Bald Mountain**, whose slopes drop 3,400ft directly into Ketchum—and cross-country runs on the 21mi **Wood River Trail System**, it remains a world-class destination.

Author Ernest Hemingway (1899-1961) spent his later years as a resident of Ketchum, where he is buried; he is remembered with a bust and epitaph at the **Ernest Hemingway Memorial** (Trail Creek Rd., 1mi northeast of Sun Valley Lodge).

Sawtooth National Recreation Area★★

Headquarters on Rte. 75, 8mi north of Sun Valley. △✕点₽ ℘208-737-3200. www.fs.usda.gov/sawtooth.

Embracing 1,180sq mi of rugged mountains—including 40 peaks of 10,000ft elevation, 1,000 lakes and the headwaters of four important rivers—this is one of the most spectacular yet least-known corners of the continental US. Route 75 climbs up the Wood River to 8,701ft **Galena Summit**★★, then descends the Salmon River drainage. To the east are the magnificent Boulder and White Cloud Mountains; to the west rise the awesome peaks of the Sawtooth Range, a dramatic granite-dominated fault scarp formed 50 million to 70 million years ago. The most developed of four large morainal lakes on the east slope of the Sawtooths is **Redfish Lake**★★, named for the sockeye salmon that traditionally spawned in its waters. A visitor center, log-cabin lodge, marina and beach attract the crowds.

Tiny **Stanley**★★ (Rtes. 21 & 75, 61mi northwest of Ketchum & 134mi northeast of Boise; ℘208-774-3411. www.stanleycc.org) is a recreation capital. Among the 100 or so hardy souls (winter snowfall averages 8ft) who call this gorgeous basin home are 23 outfitters who specialize in wilderness adventure.

Craters of the Moon National Monument★

US-20/26/93, 18mi southwest of Arco & 65mi southeast of Sun Valley. △点₽ ℘208-527-1335. www.nps.gov/crmo.

Established in 1924, this 83sq-mi preserve is a basalt jumble of fissures, lava tubes, spatter and cinder cones, an outdoor museum so intimidating, it has yet to be fully explored. So moonlike is the terrain that astronauts were trained here for lunar landings. From a low-slung stone **visitor center**, 7mi of paved road threads through the volcanic features. In late spring, the black cinder slopes are transformed into a carpet of wildflowers. Despite its apparent bleakness, the landscape is home to many birds and animals.

Glacier Park Region

One of North America's most awe-inspiring destinations is Waterton/Glacier International Peace Park, its jagged peaks, glacial lakes and U-shaped valleys straddling the US-Canada border far from major cities. Relative isolation has enhanced its wilderness charms.

Highlights

1   Historic boat cruises on **Lake McDonald** (p364)

2   Fishing and sailing on **Whitefish Lake** (p366)

3   Pioneer lifestyle at **Fort Benton** (p368)

4   Scenic Montana from the **Pintler Scenic Highway** (p370)

5   **Smokejumping history** in Missoula (p370

Glacier NP   MT

A Pristine Ecosystem

During the ice ages, glaciers plowed down Rocky Mountain river valleys, shaving mountains into horns and arêtes and gouging the valleys. Most glaciers are gone or disappearing, graphic evidence of climate change. Some glaciers flowed far enough south to impound the Clark Fork River at the present site of Lake Pend Oreille, creating glacial Lake Missoula. The inland sea spread from the Flathead region to the Bitterroot Mountains. Whenever an ice dam broke, floods raged down the Columbia River drainage to the Pacific; each time, another glacier plugged the outlet and the lake refilled. Fertile sedimentary deposits are the lake's legacy in the Mission and Bitterroot Valleys and Columbia Basin.

Lewis' and Clark's 1804-06 odyssey took them across this ruggedly beautiful land: through the Bitterroot Valley, down the Columbia drainage. Even before the Corps of Discovery returned east, mountain men were headed west into these reaches. The pioneer influx led to conflict with Native Americans whose free-roaming lifestyle disappeared into oppressive reservations. Today, visitors can see bison and eagles, meet real cowboys and Indians, and hike up near glaciers or into gold mines. The Flathead Valley of Kalispell and Whitefish has become a year-round recreation capital, with deluxe resorts, skiing, fishing, boating, biking and hiking. Visitor information for the entire region is available at www.glaciermt.com.

ADDRESSES

🛏 STAY

$$$$$ Averill's Flathead Lake Lodge – Rte. 35, Bigfork, MT. ✆406-837-4391. www.flatheadlakelodge.com. 20 cabins. Open Jun–Aug. This family-operated dude ranch, nestled in a bay on the east shore of Flathead Lake, offers a package experience of the new West. Log cottages surround a central lodge amid forestland. Visitors horseback ride fish, sail and swim at a private beach/marina.

$$$$$ Triple Creek Ranch – 5551 West Fork Rd., Darby, MT. ✆406-821-4600. www.triplecreekranch.com. 22 cabins. One of just two Relais & Chateaux guest ranches in the West, Triple Creek offers deluxe cabins with wood furnishings, and an array of on-property activities such as fishing and riding. Guests dine on gourmet preparations of seafood and game. Rates are all-inclusive, except for off-ranch excursions.

$$$$ The Coeur d'Alene – 115 S. 2nd St., Coeur d'Alene, ID. ✆208-765-4000.

TRANSPORTATION

One of the most remote places in the US from metropolitan areas, Kalispell is the gateway to Glacier National Park. **Glacier Park International Airport** (FCA; www.iflyglacier.com) has direct service from Seattle, Salt Lake City, Minneapolis and Denver. Kalispell is a 10hr drive from Salt Lake, 9hrs from Seattle.

Tours on the park's famed red "**Jammer**" open-air buses (newly refurbished and outfitted with low-pollution engines) operate daily in summer (406-892-2525; www.glacierparkinc.com).

ACCOMMODATIONS

Glacier park's famous **historic lodges**—Lake MacDonald Lodge, Many Glacier Hotel and Glacier Park Lodge (see descriptions in park text) offer memorable accommodation in or near the park and are operated by Glacier Park Inc. (406-892-2525; www.glacierparkinc.com.)

www.cdaresort.com. 336 rooms. One of America's top resorts, this golf, sailing and tennis complex offers lodgings that range from economy to 18th-story penthouses. With four restaurants and numerous amenities, it perches beside Lake Coeur d'Alene with a private beach and marina.

$$$ Pine Butte Guest Ranch – 351 South Fork Rd., Choteau, MT. 406-466-2158. http://pinebutteguestranch.com. 11 cabins. Open May–Sept. Operated by the Nature Conservancy, Pine Butte is lodged high in the foothills of the Rockies. Guests enjoy all-inclusive weeklong stays in spacious log-and-stone cabins; activities range from hiking and fishing to swimming in the solar-heated pool.

$$$ Grouse Mountain Lodge – 2 Fairway Dr., Whitefish, MT. 406-892-2525. www.grousemountainlodge.com. 143 rooms. Poised between a city park and a golf course, this classic western lodge, remodeled in 2012, features a standard hotel units to loft suites that sleep four. The decor is marked by lots of wood and stone and earth tones, and a full slate of amenities includes a spa.

$$ The Copper King Mansion – 219 W. Granite St., Butte, MT. 406-782-7580. www.thecopperkingmansion.com. 5 rooms. Built for a self-made copper millionaire in 1888, this opulent Victorian residence even offers a guided tour. It starts with the main hall's Staircase of Nations and moves to the ballroom, library and billiard room, all rich with stained-glass windows and gold-embossed leather ceilings.

$$ Grand Union Hotel – 1 Grand Union Sq., Fort Benton, MT. 406-622-1882.

Mount Gould and Grinnell Lake, Glacier National Park

Tipi on lawn of Glacier Park Lodge

© Gwen Cannon/Michelin

$$ The Duck Inn – 1305 Columbia Ave., Whitefish, MT. ✆406-862-3825. www.duckinn.com. 15 rooms. Poised on the banks of a quiet valley stream, yet close to downtown Whitefish, this inn has spacious rooms, all overlooking the water or the inn's garden. Bird song from the waterway fills the rooms.

✟ EAT

$$ Pescado Blanco – 235 First St., Whitefish, MT. ✆406-862-3290. www.pescadoblanco.com. Dinner only. **Latin American**. Though the menu embraces tacos, carne asada, fajitas and other Mexican mainstays, this Whitefish standout adds a Montana flair with elk chorizo, bison and duck enchiladas. The Mexican chocolate cake is a delight.

$$ Tupelo Grille – 17 Central Ave., Whitefish, MT. ✆406-862-6136. www.tupelogrille.com. Dinner only. **Contemporary**. It's a long way from the Mississippi delta, but this downtown restaurant buzzes each night as diners enjoy gumbo, buffalo shepherd's pie, succotash and exotic inventions like shrimp and grits, or blue corn tacos.

$$ Belton Chalet – US-2, West Glacier, MT. ✆406-888-5000. www.beltonchalet.com. Dinner only. **Regional**. Built in 1910 as a Great Northern Railway hotel, this Swiss-style chalet was filled with Arts and Crafts furniture and blazing stone fireplaces. After a major historic preservation effort, it reopened in 2000 with a handful of guest rooms and a fine-dining restaurant. The Grill prepares entrées like rainbow trout, duck Napoleon, Montana meatloaf and elk meatballs. A taproom is adjacent.

$$ The Bridge – 600 S. Higgins Ave., Missoula, MT. ✆406-542-0222. www.bridgepizza.com. **Italian and Mexican**. This neighborhood cafe has been a labor of love for its long-time owners and now the family's second generation. The bistro serves pasta, pizza, burritos, hot and pressed sandwiches and vegetarian dishes.

http://grandunionhotel.com. 26 rooms. This 1882 Gilded Age masterpiece features polished dark walnut, rich brocade fabrics and wainscoting, all restored to the standards of its glittering heyday. The **Union Grille ($$)** restaurant focuses on Montana beef, game and grains prepared in gourmet fashion; breakfast is included in room rates.

$$ Garden Wall Inn – 504 Spokane Ave., Whitefish, MT. ✆406-862-3440. www.gardenwallinn.com. 5 rooms. With clapboard siding and claw-footed tubs, this charming Colonial Revival bed-and-breakfast inn is named for the sheer cliffs that form the Continental Divide. The innkeepers, keen outdoors explorers, concoct gourmet breakfasts that might include huckleberry-pear crepes.

$$ The Sanders – 328 N. Ewing St., Helena, MT. ✆406-442-3309. www.sandersbb.com. 7 rooms. Most of the original furnishings remain in this inviting 1875 bed-and-breakfast Victorian, home for 30 years (until 1905) of frontier politician Wilbur Fisk Sanders and his suffragette wife, Harriet Fenn Sanders. Listed on the National Register of Historic Places, it has been lovingly maintained by Rock Ringling (scion of the circus family) and Bobbi Uecker.

Glacier National Park★★★

Shaped by glaciers, the Glacier Park area is characterized by rugged mountains, lakes and valleys. About 75 million years ago, a geological phenomenon known as the Lewis Overthrust tilted and pushed a 3mi- to 4mi-thick slab of the earth's crust 50mi east, leaving older rock atop younger Cretaceous rock. These mountains now rise 3,000-7,000ft above valley floors, partially forming the Continental Divide. Several major ecological regimes meet here: a wet coniferous ecosystem on the west side of the Divide is balanced by dry, sparsely vegetated terrain on the east side.

- ⌚ **Michelin Map:** 493 D 3, 4. Mountain Standard Time.
- ℹ **Info:** ✆406-888-7800 or www.nps.gov/glac
- ✪ **Don't Miss:** Going-to-the-Sun Road.
- ⌚ **Also See:** Museum of the Plains Indian.

SIGHTS
Glacier National Park★★★
Going-to-the-Sun Road off US-2, 35mi east of Kalispell. △✗⛄♿🅿 ✆406-888-7800. www.nps.gov/glac.
Known to native Blackfeet as the "Land of Shining Mountains," Glacier Park was homesteaded in the late 19C. Pressure to establish the park began in 1891 with the arrival of the Great Northern Railway; the US Congress gave its nod in 1910. The railroad built numerous delightful Swiss-style chalets and hotels, several of which still operate.

Glacier's rugged mountainscape takes its name not from living glaciers, but from ancient rivers of ice that carved the peaks, finger lakes and U-shaped valleys. The remoteness of the park's 1,584sq mi makes it an ideal home for grizzly bears and mountain goats, big-horn sheep and bugling elk. The park's glaciers have been steadily disappearing, from 100 in 1910 to 25 in 2010 to, scientists estimate, zero by 2030.

Western Approaches
Coming from Kalispell, visitors pass through the village of Hungry Horse, named for two lost horses that nearly starved one winter long ago. **Hungry Horse Dam** (West Reservoir Rd., 4mi south of US-2; ✆406-387-5241), which impounds a 34mi-long reservoir, offers grand views up the South Fork of the

Two Medicine Lake, Glacier National Park

© Gwen Cannon/Michelin

General Store at Two Medicine Lake

Flathead River, into the Bob Marshall Wilderness. A visitor center explains how the massive turbines and generators of the 564ft-high arched concrete dam produce power (summer only).

Charming **West Glacier**, a park gateway town, is an outfitting center. Amtrak trains stop at a renovated depot that now houses the nonprofit Glacier Natural History Association. **Belton Chalet** (12575 US-2 East; ℘406-888-5000; www.beltonchalet.com), built by the Great Northern Railroad in 1910, is restored and listed on the National Register of Historic Places.

Going-to-the-Sun Road★★★

52mi from US-2 at West Glacier to US-89 at St. Mary. Closed mid Oct–late May due to snow.

This National Historic Landmark may be America's most beautiful highway. Deemed an engineering marvel when completed in 1932, the narrow, serpentine roadway climbs 3,500ft to the Continental Divide at Logan Pass, moving from forested valleys to alpine meadows to native grassland as it bisects the park west to east. Passenger vehicles (size restrictions prohibit large RVs) share the route with Glacier's trademark red "jammer" buses, which have carried sightseers for more than 60 years.

Two miles from the road's beginning is **Apgar**, an assemblage of lodgings, cafes and shops at the foot of mountain-ringed **Lake McDonald★**. Like most park waters, this lake is fed by snowmelt and glacial runoff, and summer surface temperatures average a cool 55°F. The launch *DeSmet*, a classic wooden boat handcrafted in 1928, cruises from the rustic but inviting **Lake McDonald Lodge** (Mile 11; ℘406-892-2525; www.glacierparkinc.com), open summers. There's been a hotel here since 1895.

At **Trail of the Cedars★** (Mile 16.5), a wheelchair-accessible boardwalk winds through old-growth cedar-hemlock forest and past a sculpted gorge. Able-bodied hikers can amble uphill another 2mi to Avalanche Lake, fed by waterfalls spilling from Sperry Glacier. Beyond, **Bird Woman Falls** cascades from Mt. Oberlin and the **Weeping Wall★** gushes or trickles—depending on the season—from a roadside rock face.

At 6,646ft **Logan Pass★★★** (Mile 33), visitors enjoy broad alpine meadows of wildflowers and keep their eyes open for mountain goats on the 1.5mi walk to **Hidden Lake Overlook★★**. White-flowered beargrass is beautiful in summer. Ripple-marked rocks more than 1 billion years old lie along the route to the observation post.

Descending Logan Pass, travelers may stop at the **Jackson Glacier Overlook** (Mile 37) or continue to **Sun Point★** (Mile 41), where there is picnicking beside **St. Mary Lake** and a trailhead to **Baring Falls** (*1mi*).

From **Rising Sun** (Mile 45), scenic 90min **lake cruises★** aboard the 49-passenger Little Chief, built in 1925, are launched. At the eastern terminus of the road, the **St. Mary Visitor Center**, a glistening stone-and-glass facility, holds new exhibits detailing the long history of indigenous peoples in and near the park.

Eastern Valleys★★

A 21mi drive northwest from St. Mary leads to **Many Glacier★★★** (12mi west of Babboff US-89). Craggy peaks provide a memorable backdrop to the valley above Grinnell Lake. They may be reached by a 5mi hiking path (part of Glacier Park's stalwart 735mi trail network), or viewed from the landmark 1915 **Many Glacier Hotel★** (☎406-892-2525; www.glacierparkinc.com), or from a boat on sparkling Swiftcurrent and Josephine Lakes.

Two Medicine★ (13mi northwest of East Glacier Park off Rte. 49) is tucked into a carved glacial valley 38mi south of St. Mary via US-89 and has a general store and guided boat tours but no lodgings except a campground. Nearby, 8020ft **Triple Divide Peak** is the only place on the continent from which water flows to three oceans—Atlantic, Pacific and Arctic. In Browning, the **Museum of the Plains Indian★** holds a classic collection of Blackfeet, Crow and other artifacts, and modern Indian artists exhibit in two contemporary galleries (19 Museum Loop, Browning; ☎ 406-338-2230; www.iacb.doi.gov/museums).

East Glacier Park

US-2 & Rte. 49.

This small town on the Blackfeet Indian Reservation is home to the imposing 1913 **Glacier Park Lodge★** (☎406-892-2525; www.glacierparkinc.com), whose lobby is columned with old-growth Douglas fir logs. The village has hostels, bicycle rentals, outfitters and an Amtrak train depot.

Southern Boundary

Between East Glacier Park and West Glacier, a 57mi stretch of US-2 divides the park from the Great Bear Wilderness. From 5,220ft **Marias Pass** on the Continental Divide, there are superb views of the Lewis Overthrust.

Tiny **Essex** (25mi east of West Glacier), on the Middle Fork of the Flathead River, holds the **Izaak Walton Inn** (US-2; ☎406-888-5700; www.izaakwaltoninn.com), built in 1939 for rail crews. Today the half-timbered inn is a mecca for railroad fans and cross-country skiers.

Blackfeet Indian Reservation

US-2 & US-89. △✖&🄿 ☎406-338-7521. www.blackfeetnation.com.

The Blackfeet Reservation stretches east from Glacier Park across 50mi of rolling hills and prairies notorious for hot summers and wind-whipped winters. Today three Blackfeet tribes live in Montana and Alberta, ranching and farming.

EXCURSION

Waterton Lakes National Park★★

◗ Alberta Rte. 5 off Chief Mountain International Hwy. △✖&🄿 ☎403-859-5133. www.pc.gc.ca.

Glacier Park and Canada's Waterton Lakes National Park share a landscape and a history of cooperation. Together they form Waterton/Glacier International Peace Park.

Waterton Lakes Park clusters around the distinctly Canadian townsite of **Waterton Park**, on the shoreline of Upper Waterton Lake. Visitors can walk to Cameron Falls (*.5mi*), take a **lake excursion★** aboard the launch *International*, and enjoy high tea at the gabled 1927 **Prince of Wales Hotel★★** (☎403-859-2231; www.glacierparkinc.com).

Flathead Region★

Wherever the eye rests in the Flathead Valley, mountains loom. They follow the traveler like a shadow. Ice Age glaciers left behind these jagged peaks and a fertile river valley that now supports an agricultural economy. The Flathead Indian Reservation and Flathead Lake are both found in this striking land, where outdoor recreation has supplanted logging as the major industry.

⚲ **Michelin Map:** Map: 493 E 3, 4. Mountain Standard Time.

🅸 **Info:** ✆406-756-9091 or www.fcvb.org.

☺ **Don't Miss:** Kalispell.

⚲ **Also See:** The People's Center.

SIGHTS

Kalispell

US-2 & US-93 west of Glacier Park. △✕⚿🅿✆406-758-2800. www.kalispellchamber.com.

Flathead County's commercial center, this town of 20,500 melds old and new Montana. The elegant **Conrad Mansion★** (330 Woodland Ave.; ✆406-755-2166; www.conradmansion.com), a 26-room Norman-style home built in 1895, is Kalispell's crown jewel.

Whitefish★

US-93, 14mi north of Kalispell. △✕⚿🅿✆406-862-3501. www.whitefishchamber.com.

This small town of 6,500 gracefully balances its dual identity as a Western community and resort center. **Whitefish Lake★** draws anglers and water skiers in summer; 7,000ft **Whitefish Mountain Resort★** (Big Mountain Rd., 8mi north of Whitefish; ✆406-862-2900; www.skiwhitefish.com) lures snow-sport enthusiasts.

Summer visitors ride the gondola to the summit for wonderful **views★★** into Glacier National Park and the Canadian Rockies, and to hike and bike their way back down.

Flathead Lake★★

Between US-93 & Rte. 35, 11 to 38mi south of Kalispell. △

This 27mi-long lake, the largest natural freshwater lake west of the Mississippi River, offers boating, sailing and fishing with gorgeous mountain **views★**.

With its Western-theme architecture and storybook lakeside setting,

---

Where the Buffalo Roam

Sixty million bison once migrated across North America from far northern Mexico to Canada. For thousands of years they sustained generations of Plains Indians. Hides provided clothing and lodging; bones became tools and weapons; flesh and organs fed families. The herds flourished until the late 19C, when hunters slaughtered them for tongues and hides—and to erase Indian food supplies—leaving carcasses to rot.

The **National Bison Range★★** (Rte. 212, Moiese, 31mi south of Polson; ⚿🅿✆406-644-2211, www.fws.gov/bisonrange) was set aside in 1908 to preserve a small herd of buffalo, by then approaching extinction. About 350 buffalo now roam the range and provide breeding stock for private North American bison ranches, where as many as 300,000 of the great beasts are raised. Visitor center displays examine the behavior and history of these strong, temperamental animals. Drivers on the 19mi Red Sleep Mountain tour may view not only bison but also pronghorn, bighorn sheep, elk and mountain goats on more than 18,500 scenic acres.

Bigfork★ (Rte. 35, 17mi southeast of Kalispell; ⚠✕♿🅿 ☎406-837-5888; www.bigfork.org) is a center for the arts and fine dining. Galleries and gift shops line its main street, and the **Bigfork Summer Playhouse** (☎406-837-4886; www.bigforksummerplayhouse.com) draws sellout crowds to productions of comedies and Broadway musicals.

Flathead Indian Reservation

US-93 between Kalispell & Missoula. ✕♿🅿 ☎406-675-2700. www.cskt.org/vi.
Montana's Salish, Kootenai and Pend d'Oreille tribes reside on this reservation, established in 1855. Every July, traditional **celebrations★** in the villages of Elmo and Arlee welcome visitors to see Native American dancing, music and games.

The reservation's commercial center is **Polson** (US-93 & Rte. 35, 49mi south of Kalispell & 65mi north of Missoula; ☎406-883-5969; www.polsonchamber. com), a boating and outfitting hub that hugs the foot of Flathead Lake.
Six miles south of Polson, **The People's Center★** (US-93, Pablo; ☎406-675-0160; www.peoplescenter.org) relates the history of the Flathead tribes. Numerous prairie potholes, formed by glaciers 12,000 years ago, attract more than 180 bird species to **Ninepipe National Wildlife Refuge** (US-93, 15mi south of Polson; ☎406-644-2211; www. fws.gov), a 2,000-acre wetland.
The 1891 **St. Ignatius Mission★** (US-93, 29mi south of Polson; ☎406-745-2768) is graced with handsome frescoes and murals and backdropped by the majestic Mission Mountains.

Upper Missouri River★

The Missouri River played a key role in US westward expansion. Besides bringing the Lewis and Clark Expedition, fur traders, gold seekers and pioneer settlers into the region, it was part of a vast water-land route from St. Louis to the Pacific Ocean. Today, 149mi of the Missouri are a wild-and-scenic corridor rich in wildlife and pristine canyon scenes. Coursing through a land of buttes and prairies, immortalized by cowboy artist Charles M. Russell, it's the last major free-flowing remnant of an historic waterway.

- ♿ **Michelin Map:** 493 F 4. Mountain Standard Time.
- **Info:** ☎406-761-5036 http://centralmontana.com.
- **Don't Miss:** The C.M. Russell Museum.

SIGHTS
Great Falls★★

US-87 & US-89 at I-15. ⚠✕♿🅿 ☎406-770-3078. http://genuinemontana.com.
Great Falls drew national attention when explorers Lewis and Clark portaged five local waterfalls (now submerged or reduced by dams). With 59,000 residents, it is Montana's third-largest city.
Lewis & Clark National Trail Interpretive Center★★ (4201 Giant Springs Rd.; ☎406-727-8733; www.fs.fed.us/ r1/lewisclark/lcic) honors the Corps of Discovery and the Plains Indians who assisted them. Following a **film★** by director Ken Burns, visitors may explore interactive displays and exhibits that chronicle the voyageurs' odyssey. Outside, the 25mi **River's Edge Trail** entices bicyclists and walkers.
Down the road, **Giant Springs Heritage State Park★** (4600 Giant Springs Rd.; ☎406-454-5840;stateparks.mt.gov) is one of the nation's largest freshwater springs and shortest rivers—the Roe, 201ft long.

Missouri River at Great Falls, Montana

© Gwen Cannon/Michelin

Legendary artist **Charlie Russell** (1864-1926), who portrayed the vanishing American West in oils, watercolors and sculptures, made his home in Great Falls. The **C.M. Russell Museum**★★ (400 13th St. N.; ℘406-727-8787; www.cmrussell.org) features the world's largest collection of Russell masterpieces, plus the artist's home and log-cabin studio.

Not far away, Romanesque 1896 **Paris Gibson Square** (1400 1st Ave. N.; ℘406-727-8255; www.the-square.org) has a contemporary art museum and an historical society.

Fort Benton★★

Rte. 80 off US-87, 38mi northeast of Great Falls. ⛺✕♿🅿℘406-622-3864. www.fortbenton.com.

The farthest point to which steamboats could travel up the Missouri, Fort Benton developed as a river port. It was the east end of the 642mi Mullan Road to Walla Walla, Washington, linking the Missouri and Columbia River drainages. The **Fort Benton Heritage Complex**★★ (1205 20th St. at Washington Sts.; ℘406-622-5316) presents a vivid picture of Indian and settler life in the high plains' harsh conditions, including a partially complete reconstruction of the pioneer fort; the **Museum of the Northern Great Plains; Museum of the Upper Missouri;** and the **Starr Gallery of Western Art**, focusing on Karl Bodmer prints and Bob Scriver sculptures.

Upper Missouri River Breaks National Monument★

Access by river from Fort Benton. ⛺ ℘406-622-4000. wwwblm.gov/mt.

Encompassing the 149 miles of the Upper Missouri National Wild and Scenic River, this remote region has changed little since Lewis and Clark ventured through in 1805.

Designated a national monument in January 2001 and administered by the Bureau of Land Management, it is of historical, cultural, geological and ecological importance. Canoe floats from Fort Benton, guided or unguided, take modern adventurers past chalk cliffs and undeveloped shorelines still largely wilderness.

Helena★★

US-12 at I-15. ✕♿🅿℘406-449-1270. www.helenamt.com

Montana's capital, Helena perches around Last Chance Gulch, one of America's richest gold strikes. A genteel town of 29,000 with a rough-and-tumble heritage, Helena is full of old mansions and mining legends. Prominent in town are the twin-spired **St. Helena's Cathedral**★ (Lawrence & Warren Sts.; ℘406-442-5825; www.sthelenas.org) and the 1888 Queen Anne-style **Original Gov-**

ernor's Mansion★ (304 N. Ewing St.; $\mathscr{C}$406-444-4789).

Situated on a hillside facing the Helena Valley, the copper-domed **Montana State Capitol★★** (1301 E. 6th Ave.; $\mathscr{C}$406-444-4789; visit-the-capitol. mt.gov) is a grand structure with an elegant French Renaissance rotunda. Charles Russell's monumental Lewis and Clark Meeting Indians at Ross's Hole (1912) hangs here. Tours begin from the nearby **Montana Historical Society★** (225 N. Roberts St.; $\mathscr{C}$406-444-2694;

mhs.mt.gov), which displays a fine collection of Russell canvases; its Montana Homeland exhibit depicts the lifestyles of native peoples.

At **Gates of the Mountains★★** (I-15 Exit 209, 18mi north of Helena; $\mathscr{C}$406-458-5241; www.gatesofthemountains.com), the Missouri River weaves through a spectacular canyon formed from Precambrian sedimentary rock and Mississippian limestone; tours provide a river-level vantage.

Gold West Country★

About 75 million years ago, molten granite surged into the earth's crust to create the mineral-laden Boulder Batholith—the genesis of southwestern Montana's wealth and outlaw lore. Gold, silver and copper drew settlers to the area in the mid to late 19C. The charm of this historic region remains today.

SIGHTS

Butte

I-15 & I-90. ✖️♿️🅿️ $\mathscr{C}$406-723-3177. www.buttecvb.com.

An erstwhile mining town of 33,000, Butte called itself "The Richest Hill on Earth." Tunnels beneath the town, if unfurled, would stretch the length of Montana—more than 500mi.

A **trolley tour** through historic Uptown includes the **Berkeley Pit★** (east end Mercury St. off Continental Dr.), the largest truck-served open-pit copper mine in the US from 1955 to 1982. Visitors roam a reconstructed mining camp at the **World Museum of Mining★** (west end Park St.; $\mathscr{C}$406-723-7211; www. miningmuseum.org), or tour Butte's last intact mine yard, the **Anselmo Mine★** (600 block of N. Excelsior St.).

With its stained-glass windows and frescoed ceilings, the **Copper King**

♿️ **Michelin Map:** 493 E, F 4, 5. Mountain Standard Time.

ℹ️ **Info:** $\mathscr{C}$800-879-1159 or southwestmt.com.

😊 **Don't Miss:** Pintler Scenic Highway.

Mansion★ (219 W. Granite St.; $\mathscr{C}$406-782-7580; www.thecopperkingmansion.com) recalls Butte's glory days.

Deer Lodge★

I-90, 41mi northwest of Butte. ⛺️✖️♿️🅿️

A traditional ranching town of 3,400, Deer Lodge captures the attention of Old West aficionados.

At the 1,500-acre **Grant-Kohrs Ranch National Historic Site★★** (.75mi west of I-90 Exit 184; $\mathscr{C}$406-846-2070; www. nps.gov/grko), costumed Park Service rangers share the story of a ranch that once was headquarters of a four-state cattle empire.

Old Montana Prison★ (1106 Main St.; $\mathscr{C}$406-846-3111; www.pcmaf.org), provides a glimpse of yesteryear's convicts. Among five other museums are the **Montana Auto Museum★**, which features antique roadsters and novelty cars, and (across Main Street) the **Frontier Museum**, showcasing guns and saloon paraphernalia.

Bannack State Park

© Stock Connection Blue/Alamy

Pintler Scenic Highway★★

Rte. 1 between I-90 Exits 208 & 153.
⚠✕&₽.

This splendid 63mi road winds past ranches, over a mountain pass and along lakes. At one end is **Anaconda★** (Rte. 1, 24mi west of Butte via I-90; ℘406-563-2400; www.anacondamt. org), known for its Art Deco theater and a landmark smelter stack.

The highlight of quaint **Philipsburg★★** (Rte. 1, 55mi northwest of Butte; ℘406-859-3388; www.philipsburgmt.com) is the **Granite County Museum★** (155 S. Sansome St.; ℘406-859-3020), which holds the underground Granite Mountain mining exhibit and the Montana Ghost Town Hall of Fame.

The town's **Old Works Golf Club** (www. oldworks.org) features a championship golf course fashioned from an abandoned and once-toxic smelter site. Within 60mi are 21 ghost towns, the best preserved of which is the 1890s gold camp of **Garnet★★** (39mi east of Missoula via Rte. 200 & Garnet Range Rd., or 57mi northwest of Philipsburg via I-90 & Bear Gulch Rd; ℘406-329-3914; www.garnetghosttown.net).

Missoula★

US-12 & US-93 at I-90. ℘406-532-3250. www.destinationmissoula.org.

A commercial and cultural center and home to the University of Montana, Missoula is a lively town of 64,000 residents.

Built in 1877 for protection against Indians, **Fort Missoula** (South Ave. west of Reserve St.; ℘406-728-3476) served as a World War II internment center for Italians and Japanese Americans.

The **Aerial Fire Depot and Smokejumpers Visitor Center★** (5765 W. Broadway; ℘406-329-4934) explains how an elite corps of men and women fight wildfires.

EXCURSION
Bannack State Park★★

▶ South of Rte. 278, 26mi southwest of Dillon. &₽℘406-834-3413.
www.bannack.org.

A booming 1860s mining camp near the Pioneer Mountains, Bannack was Montana's first territorial capital. Its 50-plus buildings stand as abandoned when the gold played out.

Self-guided tours lead through a deserted main street that comes to life during July's **Bannack Days**, a full-dress 19C re-creation.

Coeur d'Alene Country★

In the early 1800s, fur trappers began trading for pelts with the Indians of Idaho's Panhandle. The natives proved shrewd bargainers, inspiring the trappers to say they had hearts like awls—*les coeurs d'alênes*. When the Mullan Road was completed in 1862, linking the Missouri and Columbia River watersheds, mountainous northern Idaho opened for settlement. Miners came for gold but stayed for other riches in what became one of the world's foremost regions for the production of silver, lead and zinc.

SIGHTS
Coeur d'Alene★
I-90, 32mi east of Spokane, Washington. △✕&🄿 ☎208-664-3194. www.coeurdalene.org.
The former steamship port of 45,000 is now a summer playground for jetskiers, parasailers, golfers and other recreation lovers. Beautiful **Coeur d'Alene Lake★★** extends 23mi south.

Silver Valley★★
I-90, 20 to 60mi east of Coeur d'Alene. △✕&🄿.
More than a billion ounces of silver were extracted in the 20C at **Wallace★★** (I-90 Exit 62, 49mi east of Coeur d'Alene; ☎208-753-7151; www.wallaceidaho-chamber.com), self-proclaimed "Silver Capital of the World."
At the **Sierra Silver Mine★★** (420 5th St.; ☎208-752-5151; www.silverminetour.org), retired miners demonstrate their equipment; tours include a narrated trolley ride through town. A handsomely restored train station (1901) houses railroad mementos at the château-style **Northern Pacific Depot Railroad Museum★** (219 6th St. at Pine St.; ☎208-752-0111). The **Wallace District Mining Museum** (509 Bank St.; ☎208-556-1592) shows films explaining how Idaho's mining industry evolved.

- **Michelin Map:** 493 D, E 3, 4. Pacific Standard Time.
- **Info:** www.visitnorthidaho.com.
- **Location:** The area's gateway is Spokane and its international airport.
- **Don't Miss:** Coeur d'Alene Lake.
- **Also See:** Silver Valley's mining history sites.

Kellogg★ (I-90 Exit 49, 36mi east of Coeur d'Alene; △✕&🄿 ☎208-784-0821; www.silvervalleychamber.com), Wallace's larger neighbor, has shifted haltingly from mining to tourism. Its unique **junk-art sculptures★** (by David Dose) color the landscape. Summer weekends, a gondola and chairlifts at the **Silver Mountain** ski area (610 Bunker Ave.; ☎208-783-1111; www.silvermt.com) carry visitors to the top of 6,300ft Kellogg Peak, where 360-degree **views★★** encompass parts of three states and Canada. The **Staff House Museum** (820 W. McKinley Ave.; ☎208-786-4141) features a mine model representing 135mi of tunnel.
Murray★ (Forest Rd. 9 via Forest Rd. 456, 18mi north of Wallace), a gold-rush boomtown, retains two saloons, a bank-turned-inn, and novelties on display at the **Spragpole Museum**, a bar and restaurant.
Old Mission State Park★★ (I-90 Exit 40, Cataldo, 24mi east of Coeur d'Alene; ☎208-682-3814; parksandrecreation.idaho.gov) preserves Idaho's oldest structure, the 1850 Cataldo Mission. The restored church overlooks the Coeur d'Alene River valley.
Sandpoint★ (US-2 & 95, 46mi north of Coeur d'Alene; ☎208-263-2161; www.sandpointchamber.org), Lake Pend Oreille's largest town (7.400), has a small historical museum. Nearby **Schweitzer Mountain** (Schweitzer Mountain Rd.; ☎208-263-9555; www.schweitzer.com), offers summer-weekend chairlift rides to its 6,400ft summit and fine **views★★**.

Texas

Theme Gardens at the Lady Bird Johnson Wildflower Center , Austin

Dallas–Fort Worth Area

The twin cities of Dallas and Fort Worth, together with their patchwork of suburbs, constitute the vast expanse of urbanized prairie termed the Metroplex, with a total population greater than 6 million. Though united by their physical proximity, the cities vary widely in history and character.

Highlights

1. Pay your respects at the **JFK Memorial** (p379)
2. Serious fun at **Perot Museum of Nature and Science** (p379)
3. Theme park thrills at **Six Flags** (p382)
4. Stunning collections at **Kimbell Art Museum** (p385)
5. African "safari" at **Fossil Rim Wildlife Center** (p387)

Dallas-Fort Worth

TX

The Hub of North Texas

The gleaming towers of downtown Dallas are firmly anchored in trade and commerce. Although the city is widely thought of as an oil or cattle capital, Dallas is actually a center for banking, transportation and retailing, is headquarters for a host of major companies, and was the birthplace of the integrated circuit (computer chips). Dallas also enjoys cultural prestige: Institutions such as the Dallas Museum of Art and the Morton H. Meyerson Symphony Center have made the Dallas Arts District one of the largest and most significant in the US.

Dallas' darkest moment occurred in 1963 when US President John F. Kennedy was assassinated while touring the city in a motorcade. The tragic episode is remembered at Dealey Plaza and in The Sixth Floor Museum. The city has since made a point of emphasizing its cultural sophistication and diversity – Dallas "competes" for preeminence not with Fort Worth, but Houston. Fort Worth is proud of its "Cowtown" heritage, bringing its Old West history to life in the Stockyards National Historic District and the restored downtown, known as Sundance Square. Smaller and less hurried

Dallas Skyline

than its neighbor to the east, Fort Worth offers a surprisingly diverse array of attractions beyond its Wild West flavor, including a first-rate zoo and a cluster of renowned museums in the Cultural District.

ADDRESSES

🛏 STAY

$$$$$ Hotel Adolphus – 1321 Commerce St., Dallas. ☎214-742-8200. www.hoteladolphus.com. 422 rooms. This 100-year-old creation of unabashed Baroque flamboyance and period furniture, with lacquered chinoiserie, tapestries, and chandeliers, was built by a Dallas beer baron. The crown jewel is **The French Room ($$$)**, serving creative cuisine under vaulted ceilings and gilded Rococo arches.

$$$$$ Rosewood Mansion on Turtle Creek – 2821 Turtle Creek Blvd., Dallas. ☎214-559-2100. www.mansiononturtle creek.com. 141 rooms. Once a cotton magnate's home, The Mansion has marble rotundas, elaborate decor and impeccable service. The Mansion is the flagship of the Rosewood Hotels chain. A sister inn, **Rosewood Crescent Hotel** (400 Crescent Court, Dallas; ☎214-871-3200; $$$$), has a lavish spa.

$$$$ The Ashton Hotel – 610 Main St., Fort Worth. ☎817-332-0100. www. theashtonhotel.com. 39 rooms. This downtown brick-and-stone building was built in 1915 as a private club. The six-story Italianate landmark has been refurbished into a sleek nonsmoking hotel in which every room is different. The first-floor lobby and restaurant house a collection of mid 20C artists' works.

$$$$ Le Meridien Stoneleigh Hotel – 2927 Maple Ave., Dallas. ☎214-871-7111. www.starwoodhotels.com. 158 rooms. A Jazz Age landmark (1923), this hotel has spacious apartment-style rooms with walnut and mahogany furnishings, a fitness center, a Spanish-style restaurant and an attractive Uptown location.

$$$ Stockyards Hotel – 109 E. Exchange Ave., Fort Worth. ☎817-625-6427. www.stockyardshotel.com. 52 rooms. Located in the historic cattle shipping district, this Old West hostelry recalls early Texas history: some rooms are decorated with rawhide lamps and steer skulls. The Davy Crockett Suite even boasts a coonskin cap from the days when cattle barons and rustlers sat in the saddles at the bar.

$$$ Warwick Melrose Hotel – 3015 Oak Lawn Ave., Dallas. ☎214-521-5151. www.warwickmelrosedallas.com. 184 rooms. Once a luxury apartment block, the historic (1924) Melrose boasts an understated exterior of simple brick with a carved frieze. The handsome porte cochère leads to marble floors, tall columns and recently renovated rooms. The **Landmark ($$)** serves fine Mediterranean-tinged Gulf Coast cuisine.

$$ Etta's Place – 200 W. 3rd St., Fort Worth. ☎817-255-5760. www.ettas-place.com. 10 rooms. It's in a newer building, but this B&B inn echoes the 19C ambience of Sundance Square, right down to its name: Etta Place was the Sundance Kid's mistress. Each room is furnished with Western antiques. Breakfast is a hearty repast featuring handmade sausage and quiches.

🍽 EAT

$$$ Arcodoro & Pomodoro – 100 Crescent Court, Dallas. ☎214-871-1924. www.arcodoro.com/dallas. **Sardinian.** Though many ingredients are flown in from the Mediterranean, the highly savory dishes here include regional specialties such as Texas quail in sage and grape must.

$$$ Riscky's Steakhouse – 120 E. Exchange Ave., Fort Worth. ☎817-624-4800. www.risckys.com. **American.** The interior of this local favorite resembles a street of old downtown Fort Worth. Come for Texas T-bone or chicken-fried steaks; ask about batter-dipped "calf fries," cooked to a golden brown; or the traditional Polish sauerkraut soup.

$$ The Lonesome Dove – 2406 N. Main St., Fort Worth. ☎817-740-8810. www.lonesomedovebistro.com. Closed Sun. **American.** Classically trained Chef Tim Love has turned his attention to "cowboy cuisine" at this

© Nikhilesh Haval/age fotostock

jovial Stockyards bistro. Love stuffs beef tenderloin with roasted garlic, offers two wagyu beef steaks and pairs elk loin with salsify, mushrooms and chard.

$$ Joe T Garcia's – 2201 N. Commerce St., Fort Worth. ☏817-626-4356. www.joets.com. **Mexican**. This place is the epitome of Tex-Mex, where Mexican beer is freely consumed by cowboy-clad customers on a patio that regularly fills to its capacity of 300. Visiting celebrities gobble up renowned menudos and enchiladas.

$ Sonny Bryan's Smokehouse – 2202 Inwood Rd., Dallas. ☏214-357-7120. www.sonnybryans.com. **Barbecue**. Sonny's opened in 1958 as a drive-in. The family recipes for slow-smoked brisket are a century old. Today, Texans slather Sonny's secret BBQ sauce onto spare ribs, chicken and pulled pork. Six other locations dot the DFW metroplex.

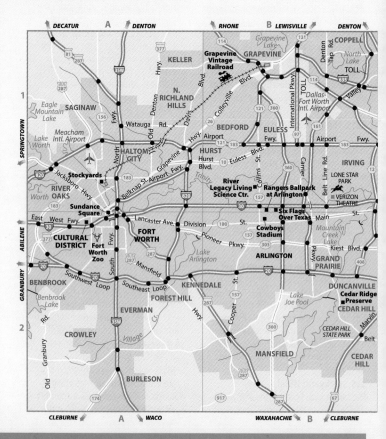

Dallas★★

Dallas has a certain familiarity even for those who haven't been to "Big D." It's the city where President Kennedy was assassinated, venue of the popular Dallas television series and movie, and home of the Dallas Cowboys football club, which fancies itself "America's team." Shoppers know the Dallas Market Center (2100 Stemmons Fwy.; t214-655-6100; www. dallasmarketcenter.com), the largest wholesale merchandise mart in the world, and the original Neiman-Marcus department store (1618 Main St.; ℘214-741-6911; www.neimanmarcus.com), an icon of Texas wealth. Museums are clustered at Fair Park, shopping dominates the West End, and Deep Ellum is a hub for nightlife.

▶ **Population:** 1,223,000.

♿ **Michelin Map:** p 376-377. Central Standard Time.

🛈 **Info:** ℘214-571-1316; ww.visitdallas.com.

◗ **Location:** Many attractions are concentrated in three areas. Museums are clustered at Fair Park, site of the largest state fair in the US each October. The Dallas Arts District is the nation's largest urban arts district. The West End Historic District, occupying renovated warehouses, holds some of the city's best shopping and nightlife.

🚫 **Don't Miss:** Dallas Museum of Art.

🕐 **Timing:** If you have kids, you'll want to allow a whole day for Arlington, home of Six Flags amusement park and some of the nation's best roller coasters.

👫 **Kids:** Six Flags Over Texas.

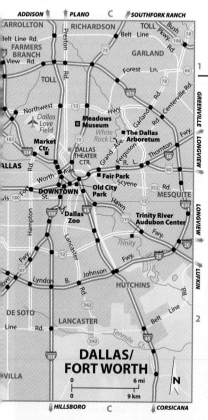

DALLAS TODAY

Perennially competing with Houston for primacy in Texas, Dallas fashions itself the premier financial and business services center of the Southwest, and a high-tech capital under the rubric "Silicon Prairie". The city's massive Arts District (below) renews the contest with Houston for cultural ascendancy as well.

A BIT OF HISTORY

Dallas began in 1841 as a trading post near a crossing on the Trinity River. By the time the US annexed Texas in 1845, the town's population had grown to 430, mostly farmers, traders and shopkeepers. It prospered as a supply station for settlers in the great westward expansion and as an agricultural center, particularly for the export of cotton. After suffering severe economic and social problems in the wake of the Civil War, during which it supported the Confederacy, Dallas rebounded as a trade center and a shipping point for the fresh meat market. In the 1870s railway and telegraph lines further enhanced its position as a hub of commerce. The Federal Reserve Bank selected Dallas as the site for a regional bank in 1911, fostering the city's role as a financial center.

Dallas' strong ties with the aviation industry began with World War I, when Love Field was founded as an air-training facility; the **Frontiers of Flight Museum** commemorates that heritage with vintage aircraft and exhibits about pioneer aviators (6911 Lemmon Ave.; ℘214-350-3600; www.flightmuseum. com). Today, although Love still operates as a commercial airport, it is overshadowed by the enormous Dallas–Fort Worth International Airport, world headquarters of American Airlines.

DOWNTOWN DALLAS★★

Downtown Dallas combines commerce and culture with shopping, dining and entertainment.

The four-story **West End Marketplace** (Lamar St. north of Pacific Ave.; www. dallaswestend.org) is a renovated warehouse with more than 50 shops, restaurants, nightclubs and a cinema complex. A few blocks farther north is a state-of-the-art sports arena, **American Airlines Center** (2500 Victory Ave.; ℘214-222-3687; www.americanairlinescenter.com), home to pro basketball and ice hockey.

Deep Ellum (Elm St. east of Good-Latimer Expwy.; http://deepellumtexas. com), a former industrial neighborhood east of downtown, now boasts a thriving nightclub scene ranging from jazz and blues to alternative music. In recent years, the scope of the avant-garde has spread beyond Elm Street (where speakeasies flourished during Prohibition) to nearby Main and Commerce streets.

Dallas Arts District★★

Main section between Ross St. and Woodall Rogers Access Rd., and St. Paul St. and the North Central Expressway. ✕&🅿 ℘214-744-6642. www.thedallasartsdistrict.org.

The Dallas Museum of Art (opposite) anchors one end of a 68-acre cultural district that's the largest in the US. Comprising museums, performance halls and parks and plazas, the district envisions numerous future developments to augment the new (2009) AT&T **Performing Arts Center** (2403 Flora St.; ℘214-880-0202; www.attpac.org). An opera house, theater and outdoor performance plaza are in place, with parks, more halls and other venues planned. The **Nasher Sculpture Center** rotates more than 300 sculptures through its indoor facility and 1.5-acre outdoor

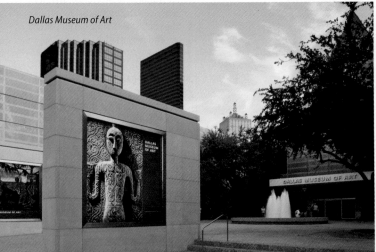

Dallas Museum of Art

© Dallas Museum of Art

garden, which holds 25 pieces at a time (2001 Flora St.; ℘214-242-5125; www.nashersculpturecenter.org).

Dallas Museum of Art★★

1717 N. Harwood St. ✗🕭♿🅿
℘214-922-1200. www.dm-art.org.
In this vast, stair-stepped building (1984, Edward L. Barnes) a collection of global scope is presented, beginning with a broad survey of human cultural evolution in the Western Hemisphere. Starting with amulets and jewelry of prehistoric civilizations, it follows creative artistry through the Spanish and British colonial periods, right up to 20C Texas. Highlights include paintings by Albert Bierstadt, Andrew Wyeth and Georgia O'Keeffe, as well as Frederic Church, Thomas Hart Benton and sculpture by James Earl Frasier.

European Painting & Sculpture★★ galleries showcase 19C canvases by Manet, Degas, Monet, Renoir, Van Gogh and Gauguin; and 20C works by Mondrian, Picasso, Braque and Modigliani. The **Contemporary Art Gallery★** presents works by Rothko, Pollock, Motherwell, Warhol and Diebenkorn.

The **Wendy & Emery Reves Collection★** features 19-20C European painting and diverse decorative arts. Its setting recalls a French Riviera villa, and it has a full room devoted to paintings and memorabilia of Sir Winston Churchill. Other exhibits covering arts of Africa, Asia and the Pacific show a wide range of world cultures.

Crow Collection of Asian Art★

2010 Flora St. 🕭 ℘214-979-6430.
www.crowcollection.com.
Real-estate magnate Trammell Crow and his wife, Margaret, built this elegant granite facility to house a renowned Asian collection of more than 500 pieces. Highlights include exquisite carved-jade pieces and a jewel-encrusted Indian marble gateway.
Nearby is the **Morton H. Meyerson Symphony Center★** (2301 Flora St.; ℘214-692-0203; www.dallassymphony.com), home of the Dallas Symphony Orchestra. The only such building designed

by I.M. Pei (1989) incorporates the Eugene McDermott Concert Hall. Pei also designed the **Dallas City Hall** (1500 Marilla St.; ℘214-670-3011).

♿♨Perot Museum of Nature and Science★

22201 N. Field St. ℘214-428-5555.
www.perotmuseum.org.
This new, precast-concrete facility (2012, Thom Mayne) was created by the family of flamboyant Texan Ross Perot, erstwhile high-tech tycoon and independent US presidential candidate. The immense cube dominates a block at the edge of the Arts District, with a glass-enclosed escalator appended to the side.
Exhibit halls cover a large range, from life sciences and energy development to cosmology and ornithology. The **Moody Family Children's Museum★** contains dozens of interactive displays designed to acquaint youngsters with practical aspects of science. A subsidiary Perot Museum at Fair Park (see below) offers abbreviated exhibits covering science.

The Sixth Floor Museum at Dealey Plaza★★★

411 Elm St. at Houston St. 🕭🅿
℘214-747-6660. www.jfk.org.
On November 22, 1963, alleged assassin Lee Harvey Oswald fired shots at US President John F. Kennedy from this level of the former Texas School Book Depository building. Today the entire 9,000sq-ft floor holds a moving tribute to Kennedy's life and career.
The southeast corner window—from which Oswald allegedly shot the president—has been re-created to look as it did when investigators discovered it, with cardboard boxes stacked to form a hiding place.
Newscaster Walter Cronkite's poignant announcement of the president's death is rebroadcast in a TV clip. Nearby is a photo of Lyndon Johnson taking the presidential oath with Jacqueline Kennedy by his side. Display cases showcase international tributes.
The Sixth Floor Museum is within **Dealey Plaza National Historic Landmark**

district, six square blocks that encompass sites important to the Kennedy assassination and its aftermath, as well as other cultural attractions.

Across the street from the museum, the **Dallas Holocaust Museum** (211 N. Record St.; ✆214-741-7500; www.dallasholocaustmuseum.org) depicts its topic by focusing on one day during World War II, April, 13, 1943.

Two blocks away, "**Old Reda**," the former county courthouse, preserves a remarkable 1892 red sandstone Romanesque building as the **Dallas County Historical Museum** (100 S. Houston St.; ✆214-745-1100; www.oldred.org). East of Dealey Plaza, **John F. Kennedy Memorial Plaza** centers on a **cenotaph**, or open tomb, designed by Philip Johnson and dedicated in 1970.

Pioneer Plaza★★

Young and Griffin Sts.

The world's largest bronze monument occupies this 4.2-acre park area north of the Dallas Convention Center.

Entitled *Cattle Drive* (1994, Robert Summers), the sculpture features 40 longhorn steers being herded by a trio of mounted cowboys down a limestone ledge, past native plants and through a flowing stream.

FAIR PARK★

Built to host the 1936 Texas Centennial Exhibition, these 277-acre grounds, a short distance east of downtown, host the largest state fair in the US (Sept-Oct), which attracts the lion's share of 7 million annual visitors to **Fair Park** (1300 Robert E. Cullum Blvd.; ✆214-426-3400; www.fairpark.org). Even during its "off-season," it bustles as a cultural center with its **Cotton Bowl** stadium (www.attcottonbowl.com); the **Music Hall at Fair Park** (909 First Ave.; ✆214-565-1116); and the **Gexa Energy Pavilion** (1818 First Ave.; ✆214-421-1111; www.livenation.com) for open-air concerts. A fairly new (2009) "performing" **fountain** adds 272 water jets to the 700ft-long Esplanade reflecting pool. Also here are numerous museums, many of them—including the Hall of State, aquarium and natural history museum—built in 1930s Art Deco style.

Hall of State

3939 Grand Ave. ♿ 🅿 ✆214-421-4500. www.hallofstate.com.

A showcase of Texas history, the limestone Hall of State is shaped like an inverted T. Larger-than-life bronze statues by Pompeo Coppini commemorate six Texas founding fathers, and ornate murals depict historical events.

Waltz across Texas

Texas music has had an outsize impact on modern music as a whole, chiefly in the classic American idioms of country music and rock 'n' roll. With Negro spirituals, Mexican ballads and Louisiana Cajun influences spicing the original stew, the state's musical heritage helped give birth to a half-dozen styles and literally dozens of stars. Scott Joplin invented ragtime, Blind Lemon Jefferson and Lightnin' Hopkins were blues pioneers, Bob Wills and Ernest Tubb were country-western pioneers, and Buddy Holly's brief career weighed heavily on rock. Their musical descendants include George Jones, Waylon Jennings, Willie Nelson, Kris Kristofferson, Roy Orbison, Stevie Ray Vaughan, Freddy Fender and the legendary Janis Joplin. The **Texas Country Music Hall of Fame** in Carthage (www.carthagetexas.com/halloffame) honors many of these artists; and there is an official state Music Office to support Lone Star musicians (www.governor.state.tx.us/music). Most would agree that the state song of Texas is not the one adopted by the Legislature ("Texas, My Texas") but the song heard at every football game and most gatherings, "The Yellow Rose of Texas."

African American Museum★

3536 Grand Ave. ♿🅿 ℘214-565-9026.
www.aamdallas.org.
This facility devoted to African-American history, art and culture occupies a two-story building (1993, Arthur Rogers) made of ivory stone with a 60ft dome in the shape of a 12C Ethiopian Orthodox cross. Its motifs symbolize pre-industrialized African cultures. Exhibits include selections from the **Billy R. Allen Folk Art Collection**, one of the best contemporary collections in the US.

♁ Perot Museum of Nature and Science

3535 Grand Ave. ♿🅿 ℘214-428-5555.
www.perotmuseum.org.
Dioramas of Texas wildlife and habitats combine with the first dinosaur discovered in this state and ecology exhibits. The entrance is marked by a bronze sculpture by Tom Tischler, based on a mammoth skeleton excavated in Dallas. More than 300 interactive displays explore scientific principles.

Texas Discovery Gardens

3601 Martin Luther King Blvd.
♿🅿 ℘214-428-7476.
www.texasdiscoverygardens.org.
An educational center for urban horticulture, this facility spans 7.5 acres of both decorative and native Texas plants. The **Butterfly House** hosts more than 250 species of African plants.

ADDITIONAL SIGHTS

♁ Dallas Heritage Village★

1515 S. Harwood St. ✗♿🅿 ℘214-413-3679. www.dallasheritagevillage.org.
This 20-acre museum village, south of downtown, contains 38 restored buildings dated 1840-1910 that were moved here from north-central Texas.
Structures include a rail depot, hotel, bank, doctor's office and school. A number of collections (tools, furniture, black and white photographs and even historic postcards) are on display.
Costumed docents carry on chores in the garden, curing shed and livestock lot of the Living Farmstead.

♁ Dallas Zoo★

650 S. R.L. Thornton Fwy., 3mi south of downtown at Marsalis Exit, I-35. ✗♿🅿
℘214-554-7400. www.dallaszoo.com.
Founded in 1888, the zoo keeps some 2,000 animals in two sections of 85 developed acres. In the larger **ZooNorth** visitors can ride camels and see bird shows. **Wilds of Africa★★**, south of Cedar Creek, has expansive habitats of different landscapes, and **Giants of the Savanna** (2010) shows off elephants, zebras, cheetahs and other animals.
The zoo also operates the **Dallas World Aquarium** (1801 N. Griffin St.; ℘214-720-2224; www.dwazoo.com), which has exhibits on Borneo, the Orinoco River rain forest, and a cenote with sharks and rays.

♁ Trinity River Audubon Center★

6500 S. Loop 12; ✗♿🅿 ℘214-398-8722.
trinityriver.audubon.org.
Carved from the wasteland of an illegal construction debris dump site, this recent (2008) park facility focuses attention on the surrounding 6,000-acre Great Trinity Forest, largest urban woodland in the US, and the many plants and animals within it. The environmentally efficient visitor center conserves water, energy and materials.

Dallas Arboretum

8525 Garland Rd. ♿🅿 ℘214-515-6500.
www.dallasarboretum.org.
This 66-acre expanse on White Rock Lake is highlighted by the **Jonsson Color Garden★**, with 20,000 azalea bushes of some 2,000 varieties. Other features are the 1940 Spanish Colonial-style **DeGolyer Home** (👁tours daily) and an annually refreshed exhibit (Mar-Dec) of a half-dozen **storybook playhouses ♁**.

Museum of Biblical Art

7500 Park Lane ℘214-368-4622.
www.biblicalarts.org.
Espousing no agenda other than exhibiting religious art and illumination in the Judeo-Christian tradition, this new (2010) facility supplants one

that burned down in 2005. Its fairly ecumenical scope includes works by Warhol, Shahn, Chagall and Kokoshcka; the Ryrie Library holds a large collection of rare Bibles.

Meadows Museum★★

Bishop Blvd. at Binkley Ave., Southern Methodist University. ℰ214-768-2516. www.meadowsmuseumdallas.org.
Its interior fashioned after Madrid's famed Prado, this small university museum houses an outstanding collection of Spanish art. Beginning with 10C Medieval and Renaissance paintings, it moves through Baroque Castilian (Velázquez) and Andalusian (Murillo) art to 18C dry-point etchings by Goya. There are 20C works by Miró and early Cubist still-lifes by Picasso.

George W. Bush Presidential Library

2943 SMU Blvd., on the campus of Southern Methodist University. ℰ214-346-1650. www.georgewbushlibary. smu.edu.
The presidency of America's first 21C leader is profiled at this new facility (2012, Robert A.M. Stern) north of downtown Dallas. Features include a full-size Oval Office replica and a 67ft-high "Freedom Hall" encircled by a video screen orienting visitors to the museum. Born in Connecticut, George Walker Bush (b.1946) lived and attended school in Midland and Houston. He was later elected Governor of Texas (1995-2000). From 2001-2009 he served as the 43rd US President, following in the footsteps of his father, 41st US President George Herbert Walker Bush.

Cedar Ridge Preserve★

7171 Mountain Creek Pkwy., 2.5mi south of I-20. 🅿 ℰ972-709-7784. www.audubondallas.org.
This 633-acre park preserves the last remaining piece of native prairie in the Dallas metroplex. Nine hiking trails wind through juniper groves, mesquite prairies, wildflower meadows and butterfly gardens. Picnicking is permitted in designated areas.

EXCURSIONS
Southfork Ranch

▶ 3700 Hogge Dr., Parker; 16mi north of downtown Dallas off US-75, Exit 30 East. ✕🅰🅿 ℰ972-442-7800. www.southforkranch.com.
This sprawling mansion was used in exterior shots for the former long-running Dallas TV series—still popular around the world. Visitors board a tractor-drawn jitney to reach the Ewing Mansion for guided tours. TV clips, star interviews and "the gun that shot J.R." highlight the "Dallas Legends" exhibit.

Arlington

▶ I-30, 16mi west of Dallas & 15mi east of Fort Worth. ℰ817-342-3888 or 800-342-4305. www.experiencearlington.org.
A city of just over 375,000 residents, Arlington is best known for its theme parks and as the home of major league baseball's Texas Rangers and the National Football League Dallas Cowboys. **The Ballpark in Arlington** (1000 Ballpark Way; ℰ817-273-5100; http://texas.rangers.mlb.com) is a 1994 structure (David M. Schwarz) in the style of early 20C ballparks; the $190 million stadium offers year-round tours.
Nearby, the huge **Cowboys Stadium** (900 E Randol Mill Rd.; ℰ817-892-5000; http://stadium.dallascowboys.com) is a 2009 state-of-the-art facility that hosts its namesake football team, as well as other events that may include a future World Cup in 2018 or 2022.

▲▲ Six Flags Over Texas★

▶ I-30 & Rte. 360. ✕🅰🅿 ℰ817-640-8900. www.sixflags.com.
The state's tallest roller coaster, the newly reconfigured "Mr. Freeze," is in this 212-acre theme park, as is the Texas Giant, rated the world's No. 1 wooden roller coaster. The 32-story "Superman: Tower of Power" ride is the tallest of its kind. The park is the flagship and original base of the Six Flags chain.
The **Six Flags Hurricane Harbor** (1800 E. Lamar Blvd.; ℰ817-265-3356; www.sixflags.com), open seasonally, boasts water rides and more than 3 million gallons of water.

Fort Worth★★

"The place where the West begins" wears its heritage like a medal. Established in 1849 as a US Army outpost on the Trinity River, Fort Worth was named for Mexican War hero William Jenkins Worth. In the 1860s the town became a shipping point for buffalo hunters on the Great Plains. No city nickname has endured like "Cowtown," a moniker adopted in the 1870s when beef cattle were driven up the Chisholm Trail from South Texas. Fort Worth was first a supply station on the way to Kansas railheads and later, with the arrival of the railway, a major terminus itself.

▶ **Population:** 736,000.
◔ **Michelin Map:** p 376-377. Central Standard Time.
▤ **Info:** ℰ817-698-3300; www.fortworth.com.
▷ **Location:** From Fort Worth westward to the Rockies lie the sere plains once inhabited only by Comanches; thus the phrase "where the West begins."
⊛ **Don't Miss:** The Kimbell and Amon Carter museums.
▲▪ **Kids:** Fort Worth Zoo; Grapevine Vintage Railroad.

A BIT OF HISTORY

With the founding of the Stockyards in 1887, the town began earning a Wild West reputation. Saloons and brothels proliferated. The infamous Hell's Half Acre district served as headquarters for **Butch Cassidy** and his Wild Bunch. By 1904, more than 1 million head of cattle had passed through the Stockyards; cattle pens extended nearly a mile; and the area was nicknamed "Wall Street of the West." During the early 20C, Fort Worth expanded and diversified, especially in aviation and oil; this prosperity was the genesis of the world-class museums in its Cultural District.

FORT WORTH TODAY

"Cowtown" now is, in many ways, everything Dallas is not, a fact both cities embrace. Development of the huge Barnett shale gas formation beneath the city has brought new energy wealth, and inaugurated the current US shale gas boom that is transforming the American energy industry.

Fort Worth is notable, too, as a city which relocated a freeway that shadowed its downtown. The city treasures its heritage, which it brands "Cowboys and Culture": at the heart of downtown Fort Worth is Sundance Square, a revitalized 20-block neighborhood named for notorious Western outlaw **Harry Longabaugh**, "The Sundance Kid." The city's museums have a distinctly Western air. But it embraces modernity, too, with a bike share program (http://fortworthbikesharing.org) with 150 miles of dedicated paths.

STOCKYARDS NATIONAL HISTORIC DISTRICT★★

An Old West flair persists in old Cowtown (ℰ817-624-4741; www.fortworthstockyards.org). A steam train, year-round rodeos and country-and-western nightlife couple with historic hotels, steakhouses and Western wear shops to give it a frontier flavor. Cowboys shepherd longhorns through the district twice a day during faux but entertaining cattle "drives." The small **Stockyards Museum** (131 E. Exchange Ave.; ℰ817-625-5082; www.stockyardsmuseum.org), in the 1902 Livestock Exchange Building, chronicles its history. At the century-old **White Elephant Saloon** (106 E. Exchange Ave.; ℰ817-624-8273; www.whiteelephantsaloon.com), patrons have left their Stetson hats nailed to the ceiling.

▲▪ Cowtown Coliseum

121 E. Exchange Ave. ♿ ℰ817-625-1025. http://stockyardsrodeo.com.
Built in 1908, the coliseum presented the world's first indoor rodeo in 1918.

Longhorn Cattle Drive

©iStockphoto.com/Kriss Russell

Cattle Drives

By the end of the Civil War, meat shortages in the East led Texas ranchers to employ new strategies to get beef to market. Most dramatic was the cattle drive: South Texas cowboys collected herds of wild range cattle ("mavericks") and drove them north to railroads in Kansas. Although the heyday of the cattle drive lasted only a dozen years, its influence persists in popular myth.

Descendants of Spanish breeds brought to the New World, Texas longhorns roamed freely over the grasslands of Texas and Mexico, numbering in the millions by the time of the first cattle drives in the late 1860s. The Chisholm Trail was the most famous of the cattle drive routes. In 1870 alone, 300,000 cattle were driven through San Antonio and Austin north to Fort Worth, the last "civilized" stop on the way.

By the late 1870s, the railroad was pushing south and west, eventually making the cattle drive obsolete. But Fort Worth visitors can witness daily cattle "drives" at the Stockyards National Historic District (p383).

Today, the twice-weekly Stockyards Championship Rodeo features bull riding, calf roping and barrel racing in which contestants compete for prizes of up to several thousand dollars; and Pawnee Bill's Wild West Show is a revival of a Western show—with rope tricks and trick riding—that first played here in 1909.

Billy Bob's Texas★

2520 Rodeo Plaza. ✕♿🅿 ℘817-624-7117. www.billybobstexas.com.
Billed as "the world's largest honky-tonk," this nightclub seats 6,000 and boasts dozens of bar stations, line-dancing lessons, two separate music stages and an indoor professional bull-riding arena. Top-line country music stars and Texas icons such as Willie Nelson perform here.

👥 Grapevine Vintage Railroad★

140 E. Exchange Ave. ℘817-410-3123. www.gvrr.com.
With the oldest "puffer-belly" locomotive in the US (c.1896), the steam train pulls Victorian coaches and open-air cars on a 75min, 21mi ride between the Stockyards and suburban Grapevine. Passengers may watch craftspeople at the Grapevine Heritage Center or attend tastings by award-winning wineries on Grapevine's historic Main Street.

SUNDANCE SQUARE★

Though its signature new pedestrian plaza (2013) is designed to resemble a European city-center square, Sundance Square refers to the heart of downtown Fort Worth, a revitalized 35-block district of brick streets lined with shops and restaurants, hotels and museums (℘817-255-5700; www.sundancesquare.com). Anchoring the district is the 1895 **Tarrant County Courthouse★** (100 W. Weatherford St.; ℘817-884-1111; www.tarrantcounty.com), patterned after the Texas State Capitol.

Often featured in the *Walker: Texas Ranger* TV series, it boasts an unusual *trompe l'oeil* paint job that gives a building extension the same appearance as the original stone structure.

The $65 million **Bass Performance Hall★** (555 Commerce St.; ℘817-212-4325; www.basshall.com), designed by David M. Schwarz (1998), occupies a full city block. It is identified by its twin 48ft limestone sculptures—trumpet-heralding angels by Marton Varo. The Bass is home to the Fort Worth symphony, ballet and opera, and the Van Cliburn International Piano Competition.

Sid Richardson Museum★

309 Main St. ♿🅿℘817-332-6554. www.sidrichardsonmuseum.org.
Five dozen paintings by Charles M. Russell and Frederic Remington are showcased in this Sundance Square museum, the personal collection of billionaire oilman Sid W. Richardson (1891-1959).

On the south side of downtown, famed architect Philip Johnson turned a vacant four-acre lot into the **Fort Worth Water Gardens★** (1502 Commerce St.), a collection of brick-lined fountains, ponds, gardens and picnic alcoves.

CULTURAL DISTRICT★★★

Trinity Park is the focus of this district, which includes five major museums, Fort Worth's zoo and botanical garden. More than 2 million visitors a year enjoy the many attractions here.

Kimbell Art Museum★★★

3333 Camp Bowie Blvd. ✕♿🅿℘817-332-8451. www.kimbellart.org.
Newly expanded (2013) to nearly double its original size, one of the country's premier art showcases now boasts 85,000sq ft of exhibit space for its remarkable collection. Architect Louis Kahn made innovative use of deflected natural light in the original 1972 building, enabling curators to subtly rearrange generous space for special exhibitions; Renzo Piano's new, $135 million addition mirrors Kahn's work with colonnaded glass and matching height.

The new pavilion hosts largely temporary exhibits, allowing the Kahn building to house the permanent collection, which includes such masterworks as Rubens' *The Duke of Buckingham* (1625); Rembrandt's *Portrait of a Young Jew* (1663); and Cézanne's *Glass and Apples* (c.1879-82). Works by Titian, El Greco, Goya, Degas, Monet, Picasso and Miró are also in the collection. While the focus is chiefly European art, rotating exhibits also feature pre-Columbian, African and Asian art.

Amon Carter Museum★★★

3501 Camp Bowie Blvd. ℘817-738-1933. www.cartermuseum.org.
This formerly small museum gained international stature with its three-fold 2001 expansion by Philip Johnson, who also designed the initial International-style building in 1961. Today it is one of the world's leading repositories of art depicting the American West, although its collection ranges farther geographically.

The original first floor is devoted to late oilman-publisher Amon G. Carter's peerless collection of 391 works by famed Western artists **Charles Russell** (1864-1926) and **Frederic Remington** (1861-1909). The latter's massive *A Dash for the Timber* is the Carter's signature painting, and its collection is unique in that visitors can compare the two artists' very different styles side-by-side. The upper level is devoted to visiting exhibits and samplings from the rest of the Carter collection, ranging from

Amon Carter Museum

© Amon Carter Museum of American Art

Thomas Moran to Georgia O'Keeffe and Grant Wood. The world-class **photography collection's** 230,000 images include works by Laura Gilpin, Eliot Porter, Richard Avedon, Ansel Adams and Robert Adams.

Modern Art Museum of Fort Worth★

3200 Darnell St. ✕&🅿 ✆817-738-9215. www.themodern.org.

The oldest (1892) art museum in Texas now resides in a modern concrete-and-glass building with 53,000sq ft of gallery space, designed by Tadao Ando (2002); it uses skylights and clerestory windows to bring natural light inside, and its pavilions seem to float on the surrounding reflecting pools.

The collection offers a thorough sampling of 20C artists, including Picasso, Rothko, Pollock, Rauschenberg, Motherwell, Warhol, Basquiat, Cindy Sherman, Ed Ruscha and others.

♟♟ Fort Worth Museum of Science and History★

1600 Gendy St. ✕&🅿 ✆817-255-9300. www.fwmuseum.org.

This recently expanded (2009) and expansive complex is both a traditional museum, with exhibits ranging from Texas butterflies to historic cameras; and a learning center.

The "Innovation Studios" portion of the complex invites families to take part in inventing, drawing, designing, exploring and creating, using hands-on activities ranging from shadow puppets to computer-aided video conferencing. Downtown (*Fire Station #1, Second and Commerce Streets*) the satellite "150 Years of Fort Worth" ranges from prehistoric times through the cowboy era to today.

National Cowgirl Museum & Hall of Fame★★

1720 Gendy St. &🅿 ✆817-336-4475 or 800-476-3263. www.cowgirl.net.

A rarely acknowledged facet of Western history receives star treatment at this 2002 facility in the Western Heritage Center. Women, who once entered and won rodeo competitions alongside men, are featured, as well as such luminaries as artist Georgia O'Keeffe, singer Patsy Cline and actress Dale Evans. The collection includes archival photos, colorful clothing and cowgirl trophies.

♟♟ Fort Worth Zoo★★

1989 Colonial Pkwy. ✕&🅿 ✆817-759-7555. www.fortworthzoo.org.

Acclaimed both for its visitor accessibility and its animal-friendly habitats, this zoo is home to some 7,000 animals of Texas and exotic species. The new (2010) **Museum of Living Art★★**, one of the world's largest herpetariums, brings visitors face to face with snakes, crocodiles, frogs, lizards and many more—

the namesake "art"—describing both their importance and perilous status. **Asian Falls** is the precinct of tigers and sloth bears. **World of Primates** permits visitors to virtually enter the gorilla habitat. **Texas Wild**★★ is a six-acre evocation of life and nature in the Lone Star State; here, visitors can try their skills at a Wild West shooting gallery, enjoy a treat in an ice-cream parlor, and meet new friends at the petting corral. WIld turkeys, river otters, horned lizards and Gulf coast marine life are among the many varied denizens that can be seen.

Fort Worth Botanic Garden★

3220 Botanic Garden Blvd. (off University Dr.). &🄿 ☎817-392-5510. www.fwbg.org.

Texas' oldest botanic garden began as a Depression-era relief program in 1933. The 110-acre gardens include more than 2,500 native and exotic species. An impressive begonia collection is in the Exhibition Greenhouse; tropical plants fill the lush, 10,000sq-ft Conservatory.

EXCURSIONS
Bureau of Engraving and Printing★

◗ 9000 Blue Mound Rd. ☎817-231-4000. wwwmoneyfactory.gov.

One of two plants at which US currency is made, this federal facility prints millions of dollars a day in paper money; tours are offered to the public on a first-come, first-served basis.

Glen Rose

◗ On US-67, 53mi southwest of Fort Worth. ☎254-897-3081. www.glenrosetexas.net.

Tucked amid oaks and cottonwoods along the Paluxy River, this erstwhile frontier town has been transformed into a weekend getaway center with galleries, cafes and small inns.

Nearby, **Fossil Rim Wildlife Center**★ (2155 County Rd. 2008; ☎254-897-2960; www.fossilrim.org) is a fascinating 1,700-acre safari park with herds of African antelope, giraffes, rhinoceros, ostriches and other species endangered in native ranges. The park educates visitors about the perilous status of many of its animals.

Fossilized dinosaur tracks lie in the limestone beds in and near **Dinosaur Valley State Park** (Park Rd. 59, 4mi northwest of Glen Rose; ☎254-897-4588; www.tpwd.state.tx.us); evolution opponents claim nearby human footprints lie beside dinosaur tracks, though a local resident revealed that her father had carved them in the Depression, supporting scientists who scoff at the claims.

Waco

◗ On I-35, 87mi south of Fort Worth (via I-35W) and 90mi south of Dallas (via I-35E). ☎254-750-8696. www.wacoheartoftexas.com.

A cattle- and cotton-farming center of 122,000 on the Brazos River, Waco is home to **Baylor University**, with some 15,000 students. The city's 475-foot **suspension bridge** over the Brazos (at University Parks Dr. downtown) was built in 1870 to carry cattle headed north, and supposedly served as the model for the Brooklyn Bridge 13 years later.

Texas Ranger Hall of Fame and Museum★

◗ 100 Texas Ranger Trail. (I-35 Exit 335B). ⚠&🄿 ☎254-750-8631. www.texasranger.org.

The lawmen responsible for taming Texas are remembered here. Displays include Billy the Kid's Winchester carbine, weapons packed by Bonnie and Clyde, and a gem-encrusted saddle.

Armstrong Browning Library★★

◗ 710 Speight Ave., Baylor University. &🄿 ☎254-710-3566. www.browninglibrary.org.

The library holds the world's largest collection of the works and belongings of British poets Robert Browning (1812-89) and Elizabeth Barrett Browning (1806-61). A.J. Armstrong, long-time chairman of Baylor's English department, donated his personal collection to the university. Many works of poetry are brought to life in the building's remarkable collection of stained-glass windows.

Houston Area

The largest city in Texas (fourth-largest in the US) lies just inland from the Gulf of Mexico in flat bayou country. The Houston Ship Channel has made the city the largest foreign-trade port in the United States, supporting one-third of all jobs in the region.

Highlights

1 Top-notch drama at **Alley Theatre** (p392)
2 Cullen Hall's **gems** (p393)
3 NASA **Space Center** (p395)
4 Alligators at **Brazos Bend** (p395)
5 Galveston's **beaches** (p396)

Houston
TX

City of Self-Confidence

Houston anchors a metropolitan area of more than 6 million people and is best known for its petrochemical industry. "Black gold" anchored the economy for most of the 20C. It remains a major player today, along with the medical and aerospace industries.

Houston's wealth has given the city a rich cultural life. One of the few US cities with permanent ballet, opera, symphony and theater companies, Houston is a US cultural leader. More than 30 museums are funded by local business fortunes. Professional baseball, football, soccer and basketball franchises anchor the sports scene. The Houston **AstroDome** (8400 Kirby Dr. at I-610 Loop South; www.reliantpark.com/astrodome) was the world's first domed stadium, though it may be torn down.

Galveston is primarily a resort destination. The barrier island fills in summer with Houstonians getting away from the city. Connected to the mainland by bridge, Galveston Island lies 50mi from Houston via Interstate 45.

Houston Skyline

SPINDLETOP

People had known for centuries there was oil in the ground in east Texas—indigenous tribes used the tar to caulk canoes, and pioneers often lit the sulfurous gas seeps for amusement. When petroleum began to replace whale oil as a fuel at the end of the 19C, numerous attempts to drill near Beaumont produced skimpy but tantalizing results. There was oil there, but not a lot.

So most thought, but entrepreneur Pattillo Higgins believed there was a huge reservoir underground, if only drillers could reach deep enough in the right spot. Armed with investor money and a new technology that relied on rotating drill bits, Higgins formed the Gladys City Oil and Manufacturing Company in 1892. The resulting enterprise changed human history, but it took nine years, several iterations of the company and its backers, and the arrival of drill-master Anthony Lucas.

Lucas was an early expert on salt domes, the geologic structures that harbor oil under pressure. Drilling to 575 feet on a local rise called Spindletop Hill yielded nothing, the money ran out, and skeptics scoffed at the wildcatters. New backers enabled the project to continue, but Higgins and Lucas retained virtually no share of the enterprise. The latter persisted nonetheless, and on January 10, 1901, the most famous event in oil and gas history took place when the team struck paydirt 1,139 feet underground.

The blow-out gusher rose 150 feet in the air and spewed 100,000 barrels of oil daily—thousands of times more petroleum than other wells. Crews capped the well nine days later, and the modern oil industry was born. Beaumont boomed to 50,000 residents and "black gold" replaced the allure of real gold in the public imagination. The craze spread to the rest of Texas, then Oklahoma, and thence around the world, enabling the global ascension of the internal combustion engine and the automobile.

The success of Higgins and Lucas added to the Texas mythos of hardscrabble pioneers who persist against great odds and reach goals others deride as unattainable. Oil remains a mainstay of the Houston and Texas economies, and Spindletop's history is celebrated at the Gladys City Boomtown Museum in Beaumont (Highway 69 at University Dr.; ☏409-880-1750;www.spindletop.org).

Side gusher in Spindletop Hill in early 20C

ADDRESSES

🛏 STAY

$$$ Hotel Galvez – 2024 Seawall Blvd., Galveston. ☎409-765-7721. www.galveston.com/galvez. 231 rooms. Built in 1911, the "Queen of the Gulf" has endured hurricanes and is listed on the National Register of Historic Places. Restoration uncovered grand archways and original stencilwork, and yielded rooms in rich gold and sepia.

$$$ The Lancaster Hotel – 701 Texas Ave., Houston. ☎713-228-9500. www.thelancaster.com. 93 rooms. Newly renovated in 2013, the Lancaster's lobby is filled with oil paintings, fine fabrics and overstuffed chairs. Guest rooms are undergoing overhaul as well.

Bistro Lancaster ($$) serves up Gulf Coast specialties like blue crab cakes along with plates of jumbo shrimp and corn tamales.

$$$ The Tremont House – 2300 Ship's Mechanic Row, Galveston. ☎409-763-0300. www.galveston.com/thetremont house. 119 rooms. This Wyndam chain hotel is hardly modest. Guests on the second and third floors have 15ft ceilings and 13ft windows. From a four-story glass-topped atrium lobby, a piano player sends music filtering to the balconies. Guest rooms have been recently renovated; marble baths include heated towel racks.

$$$ Hotel Zaza – 5701 Main St., Houston. ☎713-526-1991. www.hotelzazahouston.com. 315 rooms. Rebranded the Zaza after extensive renovations, the former Warwick opened in 1925. It was favored by oil barons who traveled by train to Houston for urban escapades. Located in the heart of the Museum District, the 12-story brick structure has guest rooms that are spacious and elegant.

$$ Sara's Inn on the Boulevard – 941 Heights Blvd., Houston. ☎713-868-1130. www.saras.com. 12 rooms. Rock in a wicker chair on the wrap-around porch of Sara's romantic clapboard Queen Anne inn. Many of the themed rooms have iron beds covered in lace and ruffles. The Fort Worth Room has a pine bed, stagecoach lamps and barbed-wire decorations. Breakfast is complimentary.

🍽 EAT

$$$ Américas – 1800 Post Oak Blvd., Houston. ☎713-961-1492. www.cordua.com. Closed Sun. **Latin American**. With trees and flowers, this skylit spot resembles an Amazon rain forest. Pargo Américas is the house version of Gulf snapper, crusted with fresh corn; grilled tenderloin is finished with a chimichurri sauce, and sweet soufflé-style rice pudding provides a perfect ending.

$$$ Gaido's – 3828 Seawall Blvd., Galveston. ☎409-762-9625. www.gaidos.com. **Seafood**. S.J. Gaido's great-grandchildren still peel shrimp and filet fish the old-fashioned way. The catch of the day is prepared 10 ways: Locals enjoy the Texas catfish crusted in crushed crackers and garlic, or blackened, with asiago cream sauce.

$$$ RDG Bar Annie – 1800 Post Oak Blvd., Houston. ☎713-840-1111. www.rdgbarannie.com. **Regional**. Chef Robert Del Grande, who revolutionized Houston cuisine at the now-closed Cafe Annie, opened this sleek glass and steel complex whose Grill Room brings Texas barbecue indoors with wood-grilled poultry, steaks and chops.

$$$ Hugo's – 1600 Westheimer Rd., Houston. ☎713-524-6992. http://ugosrestaurant.net. **Mexican**. Celebrated in Houston as a former illegal immigrant who worked his way from dishwasher to restaurant owner, Hugo Ortega makes his dishes as close to authentic Mexican as you'll find in the US—*barbacoa* (lamb marinated in chiles), *cabrito* (roast goat) and several molé-laden meats.

$$ Vietopia – 5176 Buffalo Speedway, Houston. ☎713-664-7303. www.vietopiarestaurant.com. **Vietnamese**. Dark wood trim and swirling bamboo ceiling fans set the tone at this upscale showcase for a cuisine brought to Texas by its many Vietnamese immigrants. Best are dishes that rely on Gulf seafood, such as shrimp sauteed with ginger and scallions, or crispy fish topped with peanuts and onions.

Houston★★

Houston embodies much of Texas' mystique, the notion that bigger is better. The city sprawls across more than 634sq mi of bayou country; the metropolitan area takes in more than 10,000sq mi and is bound by one of the most extensive highway systems in the nation. As the fourth-largest US city (after New York, Los Angeles and Chicago), Houston is a giant in international shipping, petrochemicals, aerospace and health care. It has attracted an equally diverse population; 83 languages are spoken in the metropolitan area, and a majority of the city's population is non-Anglo.

A BIT OF HISTORY

In August 1836, two New York land speculators, brothers Augustus and John Allen, navigated Buffalo Bayou from Galveston Bay. They founded a settlement and named it in honor of Gen. Sam Houston, who had vanquished the Mexican army at San Jacinto four months earlier. The new community was capital of the Republic of Texas from 1837 to 1839.

Initially beset by yellow fever and mud, Houston grew as a cotton-shipping center. After the 50mi Ship Channel was dredged in 1914, it became a major port for all types of trade. The discovery of oil nearby in 1901 triggered modern prosperity, boosted by the location of the Lyndon B. Johnson Space Center southeast of Houston in 1961.Since the oil crisis of the mid-1980s, Houston has developed a diversified economy. The 2001 Enron collapse, at that point the largest US bankruptcy ever, had only a modest dampening effect on the city's economy—in recent years it has consistently been at or near the top of the US' fastest-growing cities list.

HOUSTON TODAY

Long subject to the oil industry's boom-and-bust cycles, Houston's diversified economy is now more resistant to ups

- ▶ **Population:** 2,160,000.
- ◔ **Michelin Map:** 492 L 14. Central Standard Time.
- 🛈 **Info:** ✆713-437-5200 or 800-446-8786; www.visit houstontexas.com.
- ◖ **Location:** Houston's 8mi light rail system, the MetroRail tram, connects downtown with the Museum District.
- Ⓟ **Parking:** Ample pay lots in the Museum District serve visitors; bargain hunters can scout for spots several blocks away in nearby residential neighborhoods.
- ☺ **Don't Miss:** The Menil Collection.
- 👥 **Kids:** Johnson Space Center; Museum of Natural Science.
- ◔ **Also See:** Bayou Bend; River Oaks.

and downs, and the city ranks third in the US for Fortune 500 headquarters. Houston's metro economy is about $442 billion, and its port leads the US in foreign tonnage.

SIGHTS

Downtown is the hub of commerce and performing arts. Easy to spot on the downtown Houston skyline is the 75-story **JP Morgan Chase Tower** (600 Travis St.).

The Museum District is the location of most major museums, plus Hermann Park, the city's largest; the 700-acre **Texas Medical Center** (1155 Holcombe Blvd.; www.tmc.edu), southwest of downtown and the Museum district, is the largest health-care complex in the world; its 15 main institutions draw 7 million patients a year.

Uptown Houston, on the west side of the city, is the main shopping district, including the huge, European-style Galleria complex.

Downtown Houston★

✕&🅿 Framed by I-45 & US-59 south of Buffalo Bayou.

Buffalo Bayou, the original corridor of settlement, runs along the north side of downtown. Sam Houston Park (below) recalls this first community; above it rises a web of freeways. The commercial district runs east 14 blocks to the George R. Brown Convention Center. The Theater District (below) extends north and east of Sam Houston Park. Several 19C buildings have been preserved at **Old Market Square** (Preston, Travis, Congress & Milam Sts.); the original **Allen's Landing** (Commerce & Main Sts.) is three blocks beyond. More than 50 blocks (about 6mi) of downtown are interconnected by the growing **Houston Underground**, a tunnel system that shelters the population from summer humidity and winter rain, not to mention year-round street traffic.

Sam Houston Park★

1100 Bagby St. &🅿 ☎713-655-1912. www.heritagesociety.org.

Seven restored 19C and early 20C houses and an 1891 German Lutheran church have been relocated to this 19-acre park. Oldest is an 1823 pioneer home; most elaborate, a 17-room house built by oil pioneer Henry T. Staiti in 1905. **The Heritage Society Museum** has exhibits on five centuries of history. Nearby, the free **Art Car Museum★** honors a uniquely American art form for which Houston is the capital, including a Texas icon, a pink Cadillac (140 Heights Blvd.; ☎713-861-5526; www.artcarmuseum.com).

Theater District★

Preston Blvd. to Capitol St., both sides of Louisiana St.

Both the Houston Grand Opera, one of the country's premier companies, and Houston Ballet perform at the **Wortham Center** (501 Texas Blvd.; ☎713-487-7000; www.houstonfirsttheaters.com), noted for its six-story grand foyer. The Houston Symphony Orchestra is home in the block-sized **Jones Hall for the Performing Arts** (615 Louisiana St.;

☎713-487-7050; www.houstonfirst-theaters.com), identified by its facade of travertine marble. **The Alley Theatre** (615 Texas Ave.; ☎713-220-5700; www.alleytheatre.org), whose balcony offers a view of the city skyline, hosts one of the oldest and most highly regarded professional theater companies in the country.

Museum District★★

Houston's main cultural neighborhood lies 2mi southwest of downtown via Main Street and the MetroRail. Numerous important museums are found here close to Hermann Park. The new (2011, Yoshio Taniguchi) **Asia Society Texas Center★** is a cool, water-splashed facility with gallery space devoted to contemporary Asian-American art (1370 Southmore Blvd.; ☎713-496-9901; asiasociety.org/texas).

Menil Collection★★★

1515 Sul Ross St. &🅿 ☎713-525-9400. www.menil.org.

One of the world's foremost collections of 20C art, with an emphasis on Surrealism, is presented here. Established in 1987 for the collection of John and Dominique de Menil, the museum exhibits only a small part of more than 15,000 paintings, sculptures, photographs and books. Italian architect Renzo Piano's design has been acclaimed for its use of natural light.

The **Surrealist collection★★★** features more works by René Magritte and Max Ernst than any other museum in the world. Also represented are paintings by Cézanne, Klee and Matisse; early Cubist work by Braque, Léger and Picasso; Abstract Expressionism by Pollock and Rothko; and late 20C works by Johns, Rauschenberg, Stella and Warhol.

Other galleries hold Paleolithic carvings from the eastern Mediterranean; Byzantine and medieval works; and tribal arts of Africa, Oceania and the Pacific Northwest coast. The adjacent **Cy Twombly Gallery** (1501 Branard St.) houses 35 works by the noted Expressionist.

One block east, the **Rothko Chapel★** (3900 Yupon St.; ☎713-524-9839; www.

rothkochapel.org) (1971, Philip Johnson) holds 14 paintings (1965-66)—variations on a theme of black—by Mark Rothko. Outside in a reflecting pool stands *Broken Obelisk*, a sculpture (1967) honoring Martin Luther King, Jr. by Barnett Newman.

The Menil's **Byzantine Fresco Chapel Museum★** (4011 Yupon St.; ℘713-521-3990; www.menil.org) displays the only intact Byzantine frescoes in the Western Hemisphere.

Contemporary Arts Museum★

5216 Montrose Blvd. ✕&🅿

℘713-284-8250. www.camh.org.

Occupying a distinctive metal parallelogram (1972, Gunnar Birkerts), this cutting-edge museum offers frequently changing exhibits of modern art in two spacious galleries.

Museum of Fine Arts, Houston★★

1001 Bissonnet St. ✕&🅿

℘713-639-7300. www.mfah.org.

Founded in 1900 as the first municipal art museum in Texas, this 300,000sq ft facility is one of the largest art museums in the US. A wide-ranging permanent collection of more than 56,000 works is the inventory for exhibits in the **Audrey Jones Beck Building** (José Rafael Moneo, 2000), an austere post-Modern white-granite edifice.

Highlights include the **Beck Collection★** of Impressionist and post-Impressionist art, with works by Manet, Van Gogh, Renoir, Gauguin, Toulouse-Lautrec, Degas, Matisse and Cassatt; and the **Glassell Collection★★** of African gold. Here also are Egyptian, Greek and Roman antiquities; Renaissance and 18C art; and stunning American folk-art quilts. A fine collection of Remington works and Southwest Indian art are featured in the **Western art** collection. The original light-filled, Neoclassical **Caroline Wiess Law Building** (1924) across Main Street is devoted largely to temporary and traveling exhibits. A tunnel connects the two buildings and a popular basement cafe. Between the Law Building and the museum-operated **Glassell School of Art** (5101

Montrose Blvd.) is the **Cullen Sculpture Garden★** (1986, Isamu Noguchi).

The museum displays American decorative arts at Bayou Bend Collection and Gardens, and European decorative arts at **Rienzi** (1406 Kirby Dr.; ℘713-639-7800), including a fine collection of 18C Worcester porcelain.

♠♣ Houston Zoo★

6200 Hermann Park Dr. ✕&🅿

℘713-533-6500. www.houstonzoo.org.

Spanning 55 acres at Hermann Park, the zoo is home to 5,000 animals of 700 species. Of particular note are the expansive African Forest and Elephant enclosures, both newly expanded.

♠♣ Houston Museum of Natural Science★★★

1 Hermann Circle Dr. ✕&🅿

℘713-639-4629. www.hmns.org.

This outstanding four-floor museum requires two days to see it properly. The lavishly illustrated new **Morian Hall of Paleontology★★** exhibits more than 450 fossil specimens chronicled by time and location.

Adjacent to the Welch Chemistry Hall is a 63ft-tall Foucault pendulum. The **Wiess Energy Hall★★** features one of the world's most comprehensive exhibits on oil and natural gas. Unique high-tech displays, using virtual reality and video holography, trace petrochemical production from discovery to delivery. The **Cockrell Butterfly Center★**, a 25,000sq ft glass pyramid, houses 2,000 free-flying butterflies. **Cullen Hall of Gems and Minerals★★★** is a world-class collection of priceless specimens, dramatically illuminated. A sister exhibit, the **Smith Gem Vault★**, opened in 2006. Lifelike dioramas present wildlife of Texas and Africa's Serengeti Plain; the Strake Hall of Malacology showcases 2,500 rare seashells, mainly from the Gulf of Mexico.

The **John P. McGovern Hall of the Americas** focuses on native cultures from the Arctic to the Andes.

Lower-level exhibits are geared to school children. The **Arnold Hall of Space Science** incorporates the Challenger Learning Center, where students in a Mission Control mock-up communicate with others in a flight simulator.

The Health Museum★

1515 Hermann Dr. ♿🅿 ☎713-521-1515. www.mhms.org.

With the world's largest medical complex nearby, this educational center includes the Amazing Body Pavilion, where visitors take a walking tour of the human body, featuring a 10ft brain, a giant eyeball and a 22ft backbone.

👫 Children's Museum of Houston★

1500 Binz St. ✗♿🅿 ☎713-522-1138. www.cmhouston.org.

Some 14 exhibit areas here make applications of science fun. Among them, **Power Play** lets children climb 35ft. In **Invention Convention** they become inventors, and in **EcoStation**, kids collect bugs and identify footprints, among other activities.

Holocaust Museum Houston★★

5401 Caroline St. ♿🅿 ☎713-942-8000. www.hmh.org.

This compact but memorable museum (1996, Ralph Appelbaum and Mark Mucasey) is unmistakable for the broad, dark, brick cylinder—reminiscent of a Nazi death camp smokestack—that rises above it.

The exhibit traces Jewish history and the roots of anti-Semitism to the World War II-era Holocaust, followed by the Liberation. The **Memorial Room★** induces reflection.

ADDITIONAL SIGHTS
Bayou Bend Collection and Gardens★★

1 Westcott St. ♿🅿 ☎713-639-7750. www.mfah.org.

Part of The Museum of Fine Arts, this spectacular collection showcases 17-19C American decorative arts with 5,000 objects of furniture, ceramics, silver, paper, glass, textiles and paintings. It is housed in Bayou Bend (1927, John F. Staub), the Neo-Palladian-style former estate of governor's daughter Ima Hogg (1882-1975). On display are a silver sugar bowl crafted by Paul Revere, colonial portraits by John Singleton Copley and furniture by John Townsend.

Surrounding the home are 14 acres of woodlands and gardens.

The Galleria

5075 Westheimer St. at Post Oak Blvd. ✗♿🅿 ☎713-622-0663. www.galleriahouston.com.

Department stores, two large hotels and an ice rink (beneath an arched glass ceiling) anchor Houston's largest shopping complex. Patterned after a plaza in Milan, Italy, the center dominates

NASA Booster Rocket at the Space Center Houston

©iStockphoto.com/Dave Huss

the Uptown Houston district, west of Loop 610 and north of the Southwest Freeway.

Nearby is the 1983 **Williams Tower★** (2800 Post Oak Blvd.) one of Philip Johnson's best-known skyscrapers, and adjacent **Waterwall★★** fountain sculpture. At night, a 7,000-watt beacon sweeps the sky from the building's tip.

EXCURSIONS

👤👥 Space Center Houston★★★

▶ 1601 NASA Parkway, Clear Lake, 25mi south of downtown Houston off I-45.
✕&🅿 ☎281-244-2100. spacecenter.org.
Official visitor center of the National Aeronautics and Space Administration (NASA) Houston complex, this $70 million facility adjacent to the Johnson Space Center—the mission control, training and research facility for the US space program—offers live shows, presentations and interactive exhibits. Guided tram tours take visitors for a behind-the-scenes look at the Johnson Space Center. Live satellite links provide up-to-date information on current space flights. Exhibits include spacecraft from early *Mercury, Gemini* and *Apollo* missions; visitors may try on space helmets, touch moon rocks, use a simulator to land a shuttle or take a space walk.

At Kids Space Place, 40 interactive areas invite exploration as children ride across the moon's surface in a Lunar Rover or command a space shuttle.

👤👥 San Jacinto Battleground State Historic Site★

▶ 3523 Battleground Rd. (Rte. 134), La Porte, 21mi east of downtown Houston via Rte. 225. &🅿 ☎281-479-2431. www.tpwd.state.tx.us.
Though the Alamo is far more famous, this spot is actually more crucial to Texas history. A 570ft obelisk, covered with fossilized shellstone (1939), recalls the 1836 victory here by Texas troops, establishing their freedom from Mexican colonial rule.

An elevator takes visitors to the top of the monument for a grand view. On the ground floor is the **San Jacinto Museum**

of History, documenting Texas' formative years.

The adjacent **Battleship Texas★** (☎281-479-2431) served in both world wars before it was retired in 1948. The 573ft ship is open for self-guided tours of both its main deck and lower levels. Hard-hat guided tours into the bowels of the ship are available (☎713-827-9620).

Huntsville★

▶ Location via I-45, 69mi north of Houston. &🅿 ☎936-291-9726. www.huntsvilletexas.com.
Set in rolling pine-clad hills, Huntsville greets travelers with a 67ft statue of its most famous citizen, Sam Houston (1793-1863).

The Sam **Houston Memorial Museum★** (1836 Sam Houston Ave.; ☎936-294-1832; www.samhouston.org) depicts the colorful career of the only man to be governor of two states, Tennessee and Texas. Houston led the fight for Texas independence and its admission into the US, but refused to support the Confederacy.

Huntsville also is the home of the massive Texas State Prison complex. The **Texas Prison Museum** (491 State Hwy. 19.; ☎936-295-2155; www.txprisonmuseum.org) contains items that belonged to notorious outlaws Bonnie Parker and Clyde Barrow.

👤👥 Brazos Bend State Park★

▶ 21901 Farm-Market Rd. 762, Needville, 40mi southwest of downtown Houston via US-59 (Southwest Freeway). &🅿
☎979-553-5102. www.tpwd.state.tx.us.
One of the largest expanses of public land near Houston is the best place to see once-rare, now-common, native alligators. A hiking trail leads visitors around the huge marsh complex shared by waterfowl and gators, and along the Brazos River in undisturbed sycamore-pecan woodlands.

Galveston★

Located 50mi south of Houston, Galveston Island is both a summer getaway and a year-round historic destination. The compact barrier island—32mi long but just 2mi wide—is especially known for its beaches, miles of which were included in Texas' first beach replenishment program. In-city beaches are hectic strips where being "seen" may be the most popular sport. The city, at the eastern end of the island, focuses on a 36-block historic district. Galveston Bay, north of the island, is famed for its shrimp fishery; a bayside boardwalk in Kemah holds numerous restaurants specializing in bay seafoods.

▶ **Population:** 47,000.
◔ **Michelin Map:** 492 L 9. Central Standard Time.
▯ **Info:** ☏409-797-5145; www.galveston.com.
▷ **Location:** The farther west and south you go along the island, the less developed it becomes, culminating in a fairly wild stretch of barrier island illustrative of the pre-settlement Gulf Coast.
◉ **Don't Miss:** Galveston's opulent historic mansions.
◔ **Timing:** Figure at least 2hrs' drive time to Galveston from Houston.
👥 **Kids:** Moody Gardens.

A BIT OF HISTORY

Home to the Akokisa Indians in the 16C, Galveston Island remained unsettled by Europeans until the early 19C, when the pirate Jean Lafitte established the village of Campeche as his base. When he was forced out by the US Navy, the village was renamed, and Galveston slowly developed as a port city. Galveston became the richest city in Texas and home to many state "firsts": post office,

The Republic of Texas

Texans are proud that their state was once the independent Republic of Texas. Following the victory over Gen. Santa Anna at the Battle of San Jacinto on April 21, 1836, a new government was formed. Sam Houston, hero of San Jacinto, was elected the republic's first president in September 1836. Among his first concerns were the continued threats of attack by Indians and renewed attempts by Mexico to extend its borders across the Rio Grande into Texas.

Houston's initial efforts at establishing diplomatic relations with other countries, including the United States, failed. A breakthrough came when a trade treaty was signed with the United Kingdom. Fearing an alliance between Texas and Britain, the US recognized Texas as sovereign in 1837. Soon France, Belgium, The Netherlands and Germany also recognized the young republic.

In 1839 a permanent capital was established at the frontier village of Waterloo, renamed Austin. A national flag was adopted, featuring a single five-pointed star on a field of blue, flanked by horizontal red-and-white stripes; today, Texas continues to be known as the Lone Star State.

Texas President Houston was reelected to a second term in 1841. Much of his subsequent effort was directed toward achieving statehood within the US for reasons of defense and economy. On October 13, 1845, the people of Texas voted 4,245 to 257 in favor of annexation. US President James K. Polk signed Texas' admission to the union in December of that year. On February 19, 1846, the flag of the Republic of Texas flew over Austin for the final time.

hospital, naval base, telephone, private bank, gas and electric lights, and more. In the late 19C, thousands of immigrants made their way through the port, second only to New York's Ellis Island as a US entry point.

Galveston has suffered severely from hurricanes, in 1900, when some 6,000 residents were killed (after which, Galveston constructed a 10mi seawall and raised the level of the island), and more recently in 2008. The broad expanse of **Galveston Island State Park** (℘409-737-1222; www.tpwd.state.tx.us) begins 13mi southwest of town and extends for several miles.

SIGHTS
The Strand National Historic Landmark District★

The Strand, 20th-25th St.; visitor center, 2328 Broadway. ✕占P℘409-763-7080. www.galvestonhistory.org.

In the late 19C, The Strand was the city's business district, which became known as the Wall Street of the Southwest. Today, trolleys clang along the historic streets, transporting visitors past shops and restaurants housed in one of the nation's largest areas of Victorian commercial architecture.

The Grand 1894 Opera House (2020 Post Office St.; ℘409-765-1894; www.thegrand.com) has been restored to its appearance when it hosted such performers as Sara Bernhardt and John Philip Sousa. The **Galveston County Historical Museum** (2219 Market St.; ℘409-766-2340) recounts the island's fascinating history.

Hard by The Strand, Galveston's **Waterfront District★** embraces a still-active port; several attractions reflect its seafaring character. The **Great Storm multimedia presentation★** (Pier 21; ℘409-763-8808; www.galveston.com/pier21theatre) draws on contemporary accounts to offer a level-headed recounting of the catastrophic 1900 hurricane. The **Texas Seaport Museum** (Pier 21; ℘409-763-1877; www.tsm-elissa.org) has a restored 1877 three-masted sailing vessel, the *Elissa*, plus a database with the names of more than

133,000 immigrants who entered the US here. **The Ocean Star** (Pier 19; ℘409-766-7827; www.oceanstaroec.com) is a retired offshore drilling platform now converted to a museum; it explains how oil is found and produced from deep-sea beds.

Historic Houses

Numerous 19C homes, many along Broadway south of The Strand, are open for tours. **The Bishop's Palace** (1402 Broadway; ℘409-762-2475; www.galvestonhistory.org), a castle-like 1886 Victorian, was built for a railroad founder and later belonged to a diocesan bishop. Constructed of Texas granite, white limestone and red sandstone, it features elaborate woodwork, mantels and fireplaces. The 1895 Romanesque-style **Moody Mansion** (2618 Broadway; ℘409-762-7668; www.moodymansion.org) features a French Rococo reception room and a Classical Revival library.

Three homes are operated by the **Galveston Historical Foundation** (℘409-765-7834, www.galvestonhistory.org). The 1859 **Ashton Villa** (2328 Broadway) is a stately Italianate mansion. The 1838 **Menard Home** (1604 33rd St.), an antebellum estate of Greek Revival style, is furnished with Federal and American Empire antiques. The 1839 **Williams Home** (3601 Avenue P) is a Creole plantation house and a sea captain's home.

♟♙ Moody Gardens★★

1 Hope Blvd.; take 81st St. to Jones Rd. ✕占P℘800-582-4673. www.moodygardens.com.

Beginning in 1986 as a therapy center for patients with head injuries, Moody Gardens has expanded into a leading attraction. The glass **Rainforest Pyramid★★** is home to more than 1,700 tropical plants, fish, birds and insects. The **Discovery Pyramid** showcases the world of space through exhibits and interactive displays. The **Aquarium Pyramid★** contains 1.5 million gallons of water for marine life from the North and South Pacific Oceans, South Atlantic Ocean and Caribbean Sea.

San Antonio Area

Any attempt to understand Texans must begin in San Antonio, for here is the heart of Texas history and culture. Originally inhabited by Indians of the warlike Comanche tribe, the region was settled by Spanish missionaries at the end of the 17C. In 1836 one mission, converted to military use and known as The Alamo, became a stronghold for 189 Texas patriots who gave their lives defending the bastion against the vast forces of Mexico's General Antonio López de Santa Anna. Their sacrifice became a rallying cry, "Remember The Alamo!", for other rebels who soon defeated Santa Anna and won Texas independence.

Highlights

1 **Historic missions** (p403)
2 **Live music** in Austin (p405)
3 Hill Country **wildflowers** (p407)
4 **LBJ Ranch** (p407)
5 **Padre Island** (p409)

Crossroads of Texan History

The Hispanic presence remains strong and growing in central and south Texas, an area that claims San Antonio as its cultural, spiritual and economic hub. Spanish is heard as often as English.

Gondolas ply the waters of the Rio San Antonio, passing strollers on the cypress-shaded River Walk, which meanders past row after brightly lit row of atmospheric restaurants. From atop one of the city's newer buildings, the 750ft Tower of the Americas, you can gaze down upon some of its oldest, the quartet of 18C missions that make up San Antonio Missions National Historical Park.

An hour's drive northeast is Austin, the lively state capital. The University of Texas, the political ambience and an influx of high-tech industry have engendered a spirit of intellectual and cultural excitement. Scores of nightclubs have led Austin to become known as the "Live Music Capital of the World"—with an average of 200 live performances every night—topped off by South by Southwest (SXSW) music and a film festival held in the city each spring. South of Austin, the scenic Hill Country unfolds. Much farther south, Corpus Christi borders the Gulf of Mexico.

ADDRESSES

🛏 STAY

$$$$ The Driskill – 604 Brazos St., Austin. ☏512-439-1234. www.driskill hotel.com. 189 rooms. Double balconies, arched windows and a hand-laid marble lobby floor made downtown Austin's grandest hotel into a frontier palace. Col. J.L. Driskill's 1886 Victorian vision lives on with period furnishings, original artwork and a custom-made stained-glass dome. In the **Driskill Grill ($$$)**, diners savor entrées such as American buffalo and Texas quail.

$$$$ The Fairmount Hotel – 401 S. Alamo St., San Antonio. ☏210-224-8800. www.thefairmounthotel-sanantonio. com. 37 rooms. A small jewel of dark-red brick, carved limestone and elaborate pediments, this ornate Italianate railway hotel was built in 1906 and moved six blocks and across a bridge in 1985. All the marble finishes and soft guest-room colors survived.

$$$ Hotel Havana – 1015 Navarro St., San Antonio. ☏210-222-2008. www. havanasanantonio.com. 27 rooms. Individual room decor is unique at this 1914 Mediterranean Revival-style inn,

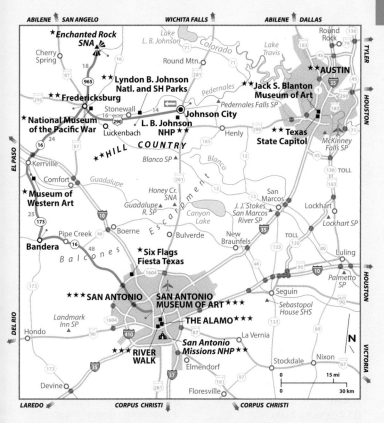

extensively renovated and reopened in 2010. It now features vintage Cuban artwork and period furnishings such as four-poster beds. Throughout are exposed brick walls and Bastrop pine floors.

$$$ The Menger Hotel – 204 Alamo Plaza, San Antonio. ☎210-223-4361 www.mengerhotel.com. 318 rooms.

A glazed iron canopy and intricate railings form the facade of the elegant Menger, built in 1859, barely a generation after the fall of The Alamo. Leaded skylights in a grand three-story lobby guide guests to opulent rooms of dark wood trim. Game has been on the **Colonial Room** ($$$) menu for a century.

The Alamo, San Antonio

© SACVB/Richard Nowitz

$$ Ab Butler's Dogtrot at Triple Creek – 801 Triple Creek Rd., Fredericksburg. ☎830-456-8335. www.abbutler.net. 2 rooms. Within this rustic country log cabin, built in 1800, are such elegant touches as a fireplace and whirlpool bath. The Dogtrot is one of several inns marketed by **Fredericksburg Traditional Bed and Breakfast Inns** (www.fredericksburgtrad.com).

$$ Dixie Dude Ranch – 833 Dixie Dude Ranch Rd., Bandera. ☎830-796-7771. www.dixieduderanch.com. 20 rooms. Spend a few nights (three minimum) at this working 1901 Hill Country ranch and you might slow down to real cowboy life. Lodgings are rustic but modern, and prices include three meals and two horseback rides a day.

$$ The Hangar Hotel – 155 Airport Rd., Fredericksburg. ☎830-997-9990. www.hangarhotel.com. 24 rooms. Housed in a hangar-like building by the Fredericksburg air strip, this unique hotel features charming 1940s decor such as rattan and leather furniture, personable service and a quiet atmosphere.

⦿/ EAT

$$$ Biga on the Banks – 203 S. St. Mary's St., San Antonio. ☎210-225-0722. www.biga.com. Dinner only. **American**. Natural light flows through a wall of windows on River Walk into Biga's modern hacienda-like interior. Design elements honor the city's cultural heritage. Chef-owner Bruce Auden's new American cuisine ranges from chicken-fried oysters to Texas venison and quail with chestnuts and juniper sauce.

$$$ Boudro's – 421 E. Commerce St., San Antonio. ☎210-224-8484. www.boudros.com. **Texas Regional**. This fine River Walk restaurant offers a bistro blend of Texas beef and Gulf Coast seafood. Diners may choose blackened prime rib with fine wine at a cozy inside table or prickly-pear margaritas on the riverside patio. River-barge dining cruises feature pecan-grilled steaks, smoked-shrimp enchiladas and guacamole made table.

$$ Altdorf Biergarten – 301 W. Main St., Fredericksburg. ☎830-997-7865. www.aldorfbiergarten-fbg.com. Closed Tue. **German**. This may be the single best place to absorb Fredericksburg's German heritage. Bavarian specialties include bratwurst, knockwurst, wiener and jaeger schnitzel, all served with sweet-and-sour potatoes, red cabbage or sauerkraut.

$ Guero's Taco Bar – 1412 S. Congress Ave., Austin. ☎512-447-7688. www.guerostacobar.com. **Tex-Mex**. This iconic South Congress Avenue, occupying a late-19C feed store, is a big part of the hip Austin scene. The kitchen serves shrimp fajitas, *huachinango* (garlic-jalapeño red snapper), and chicken three ways: chipotle (smoky jalapeño), *tampiqueño* (salsa and jack cheese) or *guanajuato* (guacamole).

$ El Alma – 1025 Barton Springs Rd., Austin. ☎512-609-8923. www.elalmacafe.com. **Mexican Regional**. Chef Alma Alcocer-Thomas brings the peppy Mexican-Continental flavors of her Mexico City youth to dishes such as the signature duck rellenos, chipotle guacamole and corn and poblano chowder. The cheery space is decorated with Mexican folk art.

$ Smitty's – 208 S. Commerce St., Lockhart. ☎512-398-9344. www.smittysmarket.com. **Barbecue**. The former Kreuz Market, Texas' erstwhile most famous barbecue, remains true to its roots: impeccable oak-smoked brisket and prime rib, smoked in a brick pit and served on butcher paper. Lockhart also offers two other famous 'cue joints, Black's (www.blacksbbq.com) and Kreuz Market (www.kreuzmarket.com).

$ Stubb's Bar-B-Q – 801 Red River St., Austin. ☎512-480-8341. www.stubbsaustin.com. **Barbecue**. C.B. Stubblefield once promised diners "Cold Beer and Live Music." His legacy lives on with nightly soul food and rhythm-and-blues. Diners may start with Texas fries or onion rings, then devour Stubb's Major BBQ plate of smoked beef brisket, sausage and ribs, ladled with C.B.'s original sauce.

San Antonio★★★

San Antonio's historic sites and museums, semitropical climate, multicultural ambience and visitor services make it a shining star of tourism.

SAN ANTONIO TODAY

Almost two-thirds Hispanic, San Antonio represents the demographic future of Texas, which is expected to hold more Latinos than Caucasians by 2020. Aside from tourism, San Antonio's economy relies on two major US military bases, the area's two largest employers.

A BIT OF HISTORY

Before Franciscan priests founded missions in the 1690s, Coahuiltecan Indians dominated the region. Two decades later, San Antonio de Bejar became a military garrison for Spain; it was a fulcrum of the Texas Revolution when The Alamo fell to Santa Anna in 1836. Following the Civil War, San Antonio boomed as a cattle center. After a devastating flood in 1921 led the city to consider turning its river into a storm sewer, conservationists raised funds to redesign the eyesore into a tourist attraction. Robert H. H. Hugman's park-like first phase was constructed in 1939-41. When the city spruced up for its HemisFair 1968 world's fair, Hugman's dream of a festive shopping and dining promenade was realized.

SIGHTS

The Alamo★★★

300 Alamo Plaza at Crockett St. ♿ ✆210-225-1391. www.thealamo.org.
The "Cradle of Texas Liberty" fronts a busy plaza downtown. Mission San Antonio de Valero—known as The Alamo (Spanish for "cottonwood")—is an enduring symbol of Texas. It was built in 1718, secularized in 1793 and occupied as a Mexican military garrison in the early 1800s. In December 1835, rebellious Texans drove Mexican troops from San Antonio and consolidated their defenses within The Alamo.

▶ **Population:** 1,383,000.
Michelin Map: p 399. Central Standard Time.
Info: ✆210-207-6700; www.visitsanantonio.com.
Location: Most attractions (Riverwalk, Alamo, Market Square, La Villita) are within easy walking distance of major downtown lodgings.
P Parking: Parking is very difficult to find around the Alamo. Best to take a taxi or walk from your hotel.
Don't Miss: The Paseo del Rio—Riverwalk.
Timing: Allow two days for San Antonio. The Riverwalk is most magical in the evening, when it's magically lit. Plan to cruise the river and have dinner at one of the innumerable waterside restaurants.

But Gen. Santa Anna, the Mexican president, led thousands of troops in an assault on the former mission two months later. The 13-day siege (February 23-March 6, 1836) was not over until virtually all The Alamo's 189 defenders – including commander William B. Travis, renowned knife fighter Jim Bowie and the legendary Davy Crockett, who left Congress for Texas' new frontier – perished. "Remember The Alamo!" became the battle cry of the war of Texas independence, which climaxed less than two months later when Gen. Sam Houston defeated Santa Anna at San Jacinto, near Houston.

Although surrounded by hustle, bustle and numerous tourist traps, the site commands quiet respect. The Alamo is an apt memorial to the courage of the men who fought for Texas in the face of insurmountable odds. Its centerpiece is **The Shrine★★★**, the former mission church, where exhibits honor the men who died here. Further exhibits in the **Long Barrack Museum★★** describe historic events leading to the siege and its aftermath.

River Walk★★★

Bridge entrances at Losoya and Commerce Sts. ✕⚡♿ ℘210-227-4262. www.thesanantonioriverwalk.com.

Also called Paseo del Rio, this verdant promenade meanders below street level through 2.5mi of downtown, weaving along both banks of a horseshoe-shaped bend in the slow-flowing San Antonio River. Sidewalk cafes, small shops, galleries and nightclubs are wedged between the arched bridges of this cypress-shaded walkway. Strollers snake like a conga line through busy areas; other stretches have a quiet, parklike atmosphere.

Work Projects Administration crews built the cobblestone and flagstone path in 1939-41 under the direction of architect Robert Hugman and engineer Edwin Arneson. The plan included the **Arneson River Theatre**, an open-air amphitheater with a stage on one side of the stream, terraced seating on the other.

The best way to view River Walk without joining the pedestrian crowds is aboard Rio San Antonio Cruises 👥 (℘210-244-5700, www.riosanantonio. com). The 60min open-air cruises feature lighthearted historical narratives by guides; the same company operates river taxis that ply the waters, as well as the opportunity to charter a boat.

La Villita★

418 Villita St., between S. Alamo & S. Presa Sts. ✕♿ ℘210-207-8614. www.lavillita.com.

At the time The Alamo was a military outpost, "The Little Village" developed as a temporary community of huts for soldiers. The Mexican surrender climaxing the Texas Revolution was signed here. Today the village is a National Historic District. Early 19C structures house artisans in studio shops, restaurants and a museum exhibit.

👥 Market Square★★

514 W. Commerce St. at Santa Rosa St. ✕♿🅿 ℘210-207-8600. www.marketsquaresa.com.

This traditional Mexican marketplace, extending across several blocks, began as an early 19C farmers' market. Later, pharmaceutical items were sold at **Botica Guadalupana**, the oldest continuously operated drugstore in central and south Texas. Today a Latin flavor persists in the shops and restaurants, including **El Mercado**, largest Mexican mall in the US. At two long-standing restaurants, **La Margarita** and **Mi Tierra**, troupes of mariachi musicians serenade diners.

Spanish Governor's Palace★

105 Military Plaza. ℘210-224-0601. www.sanantonio.gov

This National Historic Landmark near Market Square is Texas' sole surviving example of a colonial aristocrat's home. It was completed in 1749 (as the date on its massive door indicates) and restored in 1931. Self-guided tours wind through an enclosed fountain courtyard and chambers furnished with 18C antiques.

Casa Navarro State Historic Site★

228 S. Laredo St. ℘210-226-4801. www.visitcasanavarro.com.

The three refurbished buildings on this site—an adobe-and-limestone

River Walk
©SACVB/Al Rendon

house, kitchen and office—come to life on curator-led tours. Home builder José Antonio Navarro (1795-1871) was a lifelong San Antonio rancher and statesman.

👥 Tower of the Americas★

600 HemisFair Park. ✗&🅿 𝒫 210-223-3101. www.toweroftheamericas.com.
The city's finest **views★★★** are from this 750ft tower overlooking the grounds of HemisFair 1968. Visitors are whisked day and night to the 500ft level on a 1min ride in a glass-enclosed elevator. One of the tallest free-standing structures in the Western Hemisphere is 67ft higher than the Washington Monument.
Nearby, the new (2013) **Briscoe Art Museum** (210 W. Market St.; www.briscoemuseum.org) will add to the roster of Texas Western art galleries, with a focus on artists from the Lone Star State.

👥 San Fernando Cathedral★★

115 Main Plaza. &🅿 𝒫 210-227-1297. www.sfcathedral.org.
Though the cathedral dates back to 1731—it's the oldest cathedral in the US—and has played a prominent role in the city's history, the highlight here is modern: an astounding 24ft gold-leaf retablo, "Jesus Christ, Word and Sacrament," handmade in Mexico City and installed in 2003.

Institute of Texan Cultures★

801 S. Bowie St. &🅿 𝒫 210-458-2300. www.texancultures.com.
Twenty-seven ethnic and cultural groups are profiled at this HemisFair Park museum. An outdoor interpretive area replicates a 19C pioneer village.

San Antonio Missions National Historical Park★★

2202 Roosevelt Ave. &🅿
𝒫 210-932-1001. www.nps.gov/saan.
The Alamo was not the only mission in the valley of the Rio San Antonio. Four others were erected in 1720-31 near the river, which supplied water for drinking and crop irrigation by means of an *acequia* (aqueduct). The park comprises these Franciscan missions, which portray the size and scope of traditional compounds—including a church and chapel, convent, Coahuiltecan living quarters, farmland, a granary and a blacksmith. All four still support active parishes.

The chain begins at **Mission Concepción★** (807 Mission Rd. at Felisa St., 2.3mi south of The Alamo via S. St. Mary's St.). Of special note are traces of geometric designs painted by Coahuiltecans on the interior walls of the magnificent mission church (c.1731) and convent.

Mission San José y San Miguel de Aguayo★★ (6701 San José Dr, 2.2mi south of Mission Concepción) was once "Queen of the Texas Missions." San José was a major social and cultural center and home to 300 people; it remains an impressive fortress today. A bilingual Sunday-morning Mariachi Mass, featuring religious music by mariachi musicians in its 1720 chapel, highlights a visit. The national historical park's primary **visitor center** stands nearby.

Structures within the agricultural compound of **Mission San Juan Capistrano** (9101 Graf Rd., 2.5mi south of Mission San José) have been extensively restored, including the 1772 chapel, rectory and Indian quarters. Priests rescued precious icons from the 1740 church at Mission San Francisco de la Espada (10040 Espada Rd., 1.5mi south of Mission San Juan) during a 1997 fire.

San Antonio Museum of Art★★★

200 W. Jones Ave. ✗&🅿
𝒫 210-978-8100. www.samuseum.org.
This large, bright, thoroughly remodeled museum, housed in the 1904 Lone Star Brewery Company building, has impressive collections of Egyptian, Greek and Roman antiquities in its west wing; Asian works include ancient Chinese tomb figures. Among 17-18C European masters exhibited in the Great Hall are Steen, Hals and Bosch; 18-20C American works include oils by Copley, Stuart, Sargent and Homer.

Cradle of Con Carne

Market Square was the birthplace of chili con carne, the spicy beef stew that today is generally considered the state dish of Texas. Young girls known as "chili queens" first sold the concoction from small stands in the San Antonio market.

The $11 million **Nelson A. Rockefeller Center for Latin American Art★★** opened as a three-story east wing in 1998. It traces 4,000 years of Indian and Hispanic culture: pre-Columbian, Spanish Colonial, folk and modern art. An interactive education center introduces cultural history of Mexico, Central and South America. Exhibits feature Mesoamerican culture from Olmec, Maya, Aztec, Toltec and other periods, as well as Andean ceramics and gold work. Spanish Colonial works are primarily religious in nature, encompassing more than 100 paintings and objects. Folk art includes utilitarian and ceremonial pieces plus decorative items in wood, metal, ceramics, paper and textiles. Modern art features such 20C masters as Rivera, Tamaya, Torres-Garcia and Siqueiros.

♠♣ Brackenridge Park

3500 N. St. Mary's St. ✕&🅿
℘210-207-7275.
A popular picnic destination, the 343-riverside-acre park is home to the **San Antonio Zoo and Aquarium** (3903 N. St. Mary's St.; ℘210-734-7184; www.sazoo-aq.org), lodged in a former rock quarry. Nearby, the **Japanese Tea Garden** (3800 N. St. Mary's St.) offers lush flowers, climbing vines and tall palms alongside koi-filled pools.

♠♣ Witte Museum★

3801 Broadway. &🅿℘210-357-1900.
www.wittemuseum.org.
The Witte showcases human and natural history and culture, from anthropology to fashions and decorative arts. Exhibits in the main building (1926,

Robert M. Ayres) include **Texas Wild★**, which depicts the state's ecological zones. **Ancient Texans★★** focuses on the Lower Pecos culture of the Rio Grande Valley. A half-dozen relocated pioneer homes share grounds behind the museum. The **H-E-B Science Treehouse★** (1997, Lake/Flato) has four levels of science exhibits, perched over the San Antonio River on concrete oak trees created by sculptor Carlos Cortes.

San Antonio Botanical Garden★

555 Funston Pl. ✕&🅿℘210-207-3250.
www.sabot.org.
Within these 33-acre gardens, the **Lucile Halsell Conservatory★★** is the centerpiece. The 90,000sq ft cluster of individual glass houses was tucked into the earth around a courtyard sunk 16ft underground to escape the hot Texas summers.

McNay Art Museum★★

6000 N. New Braunfels Ave. &🅿
℘210-824-5368. www.mcnayart.org.
A world-class collection of 19C and 20C European and American art occupies this 24-room Spanish Mediterranean-style manor (1926, Atlee B. & Robert M. Ayres), former home of oil heiress and art collector Marion McNay. Galleries surround a landscaped garden patio or overlook the courtyard from balconies. The collection is strong in post-Impressionist French art.

Five decades of Picasso's works are in three rooms; 20C paintings by Braque, Matisse, Modigliani and Chagall also are presented. American Modernist works include O'Keeffe, Dove, Pollock, Hockney and Motherwell.

EXCURSION

♠♣ Six Flags Fiesta Texas★

🌑 17000 I-10 West. ✕&🅿
℘210-697-5050. www.sixflags.com.
This popular theme park showcases the music of Texas, from 50s rock 'n' roll to Tejano to German polka. Shows are interspersed with thrill rides and water rides, especially popular in summer.

Austin★★

The Texas capital, located between the rolling Hill Country and fertile farmland, has a vibrant cultural life and a young population that includes 52,000 University of Texas students. Founded in 1835 as Waterloo, it became the seat of government upon independence, changing its name to honor statesman Stephen F. Austin. Austin city experienced steady growth that included construction of a new state capitol in 1888. The city was plagued by flooding along the Colorado River until a series of flood-control dams were constructed in 1938, forming the chain of Highland Lakes that includes Town Lake and Lake Austin.

▶ **Population:** 842,000.
🚻 **Michelin Map:** p 399.
Central Standard Time.
📠 **Info:** ✆512-474-5171 or 866-462-8784; www.austintexas.org
👁 **Don't Miss:** Congress Avenue Bridge bats.
👥 **Kids:** Barton Springs Pool.

AUSTIN TODAY

Austin balances its serious role as seat of state government with the youthful exuberance of the university, its vibrant cultural life and a newfound identity as high-tech center. The **Sixth Street Entertainment District**, extending seven blocks from I-35 to Congress Avenue, has dozens of clubs that have built Austin's reputation as a mecca for live music, with more than 200 separate performances some nights.

The world's largest urban **colony of bats** (more than 1 million Mexican free-tail bats) nestles beneath downtown Austin's Congress Avenue bridge March to October, flying out each evening at dusk to the joy of throngs of wildlife watchers. The nearby **Barton Springs Pool** (👥 2101 Barton Springs Road, in Zilker Park; ✆512-476-9044; www.austintexas.gov), fed by huge underground springs, is one of the most popular places in Texas to cool off on hot days. Also in the city are the **Austin Museum of Art at Laguna Gloria** (3809 W. 35th St.; ✆512-458-8191; http://thecontemporaryaustin.org), with a collection of 20C American art; the **Elisabet Ney Museum** (304 E. 44th St.; ✆512-458-2255; www.ci.austin.tx.us), 19C studio of Texas' first sculptor; and the **Umlauf Sculpture Garden and Museum** (605 Robert E. Lee Rd.; ✆512-445-5582; www.umlaufsculpture.org), showcasing the work of 20C sculptor Charles Umlauf.

SIGHTS

Texas State Capitol★★

Congress Ave. at 11th St. ✕♿🅿
✆512-463-5495. www.tspb.state.tx.us.
Dominating Austin's skyline, the Renaissance Revival-style capitol was built in 1888 (Elijah E. Myers) of red granite and limestone. Over 302ft in height, it is 14ft taller than the US Capitol.
📣 Guided tours, departing from the south foyer, visit the chambers of the state legislature, which meets in odd-numbered years from January through May. In the foyer, statues by 19C sculptor Elisabet Ney memorialize founding fathers Stephen Austin and Sam Houston; paintings by W. H. Huddle portray Davy Crockett at The Alamo and the surrender of Santa Anna at San Jacinto. A terrazzo floor, depicting the Lone Star of the Republic of Texas surrounded by the coats of arms of other nations whose flags have flown here, is the centerpiece of the rotunda. The **Capitol Complex Visitors Center** (112 E. 11th St.; ✆512-305-8400) is at the southeast corner of the exquisite, 22-acre grounds. The center is housed in the former General Land Office Building (1857), oldest surviving state building in Texas. Inside, a theater shows *A Lone Star Legacy: The Texas Capitol Complex*, a 23min film narrated by famed Texas newsman Walter Cronkite.

Lyndon Baines Johnson Presidential Library and Museum★★

2313 Red River St. University of Texas. ♿🅿 ✆512-721-0200. www.lbjlibrary.org.

Located on the UT campus, this monumental facility honors the Hill Country's most famous native son. Lyndon Johnson (1908-73) served as US president following John F. Kennedy's assassination; his turbulent term (1963-69) was marked by the Vietnam War and civil-rights movement. The eight-story library (1971, Skidmore, Owings and Merrill), constructed of travertine marble, is the repository for all presidential documents produced during the LBJ administration—more than 45 million pages.

Three floors are open to the public. Tours begin with a 23min film on LBJ's childhood in the Hill Country, his political life in the House and Senate, and his White House years. Accompanying exhibits place his life in the context of US history, including a new exhibit, the **Social Justice Gallery★★**, which features ordinary Americans and the effect on their lives of Johnson's policies. The library offers a frank perspective on Johnson's era, not shirking the great controversies of his presidency. On the eighth floor, Johnson's Oval Office at the White House is replicated.

Bob Bullock Texas State History Museum★

1800 N. Congress Ave. ✗♿🅿 ✆512-936-8746. www.thestoryoftexas.com.

Named after an illustrious Texas lieutenant governor, this sunset-red expanse of granite, framed by a 35ft-tall bronze star and the six flags of Texas, has three floors of exhibits on the state's geographical and cultural regions, its human history, and juxtaposes the Texas cowboy myth against the realities of ranching and oil-exploration.

Jack S. Blanton Museum of Art★★

200 E. Martin Luther King Jr. Blvd., University of Texas. ♿🅿 ✆512-471-7324. www.blantonmuseum.org.

The Blanton's permanent collection of more than 13,000 works ranges from ancient to contemporary art. The ground floor features the **Mari & James Michener Collection** of 20C American art; donated by the late novelist and his wife, it offers hundreds of modern masterworks, from Cubist to Abstract Expressionist.

The **C.R. Smith Collection** of 19C American art includes Henry Farny's 1899 portrait of Sitting Bull and works by Bierstadt, Moran and Russell. The **Suida-Manning Collection** on the second floor has important Renaissance and Baroque art, including works by Rubens and Veronese. The **Latin American Art** gallery presents contemporary work from artists in Central and South America. An original 15C Gutenberg Bible, one of the few copies in the US, is displayed on the ground floor of the Ransom Center.

Lady Bird Johnson Wildflower Center★★

4801 La Crosse Ave. ✗♿🅿 ✆512-232-0100. www.wildflower.org.

Created by the former First Lady in 1982—her legacy is beautifully visible along Texas highways during April's wildflower extravaganza—this facility is dedicated to conserving and promoting the use of indigenous plants, including 650 species native to Texas.

The 279-acre site includes an arboretum, over 175,000 plants in research, display and botanical theme gardens (ablaze with color particularly Apr–May) as well as natural grasslands and woodlands, an observation tower, stone cisterns, aqueducts, courtyards and nature trails. In 2013 the 16 acre **Mollie Steves Zachry Texas Arboretum** was opened, with a focus on trees. In spring 2014 the 4.5 acre Luci and Ian Family Garden is scheduled to debut. The latter will double the center's maintained garden space.

Hill Country★★

The scenic Hill Country northwest of San Antonio was shaped 30 million years ago when the earth buckled and kicked up strata of limestone and granite into rugged hills and steep cliffs. Rivers, lakes, limestone caves and other natural attractions mark the region's 25,000sq mi.

A BIT OF HISTORY

The Hill Country was originally home to several Indian tribes, including Apache, Tonkawa and Comanche. Republican (1836-45) and early statehood periods were marked by immigration from the eastern US, France, Denmark, Sweden, Czechoslovakia and especially the German Rhine states.

Today the Hill Country's character is largely the legacy of a German small-landholder tradition.

🚗 DRIVING TOUR

2 days, 226mi.

▷ Take US-281 from San Antonio 63mi north, or US-290 from Austin 48mi west, to Johnson City.

Johnson City

Though named for Sam Ealy Johnson, grandfather of former US President Lyndon Baines Johnson, attractions in this small community of 1,200 people today focus on "LBJ," its most famous son.

Lyndon B. Johnson National Historical Park★★

Ave. G & Ladybird Lane. ♿ 🅿 ✆830-868-7128. www.nps.gov/lyjo.
The life and family heritage of LBJ (1908-73) is portrayed in exhibits at the **Visitor Center**. The **LBJ Boyhood Home** (Elm St. & Ave. G; 🚶‍guided tour only) has been restored to its 1920 appearance and furnished with family heirlooms. The **Johnson Settlement** (west end of Ladybird Lane) preserves the tiny log home and outbuildings of cattle

- 🕐 **Michelin Map:** p 399. Central Standard Time.
- 🔲 **Info:** www.fredericksburg-texas.com; www.kerrville
- ▷ **Location:** The Balcones Fault, the uplift that is the boundary of the Hill Country, runs just west of Interstate 35 from San Antonio most of the way to Fort Worth.
- 🔎 **Don't Miss:** Fredericksburg; wildflower season in April.
- 🕐 **Timing:** Though this drive can be done in two days, it's wonderful to linger at the many small inns in the region. Best times to visit are spring, when the region is painted with fields of bluebonnets, coreopsis and paintbrush; and autumn, when oak, sycamore and sumac infuse the plateau with color. Summer days are hot and humid, winter is often chilly and overcast.

rancher Sam Johnson and his brother, Tom, in the 1860s.

▷ Continue 14mi west on US-290.

Lyndon B. Johnson National and State Historical Parks★★

US-290, Stonewall. ♿ 🅿 ✆830-644-2252. www.tpwd.state.tx.us.
LBJ's "Texas White House" —the president's pastoral ranch beside his beloved Pedernales River—is the attraction at these combined parks, which span 1,200 acres. Buses depart from the State Park Visitor Center; those awaiting a 🚶‍tour can view a film and displays on Johnson's life. The 90min National Park Service tour travels to the **LBJ Ranch**, stopping at the one-room Junction School where Johnson began his education. The president's office, living room and dining room at the Texas White House hold LBJ memorabilia. An airstrip, cattle barns, LBJ's reconstructed birthplace home and the family cem-

etery where he is buried complete the tour. Private vehicles must obtain a permit at the Visitor Center to drive on the ranch.

Within the state-park boundary is the 1918 **Sauer-Beckmann Living History Farm**, furnished in period style and manned by costumed interpreters who perform the daily chores of a c.1900 Texas-German farm family.

Continue another 16mi west on US-290 to Fredericksburg.

Fredericksburg★★

This community of 11,000 was settled in 1846 by 120 German pioneers who ventured to Texas in response to a land-grant program. Their heritage persists along wide streets lined with picturesque homes of native limestone, Fachwerk and Victorian gingerbread. Such annual festivals as Oktoberfest pack the lanes with revelers. Wineries welcome visitors the rest of the year.

Historical artifacts are displayed in the **Vereins Kirche Museum** (100 block W. Main St.; 830-997-7832; http://pioneermuseum.net) and the **Pioneer Museum Complex** (325 W. Main St.; 830-990-8441; http://pioneermuseum.net). Eighty-three buildings are designated sites in Fredericksburg's 30-block historic district; many have been converted to B&Bs. Just outside Fredericksburg is the fabled-in-song **Luckenbach★**, an entire "town" devoted to its namesake 1849 general store, dance hall, and the outdoor stage (www.luckenbachtexas.com) where Texas troubadors have been performing for more than a century.

National Museum of the Pacific War★

340 E. Main St. 830-997-8600. www.pacificwarmuseum.org.

The only museum devoted to the World War II's Pacific theater, this newly expanded site comprises a museum housed in a curiously shiplike 1852 hotel and adjacent grounds. Much of the complex honors Admiral Chester Nimitz, a World War II hero and Fredericksburg native. Nimitz became Commander-in-Chief of US Pacific forces in December 1941, and directed 2.5 million troops until 1945. The 2009 limestone and glass **George W. Bush Gallery★** leads visitors on a comprehensive timeline through the Pacific War. Adjacent is the **Garden of Peace★**, a classic Oriental garden presented in respect of Nimitz by the people of Japan.

Drive 18mi north on Ranch Rd. 965.

Enchanted Rock State Natural Area★

16710 Ranch Rd. 965. 830-685-3636. www.tpwd.state.tx.us.

This state park contains one of the largest stone formations in the West, a 640-acre granite outcrop. The ascent takes about an hour, and hikers are rewarded with a magnificent **view★★** of the Hill Country. The trail around the rock leads through oak woods and quiet prairie.

Return to Fredericksburg and take Rte. 16 for 24mi south.

Museum of Western Art★

1550 Bandera Hwy. (Rte. 173) Kerrville. 210-896-2553. museumofwesternart.com.

This hilltop museum features work by 26 contemporary Western artists, including Gordon Snidow of New Mexico and Robert Scriver of Montana, whose paintings and sculptures capture the spirit and traditional lifestyle of the West. The building (1982, O'Neill Ford), constructed in Mexican style of 18 brick domes, surrounds an open sculpture garden.

Continue on Rte. 173 south 25mi.

Bandera

Bandera claims to be "The Cowboy Capital of the World" (www.banderacowboycapital.com). Rodeos are scheduled weekly from May to September. Local dance halls fill with two-steppers, clad in jeans and cowboy hats, dancing to country-western music most nights.

Return to San Antonio on Rte. 16.

Corpus Christi★

Where the South Texas plains meet the Gulf of Mexico, the thriving harbor city of Corpus Christi nestles beside broad Corpus Christi Bay. Its calm waters, shielded from the wind-whipped gulf by the sandy, reef-like barrier of Mustang and Padre Islands, have made "Corpus" one of the busiest ports in the US and the home of one of its largest naval air bases.

▶ **Population:** 312,000.
Michelin Map: 492 K 15. Central Standard Time.
Info: ℘361-561-2000 or 800-766-2322; visitcorpuschristi.org.
Don't Miss: USS *Lexington*.
Kids: Texas State Aquarium.

SIGHTS

Museum of Science and History★

1900 N. Chaparral St. ℘361-826-4667. www.ccmuseum.com.
Highlights of the museum are a replica of Columbus's ship the Pinta, and an exhibit devoted to the shipwreck treasure—gold and coins—from two Spanish galleons that foundered nearby in 1554.

Texas State Aquarium★

2710 N. Shoreline Dr. ℘361-881-1200. www.texasstateaquarium.org.
Gulf of Mexico marine life are at "home" in ecosystem exhibits that include marsh and shoreline, pier and estuary. Islands of Steel replicates an offshore oil platform surrounded by nurse sharks and amberjack. Outdoors are touch tanks of small sharks and stingrays, river otters, sea turtles and a rare white alligator.

USS Lexington Museum on the Bay★★

2914 N. Shoreline Blvd. ℘361-888-4873. www.usslexington.com.
This mammoth World War II aircraft carrier, berthed near the aquarium across the Harbor Bridge from downtown, was the most decorated carrier in US Navy history. Today "The Lex," its main deck larger than three football fields, offers self-guided tours.

Padre Island National Seashore★★

⚠️♿🅿℘361-949-8068. www.nps.gov/pais.
This 70mi of undeveloped beach—longest such barrier island preserve in the world—stretches south from Corpus Christi to Port Mansfield, the southern 55mi of it impassable to all but four-wheel-drive vehicles.
Park Road 22— an extension of South Padre Island Drive (Rte. 358), which crosses the JFK Bridge and Causeway 25mi east of Corpus Christi—ends just past **Malaquite Beach Visitor Center** (20420 Park Rd. 22). The northern 10mi of national seashore offer a taste of the vast sand-and-shell beaches, dunes and grasslands beyond.

EXCURSION
King Ranch★

◯ 39mi south of Corpus Christi via Hwy. 141W, Kingsville; take US-77 to Rte. 141, turn right (west) onto King Ave., proceed 3mi to blinking light; follow signs from ranch gate (on left) to visitor center. 🅿℘361-592-8055. www.king-ranch.com.
One of the largest US cattle ranches, King Ranch sprawls across 1,300sq mi. It was founded in 1853 by steamboat pilot Richard King, whose sixth-generation descendants still own the ranch. Once largest in the US, it has been superseded by Parker Ranch in Hawaii.
Highlights of a 90min bus tour include the grave of horse-racing's 1946 Triple Crown winner, Assault, and a weaver's cottage where dozens of Texas ranch brands—including King's own distinctive "running W"—are on display.

Great Plains

Beardtongue and Needle and Thread Grass,
Badlands National Park, South Dakota
© National Park Service

Black Hills Region

Rolling hills seem to go on forever in the northern Great Plains, punctuated only by an occasional ranch house or barn. Here and there, a cowboy may ride over the crest of a hill, sheepdogs in the lead, to find 100 head of cattle in a draw. Multiple thunderstorms move through the expanse of sky like ships adrift in a deceptively placid sea. High buttes that once were landmarks for westbound pioneers interrupt these wide-open spaces like ancient ruins.

Highlights

1 Icons in stone at **Mt. Rushmore** (p415)

2 Peaceful pines at **Custer State Park** (p416)

3 History in the wind at **Little Bighorn Battlefield** (p418)

4 Folk art at **Corn Palace** (p420)

5 Wild plains and canyons at **Theodore Roosevelt National Park** (p421)

Sculpted Land

The dominant landforms in the region are the Black Hills and the Badlands of South Dakota. Sacred to many High Plains Indian tribes, especially the Sioux, the Black Hills of western South Dakota were forced 60 million years ago to heights of 14,000ft. Ravaged by inland seas and thundering upheavals, the domed range today stands 3,000ft–4,000ft above the surrounding plains. From a distance, the heavily wooded hills appear dark: thus their name. The Black Hills are renowned for their caves. The same geological forces that caused them to uplift cracked the limestone layers deposited by a previous inland ocean. Water seeped in, slowly wearing down the rock into a maze of passages. The "racetrack" of limestone that circles the granite core is strewn with hundreds of miles of ancient caverns, constituting the second-longest cave system in the world. Eight caves are developed for public viewing.

East of the hills, across the Cheyenne River, erosion of sedimentary stone in the past 500,000 years created the Badlands.

ADDRESSES

🛏 STAY

$$$ The Hotel Alex Johnson – 523 6th St., Rapid City, SD. ☎605-342-1210. www.alexjohnson.com. 143 rooms. Alex Johnson built his seven-story hotel in 1928 as a showplace for Sioux culture, with hand-painted buffalo tiles and a chandelier of spears. Each floor today honors a tribe. The Vertex Sky Bar, on the hotel's 11th floor has expansive views, cocktails and walleye and buffalo.

$$$ State Game Lodge – US-16A, Custer State Park, SD. ☎605-255-4541. www.custerresorts.com. 69 units. Built in 1920, this erstwhile presidential retreat has stately lodge rooms, motel units and intimate cabins. The **Historic Pheasant Dining Room** (☎605-255-4541; **$$$**) offers creative preparations of game dishes.

$$ The Historic Franklin Hotel – 700 Main St., Deadwood, SD. ☎605-578-3670. www.silveradofranklin.com. 81 rooms. Part of a casino complex, the Franklin has existed since 1903. Rooms are dedicated to movie stars, presidents and rodeo riders. In the antiques-laden lobby is a hand-operated elevator; Durty Nelly's is Deadwood's oldest gaming hall.

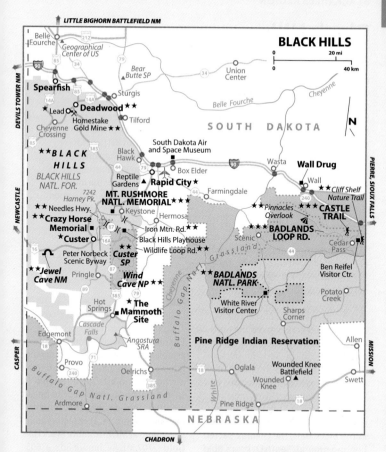

BLACK HILLS

$$ Spearfish Canyon Lodge – 10619 Roughlock Falls Rd., Lead SD ☎605-584-3435 www.spfcanyon.com. 54 rooms. Soaring timbers rise above a river-rock fireplace in the great room of this classic lodge. Suites offer Jacuzzi tubs and decks with canyon views.

$ Rough Riders Hotel – 3rd Ave. & 3rd St., Medora, ND. ☎701-623-4444. www.medora.com. 9 rooms. Teddy Roosevelt used to dine on bison and other game at this hotel, built in 1883 and restored in 1962. Every air-conditioned room has antiques and TV. Cheaper off-season rates include meals.

ⴵ/ EAT

$$ La Minestra – 106 E. Dakota St., Pierre, SD. Closed Sun. ☎605-224-8090. www.laminestra.com. **Italian**. Mark Mancuso weaves his culinary spell in an open kitchen behind an antique mahogany bar. Old World flavor permeates the

cafe; the building was constructed in 1896 as a funeral parlor. The menu features homemade pastas, eggplant Parmesan, steaks and seafood.

$$ Peacock Alley Bar & Grill – 422 E. Main Ave., Bismarck, ND. ☎701-255-7917. www.peacock-alley.com. **American**. The floral decor doesn't quite mesh with the framed photos of early boxing champions, but contradictions are right at home among the politicians who frequent this 1930s hotel lobby near the state capitol. The eclectic menu ranges from burgers to four kinds of steak.

$$ Powder House – US-16A, Keystone, SD. Open May–Oct. ☎605-666-4646. www.powderhouselodge.com. **American**. This log cabin hid bootleg liquor under its tin roof in the 1930s. Today, spirits are served on big oak tables, along with breaded mushrooms, prime rib, and buffalo stew in a homemade bread bowl.

Black Hills★★

The Black Hills uplift, 125mi long and 65mi wide, has a rugged core of granite spires, knobs and mountains. It is flanked in the west by a limestone plateau, framed by the Cheyenne and Belle Fourche Rivers and the appropriately named Red Valley. The region's urban center, and Black Hills gateway, is Rapid City.

A BIT OF HISTORY

The area's human history goes back 11,000 years. Ancient mammoth hunters were followed by nomadic tribes. For centuries these ponderosa-clad hills have been sacred to Native Americans—they call them Paha Sapa, "hills that are black." The Lakota Sioux, having domesticated horses, ruled the northern plains until European fur-trading posts arose on the Red and Missouri Rivers. In the 1850s, homesteaders moved in; European immigrants and the railroad followed. After a member of Lt. Col. **George Armstrong Custer's** expedition discovered gold in 1874 in the Black Hills, the Lakotas' sacred hunting ground, South Dakota's gold rush began. The treaty that had granted them this territory in perpetuity was ignored as prospectors rushed in to grab the earth's treasure. This intrusion inevitably led to conflict.

The Sioux and Cheyenne prevailed at the Battle of the **Little Bighorn** in nearby Montana in 1876, but that was their final hurrah. The massacre at **Wounded Knee** (see p420) in 1890 completed the subjugation of Native tribes. In 1897 President Grover Cleveland established the Black Hills Forest Reserve, later Black Hills National Forest. Until it closed at the end of 2001, the Homestake Gold Mine in Lead was the world's oldest continuously operated gold mine.

The 20C has seen the growth of tourism, triggered by the sculpting of Mt. Rushmore and the establishment of several national parks in the area.

- 🕭 **Michelin Map:** p 413. Mountain Standard Time.
- 🗎 **Info:** ℘605-355-3600; www.blackhillsbadlands.com.
- 🕭 **Don't Miss:** The Mt. Rushmore and Crazy Horse memorials. Little Bighorn Battlefield.
- 🕓 **Timing:** Plan on a full day to visit Rushmore and Crazy Horse: the morning for the first and afternoon for the latter, which are about a half-hour apart.
- 🧑‍🤝‍🧑 **Kids:** The Journey Museum.

SIGHTS

Rapid City★

US-16 & Rte. 79 at I-90. ✗♿🅿 ℘605-718-8484. www.visitrapidcity.com.

The principal Black Hills community was established on a foundation of mining, lumber and ranching; trade and tourism now support its 70,000 people. In 1876, Frenchman Henri LeBeau began creating gold designs that remain a regional trademark. Free factory tours are offered at **Mt. Rushmore Black Hills Gold** (2707 Mt. Rushmore Rd.; ℘605-343-2226).

Downtown Rapid City launched a major urban art project that marks street corners with life-size bronze sculptures of every US president.

In **Memorial Park** (444 Mt. Rushmore Rd.), just north of downtown, stands a Berlin Wall exhibit. **Dinosaur Park** 🧑‍🤝‍🧑 (Skyline Dr. W. off Quincy St.; ℘605-343-8687) features concrete replicas of prehistoric beasts, including a brontosaurus visible miles away. The **Stavkirke** (Chapel Lane Dr. off Jackson Blvd.) was built in 1969 as a replica of a 12C Norwegian stave church. **South Dakota Air and Space Museum** (Ellsworth Air Force Base, I-90 Exit 66; ℘605-385-5189, www.sdairandspacemuseum.com) displays stealth bombers and other aircraft.

MOUNT RUSHMORE NATIONAL MEMORIAL★★★

👥 Rte. 244, 3mi west of Keystone. ✕♿🅿 ✆605-574-2523. www.nps.gov/moru.

Carved on the face of a granite cliff over 14 years (1927-41) by **Gutzon Borglum**, the son of Danish immigrants to the US, Mt. Rushmore is his "shrine to democracy," and one of the most iconic images of America around the world, drawing 3 million visitors a year. Borglum chose to depict four US presidents: **George Washington**, first president; **Thomas Jefferson**, author of the *Declaration of Independence*; **Abraham Lincoln**, who ended slavery; and **Theodore Roosevelt**, America's greatest conservation leader, and a lifelong

Avenue of Flags

fan, sometime resident and advocate for the American West.

The **Avenue of Flags**, representing every US state and territory, leads 700ft to the **Lincoln Borglum Museum**. Ten-foot historical photos and storyboards tell the story of the making of Mt. Rushmore. The **Presidential Trail** (*.5mi*) takes walkers to the talus slope of the mountain and Borglum's own Sculptor's Studio; along the way, a Native American **heritage village** depicts the lifestyles of the Lakota, Nakota and Dakota tribes who have lived here for centuries.

Mount Rushmore National Memorial

👥 The Journey Museum★★

222 New York St. 🚹🅿️ 𝒫605-394-6923. www.journeymuseum.org.

State-of-the-art multimedia techniques relate the 2.5-million-year history of the Black Hills region through the collections of five museums, including the **Sioux Indian Museum★★** of the US Department of the Interior; the **Duhamel Collection of Native American Artifacts**, and **Minnilusa Pioneer Museum★★**. Provocative displays offer insight into the minds of Indian warriors and the secrets of the Sioux nation's sacred Black Hills.

Crazy Horse Memorial★★

US-16/385, 4mi north of Custer. ✖️🚹🅿️ 𝒫605-673-4681. www.crazyhorsememorial.org.

The world's largest sculptural undertaking features the emerging 563ft-high image of Sioux Chief Crazy Horse (c1840-77), battle leader at the Little Bighorn. The warrior's face, higher than the Sphinx, was completed in 1998.

The colossal carving-in-progress began in 1948 after sculptor Korczak Ziolkowski (1908-82) was invited by Sioux chiefs to create a work to complement Mt. Rushmore; the Sioux wanted "the white man to know the red man has great heroes, too." Ziolkowski's widow and children carry on the project. Ongoing blasting work is a big visitor draw.

Native artisans demonstrate their skills in the **Native American Educational and Cultural Center★** at the foot of the mountain. The nearby **Indian Museum** of North America presents traditional crafts and historic sepia-tone photos.

Custer★

US-16 & 385. ✖️🚹🅿️ 𝒫605-673-2244. www.custersd.com.

Established during the 1870s gold rush near George Custer's original encampment, this hill-embraced town of 2,000 perpetuates the historic flair of the late 19C. A highlight is the **National Museum of Woodcarving** (3mi west on US-16; 𝒫605-673-4404; www.blackhills.com/woodcarving/; closed Nov–Apr), which displays humorous caricature scenes by more than 20 carvers.

Jewel Cave National Monument★★

US-16, 13mi west of Custer. 🚹🅿️ 𝒫605-673-8300. www.nps.gov/jeca.

Since prospectors discovered the cave in 1900, spelunkers have mapped more than 120mi of passages, a mere two percent of what is estimated.

The 80min **scenic tour★** starts with a 234ft elevator descent. Visitors then follow a concrete path and aluminum stairways to 370ft below the surface, where it is a constant, cool 49°F. Massive chambers glitter with elongated crystals of dogtooth spar and nailhead spar. A **lantern tour** and 4hr **spelunking tour** are offered also.

Custer State Park★★

US-16A & Rte. 87. Park headquarters 23mi south of Mt. Rushmore. ⛺️✖️🚹🅿️ 𝒫605-255-4515. http://gfp.sd.gov/state-parks.

Wild Bill Hickok

US marshal and army scout James Butler Hickok confessed to having killed between 15 and 100 men before he was 27, "but I never, in my life, took any mean advantage of an enemy." Sharp-shooting Wild Bill was in Deadwood for only 67 days, but his legacy colors the city and indeed, the Black Hills to this day. Hickok's murder is reenacted in a mini-drama at **Old Style Saloon No. 10** and in a diorama, complete with honky-tonk music and gunshots, at the **Journey Museum** in Rapid City. Wild Bill Hickok is buried in **Mt. Moriah Cemetery★**, Deadwood's "Boot Hill," next to Martha "Calamity Jane" Canary, America's most famous bullwhip-toting dame. One-hour trolley tours depart Main Street for the cemetery.

©Sturgis Motorcycle Museum & Hall of Fame

Exhibits at the Sturgis Motorcycle Museum & Hall of Fame

Sturgis Rally and Races

South Dakota is home to one of the largest motorcycle rallies in the world. Each August, 400,000 riders meet in Sturgis (population 6,600; www.sturgis.com), 27mi northwest of Rapid City. In 1938 motorcycle-shop owner J.C. "Pappy" Hoel held the first rally with 19 racers. Today poker runs, drag races, hill climbs, road tours and riding exhibitions are among events on a full seven-day schedule.

Even nonbikers attend to see what's new in the motorcycle world and to view more than 100 antique bikes—including the oldest unrestored running 1907 Harley-Davidson and actor Steve McQueen's 1915 Cyclone—at the **Sturgis Motorcycle Museum & Hall of Fame** (2438 Junction Ave.; ✆605-347-2001; www.sturgismuseum.com).

This state park encompasses 111sq mi of grasslands, prairie swales, forest and granite peaks. Elk, deer, pronghorn, bighorn sheep and a bison herd of 1,400 are at home among wildflowers, cacti, pine and spruce.

Three scenic driving routes wind through the park, two of them segments of the 66mi **Peter Norbeck Scenic Byway** (US-16A, Rtes. 87, 89 & 244). The 18mi **Wildlife Loop Road★★** runs south and west from the rustic, 1920 State Game Lodge to Blue Bell Resort, offering vistas of the park's resident "begging" burros. The 17mi **Iron Mountain Road★★ (US-16A)** includes pigtail bridges designed in the 1930s to span steep climbs in short distances. Three narrow tunnels frame Rushmore as drivers pass through. Granite peaks—including 7,242ft Harney Peak, highest in South Dakota—flank the 14mi-long **Needles Highway★★** (Rte. 87).

Wind Cave National Park★★

US-385, 10mi north of Hot Springs & 22mi south of Custer. ⚠ ♿ 🅿 ✆605-745-4600. www.nps.gov/wica.

Although Indian legends addressed holes that "blew wind," the cave's recorded discovery came in 1881. Ranger-led tours range from the 1hr, 150-stair **Garden of Eden Tour** to the 4hr, lots-of-crawling **Wild Cave Tour**. Unique honeycomb-like boxwork is Wind Cave's trademark; created by calcite left by dissolved limestone, boxwork was named for its resemblance to old postal sorters—a diagonal crisscross of fragile-looking lines of calcite protruding from walls.

The Mammoth Site★

US-18 Bypass, Hot Springs. &🅿𝒫605-745-6017. www.mammothsite.com.

Some 26,000 years ago, the collapse of a sinkhole created a 60ft-deep death trap for Pleistocene mammals, including 61 mammoths. The silt-filled hole was revealed again in 1974. 👁️‍🗨️Today this trove of Ice Age fossils delights visitors, who get a primer on earth history during a 30min guided tour.

Deadwood★★

US-14A, 13mi west of Sturgis. ✕&🅿
𝒫800-999-1876 or 605-578-1876. www.deadwood.org.

By 1876, 25,000 people had swarmed to Deadwood Gulch. Fortune seekers, cavalrymen, Chinese laborers and gun-slinging gamblers established a main street of tents, banks, saloons and brothels. Today the buildings are shops, restaurants and, well, gaming halls lining **Main Street★★**. At the **information center (753 Main St.)**, visitors can pick up a "Historic Deadwood Walking Tour" map. The **Adams Museum★** (54 Sherman St.; 𝒫605-578-1714; www.adamsmuseumandhouse.org) holds a 7.75oz gold nugget found in 1929. The nearby **Adams House★** (22 Van Buren St.) is an 1892 Queen Anne-style mansion. In the **Old Style Saloon No. 10** (657 Main St.; 𝒫605-578-3346), role players "gun down" Wild Bill Hickok daily. The **Broken Boot Gold Mine** ▲♟ (Upper Main St. & US-14A; 𝒫605-578-1876; www.brokenbootgoldmine.com) offers underground tours and gold panning.

Homestake Gold Mine★★

160 W. Main St., Lead, 3mi southwest of Deadwood. 🅿𝒫605-584-3110. www.homestakevisitorcenter.com.

The world's oldest continuously operated gold mine, until it closed in 2001, lies uphill from Deadwood in the town of **Lead★** (pronounced LEED), whose old miners' homes crawl up steep hillsides. By 1945, 40 million tons of ore had been taken out. 👁️‍🗨️Surface tours of the **Open Cut★★**, an enormous pit 1,800ft wide, 4,500ft long and 968ft deep, are still offered (*May–Sept*).

Spearfish★

US-14A at I-90, 50mi northwest of Rapid City. ✕&🅿𝒫605-642-2626. www.spearfishchamber.org.

Spearfish's historic district centers on its 1906 opera house. The **High Plains Western Heritage Center** (825 Heritage Dr.; &🅿𝒫605-642-9378; www.westernheritagecenter.com) has exhibits that honor Native Americans and early pioneers. **Spearfish Canyon★★** is a scenic byway through the native forests.

EXCURSIONS

Devils Tower National Monument★

▶ Wyoming Rte. 110 off Rte. 24; 10mi south of Hulett WY & 52mi southwest of Belle Fourche SD via Rte. 34. ⚠&🅿
𝒫307-467-5283. www.nps.gov/deto.

Sacred to Native Americans, this fluted monolith rises 867ft; the top covers 1.5 acres. It is the core of an igneous intrusion that became exposed as surrounding sedimentary rock eroded. The first ascent of the peak was made on July 4, 1893; today 5,000 climbers a year challenge its vertical rock walls (🧗climbing prohibited in June). The butte is worth the bother, especially for those who hike the paved 1.3mi **Tower Trail★** around its base.

Little Bighorn Battlefield National Monument★★

▶ US-212, Crow Agency MT; 15mi south of Hardin MT & 201mi northwest of Belle Fourche SD. &🅿𝒫406-638-2621. www.nps.gov/libi.

At this now serene spot, one of North America's most famous battles was fought June 25-26 1876, Lakota Sioux and Cheyenne warriors killed 272 US cavalrymen, including Lt. Col. George Armstrong Custer. Natives know the conflict as the Battle of Greasy Grass; Americans refer to it as Custer's Last Stand. It was the last major victory for Native Americans in the western US. Visitors peruse the maps, photos and dioramas in the **visitor center and museum**. A stroll across the pleasant, grassy hill reveals plaques marking the sites where various fighters fell.

Badlands★★

The play of dawn's light tints the rock faces a gentle bluish-pink that warms to red, gradually covering existing layers of purple shale, chestnut sand, orange iron oxide and white volcanic ash. While the Badlands boast a remarkable geological history, it is the rare and not-so-subtle beauty of a landscape that changes seasonally, and even hourly, that visitors are compelled to see again and again.

- **Michelin Map:** p 413. Mountain Standard Time.
- **Info:** ℘605-279-2665; www.wall-badlands.com.
- **Don't Miss:** Badlands National Park; the Wounded Knee Museum.
- **Kids:** Wall Drug.

A BIT OF HISTORY

The term "Badlands" was bestowed by the Lakota Sioux. French trappers referred to the country as *les mauvaises terres à traverser*: "bad lands to cross." Fossils as old as 77 million years have been unearthed here; of note are those of early mammals, such as the rhinoceros-like brontotheres from the Eocene era. The range of spires and sawtooth ridges—a sculpted mudstone wall roughly 1,000ft at its highest—runs 90mi from South Dakota into Nebraska, bounded on both sides by prairies.

SIGHTS

Badlands National Park★★

Rte. 240 (Badlands Loop Rd.), 8mi south of I-90 Exit 110 at Wall, 51mi east of Rapid City. öf(summer only) ♿🅿 ℘605-433-5361. www.nps.gov/badl.

Most visitors see only one strip of this 375sq-mi park—the most dramatic. The 39mi **Badlands Loop Road★★★** traverses the northern rim of the Badlands, where prairie grasslands give way to buttes and hoodoos. Long blond grasses shimmer in the wind like a shaken sheet. Wildflowers speckle stream canyons, intricately carved slopes and tiny sodded buttes.

Pinnacles Overlook★★ offers a sweeping viewpoint to the south. Formations are bleached white on top, then bleed pinkish to a tawny yellow. Tiny white Hood's phlox bloom in the broad expanse of gray. The **Castle Trail★★★** (*4.5mi*) is spectacular in early morning when the moonscape valley and pointed spires get their first dose of light. The **Cliff Shelf Nature Trail★★** (*.5mi*) is popular for its shady juniper trees. The boardwalk winds through a "slump," where water retention has created an oasis.

Badlands National Park

© National Park Service

Park headquarters are at the **Ben Reifel Visitor Center** (Cedar Pass, 8mi south of I-90 Exit 131; ℘605-433-5361), at the east end of the park road. Exhibits and a film introduce visitors to the unique landscape. The **White River Visitor Center** (25mi north of Wounded Knee; ℘605-455-2878; open Jun–Aug) serves the southern end.

Pine Ridge Indian Reservation

US-18 & connecting routes south of Badlands National Park. ℘605-455-2685. www.pineridgechamber.com.

The home of the Oglala Sioux tribe (http://oglalalaotanation.org) covers nearly 3,000sq mi of western South Dakota, southeast of the Black Hills. About 20,000 Oglala live on the reservation, established in 1878 and a landmark in American Indian history.

In late 1890, two weeks after Chief **Sitting Bull** was killed during a "precautionary" arrest farther north, Chief **Big Foot** and his band left Pine Ridge to hide in the Badlands. The cavalry intercepted them. On December 29, as troops searched the band for weapons, a rifle was fired, setting off a barrage that didn't stop until Big Foot and some 250 Oglala men, women and children were dead. Thirty soldiers also died, many from their own crossfire.

A mass grave, gray stone monument and wooden highway sign today mark the privately owned **Wounded Knee Massacre site** (Tribal Rte. 27 just east of Rte. 28).

The **Heritage Center of Red Cloud Indian School** (100 Mission Dr., Pine Ridge; ℘605-867-1105; www.redcloudschool.org) showcases Plains Indians arts and crafts. Renowned Chief **Red Cloud** is buried on a hilltop overlooking the Holy Rosary Mission.

The newly expanded **Wounded Knee Museum**★★ (600 Main St., in Wall; ℘605-279-2573; www.woundedkneemuseum.org) has exhibits on the massacre and the debates about it—and about Indian culture in modern America—that persist, such as the use of Indian names as sports team mascots.

♣♠ Wall Drug

510 Main St., Wall; 51mi east of Rapid City off I-90 Exit 109 or 110. ✗♿🅿
℘605-279-2175. www.walldrug.com.
Notable mostly for the roadside billboards promoting it, Wall Drug may be the world's most famous "drug store" – or tourist trap, depending on who you ask. Behind a Western storefront is a 76,000sq-ft space with some 20 shops, filled with historical photos, 6,000 pairs of cowboy boots, wildlife exhibits and a Western art collection. In the backyard a children's play area has ice-water wells and a roaring 80ft **Tyrannosaurus**.

EXCURSION
Pierre

▶ US-14, US-83 & Rte. 34. 188mi east of Rapid City. Central Time Zone. ⚠✗♿🅿
℘605-224-7361. www.pierre.org.
Seven other towns in South Dakota are larger than the quaint state capital, located near the geographical center of the state. Some 14,000 people live in Pierre (pronounced PEER). The town lies on the Missouri River just below meandering **Lake Oahe**, which extends 231mi upstream into North Dakota. The four-story **South Dakota State Capitol** (500 E. Capitol Ave.; ♿🅿℘605-773-3765) is a modified Greek structure with Ionic columns. Built in 1910 of native fieldstone, Indiana limestone and Italian marble, it was restored in 1989.

The **South Dakota Cultural Heritage Center**★ (900 Governors Dr.; ♿🅿℘605-773-3458; http://history.sd.gov),a few blocks north of the capitol, resembles an Arikara earth lodge (1989, Blake Holman); the center couples Native American and pioneer history.

Corn Palace

▶ In Mitchell, SD; I-90, 75 mi west of Sioux Falls. ✗♿🅿℘605-995-8430.
www.cornpalace.com.
Using the most ubiquitous material at hand, corn (maize), residents of this farming community each year create a vivid mural on the walls of their community center—one of America's finest examples of the rural folk art tradition.

North Dakota★

North Dakota typifies the Great Plains—from the small lakes and forested hills of the glaciated north, where every mile has a pair of mallards in a bulrush-bordered pothole, to the rugged badlands of the Little Missouri and the rolling hills that cross into South Dakota. This is a land of climate extremes, of frigid winter blizzards and violent summer thunderstorms. But the wide-open spaces also boast a stark beauty. Outdoor recreation, prolific wildlife and vast fields of grain attract visitors from near and far.

A BIT OF HISTORY

Inhabited by Native Americans for at least 15,000 years, the state's high plains first drew European fur traders in the mid 18C. After the Louisiana Purchase in 1803, explorers **Meriwether Lewis** and **William Clark** wintered with the Mandan tribe on the Missouri River, where they were joined by **Sacagawea**, the Shoshone woman who helped guide them to the Pacific. The region developed slowly until the 1870s, when the railroad brought many wheat-farming homesteaders to the area. Statehood came in 1889. Since the late 1950s, oil derricks have dotted the landscape, and new production techniques have brought the state a 21C boom similar to that in Texas in the early 20C.

- **Michelin Map:** 491 I, J, K, 4, 5. Central & Mountain Standard Times.
- **Info:** ℘701-328-2525; www.ndtourism.com.
- **Don't Miss:** Theodore Roosevelt National Park.
- **Kids:** Fort Abraham Lincoln State Park. Little Missouri River and River Bend Overlook, Theodore Roosevelt National Park (North Unit).

SIGHTS
Theodore Roosevelt National Park★★

Off I-94 & US-85 between Medora & Watford City (3 units). △ & P
℘701-623-4730. www.nps.gov/thro.
The Little Missouri River links the 110sq mi park's South, Elkhorn Ranch and North Units, as does the 120mi Maah Daah Hey Trail. Erosion by wind, water and ice is the subtle artist, paring down softer rock, leaving behind the razor-sharp ridges and rugged buttes now called badlands. In the **North Unit★★** (US-85, 16mi south of Watford City), a 14mi scenic drive climbs to Oxbow Overlook, 500ft above the river. From here, the **Achenbach Trail** (*16mi*) approaches **Sperati Point★**, the narrowest gateway in the badlands. The **South Unit★★** (Rte. 10 Bypass off I-94, Medora, 16mi west of Belfield) is best

Little Missouri River, North Unit, Theodore Roosevelt National Park

© National Park Service

Bronze sculpture of Lewis, Clark, and Sacagawea at Fort Benton, Montana

© Photoshot

THE LEWIS AND CLARK EXPEDITION

To lead a scientific expedition into the Louisiana Territory purchased from Napoleonic France in 1803 for $11.2 million, US President Thomas Jefferson chose **Meriwether Lewis**, his personal secretary, and **William Clark,** a career soldier. Jefferson's "bargain" (Napoleon was strapped for funds) added 828,000 sq mi. to the US, doubling the size of the country in one stroke. Now, the US needed to know just what it had bought.

Though it's a myth that they were the first explorers across the continent (Alexander Mackenzie crossed Canada in 1793), it was an epic journey that fired the public imagination then and now.

The Corps of Discovery set off from St. Louis on May 14, 1804. It returned 28 months later, after traveling more than 8,000mi up the Missouri River, across the Rocky Mountains, down the Snake and Columbia Rivers, and back again. Lewis and Clark succeeded in making the unknown known to a growing nation and in opening the land to settlement. Facilities along the **Lewis and Clark National Historic Trail** (☎402-661-1804; www.nps.gov/lecl) were improved in all 11 states along the explorers' route prior to the 200th anniversary of the trek. In the Dakotas, visitors can follow the Missouri River by car, boat or foot, via interpretive signs, museums and visitor centers. The explorers negotiated passage upriver with Sioux warriors near the site of modern Pierre, at the mouth of the Bad River, in September 1804. They camped near On-A-Slant Village (now in Fort Abraham Lincoln State Park), south of modern Mandan, in October and spent that winter beside the Missouri across from its confluence with the Knife River. Exhibits at the **North Dakota Lewis & Clark Interpretive Center** (US-83 & Rte. 200-A, Washburn; ☎701-462-8535 or 877-462-8535; www.fortmandan.com) include artifacts of every tribe the party encountered between the Plains and Pacific. An art gallery contains a full set of Karl Bodmer's prints of upper Midwest Indian cultures. **Fort Mandan Historic Site** (2mi west) replicates the trapezoidal fort where the party wintered.

At **Knife River Indian Villages National Historic Site** (Rte. 37, .5mi north of Stanton; ☎701-745-3300; www.nps.gov/knri), 3mi farther upriver, a film describes the Hidatsa Mandan tribe that helped Lewis and Clark through that harsh winter. Trails weave past three buried villages and a re-created earth lodge. One village was the home of French interpreter Toussaint Charbonneau, who signed on with the expedition here, and his Shoshone wife, Sacagawea, who guided the Corps west and smoothed relations with Sioux and other tribes. When Lewis and Clark arrived here in 1804, the villages held more residents (3,000) than St. Louis did. **Sacagawea** is honored by a statue in Bismarck.

seen on a paved 36mi scenic loop drive. **Scoria Point Overlook** and **Boicourt Overlook** offer panoramas of yellow, gray and burnt-red buttes. **Wind Canyon Trail** (*.2mi*) negotiates the steep edge of a ridge. Wild horses grazing upland plateaus are a vision to behold, but prairie dogs are the darlings of the park. Behind the **South Unit Visitor Center** stands Roosevelt's Maltese Cross Cabin, restored and relocated here. At the site of **Elkhorn Ranch** (35mi north of Medora), foundation blocks are all that remain of Roosevelt's 1885 ranch.

Medora★

Rte. 10 Bypass off I–94. ✕ ♿ 🅿
𝒫 701-623-4444. www.medora.com.
This delightful frontier-style village clings to its late-19C origins with pioneer facades and a "Hi, how are ya?" spirit among its townspeople. Broadway-style productions are presented in summer at Burning Hills Amphitheater. The 26-room **Chateau de Mores State Historic Site**, built in 1883, offers guided tours.

Fort Union Trading Post National Historic Site★

Rte. 1804 (Lewis & Clark Trail) 25mi southwest of Williston. ♿ 🅿
𝒫 701-572-9083. www.nps.gov/fous.
Reconstructed, this palisaded fort sits near the confluence of the Yellowstone and Missouri Rivers. Inside, the **Bourgeois House** traces the history of the thriving trade of **John Jacob Astor's** American Fur Company.

Bismarck

I-94 & US-83. ✕ ♿ 🅿 𝒫 701-222-4308.
www.bismarckmandancvb.com.
Established as a rail camp in 1872, Bismarck boomed as a Missouri riverboat port. Now this city of 65,000 is an agricultural and oil-industry center and nexus for water sports on nearby Lakes Oahe and Sakakawea.

Its stark **North Dakota State Capitol** (600 E. Boulevard Ave.; 𝒫 701-328-2471), a 19-story limestone structure, was built in 1933. On the grounds, the 👥**North Dakota Heritage Center★** (612 E. Boulevard Ave. ♿ 🅿 𝒫 701-328-2666. history.nd.gov) contains well-interpreted history and natural history exhibits that explore the Northern Plains (under expansion, reopening in stages through 2014.) Outside is a statue of Sacagawea, *The Bird Woman* (Leonard Crunelle, 1910).

👥 Fort Abraham Lincoln State Park★

4480 Ft. Lincoln Rd. (Rte. 1806), 7mi south of Mandan. ⛺ 🅿 𝒫 701-663-4758.
www.fortlincoln.com.
This 1,000-acre park holds the house from which Lt. Col. George Custer set out in 1876 for his "last stand" at the Little Bighorn. Costumed guides offer tours of the home and other structures in Fort Abraham Lincoln, abandoned in 1891 and later restored. The **On-A-Slant Village** includes six reconstructed Mandan earth lodges used from the mid-16C to mid-18C. A restored riverboat offers cruises on the Missouri.

Teddy Roosevelt

Truly one of the outsize figures of American history, Theodore "Teddy" Roosevelt (1858-1919) was a soldier, adventurer, statesman, author, reformer, president and conservationist—and a lifelong part-time resident of the North Dakota badlands, in which his namesake national park includes his former ranch. Battle leader during the Spanish-American War in 1898, TR parlayed his fame into two terms as president (1901-1909) during which he clamped down on business monopolies, guarded food and drug safety, and cast the US presence around the world with a vastly expanded navy. Most of all, he declared preservation status for 230 million acres of public land, more than all other presidents combined. TR helped save American bison from extinction, and is the only president with a toy named for him, the Teddy bear.

Nebraska Panhandle★

Three easterly flowing rivers help define the Nebraska Panhandle that extends 135mi from the Black Hills to the Colorado border. In the north, above the White River, the white cliffs and buttes of rugged Pine Ridge extend in a 100mi arc to South Dakota's badlands. Farther south, the Niobrara River slices past 19-million-year-old fossils and through the expansive ranch and dune country of the Sand Hills. Overlooking the North Platte River, the geological formations of Chimney Rock and Scotts Bluff were significant milestones for westbound travelers. Due to the large number of fossil beds in the region and the facilities devoted to them (see below) the area has been dubbed the "Fossil Freeway."

A BIT OF HISTORY

Western Nebraska was an important 19C transition area from the Great Plains to the Rocky Mountains. The Oregon Trail followed the North Platte to Fort Laramie, Wyoming; fur merchants plied their trade farther north, on the White River. After the 1874 Black Hills gold strike, Fort Robinson was built to defend settlers and travelers from Indian attacks. The region today holds

- ⏱ **Michelin Map:** 491 I 7, 8. Mountain Standard Time.
- 🛈 **Info:** ✆308-632-2133; www.westnebraska.com.
- 👁 **Don't Miss:** Scotts Bluff National Monument.
- 👪 **Kids:** Agate Fossil Beds.

remote ranches and Lake McConaughy, Nebraska's largest recreation destination (www.ilovelakemac.com).

SIGHTS

Museum of the Fur Trade

US-20, 3mi east of Chadron. ♿🅿
✆308-432-3843. www.furtrade.org.
Some 6,000 pieces represent objects exchanged by Indians and European-Americans in the fur trade, including 300 trade guns. Behind the museum is an earthbound trading post built in 1833.

Fort Robinson State Park★

US-20, 3mi west of Crawford.
⛺✕♿🅿 ✆308-665-2900.
outdoornebraska.ne.gov.
Nebraska's largest and most historic state park covers 34sq mi in the Pine Ridge region. Established in 1874, the fort was used until 1948. Pivotal events of the Indian Wars occurred here, including the 1877 killing of Chief **Crazy Horse** and the 1879 Cheyenne Outbreak, an abortive escape attempt

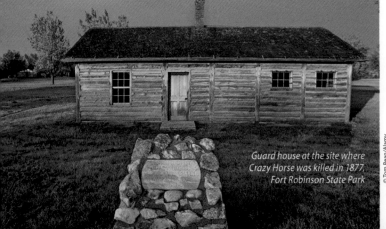

Guard house at the site where Crazy Horse was killed in 1877, Fort Robinson State Park

© Tom Bean/Alamy

The Oregon Trail

From 1842 to 1869, more than 400,000 pioneers passed west on this trail and its many branches in what is considered by historians the greatest voluntary human migration in history. The trail stretched 2,000 miles from Missouri to Oregon's Willamette Valley. Pioneers endured many hardships, but despite the mythical image of wagons circled to fend off Indian attack, the vast majority of casualties on the trail were caused by diseases such as cholera, or starvation or exposure. Though the trail is now more than 150 years old, historic trail ruts can be seen in Nebraska, Wyoming, Idaho and Oregon.

by 149 imprisoned and starving Cheyenne men, women and children. In the late 19C to early 20C, this was home to the African–American garrison known as the **Buffalo Soldiers**.

The **Trailside Museum of Natural History** (𝒫308-665-2929; http://trailside.unl.edu) includes an exhibit of bones of two mammoths, tusks locked in battle, found nearby.

👥 Agate Fossil Beds National Monument★

River Rd. off Rte. 29, 44mi north of Scottsbluff. 🔍🅿𝒫308-436-9760. www.nps.gov/agfo.

Some 3,000 acres near the Niobrara River preserve 19-million-year-old fossil remains of animals that roamed here 40 million years after dinosaurs disappeared. The **James H. Cook Collection★** of Oglala Sioux artifacts includes a whetstone that once belonged to Crazy Horse. The **Fossil Hills Trail** (*2mi*) leads to the restored 1910 homestead of Harold Cook.

Scotts Bluff National Monument★

Rte. 92, 5mi southwest of Scottsbluff. 🔍🅿𝒫308-436-4340. www.nps.gov/scbl.

Sandstone and clay bluffs stand 800ft higher than the North Platte River. Visible for many miles, the bluff was a landmark for travelers on the Oregon, Mormon, California and Pony Express trails; pioneers greeted its sight with delight, as it meant their journey across the endless plains was ending, and higher country lay ahead.

Oregon Trail Museum and Visitor Center

The Oregon Trail runs past this historic building, constructed between 1935-1949. Exhibits include works by pioneer photographer-artist William Henry Jackson, who devoted his career to depicting the westward migration.

Saddle Rock Trail

This trail (1.6mi) treats hikers to **views★★** of the North Platte Valley.

Chimney Rock National Historical Site

Rte. 92, 23mi east of Scottsbluff. 🔍🅿𝒫308-586-2581. www.nebraskahistory.org.

Westbound pioneers scrawled descriptions in their journals about this unique spire visible along both sides of the North Platte. Designated a national site in 1956, the grounds include a visitor center and museum.

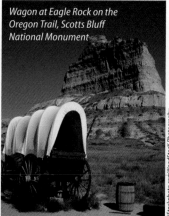

Wagon at Eagle Rock on the Oregon Trail, Scotts Bluff National Monument

©iStockphoto.com/WoodStock Photography

Kansas City Area

The mid-American prairie's rich, fertile soil generates a bounty of wheat and feed grains, supporting vast herds of cattle. Few objects obstruct the sun as it rises and sets on wide, sweeping plains that stretch endlessly to the horizons. The land's pristine beauty inspires artists, nature lovers and outdoorsmen.

Highlights

1 Swing both ways—jazz and baseball—at **18th & Vine** (p430)

2 From Rembrandt to Henry Moore at **Nelson-Atkins** (p431)

3 The buck stops here at the **Truman Library** (p432)

4 Jungle indoors at the **Henry Doorly Zoo** (p436)

5 Cold War memories at the **Strategic Air Museum** (p437)

Kansas City
KS

Modern History

Originally inhabited by Kansa (Siouan) Indians and herds of bison as broad as Rhode Island, this region's modern history began with the Lewis and Clark Expedition of 1803-06. The explorers identified a site where the Kansas River met the Missouri River as a good place to build a fort; in 1821, fur traders took their advice. By the 1830s, Westport Landing (renamed Kansas in 1850 and Kansas City in 1889) was outfitting westbound travelers with provisions, and many wagon trains began their journeys on the Oregon, California and Santa Fe Trails from here. Thousands more hopeful settlers headed up the wide Missouri on steamboats and promises.

In the pre-Civil War years, territorial Kansas was caught in controversy over slave-versus-free state status. Violent confrontations between partisans on both sides flared for years, even after "Bleeding Kansas" was admitted to the Union as a free state in 1861. Kansas City subsequently developed as a rail center. Today, the city has grown into a graceful metropolis with beauty, culture

Nelson-Atkins Museum of Art's 18ft sculptures "Shuttlecocks" by Claes Oldenburg and Coosje van Bruggen

Kansas City Convention & Visitors Association

and a healthy economy. Omaha, a 3hr drive north and the largest city in the adjoining state of Nebraska, also grew around the railroad. Today it is a grain- and livestock-shipping center well known for its fine museums and zoo, for blues, jazz and bar-becue, and as the home of famed billionaire Warren Buffett.

ADDRESSES

🛏 STAY

$$$$ Circle S Ranch & Country Inn – 3325 Circle S Lane, Lawrence, KS. Take 35th St. east off County Rd. 1045, north from US-24/59. ☎785-843-4124. www.circlesranch.com. 12 rooms. Prairie heritage reigns at the Circle S, domain since 1868 of five generations of innkeeper Mary Stevenson's family. A barn-like lodge contains a spacious homestead; visitors explore 1,200 acres of tallgrass, encountering bison and longhorn cattle, then sit for elegant prix-fixe dinners, 14mi north of Lawrence.

$$$ Hotel at Old Town – 830 E. 1st St., Wichita, KS. ☎316-267-4800. www. hotelatoldtown.com. 115 rooms. Occupying a massive 1906 former warehouse building, this charmingly restored all-suite hotel provides historic ambience (complete with

old-style piano bar) but state-of-the-art amenities including full kitchens and compact-disc players.

$$$ Hotel Phillips – 106 W. 12th St., Kansas City, MO. ☎816-221-7000. www.hotelphillips.com. 217 rooms. With a golden statue over the doorway to greet guests, this 20-story, 1935 Art Deco masterpiece was the tallest building in Kansas City at its opening. Understated decor enriches the bright guest rooms, and service is highly responsive. The 12 Baltimore cafe has free Wi-Fi and on Friday nights live entertainment featuring local jazz groups.

$$$ The Raphael Hotel – 325 Ward Pkwy., Kansas City, MO. ☎816-756-3800. www.raphaelkc.com. 123 rooms. Iron lanterns arch over the driveway and a glass foyer covers the entrance of this brick charmer facing Country Club Plaza. As the city's most elegant small hotel, the nine-story Raphael, opened in 1928, offers an old-world touch of marble tiles and wooden ceilings in the lobby, and modern amenities in all rooms. The **Chaz on the Plaza ($$$)** is one of the city's finest dining spots.

$$$ Southmoreland on the Plaza – 116 E. 46th St., Kansas City, MO. ☎816-531-7979. www.southmoreland.com. 13 rooms. Two blocks from Country Club Plaza, this c.1913 urban inn feels like a New England B&B. From its cozy Mary Atkins Room to the Clara and Russell Stover Suite, with a deck and cannonball bed dedicated to the chocolatier, guests are guaranteed quaint, vintage Americana and gourmet breakfasts.

$$ Sheraton Crown Center – 2345 McGee St., Kansas City, MO. ☎816-841-1000. www.sheraton.com/kansascity. 731 rooms. This ultra modern 40-story high rise guest tower overlooks the Crown Center and downtown Kansas City. It's sound-proof and air-conditioned.

$$ Residence Inn Kansas City Airport – 10300 North Ambassador Dr., Kansas City, MO. ☎816-741-2300. www.marriott.com. 152 rooms Near Country Club Plaza, within minutes of Crown Center, downtown, and the Power and Light District, this lodging offers freshly renovated suites and amenities.

$$ Magnolia Hotel Omaha – 1615 Howard St., Omaha, NE. ☎402-341-2500. www.magnoliahotelomaha.com. 145 rooms. This stately and historic hotel, between downtown and the bustling Old Market, is anything but cookie-cutter. Built in 1923, extensively renovated in 1996, the inn wraps around a central courtyard and reflecting pools; Oriental rugs, tapestries and oil paintings cloak its walls, and guest rooms are furnished in mahogany.

¶/ EAT

$$$ The Golden Ox – 1600 Genessee St., Kansas City, MO. ☎816-842-2866. www.goldenox.com. **American**. Hand-cut steaks at this Stockyards classic are charbroiled over hardwood in the middle of the dining room. Old photographs hang on dark wood-paneled walls, and the carpet boasts the branding iron patterns of great cattlemen. The Stockyards have closed but the Ox remains a popular local gathering place.

$$$ Justus Drugstore Restaurant – 106 W. Main St., Smithville, MO. ☎816-532-2300. www.drugstorerestaurant.com. **Regional**. Yes, this once was a drugstore, but now it serves splendid Plains cuisine based on local foods. Vermouth-braised short ribs, Duroc pork chops and lamb shoulder typify the hearty offerings.

$$$ Room 39 – 1719 W. 39th St., Kansas City, Mo. ☎816-753-3939. www.rm39.com. **Contemporary**. You can start the day with steak and eggs Benedict, or traditional biscuits and gravy, at this downtown standout, savor a fresh-made hamburger at lunch, and finish the day with seared striped bass and chorizo sausage. The nightly tasting menu focuses on produce and meat raised by area farmers.

$$$ Savoy Grill – 219 W. 9th St., Kansas City, MO. ☎816-842-3890. www.savoygrill.net. **American**. When bandleader Benny Goodman was "Stompin' at the Savoy" in the early 20C, he was on stage here. Kansas City's oldest extant restaurant opened in 1903 in the Savoy Hotel, an erstwhile luxury inn 15 years older. Six US presidents—Taft, Teddy Roosevelt, Harding, Truman, Ford and Reagan—have dined at the Savoy. Stained-glass windows, Italian tile floors and a carved oak bar remain from past eras. The fare is traditional steak and seafood.

$$$ M's Pub– 422 S. 11th St., Omaha, NE. ☎402-342-2550. www.mspub omaha.com. **American**. You still can get a kosher hot dog at M's, as you could 30 years ago. But this Old Market standby has evolved. The intimate crowd favorite boasts a 200-bottle wine list and such nightly gourmet specials as duck breast with a leek and black trumpet mushroom sauce.

$$ Vivace – 1108 Howard St. (Old Market), Omaha, NE. ☎402-342-2050. www.vivaceomaha.com. **Mediterranean**. A pioneer both in the Old Market, and in Omaha fine dining, Vivace's renovated warehouse has an ambience that is always bustling, and its design-your-own pasta dishes span 15 sauces and house-made pasta daily. Pizzas are among the best anywhere.

Kansas City★★

Located in the geographical center of the lower 48 states, Kansas City is a bustling metropolis of 2.3 million that spans the two states of Missouri and Kansas, includes two separate identically named cities, and serves as a hub for excursions into the heartland. Wide, tree-lined boulevards, more than 200 fountains and myriad parks belie the larger city's reputation as dull; it certainly isn't drab, with as many days of sunshine as Miami or San Diego.

A BIT OF HISTORY

US President **Harry S Truman** (1884-1972), painter **Thomas Hart Benton** (1889-1975) and animator **Walt Disney** (1901-66) all considered this home. Most of Kansas City isn't even in Kansas. Professional sports, jazz clubs, art museums and barbecue restaurants—a few of the things for which it's renowned— are all found mostly in the larger Missouri city.

A recent stunning addition to the Kansas City, MO, downtown skyline is the 2011 Moshe Safdie-designed **Kaufman Center for the Performing Arts** (1601 Broadway; ℘816-994-7200;www.kaufmancenter.org).

SIGHTS
Arabia Steamboat Museum★
400 Grand Blvd. ✗♿🅿℘816-471-1856. www.1856.com.
On September 5, 1856, a sidewheeler carrying 130 passengers and 200 tons of cargo sank upriver from Kansas City. Not until 1988 did treasure hunters lift the vessel (one of 289 swallowed by the Missouri River) from 45ft of mud and water. The cargo (Wedgwood china, brandied cherries, tobacco, cognac, doorknobs, pickles, boots, guns, clothing and other pioneer needs) is now on display as a living time capsule.
The *Arabia* anchors one side of **City Market** (5th St. between Wyandotte & Grand Aves.), a historic district at Kansas City's 19C riverport.

▸ **Population:** 465,000 (Missouri), 147,000 (Kansas).
Michelin Map: 492 L, 9. Central Standard Time.
Info: ℘816-221-5242, www.visitkc.com
Location: The two separate Kansas Citys are nicknamed "KCMo" and "KCK."
Don't Miss: The Jazz Museum and Negro Leagues Baseball Museum.
Kids: Science City at Union Station.
Also See: The Harry S. Truman Museum in Independence.

Crown Center
2450 Grand Ave. ✗♿🅿℘816-274-8444. www.crowncenter.com.
Surrounding the world headquarters of Hallmark Cards, this complex has 60 shops, hotels, restaurants and theaters. In the **Hallmark Visitors Center** (℘816-274-3613; www.hallmarkvisitorscenter.com), guests discover the history of the world's largest greeting-card company. At the south end of downtown, the **Crossroads Arts District★** (www.kccrossroads.org), one of the most active such areas in the US, has dozens of galleries devoted to regional and national artists, plus theaters, cafes, nightclubs and shops.

Kansas City Union Station★★
30 W. Pershing Rd. at Main St. ✗♿🅿℘816-460-2020. www.unionstation.org.
Beautifully renovated in 1999, this grand Beaux-Arts train station (1914, Jarvis Hunt), with 850,000sq ft of floor space, is second in size in the US only to New York's Grand Central Station.
Inside, exhibits and guided tours recall the building's history. Casual and upscale restaurants offer dining options for visitors to the shows and attractions in the Theater District.

Kansas City Barbecue

Kansas City is renowned for its barbecued beef, pork and chicken. The Yellow Pages and online searches list more than 60 BBQ joints. That doesn't begin to include the little roadside stands without phones; non-traditional restaurants that serve "other" dishes beside ribs; and thousands of backyard grills.

The first documented barbecuer in Kansas City was Henry Perry, who served ribs from an old streetcar barn in 1916. During Prohibition, traveling musicians working the speakeasies spread the word about barbecue. Night or day, ribs, briskets and other cheap cuts of meat were smoked, doused with sauce and served in leftover newspapers. Many of the rib joints didn't even open until midnight. Today, many don't close till well past midnight. Popular local spots include Arthur Bryant's, Gates, Hayward's and Smokehouse. The quintessential KC dish, "burnt ends," consists of the crusty tips of brisket.

👥 Science City at Union Station★

www.sciencecity.com.

Interactive exhibits cover two floors, beginning with Festival Plaza, a welcome center with a TV-newspaper laboratory. Young visitors are encouraged to walk inside a human body exhibit, design a car, train for the decathlon, track a tornado, dig up prehistoric fossils, visit a farm, and even travel to outer space.

18th & Vine Historic District★

During Prohibition (1919-33), Kansas City officials turned a blind eye to all-night speakeasies, thus attracting jazz musicians such as native son Charlie "Bird" Parker and Count Basie, who formed his band here. Some 120 nightclubs prospered, thanks in part to Tom Pendergast—a political boss who later helped launch Harry Truman's career. Liquor flowed freely; gambling, drugs and prostitution thrived. Famed musicians like Dizzy Gillespie and Big Joe Turner migrated to Kansas City to work. When the clubs closed for the evening, they retired to the **Mutual Musicians' Foundation** (1823 Highland St.; ℘816-471-5212;mutualmusiciansfoundation.org), a hot-pink bungalow that served as a rehearsal hall; today it remains a second home to jazz musicians. The best time to pack into this tiny room is after midnight Friday or Saturday, when local artists gather to jam, sometimes until dawn.

👥 The Museums at 18th and Vine★★

1616 E. 18th St. ♿🅿 ℘816-474-8463. The heritage of Kansas City's African-American community is celebrated

Negro Leagues Baseball Museum

Courtesy of the Kansas City Convention & Visitors Association

at the **Horace M. Peterson III Visitor Center**. Exhibits and a 15min film set the scene for visits to its two component museums. Across 18th Street, the renovated 500-seat **Gem Theater** (1912) hosts musical and theatrical productions.

Music memorabilia, interactive exhibits and a jukebox of jazz classics are features of **The American Jazz Museum★** (℘816-474-8463; www.americanjazz-museum.org). Special displays honor Louis Armstrong, Duke Ellington, Ella Fitzgerald and Charlie Parker. The Kansas City Institute for Jazz Performance & History teaches the nuances of swing and bebop, while **The Blue Room** (℘816-474-2929) offers live performances four nights a week.

The history of African-American baseball—from post-Civil War origins to Jackie Robinson's entry to the major leagues in 1947—is recounted in the **Negro Leagues Baseball Museum★★** (℘816-221-1920; www.nlbm.com). Designed around a baseball diamond with real-game sound effects, it features bronzes of such famous players as Satchel Paige, Josh Gibson, "Cool Papa" Bell and Buck O'Neil, longtime museum leader.

Westport Historic District

40th to 43rd Sts. at Main St. & Westport Rd. ✖&🅿℘816-531-4370. westportkcmo.com.

In 1836, when westbound wagon trains were outfitted here, Westport Landing's small population included John Sutter (central to the 1849 California Gold Rush) and scouts Kit Carson and Jim Bridger. Today, the historic brick buildings are a hip crossroads with specialty shops, boutiques, galleries, restaurants and nightlife venues.

Nelson-Atkins Museum of Art★★★

4525 Oak St., east of Country Club Plaza at Rockhill Rd. ✖&🅿℘816-751-1278. www.nelson-atkins.org.

With more than 33,000 works in 60 galleries, this recently expanded (2009) museum near Country Club Plaza is one of the finest general art museums in the US. It is renowned for Chinese antiquities, paintings by European masters, and 20C sculpture. Its American Indian galleries display one of the largest such collections in the world.

European paintings (14C-19C), sculpture and decorative arts (11C-18C) include noted works by Rembrandt, Pissarro, Gauguin, Monet and others. American works, including Thomas Hart Benton's 10-panel *The American Historical Epic* (1919-24), shares space with other 20C masters such as Miró, O'Keeffe, Picasso and Rothko. A museum highlight is an alcove devoted to seven works by famed Japanese-American sculptor Isamu Noguchi.

Highlighting the Asian collection are a Chinese temple room with a 15C carved wooden ceiling, 13C BC furnishings and porcelain, and T'ang Dynasty tomb figures. The adjacent 22-acre **Kansas City Sculpture Park★★**, one of the finest such facilities in North America, presents the largest US collection of bronzes by Henry Moore, and the museum's trademark *Shuttlecocks* by Claes Oldenburg and Coosje van Bruggen.

Kemper Museum of Contemporary Art★

4420 Warwick Blvd.; one block east of 45th & Main Sts. ✖&🅿℘816-753-5784. www.kemperart.org.

This exclusively modern facility (1994, Gunnar Birkerts) entertains and challenges. Its strictly 20C and 21C collection features Chihuly, Diebenkorn, Hockney, Johns, Motherwell, Stella and Thiebaud, and photographers Mapplethorpe and Wegman.

Country Club Plaza

450 Ward Pkwy.; between Main, Summit, Brush & W. 46th Sts. at J.C. Nichols Pkwy. ✖&🅿℘816-753-0100. www.countryclubplaza.com.

Built in 1922 as the first planned shopping center in the US, this unique 15 sq-block district features Spanish Moorish architecture of red-tiled roofs, elegant domes, ornate ironwork, romantic courtyards, statues and fountains.

♣♣ Toy and Miniature Museum of Kansas City★

5235 Oak St. ♿🅿 ✆816-235-8000.
www.toyandminiaturemuseum.org.
More than 100 dollhouses, miniatures and antique toys (including model trains) are displayed in this 38-room, 1911 mansion on the edge of the University of Missouri-Kansas City campus. Special collections feature Russian lacquer boxes and 19C folk art.

♣♣ Kansas City Zoo★★

6800 Zoo Dr., east end of Swope Park, between 63rd St. & Gregory Blvd. west of I-435. ✕♿🅿 ✆816-513-5800.
www.kansascityzoo.org.
This 200-acre zoo has more than 800 animals, lions and giraffes on the "plains of Kenya," gorillas and leopards in the tropical rain forest and kangaroos and emus in the "Australian outback." The Okavango Elephant Sanctuary lures its pachyderms to a muddy waterhole. A new polar bear exhibit features these newly endangered denizens of the far north; penguins arrived in 2013 in a their own new enclosure.

Thomas Hart Benton Home and Studio

3616 Belleview St.; two blocks west of Southwest Trafficway. ✆816-931-5722.
www.mostateparks.com/benton.htm.
This Victorian stone mansion (1903) in the Roanoke district is a state historic site where Benton and his wife, Rita, lived for 36 years. The famous painter died in his studio in 1975 when he was 85, getting ready to sign a 6ft-by-10ft acrylic he had just finished for the Country Music Hall of Fame.

EXCURSIONS
Harry S. Truman Library & Museum★★

❯ 500 W. US-24 at Delaware St., Independence. ♿🅿✆816-268-8200.
www.trumanlibrary.org.
A 20min drive from downtown Kansas City, the Truman Museum tells the story of the plain-speaking haberdasher whose terms in office (1945-53) were a bridge between World War II and the

Korean War. A 45min documentary film introduces the man. Documents and artifacts chronicle Truman's life, and an interactive theater allows visitors their input in the crucial decisions of the Truman Presidency, including dropping atomic bombs on Japan in 1945. In the courtyard are the graves of Harry (1884-1972) and his wife, Bess (1885-1982).

The house in which the Trumans lived from 1919 onward is preserved as the **Truman Home★** (219 N. Delaware St.). Tickets must be purchased at the **Harry S Truman National Historic Site visitor center** (223 N. Main St.; ✆816-254-9929; www.nps.gov/hstr).

National Frontier Trails Museum★

❯ 318 W. Pacific Ave. at Osage St., Independence. ♿🅿✆816-325-7575.
www.frontiertrailscenter.com.
Located in a 19C brick mill five blocks south of the Independence Square staging ground for travelers on the Oregon, California and Santa Fe Trails, this museum offers a primer on the westward migration. Exhibits bring to life the trials and tribulations of pioneers, as recalled in their letters and diaries.

St. Joseph★★

❯ I-29 & US-36, 60mi north of Kansas City. ✆816-233-6688. www.stjomo.com.
This friendly city of 77,000 thrives on its fame as launch pad for the Pony Express. In 1860-61, riders departed from the westernmost US rail station to deliver mail to Sacramento, CA. The riders (among them 15-year-old William "Buffalo Bill" Cody and a young James "Wild Bill" Hickok) made the 1,966mi run in only 10 days. The original stables today hold the **Pony Express Museum★** (914 Penn St.; ✆816-279-5059; www.ponyexpress.org).

The **Albrecht-Kemper Museum of Art★** (2818 Frederick Ave.; ✆816-233-7003; www.albrecht-kemper.org) harbors fine American works by Thomas Hart Benton, Mary Cassatt, Frederic Remington, Wayne Thiebaud, the Wyeth family and others.

Kansas Prairie

The producers of *The Wizard of Oz* had it all wrong in depicting Kansas in black and white. The Sunflower State may not have towering mountains or rushing ocean waves, but it has a quiet, primal beauty to captivate the senses.

◔ **Michelin Map:** 493 K, L 9, 10. Central Standard Time.

▯ **Info:** ✆785-296-2009; www.travelks.com.

▶ **Location:** The easternmost section of Kansas is actually rolling hills; the flat plains most people envision as Kansas constitute the western two-thirds of the state.

⊛ **Don't Miss:** Tallgrass Prairie Preserve.

👥 **Kids:** Cosmosphere.

A BIT OF HISTORY

Until the invention of the steel plow, this state was covered with tallgrass prairie. It was a daunting sight: a quarter-billion acres of dancing grasses, many taller than a mounted horse. Settlers eventually conquered the prairie, turning it into Kansas City, Lawrence, Wichita, Topeka and rich farmland where much of America's wheat and corn is grown. But even today, it's not hard to see why Dorothy left Oz convinced there was "no place like home" in Kansas.

SIGHTS

Lawrence★★

I-70 & US-59, 31mi west of Kansas City. ✆785-856-5282. www.visitlawrence.com.

This college town of 90,000 is a slice of mid-America. A restored 1889 Union Pacific station houses the **Lawrence Visitor Center** (N. 2nd & Locust Sts.; ✆785-856-3040). After viewing a 25min film on local history, visitors wander the nearby downtown **historic district** (Massachusetts St. & adjacent streets from 6th to 11th Sts.). The **Watkins Community Museum of History** (1047 Massachusetts St.; ✆785-841-4109) has exhibits recalling the dark day in 1863 when a renegade Confederate officer named William Quantrill led a force of 400 men in the burning of Lawrence and the murder of 200 men and boys. Three fine museums share the 1,000-acre University of Kansas campus, founded in 1866. The **Natural History Museum★ 👥** (Dyche Hall, 14th St. & Jayhawk Blvd.; ✆785-864-4450; naturalhistory.ku.edu) has dioramas of more than 250 mounted mammals. Four floors of exhibits feature fossils,

Saber tooth cat fossil, Natural History Museum

© KU Natural History Museum

including the imposing Kansas mosasaur; life on the Great Plains; and an exhibit on Indians of the plains. The **Spencer Museum of Art**★ (1301 Mississippi St.; 785-864-4710; www.spencerart.ku.edu) offers a general overview of 4,000 years of world art history, including 18C-20C European and American works, from Monet to O'Keeffe, and centuries of Chinese and Japanese paintings.

Topeka

I-70 & US-75, 56mi west of Kansas City. 785-234-1030. www.visittopeka.com. This quiet city of 128,000 centers on the limestone **Kansas State Capitol** (300 W. 10th St. at Jackson St; 785-296-3966; www.kshs.org), built between 1866 and 1903 in French Renaissance style. Gage Park contains the **Topeka Zoological Park** ♣♟ (635 SW Gage Blvd.; 785-368-9140; topekazoo.org), one of the country's finest community zoos; **Historic Ward-Meade Park** / (124 NW Fillmore St.; 785-368-3888) holds a late 19C town square and other historical buildings. Spacious, well-presented exhibits in the **Kansas Museum of History**★ ♣♟ (6425 SW 6th St.; 785-272-8681; www.kshs.org) trace state heritage, from its native cultural origins into the 1950s.

Eisenhower Center★★

200 SE 4th St. at Buckeye St., Abilene, 147mi west of Kansas City. 785-263-6700. www.dwightdeisenhower.com. Dwight D. Eisenhower (1890-1969) was a World War II hero and 34th president of the US. Raised in Kansas, he graduated from West Point. As a five-star general in the US Army, he served as Supreme Commander of the Allied Forces in World War II. He is credited, among other achievements, with initiating the interstate highway system, which today extends nearly 50,000mi in the US. After viewing a 30min orientation film guests may tour Eisenhower's boyhood home. The **Eisenhower Museum**★ displays a lifetime of memorabilia, including original oils by Eisenhower himself, an accomplished hobby painter. The Presidential Library houses documents and historical materials from his terms of office (1953-61). The Eisenhower family is entombed at the Place of Meditation. The little town of Abilene itself has a remarkable history.

Founded in the 1860s, it was the original Kansas cowtown at the end of the Chisholm Trail. Many of its 19C and early 20C homes and commercial buildings are on the National Register of Historic Places; some are open for tours.

♣♟ Rolling Hills Zoo★

625 N. Hedville Rd., Salina, 180mi west of Kansas City via I-70 Exit 244. 785-827-9488. www.rollinghillswildlife.com. A prairie oasis for world wildlife, this 95-acre conservation center is an unlikely home for threatened and endangered species. Indian and white rhinos, Amur leopards, orangutans and many other creatures thrive here. Visitors may walk refuge paths or opt for a tram ride.

Tallgrass Prairie National Preserve★★

Rte. 177, 2mi north of US-50 near Strong City, 127mi southwest of Kansas City. **P** 620-273-8494. www.nps.gov/tapr, www.nature.org.

Hauntingly beautiful, this is the only unit of the National Park System preserving the virgin tallgrass ecosystem that once cloaked the Great Plains. The 10,894-acre national preserve has a hiking trail; in summer there's a 7mi interpretive bus tour and tours of a 19C limestone ranch home, a barn and a one-room schoolhouse. The Nature Conservancy and Park Service jointly manage the preserve.

♣♟ Kansas Cosmosphere and Space Center★★

1100 N. Plum St., Hutchinson, 210mi southwest of Kansas City. ✕♿**P** 316-662-2305. www.cosmo.org. An 83ft-tall Mercury rocket greets visitors to this Smithsonian affiliate, one of the premier space museums in the US. The highlight exhibit traces the history of rocketry, beginning with the landmark Nazi V-2 rocket, carrying through the US-Soviet "space race" of the Cold War era, to current times. Numerous Russian artifacts are on display, along with the command module from the troubled *Apollo 13* mission: Cosmosphere's Spaceworks made 80 percent of the props for the Hollywood movie.

Wichita★

I-35 & I-135 at US-400, 183mi southwest of Kansas City. $\mathscr{C}$316-265-2800. www.gowichita.com.

Wichita in the 1860s and 70s was a cattle-drive hub on the Chisholm Trail. Now the largest city in Kansas with more than 368,000 citizens, it is "hip" enough that entertainer Elton John custom-orders headwear from a haberdasher (Hatman Jack's) in suburban Delano. Today's cultural hub is a broad parkland at the confluence of the Little Arkansas and Arkansas Rivers. Among the "Museums on the River" are **Exploration Place★** (300 N. McLean Blvd.; $\mathscr{C}$316-660-0600; www.exploration.org), an impressive, interactive science museum with a CyberDome Theater and motion simu-

lator; the **Old Cowtown Museum** / (1871 Sim Park Dr.; $\mathscr{C}$316-350-3323; www. oldcowtown.org), which preserves 26 structures from the 1870s; the **Mid-America All-Indian Center** (650 N. Seneca St.; $\mathscr{C}$316-350-3340; www. theindiancenter.org), whose Indian Center Museum recreates a traditional 19C village; and the **Wichita Art Museum** (1400 W. Museum Blvd.; $\mathscr{C}$316-268-4921; www.wichitaartmuseum.org), housing many American masterpieces. **Botanica: The Wichita Gardens** (701 N. Amidon St.; $\mathscr{C}$316-264-0448; www.botanica.org), has 3,600 plant species spread across a former golf course.

Sculptures by Rodin, Miró and Moore surround the **Ulrich Museum of Art** at The Wichita State University (School of Art and Design, 1845 N. Fairmount St.; $\mathscr{C}$316-978-3664; www.wichita.edu/ ulrich). The **Sedgwick County Zoo★** (5555 Zoo Blvd.; $\mathscr{C}$316-660-9453; www.scz.org), with 500 species on 247 acres, is especially noted for its snakebreeding program and recent (2009) Amur tiger exhibit.

Omaha★

Named for a Siouan tribe whose appellation means "people upstream," Omaha sits on rolling bluffs overlooking the Missouri River not quite 200mi north of Kansas City. Today, Omaha is a food-processing, transportation and telecommunications hub, perhaps best-known as the home of billionaire Warren Buffett, the eminently successful investor and philanthropist affectionately nicknamed "The Sage of Omaha."

A BIT OF HISTORY

The city was founded in 1854; in 1863, it was chosen as the eastern terminus of the transcontinental railroad. Cobblestone lanes and 1880s warehouses

▶ **Population:** 422,000.
⏱ **Michelin Map:** 491 K, L 8. Central Standard Time.
▯ **Info:** $\mathscr{C}$402-444-4660; www.visitomaha.com.
◉ **Don't Miss:** Joslyn Art Museum.
👥 **Kids:** Henry Doorly Zoo.
⏱ **Also See:** Old Market District.

survive from an era when tons of cargo were loaded onto westbound trains from Missouri River steamboats; this district, the **Old Market** (Farnam to Jackson, 10th to 13th Sts.; www.old-market.com), later became Omaha's wholesale produce district before its Victorian buildings were restored as galleries, boutiques and cafes. Horse-drawn carriages still ply the streets, giving a taste of past glory.

Among Omaha's finest estates is **Joslyn Castle** (3902 Davenport St.; ☎402-595-2199; joslyncastle.com), the 1902 Scottish baronial-style home of businessman George Joslyn and his wife, Sarah, who endowed the Joslyn Art Museum (below). The neighborhood hub remains **St. Cecilia's Cathedral** (701 N. 40th St.), a twin-spired, Spanish Mission-style house of worship.

In the first half of the 20C, President Gerald Ford (né Leslie King, Jr.) and African American leader Malcolm X (né Malcolm Little) were born in Omaha, as were the Reuben sandwich, Raisin Bran and the TV dinner (by Swansons).

SIGHTS
Joslyn Art Museum★★

2200 Dodge St. ✕&🅿☎402-342-3300. www.joslyn.org.

This pink-marble fortress is an outstanding example of Art Deco architecture, built by Sarah Joslyn in 1931 as a memorial to her husband. The collection includes works from the ancient world to the present, emphasizing 19-20C European (Degas, Matisse, Monet, Renoir) and American (Bierstadt, Moran, Cassatt, Homer, Remington, Benton, Wood, Pollock) art. Nearly 400 **Karl Bodmer watercolors★★**— of landscapes and native culture—document the Swiss artist's 1832-34 journey up the Missouri River with Prince Maximilian of Germany.

🚻 Durham Museum★

801 S. 10th St. &🅿☎402-444-5071. www.durhammuseum.org.

In its heyday, 64 trains and 10,000 people a day passed through this Art Deco-style Union Pacific Railroad station (1931, Gilbert Stanley Underwood). Now restored, it features a waiting room with gold- and silver-leaf trim, 13ft chandeliers and a classic working soda fountain, plus galleries exhibiting everything from coins to a model of the 1898 Trans-Mississippi Exhibition.

🚻 Omaha's Henry Doorly Zoo★★★

3701 S. 10th St. ✕&🅿☎402-733-8400. www.omahazoo.com.

Among the unique features of this 130-acre, world-class zoo, **Lied Jungle★★** is a 1.5-acre indoor rain-forest exhibit that pulsates with life from Asia, Africa and South America. Monkeys howl and macaws screech as visitors duck under vines and waterfalls, walk through caves and swing across rope bridges. The **Cat Complex★**, featuring 30 felines (including lions, tigers and leopards) is among North America's largest. The Scott Aquarium displays 20,000 species of fish, sharks and penguins.

The **Desert Dome**, a geodesic dome 13 stories high, depicts Africa's Namib Desert, Australia's Great Sandy Desert and North America's Sonoran Desert. The zoo's **Simmons Conservation Park and Wildlife Safari** 🚻 (16406 N. 292nd St., Ashland, off I-80 Exit 426; ☎402-944-9453), 26mi southwest of Omaha, allows visitors to drive through open habitats populated with North American animals such as bison and elk.

🚻 Boys Town★

137th St. & W. Dodge Rd., 10mi west of downtown Omaha. &🅿☎402-498-1300. www.boystown.org.

In 1917, Father Edward Joseph Flanagan borrowed $90 to rent a downtown

Joslyn Art Museum

Whooping it Up in Nebraska

Early pioneers derided the Platte River as "too thick to drink, too thin to plow." But its significance to North America's second-rarest birds—and the wildlife fans who flock to see them—belies that epithet. Each spring, as the continent's 600 or so whooping cranes head from their winter grounds along the Gulf Coast to summers in the sub-Arctic, they stop along the Platte River in central Nebraska to rest and feed, occupying sand and gravel bars along the Platte near Kearney. Hundreds of tourists head to the plains to watch the majestic birds, the Western Hemisphere's tallest cranes as they prowl nearby corn fields for leftover grain, conduct early courtship rituals, and prepare to continue their 2,500-mile journey north.

Though their numbers are still small, the cranes—nicknamed "whoopers"—have recovered from a low of just 15 birds in the 1940s. Best place for crane-viewing is the Audubon Society's Rowe Sanctuary, near Gibbon; http://rowe.audubon.org. Lodging and visitor services are available in Kearney and Grand Island.

Omaha boardinghouse as a home for the city's abused, abandoned and disabled boys.

In 1921, with many success stories under his belt, Flanagan purchased Overlook Farm, the 900 acres that make up today's Village of Boys Town (which serves girls too).

Exhibits in the Hall of History include photos, artifacts, even the Oscar that actor Spencer Tracy won for playing Flanagan in the 1938 movie Boys Town.

ᛉᐟ Strategic Air and Space Museum★

28210 West Park Hwy., Ashland, off I-80 Exit 426, 26mi southwest of downtown Omaha. ♿️🅿️ 𝒫402-944-3100. www.sasmuseum.org.

This imposing, modern (1998) glass-and-steel structure, the size of six football fields, holds examples of all 33 warplanes and each of six missiles used by the former Strategic Air Command worldwide including the SR-71 Blackbird (world's fastest plane).

ᛉᐟ Western Historic Trails Center

3434 Richard Downing Ave., Council Bluffs IA, just east of Omaha off I-80 Exit 1B. ♿️ 𝒫712-366-4900. www.iowahistory.org.

The 19C Lewis and Clark, Mormon, California and Oregon Trails are depicted here in film, photograph, artifact and interactive map.

EXCURSION
Lincoln★

▶ I-80 & US-77, 53mi southwest of Omaha. 𝒫402-434-5335. www.lincoln.org.

Nebraska's capital since 1867, Lincoln has grown into a thriving city of 221,000. Its historic center is the **Haymarket** (7th to 9th & O to R Sts., www.lincolnhaymarket.org), a c.1900 warehouse district revitalized by the National Trust for Historic Preservation. The **State Capitol** (15th & K Sts.; 𝒫402-471-0448, www.capitol.org), built in 1922-32 (Bertram Goodhue), features a mosaic dome beneath a 400ft Art Deco-style skyscraper with a 14th-floor observation deck. Outside lies a famous sculpture of Abraham Lincoln by Daniel Chester French.

The **University of Nebraska State Museum★** (Morrill Hall, 14th & Vine Sts.; 𝒫402-472-2642; www.museum.unl.edu) has a superb collection of fossil mammoths and modern elephants, plus gem, natural-history and Native American artifact displays. **Sheldon Museum of Art** (12th & R Sts.; 𝒫402-472-2461; www.sheldonartmuseum.org) focuses on 20C American art, including works by Eakins, Sargent, O'Keeffe and Rothko.

Oklahoma

It's fitting that Oklahoma means "red people" in the Choctaw language. The human history of this state revolves around its native population, largest in the US. Long before Coronado traipsed through in 1541, Osage, Kiowa, Comanche and Apache tribes had outposts in the plains. Wichitas and other sedentary tribes built mound homes in the green mountains of the east.

Highlights

1 Cattle on auction at **Stockyards City** (p442)

2 Remington, Russell and more at the **Cowboy Museum** (p442)

3 World-class Western art at **Gilcrease** (p445)

4 **Will Rogers'** homespun philosophy (p445)

5 Living history at the **Cherokee Heritage Center** (p446)

A Bit of History

After the Louisiana Purchase of 1803, the growing population of the eastern US eyed the plains as a "remedy" for what they perceived as "the Indian problem." Despite treaties with the US, Native Americans were forcibly evacuated from their homelands: most tragic was the "Trail of Tears" march to Oklahoma in 1838-39 (🔖see sidebar). For a time, Cherokees, Choctaws, Seminoles, Chickasaws and Muscogee (Creeks) lived peacefully in their new home, setting up tribal governments, schools and farms. But after the Civil War, the US government took their Oklahoma lands as "punishment" for siding with the Confederacy. In 1889, 50,000 people raced to stake their plots; cheaters staking early claims led to the state's nickname: the Sooner State.

Oklahoma City became the largest stockyard in the US. Oil was discovered in the state as early as 1901, and in 1907, Oklahoma was the 46th state admitted to the Union. Today, Indian festivals and museums are treasured fixtures, and oil money has given Oklahoma City and Tulsa world-class cultural facilities.

The End of the Trail, National Cowboy & Western Heritage Museum

© National Cowboy & Western Heritage Museum

ADDRESSES

🛏 STAY

$$$ The Colcord Hotel – 15 N. Robinson Ave., Oklahoma City. ✆405-208-4399. www.colcordhotel.com. 108 rooms. Centrally located, this 12-floor hotel was built in 1910 by a protégé of Louis Sullivan. Thoroughly modernized, rooms are equipped with the latest amenities. Morning coffee is delivered gratis, upon request, to guests In their rooms. Contemporary American cuisine is served in the restaurant, **Flint ($$)**.

$$$ Ambassador Tulsa – 1324 S. Main St., Tulsa. ✆918-587-8200. www.ambassadorhotelcollection.com. 55 rooms. This 10-story boutique hotel boasts a Mediterranean terra-cotta facade. Built in 1929, it was fully restored and reopened in the late 1990s. In the basement, **The Chalkboard ($$$)** brasserie offers sophisticated contemporary dinner cuisine.

$$$ Grandison Inn at Maney Park – 1200 N. Shartel St., Oklahoma City. ✆405-232-8778. www.grandisoninn.com. 8 rooms. A charming 1904 Victorian within walking distance of downtown Oklahoma City, this three-story B&B boasts an eclectic variety of rooms behind its mahogany woodwork and original stained glass. Rooms vary from Florentine to Victorian.

$$ Crow's Rest B&B – 3405 W. 71st St., Tulsa. ✆918-445-5115. www.thecrowsrest.com. 5 rooms. Situated west of the Arkansas River, this crisply painted farm-style house makes a quiet getaway from the city's bustle. Gardens and a small swimming pool grace the grounds Guest rooms are comfortable and nicely furnished, all with private bath.

🍽 EAT

$$$$ The Coach House – 6437 Avondale Dr., Oklahoma City. ✆405-842-1000. www.thecoachhouseokc.com. No lunch Sat. Closed Sun. **Contemporary**. Once a coach house, this restaurant recalls a European country inn. Delicate pâtés, delectable beef, fish and duck dishes, and a memorable Grand Marnier soufflé are served on linen with fine crystal and china.

$$$ Mickey Mantle's Steakhouse – 7 Mickey Mantle Dr., Oklahoma City. ✆405-272-0777. www.mickeymantlesteakhouse.com. Dinner only. **Steak and Seafood**. Honoring the New York Yankee slugger and Oklahoma native, this casually elegant restaurant, opposite the Bricktown Ballpark, is flush with baseball photos, trophies and memorabilia.

$$ Bourbon Street Cafe – 100 E. California Ave., Oklahoma City. ✆405-232-6666. www.bourbonstreetcafe.com. **Cajun-Creole**. Blackened catfish, crawfish etouffée, jambalaya, gumbo and bourbon pecan pie are a few of the offerings at this lively New Orleans-style restaurant on Bricktown Canal in Oklahoma City. Diners enjoy live jazz and Delta-toned libations.

$$ Cattlemen's Steakhouse – 1309 S. Agnew St., Oklahoma City. ✆405-236-0416. www.cattlemensrestaurant.com. **American**. Open daily at 6am In the heart of Stockyards City, this local institution is famous for hand-cut steaks cooked over hot coals, just as cowboys have done since 1910. The name changed in 1945 when the restaurant changed hands in a craps game.

$$ Mahogany Prime Steakhouse – 6823 S. Yale Ave., Tulsa. ✆918-494-4043. www.mahogany.ehsrg.com. Dinner only. **American**. The signature dish at this Tulsa standout is a 21-ounce "cowboy" ribeye, bone in, seared in a 900-degree broiler. A throwback item is the old-fashioned Midwestern "wedge" iceberg lettuce salad. Come hungry.

$ Ann's Chicken Fry House – 4106 NW 39th St., Oklahoma City. ✆405-943-8915. Closed Mon. **American**. OKC's surviving Route 66 diner remains a local landmark with the high tail fins of a pink 1950s car still parked streetside. Oklahomans visit for the chicken-fried steaks, of course.

$ Chelino's – 15 E. California Ave. (on the canal), Oklahoma City. ✆405-478-1417. www.chelinosmexicanrestaurant.com. **Mexican**. This Bricktown staple serves up authenic fare that regularly attracts the city's Hispanic customers. Fajitas, enchiladas and other traditional dishes are presented to diners in generous portions by an attentive waitstaff.

Oklahoma City★★

Oklahoma City has grown from a land-grab tent city of 10,000 to a bustling urban hub with more than a million residents in its metropolitan area. It stretches across three counties and 650sq mi on the banks of the North Canadian River, ranking it as one of the largest cities, geographically, in the US. A cowboy ambience pervades the state in art, music and wardrobe.

▶ **Population:** 591,967.
⏱ **Michelin Map:** 492 K 11. Central Standard Time.
ℹ **Info:** ☎405-297-8912; www.visitokc.com; www.travelok.com.
◈ **Don't Miss:** National Cowboy & Western Heritage Museum.
🕐 **Timing:** Allow two days, includingNorman.
👥 **Kids:** Science Museum Oklahoma.

A BIT OF HISTORY

Oil was discovered here in 1928; oil wells can still be found in the city, some formerly on the grounds of the State Capitol. Western heritage is apparent in everything from museums and restaurants to the locals' favorite garb: cowboy boots and shirts.

In 1993, residents voted more than $300 million for urban revitalization. Two years later, the shocking terrorist bombing of the city's federal building took 168 lives; the Oklahoma City National Memorial helped the recovery process. Today, that Memorial, Oklahoma Thunder NBA games, Bricktown restaurants and Myriad Botanical Gardens attract visitors and residents to the city's downtown.

SIGHTS

Oklahoma City National Memorial & Museum★★

620 N. Harvey Ave. at NW 5th St. ♿ ☎405-235-3313. www.oklahomacity nationalmemorial.org.

With its two massive gates, reflecting pool and 168 empty glass-and-granite chairs, this memorial, designed by Hans Butzer, Torrey Butzer and Sven Berg, stands as a solemn reminder of the April 19, 1995, terrorist bombing of the Alfred P. Murrah Federal Building that killed 168 men, women and children. In the **Memorial Museum,**poignant exhibits trace the tragedy. The children's area and classroom is designed to teach children about the impact of violence; a special exhibit gallery has changing displays.

Oklahoma City National Memorial & Museum

©Gwen Cannon/Michelin

Oklahoma City Museum of Art★★

415 Couch Dr. between Walker & Hudson Aves. ✖&🅿 𝓟405-236-3100. www.okcmoa.com.

This $18.5 million arts center has helped Oklahoma's oldest museum find a place on the world art stage. Architect Allen Brown's three-story limestone building incorporates Art Deco elements of the former Centre Theatre (lobby, staircase); a 10-ton, 55ft glass sculpture by Dale Chihuly dominates its atrium.

Founded in 1910, the museum's contemporary history dates from 1968, when it purchased the collection of the Washington Gallery of Modern Art upon its merger with the Corcoran Gallery of Art. Now the cornerstone of the permanent collection, these 153 pieces highlight such artists as Claes Oldenburg, Helen Frankenthaler and Richard Diebenkorn.

Myriad Botanical Gardens★

Reno & Robinson Sts. &🅿 𝓟405-445-7080. www.myriadgardens.org.

Conceived by architect I.M. Pei, this 17-acre garden, modeled after Copenhagen's Tivoli Gardens, features rolling hills, a lake and a suspended, translucent bridge, seven stories high and 224ft long. Inside are exotic plants, a skyway and 35ft waterfall, as well as a variety of animals including reptiles, birds and butterflies.

Bricktown★★

Main St. & Sheridan Ave. between E.K. Gaylord & Stiles Sts. ✖&🅿 𝓟405-236-4143. www.bricktownokc.com.

Water taxis on the 1mi **Bricktown Canal** pass lively cafes, fountains and waterfalls at this restored warehouse district recalling San Antonio's River Walk. A number of popular restaurants and bars line the canal, which is edged by landscaped walkways and benches.

Across the street, a statue of Mickey Mantle (1931-98) stands in front of the **Chickasaw Bricktown Ballpark** (Mickey Mantle Dr. & Sheridan Ave.), a modern minor-league stadium.

Stockyards City★★

S. Agnew & Exchange Sts., just south of I-40. ✖&🅿 𝓟405-235-7267. www.stockyardscity.org.

This historic cattle market has been restored to early-20C glory. See a live cattle auction (*Mon–Tue*) at the **Oklahoma National Stock Yards Company** (107 Livestock Exchange Bldg.; 𝓟405-235-8675; www.onsy.com), or watch craftsmen make saddles, boots and other Western wear: **Langston's** (2224 Exchange Ave.; 𝓟405-235-9536) has the state's best selection.

Oklahoma State Capitol★

NE 23rd St. & Lincoln Blvd. ✖&🅿 𝓟405-521-3356.

Once the capitol grounds held working oil wells that generated $8 million in revenue since first drilled; all have since been plugged. With 650 rooms, the Greco-Roman building of limestone, granite and marble features history murals and portraits of famous Oklahomans. Built in 1914-17, the capitol was not crowned with the dome of its original design; work to correct that "oversight" concluded in 2002.

Oklahoma History Center★

800 Nazih Zuhdi Dr. & 𝓟405-521-2491. www.okhistory.org.

Just east of the Capitol, this center, opened in 2005, features five galleries

© Gwen Cannon/Michelin

Myriad Botanical Gardens

Entrance, Chickasaw Bricktown Ballpark

© Gwen Cannon/Michelin

devoted to state history. The ONEOK Gallery describes the 38 tribes associated with Oklahoma, including their forced migration here in the late 19C. Exhibits include a bison-hide tipi and a wagon used in two land runs.

A few blocks from the State Capitol, the **Harn Homestead & 1889ers Museum★** (1721 N. Lincoln Blvd.; ☏405-235-4058, www.harnhomestead.com) is a 19C farm with a homestead, barn and schoolhouse, celebrating an Oklahoma pioneer who donated the land on which the Capitol building is located.

Downtown, at the intersection of Park Avenue and Broadway, the **Red Earth Museum★** (6 Santa Fe Plaza; ☏405-427-5228; www.redearth.org) features Native American cradle boards that contrast nicely with Northwest Coast totems. It organizes a Native American cultural festival each summer.

▲‼ National Cowboy & Western Heritage Museum★★★

1700 NE 63rd St. ✕👤👍🅿
☏405-478-2250.
http://nationalcowboymuseum.org.
The entrance opens onto *The End of the Trail* (1915), James Earle Fraser's famous 18ft sculpture of an Indian rider on a weary horse. To the right a hallway leads past Prosperity Junction, a re-creation

of a late-19C cattle town. Gallery highlights include: **Art of the American West** featuring works by Charles Russell, Frederic Remington and leading contemporary artists; the **American Cowboy Gallery** focuses on the working cowboy; the **Joe Grandee Museum of the Frontier West** limns the legacy of the West's traders, soldiers, conservationists and others; and the arena-like **American Rodeo Gallery** pays tribute to this colorful sport.

▲‼ Science Museum Oklahoma★★

2100 NE 52nd St. ✕👍🅿☏405-602-6664. http://sciencemuseumok.org.
This vast kids-oriented complex includes a dome theater, a planetarium, botanical gardens, and numerous interactive science exhibits. Highlights include vintage aircraft, the Oklahoma Aviation and Space Hall of Fame and NASA artifacts; a gymnastics hall of fame; and innumerable other exhibits such as a "tinkering garage" designed for children and their parents.

▲‼ Oklahoma City Zoo and Botanical Garden★

2000Remington Pl. ✕👍🅿
☏405-424-3344. www.okczoo.com.
This 110-acre park features sea-lion shows, giraffe feedings, a primate hab-

itat, a butterfly garden, "endangered species carousel" and a **Children's Zoo** with a barnyard, forest for climbing, a lorikeet habitat, and other exhibits that enlist kids in species conservation. Opening mid-2013 is a new attraction called Stingray Bay.

Norman

I-35, US-77 & Rte. 9 on south boundary of Oklahoma City. ✕⛷🅿 ℘405-321-7260. www.normanok.org.

This city of some 113,000 people has several museums on or near its University of Oklahoma campus: the **Jacobson House Native Art Center** (609 Chautauqua Ave.; ℘405-366-1667; https://jacobsonhouse.com); the **Fred Jones Jr. Museum of Art★** (555 Elm Ave.; ℘405-325-3272; www.ou.edu/fjjma); and the **Sam Noble Museum of Natural History★⛷👤** (2401 Chautauqua Ave.; ℘405-325-4712; www.snomnh.ou.edu). In 1999 Sam Noble paleontologists discovered the world's tallest dinosaur—in southeastern Oklahoma.

EXCURSIONS

Guthrie★★

◗ US-77 & Rte. 33, 32mi north of Oklahoma City via I-35. ✕⛷🅿 ℘405-282-1947. http://guthrieok.com.

Founded in 1889, Guthrie hosted territorial and state government meetings until June 1910, when the governor—in a feud with the local newspaper editor—had the state seal stolen and moved to Oklahoma City. Now with just over 10,000 citizens, Guthrie boasts a 400-block National Historic Landmark District.

First Capital Trolley (2nd & Harrison Sts.; ℘405-282-6000; www.firstcapitaltrolley.com) offers tours of the city's Victorian architecture. Other highlights include the **Oklahoma Territorial Museum** (406 E. Oklahoma Ave.; ℘405-282-1889; www.oklahomaterritorialmuseum.org) and the **Scottish Rite Temple** (900 E. Oklahoma Ave.; ℘405-282-1281), completed in 1929 with Greek, Roman, Egyptian and Assyrian architectural influences.

Anadarko

◗ US-62 & Rte. 9, 60mi southwest of Oklahoma City. ✕⛷🅿 ℘405-247-6651. www.anadarko.org.

Here in this town, the **National Hall of Fame for Famous American Indians★** (US-62) displays bronze busts of Chief Joseph, Sitting Bull and other famous Native Americans.

The **Southern Plains Indian Museum** (US-62; ℘405-247-6221) has products for sale from the **Oklahoma Indian Arts and Crafts Cooperative★**.

Wichita Mountains National Wildlife Refuge★

◗ Rtes. 49 & 115, 90mi southwest of Oklahoma City via I-44. ⚠⛷🅿 ℘580-429-3222. www.fws.gov/southwest.

Its rocky tors rising above prairie lakes, this reserve has a winding road to the top of 2,464ft **Mount Scott★**; bison and Texas longhorn cattle may be seen The eastern part holds **Holy City of the Wichitas** (℘580-429-3361; http://theholycitylawton.com), an Easter Passion Play set, handcrafted of rock.

Fort Sill National Historic Landmark★

◗ I-44 Exit 41 (Key Gate), Lawton, 87mi southwest of Oklahoma City. ✕⛷🅿 ℘580-442-5123. http://sill-www.army.mil/museum/visit.htm.

This frontier post of the Indian Wars contains original stone buildings built by the Buffalo Soldiers of the 10th Cavalry. Among them are the guardhouse where Geronimo was prisoner, and post headquarters, now the **Fort Sill Museum** (437 Quanah Rd.).

Chickasaw National Recreation Area★

◗ Rte. 7, Sulphur, 84mi south of Oklahoma City via I-35. ⚠⛷🅿 ℘580-622-7234. www.nps.gov/chic.

Ancient Indians called this area of mineral springs, streams and lakes "the peaceful valley of rippling waters." Today's visitors fish, swim, camp or hike 20mi of trails. The **Travertine Nature Center** has exhibits on history, geology and fauna.

Tulsa★

A fixture on fabled Route 66 in its 1930s-60s heyday, Tulsa has gorgeous Art Deco architecture, nationally acclaimed art museums and notable opera, ballet and symphony companies. Regularly ranked as one of the nation's top cities for quality of life, Tulsa continues to update itself, most recently with a new urban park, Guthrie Green (www.guthrie green.com), and the new Woody Guthrie Center (http://woodyguthrie center.org) honoring the Oklahoma-born folksinger. It is home to Oral Roberts University (www.oru.edu), a 263-acre Christian campus.

▶ **Population:** 393,987.
🕐 **Michelin Map:** 492 L 10. Central Standard Time.
🛈 **Info:** ℘800-558-3311; www.visittulsa.com.
👁 **Don't Miss:** Gilcrease Museum.
👥 **Kids:** Tulsa Zoo.

A BIT OF HISTORY

Tulsa dates its history from a Creek Indian conclave in 1836. The city grew as a cattle-ranching center in the 1870s but wasn't incorporated until 1898. After oil was discovered in nearby Red Fork in 1901, Tulsa boomed. Another big strike in 1905—the Glenn Pool, at that time the world's largest—made this city on the banks of the Arkansas River a center of oil exploration. Between 1907 and 1920, Tulsa's population increased tenfold to 72,000. Once dominated by petroleum-related businesses, Tulsa's economy has diversified to include aerospace, financial and high-tech industries, among others.

SIGHTS

Downtown Art Deco District★

Between 1st & 8th Sts., Cheyenne & Detroit Sts. ✕♿🅿 ℘918-576-5687. http://tulsapreservationcommission.org. The legacy of the early oil barons and a $1 million-a-month construction boom in the 1920s can be seen on a walking tour of the historic central business district. Only New York and Miami Beach claim more Art Deco buildings.
The 1927 **Philtower Building** (427 S. Boston Ave.), with its green-and-red tiled roof, monogrammed door knobs, brass elevator doors and 25ft vaulted ceilings, was once the tallest building in Oklahoma. It is linked by an underground tunnel to the 1931 **Philcade Building** (511 S. Boston Ave.), whose

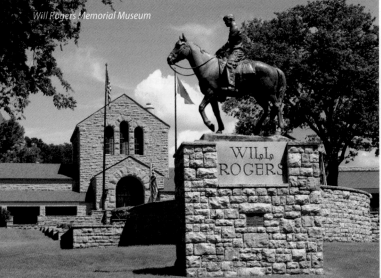
Will Rogers Memorial Museum

flamboyant Zigzag Style conceals carved-stone birds, reptiles and mammals in the terra-cotta foliage above its ground-floor windows.

The Deco style employed by the Public Works Administration in the Depression Era represented a transition from Zigzag to Streamline. Perhaps Tulsa's finest example is the 1931 **Tulsa Union Depot** (3 S. Boston Ave.), now an office complex and the **Oklahoma Jazz Hall of Fame** (℘ 918-281 8600; www.ok jazz.org).

Gilcrease Museum★★★

1400 Gilcrease Museum Rd., off US-64 west of downtown. ✘🚻♿🅿 ℘918-596-2700. http://gilcrease.utulsa.edu.

Possessing the world's largest collection of art of the American West, the Gilcrease exhibits paintings, drawings, prints and sculptures by more than 400 artists—with significant holdings of works by Frederic Remington, Charles Russell, Albert Bierstadt, George Catlin, Alfred Jacob Miller, William R. Leigh, Thomas Moran and Olaf Seltzer. It features outstanding Native American art and artifacts, including one gallery devoted to Oklahoma Indians; an interactive exhibit on Mexican art, history and culture; and myriad historical manuscripts, documents and maps. Local oilman Thomas Gilcrease (1890-1962) began collecting in 1922 when few others were interested in Western art. In 1949 he built this museum on his estate. The 23-acre grounds, perched atop a hill with a lovely view, contain theme gardens, outdoor sculpture, natural meadows and woodlands.

Philbrook Museum of Art★★

2727 S. Rockford Rd. ✘🚻♿🅿
℘918-749-7941. http://philbrook.org.

Set in 23 acres of Italian-style gardens that invite exploration, this castle-like Italian Renaissance villa (1927, Edward Buehler Delk) was the home of oilman Waite Phillips. Donated to the City of Tulsa in 1938, it today holds a renowned museum of fine and decorative arts of the Americas and Europe, Asia and Africa. The collection ranges from

Antiquities to 20C pieces, and includes Italian Renaissance oils and sculptures. Bouguereau's *The Little Shepherdess* (1889) highlights the 19C French Salon. 🍴Daily guided tours allow visitors to learn more about special exhibits and collection highlights.

👶👤 Tulsa Zoo and Living Museum★

6421 E. 36th St. N., between US-75 and US-169. ✘🚻♿🅿℘918-669-6600. www.tulsazoo.org.

The zoo's Robert J. LaFortune **WildLIFE Trek** showcases animal adaptation to cold, desert, forest and aquatic environments and includes a cave exhibit. The **Tropical American Rainforest** has jaguars and howler monkeys; at the **Elephant Encounter**, large pachyderms work and play. Researcher Jane Goodall has acclaimed the Chimpanzee Connection. A zoo train circles the park's 84 acres, and camel rides are offered seasonally.

EXCURSIONS

J.M. Davis Arms & Historical Museum★

▶ 330 N. J.M. Riggs Blvd. (Rte. 66), Claremore, 29mi northeast of Tulsa. ♿🅿℘918-341-5707. http://thegunmuseum.com.

Hotelier John Monroe Davis began to amass guns when he was 7 years old. When his collection of 20,000 guns, 1,200 steins, 70 saddles and 600 World War I posters began to consume the old Mason Hotel, the state took it over.

Will Rogers Memorial Museum★★

▶ Rte. 88, Claremore, 25mi northeast of Tulsa via Rte. 66. ⚠🅿℘918-341-0719. www.willrogers.com.

Overlooking Tiawah Valley, this limestone museum tells the story of Will Rogers' homespun life. The "Cowboy Philosopher" was a trick roper, movie star, radio commentator and newspaper columnist. Rogers (1879-1935) originally bought the 20-acre spread to build his retirement home prior to his death in an air crash.

The Trail of Tears

Despite the US treaty of 1791, which recognized the Cherokee Nation's right to ancestral lands in the Southeast, Congress in 1830 passed the Indian Removal Act. The US militia rounded up 15,000 Cherokees, along with Chickasaws, Choctaws, Creeks and Seminoles, and in 1838 moved them to a camp in Tennessee, many in shackles. In the treaty, the Cherokees had agreed to give up hunting; but they had built dwellings, farms and businesses and even published a newspaper. Yet now they were forced to abandon their ancient burial grounds. From Tennessee, in severe winter weather, they were marched at gunpoint 800mi to Indian Territory, now the state of Oklahoma. It took six months and cost more than 4,000 lives. Those who resisted were either forcibly removed or shot on sight. More than 25 percent of the Cherokee population perished. Designated in 1987 as **Trail of Tears National Historic Trail** (℘505-988-6888; www.nps.gov/trte), the route now stands as a symbol of the tragedies suffered at the hands of the US government.

The museum has statues, paintings, celebrity photos, saddles, dioramas, video kiosks and six theaters showing films in which Rogers starred.

Will Rogers Birthplace, a log-walled, two-story house at **Dog Iron Ranch on Lake Oologah** (9501 E. 380 Rd., Oologah, 12mi north of Claremore), has an airstrip, an oak barn and friendly farm animals.

Five Civilized Tribes Museum★

❍ 1101 Honor Heights Dr., Muskogee. ♿ 🅿 ℘918-683-1701. http://fivetribes.org. Housed in the former Union Indian Agency Building, built of native stone in 1875, this museum tells of the five tribes—Cherokee, Chickasaw, Choctaw, Muscogee (Creek) and Seminole —who were forcibly moved to Indian Territory (now Oklahoma) in the 19C. The museum has an art collection of more than 800 items of Native American art and sponsors several major art competitions annually.

Cherokee Heritage Center★★

❍ 21192 S. Keeler Dr., Park Hill; 6mi south of Tahlequah east of US-62. ♿🅿℘918-456-6007. www.cherokeeheritage.org. Tahlequah was the end of the "Trail of Tears" for the Cherokees. The Heritage Center, established in 1963, sits on 44 wooded acres south of town.

Permanent and temporary exhibits in the center recall tribal history and life. Modern Cherokees lead interpretive tours around a replica 1710 Cherokee Village, where craftspeople , demonstrate practices of their ancestors such as flint-knapping andbasket making. Adams Corner Rural Village represents a typical 1890s Cherokee community and includes a log cabin, schoolhouse and church.

Woolaroc Museum and Wildlife Preserve★★

❍ Rte. 123, 12mi southwest of Bartlesville via US-60. ✕♿🅿℘918-336-0307. http://woolaroc.org. Established in 1925 as the country estate of Frank Phillips, founder of Phillips Petroleum, this 3,600-acre ranch features a museum with a world-class collection of Western art, Colt firearms, cowboy gear, and Native American artifacts from 40 Indian tribes.

A spectacular lodge (Phillips' former home) and a Oklahoma oil history area share the grounds with a preserve where buffalo, elk, deer and longhorn cattle graze freely in the Osage Hills.

Northwest

Detail, *Seaform Pavilion* by Dale Chihuly,
Chihuly *Bridge of Glass*, Tacoma
Leslie Forsberg/Michelin

Seattle Area

Wedged into the northwest corner of the lower 48 states, the booming metropolis of Seattle exudes a low-key, youthful atmosphere. High-tech entrepreneurs mingle easily with rock musicians, and aerospace engineers still sport pocket protectors—along with smartphones. A futuristic skyline rises before snow-draped peaks only a couple of hours' drive away.

Highlights

1. Seattle's **Waterfront** views and seafood (p455)
2. It's all happenin' at the **Woodland Park Zoo** (p457)
3. You're on island time in the **San Juans** (p462)
4. Real **Paradise** at Mt. Rainier (p467)
5. Scenic **Lake Chelan** surrounded by vineyards (p468)

A Broad Spectrum

The surrounding state of Washington is one of the most geographically diverse in the nation. Its northern Pacific Coast is filigreed by beautiful Puget Sound and surrounded by evergreen forests (most of which have been logged at least once). Running north-south, the volcanic cones of Mounts Baker, Rainier, Adams and St. Helens define the craggy central spine of the skyscraping Cascade Mountains east of Seattle.

Long before the arrival of Europeans, coastal Indians thrived here. Their elaborately carved canoes, totems and masks attest to a culture that took advantage of abundant forests and teeming waterways. British Capt. George Vancouver made detailed charts of the Puget Sound area in 1792.

By the early 1800s, the region was included in the vast Oregon Country, and hotly contested by British and American fur-trading interests. With the steady arrival of more and more American settlers, the territory became US soil, and towns soon grew along the coast at Seattle and Port Townsend.

Today, the global scope of Microsoft, Amazon, Starbucks and Boeing maintains the area's visibility. While the state struggles to accommodate a burgeoning population, visitors continue to discover scenic splendors and urban pleasures.

ADDRESSES

🏨 STAY

$$$$ Alexis Hotel – 1007 First Ave., Seattle. ☎206-624-4844. www.alexishotel.com. 121 rooms. This luxury boutique hotel, ensconced in a historic building, combines Northwest art and over-the-top service. The Alexis embodies the high style and sleek aura of the Kimpton property that it is. The Library Bistro serves breakfast and lunch (but no dinner); an evening wine hour and morning coffee are complimentary. There's an on-site fitness center, too.

$$$$ Edgewater Hotel – 2411 Alaskan Way, Pier 67, Seattle. ☎206-728-7000. www.edgewaterhotel.com. 223 rooms. Seattle's only waterfront hotel, built atop a pier, the Edgewater is the site where the Beatles fished from the windows of Room 272 during their 1964 stay. The decor is reminiscent of a rustic mountain lodge; all guest rooms have a gas fireplace. Six Seven restaurant offers outdoor dining on Northwest cuisine while drinking in grand views of Puget Sound.

$$$$ Inn at the Market – 86 Pine St., Seattle. ☎206-443-3600. www.innatthemarket.com. 70 rooms. Embraced within Pike Place Market complex, the inn features an ivy courtyard and fifth-floor deck overlooking Puget Sound and the Olympic Mountains. Guest quarters sport simple lines and soft colors, and most have floor-to-ceiling windows. Room service arrives from the superb **Marché ($$$)** country French restaurant.

$$$$ Roche Harbor Resort – 248 Reuben Memorial Dr., Roche Harbor (San Juan Island). 360-3778-2155. www.rocheharbor.com. 75 rooms. This well-maintained long-time resort makes a great base for exploring the San Juan Islands. Accommodations range from cozy rooms in the late-19C hotel, and heritage cottages to spacious new constructions with modern amenities, all overlooking the harbor. Guests can bike quiet country roads, kayak or sail, or stroll the marina admiring its yachts.

$$$$ The Willows Lodge – 14580 NE 145th St., Woodinville. 425-424-3900. www.willowslodge.com. 84 rooms. Combining elegance and rusticity, The Willows is situated amid five acres of lush gardens in the Sammamish Valley near Seattle, and at the heart of Western Washington's wine country. Century-old Douglas fir timbers and a 30ft, double-sided stone fireplace welcome guests to the main lodge; wood decor and native art carry to the guest rooms. **The Barking Frog ($$$)** bistro serves Northwestern cuisine with Washington wines.

$$$ Hotel Murano – 1320 Broadway St., Tacoma. 253-238-8000. www.hotelmuranotacoma.com. 319 rooms. Complementing Tacoma's arts focus, Murano is a design hotel displaying a contemporary art collection in the lobby. Turquoise and orange accents add sizzle to earth-tone rooms, and the **Bite ($$)** restaurant offers Northwest fare.

$$$ Alderbrook Resort & Spa – 7101 East SR 106, Union. 360-898-2200. www.alderbrookresort.com. 77 rooms, 16 cottages. On scenic Hood Canal and surrounded by nature, this retreat offers peaceful seclusion in elegant accommodations. Rooms feature subdued natural tones of earth and forest, and all have water or woods views. Guests kayak, hike, relax or play a round at the adjoining golf course, one of the top-rated in the Northwest.

$$$ Cedarbrook Lodge – 18525 36th Ave. S., Seattle. 206-901-9268. www.cedarbrooklodge.com. 104 rooms. Cedarbrook is close to the airport, yet as far from a standard airport hotel as imaginable; it's a handsome Northwest-style lodge with lovely gardens, set in a forest. Exposed fir beams and shaped stone, airy rooms and quiet grounds give the lodge a relaxed air. Outstanding **Copperleaf ($$$)** restaurant relies exclusively on Northwest producers.

$$$ Hotel Max - 620 Stewart St., Seattle. 206-728-6299. www.hotelmaxseattle.com. 163 rooms. In the middle of downtown Seattle inside a historic building, the Hotel Max features stylish, contemporary decor with a focus on emerging and established local artists and photographers. It's two blocks from the light-rail station to the airport.

$$$ MarQueen Hotel – 600 Queen Anne Ave. N., Seattle. 206-282-7407. www.marqueen.com. 53 rooms. In a 1918 building in Seattle's Queen Anne neighborhood, north of downtown, the MarQueen is the meeting place for Old World charm and modern comfort. It's conveniently situated just a few blocks from the Seattle Center and the monorail to downtown.

$$$ Lake Quinault Lodge – 345 South Shore Rd., Quinault. 360-288-2900. www.olympicnationalparks.com. 92 rooms. On the shores of a serene mountain lake in a temperate rain forest, the lodge—with its grand brick fireplace—has been a haven for rain-soaked travelers since 1926. The **Roosevelt Dining Room ($$$)** serves steak and seafood, including local oysters and Dungeness crab.

$$$ Saratoga Inn – 201 Cascade Lane, Langley. 360-221-5801. www.saratogainnwhidbeyisland.com. 16 rooms. This charming, shingle-sided Whidbey Island inn in the artsy village of Langley has a porch with rocking chairs overlooking Saratoga Passage and the Cascade Mountains. All rooms are bright and airy, with pleasant views and gas fireplaces.

$$ The Maxwell Hotel – 300 Roy St., Seattle. ☎206-286-0629. www.the maxwellhotel.com. 139 rooms. This new (2010) hotel just blocks from the Seattle Center offers a contemporary look with bold prints and accents of orange and lime. Amenities include a swimming pool—and pineapple cupcakes, offered when checking in.

$$ Ace Hotel - 2423 1st Ave., Seattle. ☎206-448-4721. www.acehotel.com. 28 rooms. Ace Seattle is located in the heart of Belltown, near downtown and within walking distance of the Seattle Center. There are plenty of clubs for live music and DJs in the area. Occupying a historic building, the Ace features bohemian decor, and offers a cafe and bar.

♈ EAT

$$$$ Salish Lodge – 6501 Railroad Ave. SE, Snoqualmie. ☎425-888-2556. www.salishlodge.com. **Contemporary**. A steady roar persists outside this dramatic restaurant, perched on the cliff beside 268ft Snoqualmie Falls 30min from Seattle. While famed for its four-course breakfasts and its luxurious hotel and spa facilities, the lodge serves excellent cuisine such as lobster bisque, cured king salmon and roast halibut.

$$$ Elliott's Oyster House – 1201 Alaskan Way, Pier 56, Seattle. ☎206-623-4340. www.elliottsoysterhouse.com. **Seafood**. Fresh Northwest seafood is the raison d'être for this fine restaurant on a pier jutting into Elliott Bay. Oyster selections change daily; entrées include dishes such as king salmon cooked on alder planks and grilled scampi prawn risotto.

$$$ Primo Grill – 601 S. Pine St., Tacoma. ☎253-383-7000. www.primogrilltacoma.com. **American**. *Tacoma News-Tribune* readers have voted this the city's best restaurant, and owner Charlie McManus the best chef. From an apple-wood grill and wood-burning oven, McManus turns out fire-roasted shrimp, grilled pork chops, and a variety of creative pizzas and pastas.

$$$ Ray's Boathouse – 6049 Seaview Ave. NW, Seattle. ☎206-789-3770. www.rays.com. **Seafood**. Dinner only. Just past the Locks, Ray's is famed for its sunset views stretching across Puget Sound to the Olympics. But it deserves equal marks for its first-class seafood preparations, such as smoked sablefish, broiled halibut and seared sea scallops. Ray's Café, upstairs, with a deck, offers lower-priced alternatives for lunch and dinner.

$$$ Seastar Restaurant and Raw Bar – 2121 Terry Ave., Seattle. ☎206-462-4364. www.seastarrestaurant.com. **Seafood**. Located in South Lake Union, Seastar resembles an undersea garden with its glass decor and aqua accents. The star of the show is sushi, expertly prepared and presented with flavorful sauces; entrées include cedar-plank

Mount Rainier National Park

Fish vendor's stall, Pike Place Market

©iStockphoto.com/osubuckeye

roasted wild Northwest salmon and sesame-pepper crusted ahi.

$$ Flying Fish – 300 Westlake N., Seattle. ☏206-728-8595. www.flyingfishrestaurant.com. **Seafood**. Though this is a venerable Seattle institution, Flying Fish is newly situated in the city's South Lake Union neighborhood. The menu, which changes daily, puts Pacific Rim accents on fresh seafood. A popular dish is the whole fried rockfish platter, sold by the pound and served with fresh herbs and pineapple anchovy sauce.

$$ Etta's – 2020 Western Ave., Seattle. ☏206-443-6000. www.tomdouglas.com. **Seafood**. In the Pike Place Market, Etta's, one of the city's top seafood emporiums, by famed local restaurateur Tom Douglas, serves up the best crab cakes in the city and a bounty of other fresh seafood, such as Alaskan halibut served with paella made with rockfish, clams and chorizo. Wide picture windows let in the sun, as well as the market's ambience.

$$ Terra Plata – 1501 Melrose Ave., Seattle. ☏206-325-1501. www.terraplata.com. **Contemporary**. This triangular restaurant on Capitol Hill has a rustic look, with wood tables and rafters, and a summertime rooftop dining patio. Farm-to-table cuisine is offered, with a water buffalo burger and roast pig with chorizo and clams among the unique selections, accompanied by farm-fresh vegetables.

$$ The Walrus and the Carpenter – 4743 Ballard Ave. NW, Seattle. ☏206-443-395-9227. www.thewalrusbar.com. **Seafood**. This tiny restaurant, with an unlikely name—from a Lewis Carroll poem—has been designated one of the top restaurants in the nation by multiple national news media. The whitewashed walls and industrial-chic decor of the Ballard restaurant belie the bold flavors of briny local oysters and seafood, served small-plate style.

$$ Cascina Spinasse – 1531 14th Ave., Seattle. ☏206-251-7673. www.spinasse.com. **Italian**. Northern Italy's Piedmont region is the inspiration behind Spinasse, whose housemade artisan pasta—including tagliatelle with braised pheasant and huckleberries, and squash ravioli with sage—is accompanied by "secondi" ranging from trout to steak. The ambiance is romantic and rustic, with antique wooden furnishings.

$$ Ivar's Acres of Clams – 1001 Alaskan Way, Pier 54, Seattle. ☏206-624-6852. www.ivars.net. **Seafood**. Seattle icon Ivar Haglund's waterfront restaurant has been open since 1938. The fish and chips at the street-side food counter are a Seattle tradition, perfect for taking along when you ride one of the Washington State ferries that sail from the pier next to Ivar's. Inside, the dining room offers grilled salmon and whole Dungeness crab.

Seattle★★★

Blanketing high hills that overlook Puget Sound, Seattle has grown from a hard-working pioneer town into one of the nation's cultural trendsetters. Noted for its livability and natural beauty, the city is surrounded by spectacular vistas: Mt. Rainier and the Cascades south and east, the Olympic Mountains across the water to the west.

SEATTLE TODAY

Though light rains fall on the city fall through spring, they rarely dampen its youthful spirit. Ubiquitous street-corner coffee bars have encouraged a cafe society, and an abundance of Northwest seafood and produce yields a distinctive regional cuisine and world-class restaurants. In the late 20C, Seattle became a leader in high technology, thanks to local software giant Microsoft. The city's economy slumped mildly during the 2008 recession, but was buffered by its international stature and Boeing's continued strength, along with a burgeoning high-tech sector.

A BIT OF HISTORY

Though Vancouver sailed into Puget Sound and anchored within sight of Alki Point (now West Seattle) in the late 18C, no major white settlement occurred until the 1850s, when disappointed 49ers from the California gold fields and homesteaders from the Olympia area filtered north. On a typically chilly, gray November day in 1851, two small pioneer parties—one traveling overland, the other by schooner—met at Alki. Named for Chief Sealth, respected Duwamish Indian leader, the new town was platted in 1853, with commerce centering upon a sawmill built by Henry Yesler.

By the turn of the 19C, lumber barons Frederick Weyerhaeuser and William Boeing had set up shop in Puget Sound, the latter soon turning to the new technology of flight. These two industrial giants still help fuel the area's economy.

- ▶ **Population:** 635,000.
- **Michelin Map:** p 454 & p 461. Pacific Standard Time.
- **Info:** ℘206-461-5840; www.visitseattle.org.
- ▶ **Location:** Mount Rainier dominates the skyline south of Seattle; the Cascades are east, and the Olympic Mountains west, across Puget Sound. When Rainier is visible, locals say "the mountain's out," and good weather is usually at hand.
- **Parking:** Be sure to snare parking near Pike Place Market before 11am.
- **Don't Miss:** Pike Place Market, the soul of Seattle.
- **Timing:** Best to head for Pike Place Market and the aquarium in the morning, and devote the afternoon to Seattle Center.
- **Kids:** Pacific Science Center; Woodland Park Zoo.
- **Also See:** The Hiram M. Chittenden Locks in Ballard.

This formerly industrial town has given the country a zest for coffee, rock music and youthful entrepreneurship, and the region's ports continue to thrive on Pacific Rim trade.

DOWNTOWN
Pioneer Square

Generally bounded by Alaskan Way, S. King St., Fourth Ave. S. & Cherry St. ℘206-667-0687. www.pioneersquare.org.

The Pioneer Square National Historic District anchors the south end of downtown with 18 blocks of restored late 19C commercial buildings. Site of Seattle's first permanent settlement, Pioneer Square has become a sometimes boisterous nightclub district (*not safe after 9pm*).

Tracing its roots to mid-19C logging days, the area is still defined by the

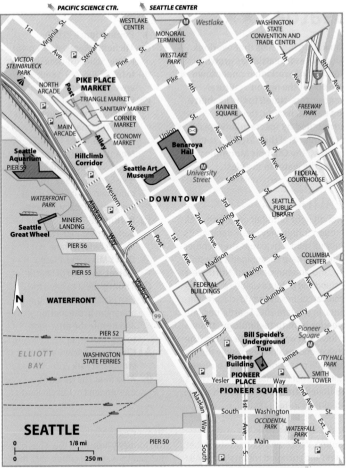

long incline of Yesler Way, the original Skid Road down which logs slid to the sawmill. A great fire destroyed most of downtown in 1889; the town pushed north and east, letting Pioneer Square lapse into a neglected "skid row" of bawdy houses and gambling dens. Proclaimed a historic district in 1969, the area now boasts galleries and restaurants, and a brick square that comes alive during the monthly First Thursday Art Walk.

The popular, humorous **Bill Speidel's Underground Tour**★ (℘206-682-4646; www.undergroundtour.com) descends into defunct tunnels below street level, where visitors learn about Seattle life up to Prohibition.

About two blocks south, the Seattle unit of **Klondike Gold Rush National Historical Park** (319 Second Ave. S.; ℘206-220-4240; www.nps.gov/klse) holds artifacts and photographs detailing the Yukon gold rush and its impact on the city. When the steamship *Portland* arrived in Seattle on July 17, 1897, laden with two tons of gold, gold fever struck the city. Films and exhibits convey the excitement of those heady days. Many residents grew rich outfitting prospectors; others shipped out for the Yukon via Skagway, Alaska, where most of this historical park is located.

🏛 Pike Place Market★★★

First Ave. & Pike St. ✕🅿 ✆206-682-7453. www.pikeplacemarket.org.

Often called the soul of Seattle, this "public market center" has been a revered city institution since 1907. Fun, feisty and infinitely appealing, the market maintains its earthy egalitarianism. An abundance of farm-fresh vegetables, seafood and flowers dazzles the eye, and dozens of professional buskers entertain clapping crowds.

An urban renewal program nearly killed the market in the early 1960s, one plan calling for it to be demolished and replaced by a giant hotel. But Seattleites, in 1971, voted overwhelmingly to preserve the market and surrounding blocks. Today a nine-acre parcel and a dozen buildings are protected in a national historic district that extends from First to Western Avenues, Union to Virginia Streets.

Hundreds of food vendors, eateries and small shops line bustling, crowded streets and alleys and fill a multilevel labyrinth of building interiors. The market's original building, the **Main Arcade** (Pike Place between Pike & Stewart Sts.), remains the hub of activity, its street-level stalls vibrant and colorful with seasonal vegetables, stands of fresh and dried flowers, and fish shops where salmon, halibut and Dungeness crabs glisten on beds of ice. A crowd often collects around **Pike Place Fish**, where mongers loudly chant the daily specials and throw fish to one another over customers' heads. Nearby **Post Alley**, an Old World-style walkway, offers shops and restaurants. Leading down to the waterfront, the **Hillclimb Corridor** is a landscaped series of stairs flanked by shops and cafes.

Seattle Art Museum★★★

1300 First Ave. ✕♿ ✆206-654-3210. www.seattleartmuseum.org.

The Seattle Art Museum's extensive, well-rounded holdings at this four-story downtown repository including arts and crafts from Korea, Japan and China; African ceremonial masks and headdresses; and Northwest Coast basketry, as well as wood and stone sculpture. Western art includes works by Rubens, Van Dyck, Lucas Cranach the Elder and Jackson Pollock. The statue out front on First Avenue, Jonathan Borofsky's *Hammering Man*, has become a Seattle icon.

Opposite the museum's Second Avenue entrance, **Benaroya Hall**★★ (200 University St.; ✆206-215-4800; www.seattlesymphony.org), is the state-of-the-art home of the Seattle Symphony.

WATERFRONT

Seattle's waterfront offers views of sailboats and ferries plying the waters of Elliott Bay, as well as souvenir shops, cafes and several top-notch attractions.

🏛 Seattle Aquarium

1483 Alaskan Way, Pier 59. ✆206-386-4300. www.seattleaquarium.org.

The recently renovated and expanded (2007) aquarium is home to fish, plants, marine invertebrates and mammals native to Puget Sound area waters. Noteworthy are the 120,000-gallon **Window on Washington Waters** and new **harbor seal** exhibits, as well as the crowd-pleasing, frolicking **sea otters**.

🏛 Seattle Great Wheel★

1301 Alaskan Way, Pier 57. ✆206-623-8600. www.seattlegreatwheel.com.

This popular new (2012) Ferris wheel with enclosed, temperature-controlled gondolas lifts visitors 175ft above the waterfront for views of downtown buildings, ferries plying the waters of Elliott Bay and the distant Olympic Mountains.

Olympic Sculpture Park★

2901 Western Ave. ✆206-653-3100. www.seattleartmuseum.org.

At the northern edge of the waterfront, this outdoor park, a part of the Seattle Art Museum, showcases large-scale, contemporary works by leading international artists such as Calder, Serra, Nevelson and Oldenburg.

Adjacent **Myrtle Edwards Park** is a narrow shoreline greenway with a 1mi path and water access.

ADDITIONAL SIGHTS
👤👤 Seattle Center★★

Generally bounded by Denny Way, Broad St., Fifth Ave. N., Mercer St. & First Ave. N. ℰ206-684-7200. www.seattlecenter.com.

The location of the 1962 world's fair, this 74-acre campus northwest of downtown now harbors theaters, the city's opera house, museums, a famous fountain and a sports arena; the complex draws more than 17 million visitors a year. Cultural festivals held nearly every weekend and two large annual music festivals—Folklife, at Memorial Day, and Bumbershoot, over the Labor Day weekend—draw throngs.

👤👤 Space Needle★★

Off Broad St. opposite Fourth Ave. N. ✕👤🅿 ℰ206-905-2100. www.spaceneedle.com.

Time has not robbed the Space Needle of its modern appearance. Embodying a 1960s vision of the future, the graceful metal tripod (1962, Victor Steinbrueck & John Graham Jr.) rises 602ft, with a revolving restaurant beneath its pinnacle. Glass-walled elevators whoosh guests to an encircling outdoor deck. Panoramic views★★ take in the city skyline, Elliott Bay, the Olympic Mountains and the Cascades.

Just north of the Space Needle entrance, the Swedish-designed Monorail★ (departs every 10min; ℰ206-905-2620; www.seattlemonorail.com) quietly travels 1.3mi to downtown's Westlake Center in less than 2min.

👤👤 Chihuly Garden and Glass★★

305 Harrison St. ✕👤🅿 ℰ206-753-4940. www.chihulygardenandglass.com.

This exciting new (2012) museum offers large-scale glass sculptures by pioneering glass artist Dale Chihuly, showcased in visually stunning settings, indoors and out. Inside the Glasshouse, a universe of red-, orange- and yellow-colored glass sculptures brighten the glass-walled building. A whimsical garden of glass "plants" as well as a cafe and bookstore add to the site's charms.

👤👤 Experience Music Project★★

325 Fifth Ave. N. at Broad St. ✕👤🅿 ℰ206-772-2700. www.empmuseum.org.

The brainchild of Microsoft cofounder Paul Allen, this psychedelically colored, notoriously unusual building (2000, Frank Gehry) pays tribute to the ever-changing dynamic of rock'n'roll with a variety of interactive exhibits. It highlights such Seattle icons as Jimi Hendrix and Kurt Cobain. Guests may strike up their own rock band in interactive activity rooms. An interesting aside, the Science Fiction Museum and Hall of Fame, probes everything from famous authors to wormholes and time travel.

👤👤 Pacific Science Center★★

Second Ave. N. at Denny Way. ✕👤🅿 ℰ206-443-2001. www.pacificsciencecenter.org.

The six interconnected buildings with striking arches dominate the south end of Seattle Center. Interactive exhibits range from the new Professor Wellbody's Academy of Health & Wellness and a virtual meteorology center to a "tech zone," outfitted with computers that enable visitors to compose, create art or try hang gliding.

Also on-site are a hall of robotic dinosaurs, a tropical butterfly house, an IMAX theater and a planetarium.

👤👤 Museum of History and Industry★★

860 Terry Ave. N. ℰ206-324-1126. www.mohai.org.

MOHAI moved into a spiffy new setting on South Lake Union in 2013, inside a historic naval armory building. Here a $90 million overhaul resulted in innovative interactive exhibits that engage visitors in the rich history of the city. Among the top attractions are a Gilbert and Sullivan-style theatrical production explaining the Great Seattle Fire of 1889, a Maritime Gallery and Boeing's first commercial airplane.

👥 Hiram M. Chittenden ("Ballard") Locks★★

3015 NW 54th St. 𝒫206-783-7059.
www.nws.usace.army.mil.

The US Army Corps of Engineers maintains this hugely popular site that links Lake Washington, on Seattle's eastern flank, with Puget Sound. It consists of two locks, a dam and spillway, a botanical garden and visitor center. Each year, 100,000 boats—pleasure and fishing craft, freight and research vessels—are "locked through," to the delight of onlookers. A **fish ladder** on the south side allows salmon to swim upstream while human visitors watch them through a sub-surface window.

👥 Woodland Park Zoo★★★

750 N. 50th St. ✕⛫🅿 𝒫206-548-2500.
www.zoo.org.

Highly acclaimed for habitats that reflect the native environments of its 1,100 animals of 300 species, this fine zoo includes 92 acres of savanna, tundra, marshland, tropical rain forest and Northwest habitat.

The largest space is an open African savanna; Asian elephants roam through a Thai village as elk graze in an Alaskan taiga. John Olmsted designed most of the original buildings in 1909. The 2-acre Bamboo Forest Reserve, with sloth bears and a tropical aviary, is the zoo's newest exhibit.

👥 Museum of Flight★★

9404 E. Marginal Way S. at Boeing Field half a mile northwest of I-5 Exit 158.
✕⛫🅿 𝒫206-764-5720.
www.museumofflight.org.

The largest air-and-space museum in the West occupies a steel-and-glass building that contains a diverse collection from early gliders to World War II bombers to space capsules. Highlights include a Space Shuttle trainer, a Concorde and the original 747. One simulator gives visitors a feel for flying and air-traffic control. The 1909 "Red Barn" relocated to this site was the hub of William Boeing's original Pacific Aero Products Company.

Seattle Asian Art Museum★★

1400 E. Prospect St., Volunteer Park.
⛫🅿 𝒫206-654-3100.
www.seattleartmuseum.org.

This Art Moderne building (1933, Carl Gould) holds a collection ranked as one of the top 10 collections outside Asia: more than 7,000 objects of Asian art, only a quarter of them on display at any one time.

Among the works exhibited in the quiet, meditative space are South Asian Buddhist and Hindu sculpture, 4,000-year-old Chinese vessels and finely wrought Japanese ceramics and temple art.

Wing Luke Museum of the Asian Pacific American Experience★★

719 S. King St. ⛫🅿 𝒫206-623-5124.
www.wingluke.org.

The fascinating but little told history of Asian immigration to the Northwest is illuminated with interactive exhibits highlighting social justice, inside a historic building. Guided tours take in the reconstructed Yick Fung mercantile, set up to look the way it did a century ago, and a historic Chinatown hotel. A Smithsonian Institution affiliate, the museum was recently named a partner of the National Park Service.

Frye Art Museum★

704 Terry Ave. at Cherry St. ✕⛫🅿
𝒫206-622-9250. http://fryemuseum.org.

A small gem, the Frye offers both a selection from its founding collection of German and American masters and challenging modern installations that focus on urban life and emerging artists.

University of Washington

Generally bounded by 15th Ave. NE, NE 45th St., Union and Portage bays.
𝒫206-543-2100. www.washington.edu.

This major university sprawls across nearly 700 acres above the banks of the Lake Washington Ship Canal, with plazas framing views of Mt. Rainier. Two excellent museums are located on the campus, and its arboretum lies nearby.

Burke Museum of Natural History and Culture★

17th Ave. NE & NE 45th St., ✕ & 🅿
𝒫 206-543-5590.
www.burkemuseum.org.
The diverse geology, archaeology and ethnology of the Pacific Rim are celebrated on two floors of exhibits. On the lower level are artifacts and photographs that highlight cultures of the Northwest Coast, the Pacific Islands, and East and Southeast Asia. The main floor examines geologic history through dinosaur skeletons, mineral specimens and an exhibit on plate tectonics.

Henry Art Gallery★

15th Ave. NE & NE 41st St. ✕ &
𝒫 206-543-2280. www.henryart.org.
One of the most progressive small museums in the US, the Henry (1927, Carl Gould) is known for embracing adventurous art, with a focus on contemporary works by Motherwell, Mapplethorpe and Robert Rauschenberg, as well as the history of photography.

Washington Park Arboretum★

2300 Arboretum Dr. E., between Union Bay & Lake Washington Blvd. E.
🅿 𝒫 206-543-8800. http://depts.
washington.edu/uwbg.
Preserving 230 acres of woodlands, the arboretum is the legacy of landscape-architect brothers John Olmsted and Frederick Law Olmsted Jr., who laid out its gardens between 1909 and the early 1930s. Trails wind past 5,500 different trees and other plants, past a Japanese garden and through a rhododendron glen and an avenue of azaleas.

EXCURSIONS

Bloedel Reserve★★

◗ 7571 NE Dolphin Dr., Bainbridge Island (35min crossing via Washington State Ferry from Pier 52, Alaskan Way).
& 🅿 𝒫 206-842-7631.
www.bloedelreserve.org.
This 150-acre reserve encapsulates the meadowlands, forests and glens of the Northwest. Native flora thrives in its own setting, amid deft and subtle landscaping.

Trails visit a marsh habitat for migratory and native waterfowl, a wetland forest, a grove of flowering shrubs, a Zen rock garden and a moss garden. The visitor center is housed in **Collinswood**, a classic French château-style home built in 1932.

👥 Tillicum Village★

◗ Tours (4 hrs.) depart Pier 55, Alaskan Way,. ✕ & 𝒫 206-622-8687.
www.tillicumvillage.com.
A commercialized but sincere attempt to celebrate Northwest native cultures, the "village"—actually a single long-house of Kwakiutl style—was built in the 1960s on small Blake Island in Puget Sound.

Visitors are treated to a cruise, followed by a traditional salmon bake, with the whole fish splayed open on cedar stakes and cooked over an alder-wood fire. Native performers offer a stage presentation based on Northwest myths, then demonstrate such traditional crafts as woodcarving.

Adjacent **Blake Island State Park** encompasses 476 acres of trees and shrubs, and 5mi of quiet beaches.

Rhododendron Species Foundation and Botanical Garden★

◗ 2525 South 336th St., Federal Way.
& 🅿 𝒫 253-838-4646.
www.rhodygarden.org.
More than 1,000 species of rhododendrons bloom along the shaded paths of this 22-acre preserve on the Weyerhaeuser Corp. headquarters campus. The Puget Sound climate is uniquely suited to these shrubs (one species is native to the region). Best months to visit are April through June, when the blooms are at their peak.

Puget Sound Area ★

Puget Sound funnels through northwest Washington state, spilling around myriad islands and into bays, inlets and straits created by long-gone glaciers. This inland sea adjoins the ever-expanding Seattle-Tacoma-Everett metroplex. While wonders such as a resident pod of orcas still ply the waters, pollution and salmon run declines threaten a natural system in which early settlers claimed one could walk across Elliott Bay on the backs of returning salmon.

- **Location:** The largest inland sea in the US, at 16,000sq mi, Puget Sound stretches north-south from the Strait of Juan de Fuca to Olympia. It's 150 miles from Olympia to Bellingham.
- **Don't Miss:** Tacoma's museum district.
- **Timing:** Plan to devote at least one day just to Tacoma.
- **Kids:** Point Defiance Zoo and Aquarium.
- **Also See:** San Juan Islands.

A BIT OF HISTORY

Until the Klondike gold rush brought worldwide attention and commerce, Seattle was not the pre-eminent city on Puget Sound; it was Tacoma. The two cities still observe a friendly rivalry, though Seattle is much larger. Everett, for its part, has long had a military presence with the US Navy.

SIGHTS

Tacoma

32mi south of Seattle via I-5. ℘253-284-3254. www.traveltacoma.com.
The 19C port and timber town of Tacoma has become a livable modern city of 202,000 people, complete with fine museums, galleries, a University of Washington branch campus and the Tacoma Dome concert venue. Timber baron mansions still line the bluffs above Commencement Bay, but the city's current identity includes the thriving downtown Museum District, a worthy rival to Seattle's downtown attractions.

Washington State History Museum ★★

1911 Pacific Ave. ✗♿🅿 ℘253-272-3500. www.washingtonhistory.org.
In nine thematic exhibit areas, life-size dioramas and voice-overs dramatize the growth of the state from earliest European-Indian encounters, through 19-20C industrialization, to modern high-tech and environmental challenges. Upper-level galleries are devoted to stimulating temporary exhibits.

Tacoma Art Museum ★★

1701 Pacific Ave. ✗♿🅿 ℘253-272-4258. www.tacomaartmuseum.org.
Spiraling upward to a top level devoted to interactive exhibits on creating art, this facility (Antoine Predock, 2003) is a striking addition to Tacoma's museum district. With a distinct focus on Northwest artists such as Jacob Lawrence and Morris Graves, it offers a regional emphasis that the Seattle Art Museum neglects. The museum's centerpiece is a gallery of works by Tacoma native and glass artist **Dale Chihuly ★** on permanent display.

Museum of Glass ★★

1801 Dock St. ✗♿🅿 ℘866-468-7386. www.museumofglass.org.
This spectacular 2002 museum, designed by Arthur Erickson, reflects the fact that Tacoma is Dale Chihuly's hometown. A distinctive 90ft-tall stainless steel cone, inspired by traditional sawmill burners and containing an interactive glass-art studio, rises above the industrial Thea Foss Waterway and connects to a rooftop plaza. Galleries

display works by contemporary glass art masters from around the world. and A collection of glass art by **Chihuly**, is presented on the 500ft-long **Bridge of Glass★**, a pedestrian passage to the Washington State History Museum and Tacoma Art Museum.

LeMay–America's Car Museum★★

1801 Dock St. ✕&🅿 ℘866-468-7386. www.lemaymuseum.org.

This 4-story museum, which opened in 2012 in the Shadow of the Tacoma Dome, is one of the largest automotive museums in the world. With striking architecture, an interactive zone and a cafe built around a 500-car collection with gems such as a 1930 Duesenberg, the LeMay goes far beyond the typical car museum.

Point Defiance Park★

Pearl St. at N. 54th St., 3mi north of Rte. 16 Exit 132. ℘253-305-1000. www.metroparkstacoma.org.

This 700-acre park rests on bluffs above Puget Sound. In addition to gardens and trails through old-growth forest, **Fort Nisqually Living History Museum★★** (Five Mile Dr.; ℘253-591-5339; www.metroparkstacoma.org) is a living-history museum within a re-created 1855 Hudson's Bay Company fort. The small **Point Defiance Zoo and Aquarium★** 🐾 (5400 N. Pearl St.; ℘253-591-5337; www.pdza.org), is notable mainly for its zoo, whose new exhibits house clouded leopards and red wolves.

Olympia

60mi south of Seattle via I-5. ℘360-704-7500; www.visitolympia.com.

Washington's modest capital centers on the striking state capitol building and the workings of state government.

Washington State Capitol★

Capitol Way between 11th & 16th Aves. ℘360-902-8880. www.des.wa.gov/services/facilities.

The white-domed capitol makes a grand statement, rising 287ft above its base. Built between 1893 and 1928, the Neoclassical building sports six massive bronze doors embossed with scenes symbolizing state history and industry. Three blocks away, exhibits at the **State Capitol Museum★** (211 W. 21st Ave.; ℘360-753-2580; www.washingtonhistory.org) focus on construction of the capitol and regional Native-American history, in a 1920s Italian Renaissance-style mansion.

Future of Flight Aviation Center★★

Rte. 526, Everett. Take I-5 north 24mi from Seattle to Exit 189; turn west 3.5mi. &🅿 ℘425-438-8100. www.futureofflight.org.

At its plant on the south side of the city of Everett, aerospace giant Boeing assembles its wide-body commercial jets—747s, 767s, 777s and the new 787. Thousands of people work here in one of the company's largest factories. Reserve tickets in advance in the summer for 90min **tours★★** that take in the cavernous Main Assembly Building and the hands-on **Airplane Design Zone**. Just outside, at Paine Field, completed jets are flight-tested.

Whidbey Island

Coupeville, on Rte. 20, is 57mi north of Seattle via I-5 (Exit 182) & Rte. 525. ℘360-929-6871. www.whidbeycamanoislands.com.

A popular weekend getaway for Seattleites, Whidbey Island arcs in a narrow 60mi curve through north Puget Sound, its bucolic tumble of hills, small towns and verdant fields interrupted only by Whidbey Island Naval Air Station.

The waterfront town of **Coupeville★**, dating from the 1850s, harbors gift shops and seafood restaurants, as well as Victorian homes built by 19C sea captains. The town is the locus of the sprawling 27sq-mi **Ebey's Landing National Historical Reserve★**, which preserves the land and spirit of an entire rural community. Headquarters are in the **Island County Historical Museum** (908 NW Alexander St.; ℘360-678-3310; www.islandhistory.org).

On the north end of the island, **Deception Pass State Park★** (Rte. 20, 23mi

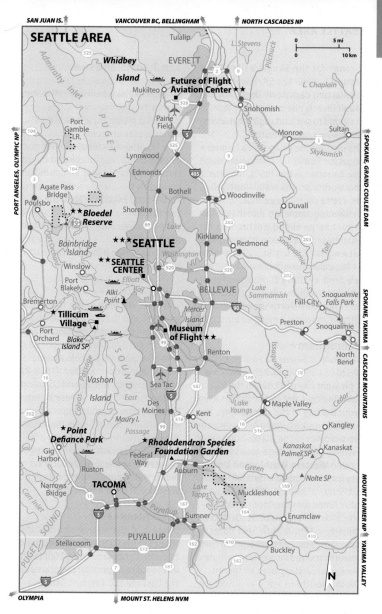

SEATTLE AREA

San Juan Is. · Vancouver BC, Bellingham · North Cascades NP

Tulalip
L. Stevens
Pilchuck
0 — 5 mi
0 — 10 km

Whidbey
Island
Mukilteo
Future of Flight
Aviation Center ★★
Paine Field
Snohomish
L. Chaplain

Everett

Port Angeles, Olympic NP

Admiralty Inlet

Port
Gamble
I.R.

Lynnwood
Edmonds
Bothell
Woodinville
Duvall
Monroe
Sultan
Skykomish

Spokane, Grand Coulee Dam

Agate Pass
Bridge
Poulsbo

★★ Bloedel
Reserve

Bainbridge
Island
Winslow

Shoreline
Kirkland
Redmond
Snoqualmie
Tolt

Lake
Washington

★★★ SEATTLE
★★ SEATTLE
CENTER
Elliott

Port
Blakely
Alki
Point
Bay
Bellevue
Lake
Sammamish
Fall City
Snoqualmie
Falls Park
Preston
Snoqualmie

Spokane, Yakima

Bremerton
Port
Orchard
★ Tillicum
Village
Blake
Island SP
Mercer
Island
Museum
of Flight ★★
Renton
North
Bend

Cascade Mountains

Vashon
Island
East
Passage
Sea Tac
Des
Moines
Kent
Maple Valley
Kangley

Maury I.

Gig
Harbor
★ Point
Defiance Park
★ Rhododendron Species
Foundation Garden
Federal
Way
Auburn
Kanaskat
Palmer SP
Kanaskat

Ruston
TACOMA
Lake
Tapps
Muckleshoot
Nolte SP

Mount Rainier NP

Narrows
Bridge
Lake
Youngs
Green

Steilacoom
PUYALLUP
Puyallup
Sumner
Enumclaw
Buckley

Yakima Valley

Olympia · Mount St. Helens NVM

N

north of Coupeville; ℘360-661-0682;
www.parks.wa.gov) occupies both sides
of Rosario Strait. Turnouts and a pedestrian walkway enable sightseers to cross
the 976ft **Deception Pass Bridge★** and
admire the turbulent tidal rapids below.
Long sandy beaches, trails through old-
growth forest and a swimming lake also
entertain visitors.

Skagit Valley

La Conner, on Rte. 534, is 66mi north of
Seattle via I-5 Exit 221. ℘360-466-4778.
www.lovelaconner.com.
This lush valley, drained by the Skagit
(SKA-jit) River flowing west from the
Cascades, is especially colorful in
spring when thousands of acres of
tulips, daffodils and **irises★★** bloom
in farms around Mount Vernon. One of
the largest commercial bulb-cultivation
districts in the world, the valley draws

throngs for the **Skagit Valley Tulip Festival** (✆360-428-5959; www.tulip-festival.org) each April. Upstream, the Skagit River is one of the best places in the world to see bald eagles in midwinter (www.skagiteagle.org).

The picturesque village of **La Conner★** edges the Swinomish Channel off Skagit Bay. Founded in the 1860s, the artists' community boasts waterfront galleries, crafts shops, three museums and a charming ambience that make it an attractive weekend destination for urbanites. The **Museum of Northwest Art★★** (121 S. First St.; ✆360-466-4446; www.museumofnwart.org) has acquired a strong reputation for its focus on Northwest masters, including Guy Anderson, Morris Graves and Dale Chihuly, as well as emerging artists.

Bellingham★

91mi north of Seattle via I-5 (Exit 256). ✆360-671-3990. www.bellingham.org.

A pleasant city of 81,000 in the Mount Baker foothills, Bellingham wraps itself around a bay of the same name. The town is both a maritime hub, as southern terminus of the Alaska State Ferry System, and a college town focused around **Western Washington University** (south of downtown via Bill McDonald Pkwy.; ✆360-650-3000; www.wwu.edu), noted for its outdoor sculpture. The **Fairhaven Historic District★** (between 13th & 20th Sts.) dates to the 1870s, a delightful mix of red brick storefronts housing cafes, galleries, bookshops and restored Victorians.

On the southern edge of town, the spacious **Spark Museum of Electrical Invention★** (1312 Bay St.; ✆360-738-3886; www.sparkmuseum.org) offers four centuries of electrical inventions in an interactive setting, with features such as a re-creation of the radio room on the Titanic and a 1915 telephone used in the first transcontinental phone call. West of Larabee State Park, on the south end of town, **Chuckanut Drive★**, affords views of the San Juan Islands (http://chuckanutdrive.com), as it wends its way south along headlands beside Puget Sound.

San Juan Islands★★

90–105mi north of Seattle; take I-5 north 65mi to Exit 230 at Burlington, then Rte. 20 west 15mi to Washington State Ferry terminal at Anacortes. ✆360-378-9551. www.visitsanjuans.com.

This 172-island archipelago was once a range of mountains, covered by glaciers during the ice ages. Lummi Indians hunted on the islands; settlers farmed and tended orchards. Now the quiet San Juans attract artists, craftspeople, writers and vacationers who come for bird-watching, whale-watching, beach-combing; it's the first place in the US to ban personal watercraft.

San Juan Island★★

The most westerly of the three main islands is also the most populous. **San Juan Island National Historical Park★** (✆360-378-2240; www.nps.gov/sajh) preserves coastal parcels associated with the joint occupation (1859-72) of the island by British and US troops during the "Pig War," a tense standoff resulting from the shooting of a swine. In the main town of Friday Harbor, the **Whale Museum★** (62 First St. N.; ✆360-378-4710; www.whalemuseum.org) is devoted to research and education on orcas, which are often seen from the west side at **Lime Kiln Point**.

Orcas Island★★

Largest of the islands, horseshoe-shaped Orcas (http://orcasislandchamber.com) bends around East Sound. Its low mountains provide panoramas of the Cascade and Olympic Ranges and Vancouver Island. More than 5,000 acres are contained within **Moran State Park★** (Horseshoe Hwy.; ✆360-376-2326; www.parks.wa.gov), which has five lakes and 30mi of hiking trails, in addition to 2,409ft Mount Constitution.

Lopez Island★

Much beloved of bike riders (rightly so), level, pastoral Lopez is lightly developed, with a selection of small inns and cafes (www.lopezisland.com). The name reflects early Spanish Northwest exploration.

Olympic Peninsula★★★

Northwestern Washington's Olympic Peninsula extends like a thumb, separating the jigsaw puzzle of Puget Sound islands and waterways from the Pacific Ocean. The glacier-sheathed Olympic Mountains rise in the central part of the peninsula, trapping wet Pacific air and creating a rain shadow to the east. This has made for a remarkable difference in rainfall between the Sequim–Dungeness Valley area on the northeast, which averages 16in a year, and the Pacific coastal valleys, which get 150in or more. Though much of the peninsula's forests are now second-growth, the valleys of Olympic National Park harbor some of the few remaining stands of old-growth rainforest in the contiguous US. Shoreward of the forests lies a strand of wonderfully wild and log-tossed Pacific Ocean beach.

- **Michelin Map:** 493 B2, 3. Pacific Standard Time.
- **Info:** ℘360-452-8552; www.olympicpeninsula.org.
- **Location:** The peninsula's main highway, US-101, encircles it; with stops, plan for a two- or three-day circumnavigation.
- **Don't Miss:** The Hoh and Quinault rainforests.
- **Also See:** Port Townsend's beautifully preserved Victorian districts.

A BIT OF HISTORY

Although Spanish voyagers first laid claim to these northwestern shores, the Hudson's Bay Company in the early 19C helped firm up Great Britain's dominance of the area. White settlement, mostly concentrated along the Strait of Juan de Fuca, did not begin until the 1850s when farming, logging and fishing took hold. The Native American presence remains strong, with some of the shoreline taken up by staunchly protected reservation land.

SIGHTS
Port Townsend★★

Rte. 20, 58mi northwest of Seattle. ℘360-385-2722. www.enjoypt.com. One of the best-preserved 19C seaports in the US, Port Townsend is chockablock with grand houses and commercial buildings with ornate touches and high ceilings. Sited at the entrance to Puget Sound, the town of 9,000 traffics in its maritime flavor and heritage, yet manages to feel authentic, rather than commercial. Fine two- and three-story stone edifices cluster along Water Street; many of them house restaurants and boutiques. On the bluff above stands a trove of Victorian homes, some converted to bed-and-breakfast inns.

Port Townsend remains a center for the marine trades: boat-building is taught (and can be observed) at the **Northwest Maritime Center★** (431 Water St.; ℘360-385-3628; www.nwmaritime.org). Much of the town is a National Historic Landmark District, and its colorful past is well documented at the **Jefferson County Historical Museum★**

Port Townsend

©iStockphoto.com/Natalia Bratslavsky

(540 Water St.; ☎360-385-1003; www.jchsmuseum.org). Visitors may partake of both history and scenery at **Fort Worden State Park★** (W St. at Cherry St.; ☎360-902-8844; www.parks.wa.gov), where the parade ground of a decommissioned fort is lined with a smart row of Victorians (some available for visitor lodging) that once quartered officers. Broad beaches frame views north to Mt. Baker and the San Juans.

Olympic National Park★★★

Access via US-101 south and west of Port Angeles. △✕&P ☎360-565-3130. Visitor center, 3002 Mt. Angeles Rd., Port Angeles. ☎360-565-3130. www.nps.gov/olym.

Designated an International Biosphere Reserve and World Heritage Site, the 1,440sq-mi park has exceptional natural beauty and remarkable diversity within its three distinct wilderness ecosystems—glaciated mountain ranges, temperate rain forests and primitive coastal beaches. The park harbors more than 300 types of birds and 70 species of mammals, among them some 5,000 Roosevelt elk, the largest herd in the world.

US Highway 101 runs around the perimeter of the national park on its east, north and west. Among its most accessible attractions is **Lake Crescent★★** (18mi west of Port Angeles), one of three large lakes in the park. Cupped within steep, forested hillsides, the deep glacial lake is popular with outdoor recreation lovers, who often base themselves at the rustic 1915 **Lake Crescent Lodge★** (416 Lake Crescent Rd.; ☎360-928-3211; www.nationalparkreservations.com). From here, a 1mi trail leads through old-growth forest to **Marymere Falls★**, a 90ft cascade. Nearby, **Sol Duc Hot Springs** offer mineral-rich bathing pools and rustic cabins for rent (www.olympicnationalparks.com).

Hurricane Ridge★★

17mi south of visitor center on Heart O' the Hills/Hurricane Ridge Rd, ☎360-565-3130.

Snowfall may close portions of the road October–late April. The winding road that climbs to the 5,230ft summit passes through dense forest and skirts vertical subalpine meadows, unfolding magnificent vistas of crenellated, snow-crusted peaks and the distant sea. Views from the top feature unobstructed perspectives on peaks, ridges and deep valleys. Paths meander through subalpine meadows blanketed in summer with low-lying sedges, grasses and wildflowers.

Hoh Rain Forest★★★

91mi southwest of Port Angeles; entrance station 12mi east of US-101. Visitor center ☎360-374-6925.

On the western side of the park, this lush, dripping, primordial world of giant cedar, hemlock and maple is draped with soft green club mosses

Hoh Rain Forest with a Roosevelt elk

©iStockphoto.com/Natalia Bratslavsky

and floored by shaggy, moldering logs. Shafts of sunlight angle into these ancient woods, casting a mystical glow and creating scenery that is eerily reminiscent of a pre-human earth, rank with life. Three short interpretive trails meander among the arboreal giants, some of them 20 stories tall, 12ft in diameter and 500 years old. The nearby **Quinault Rain Forest** offers a similar experience, though slightly less crowded.

Not far west of here, **Ruby Beach** and several other **beaches★★** around Kaloch feature offshore seastacks and shorelines that vary from narrow and rocky to wide and sandy. The ocean waters are part of the 3,300sq-mi **Olympic Coast National Marine Sanctuary**, where protected animals include sea otters, seals, migrating gray whales and the world's largest species of octopus.

Port Angeles

US-101, about 80mi northwest of Seattle. ☎360-452-2363. www.portangeles.org. Situated on the Strait of Juan de Fuca, about midway along the northern shore of the Olympic Peninsula, Port Angeles functions as a gateway to the national park, with numerous motels and small inns. A ferry service provides a link to Victoria, British Columbia, directly across the strait.

Nearby **Dungeness National Wildlife Refuge★** (15mi northeast via Kitchen-Dick Rd.; ☎360-683-5847; www.fws.org/washingtonmaritime/dungeness) encompasses serene, 5.5mi-long Dungeness Spit, a sandy hook of land that's home to a cornucopia of seabirds and marine life, and the 1857 New Dungeness lighthouse.

Neah Bay

Rte. 112, 70mi northwest of Port Angeles. Makah Indians have inhabited the Olympic Peninsula's extreme northwestern coastal region for at least 4,000 years; Neah Bay is their reservation's town. The history and culture of the tribe, which in 1999 inspired controversy when it resumed hunting whales after a self-imposed seven-decade moratorium, are brought into focus at the **Makah Cultural & Research Center★★** (Bay View Ave.; ☎360-645-2711; www.makah.com/mcrchome.html).

Seven miles west of Neah Bay, **Cape Flattery★**, named by Captain James Cook in 1788, is the northwesternmost point of the contiguous US. A forest-and-boardwalk trail (.75mi) leads to a crows-nest viewpoint with breathtaking panoramas of the cape and adjacent sea caves.

From Kalaloch south, US-101 zigzags 140mi through timberland and around long marine estuaries. Aberdeen and Hoquiam, on broad Grays Harbor, are logging ports. At the harbor's mouth, 20mi west, **Ocean Shores** is a thriving small resort town with hotels, restaurants, a tribal casino and miles of hard, flat beach that invites driving.

Long Beach Peninsula

Rtes. 100 & 103 via US-101, 165mi southwest of Seattle. ☎360-642-2400. www.funbeach.com. Stretching from the Columbia River to the mouth of Willapa Bay, the peninsula features 28mi of surf-pounded coastline. Originally inhabited by Chinook Indians, the area is famous as the place where Lewis and Clark reached the shores of the Pacific in 1805. The **Lewis & Clark Interpretive Center★★** (Cape Disappointment State Park, Rte. 100, 2mi southwest of Ilwaco; ☎360-642-3029; www.parks.wa.gov) outlines their journey of exploration and provides a view of the ironically named Cape Disappointment, where the explorers had their first, awe-inspiring look at the tumultuous Pacific.

The peninsula is famed for kite flying on its beaches and bike riding on the **Discovery Trail**. At its northern tip are the piney woods of **Leadbetter Point State Park**.

The bay itself is a vast brackish estuary that's second largest on the Pacific coast. **Willapa Bay National Wildlife Refuge** (www.fws.gov/willapa) harbors seabirds, provides a home for young salmon, and filters sediment from incoming streams. Willapa Bay oysters are famed for their quality.

Cascade Mountains★★

Separating the wet coastland from the dry, eastern portion of Washington state, the jagged spine of the Cascades runs the entire length of Washington, from Canada to the Columbia River, and down through Oregon into northern California. Several volcanoes distinguish the Cascades, including its highest peak, Mt. Rainier (14,410ft), and Mt. St. Helens (8,363ft), which erupted as the world watched in 1980. These and other major Washington volcanoes—Mt. Adams (12,276ft), Mt. Baker (10,778ft) and Glacier Peak (10,568ft)—originated only about 1 million years ago, though the Cascades began rising 25 million years earlier.

A BIT OF HISTORY

While Native Americans had forged trading trails across the Cascades, settlers found them a formidable barrier to east–west travel. Not until 1972, in fact, did the North Cascades Highway (Route 20) traverse the rugged terrain just south of the Canadian border. A patchwork of national park and forestland blankets most of these mountains, helping to protect a rich chain of wildlife and providing myriad opportunities for outdoor recreation.

SIGHTS

Mount St. Helens National Volcanic Monument★★★

164mi south of Seattle. ✆360-449-7800. Main access via Rte. 504, 48mi east of I-5 (Exit 49) at Castle Rock. www.fs.usda.gov/mountsthelens.

One of the world's most famous volcanoes, St. Helens erupted in 1980 with the intensity of 500 atomic bombs, destroying its northern flank and reducing its elevation more than 1,300ft. Today the eviscerated mountain, sur-

- ⏱ **Michelin Map:** 493 C2,3. Pacific Standard Time.
- ℹ **Info:** www.experience washington.com.
- ▶ **Location:** Touring the Cascades offers the chance to see one of the most distinct rain shadows in North America: west side valleys hold rain forest, while on the eastern slope, sometimes only miles away, arid conditions prevail.
- ⊛ **Don't Miss:** Mount Rainier and Mount St. Helens.
- 👥 **Kids:** Northwest Trek.
- ⏱ **Also See:** Leavenworth.

rounded by a 172sq mi preserve, has become a leading visitor attraction. Youngest of the major Cascade volcanoes, St. Helens was known to ancient Native Americans as Fire Mountain. Quiet through most of the 20C, the conical mountain rumbled slowly awake in spring 1980, for several weeks giving off warning quakes and hisses.

The sudden explosion on May 18 sent a column of ash 15mi into the atmosphere; poured hot rock and pumice over the countryside; devastated 250sq mi of forest; caused severe flooding, and left 57 people dead. When the eruption was over, the 9,677ft peak measured only 8,363ft.

The **Mount St. Helens Visitor Center★★** (Rte. 504, 5mi east of I-5; ✆360-274-0962) offers a fascinating live-footage film, a slide show and other worthy exhibits. From here, the 47mi drive along Spirit Memorial Highway leads to the **Johnston Ridge Observatory★★★** (Rte. 504; ✆360-274-2140), within 5mi of the volcano's crater. The devastation is still vividly apparent, though regenerated forest is starting to make a strong appearance. Acres of scorched trees, interspersed with newly planted trees, give way to the blowdown zone, where the forest was leveled by the blast.

Mount Rainier National Park★★★

Rtes. 410 & 706, about 70mi southeast of Tacoma. ☎360-569-2211. www.nps.gov/mora.

Highest volcano and fifth-highest peak in the contiguous US, Rainier is a majestic backdrop to the Puget Sound megalopolis. An arctic island in a temperate zone, the summit is covered in more than 30sq mi of ice and snow. Meltwater from its 25 glaciers filigrees the terrain with fast-running rivers and streams that course through alpine meadows, and past old-growth forests at lower elevations. Its last major eruption occurred 2,000 years ago, and though minor earthquakes at the summit are common, scientists agree there are no signs of an imminent eruption.

The **Nisqually–Paradise Road** (Rte. 706, open all year; other roads closed late Oct–late May, depending upon snowfall) enters the park at its southwest corner, twisting 19mi past streams, waterfalls and grand viewpoints to the meadows of **Paradise★★★**.

The **Henry M. Jackson Memorial Visitor Center** (☎360-569-6571) and observatory at 5,400ft provide overviews of park wildlife and geologic features.

Rustic Paradise Lodge is open for accommodations in summer. Hikes vary from the Nisqually Vista Trail (*1.2mi*) to the challenging Skyline Trail (*5mi*). **Sunrise★★★** (14mi from White River entrance, Rte. 410) is the highest point attainable by car (6,400ft) and boasts breathtaking views of Rainier (west), Sunrise Lake (east) and conical Mt. Adams (south).

👥 Northwest Trek Wildlife Park★★

Rte. 161, 6mi north of Eatonville. ☎360-832-6117. www.nwtrek.org.

This 725-acre wildlife park displays animals native to the Pacific Northwest region. Tram tours (50 min.) enable visitors to see grizzly and black bears, caribou, elk, moose, bison, bighorn sheep, great blue herons, wild turkeys and other creatures in their natural habitats.

Walk-through exhibit, several miles of nature trails, a new zip line and a children's discovery center are additional offerings.

North Cascades National Park★★

Approximately 120mi northeast of Seattle. Main access from Rte. 20, 50–100mi east of I-5 (Exit 230). ☎360-854-7200. www.nps.gov/noca.

Old-growth forests, hidden waterfalls, jewel-like lakes, alpine meadows and glaciated peaks up to 9,000ft, fill this park's 1,069sq mi; most are accessible only by foot. Its 300 glaciers account for half the icefields in the US outside Alaska. Endangered animals such as grizzly bears and wolverines inhabit the backcountry. In 1988, Congress declared 93 percent of the park's lands wilderness, affording the highest degree of federal protection. The 2,600mi **Pacific Crest National Scenic Trail** traverses the park.

Just off Route 20, which divides the park into northern and southern units, the **visitor center** (Rte. 20, 1mi west of Newhalem; ☎206-386-4495) offers films and information on fishing, hiking and backpacking. A short boardwalk trail ends at a viewpoint looking north to 6,805ft Pinnacle Peak.

Leavenworth★★

US-2 117mi east of Seattle. ☎509-548-5807. www.leavenworth.org.

In the heart of the Cascades, this Bavarian-styled mountain town is a tourist magnet, but for good reason. Clasped in a mountain fastness with a river rushing through it, Leavenworth offers year-round recreation—hiking, rafting and skiing, as well as abundant culture; the town excels at festivals, and features concerts, plays and other offerings. The town's picturesque, flower-filled streets are lined with Bavarian-theme shops, cafes and beer halls.

Eastern Washington

Open, dry and rugged, the vast expanse of eastern Washington stretches from the foothills of the Cascades to the Idaho border, and from Walla Walla north to the Okanogan highlands, and is largely lumped under the geographic term the Columbia Basin. Rivers cut deep, meandering canyons across the arid land, punctuated by irrigated fruit orchards and vineyards. Visitors who explore this grand landscape will find a wide variety of appealing natural areas, parks, museums and historic sites, as well as Washington's wine country.

A BIT OF HISTORY

Over the centuries, a parade of Plateau Indians, explorers, ranchers and farmers came through and left their respective marks. Hydoelectric power development also brought irrigation water to hundreds of thousands of acres, and the region now is a major producer of fresh fruit, potatoes, wheat, wine and vegetables, a region referred to by locals as the "Inland Empire."

SIGHTS
Spokane★

276mi east of Seattle via I-90. ℰ509-624-1341. www.visitspokane.com.
An 1880s transportation and trading center, Washington's second-largest city (210,000 residents) spreads along the wooded slopes of the Spokane River near the Idaho border. Its downtown encompasses dozens of historic buildings and a spectacular stretch of river where waterfalls crash over basalt lava cliffs. Elsewhere, residential neighborhoods line tree-shaded bluffs with well-kept Victorian mansions and Craftsman-style cottages.
Exhibits in the **Northwest Museum of Arts and Culture★** (2316 W. First Ave.; ℰ509-456-3931; www.northwestmu-seum.org) provide a concise overview of the history of Spokane and eastern Washington.

- **Michelin Map:** 493 C,D3,4. Pacific Standard Time.
- **Info:** www.experience washington.com.
- **Don't Miss:** Yakima or Walla Walla area wineries.
- **Also See:** Lake Chelan.

Riverfront Park★★

Spokane Falls Blvd. between Post & Washington Sts. ✕&ℰ509-625-6601. www.spokaneriverfrontpark.com.
Occupying both banks of the Spokane River, this outstanding park was developed for the Expo '74 world's fair. It offers rolling lawns shaded by ponderosa pines, landscaped walkways, a splendidly restored 1909 **carousel★**, a **gondola ride★★** to the base of Lower Spokane Falls, a small amusement park and an IMAX theater.

Manito Park★

Grand Blvd. & 18th Ave. &Pℰ509-625-6200. www.spokaneparks.org.
This delightful park, 2mi south of downtown, presents a Japanese garden, an immense rose garden, a perennial garden and a European Renaissance-style garden. Manito is said to mean "spirit of nature" in the Algonquian language.

Lake Chelan★★

180mi east of Seattle via I-90 on US-97A. △✕&ℰ509-682-3503. www.lakechelan.com.
This narrow, 55mi-long fjord lake nestles in a glacially gouged trough. Its upper end snakes among sawtooth peaks that soar 8,000ft high, while its lower end is one of the state's most beloved recreational playgrounds, with warm water, sand beaches and resorts, as well as apple orchards and wineries open for touring and outdoor dining.

Grand Coulee Dam★

Rte. 155, Coulee Dam, 228mi east of
Seattle via US-2. Visit interior of dam
by guided tour (50min) only. ♿🅿
℘509-633-9265.
www.usbr.gov/pn/grandcoulee.

This mammoth, 55-story-high wall of
sloped concrete stretches across the
Columbia River for nearly a mile, spanning the cliffs of a deep desert canyon.
Built by the Civilian Conservation Corps
in the 1930s, it is the largest concrete
dam in North America and the third
largest electric power producer in the
world. Lake Roosevelt, its 151mi-long
reservoir, is contained within **Lake
Roosevelt National Recreation Area**★
(1008 Crest Dr., Coulee Dam; ℘509-
633-9441, www.nps.gov/laro).

Yakima Valley★

141mi southeast of Seattle via I-90
& I-82. ℘509-575-3010.
www.visityakima.com.

A verdant river corridor, the agriculturally rich Yakima Valley stretches in
a long southeasterly arc nearly 100mi
from Ellensburg to the Columbia River.
This diverse wine-growing region is
the oldest appellation in the state,
with more than 100 **wineries** scattered
throughout the valley.

The city of Yakima itself, a commercial
hub of 93,000 people, offers two interesting museums. The **Yakima Valley
Museum** (2105 Tieton Dr.; ℘509-248-
0747; www.yakimavalleymuseum.org)
focuses on regional history and the valley's agricultural heritage; the museum's functional replica of a 1930s soda
fountain is a hit with kids. The **Yakima
Valley Trolleys** (306 W. Pine St.; ℘509-
575-1700; www.yakimavalleytrolleys.
org) is a depot for vintage electric trolley cars that take passengers on 2hr
rides through the city and countryside.
South of Yakima, the history of the
Yakama Indian tribe and its modern
transformation is presented through
dioramas, paintings and petroglyphs
at the **Yakama Nation Museum & Cultural Center**★ ♦♦ (100 Spiel-yi Loop
off US-97, Toppenish; ℘509-865-
2800; www.yakamamuseum.com). The
nearby town of Toppenish is famed for
70 **murals**★ depicting local history.

Walla Walla★★

273mi southeast of Seattle via I-90,
I-82 & US-12. ℘509-529-4718.
www.wallawalla.org.

An agricultural hub and college town of
32,000, Walla Walla is at the epicenter
of the state's highly regarded wine
industry, with several top-notch lodging options—including the renovated
1920 **Marcus Whitman Hotel**—and
well-regarded restaurants. Once the
first winery started up here in 1977
vineyards were planted and winemak-
ing burgeoned. Today there are more
than 100 wineries open for touring.

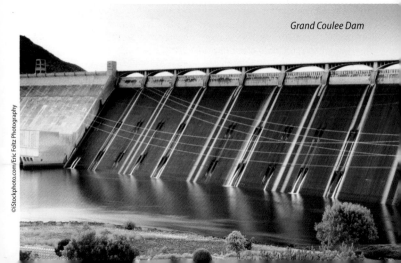

Grand Coulee Dam

©iStockphoto.com/Eric Foltz Photography

Portland Area

The commercial and cultural capital of the state of Oregon, Portland, commands a prime position straddling the Willamette River where it meets the Columbia. More than 2 million people inhabit the metropolitan area, spreading their homes across a verdant landscape of fields, rolling hills and forested ridges about 100mi upriver from the Pacific Ocean. A friendly, youthful city of unpretentious charm, Portland boasts a handsome downtown core, some 200 parks and gardens, a superb light rail system, an emphasis on sustainability, and lively neighborhoods on both sides of the Willamette.

Highlights

Portland

1 Everything's coming up roses at the **Rose Test Garden** (p476)

2 **Multnomah Falls** in the Columbia River Gorge (p477)

3 The Willamette Valley is Oregon's **Wine Country** (p478)

4 **Shakespeare** beneath the stars in Ashland (p479)

5 **Hart Mountain**, where the antelope still roam (p484)

A Rich Environment

The greater state of Oregon (OR-a-gun), bordered by California on the south and Washington state on the north, embodies the West of sweeping ranchlands, sky-thrusting mountains and a cherished independence. The snow-topped spine of the Cascade Range divides the wet maritime region of 362mi of rugged Pacific coastline and the lush Willamette (will-AM-it) Valley from the deserts of the east.

The Lewis and Clark Expedition passed through these parts in 1805-06. Fur traders followed. By 1846 a treaty with Britain established America's right to the land south of the 49th parallel; the state of Oregon was carved from the southwestern part of this new territory.

For much of the 20C to the present, Oregon has led on social reform, struggling with the clash between environmental protection and resource exploitation, and between

Portland Skyline and Mount Hood

© Portland Oregon Visitors Association

SUSTAINABLE PORTLAND

The 19C pioneers who trekked west to Oregon were adventurers willing to embrace new things. And the Willamette Valley they sought was justifiably advertised as a bountiful paradise, a land of rich earth, benign climate and great beauty. It's no surprise that their descendants, along with those who have joined in since, have become 21C pioneers in a pilgrimage toward a different bounty. Portland is determined to become the most sustainable community in the United States, a metropolitan area that uses its resources wisely, frugally and prosperously.

Portland has long been a progressive area—early 20C timber baron Simon Benson turned his fortune to community development, created a city park and helped preserve the nearby Columbia Gorge. Benson's legacy lives on in the many bubbling water fountains on downtown street corners. Former Oregon governor Tom McCall led the radical removal of Portland's old Harbor Drive waterfront freeway in the 1970s, turning the reclaimed riverfront into a delightful 29-acre park named after McCall that stretches almost a mile along the Willamette through downtown Portland.

Since then, the community has undertaken many initiatives to make Portland more environmentally friendly. The Max light rail system (begun with federal funds earmarked for freeway construction) stretches toward all four corners of the metro area, is immensely popular and well ahead of other, bigger cities. The downtown Farmers' Market was one of the nation's first, and remains one of the biggest, with more than 250 vendors; numerous neighborhood markets also offer Willamette Valley food producers a ready outlet for their goods.

Portland tops national lists for bicycling; relies on wind generation for a meaningful share of its electric power; has more LEED certified buildings (150) than any other US city, despite its small size; achieves extremely high waste diversion rates through recycling and composting; enjoys excellent air quality; and makes sustainability an official part of its municipal agenda with a city department devoted to the topic. As a result, Portland regularly wins national recognition as one of the top most-sustainable US cities.

Oregon Trail pioneers often wrote to friends and family back east of how wonderful the Willamette Valley was after they'd arrived in their hard-won paradise. Today's residents certainly agree as they pursue a hugely popular local tradition: summertime feasts served in the fields of nearby farmers. Diners enjoy the produce of the land they are visiting, are encouraged to help sustain its future, and that of the city, valley and all its resources.

For more information on Feasts in the Fields, visit www.plateandpitch fork.com. For information on sustainability in Portland, visit www. sbnportland.org.

personal liberty and social responsibility. In the western part of the state, timber and fishing have given way to agriculture, high-tech industries and tourism.

ADDRESSES

STAY

$$$$ The Allison Inn – 2525 Allison Lane, Newberg. &503-554-2525. www.theallison.com. 85 rooms. Set amid 35 acres of woods and vineyards, the first destination resort in Oregon's wine country is a sparkling wood-and-stone Northwest contemporary lodge. Guestrooms are serene and comfortable, with earth-tone decor, and highly vaunted **JORY ($$$)** celebrates the bounty of the Willamette Valley. An indoor pool is on the premises.

$$$ The Benson Hotel – 309 SW Broadway, Portland. &503-228-2000. www.bensonhotel.com. 287 rooms. Lumber baron Simon Benson completed this grand hotel in 1913, and its opulence has endured. Elaborate Austrian crystal chandeliers illuminate the marble floors and walnut walls of the lobby, and the rooms have an equally lavish ambience.

$$$ The Governor Hotel – 614 SW 11th Ave., Portland. &503-224-3400. www.governorhotel.com. 100 rooms. Murals recall the early 19C expedition of Lewis and Clark; the original stained-glass dome and tiled floor remain from 1909 construction. This classic hotel combines mahogany detailing with large and contemporary rooms, all within a grand shell.

$$$ The Nines – 525 SW Morrison St., Portland. &503-222-9996. www.thenines.com.331 rooms. Residing in one of the city's most-venerable buildings in an ideal location at the heart of the city, The Nines is a LEED silver–certified, environmentally friendly luxury hotel with a view from every room. Guest rooms are quiet and posh, with taupe walls, sparkling chandeliers and turquoise accents. **Urban Farmer ($$$)**, a contemporary steakhouse, serves Northwest fare.

$$$ Ashland Springs Hotel – 212 E. Main St., Ashland. &541-488-1700. www.ashlandspringshotel.com. 70 rooms. The lobby of this historic 1925 inn downtown is filled with cases of butterflies, shells and other natural treasures, amid tall palm trees; guest rooms are enclosed by saffron walls with botanically inspired decor. **Larks ($$$)** offers local, seasonal foods, expertly prepared, along with a solid wine list.

$$$ The Ocean Lodge– 2864 S. Pacific St., Cannon Beach. &503-436-2241. www.theoceanlodge.com. 45 rooms. Perched on the oceanfront overlooking Haystack Rock, this lodge makes a calm getaway. A two-story rock fireplace and massive Douglas-fir beams adorn the lobby. The rooms, in butter tones with fir trim, have fireplaces and views of the ocean.

$$$ Sunriver Resort – 1 Center Drive, Sunriver. &541-593-1000. www.sunriver-resort.com. 209 rooms. This classy resort boasts a larg,e deluxe hotel, numerous rental condominiums and homes, 2 golf courses, 35mi of paved bike trails, and a lovely site along the Deschutes River beneath Mount Bachelor and Paulina Peak. It's a perfect base from which to explore Central Oregon's natural attractions.

$$ Inn at Northrup Station – 2025 NW Northrup St., Portland. &503-224-0543. www.northrupstation.com. 70 rooms. Vibrant green, orange and purple colors pop at this hip urban hotel, an all-suites property with retro furniture, kitchenettes and balconies overlooking a leafy street in the trendy Nob Hill neighborhood. The Inn is situated on the streetcar line, for which guests are given free tickets.

$$ Overleaf Lodge & Spa – 280 Overleaf Lodge Lane, 2055 US-1, Yachats. &541-547-4880. www.overleaflodge.com. 54 rooms. The lodge rests on a rocky shelf close to the ocean's edge. First-floor rooms have patios, allowing easy access to tidepools. Contemporary cabins are also available. The tranquil rooms have a gas fireplace, colorful bedspreads and simple furnishings. Overleaf is an ideal launching spot for explorations of Oregon's central coast.

❦ EAT

$$$ Bluehour – 250 NW 13th Ave., Portland. ☎503-226-3394. www. bluehouronline.com. **Contemporary**. This swank Pearl District establishment is a popular spot for after-theater desserts and espresso drinks. Earlier diners can choose such dishes as oysters poached in dry Vermouth, New York steak with green peppercorn sauce and wild Oregon salmon with eggplant.

$$$ Serratto – 2112 NW Kearney St., Portland. ☎503-221-1195. www. serratto.com. **Mediterranean**. Housed in a refurbished warehouse with huge old-growth Douglas-fir beams and pillars, this Nob Hill standout specializes in Northern Italian dishes with Northwest flair, such as grilled natural ribeye with Oregon chevre-chive potato cake and grilled asparagus. The homemade pappardelle features braised wild boar and shaved peccorino.

$$$ Wildwood – 1221 NW 21st Ave., Portland. ☎503-248-9663. www. wildwoodrestaurant.com. **Northwest**. The menu changes daily at this renowned, chef-driven farm-to-table restaurant in the trendy Pearl District; the focus is on Northwest dishes such as pan-seared petrale sole with braised lobster mushrooms, or roasted pork chop with local chanterelles.

$$$ Toro Bravo – 120 NE Russell St., Portland. ☎503-281-4464. www. torobravopdx.com. **Spanish**. Patrons begin lining up before 5pm for this intimate tapas spot with big flavors. The owner's and staff's regular trips to Spain inform the diverse menu; among standouts are grilled octopus with piquillo peppers, oxtail croquettes with chili mayonnaise and top-notch paella fairly bursting with local seafood.

$$$ Ristorante Italiano – 754 E. 13th St., Eugene. ☎541-342-6963. www. excelsiorinn.com. **Italian**. An elegant Victorian steps from the University of Oregon is home to this restaurant and small inn. The menu pays heed to the slow food movement with locally grown ingredients that are chemical-free. Signature dishes include pastas such as Oregon Dungeness crab ravioli in lemon-basil cream, and ravioli filled with pear, gorgonzola and Oregon hazelnuts.

$$$ The Painted Lady – 201 S. College St., Newberg. ☎503-538-3850. www.thepaintedladyrestaurant.com. **Northwest**. This restaurant inside a tidy Victorian with white picket fence is known for its beautifully presented dishes that draw from local farms and the nearby ocean. Among the menu's mix might be crispy Netarts oysters with green-tomato remoulade, roasted wild salmon with mushrooms and English peas, or bacon-wrapped pork tenderloin with polenta.

$$ Gogi's – 235 W. Main St., Jacksonville. ☎541-899-8699. www.gogis.net. **Northwest**. Everything is made in-house at this restaurant situated inside a Victorian in the historic gold-rush town of Jacksonville. Fresh flowers and linen tablecloths create an intimate ambience, but the bistro-style food— perhaps crispy pork belly with polenta or braised lamb shank with lima beans and spinach pesto—is the star.

$$ Local Ocean Seafood – 213 SW Bay Blvd, Newport. ☎541-574-7959. www. localocean.net. **Seafood**. This seafood market and cafe on the waterfront alongside the boat harbor offers the freshest catch—whether Totten Inlet mussels, seared King salmon or Fish Wives Stew, with crab, shrimp, scallops and more. Roll-up glass doors let in the briny breezes, a perfect accompaniment to an Oregon coast meal.

$ Deschutes Brewery – 1044 NW Bond St., Bend. ☎541-382-9242. www.deschutesbrewery.com. **American**. Outdoors lovers populate this popular riverside brewery, which is the town's de facto gathering spot. From breads to sausages, the offerings are house-made. Even the burgers are hyper-local; beef cattle are fed with spent brewery grains. The gorgeous riverside setting puts this spot over the top.

Portland★★

The Willamette River, spanned by a dozen distinctive bridges, acts as a natural dividing line between the city's hilly, forested west side and flatter eastern neighborhoods. Portland is an energetic city that prides itself on a progressive, relaxed atmosphere, and is particularly noted for its eco-living and green spaces; in recent years it has become a national capital of microbreweries.

A BIT OF HISTORY

Before the 1842 opening of the Oregon Trail, American Indians, then trappers and homesteaders settled at the confluence of the Willamette and Columbia rivers. Portland burgeoned with the arrival of the railroads in the 1880s. Its river-junction location made it a shipping center; trade extended to China. The war years created demand for shipyard workers, swelling Portland's population.

Portland's downtown business district is pedestrian-friendly, and the Pearl District to the north (www.explorethepearl.com)—once run-down warehouses—has been rejuvenated with shops, cafes and residential complexes. Both are linked by the efficient Portland Streetcar (www.portlandstreetcar.org). Originally based on timber and shipping, the city's economy has been bolstered by high-tech companies, especially semiconductor firms located in the suburbs. It is now aggressively seeking to be the most sustainable city in the US.

SIGHTS

Oregon History Museum★★

1200 SW Park Ave. &℘503-222-1741. www.ohs.org.

Eight-story trompe l'oeil murals of Lewis and Clark and the Oregon Trail rise beside the entrance plaza of this archival museum. Filled with interactive displays, the new **Oregon Voices★** exhibit presents personal accounts from

▶ **Population:** 603,000.
Ⓒ **Michelin Map:** 493 B 4. Pacific Standard Time.
🗊 **Info:** ℘503-275-9750; www.travelportland.com.
◖ **Location:** Most attractions lie downtown and in Washington Park, both served by the city's exceptional light-rail system. Mount Hood, directly east of downtown, is an omnipresent landmark for direction – if it's visible.
🅿 **Parking:** Parking on the east side of the Willamette (in the OMSI lot, for instance) is cheaper than in downtown, which can be reached via a five-minute stroll across one of the city's many bridges.
Ⓐ **Don't Miss:** The Pearl District; the International Rose Test Garden in Washington Park.
Ⓛ **Timing:** Visitors strapped for time can devote one busy day to downtown (the Chinese Garden, Art Museum, Powell's Books) and the next day to Washington Park's zoo, rose garden and Japanese garden.
👥 **Kids:** OMSI is superb for kids of all ages.

Oregonians in the 1950s to today; **Oregon My Oregon★** traces state history, beginning with the 1840s Oregon Trail migration.

Portland Art Museum★★

1219 SW Park Ave. ✕&🅿℘503-226-2811. www.pam.org.

The oldest (1892) art museum on the West Coast occupies 240,000sq ft of space inside historic buildings at the heart of the city's cultural district.

The museum's **Center for Northwest Art** brings regional artists to the fore, including early 20C Oregon visitor Childe Hassam and modern master Jacob Lawrence. The **Center for Native American Art** boasts prehistoric, his-

Windsurfing the Gorge

Sailboarders have found a paradise at the Columbia River Gorge town of **Hood River** (I-84 Exit 63; www.hoodriver.org). Here, at a natural break in the Cascade Mountains, steady currents from the east meet strong winds from the west, so that summer winds average 20-25mph. Windsurfing enthusiasts discovered the gorge in the mid 1980s, and Hood River, a cozy hillside town of about 7,000 people, witnessed an adrenaline shot to its economy. There are more than three dozen sailboard retailers, distributors, and custom-board and accessory manufacturers in Hood River, which is the locus for the Columbia Gorge Windsurfing Association.

toric and contemporary crafts by North American groups. An outdoor sculpture mall features works by Henry Moore, Barbara Hepworth and Pierre-Auguste Renoir.

👥 Lan Su Chinese Garden★★★

239 NW Everett St.; 📞503-228-8131. www.lansugarden.org.

This 2000 addition to Portland's small international district is a highly stylized retreat whose high-walled courtyards, pools, walkways and meditation rooms are designed to mute the urban bustle outside its walls. Encompassing a city block (40,000 square feet), the garden's highlights include a 7,000sq ft "lake;" Tai Hu limestone rocks, 500 tons of which were shipped here from China; and hundreds of native Chinese plant species. Visitors can enjoy a respite in the garden's excellent teahouse.

Powell's City of Books★★

1005 W. Burnside St.; 📞503-228-4651. www.powells.com.

One of the most popular attractions in Oregon is this pioneering bookseller, now grown to a monolith that encompasses an entire block, an area of 1.6 acres. First in the US to mix used and new books on its shelves, Powell's today is widely considered the world's largest single bookstore. Visitors need store maps to navigate the 22 sections; particular strengths are mysteries and gardening books. With several smaller stores around the city and an online presence, Powell's claims an inventory of 4 million new, used, rare and out-of-print books.

Governor Tom McCall Waterfront Park★

Bordering SW Naito Pkwy. and the Willamette River between Marquam Bridge & Steel Bridge.

This grassy 23-acre park stretching along the Willamette was named for a governor who was a proponent of land-use planning. Among eight bridges that may be seen are the dark-green **Hawthorne Bridge** (1910), oldest operating vertical-lift bridge in the nation, and the **Steel Bridge** (1912, the world's only telescoping double-deck vertical-lift bridge).

Portland Spirit River Cruises★ (📞503-224-3900; www.portlandspirit.com) offers a wide variety of cruises year-round, departing from Salmon Street Springs. The **Portland Aerial Tram★** (www.gobytram.com) offers visitors a view of the city and snow-topped Mount Hood, as well as other peaks, during a 3min passage from the riverbank to the Oregon Health & Science University on the bluff above.

👥 Oregon Museum of Science and Industry★★

1945 SE Water Ave. ✖♿🅿
📞503-797-4000. www.omsi.edu.

This brick-and-glass building (1992, Zimmer Gunsul Frasca) inside a historic power plant on the Willamette harbors two floors of science exhibits, an Omnimax theater, a planetarium and numerous interactive exhibits.

Kids can design their own miniature sailboats and place them on a miniature lake to learn about wind power; practice structural design by building their own tiny bridges; or experience an earthquake in a simulator. Outside, the retired submarine *USS Blueback* is open for tours.

Washington Park★★

Entrances south of W. Burnside Rd. & west of SW Vista Ave. ℘503-823-7529. www.washingtonparkpdx.org.

More than 400 acres of trees, gardens, playgrounds and trails on a steep, wooded hillside west of the city embrace some of the city's top attractions, as well as many miles of trails through wooded natural areas.

International Rose Test Garden★★

400 SW Kingston Ave. 🅿 ℘503-227-7033. www.rosegardenstore.org.

One of the most significant displays of roses on the West Coast, the oldest continuously operating public test gardens for roses in the nation.boasts 7,000 roses of 550 species. The idyllic settingincludes Mount Hood looming in the background. It's

Japanese Garden★★

611 SW Kingston Ave. 🅿 ℘503-223-1321. www.japanesegarden.com.

According to the Japanese ambassador to the US, this wooded 5.5 acre garden is one of the most authentic Japanese gardens outside Japan. Ponds, waterfalls and streams, a moon bridge, ceremonial teahouse and Zen-inspired sand-and-stone garden grace the grounds.

Hoyt Arboretum

4000 SW Fairview Blvd. 🅿 ℘503-865-8733. www.hoytarboretum.org.

Within this 187-acre space are more than 1,000 species of trees from around the world and 21 trails winding through stands of magnolia, oaks and maples. In springtime the **Magnolia Trail** is among the best places to enjoy colorful blooms.

▲▲ World Forestry Center Discovery Museum★

4033 SW Canyon Rd. 🅿 ℘503-228-1367. www.worldforestry.org.

Following a $7 million renovation in 2005, this museum, originally dedicated to forestry, changed its focus to sustainability. In a 20,000sqft setting, engaging hands-on exhibits offer an understanding of the importance of forests around the world, with a focus on those of the Pacific Northwest.

▲▲ Oregon Zoo★★

4001 SW Canyon Rd. ℘503-226-1561. www.oregonzoo.org

This 64-acre zoo in a wooded canyon has five major exhibit areas with naturalistic environments for 232 species; it is a leader in conversation and breeding of endangered species. The new (2013) **California Condor** exhibit offers one of the few places to see these rare, endangered birds, the largest flying avians on the planet. A narrow-gauge train carries guests from the zoo to the International Rose Test Garden.

Pittock Mansion★★

3229 NW Pittock Dr., off NW Barnes Rd. ✕🅿 ℘503-823-3623. www.pittockmansion.org.

The most opulent historic house in Portland crests a 940ft hill in Imperial Heights. Built in 1914 (Edward T. Foulkes) for Henry Pittock, publisher of *The Oregonian* newspaper, the manse is a French Renaissance Revival-style château with 44 rooms (23 open for viewing).

Tours take in magnificent marble and woodwork, a grand staircase and luxurious early 20C furnishings.

EXCURSIONS
Mount Hood★★

US-26, 50mi east of Portland. ℘503-622-3017. www.mthoodchamber.com.

The snow-cloaked cone of Oregon's highest peak pierces the clouds at 11,239ft. In 1805 explorers Lewis and Clark were the first white Americans to set eyes on the volcanic peak, previously named by British sailors. It became a beacon to Oregon Trail travelers in the mid 19C. Their wagon ruts remain visible just west of **Barlow Pass** (Rte. 35 east of US-26).

Nearby **Timberline Lodge★** (off US-26, 6mi north of Government Camp; ℘503-

272-3311; www.timberlinelodge.com) was built by the Works Progress Administration in 1937. From here, hikers can access the 40mi **Timberline Trail★★**. **Mt. Hood Meadows★** (Hwy 35 10mi north of Government Camp; ℘503-337-2222; www.skihood.com) offers some of the best skiing in the Northwest, with broad, high-altitude meadows at the top of the mountain—the highest lift is at 7,300ft—affording views of other volcanoes in the range.

Columbia River Gorge★★

▶ I-84 from Troutdale to The Dalles, 17 to 84mi east of Portland. ℘800-984-6743. www.crgva.org.

Extending from suburban Portland to the mouth of the Deschutes River, the 455sq mi Columbia River Gorge National Scenic Area includes more than 90 waterfalls, state parks and 700ft-high cliff-edge vistas. The second-largest river in the US (after the Mississippi) slices through volcanic basalt along the Oregon-Washington border.

Providing a scenic alternative to the interstate is the **Historic Columbia River Highway★★** (US-30). Completed in 1915, it now may be driven only in two distinct sections linked by I-84: 22mi from Troutdale (Exit 17) to Ainsworth State Park (Exit 40) and 16mi from Mosier (Exit 69) to The Dalles (Exit 84). The best views are from **Portland Women's Forum State Park** (Mile 10) and the **Vista House at Crown Point★** (Mile 11; 🅿 ℘503-695-2230; www.vistahouse.com).

The gorge is a wonderland of **waterfalls**; don't miss **Multnomah Falls★★** (I-84 Exit 31; ℘541-308-1700), a mesmerizing 620ft plunge of water.

US Army Corps of Engineers visitor centers at **Bonneville Lock and Dam★** (I-84 Exit 40; ℘541-374-8820; www.nwp.usace.army.mil) and **The Dalles Lock and Dam★** (I-84 Exit 87; ℘541-296-9778; www.nwp.usace.army.mil) show how the river has been harnessed, and have fish passage viewing areas. At the **Columbia Gorge Discovery Center★★** (5000 Discovery Dr., The Dalles; ℘541-296-8600; www.gorgediscovery.org),

© Portland Oregon Visitors Association / Tim Jewett

Portland Aerial Tram and Mount Hood

visitors can use interactive devices to learn about the cataclysmic volcanoes and floods that formed the Gorge, and learn how Lewis and Clark fared on their journey down the Columbia. The **Ice Age Exhibit** life-size mammoth model is a highlight.

Fort Vancouver National Site★★★

▶ 750 Anderson St. off Mill Plain Blvd., Vancouver, WA, 8mi north of Portland. &🅿 ℘360-992-1800. www.fortvan.org.

The Hudson's Bay Company had its headquarters here in 1825-46 and the first US military post in the Pacific Northwest was founded here in 1849. **Officers Row★** includes the **Marshall House★** (1886), home to General George C. Marshall, who commanded the Vancouver Barracks from 1936-38. **Fort Vancouver National Historic Site★★★** 👥 (&🅿 ℘360-816-6230; www.nps.gov/fova) offers 👄guided tours of the reconstructed Hudson's Bay Company palisaded stockade, including a re-created carpenter shop, blacksmith shop and fur-storage facility.

Willamette Valley and Southern Oregon★★

Broad, fertile Willamette Valley is Oregon's heart. Running 110mi south from Portland to Eugene and 30mi between the Cascades and the Coast Range, this destination of Oregon Trail travelers began attracting pioneers in the 1840s. Today, despite being the state's most populated area outside metropolitan Portland, most of the area retains a rural feel: a landscape of farmland, tulip fields, hazelnut orchards and covered bridges.

- **Michelin Map:** 493 A, B 4, 5, 6. Pacific Standard Time.
- **Info:** Willamette Valley: ☏866-548-5018; www.oregonwinecountry.org; Southern Oregon: ☏541-779-4691; www.sova.org.
- **Location:** The drive from Portland to Ashland, the southernmost Oregon city on I-5 (which runs north-south) takes about 5hrs. Medford and Eugene have major regional airports. The area's best-known attractions are Crater Lake and Ashland's Shakespeare festival.
- **Timing:** May, September and October offer fine weather and fewer crowds at the Oregon Shakespeare Festival. Crater Lake can be seen best in July or August in a half-day visit.

SIGHTS

McMinnville★

43mi south of Portland on Rte. 99 West. ☏503-472-6196. www.mcminnville.org. The capital of Yamhill County is the center of the northern Willamette Valley **wine country** (☏see below), an area especially known for fine pinot noir and pinot gris. The city has an historic district and a heritage hotel, **Hotel Oregon** (www.mcmenamins.com/hoteloregon). The **Evergreen Aviation & Space Museum★★** (500 N.E. Capt. Michael King Smith Way; ☏503-434-4185; www.evergreenmuseum.org) houses the largest airplane ever built, Howard Hughes' legendary *Spruce Goose*, and a **Titan II missile**. Among additional attractions are an IMAX theater and the (2011) 10-slide **Evergreen Wings and Waves Waterpark** 🏊🧒.
From McMinnville, visitors drive quiet country roads through rolling, oak-clad hills to stop in at dozens of wineries and farmsteads.

Oregon Wine Country★★

Via Rte. 99 West off I-5, 20–40mi SW of Portland. ☏866-548-5018. www.oregonwinecountry.org.
Situated on the same latitude as France's Burgundy region, the Willamette Valley has developed into one of the finest viticultural regions in the world, with more than 300 wineries. Established in the 1960s, the industry remained relatively unknown until a pinot noir from Eyrie Vineyards did the unimaginable in a French-sponsored tasting in 1979: it outperformed several esteemed French wines. The area is also known for merlot and pinot gris; vineyards and wineries extend from McMinnville to Cottage Grove, chiefly on the west side of the valley. Many family-run operations are open for tours and tastings.

Salem★

I-5 & Rte. 99 East, 44mi south of Portland. ☏503-581-4325. www.travelsalem.com. The capital of Oregon and the state's third-largest city with some 157,000 residents, Salem traces its founding to 1840, when Jason Lee moved the headquarters of his Methodist mission to this mid Willamette Valley location. Lee's home and several other early

Shakespeare Festival

After failing to turn its lithium-rich springs into a destination spa, Ashland followed the dreams of a drama professor and converted an old bandshell into an outdoor amphitheater. There, in 1935, the city kicked off the first **Oregon Shakespeare Festival★★★** (15 S. Pioneer St.; ℘541-482-4331; www.osfashland. org). February through November, the festival stages 11 plays in its three theaters, featuring works by Shakespeare (four per season) and other classic writers, as well as contemporary works. The impressive, open-air Elizabethan Stage offers the classics beneath the stars.

buildings still stand at the **Willamette Heritage Center at the Mill★★** (1313 Mill St. SE; ✕&🅿 ℘503-585-7012; www.willametteheritage.org), a five-acre historical park that includes the 1889 **Thomas Kay Woolen Mill**, open for tours.

Downtown, the domed **Oregon State Capitol★** (900 Court St. NE; ✕&🅿 ℘503-986-1388; www.leg.state.or.us), built in 1938 (Francis Keally) in the Greek Revival style, is topped by a bronze-and-gold-leaf statue of a pioneer.

North of Salem off I-5 (exit 263), **Willamette Mission State Park** (www.oregonstateparks.org) preserves pastoral farmlands and orchards, and includes the world's largest black cottonwood tree. Nearby, at Wheatland Rd. (follow signs), the **Wheatland Ferry** is a **cable-drawn vessel** that carries cars across the Willamette.

A half-hour drive northeast of Salem, **Oregon Garden★★** (www.oregongarden.org) is an 80-acre botanical garden with 20 specialty gardens, including an Oregon white oak grove with one of the state's largest, a 100-ft, 400-year-old tree.

Forty minutes east of Salem, **Silver Falls State Park★★** (Rte. 214, Sublimity ℘503-873-8681; www.oregonstate parks.org) is Oregon's largest state park at 9,000 acres. Its highlight is the **Trail of Ten Falls**, a 7mi loop along Silver Creek that takes hikers through deep forests to 10 cascading falls.

Eugene★

Rtes. 99 & 126 just west of I-5, 108mi south of Portland. ℘541-484-5307. www.eugenecascadescoast.org.

Oregon's second-largest urban area (158,000) still has ties to its agricultural and timber-industry roots, but the **University of Oregon★** (1585 E. 13th St.; ℘541-346-1000; www.uoregon.edu) sets the pace today. Founded in 1876 and now enrolling more than 20,000 students, it is largely accountable for Eugene's thriving counter-culture, evident in its casual dress, health-food stores and environmental organizations. The UO **Jordan Schnitzer Museum of Art★★** (Memorial Quadrangle near Kincaid St.; ℘541-346-3027; http://jsma.uoregon.edu) is a fantasy of intricate brickwork with a focus on Asian art. The **Museum of Natural and Cultural History★** (1680 E. 15th Ave.; &🅿 ℘541-346-3024; www.natural-history.uoregon.edu) is a Northwest center for paleontological and archaeological research, with exhibits devoted mainly to indigenous peoples, including the local Kalapuya culture.

©Chrisboswell/Dreamstime.com

Crater Lake National Park

Crater Lake National Park★★★

Rtes. 62 & 138 west of US-97, 145mi southeast of Eugene. ℘541-594-3000. www.nps.gov/crla.

The deepest lake in the US at 1,932ft rests in the crater of a collapsed volcano. Ringed by mountains blanketed with snow much of the year, this vivid sapphire lake, 6mi in diameter, attracts hikers, geologists and those compelled by the mysterious eye-like blue caldera. The cataclysmic eruption of Mt. Mazama 7,700 years ago hurled more than 18 cubic miles of pumice and ash into the air and surrounding landscape. The collapsed mountain created a bowl-shaped caldera that filled with snowmelt.

Most visitors take the awe-inspiring 33mi **Rim Drive★★**, which circles the lake and has spectacular **views**. Among the best are those from **Sinnott Memorial Overlook** (Rim Village, south side of lake) and **Cloudcap**, highest point on the Rim Drive (7,865ft). Better yet is the perspective from atop 8,929ft **Mount Scott★★**, requiring a strenuous 5mi round-trip hike to the park's highest summit. A 7mi spur road off Rim Drive leads to **The Pinnacles★**, 80ft tall hollow fossilized fumaroles.

There are ample other attractions here, including hikes through mid-elevation pine forests, and the famed boat tour to **Wizard Island★**, a small knob in the middle of the lake.

The historic (1915) **Crater Lake Lodge** offers cozy rooms and rockers on a wide veranda; the refurbished wood lodge is perched on the crater rim with excellent views (www.craterlakelodges.com).

Ashland★★

Rte. 99 at I-5 Exit 14, 180mi south of Eugene. ℘541-482-3486. www.ashlandchamber.com

This town of 20,000 on the northern flank of the Siskiyou Mountains is the home to Southern Oregon University and a premier cultural center. The **Oregon Shakespeare Festival** (⊙see p479) is just one of several thriving theater groups. Bubbling Ashland Creek rushes through town, with public fountains spouting the naturally carbonated **lithium water** piped in from nearby mineral springs for which the city is known. Numerous small inns and B&Bs occupy refurbished historic homes and buildings, along with a wide variety of shops and cafes.

Lithia Park★ is a 93-acre preserve of gardens, woods and picnic areas that follows Ashland Creek up into the Siskiyou foothills; above, **Mount Ashland** is the only municipally owned ski area in the West.

Jacksonville★★

Rte. 238, 14mi northwest of Ashland. ℘541-899-8118. www.jacksonvilleoregon.org.

Enveloped by rolling, pine-clad hills, Jacksonville, an 1850s gold-rush town, is a National Historic District with numerous 19C brick storefronts and Victorian homes.

A **visitor center** (185 N. Oregon St.) has walking-tour maps. The summer-long **Britt Festivals★★** (℘541-779-0847; www.brittfest.org) offers first-rate classical, blues, jazz, world and pop music under the stars. Nearby, the **Applegate Valley Wine Trail★** (www.applegatewinetrail.com) showcases nearly 20 small wineries throughout the scenic valley.

Oregon Caves National Monument★★

Rte. 46, 20mi east of Cave Junction & 92mi west of Ashland via I-5 & US-199. ✕⯐℘541-592-2100. www.nps.gov/orca.

This web of marble and limestone chambers is bejeweled with stalactites, stalagmites and other wondrous calcite formations in 3mi of known passageways. On 90min tours, visitors traverse a half-mile route, climbing 500 stairs, ducking through low-ceilinged tunnels and entering chambers like Watson's Grotto and the Ghost Room.

Above ground, the park preserves stands of magnificent old growth forest; the steep **Big Tree Trail★** (*3mi*) leads to the widest-girth Douglas fir in Oregon.

Oregon Coast★★★

The 362mi Oregon coastline is a scenic blend of wave-swept rocks and sandy beaches. Even the few places where homes and businesses border the shore are nature's province: a 1967 state law made all Oregon beaches public. Though much of the forest just inland has been heavily logged, a tall border of spruce and cedar presses up to the shore, forming a key part of the coastal ecosystem.

- **Michelin Map:** 493 A, B, 4 A 5, 6. Pacific Standard Time.
- **Info:** ✆541-574-2679; www.visittheoregoncoast.com.
- **Location:** US-101, the main highway traversing the coast, skirts the shore several miles from the water. Visitors reach beaches and headlands through state parks on the west side of the highway.
- **Don't Miss:** Heceta Head.
- **Timing:** July and August can be foggy months on the Oregon Coast.
- **Kids:** The Oregon Coast Aquarium.

SIGHTS
Astoria★★

US-26, 30 & 101, 96mi northwest of Portland. ✆503-325-6311. www.oldoregon.com

Founded as a fur-trading post in 1811, Astoria was the first US settlement west of the Rocky Mountains. By the 1850s it was a thriving port at the mouth of the Columbia River.

The town of 10,000 remains a busy port. Six galleries of exhibits at the **Columbia River Maritime Museum★** (1792 Marine Dr.; ✆503-325-2323, www.crmm.org) tell the seafaring heritage of this area, and explore the shipwrecks and role of the Coast Guard.

The 125-foot **Astoria Column** (www.astoriacolumn.org) is patterned after Trajan's Column in Rome; it's 164 winding steps to the top, but views from its 600-ft elevation take in the Columbia River's mouth and distant mountains. **Fort Clatsop National Memorial★★** (6mi southwest off US-101; ✆503-861-2471; www.nps.gov/lewi) preserves the site where Lewis and Clark spent the winter of 1805-06, which the explorers declared their most miserable; the recreated fort is redolent of smoked meat, dried skins and wet wood.

Cannon Beach★

US-101, 22mi south of Astoria & 80mi west of Portland. ✆503-436-2623. www.cannonbeach.org.

This hamlet of 1,700 caters to artist-residents and well-heeled travelers; galleries and cafes are filled with visitors in summer. **Haystack Rock** rises 235ft beyond a broad expanse of sand; beachcombers stroll the beach and peer into rocky tidepools to find colorful sea life. **Ecola State Park★★** (2mi north of Cannon Beach; ✆503-436-2824; www.oregonstateparks.org) embraces 9mi of coastline topped by old-growth forest.

Cannon Beach

© Peter Wrenn/Michelin

Three Capes Scenic Drive★★

40mi from Tillamook to Pacific City, west of US-101; 63mi south of Astoria. From Tillamook, take Third St. west & follow signs. ☎503-842-7525. www.tillamookchamber.org

This delightful spin takes in dairy farms (Tillamook is famed for its cheese), bays of diving pelicans, coastal forest, seaside hamlets, dunes and vistas of the open Pacific from state parks at Capes Meares, Lookout and Kiwanda. Especially worthwhile is the drive out to Cape Meares, where an 1890 lighthouse perches on a high cliff.

Newport★

US-101, 136mi south of Astoria & 88mi west of Salem. ☎541-265-8801. www.newportchamber.org

This town of 10,000 has a tradition of agriculture, fishing and logging, along with tourism.

Across the (1936) Yaquina Bay Bridge, the **Oregon Coast Aquarium**★★ 🏊👤 (2820 SE Ferry Slip Rd., .25mi east of US-101; ☎541-867-3474; www.aquarium.org) displays 200 marine species and is rated one of the top aquariums in the country. Its exhibits focus on marine species native to Oregon waters; its massive Passages of the Deep exhibit features clear walk-through tubes, so visitors are surrounded by sharks, rays and rockfish.

About .25mi north, the **Hatfield Marine Science Center**★ 🏊👤 (2030 SE. Marine Science Dr.; ☎541-867-0100; www.hmsc.oregonstate.edu), headquarters for Oregon State University's marine-research program, offers oceanography exhibits.

Four miles up the coast, the **Yaquina Head Outstanding Natural Area**★★ (750 NW Lighthouse Dr., .5mi west of US-101; ☎541-574-3100; www.blm.gov/or) occupies an ancient finger of lava that protrudes into the Pacific. The adjacent **Yaquina Head Lighthouse**★ (1873) is, at 93ft, the tallest lighthouse in the state. Down the coast, 20mi toward Florence, **Sea Lion Caves**★★ (91560 Hwy. 101 N., Florence; www.sealioncaves.com) is the nation's largest sea cave, in which rare **Steller sea lions** congregate in large numbers. Visitors descend by elevator to a viewing platform inside the cave.

Yachats★

US-101, 159mi south of Astoria & 88mi west of Eugene. ☎541-547-3530. www.yachats.org.

The village of Yachats (YA-hots) is the gateway to the oft-photographed **Cape Perpetua Scenic Area**★★ (US-101, 3mi south; ☎541-547-3289; www.fs.usda.gov), which combines old-growth spruce forest and rocky shorelines.

Oregon Dunes National Recreation Area★★★

West side of US-101 for 48mi from Florence (186mi south of Astoria & 61mi west of Eugene) to Coos Bay. ⚠♿🅿 ☎541-271-3611. www.fs.fed.us/r6/siuslaw.

This strand of coastal dunes, some as high as 200ft, offers an ecosystem of sand, tree islands, wetlands, estuaries and beaches. From the **Oregon Dunes Visitor Center** (US-101, north end of Reedsport), rangers direct travelers to trails and overlooks. The **Siltcoos Recreation Area**★ (Siltcoos Beach Rd. off US-101, 7mi south of Florence) has a 1mi boardwalk that loops around a lagoon and the 1.2mi Waxmyrtle Trail, which ends at the ocean. Hikers on the **Umpqua Scenic Dunes Trail**★★ (US-101, 11mi south of Reedsport) enjoy a .5mi forest walk to the area's highest dunes for panoramas.

Coos Bay

US-101, 234mi south of Astoria & 109mi southwest of Eugene. ☎541-269-0215. www.oregonsbayarea.org

The largest natural harbor between Puget Sound and San Francisco Bay is a major shipping center for forest products. A waterfront boardwalk, shops and galleries attract tourists. From 150ft bluffs at **Cape Arago State Park**★ (Cape Arago Hwy., 14.5mi southwest of Coos Bay; ☎541-888-3778; www.oregonstateparks.org), one may sight whales, seals and sea lions.

Central and Eastern Oregon★

Oregon divides dramatically along the spine of the Cascades. West is a green land of farms, orchards and lush forest. East is higher, drier land, more open and less populated, with vast remote reaches of desert nicknamed the "Oregon Outback." Uplifted by tectonic forces, piled higher with deposits of lava and ash, the region was born of volcanic cataclysm and shaped by erosion.

- **Michelin Map:** 493 B, C, D 4, 5, 6. Pacific Standard Time.
- **Info:** Central Oregon: ℘541-389-8799; www.visitcentraloregon.com. Eastern: ℘541-523-9200; www.visiteasternoregon.com.
- **Location:** Bend is the commercial and visitor capital for eastern Oregon; most of the sights below can be visited using Bend as a base.

A BIT OF HISTORY

Long an Indian home, central and eastern Oregon were passed up by early pioneers en route to the fertile Willamette Valley. Later arrivals found this country excellent for ranching and mining. Natural resources still provide an economic foundation, but the region remained sparsely populated until tourism took root in outdoor recreation in the 1960s and 70s. With the growth in popularity of snow skiing, mountain biking, golf and whitewater rafting, the Bend area has attracted thousands of permanent residents seeking a low-key, recreational lifestyle.

SIGHTS

Bend★

US 20 & 97, 163mi southeast of Portland. ℘541-382-8048. www.visitbend.com.
This city of 79,000 hugs the banks of the Deschutes River. The Three Sisters mountains and other snow-capped peaks provide a stirring backdrop to the west. Early 20C buildings downtown hold restaurants and shops, as well as more than a dozen craft breweries; the Ale Trail map (www.visitbend.com) offers details and directions.
The **High Desert Museum★★** ▲▲ (US-97, 3.5mi south of Bend; ℘541-382-4754; www.highdesertmuseum.org) is an excellent small zoo and regional museum. The indoor exhibits are centered on the history of local Indian tribes and the settlement period. Outdoors, river otters frolic in a stream near a center for birds of prey. Bend has become known for its golf resorts.

Newberry National Volcanic Monument★★

Lava Lands Visitor Center, US-97 13mi south of Bend. ℘541-593-2421. www.fs.fed.us/r6.
Extending from the Deschutes River 24mi southeast to Paulina Peak, this 55,000-acre site embraces lava caves, archaeological sites and two sparkling crater lakes. The Newberry volcano last erupted 1,300 years ago; hot springs still bubble beneath lake surfaces.
The **Lava River Cave★** ▲▲ is a mile-long tube open to visitors (average temp. is 42 degrees; bring a coat), and the Lava Cast Foresta features a 1mi trail loop through molds made 6,000 years ago. The 18sq mi **Newberry Caldera★★** (Rte. 21, 25mi southeast of visitor center) is a crater that contains spring-fed Paulina and East Lakes. The only break in the steep 700-1,700ft walls of the caldera is at Paulina Falls, which drop 80ft off the outer face. Paiute Indians quarried black obsidian from the crater for tools. The 4.1mi drive to the top of 7,984ft. **Paulina Peak★★** affords panoramas that take in hundreds of miles of mountain, range and desert in every direction. Nearby, the **Big Obsidian Flow★** (1mi hike) is an entire mountainside composed of this volcanic glass.

Cascade Lakes Scenic Byway★★

West on Rte. 372, south on Forest Rd. 46, east on Forest Rd. 42. ℘541-382-8048. www.visitbend.com.

This 91mi drive passes tree-fringed lakes, rustic fishing camps and mountain trailheads. Alpine views★★★ are stunning from atop 9,065ft Mount Bachelor★ (℘541-382-2442; www. mtbachelor.com), considered one of the Northwest's best ski resorts. A chairlift operates to the summit year-round.

Hart Mountain National Antelope Refuge★★

Hart Mountain Road, 240mi southeast of Bend, 60mi northeast of Lakeview. ℘541-947-2731. www.fws.gov/sheldonhartmtn/Hart.

This remote conservation area is one of the best places to see free-roaming wild animals – deer, bighorn sheep, coyotes and pronghorn antelope, for whom the refuge was established in 1936. At nearby Steens Mountain★ (℘541-573-4400; www.blm.gov/or/districts/burns), the 52-mile Steens Mountain Backcountry Byway is the highest auto road in the Northwest. The drive affords access to the mountain's 9,700-ft summit and viewsaa of spectacular glacier-carved gorges and the Alvord Desert 6,000ft below the summit.

At the mountain's base, the Malheur National Wildlife Refuge★ (℘541-493-2612; www.fws.gov/malheur) is one of the most important stopping points for migratory birds in the West. Birdwatchers flock here to spy more than 320 species of birds such as the rare yellow-headed blackbird.

Warm Springs Indian Reservation

US-26, 108mi southeast of Portland & 55mi north of Bend.

The largest of eight native reservations in Oregon—1,000sqmi—was created in 1855 when the Wasco and Tenino bands signed a treaty ceding their rights to 10 million acres of ancient tribal lands. Its highlight is the Museum at Warm Springs★★ ▲▲ (US-26, Warm Springs; ℘541-553-3331; www.museumatwarmsprings.org), which contains Plateau Native American artifacts and a village exhibiting various dwelling types.

Smith Rock State Park★★

NE Crooked River Dr., Terrebonne, 23mi north of Bend. △ 🅿 ℘541-548-7501. www.oregonstateparks.org

Renowned for rock climbing, multicolored cliffs frame the Crooked River Canyon north of Redmond. Outcroppings of solidified magma tower 550ft above the river. Biking and hiking are also popular, allowing the opportunity to see golden eagles, prairie falcons, mule deer, river otter and beaver.

John Day Fossil Beds National Monument★★

Sheep Rock Unit, Rte. 19, 2mi north of US-26, 115mi northeast of Bend. Painted Hills Unit, Burnt Ranch Rd., 7mi north of US-26, 88mi northeast of Bend. Clarno Unit, Rte. 218, 101mi northeast of Bend. ℘541-987-2333. www.nps.gov/joda.

Preserving a small portion of the 10,000sq mi of fossil beds covering north–central Oregon, the monument holds fossilized plants and animals that lived here 50 million to 10 million years ago. The Sheep Rock Visitor Centera displays fossils of saber-tooth cats, rhinoceroses and entelodonts (bison-sized pigs). A few miles north, interpretive trails lead to Blue Basina, a natural amphitheater loaded with fossils.

National Historic Oregon Trail Interpretive Center★★

Rte. 86, 5mi east of I-84 at Baker City. ♿🅿 ℘541-523-1843. www.or.blm.gov/or/oregontrail.

Perched atop Flagstaff Hill, the museum overlooks ruts on a nearby hill made by covered wagons on the Oregon Trail. Hands-on exhibits, including historic journals, and full-scale dioramas render indelible images of the travails of early pioneers; 4mi of interpretive trails lend additional insights.

Hells Canyon National Recreation Area★★

Extending about 80mi on either side of the Oregon–Idaho border, 350mi east of Portland. Headquarters: Rte. 82, Enterprise. ✆541-426-5546. www.fs.fed.us/wallowa-whitman.

The Snake River carves the boundary between Oregon and Idaho through the deepest canyon in North America. Dark cliffs and grassy foothills tumble 6,000–8,000ft from the Wallowa Range and Seven Devils Mountains to the north-flowing river at its heart.

The canyon flooraa may be reached below Hells Canyon Dam (via Rte. 86, 91mi east of Baker City). From here, the only way to proceed is by boat or on foot. With whitewater rafting companies and jet boat operators offering river excursions, running the river has become almost routine, if still challenging. The best canyon overlooks are from Oregon's 208mi **Wallowa Mountains Loop★★** (from LaGrande, on I-84, drive northeast on Rte. 82 through Enterprise and Joseph to Rte. 350, south on Rte. 39, then west on Rte. 86 through Halfway to Baker City; ✆541-426-5546).

Nez Perce National Historical Park★

The park comprises 38 sites in four states, including the 1877 battlefields and locations important to tribal legend. The Nez Perce tribe's story is documented at the main visitor center and museum (US-95, Spalding, Idaho, 14mi east of Lewiston; ✆208-843-7001; www.nps.gov/nepe), along with the **Spalding-Allen Collection★★** of artifacts and hide clothing decorated with porcupine quills and dentalia shells, dating from 1836.

Pendleton

US-395 & Rte. 11 at I-84, 209mi east of Portland. ✆541-276-7411. www.pendletonchamber.com.

Tucked along the Umatilla River, this city is renowned for its wool blankets; tours of historic **Pendleton Woolen Mills★** (1307 SE Court Pl.; ✆541-276-6911) look at the production process.

The **Round-Up Hall of Fame★** (Round-up Grounds, I-84 Exit 207; ✆541-276-2553; www.pendletonroundup.com) commemorates the town's annual event and its participants; a highlight is the nighttime pageant, which portrays early life in a wild West town.

Tamastslikt Cultural Institute★

Rte. 331, Mission, 7mi east of Pendleton. ⚠✗⚹🅿 ✆541-966-9748. www.tamastslikt.org.

On the Umatilla Indian Reservation, this museum tells the story of the Cayuse, Umatilla and Walla Wallas. Exhibits and the Living Culture Village detail their salmon-based lifestyle.

John Day Fossil Beds National Monument

Alaska

Alaska

Alaska is more than twice the size of Texas, the next largest US state, and is bigger than all but 16 of the world's nations. It claims the 16 highest peaks in the US, 100,000 glaciers, 3 million lakes, 3,000 rivers, 3.3 million acres of state parks and 47,300 miles of coastline. A huge jagged knob at the northwestern corner of North America, "The Great Land" spans 2,350mi from the border of Canada to the western tip of the Aleutian Islands in the Pacific Ocean. Separated from Siberia by a mere 51mi of water, Alaska lies 500mi northwest of the nearest US mainland state, Washington. Only 731,000 people live in this vast (570,640sq mi) state, ranking it last in population density—though strong employment has brought it many new residents in recent years.

Highlights

1 "Meeting" a bald eagle at **Alaska Raptor Center** (p493)
2 Sensational vistas from the **Alyeska Tram** (p496)
3 Watching sea otters at **Alaska Sealife Center** (p498)
4 Spectacular flightseeing at **Gates of the Arctic** (p502)

Frozen Wilderness of Riches

Sometime between 15,000 and 30,000 years ago, nomadic bands crossed an exposed land bridge from Asia to America; Alaska thus became a major gateway to this new world.

Native groups were well established by the time Europeans arrived in the 18C. Driven by high prices for sea otter furs, the Russians developed a trade empire that stretched to California. As hunting hastened the collapse of the otter population, the Russians withdrew, selling the vast Alaska territory to the US in 1867 for $7.2 million.

Though many considered Alaska a frozen wasteland, the glitter of gold swelled settlement, with rushes to Juneau (1880), Skagway and the Klondike (1897-98), Nome (1899) and Fairbanks (1902). A much larger buildup occurred during World War II with construction of the Alaska Highway, linking Canada and the lower 48 to Fairbanks through 1,500mi of wilderness.

Statehood in 1959 brought recognition of the state's riches and strategic importance, as well as a need to grapple with a complex web of Native claims, developers' and conservationists' interests crystallized by construction of the $8 billion Trans-Alaska oil pipeline in 1977. More than one-quarter of Alaska's land is protected as park, refuge and wilderness, from coastal mountains and fjords to tundra and bear-haunted forests. Management of this natural wealth provokes nearly constant ongoing controversy.

ADDRESSES

Numerous lodges are located in and around national parks and in gateway cities. For more information, contact **Alaska Tour and Travel** (☏907-245-0200; www.alaskatravel.com). For **bed-and-breakfast reservations**: Alaska Private Lodgings (☏907-235-2148; www.alaskabandb.com). For a list of public **campgrounds** and maps, contact the Alaska Travel Industry Association.

Motels along highways usually have a cafe, gasoline and repair facilities. Call for availability, especially Oct–mid May. Sights and services are listed in *The Alaska Milepost*, available in bookstores or directly from *The Milepost* (☏907-272-6070; www.milepost.com).

In a state with few roads, spectacular landscapes, wildlife and outdoor recreation, remote wilderness lodges are a key part of the Alaska travel experience. Reached by floatplane or boat, these outposts vary from luxurious lodges with deluxe amenities to rustic cabins on distant shores. Wanting to preserve their fabulous surroundings, and operate as efficiently as possible, many are pioneers in self-sufficiency and sustainability. **Alaska Wildland Adventures**, for instance, recently installed a small hydro plant at its Kenai

GETTING THERE

Main airports in Alaska are **Anchorage International Airport (ANC)** (☎907-266-2526; www.anchorageairport.com), **Fairbanks International Airport (FAI)** (☎907-474-2500; www.dot.state.ak.us/faiiap) and **Juneau International Airport (JNU)** (☎907-789-7821; www.juneau.org/airport). **Alaska Airlines** (☎800-252-7522; www.alaskaair.com) offers the most flights to and within Alaska; JetBlue, Delta and United also serve Anchorage.

In-state airlines include **ERA Aviation** (☎907-266-8394 or 800-866-8394; www.flyera.com) and **Peninsula Airways** (☎907-771-2640 or 800-448-4226; www.penair.com).

Alaska Railroad Corp (☎907-265-2494 or 800-544-0552; www.alaskarailroad.com) links Seward, Anchorage, Denali National Park and Fairbanks; journeys on the train are memorably scenic odysseys.

There is a bus service between Anchorage, Fairbanks and Whitehorse, in Canada's Yukon Territory, via **Alaska Direct Bus Line** (☎907-277-6652 or 800-770-6652; www.alaskadirectbusline.com). Scheduled **ferry** service from Bellingham WA to Juneau and other ports in Alaska is provided by the **Alaska Marine Highway System** (see page 498). Reservations are required. For **cruise** companies, consult the Alaska Travel Industry Association (opposite).

SIGHTSEEING

Alaska Travel Industry Association (☎907-929-2200; www.travelalaska.com).

Adventure Tourism: Alaska Travel Adventures (☎907-789-0052; www.alaskaadventures.com); Alaska Wildland Adventures (☎907-783-2928; www.alaskawildland.com).

Biking: Alaskan Bicycle Adventures (☎907-245-2175; www.alaskabike.com).

Escorted tours: Gray Line (☎888-452-1737; www.graylinealaska.com).

Multi-sport excursions: REI Adventures (☎253-437-1100; www.rei.com/travel).

For more information on adventure travel, contact the **Alaska Wilderness Recreation & Tourism Association** (☎907-258-3171; www.awrta.org) or the Alaska Public Lands Information Center (☎907-271-2737; www.alaskacenters.gov).

CLIMATE

Though outsiders often suspect Alaska is a perpetually cold land of snow and rain, pleasant temperatures are the norm May–Sept (except in the Arctic) and the weather can become steamy in the interior in summer. The record high is 100°F, at Fort Yukon. Daytime highs in July average 73°F in Fairbanks, 65°F in Anchorage and 64°F in Juneau. However, nights are always cool, and rain showers are possible year-round. And even if you don't need a jacket for warmth, insects (yes, the tales are true) make it a good idea.

Backcountry Lodge to minimize use of diesel power (www.alaskawildland.com). Among hundreds of remote outfitters and lodges, more than 300 belong to **Alaska Wilderness Recreation & Tourism Association** (☎907-258-3171; www.awrta.org), which emphasizes sustainable, responsible tourism and local economic benefit. An Alaska wilderness retreat truly allows visitors to experience the marvels that keep Alaskans proud to live where they do. For EAT suggestions, see top of p502.

🏨 STAY

$$$$$ Great Alaska Adventure Lodge – 33881 Sterling Hwy., Sterling. ☎907-262-4515. www.greatalaska.com. 22 rooms. Open mid Apr–mid Sept. The front door of this timber lodge swings open into Kenai National Wildlife Refuge. Package visits may include fishing, canoeing, kayaking, hiking, wilderness overnights and bear viewing.

$$$$ Alaska's Capital Inn –113 W Fifth St. , Juneau. ☎907-588-6507. www.

alaskacapitalinn.com. 7 rooms. Poised atop the hill overlooking downtown Juneau, this B&B sits within a 1906 Edwardian style house. Both the public areas and guest rooms are furnished with period appointments like potbelly stoves, pedestal beds and handmade quilts. A lavish hot breakfast of say, sourdough pancakes, is included in the rate.

$$$$ Hotel Captain Cook – 939 W. 5th Ave., Anchorage. ☎907-276-6000. www.captaincook.com. 547 rooms. With spectacular views of Cook Inlet and the Chugach Mountains, this high-rise was Alaska's first luxury inn. **The Crow's Nest** (**$$$**), on the 20th floor, serves fresh seafood.

$$$ Glacier Bay Country Inn – 35 Tong Rd., Gustavus. ☎907-697-2288. www.glacierbayalaska.com. 5 rooms, 5 cabins (per person, meals inclusive). Open mid-May–mid-Sept. Guests are rewarded by the solitude of this rambling inn, isolated in meadows of wildflowers. Guests spend days fly fishing and whale-watching.

$$$ Seward Windsong Lodge – Mile 0.5 Exit Glacier Rd., Seward. ☎907-224-7116. Closed in winter. www.sewardwindsong.com. 180 rooms. Located near the Exit Glacier just outside Seward, this large lodge is a center for activities such as hikes to the glacier and scenic cruises; the lodge's restaurant, Resurrection Roadhouse, is a leading practitioner of Alaskan Regional cuisine.

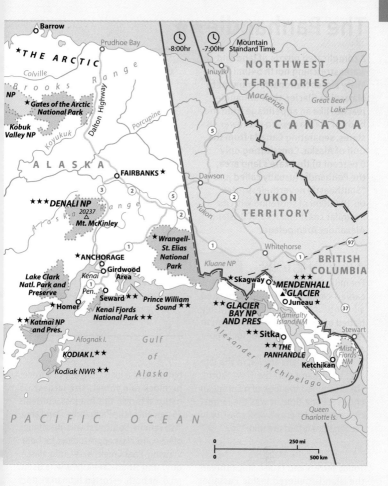

$$$ Kantishna Roadhouse – Kantishna, Denali National Park. *☎*907-374-3041. www.kantishnaroadhouse.com. 32 rooms and cabins. Closed winter. Poised along Moose Creek at the end of the Denali Park Road, this accommodation offers cozy lodging and expert guidance on park adventures; packages include all meals and transportation by bus to the lodge.

$$$ River's Edge Resort – 167 S. Franklin St., Fairbanks. *☎*907-474-0286. www.riversedge.net. 86 cottages, 8 suites. Open May–Sept. Set on the banks of the Chena River, River's Edge offers full-service hotel suites and cottages, each with private patios, in a pastoral setting. Guests can canoe or fish from the riverbank.

$$ The Oscar Gill House – 1344 W. 10th Ave., Anchorage. *☎*907-279-1344. www. oscargill.com. 3 rooms. This 1913 pioneer home was on the demolition block when Mark and Susan Lutz bought it for $1 in 1993 and moved it to a lot facing the Delaney Park Strip. Two of the three rooms share a bathroom. A family-style breakfast is included in the rate.

$ Talkeetna Roadhouse – N. Main & C St., Talkeetna. *☎*907-733-1351. www. talkeetnaroadhouse.com. 7 rooms, one cabin. With a crackling fire in the woodstove, wood-frame angles not quite 90 degrees, cozy bunkbeds, private rooms and cottages, this 1914 lodge is a Denali-area institution. The bakery draws fans from as far as Anchorage for its soups and breads.

The Panhandle★★

A complicated puzzle of land and water stretching north 540mi from Misty Fiords National Monument to Malaspina Glacier, the Panhandle reaches like an appendage from the body of Alaska toward the lower 48 states, separating Canada from the Gulf of Alaska. Constituting only 6 percent of the state's land area, the Panhandle (usually called just "Southeast") nevertheless totes up 10,000mi of shoreline with its irregular coast and its 1,000-island Alexander Archipelago.

- **Michelin Map:** 930 Inset. Alaska Standard Time.
- **Info:** www.alaskainfo.org.
- **Location:** Juneau, capital of Alaska, is two-thirds of the way up the nearly 600-mile stretch of fjords, islands and mountains that compose the Panhandle. The only roads in the area reach Skagway and Haines from Canada's Yukon.
- **Don't Miss:** Glacier Bay; Sitka.
- **Timing:** Cruise-line tours typically stop a full day in Juneau, Ketchikan, Skagway and Sitka. Onshore activities arranged through local visitor bureaus may be more affordable.

A BIT OF HISTORY

For millennia Tlingit (*KLINK-it*) Indians carved cedar canoes and harvested a bountiful living from the sea. They traded otter furs and dried salmon to Athabascans of the Interior for copper and caribou skins.

When the Russians arrived in the late 18C, their capital in the New World, Sitka, acquired the look of a European enclave. For a time, it was the largest city on North America's west coast, until the Russians left in the mid-19C.

THE REGION TODAY

Today ferries and cruise ships thread the island-sheltered Inside Passage; an Alaska cruise is a dream vacation for millions. While fishing is still the main industry in most Panhandle areas, tourism and timber production also bolster the economy. Nearly half the old-growth trees of the Tongass National Forest had been clear-cut before restrictions came to its rescue in the 1990s. The island-strewn landscape is backed by coastal mountains that crest at more than 18,000ft, the highest maritime range in the world. Though almost all are receding, glaciers slip from the heights to deep fjords where seals and sea lions bask and seabirds nest on granite islands.

The region receives some of the heaviest rainfall in North America, which, coupled with a sea-tempered climate, has created a lush covering of spruce-hemlock rain forest. The largest US national forest, the Tongass, contains 75 percent of the Panhandle's land area. Two remote Southeast wildlife venues offer world-class opportunities for **bear-viewing**: Pack Creek (www.adfg.alaska.gov) and Anan Creek (www.fs.usda.gov). At both, escorted human visitors can see bears harvesting salmon, often only a few yards away. Guided tours to Pack Creek depart from Juneau; to Anan, from Wrangell and Ketchikan; consult visitor information in either town to arrange tours.

SIGHTS
Ketchikan

285mi south of Juneau. ℘907-225-6166. www.visit-ketchikan.com.
The southernmost town in Alaska (with 8,000 residents) and one of the wettest, Ketchikan bills itself the salmon capital of the world and welcomes dozens of cruise liners each summer. Its somewhat tawdry **Creek Street Historic District** preserves a boardwalk that, until 1954, was a red-light district.

Several attractions honor the Tlingit, Haida and Tsimshian cultures. The **Totem Heritage Center★★** (601 Deermount St.; ℘907-225-5900; www.city.ketchikan.ak.us) displays nearly three dozen 19C totem poles salvaged from abandoned villages. **Saxman Native Village★** (S. Stedman St.; ℘907-225-4846; www.capefoxtours.com) offers tours that cover the tribal longhouse, schoolhouse, carver's shed and a park punctuated with 28 totem poles. Visitors may watch master carvers at work and view native dance performances at the longhouse. The fairly new (2008) **Potlatch Totem Park★**, 10mi north of Ketchikan (9809 Totem Bight Rd.; ℘907-225-4445; www.potlatchpark.com) features the work of on-site carver Brita Alander, a rising star among Native artists.

Southeast Alaska Discovery Center

50 Main St., Ketchikan. ℘907-228-6220. www.alaskacenters.gov.
This branch of Alaska's Public Lands Information Centers, managed by Tongass National Forest, includes displays on Southeast's unique landscape. It's also the information center for Misty Fiords National Monument, a 3,570sq mi preserve of lushly forested mountains, glacial fjords flanked by 3,000ft granite cliffs, and mist-enshrouded islands rich in wildlife. This park holds hidden waterfalls, spouting whales and spruce-top eagle aeries for visitors who boat its shores and hike its dense forests. (🚗*Boat or plane access only to monument*).

Sitka★★

136mi southwest of Juneau. ℘907-747-5940. www.sitka.org.
This historic town lies on the west side of Baranof Island, a balmy setting with generally mild weather. Tlingit life was uninterrupted for millennia until Russian traders in 1799 established a fortress and solicited Native help in fur trapping. But in 1802 Tlingits attacked the redoubt and killed nearly all the Russians. The Russians returned two years later, outfought the Tlingits and began displacing Native clan houses with fort-like dwellings.

Upon the sale of Alaska to the US in 1867, Sitka became the new territorial capital. Juneau claimed that office in 1906. **St. Michael's Cathedral★★** (Lincoln St. & Cathedral Way.; ℘907-747-8120), symbolizes Sitka's Russian heritage; it was rebuilt in 1976 on the site of the original 19C church, destroyed by fire. Parishioners saved from the flames a remarkable collection of **gold icons★★**, on display in the new church. Now with a population of 9,000, Sitka holds all the charms of an old seaside village. The **New Archangel Dancers**, an all-female troupe, entertain visitors while preserving the town's Russian heritage (℘907-747-5516; www.newarchangeldancers.com).

Sitka National Historical Park★★★

106 Metlakatla St.; Bishop's House at Monastery & Lincoln Sts. ℘907-747-0110. www.nps.gov/sitk.
This 107-acre park has two parcels. Exhibits at the visitor center, at the mouth of the Indian River, examine the cultural clash created by the arrival of Europeans. The adjacent **Fort Site** recalls the 1804 Battle of Sitka.
A 1mi loop trail through a spruce forest passes the clearing where a Tlingit fort stood. Along the trail, nestled in the trees, is one of the finest collections of **totem poles★★★** in the US. The long, ocher **Russian Bishop's House★★** (1843), near downtown, was sturdily built by Finnish shipwrights.

Sheldon Jackson Museum★

104 College Dr. ℘907-747-8981. www.museums.alaska.gov.
The oldest museum in Alaska anchors the campus of Sheldon Jackson College. Bentwood baskets, ivory tools, painted drums and other artfully executed pieces represent the major Native groups—Southeast and Athabascan Indians, Aleuts and Native Alaskans.

Alaska Raptor Center★★

1000 Raptor Way (half mile east of Sitka). ℘907-747-8662. www.alaskaraptor.org. This rehabilitation/research facility is devoted to birds of prey such as bald eagles. Visitors learn about and "meet" them up close.

Juneau★

650mi southeast of Anchorage. ℘907-586-2201 or 888-581-2201. www.traveljuneau.com.

Tucked along a slim strip of land between Gastineau Channel and high mountains, the capital of 33,000 is accessible only by air or sea. Juneau somewhat resembles a quaint European city, its narrow streets curving up from the waterfront. The discovery of gold in 1880 led to the establishment of a town site that became the territorial capital in 1906. Today it is also a cruise center, with nearly 1 million passengers arriving each summer.

Near the cruise-ship terminal, the **Mt. Roberts Tramway★★** (490 S. Franklin St.; ℘907-463-3412; www.mountrobertstramway.com) ascends 1,880 vertical feet to views of town and harbor. A short stroll from People's Wharf, through the heart of the historic district on Franklin and Main Streets, brings visitors to the **Alaska State Capitol** (4th & Main Sts.; ℘907-465-2479), ornamented with marble quarried on Prince of Wales Island.

Alaska State Museum★★

395 Whittier St. ℘907-465-2901. www.museums.alaska.gov.

This extensive facility holds more than 23,000 artifacts and works of art, encompassing the state's Native cultures, and its post-contact history. *The museum is building an entirely new facility expected to open in 2016 and will be closed until then.*

Mendenhall Glacier★★★

Mendenhall Loop Rd., 13mi northwest of downtown Juneau via Egan Dr. ℘907-789-0097, www.fs.fed.us/r10/tongass.

An easily accessible wonder, this 1.5mi-wide glacier arcs 11mi from the Juneau Icefield down to Mendenhall Lake. A short trail leads to the water's edge, while the 3.5mi **East Glacier Loop** brings hikers close to a huge waterfall. The river of ice is retreating about 200ft per year.

Glacier Bay National Park★★

Gustavus, 65mi west of Juneau. ℘907-697-2230. www.nps.gov/glba.

Encompassing 4,297sq mi, Glacier Bay showcases views of ice-clad mountains,

a rich variety of marine and land animals, and miles of wilderness. The original glaciers, however, have retreated more than 60mi in two centuries, and are still retreating. UNESCO declared this natural kingdom a World Heritage Site in 1992; today it provides implacable testimony of climate change.

When explorer George Vancouver sailed past in 1794, he saw only an icy shoreline, with barely an indentation to suggest a retreating glacier. The first person to seriously study the area and bring it to attention, naturalist John Muir traveled here in 1879. Inside Passage cruise ships first came calling in the 1970s.

Services are provided at the Bartlett Cove park headquarters, and in the nearby community of Gustavus (www.gustavusak.com).

Unforgettable day-long cruises★★ depart Bartlett Cove each morning. In the lower bay, naturalists point out sea otters at play; humpback whales breaching, their tails fanning as they dive; and pods of orcas rolling like black and white waves. Tours pause at Marble Island★★ where thousands of kittiwakes, puffins, cormorants, murres and other birds noisily commune on the rocks, and sea lions snort and nose each other for better places in the sun. At the head of the bay, spectacular glaciers rear up 200ft; sightseers may witness tremendous splashes as chunks of ice calve into the water.

Skagway★

80mi north of Juneau. ☏907-983-2854. www.skagway.com.

Positioned at the northern end of the Inside Passage, Skagway was the rollicking frontier town through which gold seekers passed on their arduous way up the 33mi **Chilkoot Trail** to the Yukon goldfields in 1897-98. To prevent their perishing in the wilderness, prospectors were required to carry one ton of supplies over the pass, which meant 40 back-breaking ascents.

Klondike Gold Rush National Historical Park★ (2nd Ave. & Broadway; ☏907-983-9200; www.nps.gov/klgo) preserves the Chilkoot Trail (now a recreational byway) and the historic district, with its false-fronted buildings and wooden sidewalks. Brothels and gambling dens are now shops and eateries. Next to the visitor center, the park **museum★** holds period artifacts, from gold pans to journals.

The narrow-gauge, 41mi **White Pass & Yukon Route Railway★★** (2nd Ave. & Spring St.; ☏800-343-7373; www.wpyr.com) takes tourists through scenery traversed by prospectors.

Mendenhall Glacier
Used by permission, U.S. Forest Service

Anchorage★

Sprawled over the one piece of flat ground between Cook Inlet and the sharp peaks of the Chugach Range, Alaska's largest city holds nearly half the state's population. As the state's center of commerce and culture, the city welcomes both business travelers and tourists. Anchorage residents are devoted to recreation, and take advantage of one of the most extensive, off-street trail networks in the US.

▶ **Population:** 295,000.
◔ **Michelin Map:** 930 Inset. Alaska Standard Time.
▮ **Info:** ℘907-257-2363; www.anchorage.net.

A BIT OF HISTORY

Starting as a tent city of pioneers and rail workers in 1914, Anchorage grew into a frontier city. Fort Richardson and Elmendorf Air Force Base helped push population over 30,000 by 1950. Cold War defense-system headquarters added to the city's growth. The earthquake of 1964 rocked Anchorage to its foundations. Rebuilding invigorated the city with new life, as did oil development in Prudhoe Bay. Anchorage's airport is an international hub for commercial air shipping.

SIGHTS

▲▲ Anchorage Museum★★★

121 W. 7th St. ℘907-929-9200. www.anchoragemuseum.org.
Covering most of a city block, this newly expanded (2010) repository of history, ethnography, science and art presents an in-depth look at Alaskan culture. The first-floor art collection highlights canvases★ by Sydney Laurence (1865-1940), Alaska's most famous painter. The vast Alaska Gallery displays historical objects of Indian, Aleut and Native Alaskan lifestyles, proceeding into the era of European contact. A highlight is the life-size diorama of an 18C Aleut house of whalebone, grass and sod. The new **Smithsonian Arctic Studies Center gallery**★★★ includes 600 rare objects such as a 19C Tlingit war helmet and Athabascan tunic, with expansive coverage of all Alaska (and eastern Siberian) Native cultures.

Alaska Native Heritage Center★★★

8800 Heritage Center Dr. ℘907-330-8000. www.alaskanative.net.
A free shuttle brings visitors to the center from downtown locations, mid-May to Labor Day. Occupying a pastoral 26-acre site flanking a picturesque small lake, with cottonwoods and birches tossing in the breeze, this extensive facility allows visitors to learn about Alaska's 11 major indigenous cultural groups, ranging from the well-known such as Inuit to the little-known Alutiq.

EXCURSION
Girdwood Area

◗ 37mi southeast of Anchorage via Seward Hwy. (Rte. 1).
The Seward Highway takes motorists from Anchorage along **Turnagain Arm**, whose 38ft bore tide in spring is the second-greatest in North America.. The **Alyeska Resort Aerial Tram**★★ (Alyeska Hwy., 3mi east of Girdwood; ℘907-754-2111, www.alyeskaresort.com) whisks visitors 2,300ft to the top of one of North America's premier ski mountains for **views**★★ of Turnagain Arm and ice-bitten peaks. Nearby **Crow Creek Mine** ▲▲ (Crow Creek Rd., 2mi east of Girdwood; ℘907-229-3105; www.crowcreekmine.com) has weathered buildings from the gold-rush era. The **Visitor Center** at **Portage Glacier**★ (5.5mi east of Seward Hwy., Mile 1, Portage Glacier Rd.; ℘907-783-2326; www.fs.fed.us/r10/chugach) offers a short course on glacial geology; on 1hr **boat tours**, visitors may see Portage Glacier calve. The **Alaska Wildlife Conservation Center**★ offers a chance to see bears, moose, caribou, musk oxen and more up close (Mile 79, Seward Hwy.; ℘907-783-2025; www.alaskawildlife.org).

South-Central Alaska ★★

South of the Alaska Range, the land gentles into fertile valleys and rolling forests, then suddenly buckles into another cordillera of glacier-capped peaks along the Gulf of Alaska. Land, sea and sky meet in grand proportion in this diverse region where goats clamber on steep cliffs in sight of spouting whales, and fishing villages reap the bounty of tens of millions of spawning salmon.

⌚ **Michelin Map:** 930 Inset. Alaska Standard Time.

🛈 **Info:** ✆907-262-5229; www.kenaipeninsula.org.

▶ **Location:** Most of the area is reached through Rte. 1, the Seward Highway, south out of Anchorage, roughly a 4hr drive to Homer; but Valdez, at the northern tip of Prince William Sound, is 6hr in the other direction on Rte 1.

👁 **Don't Miss:** Homer, a haven for artists and free spirits.

A BIT OF HISTORY

The ice-free ports of Valdez (*val-DEEZ*), Cordova, Seward, Homer and Kenai were staging points for exploitation of copper, coal and gold. In the early 20C, the railroad linked Seward with Anchorage, but not until the 1950s did a highway traverse the 225mi from Anchorage to Homer. On the **Kenai Peninsula**, south of Anchorage, knife-ridged mountains rise directly from the sea. Clouds accumulate in the moist sea air, saturating the coastline in summer with light but frequent rains.

The region is recovering from the Exxon Valdez oil spill of 1989, which affected more than 1,500mi of shoreline from Prince William Sound to Kodiak Island.

SIGHTS

Seward ★★

Seward Hwy. (Rte. 9), 130mi south of Anchorage. ✆907-224-8051. www.sewardchamber.org.

A spirited town of bright stucco-and-clapboard bungalows and fewer than 3,000 citizens, Seward rests at the head of mountain-rimmed **Resurrection Bay★**. Starting in 1902 as the southern terminus of the Alaska Railroad, Seward became known as the "Gateway to Alaska." Today visitors can board the train for a 4hr trip to Anchorage (www.alaskarailroad.com), shop and eat at the **Small Boat Harbor**, watch fishermen returning with their catches, and take wildlife cruises into the bay.

Dogsled Racing

A team of huskies mushing across a frozen landscape is a quintessential Alaska image. More than 4,000 years ago, nomadic Natives enlisted malamutes to help pull loads and reach hunting and fishing grounds. Their stamina and sense of direction made them invaluable to later explorers. Jack London's 1903 classic, *The Call of the Wild*, described gold seekers using dogs to haul equipment and provisions. In 1967, during Alaska's centennial celebration, a race was held to commemorate the Iditarod Trail, a route used in 1925 to relay diphtheria serum to Nome. Today, Anchorage is the March starting point for the 1,049mi **Iditarod**. The route spans tundra, frozen rivers and icy mountain ranges, with winners typically reaching Nome in just over nine days. Improved equipment, trail conditions, breeding and training have whittled the course time from 20 days in 1973. Many other mushing races, from shorter sprints in Anchorage and Fairbanks to little-known races in remote locales, capture dogsled-fanciers' interest. Many consider the 1,000mi Fairbanks-to-Whitehorse Yukon Quest in February a tougher challenge than the Iditarod.

🐾 Alaska SeaLife Center★★★

301 Railway Ave. ℘907-224-6300 or 7908. www.alaskasealife.org.

This modern research, rehabilitation and education facility was funded as a result of a legal settlement from the *Exxon Valdez* spill, and offers an even-handed explication of the continuing effects of the disaster.

Viewing platforms allow visitors to gaze into pools for sea lions, seals and sea otters; marine birds have a rock pool and cliffs. Touch tanks hold vividly colored sea stars and evanescent nudibranchs. Various marine life encounters, such as a Puffin Encounter, and an Octopus Encounter, are scheduled seasonally.

Kenai Fjords National Park★★

Visitor center at Small Boat Harbor on 4th Ave., Seward. ℘907-422-0500. www.nps.gov/kefj.

Covering 1,045sq mi of coastal fjords and glacier-clad mountains on the southeastern side of the Kenai Peninsula, this park preserves a wilderness where thousands of marine mammals and seabirds find sanctuary. More than 30ft of snow a year replenish the 300sq mi Harding Icefield, which feeds 30 glaciers—most receding.

Boat tours vary from 2hr 30min cruises around Resurrection Bay to 9hr voyages down the coastline to Harris Bay and Northwestern Glacier. Wildlife sightings range from murres and horned puffins to sea otters and humpback whales.

On the north side of the park, the **Exit Glacier★★** area (Exit Glacier Rd., 9mi west of Seward Hwy.; first 4mi paved) has a network of trails to bring visitors close to the 3mi-long river of ice. The **Glacier Access Trail** (*1mi*) is an easy stroll to glacial viewpoints.

The more strenuous **Harding Icefield Trail★** (*3.5mi one-way*) ascends 3,000ft to spectacular views of the vast icefield. From this frozen sea jut jagged nunataks, an Native Alaskan word meaning "lonely peaks."

Alaska by Sea

Voyaging by water can be a memorable part of an Alaskan vacation, and many travelers consider an Alaska cruise a lifetime experience. Alaska commercial cruises depart from Seattle or Vancouver, Canada, and take up to 10 days to travel the Inside Passage through British Columbia to Southeast. Ketchikan, Sitka, Juneau and Glacier Bay are the major stops; some ships visit Yakutat Bay and the spectacular Hubbard Glacier. Though most major lines have Alaska itineraries, the two long-time leaders are **Holland America** (www.hollandamerica.com) and **Princess** (www.princess.com), which operate big ships in the 2,000-passenger range. More information on big-ship cruising can be found at www.akcruise.org. A delightful alternative is offered on the small-ship voyages of **Un-Cruise** (www.un-cruise.com) and **Alaskan Dream** (www.alaskandreamcruises.com), both of which emphasize thoughtful shore excursions, wildlife watching, cultural exploration and education about the region's natural environment.

The **Alaska Marine Highway System** (℘907-465-3941 or 800-642-0066; www.alaska.gov/ferry) is used by commuters and sightseers alike. The ferry system links 17 towns in the Panhandle; south-central Alaska and the Aleutian Islands; and Bellingham, Washington, with major stops along the Inside Passage, making for a less expensive travel option than luxury cruises or commercial airlines. Naturalists often are on board in the summer to explain marine mammal and bird life. Comfortable overnight cabins may be available. Those planning to book a cabin, or to transport a car in summer, should reserve many months ahead.

Homer★

Sterling Hwy. (Rte. 1), 225mi southwest of Anchorage. ℘907-235-7740. www.homeralaska.org.

Guarding the entrance to Kachemak Bay in the lower Kenai Peninsula, the individualistic town of Homer is framed by Cook Inlet and the jagged graph of the Kenai Mountains. For decades it has attracted artists, retirees, fishermen and more recently, tourists; the permanent population is 5,000. The 4.5mi **Homer Spit** harbors an extensive commercial and recreational fishing industry.

Pratt Museum★

3779 Bartlett St. ℘907-235-8635. www.prattmuseum.org.

A first-rate collection of art and natural history, the Pratt offers a gut-wrenching exhibit on the Valdez spill, an interesting display about the ongoing spruce-beetle epidemic, and a hands-on video monitor for viewing nesting birds on nearby Gull Island via remote-control camera.

Halibut Cove★★

Access by Danny J ferry (4hr 30min tours) from the Homer Spit Marina. ℘907-226-2424. www.halibut-cove-alaska.com.

A 32-person ferry takes locals and tourists to this tranquil curve of beach backed by a lagoon dotted with houses on stilts. Stroll the boardwalks, visit the handful of galleries and one of the only floating post offices in the country, and absorb the beauty of a watery paradise. Guided hiking, fishing trips and glacier kayaking can be arranged from several of the lodges.

Prince William Sound★★

℘907-835-4636. www.valdezalaska.org.
Basking in the protective embrace of the Chugach Mountains on the north and the Kenai Peninsula on the west, Prince William Sound offers a quiet 15,000sq mi seascape for kayaking, cruising and studying marine wildlife. One road links the Sound with the Interior—the scenic Richardson Highway to **Valdez**, a port at the end of the Trans-Alaska Pipeline serving the giant oil tankers.

Wrangell-St. Elias National Park★

Headquarters at Mile 105.5 Old Richardson Hwy. (Rte. 4), Copper Center, 10mi south of Glenallen. ℘907-822-5234. www.nps.gov/wrst.

A magnificent wilderness of glaciers, streams and towering snow-crowned peaks, the park's 20,600sq mi make it the largest US national park, but one of the most inaccessible. Bigger than Switzerland, the park tops out at 18,008ft **Mount St. Elias**, second-highest mountain in the US. Along with Glacier Bay National Park, and Canada's Kluane/Tatshenshini complex, it is part of the largest international UNESCO World Heritage Site complex, and includes North America's largest icefield.

EXCURSIONS
Kodiak Island★★

❍ 250mi southwest of Anchorage; multiple daily flights from Anchorage. ℘907-486-4782. www.kodiak.org.

Alaska's scenic "Emerald Isle" is a vast wilderness most of whose 3,588 square miles encompass the **Kodiak National Wildlife Refuge★★** (www.fws.gov/refuge/kodiak), home of 3,000 Kodiak brown bears, the largest subspecies of brown bear and largest land-based carnivore on earth.

The **Russian Orthodox Holy Resurrection Cathedral** bears witness to the town's long history: Kodiak was briefly the capital of Russian America from 1792 until Sitka supplanted it in 1808. The 6,500 residents at the island's north end have set a goal of becoming one of the most sustainable communities in the country; six huge wind turbines on a ridge above town supply a large portion of Kodiak's power. Floatplane operators offer tours into bear country, and drives around the modest road network yield beautiful vistas in every direction.

Katmai National Park★★

❍ Field headquarters, King Salmon; 290mi southwest of Anchorage. ℘907-246-3305. www.nps.gov/katm.

Katmai embraces 6,250sq mi at the head of the Alaska Peninsula. Volcanic eruptions in 1912 poured molten rock into a once-green valley, after which steam and gases emitted from thousands of vents. Four years later, a National Geographic Society team saw these fumaroles spewing smoke and steam and named the 40sq-mi area the **Valley of Ten Thousand Smokes★**. The smokes have trailed off, yet wisps are sometimes visible.

Katmai is known for its Alaskan brown bears, which may exceed 1,400 pounds. Viewing platforms at **Brooks Camp** and **McNeil River State Game Sanctuary★** enable visitors to observe bears up close. Human visitation at McNeil is limited by lottery (www.adfg.state.ak.us).

Interior and the Arctic★

A great rolling plateau sandwiched between the Alaska and Brooks Ranges, the Interior has long been a haven for wildlife. Much in the landscape has remained the same for millennia. The taiga— a forest of spruce, alder and willow—supports a chain of mammalian life from bear and moose down to snowshoe hare and lynx. Birds in their millions migrate through, as they have for thousands of years, wings drumming, responding to the call of the north— for them, the protein-rich insects that so plague human visitors.

A BIT OF HISTORY

The Interior surged in population during the 1890s gold rush as prospectors made their way to Canada's Klondike along the Yukon River. The grittiest stayed, turning log-cabin settlements into a few sparse towns. One of them, Fairbanks, grew into a small city that is now home to a main branch of the University of Alaska.

North of the Interior sprawls the vast and forbidding Arctic, a little-traveled region that occupies nearly a third of Alaska and claims very few human residents. In this land of extremes, the sun never sets in the summer and never rises in the winter. A major mountain chain, the Brooks Range, arcs across its midriff; frozen deserts dot the hinterlands; shimmering streams etch sinuous

- ♿ **Michelin Map:** 930 Inset. Alaska Standard Time.
- 🛈 **Info:** ✆907-457-3282; www.travelalaska.com.
- ▶ **Location:** From Fairbanks, the hub of Alaska's interior, it's an 8hr drive to Anchorage; roughly 3 days on the Alaska Highway to Fort St. John, Canada; and 18hr on the Dalton Highway to Prudhoe Bay.
- ☺ **Don't Miss:** A flightseeing tour of Gates of the Arctic National Park. Muskox and caribou can be seen (summer only) at the Large Animal Research Station in Fairbanks (Yankowich Rd., 2mi northwest of the airport; ✆907-474-5724; www.uaf.edu/lars).
- 👥 **Kids:** In Fairbanks, Pioneer Park and Riverboat Discovery.

patterns across the tundra. In the brief summer wildflowers bloom bravely and caribou thunder north to calving grounds.

INTERIOR
Fairbanks★
Alaska Hwy. (Rte. 2) & George Parks Hwy. (Rte. 3), 358mi north of Anchorage. ✆907-456-5774. www.explorefairbanks.com.
Spread among rolling hills along the Chena River, Alaska's second-largest

city (32,000 people; 100,000 in the surrounding borough) is the hub for the Interior. Beginning as a trading post for gold miners in 1901, the town prospered with the building of military installations in World War II and the Trans-Alaska Pipeline in the 1970s. A resourceful and often eccentric citizenry copes with brutal winters—tempered by the spectacle of the northern lights—and opens its arms to the nightless days of summer.

The city's **Morris Thompson Cultural and Visitors Center★★** holds a compact but informative interpretive gallery explaining traditional indigenous, pioneer and modern life in the North (101 Dunkel St.; &907-459-3700; www.morristhompsoncenter.org). **Creamer's Field★★** is a former in-city dairy farm turned lovely preserve for hiking and birdwatching (1300 College Rd.; www.creamersfield.org).

♙♟ Pioneer Park★

Airport Way & Peger Rd. &907-459-1087. http://co.fairbanks.ak.us/pioneerpark. This 44-acre history theme park holds the National Historic Landmark *SS Nenana*, a restored sternwheeler that plied the Yukon River from 1933 to 1952. There are also historic wooden buildings, now gift shops and snack stands.

♙♟ Riverboat Discovery★

Steamboat Landing, 1975 Discovery Dr. &907-479-6673. www.riverboat discovery.com. A 20mi (*3hr*) cruise down the Chena and Tenana Rivers is enlivened by sled-

dog demonstrations and a re-created Athabascan Indian village.

Museum of the North★★★

907 Yukon Dr., University of Alaska Fairbanks campus. &907-474-7505. www.uaf.edu/museum. The outstanding collection of Alaskan art and indigenous artifacts at this institution on a ridge overlooking Fairbanks is of world-class magnitude. The **Rose Berry Alaska Art Gallery★★★**, home of many priceless pieces, including the 2,000-year-old, carved ivory Okvik Madonna, is the single best such collection in the state. The **Gallery of Alaska★** depicts the state's history, ecology and landscape.

Denali National Park★★★

George Parks Hwy. (Rte. 3), Denali Park; 125mi south of Fairbanks & 240mi north of Anchorage. &907-683-9532. www.nps.gov/dena. The main visitor center is located at Mile 1.5mi of the park road. At 9,375sq mi, Denali offers an incomparable cross section of the untamed Alaska Range, including the highest peak in North America, 20,237ft **Mount McKinley**, commonly known as "Denali," an Athabaskan word meaning "the high one" or "the great one." The park's geography varies from spruce forest to grassy tundra to austere granite pinnacles mantled in snow and ice. Glaciers have scoured cirques, and chiseled ridges and steep valleys, to create a remote Olympian landscape that often appears to float in a world of its own above the clouds.

Gates of the Arctic National Park

©Leslie Forsberg/Michelin

Alaskan Regional Cuisine

Long limited to crab, salmon and halibut, Alaska's chefs are fashioning an inventive regional cuisine all its own that incorporates many other seafoods—spot prawns, sablefish, oysters—as well as bison, blueberries, reindeer and home-grown produce, marketed under the "Alaska Grown" brand. Notable purveyors include Resurrection Roadhouse in Seward; Marx Brothers Café, Seven Glaciers Restaurant, Orso, Kincaid Grill and Snow City Café in Anchorage; Ludvig's Bistro in Sitka and The Rookery in Juneau. In addition, Heritage Coffee in Juneau, Kaladi Brothers in Anchorage and Alaska Coffee in Fairbanks all supply exceptional locally roasted coffee throughout the state. For more information on Alaska Grown, a state program, visit dnr.alaska.gov.

Set aside as a refuge in 1917, the park harbors 37 mammal species and 157 bird species. Moose, wolves and grizzly bears roam. Caribou graze the tundra; Dall sheep dot the uplands.

McKinley is the single largest exposed mountain in the world. Rising 18,000ft above the lowlands of **Wonder Lake**, it is 7,000ft higher than Everest from base to summit.

Early mornings and visits in March provide the best chance to view the often cloud-covered peak. Private vehicle travel in the park is restricted; **shuttle-bus tours** cross forested taiga and open tundra, offering opportunities for wildlife sightings. Few trails cross this wilderness park.

THE ARCTIC★

Spreading from Canada 700mi to the Chukchi Sea, the Arctic's northern border is the frigid Beaufort Sea. The dominating feature rises just north of the Arctic Circle—the ancient Brooks Range, with its 9,000ft peaks running east to west in endless, sharp spires. The **Dalton Highway** from Fairbanks to Prudhoe Bay (www.prudhoebay.com) is one of just two through roads in North America that cross the Arctic Circle. Driving the Dalton is one of North America's last true wilderness road adventures, a 17-hour odyssey that requires both endurance and planning: the highway has very few visitor facilities; oil field facilities can be visited during commercial tours only.

Gates of the Arctic National Park★

Headquarters, 4175 Geist Rd., Fairbanks. ℘907-457-5752. Field office, Bettles; 180mi northwest of Fairbanks. ℘907-692-5494. www.nps.gov/gaar. Bush pilots fly visitors to this sprawling (12,816sq mi) national park, with no formal trails or facilities, in the Brooks Range. Guided adventures, booked well in advance, begin either in the Inupiaq village of **Anaktuvuk Pass** or in the century-old trading village of **Bettles**.

Barrow

500mi north-northwest of Fairbanks. ℘907-852-5211. www.cityofbarrow.org. Northernmost town in the Western Hemisphere, this Inupiaq community of 4,500 citizens clings to a treeless tundra on the edge of the Arctic icepack. The Inupiaq have lived in these climes for 1,500 years; archaeologists are excavating an ancient village near downtown.

Kotzebue★

450mi northwest of Fairbanks. ℘907-442-3401. www.cityofkotzebue.com. Alaska's most populous Native community (3,100 residents, 70 percent native), Kotzebue is a thriving indigenous cultural hub. Its new (2010) **Northwest Arctic Heritage Center★** (www.nps.gov/kova) depicts human survival for millennia in this unrelenting environment, and is headquarters (℘907-442-3890) for three remote, pristine park wildernesses: **Noatak National Preserve, Kobuk Valley National Park**; and **Cape Krusenstern National Monument**.

ALASKA'S ARCTIC WILDLIFE

The semiaquatic **polar bear** is one of the most elusive large predators. Living on ice floes in the far north, this fierce ursine hunts walruses, seals and whales, sometimes waiting hours for prey to surface at a breathing hole. More than 3,000 polar bears inhabit Alaska, but disappearing sea ice led the US government to declare the animals a threatened species in 2008.

Polar bear and her cubs

© John Pitcher/Bigstockphoto.com

Unlike polar bears, **grizzly bears** eat food other than meat, often grazing on blueberries near Antigun Pass off the Dalton Highway. Though not as large as the brown bears of Alaska's south coast, Arctic grizzlies can top 900 pounds. The heaviest polar bears weigh about 1,200 pounds. Alaskan **brown bears** may exceed 1,400 pounds, with those on Kodiak Island the largest land-based predators on earth.

Reintroduced to Alaska from Greenland in 1935 and today numbering about 2,300 in the Great State, **musk oxen** are exceptionally adapted to extreme cold. A layer of fat topped by thick skin, a heavy undercoat and silky hair 15-20in long keeps them comfortable at -80ºF. Their wool, or qiviut, is prized for its softness and warmth. Chief among their enemies, **wolves** hunt in packs on the dry alpine tundra. When under attack, the musk oxen herd will circle up like a wagon train, shaggy heads facing defiantly outward.

Magnificent barren-ground **caribou** migrate in summer across cold rivers and through mountain passes, their herds sometimes running in the thousands. Zoologically the same species as Scandinavia's reindeer, Alaska's best-known caribou belong to the famous Porcupine herd. More than 120,000 of these animals migrate each year between northern Canada and the Arctic National Wildlife Refuge, and their fate is one of the key issues affecting oil development proposals in the refuge.

Caribou, Denali National Park

© Andrew Coleman/iStockphoto.com

Hawaii

King Kamehameha statue
© Douglas Peebles / age fotostock

KAMEHAMEHA THE GREAT

Hawaii

The very word "Hawaii" evokes romantic and magical images. The chain of 132 volcanic islands, many no more than rocky bird sanctuaries, stretches 1,600mi across the Pacific Ocean some 2,500mi southwest of Los Angeles, at a similar latitude to Mexico City. The eight principal islands are clustered at the southeastern end of the archipelago, across a little more than 500mi.

Highlights

1 **Iolani** is the only royal palace in the US (p512)

2 **Pearl Harbor Monument** marks a "date...in infamy" (p516)

3 Kauai's **Na Pali Coast** dazzles the eye (p519)

4 Explore an extinct volcano at **Haleakala** (p521)

5 Lava meets the sea at **Kilauea** (p527)

A Bit of History

Seven of the islands—with a total land area of 6,422sq mi—are inhabited. The largest and geologically youngest is Hawaii, aka "The Big Island." Oahu, home of Pearl Harbor and the state capital of Honolulu, is by far the most populated island, with more than 976,000 of the state's 1.4 million people.

Native Polynesians, the first of whom migrated to Hawaii from the Marquesas Islands sometime after AD 400, simply called their world *'aina*, the land, as opposed to *kai*, the sea. British Captain James Cook, the first European to sight the islands in 1778, named the archipelago the Sandwich Islands, after his sponsor the Earl of Sandwich.

The Island of Hawaii was the home of the king of Hawaii, King Kamehameha I (c.1758-1819), who united the other islands under his conquering rule. The monarchy lasted less than a century before an armed takeover by Protestant missionaries, traders, whalers and sugar planters led to change. Briefly a republic (1893-98), Hawaii was annexed as a US territory in 1898 during the Spanish-American War.

The most dramatic 20C event was the 1941 Japanese bombing of Pearl Harbor, propelling the US directly into World War II. After the war, new air service enabled tourism on Waikiki Beach to boom; later other islands joined the boom. Hawaii became the 50th US state in 1959; and proudly claims native son US president Barack Obama. Hawaii's mid-Pacific location has given it a rich ethnic mix. No single race constitutes a majority; a quarter of residents identify as two races or more. Large groups include Caucasians, Japanese, Filipinos, Koreans, African-Americans and Pacific Islanders other than Native Hawaiians; the latter now represent 6 percent of islanders.

Today, with more than 8 million visitors a year, Hawaii relies on tourism as the largest employer and revenue generator ($14 billion). Aside from the US, most visitors come from Japan—almost 3 million. For all, the peaceable spirit of aloha is evident in the general good will of all Hawaiian islanders.

ADDRESSES

🛏 STAY

$$$$$ Four Seasons Hualalai – 72-100 Kaupulehu Dr.; Kailua-Kona, (Big Island). ☏808-325-8000. www.fourseasons. com/hualalai. 243 rooms. An intimate bungalow-style resort, this lush retreat melds easily with the natural environment. Guests swim in a saltwater lagoon to cool off after sunning on the beach. **'Ulu Ocean Grill's** fresh-sheet menu (**$$$**) features 75 percent Big Island ingredients, such as grass-fed beef and wok-fried opah with local mushrooms.

$$$$$ Grand Wailea – 3850 Wailea Alanui Dr. , Wailea (Maui). ☏808-875-1234. www.grandwailea.com. 780 rooms. A $30-million art collection greets visitors to this spectacular hotel on 40 beachfront acres. An elaborate spa, a poolside water playground, seven distinct tropical gardens and four

GETTING THERE

Hawaii's main airports (www.hawaii.gov/dot/airports) are reached from the US mainland by numerous major airlines and by **Hawaiian Airlines** (℘808 838-1555 or 800-367-5320; www.Hawaiianairlines.com). **O'ahu:** Honolulu International Airport (HNL) (℘808-836-6411; http://Hawaii.gov/hnl), has service from most major mainland hubs. Outer islands are served chiefly from US West Coast hubs such as Los Angeles, Seattle, San Diego and San Francisco. **Kaua'i:** Lihue Airport (LIH) (℘808-274-3800). **Maui:** Kahului Airport (OGG) (℘808-872-3830). **Big Island:** Kona International Airport (KOA) (℘808-327-9520).

GETTING AROUND

Inter-island flight times average 40min. Hawaiian Airlines (above), **go!** (℘888-435-9462; www.iflygo.com) and **Island Air** (℘808-484-2222 or 800-652-6541; www.islandair.com) provide extensive inter-island coverage. **Pacific Wings** (℘888-575-4546; www.pacificwings.com) has scenic tours in addition to flights among Oahu, Maui, Molokai and the Big Island. The **Moloka'i Princess** passenger ferry plies the waters between Lahaina and Moloka'i several times daily (℘877-500-6284; www.molokaiferry.com); similar service is provided between Lahaina and Lana'i by **Expeditions** (℘800-695-2624; www.go-lanai.com). The routes of TheBus, Oahu's **mass transit system** ($2.25/ride), cover the full island (℘808-848-5555; www.TheBus.org). Waikiki Trolley (www.waikikitrolley.com) has four lines linking Waikiki and downtown Honolulu with other attractions.

VISITOR INFORMATION

Hawaii Convention and Visitors Bureau (℘808-923-1811 or 800-464-2924, www.gohawaii.com). Individual islands: **O'ahu Visitors Bureau** (℘877-525-6248; www.visit-oahu.com); **Kaua'i Visitors Bureau** (℘800-262-1400; www.kauaidiscovery.com); **Maui Visitors Bureau** (℘800-525-6284; www.visitmaui.com); **Big Island Visitors Bureau** (℘800-648-2441; www.bigisland.org).

ACCOMMODATIONS

Lodging options range from world-class resorts to small hotels and bed-and-breakfasts. Package deals often include hotels, car rentals and airfares. Hawaii-born **Outrigger Hotels** operates two dozen properties throughout the islands (www.outrigger.com).
Another delightful and very practical option is to rent a fully furnished condominium, of which there are thousands; the most comprehensive operator is **Aston Hotels & Resorts** (℘808-924-2924 or 877-997-6667; www.astonhotels.com).
Also, **Go Condo Hawaii** (℘800-351-1330; www.gocondohawaii.com).
Reservation services: Affordable Paradise Bed & Breakfast (℘808-261-1693; www.affordable-paradise.com); Hawaii's Best Bed & Breakfasts (℘808-885-4550; www.bestbnb.com);
Hostels: Hostelling International Honolulu (℘808-946-0591; www.hostelsaloha.com or www.hostels.com or www.hiusa.org. **Camping:** Most counties require camping permits. For more information, contact the regional visitors bureaus.

---

nearby golf courses compete for visitor attention. Spectacular sunsets enliven **Humu ($$$)**, a thatch-roof bistro that attracts a diverse clientele.
$$$$$ Halekulani – 2199 Kalia Rd., Honolulu (Oahu). ℘808-923-2311. www.halekulani.com. 453 rooms. One of the top hotels in the world, the graceful Halekulani presides over the shores of Waikiki Beach like an elegant grande dame. Spacious rooms overlook the Pacific Ocean from towers as lofty as the

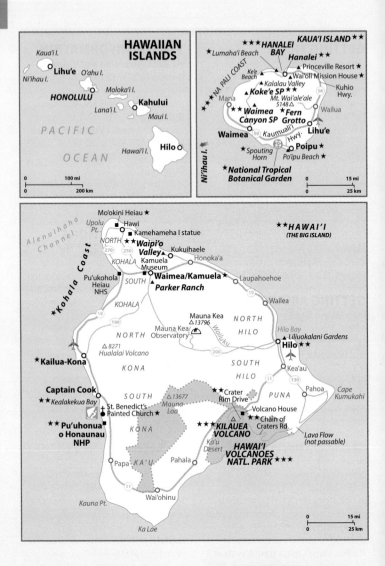

patrons. The service is top-drawer. For dining, both **La Mer** (**$$$$**) and **Orchid** (**$$$$**) are worth a visit.

$$$$$ St. Regis Princeville Resort – 5520 Ka Haku Rd., Princeville (Kauai). ℘808-826-9644. www.stregis princeville.com. 252 rooms. This huge St. Regis resort commands a dramatic view over the rugged cliffs of Hanalei Bay on Kauai's north shore. Every activity under the sun is offered here, including visits to the legendary Na Pali coast.

$$$$$ The Royal Hawaiian – 2259 Kalakaua Ave., Honolulu (Oahu). ℘808-923-7311. www.royal-hawaiian.com. 527 rooms. Still chic as ever, the storied Pink Palace of the Pacific was a Hollywood playground when built in the Spanish-Moorish style in 1927. The mai-tai is said to have been created in the hotel's eponymous bar.

$$$$$ Travaasa Hana – 5301 Hana Hwy. ℘808-248-8211. http://travaasa.com/hana. 70 cottages and suites. This peaceful luxury inn's spacious, airy villas hug a green hillside overlooking

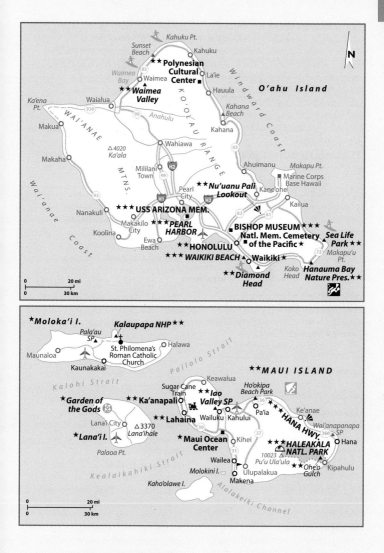

the sea. The immaculate grounds hold lush gardens. The serene dining room overlooks Hana Bay; guests feast on an array of local fruit, produce and seafood, such as lilikoi-glazed fish.

$$$$ Outrigger Waikiki on the Beach – 2335 Kalakaua Ave., Honolulu (Oahu). ✆808-923-0711 www.outrigger.com. 530 rooms. Flagship of a Pacific regional hotel group, this hotel offers such unexpected frills as classes in Hawaiian history, music and healing, and nightly Broadway-style showroom concerts. **Duke's Waikiki ($$$)**, honoring early

20C sportsman Duke Kanahamoku, is the top restaurant/lounge, overlooking the spot where Duke rode his largest wave—a 30ft swell named Bluebird.

$$$ Lahaina Inn – 127 Lahainaluna Rd., Lahaina (Maui). ✆808-661-0577. www.lahainainn.com. 12 rooms. Once a whaling town, Lahaina offers a charming counterpoint to the luxury hotels on much of Maui. This fine old inn, built as a mercantile in 1938, is the jewel of Lahaina, stuffed with antique wooden furniture and more than a couple of tall tales.

$$$ The Manoa Valley Inn – 2001 Vancouver Dr., Honolulu (Oahu). ℘808-947-6019. www.manoavalleyinn.com. 7 rooms. A 1919 post-Victorian in a leafy neighborhood near the University of Hawaii, this inviting bed-and-breakfast was restored in the late 1970s and filled with period antiques. All rooms feature four-poster beds; some share bathroom facilities.

$$$ Waimea Plantation Cottages – 9400 Kaumualii Hwy., Waimea (Kaua'i). ℘808-338-1625. www.waimea-plantation.com. 53 cottages. Charming early 20C sugar workers' bungalows stretch among 27 acres of coconut groves along a black-sand beach on Kauai's west side. Units with full kitchens and televisions are perfect for families.

⊱/ EAT

$$$ Merriman's – Opelo Plaza, 65-1227 Opelo Rd., Kamuela (Big Island). ℘808-885-6822. www.merrimanshawaii.com. **Hawaiian Regional**. One of the birthplaces of Hawaiian regional cuisine, Merriman's draws on the varied cultural palette of Hawaii. Wok-charred ahi tuna is the signature dish of chef Peter Merriman.

$$$ Pacific'O – 505 Front St., Lahaina (Maui). ℘808-667-4341. www.pacific omaui.com. **Pacific Rim**. Delectable cuisine that ranges from tandoori-spiced seafood to peppered beef is served outdoors beside the crashing surf. Chef James McDonald's selections include seaweed-wrapped tempura fried fish.

$$$ Roy's Restaurant – 6600 Kalanianaole Hwy. Honolulu (Oahu). ℘808-396-7697. www.roysrestaurant. com. **Hawaiian fusion**. Celebrity chef Roy Yamaguchi fires up dishes like opakapaka in macadamia nut sauce and roasted duck with passion fruit. This location was the first of dozens of Roy's outlets worldwide.

$$$ Hula Grill – 2435 Kaanapali Pkwy. Lahaina (Maui). ℘808-667-6636. www.hulagrillkaanapali.com. **Hawaiian Regional.** With a lively setting along the Kaanapali Beach promenade, nightly music and an expertly executed Hawaiian Regional menu, Hula's always packed. The daily catch is grilled over *kiawe* (mesquite), and the coconut seafood chowder offers a sumptuous full meal.

$$ Leoda's Kitchen – 820 Olowalu Village Rd. (just off Rte 30, approaching Lahaina). Maui. ℘808-662-3600. www. leodas.com. **Hawaiian Regional**. What began as a roadside bistro focusing on baked goods—famously, handmade pies—has evolved into a full-scale breakfast and lunch shrine with impeccable sandwiches, salads and of course, pastries, bread and pies.

$$ Brennecke's Beach Broiler – 2100 Hoone Rd. Poipu Beach (Kaua'i). ℘808-742-7588. www.brenneckes.com. **Seafood and Steak**. This casual, upbeat restaurant facing Poipu Beach Park is noted for its fresh fish, prime rib and ribeye steaks—and for its excellent salad bar.

$$ Bite Me Fish Market –74-425 Kealakehe Pkwy, Kona. (Big Island). ℘808-327-3474. www.bitemefish market.com. **Seafood**. Founded by a local charter fishing captain, this harborside cafe offers many kinds of fish rarely seen in mainstream restaurants— such as opah, monchong, ono, hebi and others. The daily specials, based on what they're catching, are your best choice.

$$ Keo's in Waikiki – 2028 Kuhio Ave., Honolulu. ℘808-951-9355. www.keos thaicuisine.com. **Thai**. Preeminent Thai chef Keo Sananikone has five local restaurants; this one is nearest to major hotels. Main courses include curry dishes, seafood selections like Indonesian shrimp in peanut sauce, and crispy mahi-mahi. Grilled country game hen and Bangkok duck are among the house specialties.

Honolulu ★★

Honolulu sprawls across the southeast quadrant of the island of O'ahu. The world's largest Polynesian city is a bustling modern metropolis of skyscrapers and traffic, extending from Waikiki's surf-washed beaches to the 3,000ft crest of the jungle-swathed Ko'olau Range. Here the first missionaries assembled their Hawaiian congregations, the only royal palace in the US was erected, and nine decades of sun-worshipers have since spread their beach towels.

▶ **Population:** 976,000.
◔ **Michelin Map:** p 509. Hawaiian Standard Time.
▯ **Info:** ℘808-524-0722; www.visit-oahu.com.
◉ **Location:** Small as Oahu is, its climate varies widely: the farther west you go from downtown Honolulu, the less rain.
☺ **Don't Miss:** The Bishop Museum.
👫 **Kids:** Sea Life Park; Children's Discovery Center.

A BIT OF HISTORY

Officially, all of Oahu (oh-AH-hoo) is the City and County of Honolulu (hoh-no-LOO-loo). But the 608sq mi island is far from entirely urbanized. There are fertile farms, mountain rain forests, and green vistas of pineapple and sugar fields. One-quarter of Oahu's land is occupied by military bases representing more than 38,000 Army, Navy, Air Force and Marine personnel. Many are based at Pearl Harbor, a deep slot in the south-central coast of the island. Across the Ko'olau range from Honolulu extends the lush Windward Coast of the island, with its suburban communities of Kailua and Kan'eohe. West of Pearl Harbor is the drier Wa'ianae Coast and the big-wave beaches of Makaha. A route through the agricultural center of Oahu leads to the North Shore, fabled for its country living and renowned surfing venues like Sunset Beach and Waimea Bay.

SIGHTS

Downtown Honolulu ★★

Honolulu Harbor to Vineyard Blvd. between Ward Ave. & River St.
While Waikiki, with its beach, hotels, restaurants and nightclubs, may be the traditional center of Hawaii's tourism industry, downtown Honolulu is the hub of history.

Native Hawaiian Sovereignty

When Queen Lili'uokalani was forcibly ousted as the last Hawaiian monarch by armed American colonists in 1893 (over fierce objections by US president Grover Cleveland) a long tradition of Hawaiian sovereignty ended that many of the 375,000 Native Hawaiians believe should be revived. Though the US government formally apologized in 1993 for the armed overthrow, activist groups seek various forms of autonomy or outright independence.
Some proposals would set aside parts of the islands as Native Hawaiian "nations" enjoying autonomy similar to Indian tribes on the mainland; other more radical voices envision complete independence (www.hawaii-nation. org). Various reparations schemes have been advanced, without resolution. A number of inland valleys on several islands are generally recognized as "Hawaiian" territory in which *haoles* (non-Hawaiians) ought not venture. "Do not covet the little vineyard... so far from your shores," Lili'uokalani pleaded to Americans long ago—a voice not completely stilled more than a century later.

Mission Houses Museum★★

553 S. King St. at Kawaiahao St. &808-447-3910. www.missionhouses.org.
The modest, wood-frame house, oldest Western-style structure in Hawaii, was brought in pieces by ship around Cape Horn and assembled in 1821 by the first American Calvinist missionaries, with Hawaiian assistance. Tours take in two other 19C historic houses.

Kawaiahao Church★

957 Punchbowl St.
&808-469-3000. www.kawaiahao.org
Designed by its first minister in 1837, this church was constructed of coral blocks cut and carried from a reef off Honolulu Harbor. The setting for 19C royal coronations, weddings and funerals is revered by isle residents. Visitors are welcome at the Sunday sermon, given partly in the Hawaiian language.

Iolani Palace★★★

S. King & Richards Sts.
&808-522-0832. www.iolanipalace.org.
This Rococo structure is the only royal palace in the US. King David Kalakaua, back from travels in Europe, erected it in 1882; its last royal occupant was Queen Lili'uokalani, whose government was overthrown in 1893.

Tours of the palace's first and second floors, guided or self-led, reveal the late Victorian elegance favored by Kalakaua and Lili'uokalani. Don't miss the Throne Room. The basement holds the Hawaiian crown jewels, the restored kitchen and the chamberlain's office.
Across King Street is a statue of **Kamehameha the Great** (Kamehameha I). A modern statue of **Lili'uokalani** stands on the other side of the palace, facing the capitol.

Queen Emma Summer Palace★

2913 Pali Hwy. &808-595-3167.
www.daughtersofhawaii.org.
Emma, wife of King Kamehameha IV, was of Hawaiian-British heritage and thus was an early symbol of cosmopolitanism in the isles. Royal Hawaiian and personal artifacts are displayed in her Victorian-era Nuuanu Valley retreat.

Hawaii State Capitol★

S. Beretania St. between Richards & Punchbowl Sts. &808-586-0146.
www.capitol.hawaii.gov.
Designed and built in 1969, the capitol has pillars that resemble palm trees. The sloping exteriors of the House and Senate chambers project from a pool, reminiscent of volcanoes rising from the sea.

Downtown Honolulu

© Brigitta L. House/Michelin

HAWAIIAN CULTURE

About nine percent of Hawaii's population call themselves Hawaiian, although the number with pure Hawaiian blood may be less than one percent – perhaps about 10,000. Many Hawaiians died in the 19C from introduced diseases. Over the past 150 years, they intermarried easily, especially with Caucasians (haoles in Hawaii) and Chinese. But their influence on the islands goes far beyond their numbers. Some of the best-known aspects of Hawaiian culture—music, dance, food and the welcoming aloha attitude—have been absorbed by all.

For at least 1,000 years, the Polynesian Hawaiians lived alone in the islands. They came in great double-hulled canoes—first from the Marquesas Islands between AD 400 and 750, later from Tahiti about 1100—and built houses of thatched grass. Their lives revolved around fishing, cultivating taro and sweet potatoes, gathering fruit and raising pigs. They had a sophisticated knowledge of astronomy, navigation and ocean ways, and an appreciation for the effect of the seasons on farming and harvesting. They imbued birds, fish and inanimate objects with supernatural powers. Things that were sacred were labeled as kapu, or forbidden.

As centuries passed, the Hawaiians ceased to build large ocean-going vessels. Stories of their former lands became songs and chants. They retained the basic spoken Polynesian language, adapting it to their own needs; ancestors and ancient gods were remembered through recitation of genealogy.

After 1820, American missionaries transliterated Hawaiian to make it a written language, reducing the number of consonants to just seven – *h, k, l, m, n, p* and *w*. The Hawaiian language today is undergoing a huge renaissance, with many school pupils educated in Hawaiian alone up to seventh grade, and ever-growing use of the language among adults as well.

Many other cultural aspects developed after contact with the West. Hawaiians embraced the diatonic musical scale and harmonies introduced by missionaries for singing hymns. From Spanish-speaking cowboys (*paniolo*) on the Big Island and Maui, Hawaiians learned guitar; they loosened the strings to change the tuning and invented the lovely "slack-key" style of playing.

When Portuguese immigrants arrived in the late 19C, Hawaiians learned to play the four-stringed *braga* and renamed it the ukulele. Along with a drum, it was played to accompany the hula. Performed with fierce rhythms—and only by men in ancient Hawaii, where it was a quasi-religious ritual—hula evolved into a graceful dance for women. (Grass skirts were a 20C tourist-trade import from Micronesia; dancers were traditionally clad in ti leaves.)

The traditional luau outdoor feast—complete with a *kalua* pig roasted in an *imu* (underground oven)—may be the best way to sample typical island foods. Expect to be served *poi* (taro-root paste, offered fresh or fermented), *laulau* (steamed meat, fish and taro leaves wrapped in ti leaves), *lomi-lomi* (salted salmon mixed with tomatoes and onions) and *haupia* (coconut pudding).

Honolulu Museum of Art★

900 S. Beretania St. at Ward Ave.
✗⚙🅿 📞808-532-8700.
http://honolulumuseum.org.

A few blocks east of the capitol, this airy building has open courtyards and an excellent collection of Asian art, including Japanese woodblocks presented by late author James Michener. The Doris Duke Theatre is the island's best-loved independent cinema, showing arthouse, Hawaiian and international movies.

Aloha Tower Marketplace★

1 Aloha Tower Dr. ✗⚙🅿 📞808-566-2337. www.alohatower.com.

Once Hawaii's tallest building, this 10-story spire has greeted five generations of cruise-ship passengers since 1921. Between the harbor and Waikiki, just off Ala Moana Boulevard, the **Hawaii Children's Discovery Center** 👤👤 (111 Ohe St; 📞808-524-5437; www.discoverycenterhawaii.org) focuses on the islands' wide ethnic diversity. Interactive exhibits allow kids to explore their own bodies and learn what being an adult entails.

Waikiki★

Ala Wai Canal to Diamond Head, east of the Ala Wai Yacht Harbor.

Once a lounging place for Hawaiian royalty, the 2mi-long suburb of Waikiki (literally, "spouting water") is recognized by the forest of towers created by its hotels. **Waikiki Beach★★★** remains one of the best places in the world to learn surfing, a sport invented here hundreds of years ago. At Waikiki Beach Center stands a statue of **Duke Kahanamoku** (Kalakaua Ave. near Kaiulani Ave.), Hawaii's three-time Olympic swimming champion (1912-20), who introduced surfing to California and Australia. Non-surfers may ride the waves in an outrigger canoe or take a cruise on a sailboat that casts off right from the shoreline. Opposite the beach, visitors have browsed through small shops and stands in the **International Market Place★** (2330 Kalakaua Ave.; 📞808-971-2080), under and around the same giant banyan tree for half a century.

The **Moana Hotel★** (2365 Kalakaua Ave.; 📞808-922-3111; www.moana-surfrider.com), now contained within the Westin Moana-Surfrider, has been restored to 1901 Victorian elegance. The **Royal Hawaiian★** (2259 Kalakaua Ave.; 📞808-923-7311; www.royal-hawaiian.com), Waikiki's "Pink Palace," is a Moorish building constructed in 1925, when most visitors came to Hawaii on ocean liners to stay for a month or longer.

At the east end, 140-acre **Kapiolani Park** encompasses the **Honolulu Zoo★** (151 Kapahulu Ave.; 📞808-971-7171; www.honoluluzoo.org) and **Waikiki Shell**, venue for open-air concerts. Denizens of the deep are observed at the well-designed **Waikiki Aquarium★** (2777 Kalakaua Ave.; 📞808-923-9741; www.waquarium.org). The third-oldest aquarium in the US features more than 500 species of Pacific marine life, including the melodically named

Waikiki Beach with Diamond Head

© Brigitta L. House/Michelin

humuhumunukunukuapua'a, Hawaii's state fish.

Diamond Head★★

Diamond Head Rd., .5mi east of Waikiki. The famous backdrop in photos of Waikiki Beach is this extinct volcanic crater. The 760ft summit is easily climbed by a **trail** (*.7mi*) that begins on the crater floor. Part of the route tunnels through old World War II fortifications, so a flashlight is advised. It's hot, so bring plenty of water.

National Memorial Cemetery of the Pacific★

Ward Ave. & Prospect Dr. ☏808-532-3720. www.cem.va.gov.
Occupying an extinct crater known simply as Punchbowl, this "Arlington of the Pacific" is the final resting place for more than 40,000 US military personnel. Many visit the graves of World War II correspondent Ernie Pyle and Hawaii astronaut Ellison Onizuka, who died in the *Challenger* space-shuttle disaster of 1986.

Bishop Museum and Planetarium★★★

1525 Bernice St. ☏808-847-3511. www.bishopmuseum.org. Closed Tuesdays.
The premier treasury of the past in Hawaii—and indeed, in the Pacific—is somewhat off the beaten path in the Kalihi district. Most archaeological and anthropological work done in Polynesia today is based here, and the Bishop Museum's collection of Hawaiiana is unequaled.
A dozen structures make up the museum. The original turreted stone building, the imposing Victorian known as **Hawaiian Hall**★, was built in 1898-1903.
Stairways and corridors lead to collections of regalia from the 19C Hawaiian monarchy, including crowns and feathered capes. Icons of gods carved from native koa wood are exhibited with woven pandanus mats and shark-tooth drums. Other galleries present the bygone whaling era, pan-Polynesian

and Asian cultures. The fine natural-history collection is particularly strong on bird and marine life.
Native Hawaiian arts and crafts—including hula dancing, lei making and quilting—are demonstrated daily.

Nuuanu Pali Lookout★★

Nuuanu Pali State Park, Pali Hwy. (Rte. 61). Oahu's premier viewpoint offers a wonderful (if windy) vista over the Ko'olau Range and the windward side of the island; it also has great historical significance. Kamehameha I drove the army of Oahu up to this point in 1795. When opposing warriors began falling by the hundreds over the 1,000ft-high cliff (*pali*, in Hawaiian), the battle and the island were won.

Hanauma Bay Nature Preserve★★

Koko Head, Kalanianaole Hwy. (Rte. 72), 12mi east of Waikiki. ✗🅿 ☏808-396-4229. www1.honolulu.gov/parks. The park limits the number of visitors; arrive early in the morning to assure entry.
An extinct volcanic crater with its seaward side recaptured by surf, this turquoise-hued cove is a favorite destination in Hawaii for snorkelers to view colorful reef fish and other marine life. Film buffs remember it in *Blue Hawaii* with Elvis Presley (1962).

👤👤 Sea Life Park★★

Makapuu Point, Kalanianaole Hwy. (Rte. 72), 15mi east of Waikiki. ✗♿🅿 ☏808-259-2500. www.sealifeparkhawaii.co
A 300,000-gallon aquarium features a spiral ramp that circles a giant, 18ft high **Hawaii Reef Tank** inhabited by over 2,000 marine creatures, including colorful reef fish, sting rays and sharks. Other exhibits feature penguins, monk seals, sea lions, dolphins, and the world's only known captive **wholphin**—a dolphin-whale cross-breed. Kids particularly enjoy the **dolphin and sea lion discovery** programs, in which they can interact with these charismatic marine mammals. The thrice-daily **sea turtle feeding** focuses attention on these gentle endangered giants.

Pearl Harbor★★★

6mi west of downtown via H-1 Freeway & Kamehameha Hwy. (Rte. 90).

Here on December 7, 1941, more than 2,300 servicemen were killed in a surprise early morning Japanese air attack on the US naval fleet. Eighteen ships, including six battleships and three destroyers, sank in the greatest US military disaster. President Franklin Roosevelt declared it "a date which will live in infamy" as he plunged the nation into World War II. The entire complex is now part of a three-state **National Monument** combined under the name "Valor in the Pacific," which focuses on the events leading up to the attack through to the signing of the peace treaty in Tokyo Bay.

Visitors should be aware that strict **security measures** in the Pearl Harbor area restrict use of bags, packs and other such items. As a site of huge loss of life, respectful attire is encouraged (no swimwear).

USS Arizona Memorial★★★

1 Arizona Memorial Dr. &P 808-422-3300. www.nps.gov/usar.

Floating over the hulk of a sunken battleship, the concave, 184ft white-concrete bridge marks the permanent tomb of 1,177 sailors killed in the Pearl Harbor attack. Each victim's name is inscribed in white marble on one wall. The macabre outline of the ship's hull is visible below. Movies and exhibits detail the 1941 attack, following which launches depart on a first-come, first-served basis from the shoreline **visitor center**.

USS Bowfin Submarine Museum & Park★

11 Arizona Memorial Dr. &P 808-423-1341. www.bowfin.org.

A walk through the Bowfin, credited with sinking 44 Japanese ships, helps modern-day visitors understand the tight quarters of World War II submarines. Tickets are sold for visits to the nearby **USS Missouri★** (808-423-2263; www.ussmissouri.org), the massive battleship on which the Japanese surrender was signed in Tokyo Bay on September 2, 1945. The **Pacific Aviation Museum** (Hangar 37, Ford Island, 319 Lexington Blvd.; 808-441-1000; www.pacificaviationmuseum.org) honors the role aircraft played in World War II, including Japanese Zero attack planes and the B25 bombers used by Doolittle's Raiders.

EXCURSIONS

Polynesian Cultural Center★★

55-370 Kamehameha Hwy. (Rte. 83), Laie, 27mi north of Honolulu. ✕&P 808-293-3333. www.polynesia.com.

The Church of Jesus Christ of Latter-day Saints (the Mormons) has had a strong presence in Hawaii since 1919. In 1955, the church established a college, now a campus of Utah's Brigham Young University. Students from all over Oceania attend classes, earning tuition by working or performing at the Cultural Center. Visitors can spend an entire day wandering through the "villages" of Hawaii, Samoa, Tonga, Tahiti, the Marquesas, Fiji and Aotearoa (Maori New Zealand), capping the evening with a spectacular 90min show of Polynesian culture.

The young staff members, in traditional dress, exhibit and teach skills such as making tapa cloth, weaving pandanus leaves, opening coconuts, and playing the ukulele.

Waimea Valley★★

Kamehameha Hwy. 59-864 Kamehameha Hwy., Hale`iwa (Rte. 83), 7mi east of Hale'iwa & 31mi north of Honolulu. 808-638-7766. www.waimeavalley.net.

Once a money-losing "adventure park," this beautiful valley on Oahu's windward (wet) side has been transformed into a conservation park devoted to preserving the valley's lush ecosystem, under the banner of a private nonprofit corporation.

Visitors can stroll serene paths, admire native plants and birds, enjoy more than a dozen different **theme gardens**, and marvel at the waterfall and pool that are the park's centerpiece. A cafe and gift store help raise funds to continue the valley's preservation.

Kauai★★

Known to locals as "The Garden Island," lush and tropical Kauai (kaw-wy-ee) has a less developed atmosphere than the other three main islands.

GEOLOGICAL NOTES
Centered on a single extinct volcano, **Mt. Waialeale** (5,148ft)—often the wettest spot on earth with average annual rainfall of 460in—Kauai is geologically the oldest inhabited Hawaiian island. It has been eroded to the point it has several rivers, the only island so blessed. It also is more separated physically from the other main islands: Oahu, Kauai's nearest significant neighbor, is out of sight about 90mi over the horizon. Kauai was the only island not won in battle by Kamehameha I: it was ceded almost amicably by King Kaumuali'i in 1810. The isle is said to be the home of the menehune, a leprechaun-like people who once served the taller Polynesians.

Most visitors arrive at Lihue, seat of Kauai's county government and its largest town. Two routes circle most of the island. The **Kaumualii Highway** (Rte. 50) heads in a westerly direction, with spur roads to Poipu Beach and Waimea Canyon. The **Kuhio Highway** (Rte. 56) rounds the island to the north from Lihue, winding past the community of Hanalei. Despite the torrents that deluge the peak of the island, many of the beaches get as little as 10in of annual rainfall.

SIGHTS
Lihue
The urban hub of Kauai is this small town of 5,900. Its **Kaua'i Museum** (4428 Rice St.; 𝒫808-245-6931; www.kauai-museum.org), which traces early island history, has excellent collections of traditional quilts and gourd calabashes. **Kilohana Plantation** (Kaumuali'i Hwy.; 𝒫808-245-5608; www.kilohanakauai.com) preserves a 1935 sugar plantation and mansion.

- 🕭 **Michelin Map:** p 508. Hawaiian Standard Time.
- ▪ **Info:** 𝒫808-245-3971; www.kauaidiscovery.com.
- ▷ **Location:** As on all the islands, the northeast shore is the windward (wet) side, and the southwest shore is dry.
- ⊕ **Don't Miss:** Kokee State Park.
- 🕐 **Timing:** It takes about six hours to circumnavigate the entire island, from Kee Beach to Kokee State Park.
- 🕭 **Also See:** Waimea Canyon.

Poipu★
Poipu Rd. (Rte. 530); 12mi southwest of Lihue. 𝒫808-742-7444. www.poipubeach.org.

A natural tunnel of swamp mahogany trees leads drivers down Maluhia Road (Rte. 520) into the 1835 plantation village of Koloa and on to **Poipu Beach★** on the south coast. A public park adjoins a string of resort hotels. Down the shoreline to the west is a natural feature called **Spouting Horn★** (Lawai Beach Rd.). Ocean waves push through the remains of an ancient lava tube and a spout of water shoots skyward. A nearby hole doesn't blow water, but just air, making odd noises.

National Tropical Botanical Garden★
Lawai Beach Rd. opposite Spouting Horn. ♿🅿 𝒫808-332-7324. www.ntbg.org.

The 252-acre **McBryde Garden** has the world's largest collection of native Hawaiian flora, plus other rare Pacific species. Adjacent **Allerton Garden** has more than 80 additional landscaped acres. There are also a research library and herbarium here.

Affiliated gardens are on Kauai's north shore (Limahuli Garden and Preserve, near Haena) on Maui (Kahanu Garden, in black volcanic soil near Hana), and two preserves on the Big Island.

Lumahai Beach

© Dennis Hallinan/Alamy

Kauai Beaches

One of Kauai's beaches is perhaps the most-oft depicted in the world—Lumahai Beach, on the north shore, is a gorgeous comma of golden sand where the movie *South Pacific* was filmed, and has thus been featured on hundreds of posters and postcards. Alas, it is subject to dangerous currents and is usually not safe. Ke'e Beach, at the end of the road past Hanalei, is a sensational sunset-viewing spot, and a reef-sheltered locale for snorkeling. Other good north island beaches include Hanalei Bay and Kalihiwai. On the south side, Poipu, Hanapepe and Waimea beaches are good options.

As on all the islands, all beaches are public property and even the most exclusive resorts are required to have a public access pathway (though the signs indicating these can be hard to spot). And the seasonal weather rules prevail: north and west shores are exposed to high seas October through April, while south and east shores are usually calm; the reverse is true May–September. But always check forecasts and only enter the water at lifeguarded beaches if you are not a confident swimmer, reading warning signs posted near the shore and heeding the advice, "when in doubt, don't go out." Waves come in sets—it can look calm for 20 minutes between dangerous sets of huge waves.

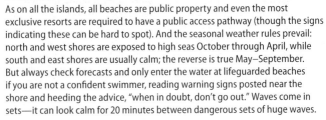

Waimea Canyon State Park★★
Koke'e Rd. (Rte. 550) via Waimea Canyon Dr. www.hawaiistateparks.org.
Called the "Grand Canyon of the Pacific," Waimea Canyon's size and depth are startling for a small tropical island. From the principal lookout, about 13mi uphill from Waimea, vivid pinks, greens and browns accent the contours of three tributary canyons.

A distant waterfall tumbles 800ft over a cliff; the ribbon-like Waimea River, draining rainy Waialeale, weaves a course 3,000ft below. Access to the canyon is only by trail.

Koke'e State Park★★
Koke'e Rd. (Rte. 550); 19mi north of Waimea. www.hawaiistateparks.org.
A cool mountain oasis, this lovely forested park boasts a small **natural-history museum** (*𝒫* 808-335-9975; www.kokee.org) and access to 45mi of hiking trails, one of which visits the unique ecosystem of the ever-misty **Alakai Swamp**. At the end of the road, at 4,000ft elevation, a dramatic overlook

of the **Kalalau Valley** (below) makes it clear why no road will ever completely encircle Kauai. The steep mountains and deep valleys of the **Na Pali Coast★★★** are too rugged to be breached. The park's lodge operates a dozen rustic **housekeeping cabins** (𝒫808-335-6061; www.thelodgeatkokee.net).

Fern Grotto★

174 Wailua Rd., Kapaa; off Kuhio Hwy. (Rte. 56) 6mi north of Lihue. 𝒫866-482-9775. www.ferngrottokauai.com.
Live ferns hang naturally from the roof of a cave, reached by 40-min boat tours that begin near the mouth of the broad Wailua River. Accompanied by hula dancers, singing, guitar-playing boat-men favor passengers with renditions of the "Hawaiian Wedding Song" and other melodies, which the acoustics of the natural amphitheater enhance.

Hanalei★★

Kuhio Hwy. (Rte. 56); 33mi northwest of Lihue.
The road to the north shore passes the expansive **Princeville Resort Kauai★** (5520 Ka Haku Rd., www.princeville. com). Large trucks and tour buses can't get much farther than this, restricted by the load limit on a narrow, rickety old bridge. That suits the residents of sleepy Hanalei just fine.
Fishing, swimming and other water sports at **Hanalei Bay★** seem to be the extent of high-energy activity. Those who enjoy local history can visit the **Waioli Mission House★** (Kuhio Hwy.; 𝒫808-245-3202; www.hawaiimuse-ums.org), built in 1831 by missionaries and now furnished with period pieces. A little west of Hanalei is **Lumahai Beach★**, the golden strand where Mitzi Gaynor tried to "Wash That Man Right Out of My Hair" in the 1958 movie *South Pacific*. The end of the road is **Ke'e Beach**, which offers swimming and snorkeling inside its reef, and is a hugely popular spot for sunset viewing. This is the starting point of a remarkable 11mi trail along the rugged cliffs of the Na Pali Coast into the Kalalau Valley, a memorable trek for properly outfitted, fit hikers.

EXCURSION
Niihau

From various points west of Waimea, people can see, 18mi offshore, the 72sq mi "Forbidden Isle" of Niihau (*NEE-ee-how*). The owners of the island are fiercely protective of the 200-or-so native Hawaiians who still live there without most modern conveniences, speaking their traditional language. Niihau may only be visited on a private helicopter tour (Niihau Helicopters; 𝒫877-441-3500; www.niihau.us) run by the Robinson family, which has owned the island and its sheep ranch since 1864.

Kalalau Hiking Trail, Kauai
©Gavin James/Bigstockphoto.com

Maui★★

The demigod Maui, whose exploits have been celebrated throughout Polynesia for a millennium or longer, is the source of this popular island's name. On "his" island, Hawaiians say he once inaugurated a Stone Age daylight savings time, ascending the dormant volcano Haleakala (literally, "house of the sun") to capture the sun itself as it rose from the crater. According to legend, the sun promised Maui that henceforth it would move more slowly across the sky so that Maui's sister could thoroughly dry her tapa cloth in its rays. Two mountain masses dominate Maui, Hawaii's second-largest island (729sq mi). Haleakala caps east Maui, while the highly eroded West Maui Mountains form the center of the other section. In ancient geological time they were two separate islands. Eventually, when the sea level dropped, an isthmus formed between them. Today much of this fertile central flat area is taken up with fields of sugar cane.

- **Michelin Map:** p 509. Hawaiian Standard Time.
- **Info:** ✆808-244-3530, www.visitmaui.com
- **Don't Miss:** Haleakala National Park
- **Also See:** Lahaina.

SIGHTS

Central Maui★

The twin towns of **Wailuku** and **Kahului**—the latter the site of Maui's main airport—occupy the north-central coast. (Together, their population is about 40,000.) At the 1842 **Bailey House** (2375-A Main St., Wailuku; ✆808-244-3326; www.mauimuseum.org), the Maui Historical Society has a museum of artifacts. The **Alexander & Baldwin Sugar Museum** (3957 Hansen Rd., Puunene; ✆808-871-8058; www.sugarmuseum.com), in a late 19C sugar-mill superintendent's residence, details the history and future of sugar production in Hawaii.

For a broad agricultural perspective, the 120-acre **Maui Tropical Plantation★** (Honoapiilani Hwy., Waikapu; ✆808-244-7643; www.mauitropicalplantation.com) offers walking and tram tours of crops of sugar, pineapple, macadamia nuts, coconuts, guavas, bananas, passionfruit, Maui onions, coffee and more. The major resort areas of central Maui, **Wailea** and **Makena** encompass a group of charming beaches with fine hotels, golf courses and championship tennis courts. **Kaanapali Beach Resort**, just past Lahaina, has several times been cited as having the best beach in America.

Iao Valley State Park★★

Iao Valley Rd. (Rte. 320), 5mi west of Wailuku. ♿ P www.hawaiistateparks.org.

Iao is the reason Maui was nicknamed the "Valley Island." The bright green cliffs and burbling stream at the eroded core of an age-old volcano have made it a popular picnic and hiking venue. **Iao Needle★★**,a basaltic spire that rises 1,200ft above the lush valley floor, is its highlight. A 6mi trail meanders beneath cliffs that spout spectacular waterfalls after heavy rains.

Maui Ocean Center★

192 Ma'alaea Rd., Ma'alaea. ✕♿P✆808-270-7000. www.mauioceancenter.com.

Exhibits in this highly rated aquarium take visitors from Hawaii's sandy shores to deep ocean trenches, pausing en route to study colorful reef life.

Exhibits include a touch pool, a green sea turtle pool, a hammerhead shark "harbor," a whale discovery center and an acrylic tunnel demonstrating life in the open ocean. A special gallery holds sea jellies, beautiful artworks of the ocean.

Lahaina★★

Honoapiilani Hwy. (Rte. 30). ℘808-667-9175. www.visitlahaina.com.

For nearly two centuries, this quaint community of 11,000 has been the center of activity in west Maui. The town figured prominently in *Hawaii*, author James Michener's novelized history. Along its waterfront, Lahaina exudes an atmosphere reminiscent of the 19C when pious missionaries and rollicking whalers vied for the loyalty of the native Hawaiian population.Whales are still an attraction (Nov–Jun). In the 9mi-wide channel between Lahaina and **Lanai** (℅see Excursions), the great creatures play, mate and give birth before migrating to northern waters for the summer. ⚓Lahaina walking tours begin under a giant **banyan tree★** planted in 1873. It spreads over an entire town square, about two-thirds of an acre. The 1901 **Pioneer Inn** (658 Wharf St.; ℘808-661-3636; www.pioneerinnmaui.com) is one of the oldest hotels still operating in the islands. Across Front Street, the former home of Lahaina's medical missionary is the **Baldwin Home★** (120 Dickenson St.; ℘808-661-3262; www.lahainarestoration.org). Dr. Dwight Baldwin is credited with saving much of the local population in the 1850s when he vaccinated hundreds against a smallpox epidemic, after waves of whooping cough, measles, dysentery and influenza had decimated islanders in the late 1840s.

Kaanapali★

Honoapiilani Hwy. (Rte. 30), 3.5mi north of Lahaina. ℘808-661-3271. www.kaanapaliresort.com.

Hawaii's first planned resort community (1963) features a shopping area called **Whalers Village** (2435 Kaanapali Pkwy.; ℘808-661-4567; www.whalersvillage.com), with a museum based on old-time whaling. The **Sugar Cane Train** (17 Kakaalaneo Dr., Lahaina; ℘808-661-0080; www.sugarcanetrain.com) makes the 6mi run between Kaanapali and Lahaina, with a singing conductor.

Haleakala National Park★★★

Haleakala Hwy. (Rte. 377), 36mi southeast of Kahului. ✕占🅿℘808-572-4400. www.nps.gov/hale.

The dormant volcano Haleakala (ha-LAY-uh-ka-lah) completely dominates east Maui. The desolation of its crater valley—7.5mi long, 2.5mi wide and 3,000ft deep—has been compared to the mountains of the moon. Here and there sprouts a silversword, an agave-like relative of the sunflower that extends a 6ft stalk of small red flowers once a human generation, then promptly dies. Among the lava flows walks Hawaii's state bird, the nene, the world's rarest goose. Thirty miles of trails criss-cross the crater floor.

On the often-chilly mountaintop, the **Haleakala Observatory** holds scientific and military technical installations.

Haleakala National Park, Maui

© Brigitta L. House/Michelin

Maui Beaches

Maui bears the distinction of often dominating best-beach lists—Kapalua Bay won the title in the first annual selection by "Dr. Beach" (Stephen Leatherman), a Florida-based shore scientist (www.drbeach.org). Long stretches of golden sand, many protected by Molokai Island's bulk 15 miles offshore, typify Maui's resort communities along Kaanapali. Other prize-winning beaches include Hamoa, Fleming, Wailea and Kaanapali.

Makena ("Big") Beach and Kealia are two long sandy beaches in south Maui with little development along the shore. The three Kama'ole beach parks along South Kihei Road in Kihei are family-oriented, with lifeguards and facilities such as bathrooms and showers, and expansive grassy fields ideal for picnicking. Like the Big Island, Maui also has a few black sand beaches, most famously Hana Bay at the end of the long, scenic drive to the windward side of the island, while Kanaha and Ho'okipa Beach Parks are two of the world's best windsurfing beaches. As on every island, all beaches are public.

Hana Highway★★★

⚠ Rte. 360.

Motorized adventurers need an early start to reach the east end of Maui via this narrow, winding 53mi road. Three miles past **Pa'ia**—an old sugar-plantation town, 7mi east of Kahului—it passes **Ho'okipa Beach Park**, a famed windsurfing venue. A good picnic stop is **Puohokamoa Falls**, 22mi before **Hana**, a serene little village on an attractive bay. Dedicated explorers may continue to **Ohe'o Gulch★★** (Pulaui Hwy., 10mi south of Hana; ℘808-248-7375, www. nps.gov/hale) in the Kipahulu District of Haleakala National Park. A series of small waterfalls tumble from the southeast flank of Haleakala, feeding from one pool to another. The simple marble grave of famed aviator **Charles Lindbergh** (1902-74) rests on a promontory in the churchyard of the 1850 Palapala Hoomau Hawaiian Church, 1.2mi past Ohe'o Gulch.

EXCURSIONS

Lanai Island★

www.visitlanai.net.

Lanai (lah-NAH-ee) was once known as the "Pineapple Isle." From 1922 until the early 1990s the Dole Company made the 141sq mi island the single largest pineapple plantation in the world. Two resort hotels now anchor the economy for the 3,100 isle residents. Few paved roads cross Lanai, so visitors must rent a four-wheel-drive vehicle to explore places like **Lana'ihale** (Munro Trail east of Lanai City), the 3,370ft island summit; and **Garden of the Gods** (Polihua Rd. northwest of Lanai City), dominated by strange volcanic rock formations.

Molokai Island★

℘808-553-5221.

www.molokai-hawaii.com.

Molokai (MOLE-oak-eye) is known as the "Friendly Isle." Its hub is the quiet port village of **Kaunakakai**, whose clapboard main street is reminiscent of a 19C Old West town. Murphy's Beach, off Highway 450, is fine for snorkeling.

Kalaupapa National Historical Park★★

Kalaupapa. ℘808-567-6802.

www.nps.gov/kala.

This unique site encompasses a 13.6sq-mi peninsula separated from the rest of Molokai by a 1,600ft cliff. To create an isolation colony for victims of Hansen's Disease (leprosy), Molokaians were relocated in 1865. In 1873, Father Damien de Veuster, a Belgian priest, worked among the infected. His original **St. Philomena's Roman Catholic Church** stands above the ruins of the village of Kalawao. Elderly leprosy patients, who pose no threat to visitors, live at Kalaupapa. Access is by small plane, private boat, foot or **mule** (℘808-567-6088; www.muleride.com).

Hawaii (The Big Island)★★

The Big Island is aptly named. It measures 4,038sq mi—nearly twice as large as the rest of the major islands combined. Because volcanic eruptions regularly add more lava to the shoreline, it is actually increasing in size. For all its bulk, however, it is sparsely populated, with 189,000 residents.

ISLAND OF CONTRASTS

Two volcanic mountains dominate the landscape. In the north, Mauna Kea (13,796ft), long dormant, is home to several astronomical observatories. In the south, Mauna Loa (13,677ft) is usually dormant. The active Kilauea Volcano, however, spews lava from the lower slopes of Mauna Loa. As the birthplace of Kamehameha I, and the site of Cook's ill-fated final visit, the Big Island is rich in traditional Hawaiian history. The separate coasts of the Island of Hawaii are readily distinguished by their climates: The drier Kona side is on the west; the much wetter Hilo side is east of the volcanoes. Most major resorts are on the Kona and adjoining Kohala coasts.

- ⚅ **Michelin Map:** p 508. Hawaiian Standard Time.
- ⚅ **Info:** ☏800-648-2441; www.bigisland.org.
- ▷ **Location:** It's easy to keep track of where you are, as the island's twin summits, Mauna Loa and Mauna Kea, are always in sight.
- ⊛ **Don't Miss:** Hawaii Volcanoes National Park.
- ⊙ **Timing:** The "Big" island is aptly named—it takes many hours to drive from Kona to Hilo. Plan adequate time for journeys around the island.
- ⚅ **Also See:** Waipio Overlook.

SIGHTS
Kailua-Kona★

The center of commercial activity in Kona is the sometimes-frenetic town of Kailua, called Kailua-Kona to differentiate it from Kailua, Oahu. Offshore waters provide some of the best deep-sea fishing in the world.

Kailua was the first capital of the Hawaiian Islands: Kamehameha I made his home here. A scaled-down representation of Ahu'ena Heiau at **Kamaka-**

Great Wall, Puuhonua o Honaunau National Historical Park

© Brigitta L. House/Michelin

Kaunaoa Beach, Kohala Coast

©Stephan Hoerold/iStockphoto.com

Hawaii Beaches

It's a myth the Big Island has no really good beaches. The Kohala Coast has many glorious strands of golden sand, some reached only by hiking modest trails across lava beds, and thus blissfully uncrowded. Anaehoomalu Bay, behind the Waikoloa Marriott, is a gentle seaside enclave where adventurous swimmers can meet resident sea turtles; and Hapuna Beach State Park is also inviting. Kona Coast State Park has two great beaches, if you don't mind jet noise from the nearby Kona Airport.

The Big Island's famous black sand beaches are generally closer to Kilauea—most notably, Punalu'u Beach State park south of Kailua, where you can observe green sea turtles sunbathing on the warm sand. Ensure you don't distress the turtles and never touch them as they are an endangered species without the immune system to protect against infection from humans. Removing black sand from the beaches is illegal and punishable by law. As on every island, all Hawai'i beaches are public.

honu, the king's final residence (75-5660 Palani Rd.), occupies the hotel grounds beside the pier; the adjacent Kona Beach Hotel has an extensive display of paintings by revered Hawaiian historical artist **Herb Kane** in the lobby. The ruler died there in 1819. The 1838 **Hulihe'e Palace★** (Ali'i Dr.; ℘808-329-1877, www.huliheepalace.net) was a retreat for later monarchs.

Opposite stands **Mokuaikaua Church★**, Hawaii's first Christian church, built by missionaries from Boston, Massachusetts, in 1837. A scale model of the ship, *Thaddeus,* that brought them here is one of the artifacts on display.

Captain Cook

Mamalahoa Hwy. (Rte. 11), 14mi south of Kailua.

This village is named for the British explorer who introduced the world to Hawaii. The **Kona Coffee Living History Farm** (Mamalahoa Highway; ℘808-323-3222; www.konahistorical.org) depicts the lifestyle of early Japanese coffee plantation workers. A short road leads downhill to **Kealakekua Bay★**, site of Cook's visit and death in 1779. The road ends near **Hikiau Heiau** (Napo'opo'o; www.Hawaiistateparks.org), a reconstruction of an ancient sacred site. The bay is now a marine reserve, popular for snorkeling.

Pu'uhonua o Honaunau National Historical Park★★

Rte. 160, Honaunau Bay, 22mi S of Kailua. ♿🅿 𝒫808-328-2288. www.nps.gov/puho.

Until the early 19C, this walled site was sacred, a sanctuary for Hawaiians who violated the *kapus* of society. If the transgressors could gain entry to the *pu'uhonua* (place of refuge), they were safe from punishment, as a *kahuna* (priest) would absolve them of their sin. Pacifists and defeated warriors also found refuge here.

Today a trail (*.5mi*) leads from a visitor center past several archaeological sites, including a reconstructed temple, and thatched huts where traditional crafts are demonstrated.

Uphill about 2.5mi from the historical park, a side road leads to **St. Benedict's Painted Church★** (follow signs from Rte. 160), decorated long ago by its Belgian priest (👈see Kalaupapa National Historical Park, above), whose amateur trompe l'oeil gave his remote congregation an idea of how a grand European cathedral looked.

Kohala Coast★

Queen Ka'ahumanu Hwy. (Rte. 19, South Kohala) & Akoni Pule Hwy. (Rte. 270, North Kohala). 𝒫800-318-3637. www.kohalacoastresorts.com.

North of Kailua, along the edge of a lava desert, is a series of impressive resorts. The **Hilton Waikoloa Village** (69-425 Waikoloa Beach Dr., Waikoloa; 𝒫808-886-1234; www.hiltonwaikoloavillage.com) has captive dolphins that swim and play with guests. The **Ka'upulehu Cultural Center of the Four Seasons Hualalai** (72-100 Ka'upulehu Dr., Ka'upulehu-Kona; 𝒫808-325-8000; www.fourseasons.com/hualalai) offers interactive history programs. **Mauna Kea Beach Hotel** (62-100 Mauna Kea Beach Dr., Kohala Coast; 𝒫808-882-7222; www.princeresortshawaii.com) was the first resort here, built by Laurence S. Rockefeller in 1965, and famed for its open-air design and Wright-esque angular sweep.

Pu'ukohola Heiau National Historic Site (.2mi north of intersection of Rtes. 19 & 270, Kawaihae; 𝒫808-882-4610; www.nps.gov/puhe) was built as a temple around 1550 and reconstructed in 1791 by Kamehameha I, who killed his last rival here to become supreme chief.

Captain James Cook

No name is more synonymous with exploration in the Pacific than that of Captain James Cook. He made three voyages between 1767 and 1779, and is credited with discovering nearly all there was to be found in this vast ocean.

Born in Yorkshire, England, in 1728, Cook escaped a humdrum life by joining the British navy. He gained acclaim as a navigator and cartographer, and at 40, was commissioned to lead an expedition to Tahiti to observe the transit of Venus across the sun. This voyage extended from 1767 to 1771; Cook discovered several islands and mapped the New Zealand and Australian coasts.

On his second voyage (1772-75), Cook circumnavigated the earth while searching vainly for the fabled "great southern continent," a theory popular in Europe. He did discover Tonga, New Caledonia and Easter Island.

Cook failed in his third voyage (1776-79) to find a northern passage from the Pacific to the Atlantic, though he traced the west coast of North America from Oregon to the Arctic. When he discovered Hawaii, Big Island natives first welcomed him warmly, perhaps mistaking him for the peripatetic god Lono. But Cook and several of his men were killed in a skirmish that remains controversial: was it simple aggression, or was he being treated as a god? A white obelisk marks the spot where the navigator is believed to have fallen.

The **Mo'okini Heiau★** (1.5mi on dirt road at Upolu Airport turnoff from Rte. 270), dating from AD 480, overlooks the Alenuihaha Channel 19mi north of Kawaihae. Nearby is the **King Kamehameha I Birth Site** (.3mi farther on same road). The islands' conqueror may have entered the world on the birthing stones here in 1758, the year of Halley's Comet, as legend tells of a great light in the night sky at his birth.

The old plantation village of **Hawi** is sprucing up with galleries, boutiques and cafes. Outside Kapa'au Courthouse stands a nine-ton, bronze **Kamehameha I statue** (Rte. 270).

Waimea/Kamuela★

Kawaihae Rd. (Rte. 19) & Mamalahoa Hwy. (Rte. 190),

Straddling a saddle between the Kohala Mountains and Mauna Loa, this pleasant town still retains its cattle ranching roots. With 350sq mi and more than 30,000 head of cattle, the **Parker Ranch** (66-1304 Mamalahoa Hwy.; ℘885-7311; www.parkerranch.com) once comprised the largest contiguous ranch in the US. It's still a working ranch; visitors may tour two historic homes at ranch headquarters (closed weekends), and browse a **store** (www.parkerranchstore.com) selling souvenirs and local products. The ranch was a land grant from Kamehameha I to John Palmer Parker, a Massachusetts sailor who married a Hawaiian princess. The ranch is now owned and operated by a foundation devoted to its preservation and to raising funds for local charities. The nearby **Kamuela Museum** (Rtes. 19 & 250; ℘808-885-4724; www.Hawaii-museums.org) is housed in a renovated historic schoolhouse and offers an eclectic collection of artifacts and locally produced art.

The **Anna Ranch Heritage Center★** (65-1480 Kawaihae Rd.; ℘808-885-4426; www.annaranch.org) is a delightfully restored window into the life of another descendant of Big Island pioneers, Anna Leialoha Lindsey Perry-Fiske (1900-1995). ☎Tours take visitors through the house and gardens, with their peaceful, breezy beauty.

Waipio Valley★★

Overlook at end of Rte. 240, 8mi north of Honokaa off Mamalahoa Hwy. (Rte. 19).

This spectacular wedge-shaped valley measures 6mi long and 1mi wide, and is flanked by 2,000ft cliffs that funnel ribbon-like waterfalls into streams emerging on a sandy ocean beach. It is accessible only by foot or commercial tour in four-wheel-drive vehicles.

Most travelers view it from a dramatic overlook near the small village of **Kukuihaele**. Inhabited for 1,000 years, the lush valley was once home to 4,000 or more Hawaiians.

Lava flow, Hawai'i Volcanoes National Park

© National Park Service

Hilo★★

www.gohilo.com.

The island's seat of government is this east-shore city of 44,000. Rebuilt after disastrous tsunamis (tidal waves) in 1946 and 1960, the community has a hodgepodge look. New homes and businesses have been constructed on higher ground, farther from the water. Early 20C commercial buildings, seemingly frozen in an age of hand-cranked cash registers and creaking wooden floors, mark the original downtown. The **Lyman Mission House and Museum** (276 Haili St.; ℘808-935-5021; www.lymanmuseum.org) is a restored 1839 missionary's home.

With 136in annual rainfall, Hilo is a floral center, especially for anthuriums and orchids. Many hotels sit near the rocky shoreline of Hilo Bay, along tree-lined Banyan Drive and **Lili'uokalani Gardens**, named for the last queen. Some have views of **Mauna Kea**, occasionally crowned by snow, to the northwest.

Hawai'i Volcanoes National Park★★★

Mamalahoa Hwy. (Rte. 11), Volcano, 28mi southwest of Hilo. ℘808-985-6000. www.nps.gov/havo.

This World Heritage Site is one of the few places to visit a live volcano. At the **Kilauea Visitor Center★★**, tourists may inspect exhibits and learn from rangers how to view the craters safely. **Volcano House** (℘808-441-7750; www.hawaiivolcanohouse.com), a rambling wooden hotel dating to 1941, sits on the brink of Kilauea Caldera, at 4,000ft elevation. Dangerous gases called "vog" (volcanic fog) rise from the caldera's deep **Halemaumau Crater★★**, which erupted most recently in 1982 and likely will again. On his 1866 tour of Hawaii, Mark Twain wrote that the lake of molten lava he found there "was like gazing at the sun at noon-day."

The **Crater Rim Drive★★** girdles the great pit and offers an opportunity to see (and smell) the fumes; danger-

© Brigitta L. House/Michelin

Waipio Valley

ous sulfur dioxide levels have closed much of the drive. Along the drive, the **Thomas A. Jaggar Museum★** (3mi west of Volcano House) presents geological exhibits, and the 450ft-long **Thurston Lava Tube★** (2mi east of Volcano House) beckons visitors.

Although the **Kilauea Volcano★★★** has been erupting since 1983, it is generally unseen. The 2,000°F molten magma moves through miles of lava tubes under the surface, and only where it breaks out near the island's southern shore is it visible; long hikes or boat tours are needed to reach active flows. Rangers advise which hiking path is safe enough to approach the lava.

The 23mi **Chain of Craters Road★★**, extending off Crater Rim Drive 4mi southeast of Volcano House, passes by old flows and reaches the shore near the place where a 2001 flow erased the end of the road.

INDEX

G

H

INDEX

INDEX

INDEX

Y

Z

🛏️ STAY

🍷 EAT

Thematic Maps

Maps and Plans

Companion Publications

Map 585 Western USA and Western Canada
Large-format map providing detailed road systems; includes driving distances, interstate rest stops, border crossings and interchanges.
♦ Comprehensive city and town index
♦ Scale 1:2,400,000 (1 inch = approx. 38 miles)

Map 761 USA Road Map
Covers principal US road network while also presenting shaded relief detail of overall physiography of the land.
♦ State flags with statistical data and state tourism office telephone numbers
♦ Scale: 1:3,450,000 (1 inch = approx. 55 miles)

North America Road Atlas
A geographically organized atlas with extensive detailed coverage of the USA, Canada and Mexico. Includes 246 city maps, distance chart, state and provincial driving requirements and a climate chart.
♦ Comprehensive city and town index
♦ Easy to follow "Go-to" pointers

★★★ **Worth the trip**
★★ **Worth a detour**
★ **Interesting**

Sight Symbols

▭ ‡ ⊡	Church, chapel – Synagogue	▨	Building described
○	Town described	▨	Other building
AZ B	Map co-ordinates locating sights	▪	Small building, statue
▪ ▲	Other points of interest	● ⁂	Fountain – Ruins
✕ ∩	Mine – Cave	🅵	Visitor information
🗡 🔺	Windmill – Lighthouse	⬭ ⚓	Ship – Shipwreck
☆ ♠	Fort – Mission	※ Ψ	Panorama – View

Other Symbols

🛡	Interstate highway (USA)	🛡	US highway	(180)	Other route
🍁	Trans-Canada highway	🛡	Canadian highway	🛡	Mexican federal highway
══	Highway, bridge				Major city thoroughfare
══	Toll highway, interchange				City street with median
══	Divided highway				One-way street
──	Major, minor route				Pedestrian Street
15 (21)	Distance in miles (kilometers)			⇌ ≡⇌	Tunnel
2149/655	Pass, elevation *(feet/meters)*				Steps – Gate
△6288(1917)	Mtn. peak, elevation *(feet/meters)*			⚠ 🗼	Drawbridge - Water tower
✈ ✈	Airport – Airfield			🅿 ✉	Parking – Main post office
⛴	Ferry: Cars and passengers			🖼 ✚	University – Hospital
⛴	Ferry: Passengers only			🚂 🚌	Train station – Bus station
← ⊂	Waterfall – Lock – Dam			● 🚇	Subway station
— ·· — ·· —	International boundary			❶ 🔭	Digressions – Observatory
- - - - -	State boundary			⊡ 🔲	Cemetery – Swamp

Recreation

▪-○-○-○-○-	Gondola, chairlift	⊂⊃ ▶	Stadium – Golf course
🚂	Tourist or steam railway	⊛ ▭ ▨	Park, garden – Wooded area
⛵ ⚓	Harbor, lake cruise – Marina	🕊	Wildlife reserve
🏄 🏄	Surfing – Windsurfing	🕊 Ψ	Wildlife/Safari park, zoo
🤿 🛶	Diving – Kayaking	- - - - -	Walking path, trail
🎿 🎿	Ski area – Cross-country skiing	🚶	Hiking trail
	Kids Sight of special interest for children		

Abbreviations and special symbols

NP	National Park	NMem	National Memorial	SP	State Park
NM	National Monument	NHS	National Historic Site	SF	State Forest
NWR	National Wildlife Refuge	NHP	National Historical Park	SR	State Reserve
NF	National Forest	NVM	National Volcanic Monument	SAP	State Archeological Park

🛡	National Park	🛡	State Park	🛡	National Forest	🛡	State Forest

All maps are oriented north, unless otherwise indicated by a directional arrow.

The Michelin Adventure

It all started with rubber balls! This was the product made by a small company based in Clermont-Ferrand that André and Edouard Michelin inherited, back in 1880. The brothers quickly saw the potential for a new means of transport and their first success was the invention of detachable pneumatic tires for bicycles. However, the automobile was to provide the greatest scope for their creative talents. Throughout the 20th century, Michelin never ceased developing and creating ever more reliable and high-performance tires, not only for vehicles ranging from trucks to F1 but also for underground transit systems and airplanes.

From early on, Michelin provided its customers with tools and services to facilitate mobility and make traveling a more pleasurable and more frequent experience. As early as 1900, the Michelin Guide supplied motorists with a host of useful information related to vehicle maintenance, accommodation and restaurants, and was to become a benchmark for good food. At the same time, the Travel Information Bureau offered travelers personalised tips and itineraries.

The publication of the first collection of roadmaps, in 1910, was an instant hit! In 1926, the first regional guide to France was published, devoted to the principal sites of Brittany, and before long each region of France had its own Green Guide. The collection was later extended to more far-flung destinations, including New York in 1968 and Taiwan in 2011.

In the 21st century, with the growth of digital technology, the challenge for Michelin maps and guides is to continue to develop alongside the company's tire activities. Now, as before, Michelin is committed to improving the mobility of travelers.

MICHELIN TODAY

WORLD NUMBER ONE TIRE MANUFACTURER
- 70 production sites in 18 countries
- 111,000 employees from all cultures and on every continent
- 6,000 people employed in research and development

Moving
for a world

Moving forward means developing tires with better road grip and shorter braking distances, whatever the state of the road.

CORRECT TIRE PRESSURE

RIGHT PRESSURE

- Safety
- Longevity
- Optimum fuel consumption

-0,5 bar

- Durability reduced by 20% (- 8,000 km)

-1 bar

- Risk of blowouts
- Increased fuel consumption
- Longer braking distances on wet surfaces

forward together
where mobility is safer

It also involves helping motorists take care of their safety and their tires. To do so, Michelin organises "Fill Up With Air" campaigns all over the world to remind us that correct tire pressure is vital.

WEAR

DETECTING TIRE WEAR

The legal minimum depth of tire tread is 1.6mm.
Tire manufacturers equip their tires with tread wear indicators, which are small blocks of rubber moulded into the base of the main grooves at a depth of 1.6mm.

Tires are the only point of contact between the vehicle and road.

The photo below shows the actual contact zone.

If the tread depth is less than 1.6mm, tires are considered to be worn and dangerous on wet surfaces.

NEW TIRE

WORN TIRE
(1,6 mm tread)

Moving forward
means sustainable mobility

By 2050, Michelin aims to cut the quantity of raw materials used in its tire manufacturing process by half and to have developed renewable energy in its facilities. The design of MICHELIN tires has already saved billions of litres of fuel and, by extension, billions of tons of CO2.

Similarly, Michelin prints its maps and guides on paper produced from sustainably managed forests and is diversifying its publishing media by offering digital solutions to make traveling easier, more fuel efficient and more enjoyable!

The group's whole-hearted commitment to eco-design on a daily basis is demonstrated by ISO 14001 certification.

Like you, Michelin is committed to preserving our planet.

Chat with Bibendum

Go to
www.michelin.com/corporate/en
Find out more about
Michelin's history and the
latest news.

QUIZ

Michelin develops tires for all types of vehicles.
See if you can match the right tire with the right vehicle…

Solution : A-6 / B-4 / C-2 / D-1 / E-3 / F-7 / G-5

THE GREEN GUIDE USA WEST

Editorial Director	Cynthia Clayton Ochterbeck
Editorial Manager	Gwen Canon
Contributing Writers	Gwen Cannon, Dayton Fandray, Leslie Forsberg, Eric Lucas, Vincent L. Michael, Connor Morrison, Carey Sweet
Production Manager	Natasha G. George
Cartography	Peter Wrenn
Photo Editor	Nicole D. Jordan
Photo Researcher	Nicole D. Jordan, Charles Anton Attebury
Interior Design	Chris Bell, Natasha G. George, Jonathan P. Gilbert
Cover Design	Chris Bell, Christelle Le Déan
Layout	Nicole D. Jordan, Natasha G. George
Cover Layout	Michelin Travel Partner, Natasha G. George

Contact Us	Michelin Travel and Lifestyle North America One Parkway South Greenville, SC 29615 USA travel.lifestyle@us.michelin.com www.michelintravel.com Michelin Travel Partner Hannay House 39 Clarendon Road Watford, Herts WD17 1JA UK ℘01923 205240 travelpubsales@uk.michelin.com www.ViaMichelin.com
Special Sales	For information regarding bulk sales, customized editions and premium sales, please contact us at: travel.lifestyle@us.michelin.com www.michelintravel.com

Michelin Travel Partner

Société par actions simplifiées au capital de 11 288 880 EUR
27 cours de l'Ile Seguin - 92100 Boulogne Billancourt (France)
R.C.S. Nanterre 433 677 721

No part of this publication may be reproduced in any form
without the prior permission of the publisher.

© Michelin Travel Partner
ISBN 978-2-067188-71-6
Printed: November 2013
Printed and bound in France - N° 201311.0163

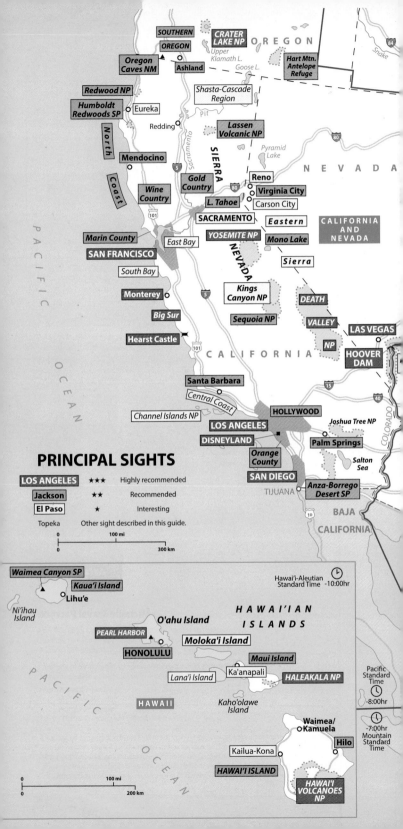

PRINCIPAL SIGHTS

LOS ANGELES	★★★	Highly recommended
Jackson	★★	Recommended
El Paso	★	Interesting
Topeka		Other sight described in this guide.

0 _____ 100 mi

0 _____ 300 km

SOUTHERN OREGON
CRATER LAKE NP OREGON
Oregon Caves NM Ashland
Upper Klamath L.
Goose L.
Hart Mtn. Antelope Refuge
Snake
84

Redwood NP
Humboldt Redwoods SP Eureka
Redding
Shasta-Cascade Region
Pit
Lassen Volcanic NP
Pyramid Lake
NEVADA
80

Mendocino
North Coast
Gold Country
Sacramento
SIERRA
Reno
Virginia City
Carson City
80

Wine Country
L. Tahoe
Eastern
CALIFORNIA AND NEVADA

SACRAMENTO

Marin County
SAN FRANCISCO
East Bay
YOSEMITE NP
Mono Lake
Sierra

South Bay
NEVADA

Monterey
5
Kings Canyon NP
DEATH

Big Sur
Sequoia NP
VALLEY
LAS VEGAS

Hearst Castle
101
CALIFORNIA
NP
HOOVER DAM
15
40

Santa Barbara
Central Coast
HOLLYWOOD
Joshua Tree NP
COLORADO

Channel Islands NP
LOS ANGELES
DISNEYLAND
Palm Springs
Salton Sea

Orange County
SAN DIEGO
TIJUANA
Anza-Borrego Desert SP
BAJA CALIFORNIA
10

Waimea Canyon SP
Kaua'i Island
Lihu'e
Ni'ihau Island

Hawai'i-Aleutian Standard Time -10:00hr

HAWAI'IAN ISLANDS

O'ahu Island
PEARL HARBOR
Moloka'i Island
HONOLULU
Lana'i Island
Maui Island
Ka'anapali
HALEAKALA NP

Pacific Standard Time -8:00hr

HAWAII
Kaho'olawe Island

-7:00hr Mountain Standard Time

Waimea/Kamuela
Kailua-Kona
Hilo
HAWAI'I ISLAND
HAWAI'I VOLCANOES NP

0 _____ 100 mi

0 _____ 200 km